lan-guage

introductory
readings

second
edition

lan-
guage

introductory
readings

second
edition

Virginia P. Clark,
Paul A. Eschholz,
Alfred F. Rosa,
Editors
University of Vermont

St. Martin's Press, New York

Library of Congress Catalog Card Number: 76-41930
Copyright © 1977 by St. Martin's Press, Inc.
All Rights Reserved.
Manufactured in the United States of America.
0987
fedcba
For information, write:
St. Martin's Press, Inc., 175 Fifth Avenue, New York, N.Y. 10010

ISBN: 312-46795-8

Since this page cannot accommodate all of the copyright notices, the three pages that follow constitute an extension of the copyright page.

ACKNOWLEDGMENTS

Part One   Language: An Introduction

p. 3   "Man the Talker," by Peter Farb. From pp. 221–225 of "Man the Talker" in *Word Play: What Happens When People Talk* by Peter Farb. Copyright © 1973 by Peter Farb. Reprinted by permission of Alfred A. Knopf, Inc.

p. 7   "The Origin of Language," by Charles L. Barber. From "The Origin of Language and the Invention of Writing" in *The Story of Speech and Language* by Charles L. Barber. Copyright © 1964 by Charles L. Barber. Reprinted by permission of Thomas Y. Crowell Company, Inc., and Pan Books.

p. 19   "The Linguist and Language," by Albert B. Cook III. From pp. 4–13 of *Introduction to the English Language: Structure and History* by Albert B. Cook III. Copyright © 1969 by The Ronald Press Company, New York, and reprinted with their permission.

p. 28   "Language, Thought, and Culture," by Peter Woolfson. St. Martin's Press, Inc., 1972. Copyright © 1972 by Peter Woolfson.

Part Two   From Animal Communication to the Human Brain

p. 43   "Language and Animal Signals," by Claire Russell and W. M. S. Russell. From pp. 159–194 of *Linguistics at Large*, edited by Noel Minnis, The Viking Press, 1971. Reprinted by permission of Dr. W. M. S. Russell, and David Higham Associates, Ltd.

p. 73   "Sarah: A Remarkable Chimp," by Victoria Fromkin and Robert Rodman. From pp. 184–188 of *An Introduction to Language* by Victoria Fromkin and Robert Rodman. Copyright © 1974 by Holt, Rinehart and Winston, Inc., and reprinted with their permission.

p. 79   "Feral and Isolated Man," by Roger Brown. From *Words and Things* by Roger Brown. Copyright © 1958 by The Free Press. Reprinted by permission of The Macmillan Company.

p. 85   "The Language of Children," by Peter Farb. From pp. 237–252 and 331–332 of *Word Play: What Happens When People Talk* by Peter Farb. Copyright © 1973 by Peter Farb. Reprinted by permission of Alfred A. Knopf, Inc.

p. 100   "The Linguistic Development of Children," by M. M. Lewis. From pp. 197–208 of *Linguistics at Large*, edited by Noel Minnis, The Viking Press, 1971. Reprinted by permission of Mrs. H. Lewis.

p. 110   "Conditioning the Uncommitted Cortex for Language Learning," by Wilder Penfield. From *Brain*, 88, Part 4 (November 1965). Reprinted by permission.

p. 122   "The Split Brain in Man," by Michael S. Gazzaniga. From *Scientific American*, 217, No. 2 (August 1967), 24–29. Copyright © 1967 by Scientific American, Inc. All Rights Reserved. Reprinted by permission of W. H. Freeman and Company.

Part Three   The History of the Language

Part Four   Words, Usage, and the Dictionary

Part Five   The Systems of Grammar

Structural, Transformational by Lyda E. LaPalombara. Copyright © 1976 by Winthrop Publishers and reprinted with their permission. Figures slightly altered.

p. 327   "Language and the Mind," by Noam Chomsky. From *Psychology Today* Magazine, February 1968. Copyright © 1968 by Communications/Research/Machines, Inc. and reprinted with their permission.

Part Six   Regional Varieties of English

p. 347   "Regional Variations," by Albert H. Marckwardt. From pp. 131–144 of *American English* by Albert H. Marckwardt. Copyright © 1958, 1969 by Oxford University Press and reprinted with their permission.

p. 358   "Dialects: How They Differ," by Roger W. Shuy. From *Discovering American Dialects*. Copyright © 1967 by the National Council of Teachers of English. Reprinted by permission of the publisher and Roger W. Shuy.

p. 384   "Grease and Greasy: A Study of Geographical Variation," by E. Bagby Atwood. From *Texas Studies in English*, 29 (1950), 249–260.

Part Seven   Social Varieties of English

p. 399   "Speech Communities," by Paul Roberts. From *Understanding English* by Paul Roberts. Copyright © 1958 by Paul Roberts. Reprinted by permission of Harper & Row, Publishers, Inc.

p. 408   "The Styles of the Five Clocks," by Martin Joos. From pp. 3–5, 11–12, 19, 23–32, 34–41 of *The Five Clocks* by Martin Joos. Copyright © 1961, 1962, 1967 by Martin Joos. Reprinted by permission of Harcourt Brace Jovanovich, Inc.

p. 416   "Sociolinguistic Factors in the History of American Negro Dialects," by William A. Stewart. From the *Florida FL Reporter*, 5, No. 2 (Spring 1967), 11, 22, 24, 26, 30, edited by Alfred C. Aarons. Reprinted by permission of the *Florida FL Reporter*.

p. 427   "Should Ghettoese Be Accepted?" by William Raspberry. From *Today's Education*, 59 (April 1970), 30–31, 61–62. Reprinted by permission of the National Education Association and William Raspberry.

p. 433   "A Checklist of Significant Features for Discriminating Social Dialects," by Raven I. McDavid, Jr. From *Dimensions of Dialect*, edited by Eldonna Evertts. Copyright © 1957 by the National Council of Teachers of English. Reprinted by permission of the publisher and Raven I. McDavid, Jr.

p. 439   "The Study of Nonstandard English," by William Labov. From *The Study of Nonstandard English* by William Labov. Copyright © 1970 by the National Council of Teachers of English. Reprinted by permission of the publisher and William Labov.

Part Eight   The Language of the Body: Kinesics and Proxemics

p. 453   "The Sounds of Silence," by Edward T. Hall and Mildred Reed Hall. Originally appeared in *Playboy* Magazine. Copyright © 1971 by Playboy. Reprinted by permission of the publisher and the authors.

p. 466   "Learning to Read Gestures," by Gerard I. Nierenberg and Henry H. Calero. From pp. 1–15 of "Acquiring the Skills for Reading Gestures," in *How to Read a Person Like a Book*. Copyright © 1971 by Gerard I. Nierenberg and Henry H. Calero. All Rights Reserved. Reprinted by permission of Hawthorn Books, Inc.

p. 477   "The Effects of Physical Appearance on Human Communication," by Mark L. Knapp. From pp. 63–75 of *Nonverbal Communication in Human Interaction* by Mark L. Knapp. Copyright © 1972 by Holt, Rinehart and Winston, Inc., and reprinted with their permission.

p. 490   "Winking, Blinking and Nods," by Julius Fast. From *Body Language* by Julius Fast. Copyright © 1970 by Julius Fast. Published by M. Evans and Company, Inc., New York.

p. 502 "Communication by Gesture in the Middle East," by Leo Hamalian. From *ETC: A Review of General Semantics*, 22 (1965), 43–49. Reprinted by permission of the International Society for General Semantics.

p. 507 "Space Speaks," by Elward T. Hall. From chapter 10 of *The Silent Language* by Edward T. Hall. Copyright © 1959. Reprinted by permission of Doubleday, Inc.

PICTURE CREDITS

p. 500 *top left:* Copyright © 1963 by Columbia Pictures Corp. All Rights Reserved. *bottom left:* Copyright © 1965 by Columbia Pictures Corp. All Rights Reserved. *right:* Rizzoli Film Distributors, Inc.

p. 501 photograph by St. Hilaire. Copyright © 1963 by Columbia Pictures Corp. All Rights Reserved.

p. 522 *top left:* photograph by Leonard Freed, MAGNUM PHOTOS. *top right:* photograph by Sergio Larrain © 1963 MAGNUM PHOTOS. *bottom:* photograph by Ron Benvenisti, MAGNUM PHOTOS.

p. 523 *top:* photograph by Rene Burri © 1965 MAGNUM PHOTOS. *center:* photograph by Leonard Freed © 1970 MAGNUM PHOTOS. *bottom:* photograph by Charles Harbutt © 1970 MAGNUM PHOTOS.

p. 524 *top:* photograph by Burk Uzzle © 1970 MAGNUM PHOTOS. *bottom:* photograph by David Margolin, from BLACK STAR.

p. 525 photograph by Ron Benvenisti, MAGNUM PHOTOS.

p. 529 advertisement courtesy of Book-of-the-Month-Club, Inc., 280 Park Avenue, New York, New York, 10017.

PREFACE

> "The limits of my language mean
> the limits of my world."
> —*Ludwig Wittgenstein*

Our language is central to everything we do; and it, more
than any other characteristic, distinguishes us from other
living creatures. Since we cannot function without our
language and since we cannot transcend our linguistic
boundaries, new discoveries and changes in language study
profoundly affect our view of ourselves and of our place in
society. In appreciating the complexities of the medium
through which we all communicate, we understand more
fully our humanity.

This new edition of LANGUAGE: INTRODUCTORY
READINGS reflects many recent changes in attitudes toward
language. In addition to bringing the book up to date, we
have sought to make the book more comprehensive in its
coverage and more practical in its classroom applications by
expanding the number of sections and sharpening the focus
of each section. The revisions include a new section on basic
concepts in language study, a new section on the history of
British and American English, an expanded unit on social
dialects, and a refocused grammar section. New selections
discuss children's acquisition of language, recent work with
chimpanzees and language, language functioning and the
human brain, sexism in English, and usage and usage

dictionaries. Also included are representative samples from dialect and somatype questionnaires.

The sections in this new edition are as follows:

1) Language: An Introduction
2) From Animal Communication to the Human Brain
3) The History of the Language
4) Words, Usage, and the Dictionary
5) The Systems of Grammar
6) Regional Varieties of English
7) Social Varieties of English
8) The Language of the Body: Kinesics and Proxemics

These eight sections, we believe, provide a basis for a meaningful study of language. The previous edition of LANGUAGE: INTRODUCTORY READINGS was the first language anthology to consider nonverbal communication an essential part of language study. Recent work in kinesics and proxemics and their interrelationships with verbal communication confirms our earlier belief that no consideration of language can be complete that does not recognize this important area. Since nonverbal communication is in large part visual, we have again included photographic materials as illustrations of the principles discussed in the text.

In selecting articles for the second edition, we have tried to achieve an evenness of sophistication and reading level. We have prized readability and, as before, have not hesitated to go beyond the standard linguistic authors and journals for the kind of material that not only challenges students but also stimulates their interest. Although there is a rationale for the arrangement of the sections, the order is by no means inflexible, and instructors may wish to establish their own sequences. We do, however, strongly recommend that the first section—"Language: An Introduction"—be assigned before any of the other sections because it provides important background material.

In addition to questions at the end of each article, which serve to focus the students' attention on specific issues in their reading, we have included a series of projects at the end of each section. These projects are designed to encourage students to go beyond their reading and to apply what they have learned. The annotated bibliographies that conclude each section are designed to aid students in working with the projects.

We are grateful to Mrs. Barbara Manchester for her careful typing of the manuscript. Special thanks go once again to our students at the University of Vermont, whose continued enthusiasm for language study and whose responses to materials included in this edition as well as in the first have been most helpful.

Virginia P. Clark
Paul A. Eschholz
Alfred F. Rosa

CONTENTS

lan-guage

introductory readings

second edition

PART ONE

Language: An Introduction

Language is not only the principal medium that human beings use to communicate with each other but also the bond that links people together and binds them to their culture. To understand our humanity, therefore, we must understand the language that makes us human. The study of language, then, is a very practical pursuit. Before embarking on this study, however, we should consider some fundamental questions: What is language? Where did language come from? How do people use language? What effect does language have on people?

The articles in this section are intended to raise some basic questions about language, identify some important issues concerning language, heighten the reader's awareness of language, and provide a context for the other areas of language study examined in this book. Specifically, the articles consider the infinite flexibility of language, the possible origins of language, some essential language concepts, the role of the linguist, and the interrelationships of language and culture—the Sapir-Whorf Hypothesis that language is culture-bound and shapes our reality.

1
Man the Talker

Peter Farb

Although the ability to use language is perhaps the most distinguishing characteristic of human beings, most people underestimate the miracle of language, the linguistic creativity involved "in the various strategies of speech interaction, in word play and verbal dueling, in exploiting a language's total resources." And this linguistic creativity is the birthright of every human being, as Peter Farb reminds us in this excerpt from his provocative book *Word Play: What Happens When People Talk.* Farb stresses the infinitely flexible nature of language and the extraordinary power that we can wield when we talk.

SOME twenty-five hundred years ago, Psamtik, an Egyptian pharaoh, desired to discover man's primordial tongue. He entrusted two infants to an isolated shepherd and ordered that they should never hear a word spoken in any language. When the children were returned to the pharaoh several years later, he thought he heard them utter *bekos,* which means "bread" in Phrygian, a language of Asia Minor. And so he honored Phrygian as man's "natural" language. Linguists today know that the story of the pharaoh's experiment must be apocryphal. No child is capable of speech until he has heard other human beings speak, and even two infants reared together cannot develop a language from scratch. Nor does any single "natural" language exist. A child growing up anywhere on earth will speak the tongue he hears in his speech community, regardless of the race, nationality, or language of his parents.

Every native speaker is amazingly creative in the various strategies of speech interaction, in word play and verbal dueling, in exploiting a language's total resources to create poetry and literature. Even a monosyllabic *yes*—spoken in a particular speech situation, with a certain tone of voice, and accompanied by an appropriate gesture—might constitute an original use of English. This sort of linguistic creativity is the birthright of every human being on earth, no matter what language he speaks, the kind of community he lives in, or his degree of intelligence. As Edward Sapir pointed out, when it comes to language "Plato walks with the Macedonian swineherd, Confucius with the head-hunting savage of Assam."

And at a strictly grammatical level also, native speakers are unbelievably creative in language. Not every human being can play the violin, do calculus, jump high hurdles, or sail a canoe, no matter how excellent his teachers or how arduous his training—but every person constantly creates utterances never before spoken on earth. Incredible as it may seem at first thought, the sentence you just read possibly appeared in exactly this form for the first time in the history of the English language—and the same thing might be said about the sentence you are reading now. In fact, if conventional remarks—such as greetings, farewells, stock phrases like *thank you*, proverbs, clichés, and so forth—are disregarded, in theory all of a person's speech consists of sentences never before uttered.

A moment's reflection reveals why that may be so. Every language groups its vocabulary into a number of different classes such as nouns, verbs, adjectives, and so on. If English possessed a mere 1,000 nouns (such as *trees, children, horses*) and only 1,000 verbs (*grow, die, change*), the number of possible two-word sentences, therefore, would be 1,000 × 1,000, or one million. Of course, most of these sentences will be meaningless to a speaker today—yet at one time people thought *atoms split* was a meaningless utterance. The nouns, however, might also serve as the objects of these same verbs in three-word sentences. So with the same meager repertory of 1,000 nouns and 1,000 verbs capable of taking an object, the number of possible three-word sentences increases to 1,000 × 1,000 × 1,000, or one billion. These calculations, of course, are just for minimal sentences and an impoverished vocabulary. Most languages offer their speakers many times a thousand nouns and a thousand verbs, and in addition they possess other classes of words that function as adverbs, adjectives, articles, prepositions, and so on. Think, too, in terms of four-word, ten-word, even fifty-word sentences—and the number of possible grammatical combinations becomes astronomical. One linguist calculated that it would take ten trillion years (two thousand times the estimated age of the earth) to utter all the possible English sentences that use exactly twenty words. Therefore, it is improbable that any twenty-word sentence a person speaks was ever spoken previously—and the same thing would hold true, of course, for sentences of greater length, and for most shorter ones as well.

For a demonstration of just why the number of sentences that can be constructed in a language is, at least in theory, infinite, show twenty-five speakers of English a cartoon and ask them to describe in a single sentence what they see. Each of the twenty-five speakers will come up with a different sentence, perhaps examples similar to these:

> I see a little boy entering a magic and practical-joke shop to buy something and not noticing that the owner, a practical joker himself, has laid a booby trap for him.
>
> The cartoon shows an innocent little kid, who I guess is entering a magic shop because he wants to buy something, about to be captured in a trap by the owner of the shop, who has a diabolical expression on his face.

It has been calculated that the vocabulary and the grammatical structures used in only twenty-five such sentences about this cartoon might provide the raw material for nearly twenty *billion* grammatical sentences —a number so great that about forty human life spans would be needed to speak them, even at high speed. Obviously, no one could ever speak, read, or hear in his lifetime more than the tiniest fraction of the possible sentences in his language. That is why almost every sentence in this book—as well as in all the books ever written or to be written—is possibly expressed in its exact form for the first time.

This view of creativity in the grammatical aspects of language is a very recent one. It is part of the revolution in ideas about the structure of language that has taken place since 1957, when Noam Chomsky, of the Massachusetts Institute of Technology, published his *Syntactic Structures*. Since then Chomsky and others have put forth a theory of language that bears little resemblance to the grammar most people learned in "grammar" school. Not all linguists accept Chomsky's theories. But his position, whether it is ultimately shown to be right or wrong, represents an influential school in theoretical linguistics today, one that other schools often measure themselves against.

Chomsky believes that all human beings possess at birth an innate capacity to acquire language. Such a capacity is biologically determined —that is, it belongs to what is usually termed "human nature"—and it is passed from parents to children as part of the offspring's biological inheritance. The innate capacity endows speakers with the general shape of human language, but it is not detailed enough to dictate the precise tongue each child will speak—which accounts for why different languages are spoken in the world. Chomsky states that no one learns a language by learning all of its possible sentences, since obviously that would require countless lifetimes. For example, it is unlikely that any of the speakers who saw the cartoon of the child entering the magic store ever encountered such a bizarre situation before—yet none of the speakers had any difficulty in constructing sentences about it. Nor would a linguist who wrote down these twenty-five sentences ever have heard them previously—yet he had no difficulty understanding them. So, instead of learning billions of sentences, a person unconsciously acquires a grammar that can generate an infinite number of new sentences in his language.

Such a grammar is innately within the competence of any native speaker of a language. However, no speaker—not even Shakespeare, Dante, Plato, or the David of the Psalms—lives up to his theoretical competence. His actual performance in speaking a language is considerably different, and it consists of numerous errors, hesitations, repetitions, and so forth. Despite these very uneven performances that a child hears all around him, in only a few years—and before he even receives instruction in reading and writing in "grammar" school—he puts together for himself the theoretical rules for the language spoken in his community. Since most sentences that a child hears are not only unique but also filled with errors, how can he ever learn the grammar of his language? Chomsky's answer is that children are born with the capacity to learn only grammars that accord with the innate human blueprint. Children disregard performance errors because such errors result in sentences that could not be described by such a grammar. Strong evidence exists that native speakers of a language know intuitively whether a sentence is grammatical or not. They usually cannot specify exactly what is wrong, and very possibly they make the same mistakes in their own speech, but they know—unconsciously, not as a set of rules they learned in school—when a sentence is incorrect.

FOR DISCUSSION AND REVIEW

1   What does Farb mean when he says that "native speakers are unbelievably creative in language," and that "linguistic creativity is the birthright of every human being on earth"?

2   Implicit in Farb's discussion of man and language is his definition of language. List the main characteristics of language as Farb sees them.

3   Who is Noam Chomsky? Why, according to Farb, is he important?

4   What evidence does Farb present to support Chomsky's claim that "no one learns a language by learning all of its possible sentences"?

5   What distinctions, according to Farb, does Chomsky draw between competence and performance?

2

The Origin of Language

Charles L. Barber

Despite the ruling of the Linguistic Society of Paris in 1886 prohibiting the presentation of papers dealing with the origin of language, speculation on this subject continues. The question of how language originated, like the question of how human life originated, has captured the imagination and commanded the attention of generations, but the answer lies lost in the aeons of prehistory. In this excerpt from *The Story of Speech and Language,* Charles L. Barber recounts the types of evidence available about the origin of language and surveys the major theories on the subject. Such a discussion seems worthwhile, not only because the subject is of interest in itself, but also because it reveals some important aspects of the nature of language.

W E ARE profoundly ignorant about the origins of language, and have to content ourselves with more or less plausible speculations. We do not even know for certain when language arose, but it seems likely that it goes back to the earliest history of man, perhaps half a million years. We have no direct evidence, but it seems probable that speech arose at the same time as tool making and the earliest forms of specifically human cooperation. In the great Ice Ages of the Pleistocene period, our earliest human ancestors established the Old Stone Age culture: they made flint tools, and later tools of bone, ivory, and antler; they made fire and cooked their food; they hunted big game, often by methods that called for considerable cooperation and coordination. As their material culture gradually improved, they became artists, and made carvings and engravings on bones and pebbles, and wonderful paintings of animals on the walls of caves. It is difficult to believe that the makers of these Palaeolithic cultures lacked the power of speech. It is a long step, admittedly, from the earliest flint weapons to the splendid art of the late Old Stone Age: the first crude flints date back perhaps to 500,000 BC, while the finest achievements of Old Stone Age man are later than 100,000 BC; and in this period we can envisage a corresponding development of language, from the most primitive and limited language of the earliest human groups to a fully developed language in the flowering time of Old Stone Age culture.

Evidence about the Origins of Language

How did language arise in the first place? There are many theories about this, based on various types of indirect evidence, such as the language of children, the language of primitive societies, the kinds of changes that have taken place in languages in the course of recorded history, the behavior of higher animals like chimpanzees, and the behavior of people suffering from speech defects. These types of evidence may provide us with useful pointers, but they all suffer from limitations, and must be treated with caution.

When we consider the language of children we have to remember that their situation is quite different from that of our earliest human ancestors, because the child is growing up in an environment where there is already a fully developed language, and is surrounded by adults who use that language and are teaching it to him. For example, it has been shown that the earliest words used by children are mainly the names of things and people ("Doll," "Spoon," "Mummy"): but this does not prove that the earliest words of primitive man were also the names of things and people. When the child learns the name of an object, he may then use it to express his wishes or demands: "Doll!" often means "Give me my doll!" or "I've dropped my doll: pick it up for me!"; the child is using language to get things done, and it is almost an accident of adult teaching that the words used to formulate the child's demands are mainly nouns, instead of words like "Bring!"; "Pick up!"; and so on.

One thing that we can perhaps learn from the small child is the kind of articulated utterance that comes easiest to a human being before he has learned the sound system of one particular language. The first articulate word pronounced by a child is often something like *da, ma, na, ba, ga,* or *wa.* The vowel is most commonly a short *ah* sound, and the consonant a nasal or a plosive. Nearly always, these early "words" consist of a consonant followed by a vowel or of a sequence of syllables of this type (*dadada,* etc.). When the child attempts to copy words used by adults, he at first tends to produce words of this form, so that "grandfather" may be rendered as *gaga*, "thank you" as *tata*, and "water" as *wawa*. This explains why, in so many languages, the nursery words for mother and father are *mama* or *dada* or *baba* or something similar: there is no magic inner connection between the idea of parenthood and words of this form: these just happen to be the first articulated sounds that the child makes, and the proud parent attributes a suitable meaning to them. Such words may also have been the first utterances of primitive man, though hardly with this meaning.

The languages of primitive peoples, and the history of languages in literate times, may throw some light on the origin of language by suggesting what elements in it are the most archaic. But again we have to be careful, because the language of the most primitive people living today is still a very ancient and sophisticated one, with half a million years of history behind it; and the earliest written records can take us back only a few thousand years. It is probable, of course, that in early times language changed more slowly than in historical times. The whole history of human culture has been one of an accelerating rate of change: it took man about half a million years to develop through the Old Stone Age to the higher material culture of the Middle and New Stone ages, but a mere 5,000 years or so for these to give way to the Bronze Age, and perhaps 1,000 for the Bronze Age to develop into the Iron Age; and since the Industrial Revolution, the pace has become dizzying. It is perhaps arguable that the rate of change in language has been parallel to that in material culture, and in that case the gap of half a million years between the origin of language and the first written records becomes a little less daunting. It remains daunting enough, however, and we must obviously be careful in theorizing about the remote past.

Still, we may be able to pick up some hints. For example, it is noticeable among primitive peoples how closely their languages are adapted to their material needs: in Eskimo, there is no single word for "snow," but a whole series of words for "new fallen snow," "hard snow," and so on; and in general a primitive people tends to have words for the specific things that are materially important to it (like the particular birds or plants that it eats), and to lump together other things (like birds or plants that it does not eat) under some generic expression. We may also find some evidence about the types of word and the types of expression which are oldest: there is a good deal to suggest that words of command (like "Give!"; "Strike!") are very archaic, since in the earliest known forms of many languages these imperative forms are identical with the simple stem of the verb, without any special ending added. Compare, for example, Latin *dic* ("say!") with *dicit* ("he says"), *dicunt* ("they say"), or *dicere* ("to say"): the form used for giving a command is the shortest, the most elementary. Some of the personal pronouns, like *me*, also seem to be very archaic, and so do vocatives (the forms of words used in addressing people).

A study of the higher animals can help us by suggesting what man was like in the prelinguistic stage, immediately before he became man. The expressive noises, signals, and gestures of the higher apes show us what man started from in his creation of language; but they cannot show us how he created language, for it is man alone who has broken through to the use of symbols: the apes, however expressive their signals may be, remain on the other side of language. Apes, of course, have smaller brains than men; and man's development, as part of his adaptive evolution, of a larger and more complex brain than any other creature was undoubtedly a prerequisite for the emergence of language.

The last source of evidence, the behavior of people suffering from speech defects, is probably the least helpful. The condition which has especially been referred to is *aphasia*, in which the power of speech is wholly or partially lost, often as a result of a brain injury. In recovering from aphasia, the patient to some extent repeats the process gone through by a child in learning to speak for the first time, and some psychologists have suggested that he also repeats the history of the human race in inventing language. It is difficult, however, to see the grounds for this belief, since language, though it uses inherited biological skills and aptitudes, is not itself a biological inheritance but a cultural one; and the kind of prehistory of language which has been constructed on evidence of this kind is not a very convincing one.

Emphasis on one type of evidence or another has led to rather different theories of the origin of language. Different authors, too, seem to mean different things when they talk about the origin of language: some are thinking especially of the prelanguage situation, and of the basic human skills and equipment that were a prerequisite for the invention of language; others are thinking more of the actual situations in which the first truly linguistic utterances took place; others again are thinking of the very early stages of language after its invention, and the ways in which it expanded its resources.

The Bow-wow Theory

One theory is that primitive language was an imitation of natural sounds, such as the cries of animals. This has been called the bow-wow theory. Supporters of the theory point to the large number of words in any language which are, it seems, directly imitative of natural sounds—words like *quack, cuckoo, peewit*. They add that many other words show a kind of "sound symbolism," enacting in sound whatever it is that they denote; examples of such words in English would be *splash, sludge, slush, grumble, grunt, bump,* and *sneeze*. It is certainly plausible to believe that a primitive hunter, wishing to tell his companions what kind of game he had found, may have imitated in gesture and sound whatever kind of animal it was—horse, or elephant, or quail; and this may well have played a part in the development of vocal symbols.

This theory, however, does not explain how language obtained its articulated structure. When we invent an imitative word like *whizz-bang* or *crump*, we use an already existing language system, with its vowels and consonants, its laws of word structure, and so on, and we make our imitative word conform to this pattern. But man in the pre-linguistic stage had no such language system, and his imitation of a horse or an elephant would simply be a whinnying or trumpeting sound, without the articulation characteristic of speech. Imitation of this kind may explain part of the primitive vocabulary, and it may have played a part in the transition from expressive cry to vocal symbol, but it cannot by itself account satisfactorily for the rise of language.

Moreover, we probably deceive ourselves about the extent and importance of sound symbolism in language. Because of our intimate knowledge of our language since our early years, and the way it is bound up with our whole emotional and intellectual life, the words that we use inevitably *seem* appropriate to what they mean, simply by constant association. It may be retorted that some groups of sounds really are appropriate to certain meanings, and this is shown by their occurrence in a number of words of similar meaning: for example, in English we find initial *fl-* in a number of words connected with fire and light (e.g., *flame, flare, flash*) and in an even larger number of words connected with a flying or waving kind of motion (e.g., *flail, flap, flaunt, flay, flicker, flog fluctuate, flurry, flutter*). But it is difficult to see any *inherent* appropriateness in the *fl-* sound for expressing ideas of flame or flickering motion: the sense of appropriateness surely arises from the fact that it occurs in all these words, not vice versa. And once a group of words like this exists in the language, new words may be coined on the same model (as perhaps happened with *flash* and *flap*), and words of similar form may develop new meanings on analogy with the members of the group (as has perhaps happened with *flourish*). But there are many other words in English which begin with *fl-*, which have nothing to do with flames or flickering, and yet which by long familiarity sound equally appropriate to their meanings, like *flange, flank, flannel, flask, flat, flesh, flimsy, flinch, flock,* and so on. It is noticeable that, when you learn a foreign language, the words that strike you as particularly appropriate in sound (or, sometimes, as grotesquely inappropriate) are very often ones that do not strike a native speaker in this way.

The Pooh-pooh Theory

A second theory of the origins of language has been called the pooh-pooh theory. This argues that language arose from instinctive emotional cries, expressive for example of pain or joy. On this view, the earliest linguistic utterances were interjections, simple exclamations expressive of some emotional state. This theory, it seems to me, suggests some of the material which language may have used, rather than the process by which it arose. The theory does nothing to explain the articulated nature of language, and it does little to bridge the gap between expressive cry and symbol. We can, indeed, imagine how, by association, an emotional cry may have become a signal: a cry of fear or of pain, for example, could easily become a signal which warned the group of danger; but this level has already been reached by the higher animals, which react to signals of this kind; the further step from trigger stimulus to symbol must also be explained. And the theory does not suggest any motivation for this development; a tremendous task like the creation of language would surely have been undertaken only under the pressure of man's needs.

The Ding-dong Theory

A third theory is the so-called nativistic theory, nicknamed the ding-dong theory. This begins from a fact we have already noticed, namely, that there is an apparently mysterious harmony between sound and sense in a language. On this basis, the theory argues that primitive man had a peculiar instinctive faculty, by which every external impression that he received was given vocal expression. Every sensory impression was like the striking of a bell, producing a corresponding utterance. The trouble with this theory is that it explains nothing: it merely describes the facts in a different terminology, and so is only a pseudotheory.

The Yo-he-ho Theory

A fourth theory, put forward by the nineteenth-century scholar Noiré, has been called the yo-he-ho theory. This envisages language arising from the noises made by a group of men engaged in joint labor or effort—moving a tree trunk, lifting a rock. We all know from experience that, while performing work of this kind, we make involuntary vocal noises. While exerting powerful muscular effort we trap the breath in our lungs by tightly closing the glottis (the vocal cords); in the intervals of relaxation between the bursts of effort, we open the glottis and release the air, making various grunting and groaning noises in the process; since a stop is released, these noises often contain a consonantal sound as well as a vowel. Vocal noises of this kind might then develop into words, meaning such things as "heave!"; "rest!"; "lift!" This theory has two great virtues: it gives a plausible explanation for the origin of the consonant-vowel structure of language, and it envisages the origin of language in a situation involving human cooperation, with adequate motivation. It also envisages the earliest speech utterances as commands, and we have already seen that there is some linguistic evidence for the antiquity of such imperative forms. Against the theory, it has been argued that it postulates too advanced a form of social cooperation: language, it is argued, would be necessary *before* men could embark on the kind of complex communal labor that the theory demands. I am not sure that this objection is very compelling: we must surely envisage language and cooperative human labor arising *simultaneously*, each making the other possible; they would continually react on one another, so that there would be a progressive development from the simplest utterances and acts of cooperation to the most complex speech and division of labor.

A variant of the theory has recently been elaborated by A. S. Diamond. He agrees that the first articulated words were commands, uttered simultaneously with the execution of violent arm movements, but argues that all the evidence shows that the most primitive words did not mean such things as "Haul!" but rather such things as "Strike!"; "Cut!"; "Break!"; He therefore envisages the rise of language in requests for assistance from one man to another in situations where maximum bodily effort was required. He does not speculate on the exact nature of these situations, but presumably they might be such things as tool making, the breaking off of tree branches, and the killing of animals during hunting. Such things might occur at a more primitive stage of human society than the communal heaving suggested by Noiré.

The Gesture Theory

A fifth theory of the origins of language takes the view that gesture language preceded speech. Supporters of this theory point to the extensive use of gestures by animals of many different kinds, and the highly developed systems of gesture used by some primitive peoples. One of the popular examples is the sign language formerly used by the Indians of North America; this was an elaborate system of gestures which was used for negotiations between tribes that spoke different languages. It is certainly true that speech and gesture are closely intertwined; the centers in the brain which control hand movements are closely linked with those that control the vocal organs, and it seems highly probable that speech and gesture grew up together. This does not prove, however, that gesture came *first*. And, while it is true that animals use gestures, it is also true that they use cries: the chimpanzee makes signals and expresses its feelings both by bodily movements and by vocal noises, and the same was probably true of early man.

An extreme form of the gesture theory argues that speech arose very late (round about 3500 BC) and was derived from early pictorial writing; this writing itself, it is argued, was derived from gesture language. I must say that I find this incredible. We are asked to believe that man lacked speech right through the Old and New Stone ages, and did not develop it until the time of the city civilizations of the early Bronze Age. But it is difficult to believe that man could have built up the elaborate cultural apparatus of the New Stone Age (agriculture, pottery, weaving, house building, religious burial) without the aid of speech; for a gesture language, however highly developed, has grave disadvantages compared with a spoken language. To use a gesture language you have to have your hands free; but as soon as man becomes a tool maker and a craftsman his hands cease to be free; and the times when primitive man needed to communicate most urgently must have been precisely the times when he had a tool or a weapon in his hand. It is in fact arguable that it was just this preoccupation of man's hands with tools and weapons that led to the increased importance of vocal language compared with gestures; and this would support the view that spoken language goes right back to the beginning of man's career as tool maker. Gesture, too, has the disadvantage that it cannot be used in the dark, or when the users are separated by obstructions like trees—a serious disadvantage for a hunting band, which would surely develop hunting calls and similar cries. Nor can a gesture be used to attract the attention of somebody who is looking in another direction, and so it has very limited value as a warning of the approach of danger. None of these disadvantages of gesture can *prove* that early man had a spoken language, but they do suggest that he had very powerful motives for creating one.

A more attractive version of the gesture theory is the *mouth gesture* theory, which was strongly argued by Sir Richard Paget and has recently been supported by an Icelandic professor, Alexander Jóhannesson. Paget argues that primitive man at first communicated by gestures; as his intelligence and technique developed he needed more exact gestures, but at the same time found that his eyes and hands were more occupied by his arts and crafts. But the gestures of the hands were unconsciously copied by movements of the tongue, lips, and mouth; and when the man was unable to go on gesturing with his hands because of their other uses, the mouth gestures continued without them, and he discovered that if air was blown through the mouth or nose the gesture became audible as whispered speech; if he simultaneously sang or roared or grunted, he produced voiced speech. To support his theory of the sympathetic movements of the speech organs, Paget quotes a passage from Darwin's book *The Expression of the Emotions:*

> There are other actions which are commonly performed under certain circumstances independently of habit, and which seem to be due to imitation or some kind of sympathy. Thus, persons cutting anything with a pair of scissors may be seen to move their jaws simultaneously with the blades of the scissors. Children learning to write often twist about their tongue as their fingers move, in a ridiculous fashion!

Language was thus produced by a sort of pantomime, the tongue and lips mimicking the movements of the hands in a gesture. As an elementary example, Paget takes the movement of the mouth, tongue, and jaws as in eating, as a gesture sign meaning "eat." If, while making this sign, we blow air through the vocal cavities and switch on voice, we produce the sounds *mnyum mnyum* or *mnya mnya*, which, Paget says, would be universally understood. Similarly, the action of sucking a liquid in small quantities into the mouth produces words like *sip* or *sup*. Paget goes on to analyze large numbers of words in terms of mouth gestures of this kind, and this work has been continued by Jóhannesson, who has examined large numbers of the basic words of the earliest known languages. Some of these analyses strike me as fanciful, and there are times when one feels that, with sufficient ingenuity, any movement of the tongue could be construed as a gesture representing anything one liked. Nevertheless, the theory has considerable plausibility, and must be taken seriously. It has the merit of accounting for the articulated nature of speech, and of giving an explanation for the way the linkage was effected between sound and meaning.

The Musical Theory

A sixth theory sees the origin of language in song, or at any rate sees speech and music as emerging from something earlier that included both. This theory was put forward by the great Danish linguist Otto Jespersen. He thought that the bow-wow, pooh-pooh, and yo-he-ho theories could all explain the origins of parts of language, but that none of them could explain the whole of it. His own method was to trace the history of language backwards, to see what the long-term trends were, and then to assume that these same trends had existed since the beginning of language. By this means he arrived at the view that primitive language consisted of very long words, full of difficult jaw-breaking

sounds; that it used tone and pitch more than later languages, and a
wider range of musical intervals; and that it was more passionate and
more musical than later languages. Earlier still, language was a kind of
song without words; it was not communicative, but merely expressive;
the earliest language was not matter-of-fact or practical, but poetic and
emotional, and love in particular was the most powerful emotion for
eliciting outbursts of music and song. "Language," he writes, "was born
in the courting days of mankind; the first utterances of speech I fancy
to myself like something between the nightly love-lyrics of puss upon
the tiles and the melodious love-songs of the nightingale." A romantic
picture.

It may be doubted, however, whether the trends in language are as
constant and universal as Jespersen thinks. His theory assumes that the
same kinds of general change have taken place in all languages throughout their history. But we know nothing of languages before the Bronze
Age; even if there has been a universal trend in language since the beginnings of Bronze Age civilization (which is by no means certain), it
does not follow that the same trend occurred in the Old Stone Age,
when man's circumstances were entirely different. Moreover, we have a
historical knowledge of relatively few of the world's languages: of the
two thousand languages spoken today, only a handful have records going back to the pre-Christian era.

The Contact Theory

Finally, mention may be made of the contact theory, which has
recently been advanced by G. Révész, a former professor of psychology
at Amsterdam. He sees language as arising through man's instinctive
need for contact with his fellows, and he works out a series of stages by
which language may have developed. First comes the contact sound,
which is not communicative, but merely expresses the individual's need
for contact with his fellows; such are the noises made by gregarious
animals. Next comes the cry, which is communicative, but which is
directed to the environment generally, not to an individual; examples
are mating calls and the cries of young nestlings in danger. Then there
is the call, which differs from the cry in being directed to an individual;
it is the demand for the satisfaction of some desire, and is found in
domestic animals (begging) and speechless infants (crying for their
mother); the call is seen as the starting point for both music and language. Finally comes the word, which has symbolic function and is
found only in man. Révész thinks that the earliest speech was an "imperative language," consisting only of commands; this later developed
into mature human language, which contains also statements and ques-

tions. Révész's sequence of stages is carefully worked out, and is made very plausible. He does not, however, explain how human language came to be articulated; and he places undue emphasis on the instinctive need for contact as a motive for the invention of language, while rather neglecting the urgent practical motives in cooperative labor which must surely have impelled early man.

The Probabilities

What are we to make of this welter of theories? It is plain that no finality is possible at present, and that it is merely a matter of weighing the probabilities. It seems to me that we should attach great weight to the question of motivation in the origin of language, since such a great intellectual achievement would hardly have been possible except under the pressure of definite needs. Since the basic function of language is to influence the behavior of our fellow men, this would favor theories that emphasize the origins of language in situations of social cooperation: such for example are the yo-he-ho theory and Diamond's variant of it. However, other theories, such as the bow-wow theory and the mouth gesture theory, can also be adapted to views of this kind. In the second place, I think we should attach great importance to the articulatedness of language, as seen for example in its vowel and consonant structure; and it seems to me the weakness of many theories that they do nothing to explain this structure; the theories that come off best on this count are the yo-he-ho theory and the mouth gesture theory. But at present we cannot reach absolute certainty.

We must also remain in doubt about the nature of the earliest language, and we do not even know if there was one original language or whether language was invented independently at several different times and places. Jespersen, we have seen, postulates a primitive language that was musical and passionate; he believes that it was very irregular; that it dealt with the concrete and particular rather than the abstract and general; that it contained very long words full of difficult combinations of sounds; and indeed that the earliest utterances consisted of whole sentences rather than single words. Somewhat similar views have been advanced by investigators who have attached great significance to the babbling stages of child speech. But Révész thinks that the earliest language consisted solely of commands; so does Diamond, who argues that these were single words and had the structure consonant-vowel-consonant-vowel (like *bada* or *taka*). The bow-wow theory, on the other hand, demands a primitive language full of imitative sounds like the howling of wolves or the trumpeting of elephants. In the absence of certainty about the origins of language, we must obviously lack certainty about the form which that language took (though the kind of language envisaged by Révész or Diamond seems more plausible than that envisaged by Jespersen).

Inevitably we remain in the realm of more or less plausible speculation as long as we are dealing with a period which has left us no record of its language. [Only when] we reach periods in which writing was practiced [are we] on much firmer ground.

FOR DISCUSSION AND REVIEW

1   Why, according to Barber, does it seem probable "that speech arose at the same time as tool making and the earliest forms of specifically human cooperation"?

2   Why does Barber give "great weight to the question of motivation in the origin of language"?

3   What types of evidence give us clues as to the origin of language? How reliable is the evidence?

4   Briefly describe each of the different theories of the origin of language. Why does the "Yo-he-ho" theory seem somewhat more attractive than the others? What do the

names that have been given to each of the theories suggest about the theories themselves?

5   In his discussion of sound symbolism in language, Barber refers to the initial fl- that occurs in a number of words connected with fire or light or with a flying or waving motion. What other examples of sound symbolism do you find in English? (Consider, for example, the initial sn-, the final -er, and the low back vowel sound as in loop.) Does sound symbolism help account for the origin of language?

3

The Linguist and Language

Albert B. Cook III

Although we all use language daily, we tend to take it for granted, never giving it a second thought. Few of us have stopped to think about what language really is. In this selection, Professor Cook of the University of Kansas examines the nature of the phenomenon that we call language and the role of the linguist in an effort to clear up misconceptions that many people have. Before reading Cook's discussion, formulate your own definitions of *linguist* and *language*. How do they compare with Cook's definitions?

To many people, a linguist is the same as a polyglot, one who can speak several languages fluently. For this reason, specialists in the field of linguistics have intermittently been looking for a better occupational word, though without success.[1] In professional usage, the linguist is a scholar who studies language objectively, observing it scientifically, recording the facts of language, and generalizing from them. The use of the term *scientific* should perhaps be soft-pedaled, because language is a human phenomenon which cannot be subclassified so neatly as the natural phenomena of the scientist; but so far as one is able to be scientific vis-à-vis human conduct, the linguist certainly adheres to the scientific method. The facts of language which he may observe include its sounds, forms, and syntactic arrangement, and from these he formulates general rules which describe how a specific language is actually used. In addition, the linguist can observe the facts of a language for the purpose of describing its historical development (historical linguistics), its regional and social differences (linguistic geography, or dialectology), its relationship to other languages (comparative linguistics), or

---

[1] The term *linguistician* has been suggested, but it is usually shouted down by those who feel that it is too fancy, or too much like "mortician." Occasionally the expression *linguistic scientist* is used interchangeably with *linguist*, but to the layman it is too close to the laboratory and the test tube.

its application to other fields, particularly education (applied linguistics). Because the field is so broad and touches so many facets of human conduct, it is a shame that so little real awareness or understanding of it has managed to percolate down to the schools.

The linguist, primarily concerned with describing the language as it is, should be differentiated from certain other scholars who are also involved, at least peripherally, in language, and usually in the field of English. These include the rhetorician, who is primarily interested in effective written or spoken communication, and the literary critic, who makes value judgments about the worth and effectiveness, the literary merit, of the works of a writer's creative imagination. It sometimes happens that an English teacher can wear all three of these hats. Your instructor in this course, insofar as he assists you in objectively viewing your language, is a linguist. But if he teaches freshman composition, too, he is a rhetorician, using in part the findings of the linguist about social reactions to language to demonstrate to his writers how best to order their prose. Finally, if he also teaches a sophomore literary survey course, he is a critic, using as the basis of his subjective judgments on literature some of the opinions of the rhetorician on what constitutes good writing. Unfortunately, the relationships aren't always this simple, for even in the most enlightened English departments, when specialization is the natural order of things the communication between the linguist and his colleagues sometimes breaks down because of misunderstanding.

Part of the misunderstanding comes from the failure of the linguist (and his lay supporters) to make completely clear his attitude toward language. Too often, he is viewed as one who believes that "everything goes" in language, that "one expression is as good as another," especially in relation to such shibboleths as *ain't*. Actually, he tries to show that in certain communities, under specified conditions, *ain't* (originally a contraction of *am not*, and thus as respectable in its parentage as *isn't* or *aren't*) is in perfectly good spoken usage by all the leading citizens. Some people, unfortunately, see red where *ain't* is concerned, and they won't wait to hear the full explanation: the linguist isn't sanctioning the use of this heinous four-letter word in communities where the leading citizens abjure it; he is simply describing the facts. Other colleagues, depressed by the linguist's descriptions of the grammatical facts of a language, feel that he is complicating things unnecessarily, particularly when they feel they themselves have a sufficient grasp of the "grammar" they learned in school. Besides, they add, with his objective views on usage and his formulaic statements of grammar, the linguist is doing great violence to the language handed down to us from Shakespeare, Milton, and Wordsworth. Finally, there are those colleagues, more amused than alarmed, who profess themselves nonplussed by the pre-occupation of some linguists (particularly those who are affiliated with the anthropology departments of major universities) with the "savage tongues" of the American Indians, or of Africa and the Far East. How, they ask, can one take techniques devised to analyze "inarticulate babblings of savages" and use them in the same way on the civilized languages of the West?

This situation is not as pervasive as it was even ten years ago, but there is still a great need for all educators, and laymen as well, to under-stand more thoroughly the work of the linguist, even if they cannot bring themselves to approve of it. Currently, this need is greatest amongst the English teachers in the public schools, who need to be shown how new language discoveries can benefit them. One place to start is with the future teachers, and the best possible footing comes from knowing what the linguist means when he uses [a term such as *language*, a term which has] suffered from multiplicity of meaning, thereby causing more confusion among the already confused laity.

Consider the term *language*. Even though this might seem silly, try to give your definition of it. Here is a word that all of us have used without a second thought, a term which is so obvious that we feel we "know" its "meaning" without inquiring further. Consequently, by now you have probably come up with an answer very much like:

(1) Language is a means of communication.

If we consider this definition for a moment, we must agree that it is just a little bit circular. Furthermore, what is the medium of this "means of communication"? We could name a variety of ways by which communication is carried on: noises in the throat, scribbles on paper, scratches on stone, semaphore, wigwagging flags, smoke signals, Morse code, hand-and-arm signals, deaf-and-dumb signs, and anything else which might "communicate something."

It is a mistake to say that everything on this list is a summation of the instances of language. Consider, first of all, something of the matter of precedence. Some means of communication are less important than others, or are based directly upon them. After pondering this list for a moment, you have probably concluded that all of the various code and signaling devices are secondary to writing—and you are right. The Morse code, for instance, is a system of dots and dashes which is based directly upon the alphabet, and thus could not be devised without the clear and familiar presence of an alphabet system. It is true that before the era of the automatic writing machines, experienced telegraphers had de-vised a rather large inventory of abbreviations and shortcuts for the commonly used words and expressions in their work, but most of us have never gotten beyond a rather rudimentary knowledge of the Morse system, acquired in our Boy Scout days. At any rate, we can agree that these systems are dependent upon writing, and only a rather obvious sort of hand-and-arm signal could be used with any ease by anyone who was illiterate.

Consequently, we are left with only two means of communication which might be judged primary: noises we make with our throats (speaking) and scribbles we make on a surface (writing). Which is primary? The answer, you would say, is very simple. Remembering that the great tradition of Chaucer, Shakespeare, Milton, the Bible, the whole of literature, is handed down to us in writing; remembering that your basic medium of learning is the written textbook; remembering all of the agony you and your composition teacher put into your written work; perhaps remembering the old injunction to "put it into writing" so that you (or someone else) will remember it—you will immediately leap to the conclusion that:

(2) Language is a *written* means of communication.

Let's look at that a little more closely. Already we can probably frame some rather vague objections to this conclusion. For instance, there are hundreds of different groups of people who have no writing system whatsoever. It is very easy to dismiss them as ignorant, primitive, savage groups, of little account in the modern world, but is it fair to say that they have no language? On the contrary, they probably communicate with one another quite as easily as we do.

Just to make the situation a little plainer, consider the following pieces of information.

1. Mankind was speaking long before the dawn of recorded history. Writing . . . is a relatively recent discovery. It is unfortunately true that we know very little about the peoples who leave behind only bits of tools or shards of pottery for archaeologists to uncover, and that "finds" like the Dead Sea Scrolls are far more spectacular, but this does not alter the historical precedence of speech over writing.

2. It is easy to be misled by the emotional appeal of great literature. Yet we must consider that such masterpieces as *Beowulf*, the Norse sagas, the Homeric epics, the "fairy tales" collected by Grimm, even a goodly part of the Bible, were all handed down intact in an oral tradition before someone decided to set them down in writing. Great literature was conceived and passed on without the benefit of writing, and it should also be remembered that the rhyme and rhythm techniques of poetry (and also of Elizabethan drama) were devised originally as aids to memory.

In connection with this, have you ever had the experience of reading to a young child one of his favorite stories? If, in the course of your reading, you skipped a passage or simply substituted a word, the chances are that you were promptly corrected. The truth of the matter is that all preliterate societies and peoples have remarkable memories and are quite able, even willing, to correct the storyteller who alters the story. Storytellers themselves were not selected for their memories—everyone had a good memory—but rather for their storytelling ability. Today, the sad truth probably is that because of our reliance upon writing, we have allowed a good portion of our faculties for memorization to atrophy.

3. But, you will argue, speech is lost the instant it is uttered by the speaker, whereas there is something permanent and lasting about writing. *Littera scripta manet,* as the old expression goes: "The written word remains." There is no denying this; but unfortunately there is a lot of writing left in the world which is scarcely more than scribbling or ornate carving, simply because there is no one around to decipher it for us. In the last chapter of his book *Lost Languages,* P. E. Cleator describes several of these written remains which give every indication of remaining unknown to us: the Cretan Linear A script, the so-called Eteocyprian script of Cyprus, the Etruscan inscriptions, the Mayan glyphs in the Yucatan, and the *rongo rongo* script of Easter Island, to name a few.[2] Those who could speak the languages inscribed have long since departed, taking with them their knowledge of the correspondence between sound and marking. Indeed, only the written word remains.

4. Finally, those of us who are poor spellers are ruefully aware of the imperfect correspondencies between our alphabet and our language. We have heard of writing systems commonly called "phonetic" in which there is a close correspondency between the letter and the sound. The systems of Spanish and Finnish come most readily to mind. But even here, the relationship is imperfect. And of course in English, there is a good deal of meaningless variation, exemplified by the diverse spelling of the *sh* sound as in *mission,* not to mention the pedantic superfluities in such spellings as *debt, psychology, knight,* and *phthisic.*

By now, I trust that you are convinced of the actual primacy of speaking over writing, and are willing to alter our definition to:

(3) Language is a *vocal* means of communication.

Thus we show that writing is a secondary language form based upon speech, and that Morse code, semaphores, Navy signal flags, deaf-and-dumb signals are all of them tertiary, based upon writing.

[2] (New York, 1959), pp. 161–177.

But still the definition is incomplete. What, for instance, is it that we are vocalizing? We don't just make a lot of noises; everything we utter is set forth in a meaningful order which we have somehow learned, and from which we depart only within narrow limits, lest we fail to communicate. In order to have communication, we must have system; otherwise we are simply making noises to no purpose. Thus we amend our definition:

(4) Language is a vocal *system* of communication.

The noises in our throats must adhere to some preconceived order and arrangement. All languages have system; the reason why languages other than our own sound like gibberish is because we have not mastered the complexity of their systems. In addition, this system has a framework of ideas built up within it, so that every utterance we make communicates these ideas to the auditor, who in turn responds by framing the same ideas, assuming we have communicated properly. Some of these ideas are lexical, conveying "dictionary" meaning, while others are grammatical, serving only the purpose of maintaining the system. We will. call the former *symbols*, and the latter *grammatical signals*, both of which we must first learn in order to react to them or utter them. Thus we can further revise the definition to read:

(5) Language is a system of vocal *symbols and grammatical signals* used for communication.

Now let's further consider the nature of the "vocal symbols" in our definition. Take for example the semantic unit *dog*. We are all agreed that this word represents for us the general idea of *Canis domesticus*, with some emotional overtones, depending upon whether we remember a faithful pet, or were bitten once by one of those snarling creatures. Now, to make the problem more complex, consider as well the semantic units *chien, Hund, perro*, which represent respectively the French, German, and Spanish equivalents of our word *dog*. Some might notice that French *chien* seems to be derived from Latin *canis* and will likewise agree that German *Hund* is cognate with the English *hound*; but beyond that no one really can see how any one of these four words innately represents an idea of "dogginess," except that the speakers of the respective languages have all agreed arbitrarily upon the relationship of utterance and concept. In fact, one might almost argue that on the face of it, the infant's spoken *bow-wow* is ideationally more meaningful than *dog*.[3] Be it as it may, *dog* is in English the adult term, and

[3] It is instructive to note that even these onomatopoetic representations differ from language to language. See Noel Perrin, "Old Macberlitz Had a Farm," *New Yorker* (January 27, 1962), 28–29; with additions in the February 24, 1962, issue, p. 125.

in recognition of the fact that it is only our tacit agreement of utterance and idea at work here, and not any innate relationship bound up in the utterance, we can further alter our definition:

(6) Language is a system of *arbitrary* vocal symbols and grammatical signals used for communication.

We have now built up the first part of our definition sufficiently well to make that last part seem weak. What is it that this system of arbitrary vocal symbols and grammatical signals can do? We have already listed communication, which suggests the imparting of ideas. But we don't simply listen passively to ideas all the time. Rather, we often find ourselves called upon to lend a helping hand, to assist in an enterprise, to rouse ourselves to action. Thus language is called upon not only for communication, but also for interaction.

But this isn't all. So far we have only implied that this is a human action. What of the so-called language of monkeys, for instance, or dolphins? Apparently they are able to communicate ideas, admittedly rather simple, and interact by means of an arbitrary vocal system. We are told that monkey colonies have signals which seem to mean danger, or food, or a predator. How does human language differ from these rude animal noises? The difference lies in the fact that whereas the monkeys can signal to one another the general concept of *food*, they are unable to communicate information and ideas which they might have acquired about the particular food in question. On the other hand, humans are able to say, "Don't eat that, it's poisonous!" (based upon the recollection of someone's sad experience, or what one has been told about someone who allegedly ate the food); or, "Don't eat that, it's not good for you" (in the situation of parent to child with a hunk of candy only a few minutes before dinner); or, "Eat that, it's good for you" (any parent speaking to any child about spinach, about which we have acquired a dubious, but time-honored notion of nutritious goodness); all the way through a scale of associations. We thus have passed on a whole complex of ideas, some of which are the result of personal experience, others of hearsay, and still others of cultural transference, even taboo. This is what makes language a purely human phenomenon, and thus we are ready to add to our definition:

(7) Language is a system of arbitrary vocal symbols and grammatical signals used for communication, *interaction*, and *cultural transmission*.

This seems pretty good, but it is still a little bit impersonal. Who, we might ask, uses this instrument for communication, interaction, and cultural transmission? Obviously, the speakers of the language, but to

refer to them in this way will force us to use in our definition the very
word we want to define. Perhaps we should take our hint from Leonard
Bloomfield: "Within certain communities successive utterances are
alike or partly alike. . . . Any such community is a *speech community*."[4] Thus we can complete our definition both by making it less impersonal and by specifying the users:

(8) A language is a system of arbitrary vocal symbols and grammatical signals by means of which *the members of a speech community* communicate, interact, and transmit their culture.

Our definition follows that of Edgar L. Sturtevant,[5] with the addition of the phrase *transmit their culture*, which, as we showed, makes
explicit the human quality of language; and the phrase *grammatical
signals*, which clarifies the difference between the lexical inventory of
the language and the nonlexical portion which orders and regulates the
system of the language. We can quote several other definitions as well
for the sake of comparison:

Language is a purely human and non-instinctive method of
communicating ideas, emotions, and desires by means of a system of
voluntarily produced symbols. These symbols are, in the first instance, auditory and they are produced by the so-called "organs of
speech."

EDWARD SAPIR, *Language* (1921)

A language is an arbitrary system of articulated sounds made
use of by a group of humans as a means of carrying on the affairs of
their society.

W. NELSON FRANCIS, *The Structure of American English* (1958)

[Language is] a system of arbitrary vocal symbols by which
thought is conveyed from one human being to another.

JOHN P. HUGHES, *The Science of Language* (1962)

Whatever the definition, it must include directly, or by close implication, all of the following attributes of language:

1. Language has system.   5. Language is noninstinctive.
2. Language is vocal.   6. Language is a social activity.
3. Language is arbitrary.   7. Language is related to culture.
4. Language is a human activity.   8. Language changes.

4 "A Set of Postulates for the Science of Language," *Language*, II (1926); reprinted
  in Martin Joos (ed.), *Readings in Linguistics* (3d ed.: New York, 1963), p. 26.
5 *An Introduction to Linguistic Science* (New Haven, 1947), pp. 2–3.

FOR DISCUSSION AND REVIEW

1   What, according to Cook, is a linguist? How is the linguist differentiated from the rhetorician and the literary critic?

2   Why does Cook feel that educators and laymen alike need to understand more thoroughly the work of the linguist?

3   Do you consider Cook's definition of "language" complete? Why or why not?

4   Summarize Cook's arguments for the actual primacy of speech over writing.

5   Illustrate with three examples the difference between "symbols" and "grammatical signals."

6   What does Cook mean when he says that language is "arbitrary," "is a social activity," "changes"?

4
Language, Thought, and Culture

Peter Woolfson

As far back as 1836, Wilhelm von Humboldt, in *Linguistic Variability and Intellectual Development*, looked at language as a tool man uses to represent ideas in sentences. His work prefigured the emphasis on the relationship between language and thought later developed by Edward Sapir in *Language* (1921) and popularized by Benjamin Lee Whorf. The so-called Sapir-Whorf hypothesis that language shapes reality is probably one of the most controversial hypotheses in linguistic anthropology and psycholinguistics. In the following article, Peter Woolfson examines the limitations and potentialities of Whorf's linguistic relativity hypothesis. Woolfson is professor of anthropology at the University of Vermont.

PSYCHOLINGUISTS and linguistic anthropologists share a common concern with the relationship between language and thought. Several questions have been raised about this relationship, but the dominant one can be stated very simply: does the language we speak determine the way we think? One well-known attempt to answer the question is the *linguistic relativity hypothesis* (also called the Sapir-Whorf hypothesis or the Whorfian hypothesis).[1] In essence, the hypothesis suggests that a given language, especially in its grammar, provides its speakers with habitual grooves of expression which predispose these speakers to see the world in ready-made patterns. Since grammars vary from language to language, it is likely that the habitual patterns of thought vary from language to language. If so, the world view of a speaker of a particular language will be different from the world view of a speaker of a different language. Although the hypothe-

[1] Benjamin L. Whorf, *Language, Thought, and Reality*, ed. J. B. Carroll (New York: John Wiley & Sons, 1964).

sis seems to affirm the view that language determines thought, one should remember that it concentrates on habitual patterns; and habitual patterns may be ignored or circumvented. What is necessary is that we become aware of these patterns by conscious introspection, scientific study, or cross-cultural comparison.

Why are habitual patterns of expression so important? We all have approximately the same set of physical organs for perceiving reality— eyes to see, ears to hear, noses to smell, tongues to taste, and skins to feel. Reality should be the same for us all. Our nervous systems, however, are being bombarded by a continual flow of sensations of different kinds, intensities, and durations. It is obvious that all of these sensations do not reach our consciousness; some kind of filtering system reduces them to manageable proportions. The Whorfian hypothesis suggests that the filtering system is one's language. Our language, in effect, provides us with a special pair of glasses that heightens certain perceptions and dims others. Thus, while all sensations are received by the nervous system, only some are brought to the level of consciousness. One of Whorf's classic examples, *snow*, illustrates the role of language in this process:

> We have the same word for falling snow, snow on the ground, snow packed hard like ice, slushy snow, wind-driven flying snow—whatever the situation may be. To an Eskimo, this all-inclusive word would be almost unthinkable; he would say that falling snow, slushy snow, and so on, are sensually and operationally different, different things to contend with; he uses different words for them and for other kinds of snow. The Aztecs go even farther than we in the opposite direction with "cold," "ice," and "snow" all represented by the same basic word. . . .[2]

Although Whorf demonstrated that different languages use words differently to classify reality, he also indicated by his techniques of illustration that these concepts can be expressed, in a language that lacks them, by other means. Thus, the different types of snow may be described by adjectival words and phrases. Using these alternatives in English grammar, he makes it possible for us to visualize the different types of snow and to perceive the differences among them. Because the differences are specifically labeled, we become conscious of them. The important point to remember is that we are not *habitually conscious* of these distinctions. But if it becomes necessary for us to perceive these distinctions, as a skier might with snow, then they would become conscious, and the vocabulary or descriptive items would follow. In the case of the skier, he borrows his terms for snow from the more specialized vocabulary of the Austrians.

2 Whorf, p. 216.

Snow, however, is an example of a word with obvious cultural and environmental emphases. In many instances the relationship between cultural emphasis and vocabulary is much less apparent. For example, Americans are a mobile people and transportation plays an extremely important role culturally in our society. And yet we use the word *go* whether we are going by foot, car, train, or plane. Germans, on the other hand, use *gehen* when they go by foot, and *fahren* when they go by vehicle. The Navaho, according to Kluckholn and Leighton, make an even more complex set of distinctions:

> When a Navaho says that he went somewhere he never fails to specify whether it was afoot, astride, by wagon, auto, train, or airplane. This is done partly by using different verb stems which indicate whether the traveler moved under his own steam or was transported, partly by naming the actual means. . . .
>
> Moreover the Navaho language insists upon another type of splitting of the generic idea of "going" to which German is as indifferent as English. The Navaho always differentiates between starting to go, going along, arriving at, returning from a point. . . .[3]

And so, although transportation is a major cultural emphasis in American society, our word *go* is certainly considerably less precise than the terms used by the Navaho for this activity. It becomes apparent, then, that even when an activity has considerable cultural emphasis, certain perceptions may be heightened by the language while others may remain dim.

Does having separate words for different aspects of a thing or an event really make a difference in our consciousness, our awareness? For example, we commonly make distinctions between the colors *purple, blue, green, yellow, orange,* and *red.* If we have special interests like painting or dress designing, we may have a much wider vocabulary which includes distinctions between shades such as "cerise," "burgundy," or "magenta." These distinctions, however, are not part of the ordinary vocabulary of the American male, for instance. Investigations show that other languages are more restricted in their color vocabulary than English. The Shona of Rhodesia have only three major terms: *cips^wuka* (orange, red, purple and some blue); *citema* (blue and some green); and *cicena* (green and yellow). The Bassa of Liberia have only two major color terms: *hui* which represents purple, blue, and green; and *zīza* which represents yellow, orange, and red.[4] In one sense, these more restricted vocabularies do not affect consciousness. If the speaker

[3] Clyde Kluckhohn and Dorothea Leighton, *The Navaho* (New York: Doubleday & Company, 1962), pp. 274–275.

[4] H. A. Gleason, Jr., *An Introduction to Descriptive Linguistics*, rev. ed. (New York: Holt, Rinehart and Winston, 1961), pp. 4–5.

of one of these languages finds it necessary to make color distinctions not indicated by his color terms, he can still express the distinction by using the objects in the environment—"that's leaf *citema*" or "that's sky *citema*," for example. On the other hand, psycholinguists like Lantz, Brown, and Lenneberg have shown that having a number of terms for color distinctions is particularly useful for remembering colors that have been seen at an earlier time.[5] The more color terms the subjects in these experiments had, the better their memories were for sorting out the colors they had seen. These examples show that there is a relationship between vocabulary, cultural emphasis, and habitual consciousness.

But does the language of a speaker provide him with a structure for seeing the world in ready-made patterns? In other words, is the Whorfian hypothesis valid? It should be obvious that the Whorfian hypothesis is just that, a hypothesis: an idea to be tested, an informed guess. In spite of numerous attempts at verification, it has never been satisfactorily proved or disproved. But it remains plausible. For example, the grammatical categories of singular and plural are important ones in English grammar, so important that they are expressed redundantly:

> One boy goes outside.
> Two boys go outside.

Plurality, in these examples, is reiterated by the use of a number word, a noun suffix, and a specific verbal form. Singular and plural are categories that can hardly be ignored. A speaker of English finds it natural to divide his universe into things that are either singular or plural. To a speaker of Taos, an American Indian language, however, this view would represent a gross oversimplification. According to Trager:

> . . . In the Taos linguistic universe there is no such simple distinction: some things are indeed unitary, and others are multiple, but some unitary things can be multiple only in sets, while others are multiple as aggregates: moreover, a set can be unitary, if it is inanimate, or it can be multiple—but then only if it is animate. . . .[6]

Thus, the Taos Indian classifies the objects in his universe differently from a native speaker of English. The Whorfian hypothesis suggests that because of this difference in classification, the Taos Indian actually sees the world differently from a native speaker of English.

The apparent relationship between grammar and world view can be seen in the basic types of sentence structures. Probably the most typical kind of sentence in English is the declarative sentence made up of a

[5] Joseph DeVito, *The Psychology of Speech and Language* (New York: Random House, 1970), p. 200.
[6] George L. Trager, *Languages of the World* (Buffalo, New York: unpublished manuscript), IV, 17.

subject, verb, and direct object and associated with our conceptual focus of an actor, an action, and the object of an action. For example, the answer to the question "What happened?" could be either

John	*dropped*	*the ball*
Subject	Verb	Direct Object
Actor	Action	Object of Action

or

The car	*hit*	*the bridge*
Subject	Verb	Direct Object
Actor	Action	Object of Action

This sentence form is so common in English that we use the form metaphorically without being the least bit conscious of imposing the form "actor, action, object of action" where it does not literally apply. As a result, English commonly produces sentences such as:

Communism	*threatens*	*Southeast Asia*
Subject	Verb	Direct Object
Actor	Action	Object of Action

Northern Chinese, however, does not ordinarily use this kind of sentence structure. If one asked a speaker of Chinese the equivalent of the question "What happened?" he would probably get the answer in the form of *topic* and *comment*. In other words, where the American would say, "John dropped the ball," the Chinese would say, "Ball-particle (type of object)-dropping." It is not necessary for the Chinese to indicate the actor or the time of the action. Speakers of English, in contrast, specify whether the action was in the past or not. However, they do have a sentence form where the actor is not specified: subject and passive verb: "The ball was dropped." Nevertheless, many speakers of English feel uneasy about this construction; it does not appear complete. Since only two of the three habitual components are present, they feel compelled to ask, "Dropped by whom?" In short, Americans and Chinese have different basic sentence structures which focus on different aspects of a situation.[7]

In order to deal systematically with the question of the validity of the Whorfian hypothesis, it is necessary to ask several other questions. First, is thought possible without speech? If it is, then at least some perceptions are possible without the mediation of language. Studies of animal behavior suggest some answers. W. H. Thorpe, an ethologist, maintains that all animals perceive—that is, anticipate and recognize.

[7] Charles F. Hockett, *A Course in Modern Linguistics* (New York: The Macmillan Company, 1958), pp. 201–203.

He writes, "Some essential ability to deal with events in time as in space is, by definition, to be expected throughout the world of living things."[8] For example, when a cat runs up a tree after seeing a dog, he exhibits this ability. The cat sees the dog (perception); it identifies the dog as dangerous (cognition); it foresees trouble (anticipation); it quickly checks its environment (evaluation); and it runs up the nearest tree (resolution). The cat does all this without the aid of language, and therefore it seems reasonable to assume that we are capable of some processes of thought without the mediation of language.

Second, are the grammars of various languages really different? Do not all languages possess features in common? Is there not a universal grammar, a general grammar of human languages? Are not the differences between languages, in reality, superficial, of little consequence in determining man's perceptions of reality? Let us look at the kinds of language universals that have been identified by Charles Hockett and Joseph Greenberg. Hockett[9] outlines thirteen design features of language, such as *semanticity* (shared associations), *arbitrariness* (non-iconicity), and *productivity* (open-endedness). Greenberg[10] discusses such universals as *multi-modality: indicative mode* (statement) and *imperative mode* (command), for example. There are, to be sure, very broad and general, universal statements about language that can be made to which no exceptions can be found. However, it is equally true that the grammars of the languages of the world show considerable variety in the devices they employ to classify reality. It is this level of classification, dissection, and organization, the level of diversity rather than universality, with which Whorf's linguistic relativity hypothesis is concerned.

Third, what effect does culture—learned and shared behavior patterns—have on the way we perceive the world? Although language is our principal means of transmitting culture from generation to generation, much of our learning, especially while we are young, takes place without explicit verbalizations: that is, much of our behavior is learned informally through observation and imitation. All kinds of sensory data may be used to recognize, classify, anticipate, and evaluate experiences. For example, a child whose first experiences of life take place within a single-roomed structure such as an igloo, tipi, or tent develops a sense of reality which is quite different from the child whose early experiences take place in a multi-partitioned structure in which his own place, the nursery, is safely insulated from the adult experiences around him. The different settings, themselves, affect the child's image of self, his rela-

[8] W. H. Thorpe, *Learning and Instinct in Animals* (Cambridge, Mass.: Harvard Univ. Press, 1958), p. 4.
[9] Charles Hockett, "The Origin of Speech," *American Scientist*, 203 (1960), 89–96.
[10] Joseph Greenberg, *Anthropological Linguistics* (New York: Random House, 1968).

tionship to others, to events, and to things. Thus culture provides many avenues for developing our perception of reality.

In spite of these questions, social scientists have attempted to devise tests for verifying the Whorfian hypothesis. One major consideration in such testing has been the nature of Whorf's evidence. Frequently, he named a grammatical device in one language and a different device for handling a similar situation in another language, and assumed that the difference demonstrated a difference in perception. This assumption is not necessarily valid. For example, French classifies all nouns as either masculine or feminine—*le soleil*, "the sun," is masculine, but *la lune*, "the moon," is feminine. Despite this classification, the Frenchman does not actually perceive these gender distinctions as real; they are simply grammatical devices. Whatever relationships these classifications once had with reality are now very remote.

In an attempt to provide a more defensible way of verifying the hypothesis, social scientists began to look for non-verbal behavioral concomitants for linguistic categories. One test, given by John Carroll, involved showing English and Hopi subjects three pictures from which they were to select the two that they felt were most alike. The pictures were based on differences in the way objects are handled. For example, one series of pictures showed three men, one unloading a carton of fruit, one spilling milk, and one dropping a coin. English subjects most often grouped the accidental actions, whereas the Hopi grouped the first two because words in their language for these actions are similar.[11]

Another experiment, conducted by Joseph Casagrande, involved Navaho and English-speaking children:

> Navaho and English-speaking children were presented with two objects which differed from each other in both form and color, for example, a blue stick and a yellow rope. They were then shown a third object which matched one of the original objects in color and the other in form, for example, a blue rope. They were asked to select one of the two original objects which best matched this third object. A number of such sets were used and the results confirmed the hypothesis. Navaho children, in the example cited above, selected the yellow rope, whereas English-speaking children selected the blue stick.[12]

When middle-class English-speaking children in metropolitan Boston were given the same test, however, there were unexpected results.[13] They made choices similar to those of the Navaho children. Apparently,

---

[11] DeVito, p. 205.

[12] DeVito, p. 206.

[13] John B. Carroll and Joseph B. Casagrande, "The Function of Language Classifications in Behavior," *Communication and Culture*, ed. Alfred Smith (New York: Holt, Rinehart & Winston, 1966), pp. 503–504.

the Boston children were accustomed to having "creative" toys to play with, toys that involve the child in manipulating objects. Certainly the results achieved in Boston weaken the conclusiveness of the original experiment. An additional problem with the validity of these tests is that they are designed to show relationships between language and behavior on a relatively concrete level, and the selection of a yellow rope or a blue stick hardly qualifies as an example of philosophical orientation. In reality, the Whorfian hypothesis has most relevance in the areas that are most difficult to pin down: philosophy, religion, ethics, and values. Behavioral concomitants on this level are difficult to find and test.

Another difficulty in testing the Whorfian hypothesis is that of controlling variables. Ideally, tests should be conducted on subjects whose backgrounds include a unilingual-unicultural environment. Unfortunately, the kind of geographic and cultural isolation necessary for this kind of environment is very rare. The modern world is one that fosters cultures which are multilingual and languages which are multicultural.

In the final analysis, Whorf's linguistic relativity hypothesis will probably remain only a hypothesis. But this does not mean that we should abandon it as a useful tool. On the contrary, by comparing patterns of grammatical usage—becoming conscious of them, studying them, and evaluating them—we will gain insights into the categories our language forces us to pay attention to, the ideas that are easy for us to express, and the ideas that are difficult to voice. We can, as Whorf put it, turn background into foreground. Thus, both science and man are served.

Bibliography

Brown, Roger. *Social Psychology.* New York: The Free Press, 1965.

Carroll, John B. *Language and Thought.* Englewood Cliffs, New Jersey: Prentice-Hall, 1964.

———, and Joseph B. Casagrande. "The Function of Language Classifications in Behavior." *Communication and Culture.* Ed. Alfred Smith. New York: Holt, Rinehart & Winston, 1966.

Chomsky, Noam. *Language and Mind.* New York: Harcourt, Brace & World, 1968.

DeVito, Joseph. *The Psychology of Speech and Language.* New York: Random House, 1970.

Fishman, Joshua. "A Systematization of the Whorfian Hypothesis." *Behavioral Science,* 5 (1960), 323–39.

Gleason, H. A., Jr., *An Introduction to Descriptive Linguistics.* Rev. ed. New York: Holt, Rinehart & Winston, 1961.

Greenberg, Joseph. *Anthropological Linguistics.* New York: Random House, 1968.

Hockett, Charles F. *A Course in Modern Linguistics.* New York: The Macmillan Company, 1958.

———. "The Origin of Speech." *American Scientist,* 203 (1960), 89–96.

Hoijer, Harry, ed. *Language in Culture.* Chicago: University of Chicago Press, 1954.

Hymes, Dell, ed. *Language in Culture and Society.* New York: Harper, 1964.

Kluckhohn, Clyde, and Dorothea Leighton. *The Navaho.* New York: Doubleday & Company, 1962.

Sapir, Edward. *Culture, Language, and Personality.* Ed. David B. Mandelbaum. Berkeley and Los Angeles: University of California Press, 1949.

————, *Language.* New York: Harcourt, Brace, 1921.

Thorpe, W. H. *Learning and Instinct in Animals.* Cambridge, Mass.: Harvard University Press, 1958.

Trager, George L. *Languages of the World.* Buffalo, New York: Unpublished manuscript.

Whorf, Benjamin L. *Language, Thought, and Reality.* Ed. J. B. Carroll. New York: John Wiley & Sons, 1964.

Woolfson, Peter, "Sapir's Theory of Language." *Language. Sciences,* No. 11 (August 1970), 8–10.

FOR DISCUSSION AND REVIEW

1 In brief, what is the *linguistic relativity hypothesis* (or *Whorfian hypothesis*)?

2 What are "habitual patterns"? According to Woolfson, why are they important to the Whorfian hypothesis?

3 At the lexical level, how does language shape perception? What evidence does the author provide on this point?

4 Is there a relationship between vocabulary, cultural emphasis, and habitual consciousness? If so, explain what the relationship is.

5 In what ways can the grammar of a language affect the way a person perceives his environment?

6 On the basis of a cat's behavior in the presence of a dog, Woolfson believes that it is "reasonable to assume that we are capable of some processes of thought without the mediation of language." Do you agree? Why or why not?

7 In what ways can culture, according to Woolfson, shape one's perception of reality? Can you think of any examples from your own experiences that show how culture influences perception? Explain.

8 Even though the Whorfian hypothesis is likely to remain a hypothesis, why does it continue to be interesting and valuable?

PROJECTS FOR "LANGUAGE: AN INTRODUCTION"

1 As Peter Farb suggests (p. 5), "show twenty-five speakers of English [e.g., the members of your class] a cartoon and ask them to describe in a single sentence what they see." Compare the sentences produced. You may wish to ditto the replies for class distribution. What conclusions can be drawn?

2 As a native speaker of English, you have several basic language competencies. For example, you can determine whether or not an utterance is a grammatical sentence. Other competencies include the ability to tell when two or more sentences are synonomous, recognize ambiguity in a sentence, and interpret completely novel utterances. Discuss these competencies in a brief essay.

3 The bow-wow theory of the origin of language indicates that primitive language was an imitation of natural sounds, such as the cries of animals. Collect a list of onomatopoeic English words, words that, in effect, support this theory. If you are fluent in another language, prepare a similar list of words for that language. How convincing is the evidence?

4 In his book The Word-a-Day Vocabulary Builder, lexicographer Bergen Evans states:

> Words are the tools for the job of saying what you want to say. And what you want to say are your thoughts and feelings, your desires and your dislikes, your hopes and your fears, your business and your pleasure—almost everything, indeed, that makes up you. Except for our vegetablelike growth and our animal-like impulses, almost all that we are is related to our use of words. Man has been defined as a tool-using animal, but his most important tool, the one that distinguishes him from all other animals, is his speech.

Do you agree with Evans's statement? Is it possible to think without language? Are there some creative activities for which people do not need speech? Write a brief essay in which you defend your position.

5 The following excerpt from Benjamin Lee Whorf's Language, Thought, and Reality suggests that language acts as a filter for our experience and as such helps shape reality for us:

> We have the same word for falling snow, snow on the ground, snow packed hard like ice, slushy snow, wind-driven flying snow—whatever the situation may be. To an Eskimo, this all-inclusive word would be almost unthinkable; he would say that falling snow, slushy snow, and so on, are sensually and operationally different, different things to contend with; he uses different words for them and for other kinds of snow. The Aztecs go even farther than we in the opposite direction with "cold," "ice," and "snow" all represented by the same basic word. . .

Using "Language Shapes Reality" as the thesis and title of a short paper, describe several incidents from your own experience that clearly exemplify the shaping power of language. For example, consider some of the recent purchases you have made. Have any of them been influenced by brand names, advertisements, or language used by salesmen? Did you ever find yourself taking or avoiding a course primarily because of its name?

SELECTED BIBLIOGRAPHY

Barnett, Lincoln. The Treasure of Our Tongue: The Story of English from Its Obscure Beginnings to Its Present Eminence as the Most Widely Spoken Language. New York: Alfred A. Knopf, 1964. (See pp. 39–78 for a thorough discussion of the theories of the origin of language.)

Bolinger, Dwight. Aspects of Language. 2nd edition. New York: Harcourt Brace Jovanovich, Inc., 1975. (Chapters of interest include "Some Traits of Language," "Origin of Language," and "Mind in the Grip of Language.")

Chafe, Wallace L. "The Nature of Language." *The National Elementary Principal,* 45 (September 1965), 10–15. (Basic discussion of language and language universals.)

Chase, Stuart. "How Language Shapes Our Thoughts." *Harper's Magazine,* April 1954, pp. 76–82. (A discussion of language as a shaper of thought with examples drawn from many different cultures.)

Francis, W. Nelson. *The English Language: An Introduction.* New York: W. W. Norton & Company, 1963. (See pp. 1–12 for a discussion of the nature of language and pp. 118–120 for a discussion of the Whorfian hypothesis and the perception of colors.)

Fromkin, Victoria, and Robert Rodman. *An Introduction to Language.* New York: Holt, Rinehart and Winston, Inc., 1974. (See pp. 1–14 for chapter entitled "What is Language?" and pp. 15–29 for chapter entitled "In the Beginning: Language Origin.")

Kluckholm, Clyde. "The Gift of Tongues." *Mirror for Man: The Relation of Anthropology to Modern Life.* New York: Whittlesey House, 1949. (An anthropologist's view of language, culture, and the Whorfian hypothesis.)

Langacker, Ronald W. *Language and Its Structure: Some Fundamental Linguistic Concepts.* 2nd edition. New York: Harcourt Brace Jovanovich, Inc., 1973. (Good but somewhat difficult discussion of basic language concepts and the influence of language on thought.)

Langer, Suzanne K. *Philosophy in a New Key: A Study in the Symbolism of Reason, Rite, & Art.* 3rd edition. Cambridge: Harvard University Press, 1956. (A classic work on the human symbol-making process and its relationship to language.)

Levitt, John, and Joan Levitt. *The Spell of Words.* Sussex, England: Darwen Finlayson, Ltd., 1959. (Contains an interesting chapter devoted to the theories on the origin of language.)

Moulton, William G. "Linguistics." *NEA Journal,* 54 (January 1965), 49–53. (Discussion of language as a code, a special kind of system used for communication.)

Myers, L. M. *The Roots of Modern English.* Boston: Little, Brown and Company, 1966. (A historical approach to modern English with an interesting chapter on the nature of language.)

Pyles, Thomas. "Facts, Assumptions, and Misconceptions About Language." *The Origins and Development of the English Language.* 2nd edition. New York: Harcourt Brace Jovanovich, Inc., 1971. (Thorough discussion of language basics.)

Robertson, Stuart, and Frederic G. Cassidy. *The Development of Modern English.* 2nd edition. Englewood Cliffs, New Jersey: Prentice-Hall, 1954. (See pp. 1–14 for a discussion of theories about the nature and origin of language.)

Salus, P. H., ed. *On Language: Plato to Von Humboldt.* New York: Holt, Rinehart and Winston, Inc., 1969. (Includes several essays on the nature and origin of language.)

Sapir, Edward. *Language: An Introduction to the Study of Speech.* New York: Harcourt Brace & World, 1949. (A classic book that explores the relationship between speech and culture.)

Sturtevant, E. H. *An Introduction to Linguistic Science.* New Haven: Yale University Press, 1947. (Contains a provocative discussion of the origin of language in the fifth chapter.)

Ullmann, Stephen. *Words and Their Use.* New York: Philosophical Library, Inc.,

1951. (Contains an excellent chapter on the symbol-making process in language.)

Whatmough, Joshua. *Language: A Modern Synthesis*. New York: St. Martin's Press, Inc., and Secker & Warburg, 1956. (Good opening chapter on the nature of language.)

Whorf, Benjamin Lee. *Language, Thought, and Reality*. Ed. John B. Carroll. Cambridge: The MIT Press, 1956. (A classic work on the relationship between language and culture.)

PART TWO

From Animal Communication to the Human Brain

Recent studies of language have shown an increasing reliance upon the research of ethologists, psychologists, sociologists, neurosurgeons, and physiologists. Clearly this reliance is the product of an awareness by linguists that language is a part of the total behavior of human beings and that their behavior, in turn, influences their language. Articles dealing with questions that were not previously considered relevant to linguistics form the subject matter of this section. For example, the topics covered include what the communication systems of animals can tell us about human language, the child's acquisition of languages, the mental processes of the bilingual, and the functions of the brain and how language is processed.

The readings that follow introduce the student to recent work in these areas. Studies show, for example, how the findings of the brain surgeon can influence foreign-language teaching and how the language of small children can give us insights into the nature of grammar. And they raise the fascinating question of the extent to which other species can learn, and use, forms of human language. There is diversity in these readings because man's behavior is complex. There is also a sense of unity because a greater knowledge of language and how it is acquired and used is a central theme of all the selections.

1
Language and Animal Signals

Claire Russell
and W. M. S. Russell

Is it language that separates human beings from the rest of the animal kingdom? Are humans the only symbol-making animals? These questions have attracted the attention and study of noted linguists and ethologists. Lengthy and detailed studies have been carried out with "talking" horses, dolphins, bees, whales, monkeys, birds, and chimpanzees. In this essay, the Russells discuss the meaning of language, survey the important work that has been done with the communication systems of the bee, the dolphin, and the monkey, and speculate about the origin of human language as we know it. As you read the selection, consider carefully the distinction the Russells draw between "true language" and "automatic signal codes."

THE IDEA that animals have their own language or languages is an old one. Folklore teems with examples, and the subject is allotted several pages in Stith Thompson's enormous *Motif-Index of Folk Literature.* Methods of learning animal languages vary widely. You can do it by wearing a magic ring, like King Solomon, or by taking a cocktail of dragon's blood, like Siegfried. But there are much simpler ways, such as having your ears cleaned out, or carrying churchyard mould in your hat. Several people have published dictionaries of animal languages. The Abbé Guillaume-Hyacinthe Bougeant, a Jesuit professor, published a glossary for several bird and mammal species in 1739, and got into serious trouble with his superiors. The French aristocrat Dupont de Nemours is famous for founding in America a firm that is one of the biggest in the world today (partly thanks to developing and making nylon). He had other interests, and in 1807 he compiled Crow-French and Nightingale-French dictionaries. In recent times, an English-Ape and Ape-English dictionary has been produced by a former assistant director of Washington Zoo called Schwidetsky. The chimpanzee word for "food," according to Schwidetsky, is *ngahk*; it is related to the German word for "nutcracking," which is *knacken*.

Language and Signal Codes

We need not really worry unduly about the linguistic relations of German and Chimpanzee. But the idea that some animals may be capable of language is far from ridiculous. As we shall see, it is a matter of serious scientific study in the later 20th century. At first sight, indeed, there seems to be a lot in common between human spoken language and the calls used by a great variety of animals. A human language can be broken down into units of sound called *phonemes*, which include consonants, vowels and certain double consonants and double vowels such as *ch* [tʃ] and *ou* [aʊ] (as in *house*). In terms of patterns of sound waves of different frequencies, a given phoneme is by no means always identical. Thus the *p* sounds in the words *pin*, *spin* and *nip* are somewhat different from each other in physical properties. But an English-speaker will recognize all of them as the *p* phoneme. English has between 35 and 45 of these phonemes, according to whether certain double vowels are counted as one or two units each. Italian has 27 phonemes, which must be a satisfactory number from the musical point of view, since Italian sounds so good when it is sung. The different human languages vary widely in number of phonemes, from 11 to 67. Any of us can make far more different sounds than this, and hence can learn other languages; but we rely on the basic number of phonemes when speaking our own language. Now animal call systems can similarly be broken down into basic signal units or calls, and the numbers of such units for different species of mammals and even birds fall roughly into the same range as do the numbers of phonemes of human languages, as is clear from the Table.

Animal Species	Number of Identified Basic Vocal Signals
Birds	
Chaffinch	12
Domestic chicken	20
European finch	20
White-throated warbler	25
Lower Mammals	
Coati	7
Brown lemur	7

Tree-shrew	8
Domestic and wild cow	8
Prairie dog	10
Pig	23
Fox	36

Dolphins

Amazon freshwater dolphin, pulsed sounds (e.g. "squawk")	7
Pilot whale, whistles	7
Pacific bottlenose dolphin, whistles	16
Pacific common dolphin, whistles	19
Atlantic bottlenose dolphin, whistles	17
Atlantic bottlenose dolphin, pulsed sounds	11

Monkey and Apes

Gray langur	10
Night monkey	10
Patas monkey	11
Cynocephalus baboons	15
Gibbon	15
Rhesus monkey	17
Howler monkey	20
Gorilla	23
Chimpanzee	25
Squirrel monkey	26
Vervet monkey	36
Japanese monkey	37

Human Languages   11–67

On this basis alone, we might be tempted to regard human languages and animal call systems as quite comparable. But the number of vocal units is nòt everything, and we need not suppose that Japanese monkeys, with 37 units, must be more sophisticated than human speakers of Hawaiian, who make do with 13. About 2300 years ago, Aristotle put his finger on the crucial point. "The articulated signs of human language," he declared, "are not like the expression of emotions of children or animals. Animal noises cannot be combined to form syllables." It is the principle of combination that makes all the difference.

Aristotle was, however, being rather dogmatic. If we are seriously to consider whether any animals have languages, we must begin by considering some properties of languages and automatic signal codes. To begin with, human spoken language is generally conveyed by sound; and, as we've just seen, many animal signals are also calls. But this is not an essential feature of either language or animal signals. There are several different types of true sign or gesture language, evolved for communication between the deaf and dumb and between monks of religious orders forbidden to talk. These sign or gesture languages are perceived through the eyes instead of the ears. Animal signal codes too are often predominantly gestures or postures to be seen by the recipient. In teaching severely handicapped children such as Helen Keller, use has been made of communication by touch, and touch signals are also widely used by animals. Human language is not normally conveyed by smell or taste, though it could conceivably be coded in this way, but elaborate chemical signals are quite common among animals and simpler ones are involved in the human perfume industry. So the use of a particular physical medium or sense is not a crucial feature of language.

Another distinction we can make also cuts across the distinction between true language and automatic signal codes. Both can convey messages about two different kinds of things, which we can sum up as *emotion* and *economics*. We can talk about how we feel about somebody else; we can also talk about natural surroundings, things, techniques and technical aspects of our life in society. In the same way an animal's signals may convey, for instance, a readiness to groom another animal's coat (emotion) or the presence of food or danger (economics). This is an important distinction, but it is no help in deciding what is or is not true language.

The use of symbols or symbolization used to be regarded as unique to human language. This is now known to be nonsense. Symbolization simply means that a set of things or events can be translated into a set of signals, with one signal for each, and that the individual who receives the signals can translate them back into the things symbolized. There is no doubt at all that animals can symbolize in this sense, both as signallers and receivers, as we shall see most clearly in the case of honeybees. A more interesting contrast is that between two kinds of symbols, *representative* and *arbitrary*. A representative symbol has something structurally in common with the thing symbolized. When a herring gull lifts his wrist joints as if about to unfold his wings, and holds his head up straight with beak pointing downwards, this actually *looks like* the beginning of a fighting attack, in which the gull would raise his wings to beat his opponent, and raise his head to peck downwards from above. The raising of the wrist joints and the position of the head are examples of *intention movements*; they symbolize attack, and act as a threat: a gull so threatened will often retreat. On the other hand, an arbitrary symbol bears no particular formal resemblance to the thing it symbolizes. Herring gulls in a conflict between the urges to attack and flee may resolve their problem by doing a third, irrelevant thing derived from some other behaviour context—a *displacement activity*, as it is called. They may, for instance, pluck at the grass as if gathering material for a nest. This does not look at all like a real attack, but it also comes to symbolize attack, and acts as a threat which may cause another gull to retreat. Niko Tinbergen has shown that intention movements and displacement activities are the basic units of signal codes in many animal species: animals thus use both representative and arbitrary symbols.

Human language relies heavily on arbitrary symbols. The sound of the word *sun*, for instance, has nothing structurally in common with the sun itself. It is true that we sometimes use representational symbols in language. In spoken language, words that symbolize sounds often resemble the sounds themselves: words such as *thunder* and *hiss* really represent what they symbolize. In American Sign Language, used by the deaf in North America, many signs are arbitrary, but the symbol for *flower* is touching the two nostrils in turn with the tip of the tapered hand, which clearly suggests smelling a flower. Representational effects of a subtler kind are important in poetry, as Pope observed in his *Essay on Criticism*.

> 'Tis not enough no harshness gives offence,
> The sound must seem an Echo to the sense:
> Soft is the strain when Zephyr gently blows,
> And the smooth stream in smoother numbers flows;
> But when loud surges lash the sounding shore,
> The hoarse, rough verse should like the torrent roar.

But, on the whole, the lavish use of arbitrary symbols is a great advantage. Only by arbitrary symbols can we represent such complicated or abstract conceptions as *Institute, Contemporary* or *Arts*. We can see this well in the special case of written language, which advanced from simple picture signs as representational symbols to arbitrary symbols for the sound units of spoken language, and hence for the things which are symbolized in turn by the patterns of sound units making up words.

In the long run, too, arbitrary symbols lend themselves most readily to the formation of many combinations and recombinations. And here we do come to a crucial feature of true language. The signal units of many animals can be put together in many different combinations. Thus the calls and facial expressions of monkeys consist of units which can be combined in many ways. For instance, rhesus monkeys, observed at Whipsnade Zoo by Vernon Reynolds, had a number of different signal units for threat, such as bobbing the head up and down, raising the eyebrows, drooping the eyelids, opening the mouth without showing the teeth, and making a low-pitched noise described as *hough*. A number of different combinations of these units could be observed, according to the intensity of aggression expressed.[1] Even the threat postures of gulls can show a number of different combinations of units signalling various in-

[1] V. Reynolds: Dissertation (University of London, 1961).

tensities of the urges to attack and flee, as Niko Tinbergen and his colleagues have shown.

But these animal signal combinations are both governed and limited by the close relation here between emotion and its expression in vocal and postural and facial symbols. Each signal is tied to a particular emotional state, and signal combinations reflect only combinations of emotions. Some combinations, for instance of units expressing extreme fear with units expressing extreme sexual desire, are simply impossible. Now any symbol units of true language can be uttered in any emotional state. Hence many new combinations become possible, and emotional rules of combination are replaced by logical ones, which we call grammar and syntax. In this way it becomes possible to form at any time totally new combinations of symbols, which the speaker may never have used before, and even combinations which no member of his language-group has ever used before. Human languages vary in their vocabularies or terms of reference, but they all have this potential flexibility. During World War II, when young East Africans were being trained for the Bantu Rifles, a problem arose because there were no words for "red" or "green" in the local language. The problem was easily solved by using the phrases *colour of blood* and *colour of leaves*. By similar means, totally new situations can be described, or totally new possibilities envisaged. This power of producing new combinations is crucial to true language.

R. J. Pumphrey has noted another advantage of detaching symbols from the direct expression of immediate emotion. An alarm call indicating the presence of a lion is given only when the calling animal is feeling the special fear associated with seeing or hearing or smelling a lion. The word *lion*, on the other hand, can be used when no lions are about. "Whereas an emotive lion is necessarily in the present, an intelligible lion could be discussed in the future or in the past; and so tradition and forward planning about lions became possible."

True language, therefore, involves the free combination of symbols limited only by logical rules of grammar and syntax, which themselves express *relations between* symbols and hence symbolize *relations between* things and individuals and events. In addition, true language must involve true communication. Compulsive utterance of signals in the absence of other individuals is not true communication. And signalling which produces automatic effects on other individuals is mere interaction. In true communication the signaller transmits information which enables the recipient to behave more freely, to have a greater range of choice and decision; so whereas interaction reduces, communication increases the variability of the recipient's behaviour. No doubt the combination of all these qualities is necessary before we can speak of true language, as opposed to an automatic code of signals.

An Animal Without True Language

Equipped with these general ideas, we can consider more exactly whether any animals have true languages. To begin with, it is worth glancing at the signal code of an animal which certainly cannot talk, namely the human infant—the word *infant* is simply the Latin root meaning "speechless." Infants have, in fact, a very simple signalling system with at most 8 sound units. These are said to correspond to phonemes, 5 vowels and 3 consonants, but they are certainly not used as elements to be combined in a language. Four kinds of infant cries have been studied in 351 infants in Sweden and Finland, by means of sound spectrographs, which display on a sort of graph called a sonagram the amount of energy produced at different sound frequencies over the time-course of a cry. Birth cries were produced only at birth. Pain cries were produced when the baby was vaccinated. Hunger cries were produced about 4 hours 20 minutes after a feed. Pleasure cries were produced when the infant, after being fed and changed, was lying comfortably in bed or in the mother's or nurse's arms. The sonagrams showed that each kind of cry varied considerably but always differed in definite ways from the other 3 kinds of cry. Each cry was uttered only in its appropriate situation, so there was no question of combining them to produce, say, a sentence like *I was hungry, now I am comfortable*, still less to describe something unusual and new. All this, perhaps, is a bit obvious. But it shows rather clearly what we mean by a simple signal code as opposed to a true language. Adults have to interpret the signals much as they try to interpret the signals of a cat or a dog.

High-fidelity tape recordings of 6 of each of the 4 kinds of cries were played to 483 adults under 50, including 349 women, and these people were asked to identify the cries as birth, pain, hunger or pleasure cries. They were far from perfectly accurate in their interpretations. Pleasure cries were easiest to recognize, with 85% correct interpretations; then came hunger cries, 68%; pain cries, 63%; and birth cries, which most people hear very rarely, with only 48% correct interpretations. Experience naturally helps in such matters. Children's nurses were better at recognizing pain and hunger cries than mothers who had only had one child each; and, not surprisingly, the top score for recognizing birth cries was obtained by midwives.

If the signals of babies are so relatively difficult to interpret, it will be clear that it takes much work and skill to understand animal signals. The great decoders of animal signal codes, such as Karl von Frisch, Konrad Lorenz and Niko Tinbergen, have had to use as much ingenuity as those of Cretan Linear B or the script of the Mayas. If we are to consider whether any animals have true languages, we shall naturally focus our attention on the most promising candidates, whose signalling is enormously more elaborate than that of human babies. These animals fall into three groups, which we shall consider in turn, beginning with the extraordinary code of the honeybees. It is simplest to describe this as a language; whether it deserves to be called a true language will appear when we have seen what it does.

The Dance of the Honeybee

In 1788, Pastor Ernst Spitzner reported a surprising fact. When a honeybee finds a good supply of honey, she returns to the hive and there performs a curious circular dance. Spitzner put out some honey, brought 2 bees to it, watched them dance on their return to the hive, and saw that many of their fellow-bees came to the honey-place. He concluded that the returning bees had somehow told their colleagues about the honey. It was a beautiful observation and a true inference, but Spitzner went no further, and it was left to Karl von Frisch, in our own age, to interpret the language of the honeybees. How he made his discoveries can be read in his books. Here we will simply summarize some of what he and Martin Lindauer and their colleagues discovered, beginning with the language of the Carniolan honeybee.[2]

When a honeybee of this race discovers a new source of honey within about 10 m. of the hive, she returns to the hive and regurgitates drops of honey which are eagerly drunk by other bees. Then she begins to dance round in a circle; first she goes one way round, then she reverses and goes the other way round, then another reverse, and so on. This is called the *round dance*. Other bees follow her about, holding their antennae against her abdomen. After dancing, she "refuels" by

[2] *Apis mellifera carnica.*

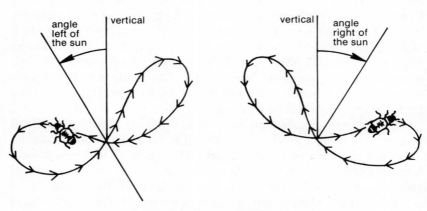

Figure 1. The round dance.

taking a drop or two of honey back from some other bee, and flies back to the food source, which in natural conditions is a flower or group of flowers. The other bees who followed the dance do not fly after her. They fly out in all directions. But, fairly soon, a lot of them find the new food source. They do so because they have smelt the scent of the flower that clung to the dancer's body, and so look for the right kind of flower. In one experiment, bees informed by a dancer found the right flowers in a section of the Munich Botanical Garden where 700 different plant species were blooming at once. The round dance, therefore, tells the other bees to go out and search the near neighbourhood of the hive; the scent on the dancer's body tells them what flowers to look for.

But honeybees can forage for food at far greater distances than 10 m. They have been known to fly more than 13 km. in search of honey. A honeybee is only about 13 mm. long, so 13 km. for a bee is the equivalent of about 1000 miles for a human being—not a bad commuting trip. But of course, even at much smaller distances, a round dance would not be much use. If the discoverer of new food told her colleagues to go out and search in all directions for several km., she might just as well save her energy. They would never find the flowers. So when a Carniolan honeybee finds food at a considerable distance from the hive, say between 100 m. and 10 km., she returns to the hive, offers the honey she has found, and then performs a different kind of number, called a *tail-wagging dance*, which is somewhat reminiscent of the Charleston or Black Bottom. She dances along in a straight line for a certain distance, wagging her tail for all she is worth and buzzing away

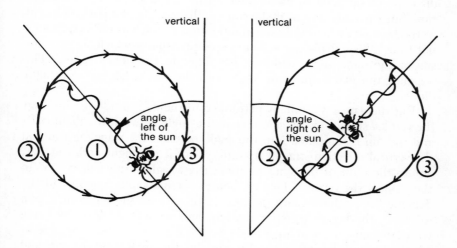

Figure 2. The tail-wagging dance. The number of times per minute the bee dances a complete pattern (1-2-1-3) indicates the distance of the food source.

by means of slight vibrations of the muscles that flap her wings in flight. It is as if she was, so to speak, flying on the spot. At the end of this *waggling run*, she stops buzzing and wagging her tail, circles round to one side back to where she started, does another waggling run, circles round to the opposite side, does a third waggling run, circles to the first side, and so on. A number of other bees follow her around, showing special interest in the waggling runs. Bees cannot hear sounds in air, but they can feel the buzzing vibrations through the surface on which the dance is done. Like the round dance, the tail-wagging dance tells the bees who follow it that there is food available, and what flowers to look for, from the smell. But it tells them much more than this. It tells them exactly how far away the flowers are, and in exactly what direction. And so, even at distances of km., the bees who study the dance can fly with precision to the spot indicated and find the honey-bearing flowers.

The distance to the food is conveyed by the tempo of the dance. A quickstep tempo means a relatively nearby food source, a slow foxtrot tempo a more distant one. To be exact, as the distance increases so does the duration of each waggling run. A single waggling run may be inaccurate, but Von Frisch and his colleagues have shown that the bees who follow the dance study several waggling runs and calculate the average duration, which they then translate into distance by a mathematical rule.

The tail-wagging dance is sometimes done on a horizontal surface just outside the hive. When this happens, the dancer indicates the direction of the food by aiming her waggling run in exactly this direction. She can only do this if she can see the sun (or the polarized light of the blue sky, which indicates the position of the sun to bees, though not to us). So actually she is taking up a position in which she sees the sun at the same angle as during her flight to the honey source. The waggling run makes the same angle with the sun as her outward flight did.

But the dance is normally performed in the dark inside the hive, on the *vertical* surface of the comb. Here the angle between the flight path and the sun is translated into the angle between the waggling run and the vertical direction straight upwards. Thus if the flight path was, say, 30° to the right of the sun's position, the waggling run will be 30° to the right of the vertical. This symbolism is remarkable enough, but the dancing bee's achievements go even further. If on the flight there is a sidewind, the bee corrects for the tendency to drift sideways by flying with her body at an oblique angle to the flight path. So the angle at which she sees the sun is not the same as the angle between sun and flight path. Nevertheless, in the dance, she makes the necessary correction, and tells the other bees the true angle between sun and flight path. More remarkable still, if she has reached her goal (and returned from it) by an L-shaped detour, she uses the angles and lengths of the 2 segments of the flight to calculate the true direction of the goal by straight-line flight, and this is the direction she conveys in her dance, although she has never flown this direct route herself. One critic objected to the idea of a bee calculating, and proposed instead "a kind of 'mixture' of the neuronal learning effects during the segments." As Von Frisch observes, this is "a statement that simply clothes the phenomena in other words."

As for the bees who are following the dance, they are working literally in the dark and can only use touch to find out the angle of the dancer's waggling run with the vertical. They translate this back into a visual angle with the sun, fly off in this direction (allowing for any bending *they* have to do to oppose a sidewind) for the distance signalled by the waggling run tempo, and look for flowers of the scent they smelled on the dancer. Many experiments by Von Frisch and his colleagues show that they duly find the food.

On 14 August 1946, Von Frisch returned from a trip in the mountains to his field base. His daughters told him they had set up a new station with sugar-water for the bees in his experimental hive, but they would not tell him where it was. He must ask the bees! Von Frisch did ask the bees (by observing their dances), and he found the feeding station. On 22 September 1951, while doing some experiments, Von Frisch noticed lively dancing going on in a hive. He decoded the dances, entered the spot indicated on a map, and found it was a place (600 m. away) where a local dealer kept his bees. An assistant went over and found the dealer had just spun down honey from some combs, and then put them out in the sun for his own bees to gather back the remaining traces of honey. The assistant told the dealer Von Frisch's bees were stealing this honey and had told Von Frisch where it was. The dealer told the assistant he had to be joking, and never did believe this story, which, however, is perfectly true.

Even all this does not exhaust the symbolism of the honeybee dances. They can also vary in liveliness and total duration. They are livelier and longer the sweeter the food, the easier it is gathered, the better the weather. When honey is short in the hive, any returning bee will be eagerly badgered for honey drops, and this stimulates her to longer and livelier dances; when there is plenty of honey in the hive, the returning bee will have to search hard for customers, and this makes for shorter and less lively dances. If, of two food sources, one is richer, fewer customers are left for bees returning from the other, so even the relative attractions of different sources are represented. All this makes for flexibility and economy of labour and a readiness to exploit a variety of flowers as each ripens. The dances do not compel a reaction from every bee that the dancer meets; as Von Frisch nicely puts it, there is a most subtle regulation of "supply and demand on the flower market."

So far we have described the language of the Carniolan race of the honeybee. Other races have different dialects. German, North African, Caucasian, Italian and Egyptian honeybees[3] all begin to indicate distance and direction at much shorter distances than the Carniolan race. Italian honeybees, for instance, start indicating these data by a modified tail-wagging dance at about 10 m., as opposed to about 85 m. in the Carniolan bees. All the races indicate distance by dance tempo, but on different scales. Thus Italian honeybees dance slower than Carniolan ones for any distance of the food source. When a colony was made up of Italian and Carniolan bees, misunderstandings arose. When Italian bees danced, Carniolan ones flew too far; when Carniolan bees danced, Italian ones did not fly far enough. Each race was using their own scale to interpret the other's dances. Bees of different species, living in India and Ceylon, the Indian honeybee, dwarf honeybee and giant honeybee,[4] show similar but more extreme differences in tempo scales. The dwarf honeybee dances in the open on top of its comb, which is unprotected from the weather, and thus on a horizontal surface; unlike all the other honeybees, she cannot translate the angle with the sun into the angle with the vertical.

Wonderful as the bee language is in its precise and elaborate symbolism, there are many indications that it is really a matter of automatic signalling and not a true language after all. One experiment will perhaps make this clear. We have mentioned that the Italian bee uses a modified tail-wagging dance at 10 m. At smaller distances, this bee uses round dances in the usual way. On one occasion Von Frisch and his colleagues put a hive of these bees on the concrete foundation of a radio tower, and brought 10 bees a distance of 50 m. straight *up* the inside of the tower to a station with rich sugar water. The 10 bees flew down to the hive and danced "most vigorously" for 4 hours. But the honeybee languages contain no symbols for "up" or "down." All the dancers could do was to perform round dances (indicating that the food source was not far away *horizontally*). Consequently their colleagues all set out and scoured round the neighbourhood of the hive at ground level. Not one of them found her way up to the feeding station high up in the tower right over the hive. In Von Frisch's words, the dancers "sent their hivemates astray—their ability to communicate broke down when faced with the unaccustomed task." Thus the bee language, unlike human languages (such as the East African one we

---

[3] A. *m. mellifera, intermissa, caucasica, ligustica* and *fasciata*, respectively.
[4] A. *indica, florea, dorsata*.

mentioned) cannot generate new combinations of symbols to describe a completely unusual event. We are bound to conclude it is not a true language. Studies of other insects suggest origins for both the round and the tail-wagging dances in automatic circling and wagging movements performed by flies and moths, respectively, without any communicative function. The moths even wag their bodies more the further they have just flown. Even the marvellous translation of sun angle into vertical angle can be seen to have developed from a widespread automatic tendency of insects to translate responses to light into responses to gravity in darkness. This arises from the simple fact that an insect can generally move upwards either by going towards the light or, of course, by going against gravity. What the honeybees have evolved from these elements is marvellous indeed, but it is not a true language.[5]

The Voice of the Dolphin

For our next candidates, we can choose animals much more like ourselves—individualistic mammals: the whales, dolphins and porpoises, notably dolphins and above all the best studied and so far the most remarkable species, the Atlantic bottlenose dolphin.[6] Dolphins are, so to speak, the monkeys of the sea: they have evolved many similar aspects of behaviour. Both groups of animals show prolonged and intense parental care for their young, and with this go very long-term relationships between mother and offspring. Amicable relations between 3 generations—grandmother, mother and daughter—have been seen among chimpanzees and in bottlenose dolphins. Male Japanese monkeys and bottlenose dolphins "baby-sit" for the females when these are other-

---

[5] The honeybee signal code introduces us to yet another distinction. The signalling of distance by waggling run duration, and the signalling of angle of flight path with sun by angle of waggling run with vertical, are both examples of *continuous* signalling. Distance and direction vary continuously, and so do the signals for them. In human languages, signalling is normally done by separate or *discrete* signal *units*, such as phonemes, combined in various ways. As we have seen, many animal signal codes are also based on combinations of discrete units, and the whole science of animal behaviour study is based on the description and observation of such units of social behaviour. Signal units may be arbitrary or representational, as we have seen in the case of human words (*sun* and *hiss*, respectively). Continuous signals could in theory be arbitrary—for instance, bees could signal a flight angle of 40° by a dance angle of 10°, an angle of 60° by 11°, 80° by 9°, and so on. But, as Stuart A. Altmann has pointed out, in such a system any slight error in signalling would lead to serious mistakes, so continuous signalling must in practice be representational, as it is in honeybees, with a real formal relationship between signals and events.

[6] *Tursiops truncatus.*

wise occupied; on one occasion, a bottle-fed baby dolphin, suffering from wind due to a badly composed formula, had his buoyancy relations upset and could not stay upright: he was cured in a rough but effective way by an adult male, who gave him a bang on the belly to empty out the wind. In both groups, mothers become so attached to their babies that they cannot be parted from them even after the baby has died of some illness. A rhesus monkey mother will carry a dead infant around till it is completely decomposed, and the same is observed in dolphin mothers, for instance one observed at sea "supporting the partially decomposed head of a dolphin young with its own head"; it "withdrew support only long enough to surface and breathe, then returned to its burden." Live dolphin infants are normally held at the surface after birth to enable them to take their first breath—for of course dolphins are mammals and need to surface regularly for air.

The prolonged parental care gives young dolphins, like young monkeys, the opportunity for a great deal of play and exploration. They make up a great variety of games. For instance, in captivity in a tank, one young dolphin will put an object over an intake jet and let it go, allowing the current of water to whirl it up towards the surface, where another youngster catches it, and immediately returns it to the jet while the first player goes up to catch it in his turn. Even as adults, dolphins, like monkeys, are highly exploratory animals.

The powerful parental urge is also extended, in both groups, to a care for the welfare and survival of other adults. In the wild, adult monkeys will remove thorns and clean wounds for each other, and a band of monkeys will rush into danger to rescue one of their number who has fallen down a well or been captured by human beings. In the open sea, adult dolphins and also many species of large whales will stand by a wounded comrade; 19th-century whalers knew this well, and would regularly wound a whale without killing it so that they could easily kill his comrades, who would not leave while he was alive; the procedure was risky, because sometimes the comrades managed to release the first victim or even attacked the whale-boats. Dolphins have extended to sick or injured adults the practice of holding the patient's head above water to let him breathe, just as they do with babies. When dynamite is exploded at sea near a school of dolphins, they will all leave the area at once. But on one occasion one dolphin was stunned by the explosion. Two comrades at once came and held the victim's head out of water; when they had to surface to breathe themselves, two others relieved them; the whole school stayed around till the stunned dolphin recovered completely, whereupon all left at once.

In captivity, under crowding stress, monkeys and dolphins can be as cruel as human beings under such pressures. Monkeys will cruelly wound and kill each other, including females and young. Dolphin adult males and females have been observed to bite juveniles and bash them against the tank wall, and one adult male bottlenose dolphin bit and bashed a small female so viciously, drawing much blood, that she had to be separated from him to save her life. But even in captivity, the care for others in distress can also be seen. J. C. Lilly found that sick dolphins often recover without treatment provided they are left with other dolphins, who support them at the surface. He found that dolphins will instantly help sick or stunned *strangers*, even of different species. On one memorable occasion, reported by D. H. Brown, a female Pacific Common Dolphin[7] was giving birth to a stillborn baby, whose fin stuck in the birth canal. Two females of *other* species acted as midwives. One of them[8] pulled out the foetus, and helped the mother to hold the stillborn baby at the surface (in vain, unfortunately). The other female[9] pulled out the afterbirth. On another occasion, Lilly reports that two bottlenose dolphins, male and female, supported a conscious adult female with a back injury at the surface for 48 hours till she recovered. They worked out 10 different methods of keeping her head out of water, the simplest being to hold her tail on the bottom in such a way that she was pushed upright. During this and similar occasions, Lilly has noted prolonged and complicated exchange of calls between the patient and his or her helpers, and it is hard to resist the suggestion that they may be exchanging requests and information in true language, or even discussing what to do.

The dolphin brain resembles the human brain in being very large and having its cerebral cortex (surface layer) very wrinkled, and in certain other respects.[10] But some say the cortex is so wrinkled only for mechanical reasons, because it is very thin, and that in fine structure of layering it is simpler and cruder, and has a lower density of nerve cells, than that of a rabbit. So if we seek for evidence from the dolphin brain about the dolphin's capabilities, we are back where we started. The behaviour observations, however, are so suggestive that in the past two decades people have been seriously studying the calls of the dolphins to find out whether they are a true language.

Dolphins are extremely vocal animals. As Gregory Bateson has put it, "adaptation to life in the ocean has stripped the whales of facial

---

[7] *Delphinus bairdi.*

[8] *Lagenorhynchus* species.

[9] *Pseudorca* species.

[10] Nearly all of the dolphin cerebral cortex, like that of man, is made up of the most recently evolved kind of structures (neocortex); but this may only be because the older structures are related to the sense of smell, which is much reduced in these sea animals. It is also said that large areas of the dolphin cortex, as of the human cortex, are not directly concerned with control of muscular activity.

expression." Their heads and bodies are naked, rigid and streamlined, and anyway visibility under water is probably usually not good enough to recognize subtle facial expressions or bodily postures. So nearly all their signalling is by sound. It seems likely from records of their calls that they produce discrete vocal signal units in more elaborate sequences or combinations than any other animals, though this leaves open the question whether the rules of combination are emotional or truly logical, with grammar and syntax.

Dolphin calls are of three kinds. They produce sequences of clicks. These are probably used mainly for echolocation ("sound radar") but to some extent for signalling also—among sperm whales, where click sequences are the only calls, they are almost certainly used for signalling. The two other kinds of dolphin calls are pulsed sounds (such as squawks and mews) and whistles, and both these are certainly signals. The pulsed sounds are easily recognized as different-sounding unit calls. The analysis of the whistles can be done by exactly the methods used to analyse certain human languages.

A number of human languages, in North America, East Asia, and Africa south of the Sahara, are said to be *tonal*. That is, much of the meaning of the words is carried by the relative *pitch* at which they are uttered. There are a varying number of pitch levels or *registers*, higher or lower. The voice goes up or down so that syllables are *relatively* higher or lower, and it is the difference or contrast and not the absolute pitch that matters; hence women and boys can talk on average at a higher pitch than men without misunderstandings. Tone may be so important that a language can be almost completely intelligible without hearing vowels and consonants at all. Hence many African tribes construct drums with the same number of registers (pitch levels) as their languages, and can transmit long conversations over long distances by drumming. The distinguishable units of tone languages are often *glides*, in which the voice goes up, down, up and down, down and up, starting and ending at different levels, changing pitch faster or slower, and so on. These units can be represented on paper as *contours*, in which a line goes up and down to represent rising and falling pitch; a contour in the shape of the letter V, for instance, would mean that the voice gets lower and then suddenly rises again in pitch by the same amount; and all other variations can be represented in this sort of way. A similar method was used for writing down music in Georgia in the 8th to 11th centuries A.D.

Some peoples speaking tonal languages have also evolved actual whistling languages which they use in addition. Whistling languages have been studied on Gomera Island in the Canaries, in the village of Aas in the French Pyrenees, and among the Mazatecos, Zapotecos and Tlapanecos of Mexico. Among the Mexican peoples, only the men whistle. It is considered bad form to raise the male voice, so the men began to communicate over the mountain trails by whistling. Women do not normally whistle, but they understand the language and can demonstrate it (with a certain embarrassment). G. M. Cowan heard a young man whistle to a girl for several minutes. It was far more detailed than a wolf whistle, and she understood every word he whistled—finally she answered him back furiously in ordinary words. These whistling languages can also be represented as sets of contours.

John J. Dreher and René-Guy Busnel have tried to study dolphin whistling as if it were a human tonal or whistled language (respectively). The idea is to represent each different whistle unit by a contour, and then try to decipher whole sequences of contours as if one were deciphering sequences of hieroglyphs from some ancient script, or, for that matter, the Georgian medieval musical contour notation, which actually has been deciphered from Georgian musical documents preserved in the monasteries of Mount Athos and Mount Sinai. Such decoding methods depend on analysing the frequency of different units and how they combine together. In addition, of course, since this is a living language, or at least a living signalling system, the occurrence of each different sound unit and each combination can be related first to what is happening to the signalling dolphin, and second to what other dolphins do in response. Both whistles and pulsed sounds have been studied in this way in Atlantic bottlenose dolphins, and Dreher has also played different whistle units back to dolphins and obtained different complicated responses in the form of actions and long sequences of calls. So far a number of units have been related to simple emotional situations, such as the distress call, a whistle of falling pitch, and the sex yelp of the male. But these are quite on a par with the simple automatic signal codes of many animals. Little progress has yet been made in deciphering long sequences of calls. J. C. Lilly, and later T. G. Lang and H. A. P. Smith, have recorded long exchanges of calls between pairs of dolphins who could not see each other. But many animals will exchange vocal signals, and there is no certain evidence that these are real conversations, though there is some indication that a dolphin can distinguish the naturally changing calls of another dolphin from repeated playback of a standard dolphin call recording.

It was against this background of uncertainty that Jarvis Bastian, in 1966, reported on a highly imaginative experiment. Two Atlantic bottlenose dolphins, a male and a female, were kept in a large tank and trained to work together in pressing paddles to be rewarded by an automat which disgorged fish when the proper paddles were pressed. At a certain stage in the complicated sequence of training procedures, the tank was divided by an opaque partition, with the male on one side and the female on the other. The arrangement was then as follows. Both the male and the female were warned by lamps being switched on that the game was ready to begin. Then another lamp was switched on to give *either* a continuous *or* a flashing light. In the former case, the right-hand paddle must be pressed, in the latter case the left-hand paddle. Now the female could see this signal lamp, but the male *could not see either the lamp or her*. Both dolphins got fish if, and only if, the *male first* pressed the correct paddle on his side of the tank, and *then the female* pressed the correct paddle on her side, there being a pair of paddles for each of them. So the male had to press the correct paddle without seeing the lamp that signalled which paddle to press.[11] On the face of it, he could only do this if *the female told him, by her calls, which paddle to press, when she saw whether the lamp was flashing or steady*. Nevertheless, over many thousands of runs, the male pressed the correct paddle and the dolphins succeeded in earning their reward on more than 90% of the tests. Analysis of the female's calls indicated that she made different pulsed sounds when her lamp was flashing and steady, responding sooner, longer and at faster pulse rate to the steady light; it is quite possible the male, hearing her, could tell the difference between the two kinds of call. The dolphins' success was only prevented if *either* the female was not rewarded with fish (as happened accidentally in two test series through a defect of her automat), *or* her signal light was hidden from her as well as from the male, *or* the barrier between male and female was made sound-proof. It seems certain from this amazing experiment that *in some sense* the female was telling the male whether the light was flashing or steady, so that he could press the correct paddle in response.

Was this true language? The dolphins were surely presented with a most unusual and novel situation and problem, and, unlike the honeybees, they solved it. Were they using a new combination of symbols to deal with this problem in communication? In 1966, the answer was uncertain. But alas! in 1969 Bastian published further findings. It now seemed all too clear that true language was not involved after all. Apparently the female went on giving her different calls in response to flashing and steady light when the barrier was taken down, the male could see the light himself, and the calls were quite superfluous. And she went on doing it after this even after the male had been taken out of the tank before her very eyes and she was "talking" all by herself. This and other detailed evidence made it extremely likely that the female had become conditioned to giving different calls in response to the

---

11 Very elaborate control experiments ensured that the male could not be guided by noises from the lamps or even by echolocation to find which paddle the female was nearest to, for putting the paddles far apart or side by side made no difference to the results.

different light signals, because this *worked* in getting her fish, without realizing that it worked by telling the male what to do; and that the male had become conditioned to pressing different paddles in response to the two different calls of the female, because this also *worked* for him, without realizing why she gave these calls. This is pretty remarkable in itself, and the male did make a very quick transfer from using visual clues (when he could see the signal lamp) to using sound clues (when he could only hear the female's calls); people have said in the past that this easy juggling between the senses was necessary for human language and not present in animals. But, after all, we cannot speak of true language where both signalling and reaction were conditioned and compulsive and not a true communication between individuals. So the dolphins, so far, like the bees, cannot be said to have a true language. There have been other indications that these enigmatic animals may not be quite so bright as they sometimes appear. One female bottlenose dolphin had a 5-foot leopard shark[12] in a tank with her. She apparently mistook it for a baby dolphin, and held its head repeatedly above water. Dolphins breathe in air, but sharks are fishes and breathe in water, and within a day the wretched shark had suffocated and died. So far this could have been the intelligent use for killing a shark of a technique evolved for saving baby dolphins. But the dolphin really was making a mistake, it seems, for she carried the dead shark about for 8 days as if it were a dead infant, fed little as if in mourning, and would not let divers take the carcass away till it was decomposed. It seems inescapable that this particular dolphin was not very bright, unless she was as short-sighted as Mr. McGoo.[13]

The Monkey's Paw

After honeybees and dolphins, it is natural to turn back to what have always seemed the most hopeful candidates for true animal language, the monkeys and apes (for convenience, we refer to both as *monkeys*). Though, as we have seen, monkeys have much in common

---

12 *Triakis semifasciatum.*

13 But before dismissing dolphin capabilities altogether, we must make one reservation. As Dreher and Evans have pointed out, not all the work being done on dolphins is being published: much of it is enveloped in, military secrecy. Already in 1963, L. Harrison Matthews, then Director of the London Zoo, remarked that "some people are proposing to prostitute their biological work on the Cetacea and involve the animals in human international strife by training them as underwater watch-dogs to guard naval installations from frogmen, or to act as unmanned submarines. Intelligent as the animals may be, they are, unfortunately, not sufficiently intelligent to refuse cooperation and treat their trainers to some of those characteristic underwater noises which, if produced in the air, would be regarded as gestures of contempt."

with dolphins, they differ from them strikingly in at least one respect. They have agile bodies and mobile faces. Most species have considerable repertoires of calls, and some species living in dense forest rely heavily on these. But many species live partly on the ground and/or in relatively open country, where visibility is good; and these include the species we know most about. Among these monkeys, visual signals, made by gesture, posture and facial expression, are far more important than vocal signals made by calls. Thus in the rhesus monkey[14] colony studied by Vernon Reynolds at Whipsnade Zoo, 73 signal units could be distinguished. Of these 63 were visual signals, and only 10 were calls. In another rhesus community, Stuart A. Altmann recorded a total of 5504 signalling events. Only 5.1% of these social signals involved calls (with or without accompanying gestures), and only 3% consisted of calls alone. Comparable counts have not been made for chimpanzees, among whom the richness and sensitivity of facial expression are considerably greater than among rhesus monkeys.

Unlike the honeybee code, which concerns itself entirely with information about economics—whereabouts of food, weather conditions, state of the hive's food reserves, and so on—monkey signalling is mainly concerned with emotional states and events and interpersonal relationships. Thus 36 vocal units have been distinguished in vervet monkeys[15] by Thomas T. Struhsaker, working in the Amboseli Reserve of Kenya. Only 7 of these refer to events in the natural surroundings (sighting, approach or sudden movement of various kinds of predatory animals); 3 are not really signals (coughing, sneezing, vomiting); the other 26 all refer to different social situations (such as a subordinate monkey appeasing a dominant one nearby, a female protesting she is not in the mood for sex, or several monkeys warning of the approach of a "foreign" group of the same species).

In Struhsaker's study of the vervet monkeys, he found that the calls occurred in at least 21 different situations, and produced at least 22 different responses in the monkeys who heard them. As with the dolphins, studies of the situations evoking different signals and their effects on other individuals have been made in many monkey species, in this case for visual as well as vocal signals. One result of great interest has been the finding that different communities of the *same species* may have different signal codes. This is a special case of the fact that different communities of the same monkey species differ in many aspects of their behaviour, including diet, way of getting food, and even mating taboos. Thus among Japanese monkeys[16] one community scratches up

---

14 *Macaca mulatta.*
15 *Cercopithecus aethiops.*
16 *Macaca fuscata.*

edible roots, another invades rice-fields, others do neither. It appears that young monkeys acquire the customs of their band by imitation and because some of their actions are encouraged, others discouraged, by mothers and leaders. Occasionally a new habit is adopted by a young monkey and accepted by his or her mother, and gradually spreads through the kinship group in the mother's line, and eventually to the whole band (except some of the older monkeys who, like old dogs, will not learn new tricks), being afterwards transmitted to subsequent generations. This has happened, for instance, in a band on Kōshima Island, with the practices of washing sweet potatoes before eating them and separating wheat grains (supplied by human observers) from the sand on which they have fallen by washing out a handful of grain and sand in water. In this way each band has its own *culture*, and this includes its own signal units. The Kōshima monkeys have acquired a completely new gesture for asking for food. A rhesus monkey community in Regent's Park Zoo used regularly to smack their lips as a friendly gesture and to execute a kind of press-up by bending and stretching their arms as a form of threat; neither gesture was ever seen in the rhesus community at Whipsnade.

Monkey signal codes have been much more studied than those of dolphins, and we know enough about them to be quite sure that they are simply automatic codes of signals which, as we saw earlier, are combined only according to emotional and not according to logical rules. Monkeys certainly have not evolved true languages. But so many combinations are at least possible, and monkey behaviour is so variable and exploratory, that several scientists have tried seriously to teach a *human* language to chimpanzees, the most variable and exploratory of them all. It has long been known that chimpanzees can respond separately to as many as 60 different human words. But then even a seal can do so to 35 words, and an elephant to 20. The real test is whether chimpanzees can be taught to use human words themselves, and to combine them, in appropriate ways. A very intensive attempt to teach a chimpanzee to talk was made some years ago by a married couple, both scientists, K. J. and Cathy Hayes. They adopted a baby chimp called Viki, and brought her up in their house exactly as if she were a human child, but using in addition the most sophisticated methods of teaching available. The result was disappointing. After 6 years of great effort and ingenuity, Viki had learned to utter only 4 sounds resembling English words. From this and other studies, it looked as if chimpanzees cannot be taught a human language.

So matters stood until June 1966, when another scientist couple, R. A. and Beatrice T. Gardner, began work at the University of Nevada with a female chimpanzee between 8 and 14 months old, whom they named Washoe after the county where the University is situated. Benefiting from the Hayes' experience, the Gardners had had an imaginative new idea. We have seen that most monkeys rely more on visual than on vocal signals. Even the actual vocal apparatus of chimpanzees is very different from man's. So instead of trying to teach *spoken* English, the Gardners decided to teach Washoe American Sign Language, as used by the deaf in North America, in which English words or concepts are represented by signs made with the hands; some of these symbols are representational, others are arbitrary, and all can be combined according to principles of English grammar and syntax. The Gardners and their colleagues brought up Washoe in shifts so that she never lacked for affectionate human company. They played all sorts of games with her and seem to have given her a very good time. All the time they were chattering among themselves in Sign Language, for it is known that simply being exposed to adults talking helps human children to learn to talk. They encouraged Washoe to imitate them, prompted her to get a sign right by repeating it themselves or by placing her hands in the right position, introduced plenty of toys and other objects to increase her vocabulary, encouraged her to "babble" with her hands, as a child does with his voice, and rewarded her for correct usage by tickling her, which she greatly enjoyed.

The results of all this were as follows. After 22 months of teaching, Washoe could use 34 words correctly in the appropriate circumstances. (She was only counted as knowing a word if three observers independently saw her use it correctly and without prompting). Whenever Washoe learned a new word, she very soon and quite spontaneously transferred it from a particular object, such as the key of a cupboard, to a whole class of objects, such as all keys. She would spontaneously call the humans' attention to objects by making the correct signs. She used the sign for "dog" when she saw a picture of a dog or even heard a dog bark without seeing it; evidently, like the dolphins, she had the capacity, previously supposed to be unique to man, of transposing patterns from one sense to another.

All this is remarkable, but Washoe did more. Without any prompting and apparently quite spontaneously, as soon as she had about 10 signs in her repertoire, Washoe began to *invent combinations* of signs and use them in a perfectly appropriate way. Among combinations which she invented are:—*open food drink*, for opening the refrigerator; *go sweet*, for being carried to a raspberry bush; *open flower*, to be let through the gate to a flower garden; and *listen eat*, at the sound of an alarm clock signalling meal-time. Just before the Gardners published their first results (in August 1969), Washoe had learned the pronouns *I-me* and *you*, "so that combinations that resemble short sentences have begun to appear." It only remains to add that Washoe's learning was accelerating—she had learned 4 signs in the first 7 months, 9 in the next, and 21 in the last 7 months.

Since Washoe unmistakably combines and recombines signs to describe objects and situations new to her in perfectly appropriate ways, this wonderful experiment seems to have established beyond doubt that a chimpanzee is capable of learning true language. True, at 3 years of age, she only has 34 words; at the equivalent age in terms of development, namely 5 years old, the average human child has a vocabulary of hundreds of words and makes sentences averaging 4.6 words in length. Sheer numerical differences of this kind may be important for the potentialities of human language. But the Gardners' achievement remains epoch-making. An animal has been taught to use true language, to communicate with human teachers.

The Origin of Language

So far, however, we have no evidence of any animals spontaneously evolving true language without anybody to teach them. Man *did*. How, and when, did this happen? What are the origins of human language? Our study of animal signals may help in some ways towards answering these questions.

How old is human language? Obviously it is at least as old as writing. The art of writing evolved rapidly in ancient Iraq between 3500 and 2900 B.C. A series of tablets from Erech, Jamdat Nasr, Ur and Fara tell the story of a transition from pictured objects and numbers to true writing with conventional signs for the syllables of the spoken language. But of course, even the first stage presupposes language itself, which must therefore be older than 3500 B.C. Much earlier than this, some time between 9000 and 6500 B.C., there lived at Ishango, on the shores of Lake Edward in the Congo, a people, apparently Negro, of great technological achievement for their time. The excellent bone harpoons they manufactured were exported as far as the Upper Nile and almost to the coast of West Africa. A bone tool-handle found at Ishango is marked with 3 series of notches grouped together in sets. One series has 11, 13, 17 and 19 notches—the 4 prime numbers between 10 and 20. Another has groups suggesting multiplication—3 and 6, 4 and 8, 10 and 5 and 5. The third series has 11 $(10 + 1)$, 21 $(20 + 1)$, 19 $(20 - 1)$ and 9 $(10 - 1)$, suggesting a decimal system. If these people really had a number system, they certainly must have talked, and we can put the age of language back to at latest 6500 B.C.

Now let us go back to the other end of man's story. Man-like beings who made and kept stone tools seem to have been at Olduvai Gorge in Tanzania 1,750,000 years ago, to judge from potassium dating. Now human language is connected with another peculiarity of man: his brain functions in an asymmetrical way. Language is controlled by the left side of the brain in 97% of human adults. The asymmetry also appears in the fact that most people are right-handed, whereas in monkeys right- and left-handedness appear to be about equally common. E. H. Lenneberg has suggested, for complicated reasons, that there is a *necessary* connection between the two things, language and an asymmetrical brain. Washoe has, perhaps, proved him wrong in one way; but the idea may still be relevant for the *initial spontaneous evolution* of language, as opposed to the capacity to learn it. It is said that the earliest human stone tools show evidence of a predominance of right-handed tool-makers; so if Lenneberg is right, man had the potentiality of developing language from his earliest beginnings.

But did he develop it at once? For nearly all of his 1,750,000 years, man continued to make simple hand-axes and flake tools. All these crude stone implements look virtually alike to those of us who are not experts in prehistoric archaeology; there is scarcely any obvious difference between hand-axes hundreds of thousands of years apart. Then, suddenly, in the last Ice Age, about 100,000 years ago, there was a breakthrough: people began to manufacture more and more elaborate stone and bone tools in greater and greater diversity. To us, the conclusion has seemed inescapable that this efflorescence was made possible by the emergence of true language.

We reached this conclusion a few years ago, and have since found we are not the first to reach it. In 1951, in his Inaugural Lecture as Derby Professor of Zoology in the University of Liverpool, R. J. Pumphrey presented just this hypothesis. Throughout those hundreds of thousands of years, he wrote, "the hand-axe and flake cultures show an extraordinary conservatism of type and an improvement in the technique of manufacture so gradual as to make the intervention of what we should call 'reason' unlikely in the extreme. . . . And then in the last Ice Age the picture changes . . . with dramatic suddenness." Pumphrey had already stressed the relationship between true language and planning for the future ("forward planning about lions"). He noted that in the last Ice Age a wide range of stone tools began to be designed and made *to make other tools* by boring, scraping, cutting and polishing bone and antler, "clear evidence of an objective reached through a planned and orderly succession of *different* operations." And so, he suggested, "characteristically human speech" appeared about 100,000 years ago in the last Ice Age.

A similar idea had apparently suggested itself independently to the Australian archaeologist V. Gordon Childe. In an article published in 1953, he too noted the enormous acceleration of technical progress in the last Ice Age, and concluded that this "apparent change in tempo might reasonably be attributed to the increasing use of a more flexible system of symbols with which to 'operate in the head' as a substitute for physical trial-and-error processes."

Suppose that true language did originate in or just before the last Ice Age: we have still to consider what stimulated this momentous development. Now we have seen that monkey bands are regulated by automatic codes of signals, and that these signal codes *vary* between bands of the same species. This creates no new problems of communication, for when monkey bands meet they do not normally mix, interacting only by a set of common threat signals, simpler than those used within the band. When bands of howler monkeys meet, for instance, each band sets up a howl, and the louder band must be the larger; the smaller and less noisy band discreetly withdraws. Human beings originally moved about in similar small groups, and there was probably comparatively little contact between these groups. While still living under these conditions, they developed the manufacture of durable tools. They could very well manage to continue to function thus, tools and all, on the basis of automatic monkey-like codes of signals. Chimpanzees are known to shape sticks and straws to size, for fighting leopards and for luring termites out of their nests, respectively.

But about 300,000–400,000 years ago, man achieved control of fire, gathered on lavafields or from lightning brush fires and carefully kept burning, and some time between then and the last Ice Age he discovered how to *light* fires himself. These tremendous advances gave him a new control over his environment, notably in defence against predators and protection from the cold; the world human population increased considerably, and spread out over the continents, invading temperate and even colder regions for the first time. Now there were many more small groups, and more likelihood of their meeting frequently. Moreover, tools at last began to become gradually more elaborate and diversified from group to group. With this frequent contact between groups, and this incentive to borrow and copy each other's tools, a new development began. The old automatic signal codes would not work *between* groups (compare the Carniolan and Italian honeybees). The automatic noises and gestures that had formerly sufficed would eventually have to be replaced by *words*—overriding and controlling automatic moods—intelligible and intelligent between groups with different cultures. In this way man was stimulated to break the link between signal and automatic mood, and begin the logical combination of signals, or true language. Claire Russell has shown that a connection between the dawn of language and contact between culturally different groups can be detected in myths from several parts of the world. Gordon Childe has summarized the considerable evidence for trade and technical influence, and hence for communication, between culturally different groups great distances apart in the last Ice Age. So we may plausibly suppose that increasing contact between culturally separate groups was the stimulus for the evolution of true language. Even today, intercultural relations can stimulate new combinations of words—as in the case cited earlier of East African recruits and the phrases *colour of blood* and *colour of leaves.*

It remains to ask, why vocal rather than sign language, especially since chimpanzees and other advanced monkeys are, as we have seen, so geared to visual signals? Now we have also seen that where visibility is poor, calls predominate, as in dolphins or monkeys of dense forest. Martin Moynihan studied a Central American monkey active at night —the night monkey.[17] Though this species has only 10 calls, it has even fewer visual signals, and uses the calls far more. Now human eyes are not much use at night, and one of the results of man's control of fire was a new ability to continue his activities after sundown. Kenneth Oakley has suggested that "the lighting aspect of fire was probably almost as important as its heating aspect in extending man's range northwards." But visibility is *far from perfect* on a dark night around a flickering fire, and we may suppose that, as man became active at night, the value of vocal signals would greatly increase. So, we may conjecture, when true language appeared, it was conveyed by voice and not by gesture, until the deaf and their teachers, and certain monks, evolved sign languages to translate existing spoken ones.

The Future of Language

Finally, let us return to our contrast of economic and emotional information. We have seen that monkey signalling is heavily biased towards emotion. With the coming of true language in man, the balance tipped towards economics. For purposes of handling tools, techniques, science, our natural surroundings, language has come a long way since the last Ice Age, and made possible the achievement of many marvels, from bone harpoons to moon-walks. But for purposes of communicative mood, for conveying subtle and sophisticated aspects of emotion and human relationship, language was, and still is, only developed to a rudimentary degree. We continue to convey emotion by crude, often unconscious, automatic signal codes, carried by "calls"— our *tone of voice* when speaking—or by the posture changes, gestures and facial expressions with which we are interacting all the time—as you can easily see by turning off the sound on your television set during an interview, discussion or documentary. These signals vary from group to group, transmitted as a crude and automatic culture in the monkey

[17] *Aotus trivirgatus.*

way, while true language is transmitting its creative culture of accumulated knowledge. The gesture we call beckoning means a summons in Britain, a dismissal in Italy, a deadly insult in Malawi—such variation is an obvious source of cross-purposes. In an isolated Scandinavian village, a scientist noticed that everyone bowed to a certain whitewashed wall. They did not know why—they did not even know they were doing it till he asked. He removed the whitewash, and found a religious ikon, *centuries* old. How is such a pattern transmitted? We once saw, on documentary film, a Japanese mother in traditional dress with her baby on her back, bowing to a Shinto shrine. As she bowed, she put her hand behind her own head and *pushed the baby's head down.*

Language itself is involved in this automatic signalling, through tone of voice and also accent, which differs from group to group like other patterns, and forms the basis for crude stress behaviour of a highly automatic kind. At worst, it directs violence: the ancient Israelites are said to have massacred, on one occasion, all who could not pronounce the word *shibboleth*; the medieval Sicilians, rising against the French, killed all who could not pronounce the word *ciceri*. At mildest, such signal differences may affect cultural cross-mating, as neatly indicated in the Ira Gershwin lyric—"You say potartoes and I say potaytoes, You say tomartoes and I say tomaytoes, Potartoes, potaytoes, Tomartoes, tomaytoes, Let's call the whole thing off."

Our very talking may be as compulsive and conditioned as that of Bastian's female dolphin: humans, too, are liable to talk when alone, and often when two apparently converse, neither is listening to the other or really concerned whether the other listens to them. We may also be conditioned by words—and conditioning is the reduction of variability of behaviour, whereas learning is the increase of variability. Russian scientists have "trained" human individuals to blink in reaction to spoken sentences. The sentences worked as a conditioning signal even if the word order was reversed, just as the song of a robin has been recorded, reversed and played back (by the French scientists Bremond and Busnel) to another robin, who reacted exactly as to the usual song. Language is here debased to the level of a crude signalling system. And all these many indications of deficiency and degradation of language appear far more when we discuss emotion than when we discuss technical matters. Indeed language has so far been of little help in relieving the sense of emotional isolation from which humans have always suffered. "What are the sorrows of other men to us" wrote Daniel Defoe, "and what their joy? . . . Our passions are all exercised in retirement; we love, we hate, we covet, we enjoy, all in privacy and solitude. All that we communicate of those things to any other is but for their assistance in the pursuit of our desires; the end is at home . . . it is for ourselves we enjoy, and for ourselves we suffer."

Mankind, then, has achieved technical wonders by means of his true language such as no animal could begin to achieve. It is now time— and high time, for we live in an age of emotional turmoil under the stress of population pressure—for man to begin to achieve wonders of emotional relationship and social harmony. Perhaps, to emancipate signals from immediate emotional impulse, the stimulus of discussing technical matters was necessary. But now we may hope to use the subtlety and power of language for true *communication* about our emotions. Art, and above all poetry, has been man's chief effort so far in this direction, and it is fitting that this series of lectures is launched by the Institute of Contemporary Arts. It is fitting, too, to end our story with a poem (by Claire Russell) about language.

Words, like pebbles galore
At the mouth of the sea,
Litter the shore
Of society.
Worn into every shape and size
Their hard reality defies
The sea's speechless agitated tongue
That lives and cries
Upon the wind, unsung.

I wonder what these words are for
That I pick up along the shore;
I wander restlessly to seek
For pebbles of reality,
I wander restlessly along the shore to speak
Against the stormy agitated feelings of society.
But the storm defies
The pebbly scientific tongue
And a voice that dies
Upon the wind, unsung.

Pebbly words galore
Litter the shore,
While speechless feelings seek
To speak;
And a voice that lives and cries
With an agitated tongue
Echoes a voice that ever lives and dies,
As waves upon the wind, a far off magic legend that is sung.

Further Reading

1. Babies

Irwin, O. C.: *Infant Speech, Scientific American Reprint* 417 (San Francisco, 1949).

Wasz-Höckert, O.; Lind, J.; Vuorenkoski, V.; Partanen, T.; Valanné, E.: *The Infant Cry* (London, 1968), with 45 rpm record.

2. Bees

Von Frisch, K.: *The Dance Language and Orientation of Bees*, translated by L. E. Chadwick (London, 1967).

3. Whales, Dolphins and Porpoises

Andersen, H. T. (Ed.): *The Biology of Marine Mammals* (New York and London, 1969).

Busnel, R. H. G. (Ed.): *Animal Sonar Systems: Biology and Bionics*, Vol. 2 (Jouy-en-Josas, France, 1966).

Norris, K. S. (Ed.): *Whales, Dolphins and Porpoises* (Berkeley and Los Angeles, 1966).

Tavolga, W. N. (Ed.): *Marine Bio-Acoustics* (Oxford, London and New York, 1964).

4. Monkeys and Apes

Altmann, S. A. (Ed.): *Social Communication among Primates* (Chicago and London, 1967).

Devore, I. (Ed.): *Primate Behavior* (New York and London, 1965).

Gardner, R. A. and Gardner, B. T.: "Teaching Sign Language to a Chimpanzee," *Science* 165, pp. 664–72 (15th August, 1969).

Morris, D.: *The Naked Ape* (London, 1967).

Moynihan, M.: *Some Behaviour Patterns of Platyrrhine Monkeys. 1. The Night Monkey* (Aotus trivirgatus) (Washington, 1964).

Russell, C. and Russell, W. M. S.: *Violence, Monkeys and Man* (London, 1968).

Southwick, C. J. (Ed.): *Primate Social Behaviour* (Princeton and London, 1963).

5. Language and Animal Signals: General

Cornwall, I. V.: *The World of Ancient Man* (London, 1964).

Count, E. W.: "An Essay on Phasia: on the Phylogenesis of Man's Speech Function," *Homo* 19, pp. 170–227 (1969).

Gerard, R. W.; Kluckhohn, C. and Rapoport, A.: "Biological and Cultural Evolution: Some Analogies and Explorations," *Behavioral Science* 1, pp. 6–34 (1956).

Hastings, H. (Ed.): *Abbé Bougeant: Amusement Philosophique sur le Language des Bêtes* (Geneva and Lille, 1954).

Heinzelin, J. de: "Ishango," *Scientific American Reprint* 613 (San Francisco, 1962).

Hockett, C. D.: "The Origin of Speech," *Scientific American Reprint* 603 (San Francisco, 1960).

Kalmus, H.: "Ethnic Differences in Sensory Perception," *Journal of Biosocial Science* Supplement 1, pp. 81–90 (1969).

Lenneberg, E. H.: *Biological Foundations of Language* (New York and London, 1967).

Métraux, G. S. and Crouzet, F.: *The Evolution of Science* (London, 1963).

Oakley, K.: "Fire as Palaeolithic Tool and Weapon," *Proceeding of the Prehistoric Society* 21, pp. 36–48 (1955).

Pike, K. L.: *Tone Languages* (Ann Arbor, 1948).

Pumphrey, R. J.: *The Origin of Language* (Liverpool, 1951).

Russell, C.: *Forbidden Fruit* (Stockholm, in press).

———— and Russell, W. M. S.: *Human Behaviour: a New Approach* (London, 1961).

Russell, W. M. S.: "Animals, Robots and Man; Signals and Shibboleths," *The Listener* 68, pp. 169–70, 207–8, 213 (2nd and 9th August, 1962).

————: *Man, Nature and History* (London, 1967).

Smith, F. and Miller, G. A. (Ed.): *The Genesis of Language* (Cambridge, Mass., and London, 1966).

Thompson, S.: *Motif-Index of Folk-Literature* Volume 1 (Helsinki, 1932).

Tinbergen, N.: *The Herring Gull's World* (London, 1953).

————: *Social Behaviour in Animals* (London, 1953).

Woolley, Sir Leonard: *The Beginnings of Civilization* (London, 1963).

FOR DISCUSSION AND REVIEW

1 According to the Russells, what do human spoken language and the calls used by a great variety of animals have in common?

2 What is a *phoneme*?

3 The Russells refer to two categories of symbols, *representative symbols* and *arbitrary symbols*. What distinctions are made between them? In what way are these concepts useful or valuable?

4 The Russells state that the "power of producing new combinations is crucial to true language." Explain this statement by using several examples or illustrations.

5 What do the Russells mean by "true language"? How do they differentiate it from "automatic signal codes"? Do you agree with their distinction? Explain.

6 Discuss the symbolism involved in the bee's "round dance" and "tail-wagging dance." Why do the Russells say these dances are not true language?

7 What is your opinion of the Russells' theory concerning "the origin of language"? Explain.

8 Why, according to the Russells, have man's messages tended to be "economic" and not "emotional"? Do the Russells offer a solution for this probelm? Discuss.

2

Sarah: A Remarkable Chimp

The most interesting work to date in the effort to teach a chimpanzee a complicated language system has been done by Ann and David Premack with Sarah at the University of California, Santa Barbara. In the following selection, Professors Fromkin and Rodman discuss Sarah's many "language" achievements. Although these achievements certainly do not disprove the idea that only humans possess language, they do show that chimpanzees have more linguistic ability than had previously been believed.

Victoria Fromkin and Robert Rodman

A REMARKABLE CHIMP, named Sarah, is now being taught a language very similar to English by David Premack, a psychologist at the University of California, Santa Barbara.[1] The units of Sarah's "language" consist of differently shaped and colored plastic symbols which are metal-backed. Sarah and her trainers "talk" to each other by arranging these symbols on a magnetic board. Sarah has been taught to associate particular symbols with particular meanings. These symbols are the "words" or "morphemes"[2] of Sarah's language. Thus a small red square means "banana" and a small blue rectangle means "apricot." Some of these symbols are shown in Figure 1. These and others reveal that Sarah has words for nouns, adjectives, and verbs. She even has symbols for abstract concepts like "same as" and "different from," "negation," and even a symbol to represent "question."

The forms of these symbols are *arbitrarily* related to their meanings. For example, the color red is represented by a gray chip, and the color yellow by a black chip. Sarah has learned the concepts "name of" and "color of." Premack is able to ask Sarah for "the color of name of blue" (that is, the color of the plastic chip that means "blue"). Sarah selects

---

[1] Ann James Premack and David Premack, "Teaching Language to an Ape," *Scientific American* (October 1972).

[2] For a definition of *morpheme*, see note on p. 224.

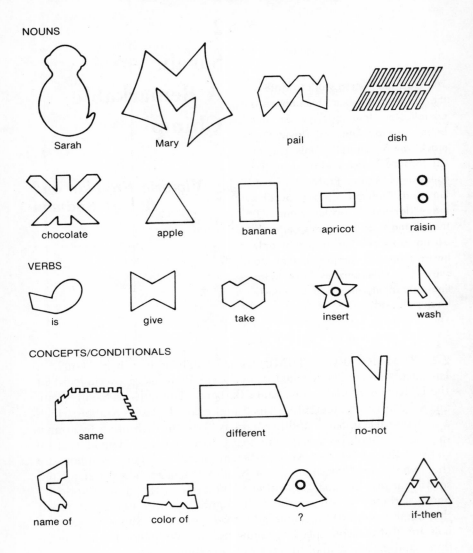

Fig. 1. Plastic symbols that varied in color, shape, and size were chosen as the language units to be taught to Sarah. The plastic pieces were backed with metal so they would adhere to a magnetic board. Each plastic symbol stood for a specific word or concept. A "Chinese" convention of writing sentences vertically from top to bottom was adopted because at the beginning of her training Sarah seemed to prefer it. Sarah had to put the words in proper sequence, but the orientation of the word symbols was not important. Actually, most of these symbols were colored. (Adapted from "Teaching Language to an Ape" by Ann James Premack and David Premack, *Scientific American*, October 1972. Copyright © 1972 by Scientific American, Inc. All rights reserved.)

the gray plastic chip which means "red," since red is the color of the chip that means "blue." We can see that Sarah is even capable of using language as a metalanguage to describe her language. If you're confused, remember that a "dumb" chimpanzee named Sarah has no difficulty with this task.

Indeed, such "conversations" occasionally bore Sarah. During a particularly tedious drill one time, Sarah reached out and stole all the plastic tokens. Then, as if to suggest "let's get the whole thing over with," she wrote out all the questions she was being asked as well as the corresponding answers. This was very clever, showing that Sarah knew the questions and the answers. But she did not (and probably could not) write out "no questions" even though she had a "word" for "no" and one for "question." She is able to form new sentences, but only in the exact form of those she has been carefully taught.

Yet, Sarah seems to have mastered some rules of syntax. And like children, no one specifically teaches her these rules. She must generalize from the data. For example, given the sentence *If Sarah put red on green, Mary give Sarah chocolate*, Sarah will dutifully place a red card on top of a green card and collect her reward. The sentence *If Sarah put green on red, Mary give Sarah chocolate* also evokes the correct response. Sarah is quite obviously sensitive to word order—that is, the "syntax" of the sentences.

Sarah is also able to understand some complex sentence structures. She was taught to respond correctly to sentences such as *Sarah insert apple pail* (that is, "Sarah, insert the apple in the pail"), *Sarah insert banana pail, Sarah insert apple dish,* and *Sarah insert banana dish.* These sentences were then combined into *Sarah insert apple pail Sarah insert banana dish.* Sarah performed both tasks. Then a "transformational rule" was performed on this sentence by the trainer, which deleted the second occurrence of *Sarah insert. . . .* This transformed sentence given Sarah was *Sarah insert apple pail banana dish.* Sarah still performed the complicated instruction, showing that she "understood" the "underlying" compound sentence. She correctly grouped together *apple* with *pail* and *banana* with *dish* rather than incorrectly grouping *pail* with *banana*, and she did not put the apple, pail, and banana in the dish, as the word order would suggest. Thus we see that when Sarah processes a sentence she does more than link words in simple linear order. She imposes a hierarchical structure, just as we do. Sarah's grammar apparently possesses a transformational rule, which associates Figure 2 with Figure 3.

Does Sarah disprove the notion that only humans can learn language? Sarah's language certainly seems to include many of the properties of human language: arbitrariness of the linguistic sign,

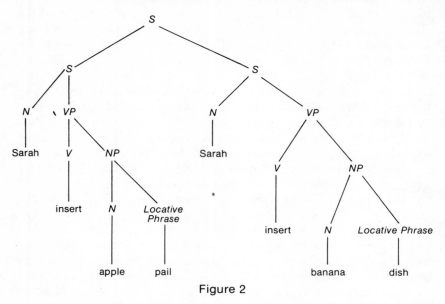

Figure 2

"open-endedness" or "creativity," hierarchical structure, transformational rules.

One major difference between the way Sarah has learned her language and the way children learn theirs is that each new rule has been introduced in a deliberate, highly constrained way. When parents speak to children they do not confine themselves to a few words in a particu-

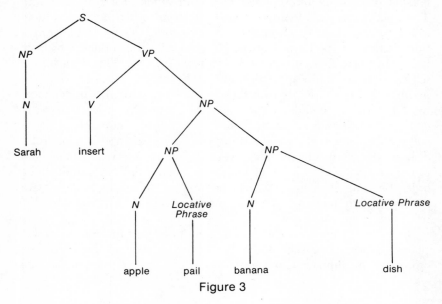

Figure 3

lar order for months, rewarding the child with a chocolate bar or a banana each time the child correctly responds to a command. Nor do they wait until the child has "mastered" one rule of grammar before going on to a different structure.

Young children require no special training. Children brought up with little adult "reinforcement" or encouragement will acquire all the complexities of their language. This is demonstrated by children brought up in orphan homes or institutions. Of course, exposure to language is required. Feral children such as those raised by animals do not learn language. . . . Normal children, while they require exposure to language, are not taught language the way Sarah is being taught.

Furthermore, Sarah does not "initiate" any conversations. Her use of the language being taught her is in response to her trainers' questions. Sarah responds because she is rewarded. The reward may be food, or it may be approval from her trainers. She does not use language the way humans do.

It would be interesting to see what would happen if another chimp were taught Sarah's language. Would they communicate with each other using this language? And if they were mated and bore baby chimps, could they teach their babies the new chimp language? If such could happen we would then know the origin of "Chimpanese."

The differences between Sarah's language acquisition and that of normal human children in no way negate the great achievement on Sarah's part and also on the part of Dr. Premack. At this time we do not know how much more Sarah will learn. We do know that a child by the age of four has already learned complex rules and a grammar qualitatively beyond what Sarah has mastered.

When we try to compare Sarah's language with human language we immediately perceive the impossibility of separating linguistic ability from general intelligence. The human animal appears to possess a brain capable of far greater analytic and synthetic abilities than does the chimpanzee, or any other animal. "Stupid" humans are far "smarter" than "smart" chimpanzees. If language is the result of superior brain mechanisms, then the kind of language learned and used by humans remains unique to the species.

If language is defined merely as a system of communication, then language is not unique to man. There are, however, certain characteristics of human language which are not found in the communication systems of any other species. A basic property of human language is its creative aspect—a speaker's ability to string together *discrete units* to form an *infinite* set of "well-formed" sentences. Furthermore, children need not be taught language in any controlled way; they require only linguistic input to enable them to form their own grammar.

The fact that deaf children learn language shows that the ability to hear or produce sounds is not a necessary prerequisite for language learning. And the ability to "imitate" the sounds of human language is not a sufficient basis for the learning of language, since "talking" birds imitate sounds but can neither segment these sounds into smaller units nor understand what they are imitating.

Birds, bees, crabs, wolves, dolphins, chimpanzees, and most other animals communicate in some way. Limited information is imparted, and emotions such as fear, and warnings, are emitted. But the communication systems are fixed and limited. They are *stimulus-bound*. This is not so of human language. Experiments to teach animals more complicated language systems have historically failed. Recently, however, some chimps have demonstrated an ability to master some subset of a human language. It is possible that the higher primates have the limited ability to be taught *some* complex rules. To date, however, language still seems to be unique to man.

FOR DISCUSSION AND REVIEW

1   What are the "words" of Sarah's language? Can she deal with abstractions?

2   What do Fromkin and Rodman mean when they say that Sarah's "symbols are *arbitrarily* related to their meanings"?

3   A metalanguage is a language that is "potentially self-reflexive," that is, a language that can be used to talk about itself. Sarah can use language as a metalanguage. Why is this ability so important?

4   How "creative" is Sarah's use of language? Explain.

5   What properties of human language does Sarah's language seem to possess?

6   According to Fromkin and Rodman, how does a young child's acquisition of language differ from Sarah's? How do their uses of language differ?

3

Feral and Isolated Man

Roger Brown

There is for "civilized" people an aura of exoticism and fascination surrounding humans who are wild or "uncivilized." We measure ourselves against such individuals and hope to see revealed in them some of the reasons for our own behavior. Studies of feral and isolated humans also hope to tell us something about the acquisition of language. However, one of the major problems in the studies of such individuals is the determination of those factors that are hereditarily linked and those that are the product of environment. In the following article, Roger Brown reviews nine of the major specimens of feral and isolated man found to date in the light of those forces most influential on behavior.

IN THE TENTH edition of his *Systemae Naturae*, published in 1758, Linnaeus listed *Homo Ferus* (L. wild man) as a subdivision of the genus *Homo Sapiens*. The defining characteristics of feral man, succinctly listed by Linnaeus, were *tetrapus, mutus, hursutus*. There were nine historical records of wild men available to the great taxonomist. These included the Hessian wolf-boy of 1349, the Lithuanian bear-boy of 1661, and Wild Peter of Hanover of 1724. Since Linnaeus' time about thirty additional cases have accumulated. These cases have generally conformed to two of Linnaeus' specifications: They have lacked speech and have gone on all fours. The majority have not been especially hirsute and that characteristic does not help define feral man. An attribute not mentioned by Linnaeus, but reliably found in these cases, is the depression of sexuality. It appears, like speech, to be a function that a society must develop. Within the class of feral men a distinction should be made between those known to have been nurtured by wild animals and those who lived on their own in the wilds.

It must be assumed that these latter cases lived in human society until they were old enough to wander off and look after themselves. They fall between true feral man and cases of extreme isolation. It has sometimes happened that a child has been shut away from human society except for routine feeding. These cases, living with minimal human aid, are called isolated man.

Feral and isolated man interest the psychologist, philosopher, and sociologist because they provide an important natural experiment on the relative importance of genetic and environmental factors in the determination of all aspects of human behavior. The importance of feral man to the science of man was perceived long ago. Lord Monboddo proclaimed the discovery of Wild Peter of Hanover to be more important than the discovery of 30,000 new stars. Wild Peter was brought from Hanover to England by King George so that he might be used to test the doctrine of innate ideas. The king presented Peter to the enlightened princess of Wales and she placed him in charge of Dr. Arbuthnot, that good friend of Pope and Swift.

While Peter began the tradition of scientific interest in feral man, he also, unfortunately, began an equally hardy tradition of scientific difficulty in interpreting the data so obtained. There was, first of all, the problem of determining the exact circumstances of Peter's earlier life. From a number of sources it seems clear that he had lived for some time in human society. He was probably the child of a certain widower whose second wife drove Peter from the house. There was, secondly, the problem of estimating Peter's native intelligence. The behavior of feral man somewhat resembles that of the ament living in human society. If one cannot decide whether or not these cases are congenitally deficient, the results obtained are all open to the following directly opposed interpretations.

The extreme environmentalists, like Rousseau, have found in feral man proof of the infinite plasticity of man. The feral cases violate all parochial notions of human nature and prove that human nature is created in society and may take any form that society dictates. However, the extreme environmentalist cannot deny the importance of genetic factors since, as Zingg remarks, there is something lacking to make this case complete—a wolf or dog who has been trained to human behavior. He can acknowledge that the character of the species sets limits on behavioral development but that, within these limits, environment is the principal factor.

The student who is inclined to give more importance to heredity will interpret the cases of feral man quite differently. He believes them all to be congenitally feeble-minded; their behavior simply demonstrates the strong determining power of innate intelligence. Aments, whether in human or wolf society, are much alike. To be sure some feral cases have recovered and demonstrated considerable learning ability, but these cases cannot have been true aments, in the opinion of the men backing heredity. Their recovery proves that when there is no genetic deficiency the most unfavorable environment has only a temporary handicapping effect. With this uncertainty about native intelligence the environmentalist cannot prove that genetically normal human specimens are rendered permanently inhuman by the lack of society in their early years. Those that remain *mutus* and *tetrapus* may be feeble-minded. Those that recover have not remained inhuman. The environmentalist points out, with irritation, the improbability that all feral cases would be feeble-minded. The heredity-man counters that the feeble-minded child is just the one to be driven out of his home or exposed to wild beasts and furthermore, not all feral men are assumed to be feeble-minded—only those who do not recover. In the opinion of the environmentalist, anyone who thinks that a child who has survived in the wilds on his own initiative could possibly be feeble-minded . . . —the man who thinks that must himself be suspected of feeble-mindedness. We tiptoe out and softly close the door behind us. Let us look at several of the best documented cases to see if they do not teach something more modest than the truth about human nature, perhaps something about the nature of language.

The Wild Boy of Aveyron. The case of Victor, the wild boy of Aveyron, [is described in the Introduction to Brown's book]. Victor was about twelve years old when he was captured in the Caune Woods and Dr. Itard tried for five years to teach him to speak and read. Victor succeeded in understanding a large number of words and phrases but he could produce no speech except the two exclamations: *"Oh, Dieu!"* and *"Lait!"* These came out, in very imperfect form, quite early in training. The discrepancy between the boy's achievements in reading and in speech production requires some explanation.

It is conceivable that Victor's mentality was adequate to the full use of language and that he was simply held back by inability to master the business of articulation and phonation. Perhaps the impulse to babble which is so evident in infants operates on a maturational timetable such that it must receive social support when the readiness is there or the impulse will die. The pecking response in chicks is an example of this kind of timed skill. A bright spot elicits the pecking response in newborn chicks. When chicks were raised in the dark and fed by dropper for fourteen days it was found that they would not peck though exposed to daylight. The original study includes a dramatic photograph of a starving chick standing in the midst of a pile of grain—not pecking! Itard's experience with Victor suggests that speech in man, like pecking in chicks, may require social reinforcement at the crucial age when the impulse is ripe or else it will not develop at all. To evaluate this proposal we will look at other cases of feral and isolated man.

Kamala and Amala. Since 1850, at least, there have been constant reports of wolf-children in India. Some of the Indian people have a superstitious reluctance to kill wolves and there has also been a practice of exposing unwanted children. Most of those carried off have certainly been killed but occasionally the child is taken to the wolf den and survives for a time as an extra cub.

In 1920 the Rev. A. L. Singh was told of a *manushbhaga*, a man ghost, haunting a certain Indian village. The ghost had been seen in the company of wolves going in and out of a giant dead ant hill which the animals presumably used as a den. Singh had a shooting platform built over the hill. He and some natives watched there one night and saw a procession of mother wolf and cubs, two of which looked human though they went on all fours and had long matted hair. The local natives would not dig out the hill but Singh brought in some more willing workers. The mother darted out to attack the invaders, and was killed. In the den itself they found a monkey ball of four little creatures clinging together—two cubs and two little girls.

Kamala was about eight years old and Amala only one and one-half. They were thoroughly wolfish in appearance and behavior: Hard callus had developed on their knees and palms from going on all fours. Their teeth were sharp edged. They moved their nostrils sniffing food. Eating and drinking were accomplished by lowering their mouths to the plate. They ate raw meat and, on one occasion, killed and devoured a whole chicken. At night they prowled and sometimes howled. They shunned other children but followed the dog and cat. They slept rolled up together on the floor.

Amala died within a year but Kamala lived to be eighteen. Both children's bodies were covered with sores when they were captured. Mrs. Singh healed these and softened their skins with oils and massage. She fed and bathed and caressed Kamala and evidently was the means of her socialization. The first sign that Kamala had become "involved" with a human being appeared when Mrs. Singh returned from a trip and Kamala ran to her with evident affection. In time Kamala learned to walk erect, to wear clothing and even to speak a few words.

Because Amala learned to talk a little, and promised to learn more, we cannot believe that continuous social support of infantile babbling is an essential pre-requisite to speech. Vocalization survived in her as an operant response while it did not for Victor. It is, of course, possible that Kamala lived for a longer time with adults than did Victor and so received more reinforcement for vocalizing. The situation, however, was the reverse. Victor was not found in the care of animals but was living alone. A child could survive outside of human society at an earlier age if it was in the society of some animal than would be possible if it had to shift for itself in the wilds. Victor is likely to have remained longer at home. It seems that speech is possible even when left dormant for many childhood years. Victor's failure was probably due to some specific impairment—probably of hearing. The facts on several cases of extreme social isolation will reinforce these conclusions.

Cases of Extreme Social Isolation. In 1937, in Illinois, the child Anna was discovered tied to a chair in a second floor attic-like room. She was nearly six years of age, emaciated, and speechless. She had received absolutely minimal attention since her birth, had been fed almost exclusively on cow's milk, seldom moved from her chair, and never instructed in anything. Anna was an illegitimate child whose mother had hidden her away to avoid the anger of the child's grandfather.

The child was taken to a county home for retarded children and, after a year and a half there, removed to a private home. Anna lived for only four more years. In that time she learned to walk, to dress herself, to play simple games with other children, and to speak a little. She could call attendants by name and had a few sentences to express her desires. The school report on Anna expressed the opinion that she was probably congenitally feeble-minded. This diagnosis is strengthened by the fact that Anna's mother proved to be a middle-grade moron with an IQ of 50 on the Stanford revision of the Binet-Simon scale. The probability that feral and isolated children who have learned little or no speech were feeble-minded is increased by the remarkable achievements of another isolated child—Isabelle.

Isabelle was found in Ohio at about the same time as Anna. Isabelle was also nearly of an age with Anna, being six and one-half at the time of her discovery. She was the illegitimate child of a deaf mute, and mother and child had lived most of the time in a darkened room away from the rest of the family. Isabelle behaved in many ways like a wild animal. She was fearful and hostile. She had no speech and made only a croaking noise. At first she seemed deaf, so unused were her senses.

Isabelle was taken away and given excellent care by doctors and clinical psychologists. Although her first score on the Stanford-Binet was nineteen months, practically at the zero point of the scale, a program of speech training was, nevertheless, undertaken. A week of intensive work was required to elicit even a first vocalization. Yet a little more than two months later she was beginning to put sentences together. Nine months after that, she could identify words and sentences on the printed page and write very well. Isabelle passed through the usual stages of linguistic development at a greatly accelerated rate. She covered in two years the learning that ordinarily occupies six years. By the age of eight and one-half Isabelle had a normal IQ and was not easily distinguished from ordinary children of her age. In this case speech behaved like many other human and animal performances; the delayed subject progressed at an accelerated rate, presumably because of her maturity.

The case of Isabelle strongly suggests that a child with good congenital intelligence can overcome the mutism caused by social isolation. It is possible that Anna would have done as well with equally expert tutelage but it seems likely that Anna was not Isabelle's equal in congenital intelligence. We do not yet know how many years of social isolation it is possible to overcome with speech training. The excellent results with Isabelle indicate that as many as six and one-half years of isolation can be made up. The moderate success with Kamala (carried on by less expert teachers) suggests that much may be done to offset even eight years of isolation from the human community.

Neither feral nor isolated man creates his own language these days, but must not such a man have done so once in some prehistoric time and so got language started? Actually the circumstances in which language must have begun represent a combination for which we can provide no instances. We have animals among themselves, animals in linguistic communities, and humans among animals, and in none of these cases does language develop. We have humans raised in linguistic communities and, in these circumstances, language does develop. What about a human born into a human society that has no language? We don't know of any such societies and so we don't know of any such individuals. But these must have been the circumstances of language origination. We shall be better able to guess what happened in these circumstances, intermediate between the primate community and the linguistic community, when we are clearer about the lines of phyletic advance that lead toward language function.

FOR DISCUSSION AND REVIEW

1   What three characteristics did Linnaeus use to differentiate *Homo Ferus* and *Homo Sapiens*? Which characteristic is not helpful in defining feral man? Is there a characteristic Linnaeus fails to mention? Explain.

2   What is the difference between feral and isolated man?

3   Human beings are social creatures. What problems or complications arise because of this fact when we attempt to determine how language is acquired?

4   Brown says, "We have animals among themselves, animals in linguistic communities, and humans among animals, and in none of these cases does language develop." Is it the linguist's conclusion that language is human? Explain.

5   Discuss the pros and cons of the heredity-environment issue as posed in Brown's essay.

4
The Language of Children

Peter Farb

Although we usually do not think much about it, children's ability to learn their native language before they reach the age of five or six and without systematized instruction is a remarkable achievement. Until recently, little research has been done in this area. Noam Chomsky's ideas about language, however, have heightened interest and stimulated research in the field of language acquisition. In the following selection from *Words at Play*, Peter Farb examines the remarkable abilities of children to acquire language, calling our attention to aspects of this phenomenon that we know about but whose significance we probably have not considered. "The unfolding of a child's language," as Farb emphasizes, "is a wondrous thing to listen to."

CAROLUS LINNAEUS, the eighteenth-century inventor of the system of classification of living things still in use, listed *Homo ferus*, Latin for "wild man," as a subdivision of our species, *Homo sapiens*. The characteristics of the feral form of human life, he declared, were hairiness, walking on all fours—and lack of speech. When Linnaeus made his classification, he knew of ten cases of "wolf children" abandoned by their parents to fend for themselves and purportedly nurtured by wild animals. Since then upward of thirty more cases have been thoroughly documented, although it has never been demonstrated that these children were reared by wolves or by any other animals. Scientists and philosophers early recognized the importance of "wolf children," because such wild creatures provide natural experiments in the way man develops his behavior when isolated from society. In fact, the capture of "Wild Peter" in Hanover, Germany, in 1724, led a scientist to proclaim that he was more important than the discovery of thirty thousand new stars. When the twelve-year-old "Wild Boy of Aveyron" was captured in 1797 in France, contemporary readers of Rousseau anticipated that he would display the virtues of the "noble savage" uncontaminated by civilization. Scholars anxiously awaited his first words, which they conjectured would be man's "natural" language, most probably Hebrew. They were disappointed. The Wild Boy was not particularly hairy, as Linnaeus claimed, but he did trot along on all fours—and he was inarticulate.

A young French physician, J. M. G. Itard, expressed the belief that the speechless Wild Boy of Aveyron was not an "incurable idiot," as a leading scientist of the time had concluded. Itard set out to instruct the boy, whom he named Victor, in language. After five years of extraordinary patience, Itard showed that Victor possessed a capacity to learn many things—but not language. Victor did manage to understand a few simple words and phrases and to read written commands, but he never did learn how to speak. In contrast, a six-year-old abandoned girl, discovered in Ohio in the 1930s, was also instructed in language; in only two years she progressed through six years of language learning. By the time she was eight and a half, she had so accelerated her acquisition of language that her speech was little different from that of other girls her age. Although a few doubts remain to this day whether or not Victor was mentally deficient, he apparently failed to learn speech because he had missed the opportunity at a critical age. By the time he was captured as a twelve-year-old, his ability to speak could never again be recovered.

A complete contrast to wolf children, abandoned to fend for themselves in the wild, are normal children reared by doting parents. But the notion that children learn to speak merely by imitating their parents, somewhat like intelligent parrots, is sheer folklore. Unlike parrots, children are linguistically creative at a very early age. They say all kinds of things they have never heard previously from adults, and they often put together combinations of words which they use in speech situations novel to those utterances. For example, one linguist tape-recorded the following sequence of prattles by a three-year-old child before sleep.

pig (repeated many times)
big
sleep
big pig sleep now

The linguist was certain that the child had never encountered the final utterance in a storybook or heard it in conversation. For that child, it was a totally new creation.

Parents usually do not realize that they unconsciously speak differently to children, even those six or seven years old, than they do to adults. They exaggerate changes in pitch and sometimes they speak almost in singsong; they utter their words more slowly; they use simple sentence structures. And the sounds of their speech are much more precise, as seen, for example, in the pronunciation of *butter*. Most English-speaking adults talking to other adults pronounce it almost as if it were spelled *budder*, but in speaking to a child they usually use the strong *t* sound of *table*. Such careful attention to speech when talking to children is, however, different from the baby-talk words like *choo-choo* and *itsy-bitsy*. Baby talk, rather than representing a "natural" vocabulary that a child instinctively uses, actually is taught to children by adults—who, after a few years, then force the children to stop using it. Baby talk is simply a variation of the adult language, invented by adults for the sole purpose of talking to very young children. Once baby talk becomes part of the language system of speech communities, it persists for long periods. Some Latin baby-talk words are still being used in Romance languages after two thousand years, like today's Spanish *papa*, "food," which derives from the Latin word *pappa*.

The Comanche Indians of the North American Plains began to teach their children a rich vocabulary of special baby-talk words when they reached about one year of age. But shortly after the child learned baby talk, he was discouraged from using it. By the age of five he was supposed to switch to normal, adult language, but if he failed to make the transition at the appropriate time, he was ridiculed for his childish ways. Comanche baby talk used a limited number of the more simple sounds in the language, such as *p*, *b*, *m*, *t*, *d*, *k*, and a few basic vowels. The words were almost always reduplicated—that is, a single syllable was repeated. For example, Comanches transformed their adult word *pia*, meaning "mother," to *pipia* when speaking to children, much as English-speaking children are taught to say *nighty-night*.

Comanche baby-talk vocabulary reveals not so much what the children were interested in saying as what the attitudes of the adult culture were. Most of the baby-talk vocabulary seems preoccupied with words for snakes, fire, wounds, darkness, and mythological bogeymen—all obviously intended to frighten the child—and with words that admonish the child to control his actions and to be obedient. The same baby word, *asi*, could be used by the child to say that he had a bowel movement, to point out feces or anything else that Comanche society deemed filthy, to complain about a bad smell, or to talk about his penis. The equating of disgust with feces, dirt, and the genitals in baby talk says nothing about Comanche children but rather indicates adult attitudes toward the human body.

Baby-talk vocabulary has been compared in six quite different languages from around the world: two major European languages (English and Spanish), two major languages of Asia with strong literary traditions (Arabic and Marathi), one language of a small nonliterate community in Siberia (Gilyak), and one language of a small nonliterate community in North America (Comanche). The actual baby-talk words in the six languages were, of course, different; nevertheless, the vocabularies revealed surprising similarities in linguistic characteristics. All the languages simplified clusters of consonants (as English speakers do when they substitute *tummy* for *stomach*); they replaced *r* with some other consonant (such as *wabbit* for *rabbit*); they reduplicated syllables (*choo-choo, wee-wee*); and most of the languages dropped unstressed syllables (as when *goodbye* becomes *bye*). The six languages altered words to form diminutives (such as the English *y* in *doggy, horsey,* and *dolly*) and substituted words to eliminate pronouns (*Daddy wants* instead of *I want*). We might expect that people from six widespread cultures would want to talk about different things with their children —but the items in the baby-talk vocabularies were very much the same. Almost all the words referred to bodily functions, good or bad behavior, sensations like hot and cold, names of common animals, and kinship terms for close relatives.

Since children are not born to speak baby talk, what could possibly be the explanation for its prevalence around the world? Most adults in the six cultures claimed that baby talk made it easier for children to learn to speak. It is indeed true that in most cases baby-talk words have simpler consonant arrangements and fewer vowels than adult language. On the other hand, some baby-talk systems, such as that of Arabic, employ difficult sounds which children do not ordinarily master until they have considerable experience in speaking the adult language. And is it really easier for an English-speaking child to say *itsy-bitsy* than *tiny*? Despite such exceptions, folk wisdom about baby talk apparently is correct; it does give children practice in speaking. Baby talk presents the child with a stock of simple utterances, and reduplication increases practice in their use. These utterances can gradually be discarded when adult words begin to be used, by which time they have served their purpose.

Reduplication does, however, persist into adult speech, to a much greater extent in some languages than in English, which has comparatively few examples like *helter-skelter, fiddle-faddle, hocus-pocus, mish-mash,* and *teeny-weeny.* Other languages sometimes make reduplication serve functional uses, as when Indonesians say *igi-igi-igi-igi* to emphasize the idea of "multitudes," and when the Ewe of Africa form the reduplicated *gadagadagada* to express intensity, in this case the heat of a fire. Chinese in particular has found uses for reduplication with various parts of speech. A reduplicated noun adds the meaning "every," as when *tian,* "day," becomes *tiantian,* "every day." Reduplication applied to verbs adds a transitory meaning to the action: *zou* means "to walk," but *zouzou* signifies "to take a walk." Adjectives are converted to adverbs by reduplication plus the addition of the suffix -de—as when *kuai*, "quick," becomes *kuaikuaide*, "quickly."

The most common sounds in baby talk—the consonants made with the lips, such as *p*, *b*, and *m*—are the first ones the child can make, probably because the lips are used early for nursing. The next three consonants a child learns are formed with the teeth and gums—*t*, *d*, and *n*—and they are almost as important in the early stages of speech as the first three. So it is not surprising that the earliest words infants speak are those like *papa*, *dada*, *baba*, *mama*, and *nana*. At first children simply utter these sounds without reference to any particular people—and so most parents are incorrect when they believe the sounds refer to a recognition of father, brother, mother, and nursemaid. A sampling of "mother" and "father" words from a variety of languages shows the importance of the six consonants which are learned first:

	"MOTHER" WORDS	"FATHER" WORDS
French	*mère*	*père*
Welsh	*mam*	*tad*
Turkish	*ana*	*baba*
Hebrew	*ima*	*aba*
Russian	*mat*	*otyets*
Mongolian	*eme*	*echige*
Crow Indian	*masake*	*birupxe*

The cause for the similarities in "mother" and "father" consonants is in dispute, but the explanation is more apt to lie in the universal way that children learn to speak rather than in some common origin of these languages in the very distant past.

Child-development specialists occasionally argue over whether or not adults should speak baby talk to their children. Some believe that it retards the child in developing normal language; others feel that baby talk affords good practice in producing sounds. Apparently, speaking baby talk does no harm, and it may even be a valuable aid in the early stages of acquiring a language. On the other hand, if a child continues to speak it beyond the first several years of life, it may retard his speech at a babyish level.

Neither the grunts of wolf children nor the adult-imposed system of baby talk reveals anything about the way in which almost all children, healthy and reared within a social framework, acquire their language. Most communities have long believed that the human infant comes into the world inarticulate—and in fact the very word *infant* is derived from a Latin word that means "speechless." In an obvious way this belief is correct. The cry of an infant at birth, the pain cry when being vaccinated, the hunger cry several hours after a feeding, and the pleasure cry when being held—these expressions of emotions certainly are not language. They are like ape calls in that they are uttered only in immediate contexts and they are never combined.

Yet the infant emits a cry—and soon the hospital nurse, later his mother, responds in a way that is pleasurable to him. The infant has learned that language is a social instrument that evokes a response from other human beings. In the first days of life the child is already responsive to a sound and tries to move his head toward its source. Only a few weeks later he responds to the high-pitched female voice more readily than to any other sound. Soon the infant coos and babbles and makes other noises, and he notes that his mother reacts to each in a different way. The child has learned the appropriate use of speech in various situations.

Children normally begin to speak as early as eighteen months, occasionally as late as twenty-eight months; in the exceptional case of Albert Einstein, the onset of speech did not occur until he was nearly three years old. Certainly all mothers have not mutually agreed that it is time to teach infants to talk when they are approximately two years old. But the effort to learn what triggers a child's speech is somewhat like a problem presented to engineering students. They are shown the outside of a black box, with input wires leading to it and other wires leading out that produce an electrical result. The students must then try to infer the internal wiring of the box solely on the basis of the input-output relationships. The child's mind presents a similar sort of problem. It is a black box (or "language-acquisition device," as it has been called) that cannot be looked into in the living child. The linguist knows only that the language-acquisition device receives input in the form of relatively few utterances, which emerge as utterances in accordance with the grammar of the child's native tongue. Furthermore, the mysterious device in the child's mind works wherever he happens to spend the first several years of life, with the result that the language he learns is that of his native community.

Noam Chomsky has given fresh insights to psychologists and linguists who are attempting to discover how the language-acquisition device works. In an earlier period of psycholinguistic research, many psychologists were influenced by behaviorists such as B. F. Skinner and Ivan P. Pavlov. The behaviorists visualize the child's mind at birth as a blank slate which lacks any inborn capacity to acquire language. The fact that the child does eventually speak is attributed solely to training, in much the same way that an animal can be conditioned to learn by offering it rewards and other reinforcements. The behaviorists think in terms of the child as building up his language piece by piece in accordance with the orders given by the adult generation, which rewards him when he speaks correctly and ridicules him when he speaks incorrectly. This view looks upon learning language as little different from learning correct table manners. Chomsky instead regards language as a creative instrument that is the birthright of all healthy human children, who acquire it as a by-product of growing up, simply by exposure to it. They are born with a blueprint for language which they use to analyze the utterances heard in their speech community and then to produce their own sentences. To Chomsky, the influence of training is minimal—a view which is the direct opposite of behaviorist theories that a child learns the grammar of his language as a result of social pressures, conditioning, or simply the trial-and-error imitation of adults.

Chomsky feels that his theory can account for a basic and mystifying fact about language acquisition. The child hears a relatively small number of utterances, most of which are grammatically incorrect or misunderstood—yet, on the basis of this scanty and flawed information, in his preschool years and with no special instruction, he discovers for himself the complex grammatical rules of his speech community. This fact can be explained only by assuming that the child is born with competence in the structure of language, in the same way that a child is genetically endowed at birth with numerous other abilities that make him human. The situation is somewhat like learning to walk. The child possesses at birth the blueprint for the muscular coordination that he will develop later in order to walk. No one tells him how to lift his legs, bend his ankles or knees, or place his feet on the ground. He does not consciously arrive at the skill of balancing himself on his legs, any more than a three-year-old consciously figures out the rules for grammatical transformations. The child walks and the child talks—and in neither case does he know exactly how he did it.

A simple example of the way in which a child can be seen putting together the rules for his language's grammar is the English word *hisself*, an "erroneous" form of *himself* which most children use until about the age of four, despite attempts by parents to correct them. So persistent is this "error" that it has been known since the time of Chaucer and survives in several dialects of English. What is the explanation for its persistence? And why is it constructed by children who usually have never heard it before? The answer is that *hisself* strictly follows the rules of English grammar that the child is acquiring. *Hisself* is a reflexive pronoun like *myself*, *yourself*, and *herself*—each of which is formed by combining the possessive pronoun *my*, *your*, or *her* with *self*. The masculine possessive in this set is *his* and therefore, when combined with *self*, should rightly produce the reflexive *hisself*. But English is inconsistent in this instance, as all languages are in one instance or another, and the preferred form is *himself*. So children, by insisting upon *hisself* until the age when they acquire knowledge about the irregularities of English, show that they have internalized a basic rule of their grammar and follow it for a long time, despite adult attempts to correct them.

Strong evidence supports Chomsky's view. Only human children learn to speak, thus indicating that some sort of blueprint for language must be transmitted from generation to generation in our species. And human children everywhere develop a language without instruction, unless they are isolated as "wolf children" during the critical acquisition years or unless they suffer from extreme mental deficiency. Bright children and stupid children, trained children and untrained children, all learn approximately the same linguistic system. Some street urchins do not have parents to instruct them, but they learn to speak nevertheless —and, as can be seen in international cities like Tangiers and Singapore, the homeless child may speak several languages fluently. (Imperfections in pronunciation or vocabulary are insignificant when compared with the tremendous accomplishment of acquiring the complex rules of a language.) But the same thing cannot be said about developing other skills, such as arithmetic or playing a musical instrument, both of which require long years of training. Even though two violin students take lessons from the same teacher and devote equal time to practice, one may become merely a good player while the other bcomes a virtuoso. Natural endowments for the skill of violin-playing vary, but all children show equal aptitude for language in their early years.

At the same time that the child is acquiring grammatical rules, he is also learning rules for the correct use of his language in the various speech situations of his community. By the age of two or so, children already use speech to get what they want, to talk about things they know will interest the listener, and to influence the social behavior of others. They know some of the occasions on which it is proper to shout or to whisper; they know that it is permissible to say *gimme* to certain people but that they should use *please* in other speech situations; they have some idea of differences in age and rank of listeners and the kinds of speech appropriate with a child or an adult, with a stranger or a neighbor. Only a little later children begin to play word games and to make up nonsense rhymes—clear evidence that they have already internalized the rules and can exploit the alternative possibilities of their language. Although most children acquire their grammar at a steady rate, largely insulated from major influences in the social environment, learning the appropriate use of language depends upon the speech community in which the child grows up and the social group to which he belongs. Children from various social classes differ considerably in their abilities to talk about certain things, and to do so in the appropriate situations. Middle-class white children in the United States usually place a high value on the ability to read at an early age; lower-class black children, on the other hand, may consider such a skill irrelevant and are likely to emphasize nimbleness in verbal encounters.

The age at which a child is considered capable of understanding speech varies greatly from culture to culture. Most Europeans feel that children cannot comprehend what is said to them until they are a year or so old. In contrast, the Ashanti of Ghana believe that a fetus possesses the ability to understand speech and they sometimes address question to it in the womb. Psycholinguists now know that infants are aware of speech at a very early age, although not so early as the Ashanti believe. Before the age of one month, the child associates the sound of the human voice with pleasurable sensations, such as feeding, fondling, and the changing of diapers. Very soon afterward the child detects different emotional attitudes in the speaker's tone of voice and responds by smiling or crying. A two-month-old infant in an English-speaking community can often discriminate between the sounds *p* and *b*, which is a very exact discrimination indeed. A child's language gradually unfolds in a sequence of stages of development during the first few years of life. A parent can say to a child *Speak only when spoken to*, and the child may obey—but the language-acquisition device in the child's brain will not obey. Biology does the work, and fond parents can add little except simply to talk within earshot of the child. The course of language for most normal children, regardless of the speech communities they are born into, is thought to be keyed to motor development—as seen below in one possible correlation—although some researchers believe it is keyed to a child's general cognitive development.

When supports head while lying on stomach (*age about three months*): The infant responds to speech by smiling and by making the gurgling sound known as "cooing," which is vowel-like and has pitch.

When plays with a rattle placed in hands (*about four months*): The infant turns his head and eyes to seek the source of a speaker's voice. He adds chuckling noises to cooing.

When sits propped up (*above five months*): The vowel-like cooing sounds now become interspersed with consonant-like sounds.

When can bear weight if held in a standing position (*about six months*): Cooing changes to babbling of one-syllable utterances like *ma, mu, da, di*, and so on.

When picks up objects with thumb and forefinger (*about eight months*): Reduplication, such as *mama* or *dada*, becomes frequent. Strings of sounds are expressed with emphasis and seem to signal emotion. Intonation, as heard in adult questions and exclamations, becomes noticeable.

When pulls self to standing position (about ten months): Bubble-blowing and other sound play is now added to vocalizations. The infant apparently tries to imitate sounds but is rarely successful. He begins to discriminate between words by reacting differently to various utterances.

When walks held by one hand (about one year): The infant definitely understands some words and attempts to carry out simple commands. He can also speak a few words.

When creeps down stairs backward (about one and a half years): The child is now on the threshold of speech and displays a much greater understanding of what is said to him. His vocabulary consists of between three and fifty words, although little attempt to communicate information is made as yet. He can utter brief stock phrases, such as *thank you*, but he does not attempt to join these into more complicated statements.

When walks up or down stairs (about two years): The typical child now has a vocabulary of more than fifty words and can name almost everything he has daily contact with in the home or on walks. Rather than repeating stock phrases, he often utters two-word phrases which are his own creation. Language acquisition gains momentum and a definite interest in words is displayed.

When jumps with both feet (about two and a half years): Vocabulary increases very rapidly and new words are added daily. Babbling ceases. Utterances are intended to have communication value, and the child is frustrated when he is not understood. He seems to understand almost everything said to him, and he responds with statements up to five words in length.

When rides tricycle (about three years): This stage marks the end of the naming explosion, at which time the child has a vocabulary of about a thousand words. He probably understands an additional two or three thousand words he has not yet learned to use. The grammatical complexity of the utterance is about equal to that of colloquial adult speech, although numerous errors occur.

When catches ball in arms (about four years): The child has now mastered the essentials of his native tongue.

A child of four has performed an awesome intellectual feat. He has not merely learned the names of things; he has acquired an entire linguistic system that enables him to create sentences for the rest of his life. If among the words a child knows are *hill, water, Jill, fetch, Jack, pail,* and *go*, he may eventually put them together into a sentence like *Jack and Jill went up the hill to fetch a pail of water.* Think for a moment how remarkable this sentence is. The child has taken a random assortment of words and given them order. *Jack* and *Jill* do not appear just anyplace in the sentence, but at the beginning of it, where they are made to serve as the subjects of the verb *go*. Equally important, the child added what are known as "markers" in the form of functor words (*and, up, the, to, a, of*). Functors identify the different classes of words (as when *the* or *a* indicates that a noun follows); they specify relationships between words (*and*, for example, ties together *Jack* and *Jill*); and they signify meanings by the tense of the verbs. If the child had arranged the same words differently—such as *Jack fetched Jill's pail of water and went up the hill*—he would have used other markers (*-ed* and *-'s*) and a different word order. The child knows unconsciously that he should not use the markers in the second sentence to construct the first kind of sentence, since his grammar tells him that a sentence like *Jack and Jill's went up the hill to fetched a pail of water* is an impossible creation in English.

Considerable dispute exists as to exactly how a child of four or five attains such remarkable proficiency in these, and even more difficult, grammatical tasks. One explanation is that the child codes the words he learns into grammatical classes, thereby eliminating the necessity of knowing the grammar of each word in his vocabulary. For example, if a child possesses a category that he codes as "nouns," then he recognizes words belonging to this class whenever they occur. He knows that they can be used only in certain ways in sentences and that they are associated with certain markers (such as *the* and *a*). He also realizes that not all words in English are equal. Some content words (such as *Jack, Jill, went,* and *hill* in the nursery rhyme quoted in the previous paragraph) carry important burdens of meaning, while other, functor words (*and, up, the,* and so on) can be eliminated with a high probability that the message will still be understood. Adults employ the distinction between content and functor words when they send a telegram and eliminate "unnecessary" words. The telegram ARRIVING KENNEDY SEVEN TONIGHT AMERICAN easily enough translates as *I will be arriving at Kennedy Airport at seven o'clock tonight on American Airlines.* "Telegraphic" English communicates very well because it retains the content words like *arriving* and *Kennedy* that one would have difficulty in guessing and eliminates those that can easily be guessed (*I, at, on*). Content words alone are usually sufficient to tell the story, but functor words alone are gibberish.

Young children employ much the same sort of telegraphic speech when they say *Where baby?* for *Where is the baby? Where* and *want* are among the most common "operator" words of children at certain ages, although most children go through fads in their preferences for particular operators. They fasten on a favorite operator and then use it with a variety of other words belonging to a single class, in that way learning the entire class. For example, a child who for a time regards *want* as a favorite operator will employ it with most of the nouns he knows to create two-word sentences like *want outside, want doggy,* and *want milk.* Children are also very exact in discriminating between the noun class, which refers to things, and the verb class, which refers to actions. In a typical experiment, preschool children were given a selection of pictures and then asked to associate them with nonsense words. When they heard *a sib,* they immediately reached for pictures that showed a single object, thereby indicating that they had put *a sib* into the class of singular nouns. When asked to show *some sibs,* they reached for pictures of confetti-like material (the class of plural nouns). And when asked to find something *sibbing,* they selected pictures showing action (the class of verbs). Since the words themselves were meaningless, the children obviously made correct choices because grammatical clues helped them to recognize that the words belonged to certain classes.

By the age of four, the child is well on the way to knowing these and other aspects of grammar. During the next several years, this knowledge is consolidated, becomes automatic, and is extended to include words with irregular patterns (*men* and not *mans* as the plural of *man*). A six-year-old child may use *he bought* and *he buyed* interchangeably, but he usually corrects himself, showing that he knows the proper form even though he does not yet employ it automatically. Surprisingly, some features of language that appear to be simple are not learned until quite late. One such is the "tag question"—as in *The doggy can come in the house, can't he?*—which is very complex because the tag (*can't he?*) is determined completely by the structure of the declarative sentence to which it is attached and for which it requests confirmation. If the declarative sentence had instead been *The doggy will come home,* then a different kind of tag question would be needed: *won't he?* (The problem does not arise in French and German where the tag questions—*n'est-ce pas?* and *nicht wahr?* respectively—do not vary; English also has several invariant forms, among them *right?* and *huh?*) Think of the complex grammatical operations a child has to perform to produce the apparently simple *The doggy can come in the house, can't he?* First of all, the child has to convert the subject of the declarative sentence (*The doggy*) into a pronoun (*he*)—not just any pronoun but one which is masculine, third person, and in the nominative case. Next, the tag must be made negative by adding *not* or its contraction *n't* to the auxiliary verb *can,* and then be made a question by reversing the order of *he* and *can't.* Finally, the child has to delete from the tag *come in the house*—that is, all of the verb phrase in the declarative sentence except for the auxiliary *can.*

The child continues to refine his speech in this way until about the age of ten, by which time he has internalized all the complicated rules of his native grammar. Children soon outgrow their ability to acquire language with little effort, as is realized by high-school students and adults who try to master a language in addition to their mother tongue. Whether or not a child will speak a foreign language with an accent depends largely upon the age at which he learns the second language. A child who enters a foreign speech community by about the age of three or four learns the new language rapidly and without the trace of an accent. During the next several years, such facility declines slightly. But then, around the age of puberty, an irreversible change takes place, and practically every child loses the ability to learn a second language without an accent.

The unfolding of a child's language is a wondrous thing to listen to, as every parent knows. Working with an extremely limited vocabulary, poorly pronounced, and the meanings only dimly understood, the child produces the grammar of his language. No amount of reward, praise, or punishment makes him do a substantially better or worse job. He of course makes many errors at first, but eventually he puts together a grammar that is equal to the grammar of the people in his speech community who talked to him and played with him during the critical years of language acquisition. As in the development of his personality, the child has used his innate potential to create something very much like that of other people in his community, yet also something uniquely his own.

References

The story of Victor is told by J. M. G. Itard, *The Wild Boy of Aveyron* (Englewood Cliffs, N.J.: Prentice-Hall, 1962).

Much of my material on the innateness of language is from Eric H. Lenneberg, "On Explaining Language," *Science*, 164 (1969), 635–643; see also his *Biological Foundations of Language* (New York: Wiley, 1967), 135–139. Noam Chomsky's argument with the behaviorists is clearly stated in his "Review of B. F. Skinner's *Verbal Behavior*," *Language*, 35 (1959), 26–58. Charles F. Hockett, *The State of the Art* (The Hague: Mouton, 1968) and George Steiner, *Extraterritorial: Papers on Literature and the Language Revolution* (New York: Atheneum, 1971) present detailed criticisms of Chomsky's theories. A valuable discussion of how children acquire social skills in the use of language at the same time that they acquire their grammar is Susan Ervin-Tripp, "Social Backgrounds and Verbal Skills," in Renira Huxley and Elisabeth Ingram, eds., *Language Acquisition: Models and Methods* (New York: Academic Press, 1971). The path of normal language development in the child is abridged from Lenneberg (1967), pp. 125–135, with some valuable insights taken from Peter D. Eimas et al., "Speech Perception in Infants," *Science*, 171 (1971), 303–306. Tag questions and the example of *hisself* are discussed by Roger Brown, "Development of the First Language in the Human Species," *American Psychologist*, 28 (1973), 97–106, in an important paper on recent trends in the study of language acquisition. The literature about the way children acquire language is immense and fascinating; unfortunately, space limitations allowed only major themes to be presented in this book. The papers in Ursula Bellugi and Roger Brown, *The Acquisition of Language* (monograph of the Society for Research in Child Development, 1964) are valuable, as are those by Frank Smith and George A. Miller, *The Genesis of Language* (Cambridge, Mass.: M.I.T. Press, 1966) and all of the following by Eric H. Lenneberg, "The Biological Foundations of Language," in Mark Lester, ed., *Readings in Applied Transformational Grammar* (New York: Holt, Rinehart & Winston, 1970); "On Explaining Language," *Science*, 164 (1969), 635–643; *Biological Foundations of Language* (New York: Wiley, 1967); "A Biological Perspective of Language," in Eric H. Lenneberg, ed., *New Directions in the Study of Language* (Cambridge, Mass.: M.I.T. Press, 1964), which itself is useful. See also Robert D. King, *Historical Linguistics and Generative Grammar* (Englewood Cliffs, N.J.: Prentice-Hall, Inc., 1969), pp. 66–78; Carol Chomsky, *The Acquisition of Syntax in Children from 5 to 10* (Cambridge, Mass.: M.I.T. Press, 1969); Susan M. Ervin and W. R. Miller, "Language Development," in Joshua A. Fishman, ed., *Readings in the Sociology of Language* (The Hague: Mouton, 1969); Susan M. Ervin, "Imitation and Structural Change in Children's Language," in Eric H. Lenneberg, ed., *New Directions in the Study of Language* (Cambridge, Mass.: M.I.T. Press, 1964); and Roger Brown and Ursula Bellugi, "Three Processes in the Child's Acquisition of Syntax," pp. 131–162 in the Lenneberg anthology just cited. Technical discussions of many aspects of language acquisition are in Renira Huxley and Elisabeth Ingram, eds., *Language Acquisition: Models and Methods* (New York: Academic Press, 1971). A very important book on the subject—Roger Brown, *A First Language* (Cambridge, Mass.: Harvard University Press, 1973)—appeared just as this book was going to press.

FOR DISCUSSION AND REVIEW

1 Compare Brown's discussion of *Homo ferus,* especially Victor, with that of Farb. Do Brown and Farb emphasize different aspects of this phenomenon?

2 Farb asserts that parents "unconsciously speak differently to children. . . ." Give some specific examples of such differences. Do you speak differently to young children than you do to adults? If so, how? If you do speak differently to children, were you aware of this behavior before reading Farb's article?

3 According to Farb, what is "baby talk"? What functions, if any, does it serve? What do comparisons of baby-talk vocabulary in different languages reveal? What explanation does Farb offer for the world-wide prevalence of baby talk?

4 What is reduplication? Give three examples from English (or from another language that you know well) that are not mentioned by Farb.

5 What are the six most common sounds in baby talk? How does Farb account for their frequency? The same sounds seem to occur most frequently across cultures and among unrelated languages; what are some of the implications of this fact?

6 Farb mentions four distinct cries of infants (among which, studies have shown, mothers and nurses can easily distinguish). What are they?

7 Explain Farb's analogy between the child's mind and a black box in an engineering problem. What does he mean by the term *language-acquisition device?*

8 How do behaviorists like Skinner

and Pavlov visualize the process of language learning? How do their views differ from those of transformationalists like Chomsky (who would, incidentally, speak of "language acquisition," not "language learning")?

9 Explain Farb's analogy between learning to walk and learning to talk.

10 Describe the stages through which children pass as they develop their ability to understand the speech of others. Give an approximate indication of the different ages involved.

11 Some psychologists and linguists believe that the development of language is linked to the development of motor skills. What does Farb say about this connection?

12 What is the importance of "grammatical classes" (roughly, parts of speech) in language acquisition? Distinguish between "content words" and "functor words"; give three examples of each.

13 What does Farb mean by the term operator words? How do children use such words?

5

The Linguistic Development of Children

M. M. Lewis

The complex process of language acquisition has long been of interest to scholars in many fields. The connection between the noises of babies —their cries, coos, and babblings —and the language of adults is crucial to an understanding of this process. In a lecture presented to the Institute of Contemporary Arts, M. M. Lewis first gives a brief background sketch of the history of the study of language acquisition, and theories of reinforcement and conditioning developed by scientists like Ivan Pavlov and B. F. Skinner, and then discusses the revolutionary ideas of Noam Chomsky.

The Roots of Language

Wᴴᴬᵀ ARE we talking about this evening? This: . . . the infant, mewling and puking in his nurse's arms. I don't know about puking; what I can say is that there is nothing more important for a child than his mewling. His crying is the beginning of his language. On his very first day, as soon as he cries and his mother comes to him, we have the basic pattern of language between people—one person utters sounds and another responds.

It is on his first day also that a child often shows that he is already aware of sounds. Recent investigations have demonstrated, as early as this, an "auditory orienting reflex"—a movement of the child's head towards the source of a sound.[1] Within a couple of weeks this has usually become more specific: the child responds more readily and more regularly to a high-pitched human voice than to any other auditory stimulus.[2] And of course the most frequent high-pitched human voice is his mother's.

[1] R. H. Walters and R. D. Parke: "The Role of the Distance Receptors in the Development of Social Responsiveness," in L. P. Lipsitt and C. S. Spiker: *Advances in Child Development and Behaviour* (1965), p. 75.

[2] *Ibid*, p. 65.

During these early days a child not only cries; he coos. When he is hungry or uncomfortable he cries; when he is content and comfortable he coos.[3]

The next new thing to come from the child—different from his crying and his cooing—is his babbling. Often as early as his sixth week he will be heard uttering strings of sounds, repeating them with a rhythm and intonation, apparently for the pleasure of making them; playing with sounds.[4]

He cries or coos or babbles; to each of these his mother is likely to respond in a specific way. He cries and she attempts to alleviate his discomfort; he coos and she comes and smiles and perhaps pets him; he babbles and she may well encourage him by joining in, imitating him in fun, so that in turn he imitates her.

The simple pattern of interchange is enlarged as the child begins to respond to speech in its situation. These are the rudiments of comprehension; how far back in his history they begin it is impossible to say. His earliest response to *Baby, Milk!* may be to his mother's voice as an auditory stimulus specific to him as a human infant. From this there will be a transition to the time when he responds to the phonemic form of *milk* in the situation in which he hears it, the context of circumstances, even when he can see neither the speaker nor the milk.

While these are the rudiments of meaning in what a child hears, there are also rudiments of meaning in what he utters. From the beginning, his crying and his cooing have each of them its own context of situation in the child himself—discomfort, distress when he cries, contentment when he coos. This, of course, is not to say that at the beginning he himself is aware of the connection between his crying and discomfort, or his cooing and contentment. But we who are with him have to recognize, from a very early moment, the rudimentary semantic content of his crying or his cooing. His babbling has another place in his development: he plays, practises, experiments.[5]

Advance in Early Childhood

The speed of linguistic development is phenomenal. By the end of the third year most children have a working command of a good many of the phonemic and syntactical structures of the mother tongue and of their use and comprehension in communication. Five years later this has normally extended to the whole range of the structures of the lan-

---

[3] M. M. Lewis: *Language, Thought and Personality in Infancy and Childhood* (1963), pp. 16–19.
[4] *Ibid*, p. 20.
[5] *Ibid*, pp. 20–22.

guage; what has yet to come is an increase in the size and scope of vocabulary and in the complexity of syntax; above all, in the development of the complex relationships between the structural and the semantic systems of the language.[6]

All this has been seen by mothers and others from time immemorial; seen, but rarely observed. Not the least remarkable thing about children's linguistic development is that we know so· little about it. Today we have barely reached the centenary of the first systematic studies. One of the pioneers is Darwin, who made a record of his son as early as 1840, though he refrained from publishing it until 1877.[7]

During the greater part of the present century, while there has been a stream of sporadic attempts at description and interpretation, gaps have remained unfilled. But now, suddenly, in the last few years, there has burst upon us an explosion of concern, thought and observation. This is one of the major products of modern psycholinguistics, from which the name of Noam Chomsky is now inseparable.

Chomsky has been hailed as the herald of revolution in the study of language, as the Einstein of modern psycholinguistics. Here we ask what he has to say to us about the development of language in children.

Half-a-Century of Study

Chomsky offers hypotheses which have injected fresh vigour into observation and experiment by a variety of workers. What is new in these hypotheses is best seen in the perspective of the ideas current before he arrived.

We go back to the beginning of the century, to the pioneers, William and Clara Stern, whose book *Die Kindersprache* first appeared in 1908. They take as the fundamental explanation of linguistic development the principle of "convergence": the interaction between what comes from the child—the drive in him to use language (Sprachdrang) —and what comes to him from his linguistic environment.[8] This would no doubt seem to many even today irrefutable if innocuous. But it soon proved to be altogether too broad a formulation to satisfy the growing demand in psychology for precision; least palatable was the somewhat mystical hypothesis of an inborn "drive."

During the following half-century the main line of thought about linguistic development took a different course. In the U.S.A., under the influence of studies of the processes of learning; in the U.S.S.R.,

[6] M. C. Templin: *Certain Language Skills in Children* (1957), p. 141.
[7] C. Darwin: "The Biography of an Infant," *Mind*, II (1877).
[8] C. and W. Stern: *Die Kindersprache* (1908), p. 123.

under the influence of Pavlov; in both, the balance of "convergence" shifted to a heavier emphasis on the outside forces acting upon the child. In the U.S.A. the development of language was seen by many as the reinforcement of a child's responses to others. There was a solid movement of thought in this direction, among philosophers, sociologists and linguists no less than among psychologists. Of these we may name Skinner as one of the latest as well as one of the most thoroughgoing exponents of the function of reinforcement in linguistic development.[9]

The parallel with work in the U.S.S.R. on conditioning is too obvious to need more than a mention. The genesis of language was one of the main preoccupations of Pavlov because of its far-reaching relationships with every aspect of human behaviour. Pavlov envisaged language as the "second signal system," established by the conditioning of primary conditioned reflexes.[10] The fertility of this concept of linguistic development is attested by the quantity and quality of the work carried out under its influence by such men as Vigotsky and Luria.

The Chomsky Revolution

Reinforcement or conditioning; these were as strongly entrenched explanatory concepts as any in the history of psychology. But in 1957, five decades after *Die Kindersprache*, there appeared a treatise with an innocent title-page: *Syntactic Structures*, by N. Chomsky. Apparently addressed to professional linguists, it dealt with problems which might be regarded as of limited interest even to them: the syntactic structures of a language could be shown to be logically "generated in accordance with the rules, the grammar of the language."[11]

If this was new in linguistics, it was not obviously a revolution in psycholinguistics. But although Chomsky was careful to point out that his description of the generation of structures must not be taken as an account of actual genesis, its implications for the understanding of linguistic development soon appeared. The cat among the pigeons was seen to have sharp claws.

The pigeons were Skinner's. In a series of elegant experiments he had demonstrated that by selecting some more or less random movements of a pigeon and reinforcing a succession of these by appropriate "rewards," a complex pattern of behaviour could be set up. The behaviour of the pigeon was determined by what we did to him.

When Skinner applied the same principles to verbal behaviour in

[9] B. F. Skinner: *Verbal Behaviour* (1957).
[10] I. P. Pavlov: *Conditioned Reflexes,* trans. G. V. Anrep (1927).
[11] N. Chomsky: *Syntactic Structures* (1957).

his book of that name, his treatment seemed to many to be vitiated by a serious limitation: the suggestion that a child's linguistic development is mainly determined by what we do to him. Chomsky was roused to a ferocious polemic, reminiscent of the cut-and-thrust of seventeenth-century philosophers' battles. In a slashing review he set about clawing Skinner's book into shreds, not without some glee.[12] Not merely by negative strictures, but by positive refutations Chomsky expounded his ideas on language and linguistic development. As subsequently elaborated by him and his colleagues, they are revolutionary to this degree, that they have given a new direction to thought about language and a new stimulus to the examination of the linguistic development of children.

Back to the Past

Like many another revolutionary, Chomsky takes a step backward in order to take two forward. There was already in the U.S.A. something of an uneasy movement back to the past. It is startling to find a modern psychologist of the calibre of J. McV. Hunt "revisiting" McDougall for his insistence on primary drives as factors in development; still more, recalling one Montessori for her recognition of children's initiative and creativeness.[13]

Chomsky takes a wider sweep, back to a golden age, long before the philosophy of language was polluted by Behaviorism and S–R learning theory. He invokes a line of honourable ancestry for his ideas: Descartes and Leibniz and the seventeenth-century thinkers about language, Goethe and von Humboldt in the following century.[14] He turns to them for support as he expounds his hypotheses. From the logical genesis of language by generative processes he goes on to suggest implications for the linguistic development of children, still denying that he can offer a factual account of what actually happens.

Chomsky on Linguistic Development

Chomsky's exposition consists of six main statements:

There is an innate predisposition to achieve the mastery of language
The structures of a language are generated from primary deep structures

---

12 N. Chomsky: Review of Skinner's "Verbal Behaviour," *Language*, 35 (1959).
13 J. McV. Hunt: "The Importance of Pre-verbal Experience," in M. Deutsch *et al*: *Social Class, Race and Psychological Development* (1968).
14 N. Chomsky: *Cartesian Linguistics* (1966).

The linguistic development of children is a process of maturation
In the process of development the child is essentially creative
Imitation is a subsidiary factor in the acquisition of a language
Analogy is a complex factor in this development.
We look at these in turn.

The most fundamental and at the same time the most controversial
of Chomsky's hypotheses is that we are born with a disposition to acquire language. This he regards as peculiar to man; or, in Lenneberg's
terms, it is "species-specific."[15] In Chomsky's terms, children are born
with a potential knowledge of grammar. Nonsense? But as Chomsky
uses them, "knowledge" and "grammar" are pickwickian terms. By
knowledge he means what he also calls "competence" in language, to
be sharply distinguished from "performance." And the meaning of
"grammar" he extends to include the whole system of rules covering
the relationships of the phonemic, syntactic and semantic components
of a language. Chomsky is maintaining that we are born with an aptitude to acquire these rules, and that as linguistic development goes on
there is "a grammar which each individual has somehow and in some
form internalized."[16]

Thus "competence" is the grasp, more or less conscious, of the rules
of a language; "performance," actual linguistic behaviour which will be
—more or less—in accordance with these rules. By the systematic study
of children's performance we can infer the nature and degree of their
competence.

One of Chomsky's chief grounds for postulating innate competence
is the speed with which a child attains the mastery of the complex
system of skills that constitute a language, "on the basis of a fairly
restricted amount of evidence."[17] In passing, it may be pointed out that
Chomsky is underestimating the richness of a child's linguistic experience. A child with normal hearing, born into a society of speakers, is
surrounded by language from the moment of his birth. In his first three
years, say his first one thousand days, he must hear some millions of
words.

Is there anything new in Chomsky's insistence on the innate bases
of language? This: while it has always been recognized that there are
innate roots of *speech*, Chomsky postulates an innate competence in

[15] E. H. Lenneberg: *Biological Foundations of Language* (1967), p. 296.

[16] N. Chomsky: "Methodological Preliminaries," in L. A. Jakobovitz and M. S.
Miron: *Readings in the Psychology of Language* (1967), p. 89; N. Chomsky:
"The Formal Nature of Language," in E. H. Lenneberg: *Biological Foundations
of Language* (1967), p. 408; N. Chomsky: Review of Skinner's "Verbal Behaviour," *Language*, 35 (1959), p. 170.

[17] N. Chomsky: "The Formal Nature of Language," in E. H. Lenneberg: *Biological
Foundations of Language* (1967), p. 437.

language. Indeed, as Lenneberg has shown, language may develop in the absence of speech, even comprehension of spoken language in the absence of articulation.[18] To say that there is an innate basis of competence means that it is natural for a child growing up in a linguistic society to become linguistic.

The second main idea of Chomsky's is that competence develops out of basic innate deep structures, through a succession of transformations. The genesis of a language for a child, as Chomsky sees it, is this:

Deep structures . . . kernel sentences . . . infantile structures . . . structures of the mother tongue.

Deep structures are the hypothetical capacities inferred from a child's overt language later. It is not surprising therefore if different readers of Chomsky's exposition do not agree in their ideas of deep structures.

Chomsky would seem to suggest that while deep structures are dispositions to acquire language, they are not themselves linguistic. They are pre-linguistic; cognitive, but in forms that lend themselves to language. Chomsky concurs with Descartes' description of them as "a simple reflection of the form of thought"; and with von Humboldt's conclusion "that the force that generates language is indistinguishable from that which generates thought."[19]

To test our interpretation of Chomsky we may attempt an example of a basic deep structure and its subsequent progressive transformations into a structure of English. The argument would run on something like the following lines.

We may reasonably suppose that when an infant, even in his earliest days, sees the movement of a bird across the sky, his perception is already different from that of a dog, however intelligent. While the dog, we may suppose, has a single integral perception of the bird in flight, the child is born with more advanced cognitive capacities. His perception, we would assume, soon has the rudiments of two components—the bird and its movement. He begins to see the *bird* . . . flying, and the *flying* . . . as performed by the bird. If all this is highly hypothetical, it is what is implied by saying that a child, by contrast with a dog, begins with deep structures which will lend themselves to language.

As a child acquires words, he may begin to use them to symbolize his perception. *Bird!* he announces—more probably, *Birdie!*—later perhaps, *Bird flying!* This is a kernel sentence; so too was *Bird!* earlier; it has long been recognized that many of a child's single early words are

[18] E. H. Lenneberg: "Speech as a Motor Skill," *Child Development Monograph* (1964), p. 127.
[19] F. Smith and G. A. Miller: *The Genesis of Language* (1966), p. 6; N. Chomsky: *Cartesian Linguistics* (1966), pp. 30 and 35.

semantically sentences. From a kernal sentence there is a transformation or a series of transformations to a structure of current English: *The bird is flying*. A French child, beginning with the same basic deep structure, ends up with *l'oiseau qui vole*—not with the English schoolboy's *l'oiseau est volant*.

Chomsky's third main idea is that the linguistic development of a child is a process of *maturation*, not the imposition upon him of the forms of the mother tongue by authority from above, through conditioning, reinforcement or any other means.

This is a very important tenet in Chomsky's system and he and his colleagues have taken a great deal of trouble to demonstrate the validity of this principle of development. For support, Chomsky again goes back to von Humboldt, citing him to the effect that language grows by the maturation of relatively fixed capacities under appropriate external conditions.[20] Among Chomsky's colleagues a principal exponent of this view is Lenneberg, who adduces evidence to show that, like progress in walking, talking develops by the unrolling of tendencies already present in the child. Environment may, of course, be more or less favourable—but it is a condition, not the source, of linguistic development.[21]

The last three of Chomsky's general hypotheses expound a most important implication of the first three: that a child is creative in his linguistic development.

For Chomsky this is indeed an indispensable concept for the understanding of all human behaviour. He brings in the support of Descartes for the doctrine that "a fully adequate psychology of man requires the postulation of a 'creative principle.'" This has become so intrinsic in Chomsky's view of language that one of his exponents, McNeill, heads a paper with a title that is surely meant to be provocative: "The Creation of Language by Children."[22] This sets itself to counter the line of thought which so long had seen the development of language as a process of social influence upon the child, whether by reinforcement or conditioning or example.

What then immediately becomes unavoidable is the crucial question of the function of imitation. Nothing could be more obvious than that the linguistic differences between English and French children must be due to imitation. Chomsky asks, How far due to imitation? And he brings forward two lines of argument to show that imitation is much less important than would appear at first sight: first, the nature

[20] N. Chomsky: *Cartesian Linguistics* (1966), p. 64.
[21] E. H. Lenneberg: *Biological Foundations of Language* (1967), pp. 136, 142.
[22] N. Chomsky: *Cartesian Linguistics* (1966), p. 6; D. McNeill: "The Creation of Language by Children," in J. Lyons and R. J. Wales: *Psycholinguistic Papers* (1966).

of imitation itself as a psychological process; and secondly the relation between imitation and other factors in linguistic development.

Imitation, Chomsky points out, is not only a means by which we learn; imitation itself has to be learnt. Lenneberg enjoins us to remember "that imitation implies the learning of analytic tools, namely grammatical and phonemic rules."[23] Imitation in language thus goes far beyond mere mimicry; the child is active in that he forms for himself systems of rules and applies them. When a child has encountered a particular usage of language, his imitation consists of similar usages in similar circumstances.

More than this: the rôle of imitation, though powerful, is limited. How else can we explain some of the mistakes children make? *I taked*; *I eated*. These, and so many others, can only be due to a process that we must call reasoning by analogy, even though in saying this we realize that a good deal of the time the "reasoning" is unconscious.

The more closely we observe children the clearer does it become that in their linguistic development both imitation and analogy are at work. It is found, for instance, that some children, at a time when they are saying *I breaked*, are also saying *I broke*.[24] It is worth noticing that each of these owes something to imitation, something to analogy. *Breaked* is by analogy with such a form as *walked*, which directly or indirectly comes from imitation. *Broke* is imitated, but then used, analogically, in a new situation.

Chomsky is so anxious to stress the function of creation that he maintains that even "analogy" may be misleading; that it would be truer to say that the child behaves as though he were reasoning by analogy when in fact he is acting creatively in a new situation.[25]

Throughout Chomsky's exposition there runs this thought: to say that a child acquires language is misleading if it is taken to mean that he gathers and enlarges a stock of structures which he learns to understand and utter. It is rather that the child extends his competence over the rules of the language as he generates structures in accordance with these rules.

Language is Creation

Chomsky's six hypotheses are likely to have important influences on our knowledge of children's linguistic development. As hypotheses some are open to direct verification, others not.

23 E. H. Lenneberg: "Speech as a Motor Skill," *Child Development Monograph* (1964), p. 122.
24 S. M. Ervin: "Imitation and Structural Change in Children's Language," in E. H. Lenneberg: *Biological Foundations of Language* (1964), p. 179.
25 N. Chomsky: *Cartesian Linguistics* (1966), p. 12.

The first—the innate basis of competence—can be tested only indirectly, by inference from the observed facts of children's development. The second hypothesis—the generation of the structures of a language—lends itself somewhat more readily to verification, but only through careful and even subtle experiment and controlled observation.

The hypothesis of maturation as the process of development is rather better supported by available data, particularly of the kind presented by Lenneberg; and it gains some additional force from its agreement with Piaget's principle of the biological adaptation of the child to his society.

The last three hypotheses of Chomsky's are of a different kind. The creativeness of the child and the functions of imitation and analogy in his linguistic development—these are descriptive of actual "performance," so that their validity rests on the systematic observation of children, supplemented where possible by experiment. Both observation and experiment have been given a powerful impetus by the discussions of Chomsky and his colleagues; and it is to the work in the field that we look for the closure of the gaps in our knowledge of the linguistic development of children. We may hazard the prediction that more will be found to depend on a child's linguistic environment than Chomsky seems inclined to allow.

In the meantime let us record a new outlook on the nature of language itself. There is a new creed. Its major tenets have nowhere been stated so clearly as by Miller who, among the disciples of Chomsky, may rank as the apostle of common sense. In an admonitory epistle to the psychologists he announces a revelation: "Language is exceedingly complicated." And he makes his confession of faith: "I now believe that mind is something more than an Anglo-Saxon four-letter word; human minds exist."[26]

FOR DISCUSSION AND REVIEW

1 Why, according to Lewis, is there "nothing more important for a child than his mewling"?

2 What are the three early stages of linguistic development in a child, as seen by Lewis? Explain the importance of each.

3 What are Noam Chomsky's six main hypotheses concerning linguistic development in a child? In what ways are they "revolutionary"?

4 Chomsky says that "imitation is a subsidiary factor in the acquisition of a language." How would B. F. Skinner and other behaviorists react to this statement? Does Brown's dis-

[26] G. A. Miller: "Some Preliminaries to Psycholinguistics" in R. C. Oldfield and J. C. Marshall: *Language* (1968), p. 212; G. A. Miller: "Some Psychological Studies of Grammar" in L. A. Jakobovitz and M. S. Miron: *Readings in the Psychology of Language* (1967), p. 217.

cussion of feral and isolated man (pp. 79–84) provide any insights? Discuss.

5 People have a tendency to demean imitation. Is imitation as simple a process as has been supposed? Explain.

6 What does Chomsky mean when he says "man is born with a disposition to acquire language"? What distinctions does Chomsky make between *knowledge* and *grammar*, and between *competence* and *performance*?

6
Conditioning the Uncommitted Cortex for Language Learning[1]

Wilder Penfield

We are now beginning to realize in this country that the best time to learn a language is when we are young. This conclusion would appear to be common sense, since we know that children of every language community learn their own language with no difficulty. The reasons we have given for learning languages when we are young have not, however, been empirical or very logical. In the following article, Wilder Penfield, a neurosurgeon, gives physiologically sound evidence for the belief that languages should be taught before the age of twelve. His research on the uncommitted cortex of the brain, that area of the brain that develops as a speech and perception center, reveals that it must be developed early and that its proper development may, in fact, influence performance on intelligence tests.

IN THIS changing modern world, it is most urgent for a "well-educated" man to master one or more secondary languages. Once it was

[1] A part of this communication was published in different form in *The Atlantic Monthly*, Boston, July 1964, vol. 214, p. 77, entitled *The Uncommitted Cortex*.

the dead languages. Now it is the living languages that are important. This calls for change in the plan of education. The following discussion of the neurophysiology of speech and its relation to language-learning was prepared for this volume of *Brain*, which honours a neurologist, F. M. R. Walshe. But it is not written for neurologists. It is intended for educators and parents, in the hope that it may help them to adjust school curricula and home instruction to the changing physiology of the brain of childhood.

The human brain is not a previously programmed calculator. It is a living, growing, changing organ. It can even carry out its own repairs to some extent. But it is subject to an inexorable evolution of its functional aptitudes. No one can alter the time schedule of the human brain, not even a psychiatrist, or an educator. The built-in biological clock tells the passage of learning aptitudes and the teacher's opportunity.

When I was in India in 1957, visiting some of the universities under the Commonwealth Colombo Plan, I received a startling invitation from the Department of Education—to give a series of two broadcasts over the All-India Radio on the teaching of secondary languages. Some educator, I reflected, must indeed be desperate! It might well have been so, for the Government of India had laid at the door of the Ministry of Education the task of teaching the people Hindustani and English, although the mother-tongue of the majority was something else. The request was startling to me, not because the problem was new but because an educator had turned to a neurosurgeon.

My wife tried to reassure me by pointing out that our own children had gained a satisfactory command of two added languages. We had done no more than to have them hear German and French well-spoken in their early childhood. Was it, after all, as simple as that? I gave the broadcast and the Department of Education had 10,000 copies of it printed and distributed to the teachers of India. This seemed to leave me with no avenue for retreat. But fortunately this has not been necessary.

For my own part, I had heard no foreign tongue before the age of 16. After that, I studied three modern languages for professional purposes but spoke none well. Before beginning the study of medicine, I even spent a whole year teaching German and was paid for it in an otherwise efficient boys' school. It was, I fear, very poor language teaching. I handed on, as best I could, the words and the grammar I had learned at Princeton to boys who were between 15 and 18 years of age.

On the other hand, my own children learned to use German and French without apparent effort, without foreign accent, and without the long hours of toil that I had sacrificed to language study. They did well what I did badly. There must be a physiological explanation for the difference (unless these children were vastly more intelligent than their father!).

Before saying anything more about the children or the broadcast in India, perhaps the reader will follow me in a short detour. I have had a remarkable opportunity to study speech mechanisms, language learning and bilingualism. Most of my clinical career has been passed in Montreal where my patients were, half of them, French-speaking and half English-speaking. I have seen children, below the age of 10 or 12, lose the power of speech when the speech convolutions in the left hemisphere of the brain had been destroyed by a head injury or a brain tumour. I have seen them recover after a year of dumbness and aphasia. In time, they spoke as well as ever because the young child's brain is functionally flexible for the start of a language. They began all over again. Occasionally when such children had become epileptic because of the brain injury, we were able to study what had happened, while we were trying to cure them. In every case, we found they had established a speech centre located on the other side of the brain in what is called the non-dominant hemisphere. (In a right-handed person, the left hemisphere is normally dominant for speech. That is, it contains the whole specialized speech mechanism.)

When the major speech centre is severely injured in adult life, the adult cannot do what he might have done as a child. He may improve but he is apt to be using the remaining uninjured cortex on the side of the injury. He can never establish a completely new centre on the non-dominant side, as far as our experience goes. That is not because he is senile. It is because he has, by that time, taken over the initially uncommitted convolutions on the non-dominant side of his brain for other uses.

Grey matter is made up of many millions of living nerve cells that are capable of receiving and sending electrical impulses. The cerebral cortex, which is the thick layer of grey matter covering the outer surface of the brain, has been called "new" since it is found to be more and more voluminous as one ascends the philogenetic scale from fish to man. It covers the convolutions and dips down into the fissures between them. The underlying white matter is made up of the branching connexions of the nerve cells. They are capable of transmitting electric potentials like insulated wires. Some of the connexions pass inward from cortex into the "old" grey matter of the brain-stem (the old brain); some unite cortex and brain-stem with the eyes and ears; some pass up and down the spinal cord and along the nerves to the muscles and the skin.

Certain parts of the cerebral cortex are functionally committed from the start. The so-called "sensory cortex" and "motor cortex" can only be used for sensory and motor purposes because these parts seem to have fixed functional connexions from birth onward.

But there is a large area of cortex covering a given, large part of each of the two temporal lobes that is uncommitted at birth. This uncommitted cortex will in time be used for language and for perception. For language, it will make possible the remembrance and use of words. For perception, it will play a part in the recall of the past and the interpretation of present experience. As the child begins to perceive and to speak, electrical currents must be passing in corresponding patterns through this cortex and underlying brain. After each time of passage, it is easier for the passage of later currents along the same trail. This tendency to facilitation of electrical passage results in man's amazingly permanent records of the auditory and visual stream of his conscious life.

Now, if the posterior half of the left uncommitted cortex is used by the child for speech, as it usually is, it becomes the major speech area, or speech cortex.[2] Then the remaining three-quarters is used for interpretation of experience (interpretive cortex). Functional connexions are gradually established by the child and by the time he enters the teens the general uses of the uncommitted areas are apparently fixed for life.

Much of this information about mechanisms of speech and perception has come to us from the well-known work of others. Some has come to us unexpectedly during long operations on conscious alert patients who were kept from pain by local novocain injection into the scalp while a trap door opening was made in the skull. In the attempt to relieve each patient of his attacks of focal epilepsy, a preliminary survey of the brain was made after the exposure was completed.

A gentle electrical stimulus was applied by touching the cortex here and there with an electrode. This served to map the sensory cortex by causing sensation (visual auditory or bodily, according to which of the different areas was touched) and the motor cortex by producing crude movement of the face or tongue or limb. When an abnormality in a certain area of brain was suspected of being the cause of fits, the electrode might produce by stimulation there the characteristic beginning of the attack from which the patient sought relief. (Surgical excision of areas of bad cortex is a worth-while

[2] There are also two secondary speech areas, both of them in the frontal lobe of the dominant hemisphere: Broca's area in the third frontal convolution, and the supplementary speech area in the supplementary motor area. An adult can recover speech after aphasia of varying lengths of time when either one is destroyed. The posterior speech area (Wernicke's), established in the uncommitted temporal cortex, is the major one.

method of treatment in case conservative medical therapy has failed in the hands of experienced neurologists.)

The most precious and indispensable portion of the adult's cortex is the major speech area. It might be worth while to forfeit other areas and so lose other functions in order to gain a cure of epilepsy, but never the speech area. Thus the need of a method to map out the exact territory devoted to speech was urgent.

When the electrode was applied to the speech cortex, it did not cause a man to speak. It seemed at first to have no effect. But if the patient tried to speak while the electrode was in place, he discovered to his astonishment (and to ours at first) that he could not find his words. If shown a pencil, he knew what it was and could make appropriate movements with the hand, but he had lost the power of speaking. He was aphasic. The gentle electric current was blocking the action of the speech cortex, with its underlying connexion, without disturbing the function of the adjacent areas. When the patient was shown an object and was asked to name it, he perceived its nature, and he must have dispatched electric potentials along the brain's integrating circuits to the speech mechanism. But, to his surprise, he "drew a blank."

Normally, when the appropriately patterned potentials reach the speech mechanism, the word, by instant reflex action, is made available to consciousness—its sound, how to write it, how to speak it and how to recognize the written word. As long as the electrode continued to paralyse the action of the speech unit, none of these was possible. But as the electrode was lifted, the patient, not knowing what had been done, would exclaim, "Now I can speak! That was a pencil."

So we had a much-needed method of mapping out the major speech area exactly (and the minor ones as well). And we could remove less useful cortex right up to the speech frontier without fear of losing speech function. We mapped out the cortical area thus in hundreds of cases and acquired precise knowledge of the demarcation in each case. This took the place of anatomical conjecture. But what about the similar area in the non-dominant hemisphere and the uncommitted temporal cortex farther forward on both sides? So far, neurologists had found no clear indication of function for these areas.

Stimulation in them never produced aphasia. What were they used for? One day I stumbled on a clue. I applied the electrode to the right temporal cortex (non-dominant). The patient, a woman of middle age, exclaimed suddenly, "I seem to be the way I was when I was giving birth to my baby girl." I did not recognize this as a clue. But I could not help feeling that the suddenness of her exclamation was strange and so I made a note of it.

Several years later during a similar operation, the electrode caused a young girl to describe, with considerable emotion, a specific experience she had when running through a meadow. There is no sensation in the cortex and she could not know when I had touched the electrode to her right temporal lobe but, each time I did so, she described the experience again, and stopped when the electrode was removed. Since that day we have been on the alert and have gathered more and more cases which could be studied critically. We have now published all of them in complete summary.[3]

The conclusion is as follows: There is within the adult human brain a remarkable record of the stream of each individual's awareness. It is as though the electrode cuts in, at random, on the record of that stream. The patient sees and hears what he saw and heard in some earlier strip of time and he feels the same accompanying emotions. The stream of consciousness flows for him again, exactly as before, stopping instantly on removal of the electrode. He is aware of those things to which he paid attention in this earlier period, even twenty years ago. He is not aware of the things that were ignored. The experience evidently moves forward at the original pace. This was demonstrated by the fact that when, for example, the music of an orchestra, or song or piano, is heard and the patient is asked to hum in accompaniment, the tempo of his humming is what one would expect. He is still aware of being in the operating room but he can describe this other run of consciousness at the same time.

The patient recognizes the experience as having been his own, although usually he could not have recalled it if he had tried. The complete record of his auditory and visual experience is not subject to conscious recall, but it is evidently used in the subconscious brain-transaction that results in perception. By means of it, a man in normal life compares each succeeding experience with his own past experience. He knows at once whether it is familiar or not. If it is familiar, he interprets the present stream of consciousness in the light of the past.

Careful comparison of all the brain maps we have made shows no overlap of the boundaries that separate speech cortex (which endows a man with memory of words) and the interpretive cortex which gives him access to the memory of past similar experience and thus enables him to understand the present.

Before the child begins to speak and to perceive, the uncommitted

[3] W. Penfield and Ph. Perot—*Brain* (1963), 86, 595–696.

cortex is a blank slate on which nothing has been written. In the ensuing years much is written, and the writing is normally never erased. After the age of 10 or 12, the general functional connexions have been established and fixed for the speech cortex. After that the speech centre cannot be transferred to the cortex of the lesser side and set up all over again. This "non-dominant" area that might have been used for speech is now fully occupied with the business of perception.

The brain of the 12 year old, you may say, is prepared for rapid expansion of the vocabulary of the mother tongue and of the other languages he may have heard in the formative period. If he has heard these other languages, he has developed also a remarkable *switch mechanism* that enables him to turn from one language to another without confusion, without translation, without a mother-tongue accent.

In my broadcast to the teachers of India, I could only reason as follows: Do not turn without question to the West for your model of teaching secondary languages. Consider first the changing functional capacities of the child's brain. Most of our schools in the West begin the teaching of foreign languages by the dead-language technique. It was designed for adults learning Greek and Latin by means of word-lists and grammar. Your hope that the people of India will speak English and Hindustani as living-languages is doomed to failure if you follow this technique. The dead-language technique has its place, no doubt, but it cannot be used in the years when the child is a genius at language initiation.

But there is another method of beginning a language—the direct method that mothers use. It was used to teach foreign languages as well as the mother-tongue, in the families of ancient Ur and during the Roman Empire. It is used by some parents in the West and in the East today. Even a child's nurse or the least experienced tutor can use the mother's method for a second language. The mother does her teaching when the child's brain is ready for it. In three or four years she may only give the child a few hundred words, perhaps. But he gets the set, acquires the units, creates the functional connexions of the speech cortex. In unilingual countries the mother conducts the first stage of language learning by the direct method and the school carries on easily with the second stage—vocabulary expansion. If a nation is to be bilingual or trilingual, or multilingual, the nation's schools should adopt the mother's direct method for the first stage of foreign language teaching.

In retrospect, I am not sure whether, when I presumed to offer a solution to the teachers of India, I was speaking from scientific evidence, or as a man who had tried unsuccessfully to master secondary languages by the classical methods, or as a teacher of German who had employed the classical method, or, finally, as a father whose children had approached two second languages successfully by the mother's method. In any case, I ventured an opinion:

India's problem is not insuperable. Use the mother's method at the very beginning of formal education with teachers who can speak either English or Hindustani well and who understand kindergarten techniques. Following that, I outlined, in a rather confused manner (my thinking was less clear in this regard then than now) what is described below as *parallel bilingualism* (one language in the morning, the other in the afternoon).

But India, with her most important task of language-teaching, is far away. In other nations of the world the problem of second-language teaching is hardly less urgent, although it presents itself in varying patterns. The urgency of the problem will, I hope, excuse a parent and a clinical neurophysiologist if he addresses school teachers and parents nearer home than India.

There is a good deal of evidence to suggest that when a young child is allowed to hear a second language and learns to use only a few hundred words of that language—he becomes a better potential linguist; his uncommitted cortex is conditioned to further second-language learning. It is difficult or impossible to condition it thus later in life because the functional connexions tend to become fixed.

This would explain the reputed genius of the Swiss, the Poles and the Belgians as linguists. Most of them hear a second language in early childhood in the streets and the playgrounds, if not at home. On the contrary, the average so-called Anglo-Saxon, in Great Britain or the United States, hears only English until possibly he is taught a modern language in his teens at school.

J. B. Conant (former President of Harvard), in his recent studies of American high schools, concluded that in the best schools of today the work is satisfactory, except in one department: the teaching of foreign languages. The classical method, with its grammar and word lists designed to teach dead languages, is the indirect method of the high school. A little child cannot use it. He would only laugh at it, and yet the little child is the genius in our society for starting languages. The brain of the 12 year old is already senescent in that regard. He is ready for vocabulary expansion.

Education, to be scientific, must consider the physiology of a child's brain. When the classical method is used to start a unilingual teenage pupil or adult in the learning of second languages, the procedure is unscientific and not in accordance with the dictates of neurophysiology. With hard work, it may serve the purpose as a second-best method.

The teaching of additional living languages, as intelligent parents have managed it, ever since the society of ancient Ur became bilingual, is in accordance with the modern findings of speech physiology.

The mother's method of initiating the learning of the mother tongue is scientifically correct and successful. This is the original direct method. It conditions the child's uncommitted cortex to the set and the style of the language. Second languages can be started by the same direct method without confusion.

There are examples of early language teaching by the direct method in schools in many parts of the world. But these are still sporadic. It may serve my purpose best to describe a school in Montreal in which the mother's direct method is being well used. The school is available to children from French-speaking homes or English-speaking homes and also to children from Polish or Ukrainian-speaking families.

This is a day-school in which the method of *parallel bilingualism* is used by teachers speaking their native tongue (English or French). They are the teaching nuns of Notre Dame de Sion, 4701 Dornal Avenue, Montreal. The procedure is not at all complicated. Their school has two years of kindergarten and one of first grade. In the morning the children, aged 4 to 6, are received by English-speaking teachers and in the afternoon by French-speaking teachers or vice versa. No time is wasted teaching language as such. The children play and sing and study in one language in the morning and the other in the afternoon. They begin to read and write in two languages. If there is any difficulty in spelling, it disappears spontaneously after the manner of vanishing baby-talk. Every evening the children return to their homes to speak the mother tongue and to receive whatever home religious instruction is desired by their parents.

After two years of bilingual kindergarten and one in the first grade, children of this school have started reading and writing. They are ready to carry on in either language smoothly and without accent or confusion in some other elementary school. They could, of course, transfer to a school that used a third language. Vocabulary expansion could be provided for by reading and conversation almost any time in the first and second decades of life. When they enter middle school, high school or university, these children should be able to study the literature of second languages instead of struggling with grammar.

The child is the genius in our society when it comes to acquiring the early set, the units or the patterns of a language. The enlargement of vocabulary is another story. The 10 year old expands vocabulary as he expands his knowledge miraculously in the direction of his interests.

The secret of the child's freedom from confusion lies in the action of a conditioned reflex that works in his brain automatically from the beginning. It is what might be called the *switch mechanism*. When the English child (or adult) hears a French word or meets a French person or enters a French school, he unconsciously switches on his French "network" with its vocabulary, however meagre it may be. What he proceeds to learn is then added to the French network. In the brain, French, English and Chinese, if learned, seem to utilize the same general area of speech cortex without demonstrable separation into different areas. Every adult who speaks secondary languages is aware of this subconscious reflex which brings the word *bleistift* to his mind instead of "pencil" as he turns to a German companion, or *crayon* as he enters the class conducted in French.

It is preferable in my opinion that, in the early stages, a bilingual adult, charged with the care of a young child, should not switch back and forth too often from one language to another in conversation. But it works well to do what a bilingual mother of my acquaintance has done: establish "upstairs" in the home as a French-speaking area and "downstairs" for English. Her little children accepted it as no problem at all. Language to them is only a way of getting what is wanted or expressing constructive (or destructive!) ideas.

The first stage of language learning is always in the home. During the first two years of life, imitation of words comes only after months of hearing them.[4] Baby talk shows that the set of the brain for language is not established immediately. It takes time, and the baby's accent and the formal phrasing and organization of sentences alters gradually to that of the adult (without the need of lectures on grammar).

In our own home the two younger children heard German in the nursery from a governess who could speak nothing else. When she took them to French nursery school (aged 3 and 4) they switched to French as they entered the door and switched back again when they found her waiting outside the door at the close of the school. Our two older children, aged 8 and 9, first heard German spoken for a few months in Germany. After that they spoke German to their younger brother and sister and, on occasion, to the governess, but they were never taught the language formally. In spite of that, both older children had excellent command of the language, one for a year of university work in Munich, the other for wireless intelligence in the Second World War.

A unilingual adult, who begins the learning of a second language late, speaks it with a mother-tongue accent and tends to learn by translation. However, the adult who has previously learned some other language in childhood is apt to learn a later third and fourth language faster and probably better than a unilingual adult. It may be suggested that this greater facility of the bilingual adult is due, at least in part, to

---

[4] According to W. E. Leopold's careful study, there is a lag of two to seven months after the child first hears a word in the second year of life before he uses it in a meaningful manner. (Northwestern University Press, 4 vols., 1939–1949.)

the well developed "switch mechanism" which he acquired in child-hood. He is able to switch off the mother tongue more easily and, thus, to learn directly.

It follows, for example, that in a school district where the only for-eign native-born teachers available are Swedish or Spanish, it would be the part of wisdom to have beginning years taught in Swedish (or on a bilingual basis—Swedish in the mornings and Spanish in the after-noons). Those children who continue their schooling in English and eventually go on to college and into professional schools will be better prepared to learn the Russian and Chinese which intelligent English-speaking adults of the future will want to understand. The bilingual child, prepared for formal education by the mother and the child's nurse, or mother and a second language kindergarten, has undoubted advantage over other children whatever the second languages may have been and whatever the eventual work of the individual may prove to be.

The experience of many parents has, of course, been similar to our own, past and present. It is a common experience that when families immigrate, the children learn the new language by the direct method (without confusion) and unilingual parents learn it less well and more slowly by translation and with a mother-tongue accent. This is the supporting evidence of common sense and common experience. And yet there are those who argue that it is better for a child to establish the mother-tongue well before confusing him by exposure to a second language! The child seems to be protected from confusion by rapidly acquired conditioned reflexes and by the action of the switch mecha-nism which is a conditioned reflex.

There is other good evidence that even a limited familiarity with additional languages in the first decade endows the normal child with a more efficient and useful brain. In a study supported by the Carnegie Foundation and conducted under W. E. Lambert, Professor of Psy-chology at McGill University, it was concluded recently that bilingual children, at the 10-year level in Montreal, showed greater intelligence than unilingual children of the same age. They were examined by non-verbal as well as verbal tests.[5]

A second study has been carried out in the same department.[6] In this study, an equal number of bilingual university students was com-pared with a similar selection of unilingual students. The bilingual students scored higher in intelligence tests when those tests were verbal and also when they were non-verbal. In the bilingual society of the

[5] Peel, Elizabeth and Lambert, W.: The Relation of Bilingualism to Intelligence, Psychological Monographs, General and Applied, vol. 76, 27, Amer. Psychol. Ass'n. Washington, D.C., 1962.
[6] Anisfeld, Elizabeth Peel: The Cognitive Aspects of Bilingualism. McGill Uni-versity, Ph.D. thesis.

Province of Quebec, those who were bilingual before entering university would have heard the second language early.

In conclusion, man (to a far greater extent than other mammals) is endowed with extensive areas of cerebral cortex which, at birth, are not committed to sensory or motor function. Much of the uncommitted areas covering the temporal lobes that are not used as "speech cortex" will, in time, be used as "interpretive cortex" and so play a rôle in the process of perception. While the mother is teaching the child to understand and to use a few hundred words and teaching the child to perceive the meanings of words and experiences, she is "programming" the brain. Part of the uncommitted cortex is being conditioned or "programmed" for speech, the remaining uncommitted cortex is used as a part of the mechanism of perception. In the second decade of life, functional connexions seem to have become fixed. Vocabulary expansion and multiplication of perceptions then proceed rapidly.

The mother's method of direct language teaching can be used for second languages but this should *begin* before the age of 6 or 8 if possible. When the uncommitted cortex is thus conditioned early, the individual becomes a better linguist; the child is better prepared for the long educational climb. In the years of life that follow, the man or woman will more easily become the "well-educated" adult for which the future calls so urgently.

Teachers and parents must always share responsibility for the education of each new generation. This includes the conditioning of each child's brain. How and when it is conditioned, prepares the man for great achievement or limits him to mediocrity. A neurophysiologist can only suggest that the human brain is capable of far more than is demanded of it today. Adjust the time and the manner of teaching to the aptitudes of the growing, changing master-organ. Then, double your demands and your reasonable expectations.

FOR DISCUSSION AND REVIEW

1 What is "the uncommitted cortex of the brain"?

2 How exactly have the functions of particular areas of the brain been determined?

3 If an adult receives damage in the speech center, why is that damage usually permanent?

4 Penfield refers to a "switch mechanism" that allows a bilingual speaker to interchange languages. Does he say how this mechanism

works? Explain.

5 On the basis of limited research, Penfield claims that bilingual children perform better on I.Q. tests than unilingual children do. Can you offer an explanation for this from what you have learned from this article? Discuss.

6 Why does Penfield say that the West is not providing, or traditionally has not provided, a good model for language teaching?

5

The Split Brain in Man

Michael S. Gazzaniga

Symmetry is the rule in the human body; and for many years there was no reason to question that the human brain, too, was symmetrical. Since 1961, however, neurosurgeons, physiologists, psychologists, and linguists have been studying patients who have undergone an operation that surgically severed the corpus callosum that connects the two halves of their brains, that is, the two cerebral hemispheres. To their surprise, the investigators found that severing the corpus callosum "produced no noticeable change in the patients' temperament, personality, or general intelligence." There were, however, other changes, particularly in language production and reception but also in perception, so that Gazzaniga can speak of "the bisected-brain syndrome." In the following article, Gazzaniga describes some of these changes and explains why they lead to the conclusion that the human brain, unlike the rest of the human body, is *asymmetrical*, with most language functions localized in the left hemisphere. Most, but not all; because the right brain does have some language capabilities that are beginning to be identified, and because the right hemisphere controls most language functions in a few of the small percentage of people who are left-handed. As Gazzaniga points out, the implications of this research for linguistics are far-reaching. The research will affect work in language acquisition, in basic grammatical theory, in speech pathology, in second-language teaching—and much more.

T HE BRAIN of the higher animals, including man, is a double organ, consisting of right and left hemispheres connected by an isthmus of nerve tissue called the corpus callosum. Some 15 years ago Ronald E. Myers and R. W. Sperry, then at the University of Chicago, made a surprising discovery: when this connection between the two halves of the cerebrum was cut, each hemisphere functioned independently as if it were a complete brain. The phenomenon was first investigated in a cat in which not only the brain but also the optic chiasm, the crossover of the optic nerves, was divided, so that visual information from the left eye was dispatched only to the left brain and information from the right eye only to the right brain. Working on a problem with one eye, the animal could respond normally and learn to perform a task; when that eye was covered and the same problem was presented to the other eye, the animal evinced no recognition of the problem and had to learn it again from the beginning with the other half of the brain.

The finding introduced entirely new questions in the study of brain mechanisms. Was the corpus callosum responsible for integration of the operations of the two cerebral hemispheres in the intact brain? Did it serve to keep each hemisphere informed about what was going on in the other? To put the question another way, would cutting the corpus callosum literally result in the right hand not knowing what the left was doing? To what extent were the two half-brains actually independent when they were separated? Could they have separate thoughts, even separate emotions?

Such questions have been pursued by Sperry and his coworkers in a wide-ranging series of animal studies at the California Institute of Technology over the past decade. Recently these questions have been investigated in human patients who underwent the brain-splitting operation for medical reasons. The demonstration in experimental animals that sectioning of the corpus callosum did not seriously impair mental faculties had encouraged surgeons to resort to this operation for people afflicted with uncontrollable epilepsy. The hope was to confine a seizure to one hemisphere. The operation proved to be remarkably successful; curiously there is an almost total elimination of all attacks, including unilateral ones. It is as if the intact callosum had served in these patients to facilitate seizure activity.

This article is a brief survey of investigations Sperry and I have carried out at Cal Tech over the past five years with some of these patients. The operations were performed by P. J. Vogel and J. E. Bogen of the California College of Medicine. Our studies date back to 1961, when the first patient, a 48-year-old war veteran, underwent the operation: cutting of the corpus callosum and other commissure structures connecting the two halves of the cerebral cortex (see Figure 1). As of today 10 patients have had the operation, and we have examined four thoroughly over a long period with many tests.

From the beginning, one of the most striking observations was that the operation produced no noticeable change in the patients' temperament, personality, or general intelligence. In the first case the patient could not speak for 30 days after the operation, but he then recovered his speech. More typical was the third case: on awakening from the surgery the patient quipped that he had a "splitting headache," and in his still drowsy state he was able to repeat the tongue twister "Peter Piper picked a peck of pickled peppers."

Close observation, however, soon revealed some changes in the patients' everyday behavior. For example, it could be seen that in moving

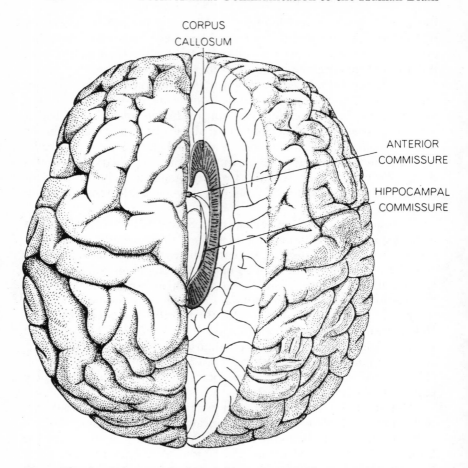

CORPUS
CALLOSUM

ANTERIOR
COMMISSURE

HIPPOCAMPAL
COMMISSURE

Fig. 1. Two hemispheres of the human brain are divided by neurosurgeons to control epileptic seizures. In this top view of the brain the right hemisphere is retracted, and the corpus callosum and other commissures, or connectors, that are generally cut are shaded.

about and responding to sensory stimuli the patients favored the right side of the body, which is controlled by the dominant left half of the brain. For a considerable period after the operation, the left side of the body rarely showed spontaneous activity, and the patient generally did not respond to stimulation of that side: when he brushed against something with his left side he did not notice that he had done so, and when an object was placed in his left hand he generally denied its presence.

More specific tests identified the main features of the bisected-brain syndrome. One of these tests examined responses to visual stimulation. While the patient fixed his gaze on a central point on a board, spots of light were flashed (for a tenth of a second) in a row across the board that spanned both the left and the right half of his visual field. The patient was asked to tell what he had seen. Each patient reported that lights had been flashed in the right half of the visual field. When lights were flashed only in the left half of the field, however, the patients generally denied having seen any lights. Since the right side of the visual field is normally projected to the left hemisphere of the brain and the left field to the right hemisphere, one might have concluded that in these patients with divided brains the right hemisphere was in effect blind. We found, however, that this was not the case when the patients were directed to point to the lights that had flashed instead of giving a verbal report. With this manual response they were able to indicate when lights had been flashed in the left visual field, and perception with the brain's right hemisphere proved to be almost equal to perception with the left. Clearly, then, the patients' failure to report the right hemisphere's perception verbally was due to the fact that the speech centers of the brain are located in the left hemisphere.

Our tests of the patients' ability to recognize objects by touch at first resulted in the same general finding. When the object was held in the right hand, from which sensory information is sent to the left hemisphere, the patient was able to name and describe the object. When it was held in the left hand (from which information goes primarily to the right hemisphere), the patient could not describe the object verbally but was able to identify it in a nonverbal test—matching it, for example, to the same object in a varied collection of things. We soon realized, however, that each hemisphere receives, in addition to the main input from the opposite side of the body, some input from the same side. This "ipsilateral" input is crude; it is apparently good mainly for "cuing in" the hemisphere as to the presence or absence of stimulation and relaying fairly gross information about the location of a stimulus on the surface of the body. It is unable, as a rule, to relay information concerning the qualitative nature of an object.

Tests of motor control in these split-brain patients revealed that the left hemisphere of the brain exercised normal control over the right hand but had less than full control of the left hand (for instance, it was poor at directing individual movements of the fingers). Similarly, the right hemisphere had full control of the left hand but not of the right hand. When the two hemispheres were in conflict, dictating different movements for the same hand, the hemisphere on the side opposite the hand generally took charge and overruled the orders of the side of the brain with the weaker control. In general the motor findings in the human patients were much the same as those in split-brain monkeys.

We come now to the main question on which we centered our studies, namely how the separation of the hemispheres affects the men-

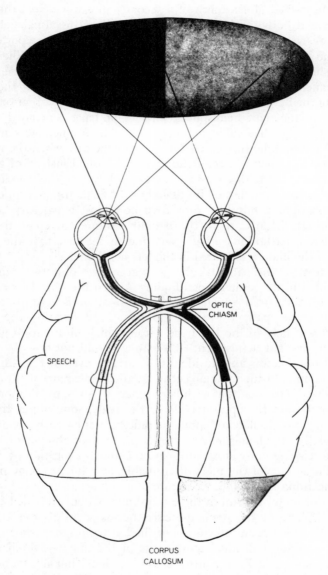

Fig. 2. Visual input to bisected brain was limited to one hemisphere by presenting information only in one visual field. The right and left fields of view are projected, via the optic chiasm, to the left and right hemispheres of the brain, respectively. If a person fixes his gaze on a point, therefore, information to the left of the point goes only to the right hemisphere and information to the right of the point goes to the left hemisphere. Stimuli in the left visual field cannot be described by a split-brain patient because of the disconnection between the right hemisphere and the speech center, which is in the left hemisphere.

tal capacities of the human brain. For these psychological tests we used two different devices. One was visual: a picture or written information was flashed (for a tenth of a second) in either the right or the left visual field, so that the information was transmitted only to the left or to the right brain hemisphere (see Figure 2). The other type of test was tactile: an object was placed out of view in the patient's right or left hand, again for the purpose of conveying the information to just one hemisphere—the hemisphere on the side opposite the hand.

When the information (visual or tactile) was presented to the dominant left hemisphere, the patients were able to deal with and describe it quite normally, both orally and in writing. For example, when a picture of a spoon was shown in the right visual field or a spoon was placed in the right hand, all the patients readily identified and described it. They were able to read out written messages and to perform problems in calculation that were presented to the left hemisphere.

In contrast, when the same information was presented to the right hemisphere, it failed to elicit such spoken or written responses. A picture transmitted to the right hemisphere evoked either a haphazard guess or no verbal response at all. Similarly, a pencil placed in the left hand (behind a screen that cut off vision) might be called a can opener or a cigarette lighter, or the patient might not even attempt to describe it. The verbal guesses presumably came not from the right hemisphere but from the left, which had no perception of the object but might attempt to identify it from indirect clues.

Did this impotence of the right hemisphere mean that its surgical separation from the left had reduced its mental powers to an imbecilic level? The earlier tests of its nonverbal capacities suggested that this was almost certainly not so. Indeed, when we switched to asking for nonverbal answers to the visual and tactile information presented in our new psychological tests, the right hemisphere in several patients showed considerable capacity for accurate performance. For example, when a picture of a spoon was presented to the right hemisphere, the patients were able to feel around with the left hand among a varied group of objects (screened from sight) and select a spoon as a match for the picture. Furthermore, when they were shown a picture of a cigarette they succeeded in selecting an ashtray, from a group of 10 objects that did not include a cigarette, as the article most closely related to the picture. Oddly enough, however, even after their correct response, and while they were holding the spoon or the ashtray in their left hand, they were unable to name or describe the object or the picture. Evidently the left hemisphere was completely divorced, in perception and knowledge, from the right.

Other tests showed that the right hemisphere did possess a certain amount of language comprehension. For example, when the word "pencil" was flashed to the right hemisphere, the patients were able to pick out a pencil from a group of unseen objects with the left hand. And when a patient held an object in the left hand (out of view), although he could not say its name or describe it, he was later able to point to a card on which the name of the object was written.

In one particularly interesting test the word "heart" was flashed across the center of the visual field, with the "he" portion to the left of the center and "art" to the right. Asked to tell what the word was, the patients would say they had seen "art"—the portion projected to the left brain hemisphere (which is responsible for speech). Curiously, when, after "heart" had been flashed in the same way, the patients were asked to point with the left hand to one of two cards—"art" or "he"— to identify the word they had seen, they invariably pointed to "he." The experiment showed clearly that both hemispheres had simultaneously observed the portions of the word available to them and that in this particular case the right hemisphere, when it had had the opportunity to express itself, had prevailed over the left.

Because an auditory input to one ear goes to both sides of the brain, we conducted tests for the comprehension of words presented audibly to the right hemisphere, not by trying to limit the original input but by limiting the ability to answer to the right hemisphere. This was done most easily by having a patient use his left hand to retrieve, from a grab

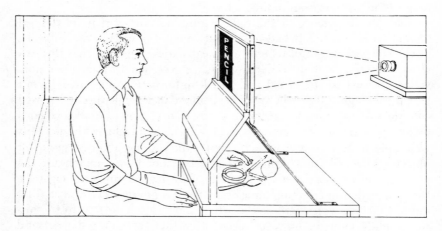

Fig. 3. Response to visual stimulus is tested by flashing a word or a picture of an object on a translucent screen. The examiner first checks the subject's gaze to be sure it is fixed on a dot that marks the center of the visual field. The examiner may call for a verbal response—reading the flashed word, for example—or for a nonverbal one, such as picking up the object that is named from among a number of things spread on the table. The objects, hidden from the subject's view, can be identified only by touch.

bag held out of view, an object named by the examiner. We found that the patients could easily retrieve such objects as a watch, comb, marble, or coin. The object to be retrieved did not even have to be named; it might simply be described or alluded to. For example, the command "Retrieve the fruit monkeys like best" results in the patients' pulling out a banana from a grab bag full of plastic fruit; at the command "Sunkist sells a lot of them" the patients retrieve an orange. We knew that touch information from the left hand was going exclusively to the right hemisphere because moments later, when the patients were asked to name various pieces of fruit placed in the left hand, they were unable to score above a chance level.

The upper limit of linguistic abilities in each hemisphere varies from subject to subject. In one case there was little or no evidence for language abilities in the right hemisphere, whereas in the other three the amount and extent of the capacities varied. The most adept patient showed some evidence of even being able to spell simple words by placing plastic letters on a table with his left hand. The subject was told to

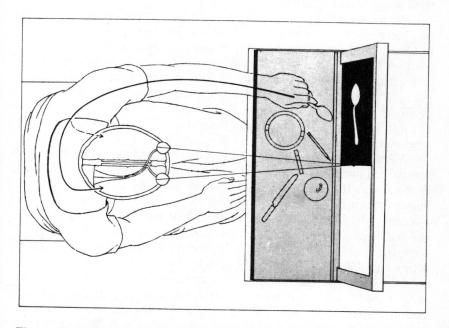

Fig. 4. Visual-tactile association is performed by a split-brain patient. A picture of a spoon is flashed to the right hemisphere; with the left hand he retrieves a spoon from behind the screen. The touch information from the left hand returns mainly to the right hemisphere, but a weak "ipsilateral" component goes to the left hemisphere. This is usually not enough to enable him to say (using the left hemisphere) what he has picked up.

spell a word such as "pie," and the examiner then placed the three appropriate letters, one at a time in a random order, in his left hand to be arranged on the table. The patient was able to spell even more abstract words such as "how," "what" and "the." In another test three or four letters were placed in a pile, again out of view, to be felt with the left hand. The letters available in each trial would spell only one word, and the instructions to the subject were "Spell a word." The patient was able to spell such words as "cup" and "love." Yet after he had completed this task, the patient was unable to name the word he had just spelled!

The possibility that the right hemisphere has not only some language but even some speech capabilities cannot be ruled out, although at present there is no firm evidence for this. It would not be surprising to discover that the patients are capable of a few simple exclamatory remarks, particularly when under emotional stress. The possibility also remains, of course, that speech of some type could be trained into the right hemisphere. Tests aimed at this question, however, would have to be closely scrutinized and controlled.

The reason is that here, as in many of the tests, "cross-cuing" from one hemisphere to the other could be held responsible for any positive findings. We had a case of such cross-cuing during a series of tests of whether the right hemisphere could respond verbally to simple red or green stimuli. At first, after either a red or a green light was flashed to the right hemisphere, the patient would guess the color at a chance level, as might be expected if the speech mechanism is solely represented in the left hemisphere. After a few trials, however, the score improved whenever the examiner allowed a second guess.

We soon caught on to the strategy the patient used. If a red light was flashed and the patient by chance guessed red, he would stick with that answer. If the flashed light was red and the patient by chance guessed green, he would frown, shake his head and then say, "Oh no, I meant red." What was happening was that the right hemisphere saw the red light and heard the left hemisphere make the guess "green." Knowing that the answer was wrong, the right hemisphere precipitated a frown and a shake of the head, which in turn cued in the left hemisphere to the fact that the answer was wrong and that it had better correct itself! We have learned that this cross-cuing mechanism can become extremely refined. The realization that the neurological patient has various strategies at his command emphasizes how difficult it is to obtain a clear neurological description of a human being with brain damage.

Is the language comprehension by the right hemisphere that the patients exhibited in these tests a normal capability of that hemisphere or was it acquired by learning after their operation, perhaps during the course of the experiments themselves? The issue is difficult to decide. We must remember that we are examining a half of the human brain, a system easily capable of learning from a single trial in a test. We do know that the right hemisphere is decidedly inferior to the left in its overall command of language. We have established, for instance, that although the right hemisphere can respond to a concrete noun such as "pencil," it cannot do as well with verbs; patients are unable to respond appropriately to simple printed instructions, such as "smile" or "frown," when these words are flashed to the right hemisphere, nor can they point to a picture that corresponds to a flashed verb. Some of our recent studies at the University of California at Santa Barbara also indicate that the right hemisphere has a very poorly developed grammar; it seems to be incapable of forming the plural of a given word, for example.

In general, then, the extent of language present in the adult right hemisphere in no way compares with that present in the left hemisphere or, for that matter, with the extent of language present in the child's right hemisphere. Up to the age of four or so, it would appear from a variety of neurological observations, the right hemisphere is about as proficient in handling language as the left. Moreover, studies of the child's development of language, particularly with respect to grammar, strongly suggest that the foundations of grammar—a ground plan for language, so to speak—are somehow inherent in the human organism and are fully realized between the ages of two and three. In other words, in the young child each hemisphere is about equally developed with respect to language and speech function. We are thus faced with the interesting question of why the right hemisphere at an early age and stage of development possesses substantial language capacity whereas at a more adult stage it possesses a rather poor capacity. It is difficult indeed to conceive of the underlying neurological mechanism that would allow for the establishment of a capacity of a high order in a particular hemisphere on a temporary basis. The implication is that during maturation the processes and systems active in making this capacity manifest are somehow inhibited and dismantled in the right hemisphere and allowed to reside only in the dominant left hemisphere.

Yet the right hemisphere is not in all respects inferior or subordinate to the left. Tests have demonstrated that it excels the left in some specialized functions. As an example, tests by us and by Bogen have shown that in these patients the left hand is capable of arranging blocks to match a pictured design and of drawing a cube in three dimensions, whereas the right hand, deprived of instructions from the right hemisphere, could not perform either of these tasks.

It is of interest to note, however, that although the patients (our first subject in particular) could not execute such tasks with the right hand, they were capable of matching a test stimulus to the correct design when it appeared among five related patterns presented in their right visual field. This showed that the dominant left hemisphere is capable of discriminating between correct and incorrect stimuli. Since it is also true that the patients have no motor problems with their right hand, the patients' inability to perform these tasks must reflect a breakdown of an integrative process somewhere between the sensory system and the motor system.

We found that in certain other mental processes the right hemisphere is on a par with the left. In particular, it can independently generate an emotional reaction. In one of our experiments exploring the matter we would present a series of ordinary objects and then suddenly

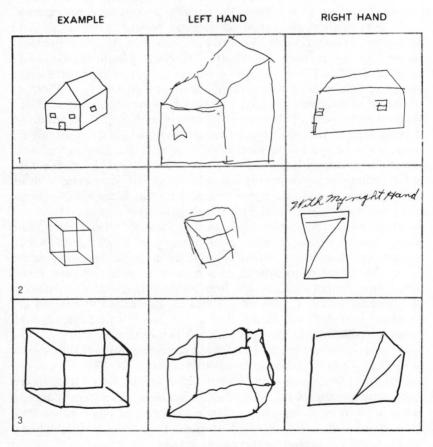

Fig. 5. "Visual-constructional" tasks are handled better by the right hemisphere. This was seen most clearly in the first patient, who had poor ispilateral control of his right hand. Although righthanded, he could copy the examples only with his left hand.

flash a picture of a nude woman. This evoked an amused reaction regardless of whether the picture was presented to the left hemisphere or to the right. When the picture was flashed to the left hemisphere of a female patient, she laughed and verbally identified the picture as a nude. When it was later presented to the right hemisphere, she said in reply to a question that she saw nothing, but almost immediately a sly smile spread over her face and she began to chuckle. Asked what she was laughing at, she said: "I don't know . . . nothing . . . oh—that funny machine." Although the right hemisphere could not describe what it had seen, the sight nevertheless elicited an emotional response like the one evoked from the left hemisphere.

Taken together, our studies seem to demonstrate conclusively that in a split-brain situation we are really dealing with two brains, each separately capable of mental functions of a high order. This implies that the two brains should have twice as large a span of attention—that is, should be able to handle twice as much information—as a normal whole brain. We have not yet tested this precisely in human patients, but E. D. Young and I have found that a split-brain monkey can indeed deal with nearly twice as much information as a normal animal (see Figure 6). We have so far determined also that brain-bisected patients can carry out two tasks as fast as a normal person can do one.

Just how does the corpus callosum of the intact brain combine and integrate the perceptions and knowledge of the two cerebral hemispheres? This has been investigated recently by Giovanni Berlucchi, Giacomo Rizzolati, and me at the Istituto de Fisiologia Umana in Pisa. We made recordings of neural activity in the posterior part of the callosum of the cat with the hope of relating the responses of that structure to stimulation of the animal's visual fields. The kinds of responses recorded turned out to be similar to those observed in the visual cortex of the cat. In other words, the results suggest that visual pattern information can be transmitted through the callosum. This finding militates against the notion that learning and memory are transferred across the callosum, as has usually been suggested. Instead, it looks as though in animals with an intact callosum a copy of the visual world as seen in one hemisphere is sent over to the other, with the result that both hemispheres can learn together a discrimination presented to just one hemisphere. In the split-brain animal this extension of the visual pathway is cut off; this would explain rather simply why no learning proceeds in the visually isolated hemisphere and why it has to learn the discrimination from scratch.

Curiously, however, the neural activity in the callosum came only in response to stimuli at the midline of the visual field. This finding raises difficult questions. How can it be reconciled with the well-established observation that the left hemisphere of a normal person can give a run-

Fig. 6. Split-brain monkeys can handle more visual information than
normal animals. When the monkey
pulls a knob (1), eight of the 16
panels light momentarily. The monkey must then start at the bottom
and punch the lights that were lit
and no others (2). With the panels
lit for 600 milliseconds normal
monkeys get up to the third row
from the bottom before forgetting
which panels were lit (3). Split-
brain monkeys complete the entire
task with the panels lit only 200
milliseconds. The monkeys look at
the panels through filters; since the
optic chiasm is cut in these animals, the filters allow each hemisphere to see the panels on one side
only.

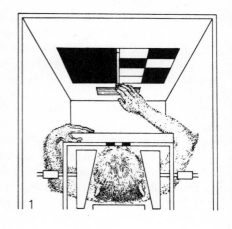

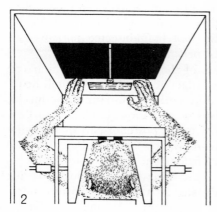

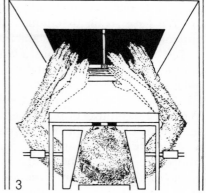

ning description of all the visual information presented throughout the
entire half-field projected to the right hemisphere? For this reason alone
one is wearily driven back to the conclusion that somewhere and somehow all or part of the callosum transmits not only a visual scene but
also a complicated neural code of a higher order.

All the evidence indicates that separation of the hemispheres creates two independent spheres of consciousness within a single cranium,
that is to say, within a single organism. This conclusion is disturbing to
some people who view consciousness as an indivisible property of the
human brain. It seems premature to others, who insist that the capacities revealed thus far for the right hemisphere are at the level of an
automaton. There is, to be sure, hemispheric inequality in the present

cases, but it may well be a characteristic of the individuals we have studied. It is entirely possible that if a human brain were divided in a very young person, both hemispheres could as a result separately and independently develop mental functions of a high order at the level attained only in the left hemisphere of normal individuals.

FOR DISCUSSION AND REVIEW

1 What is the corpus callosum? What is its function? Why is it sometimes surgically severed in human beings?

2 What effects does severing the corpus callosum have on general intelligence, personality, and temperament or disposition?

3 What immediate—and usually prolonged—effect did the operation have on patients' motor activity and sensory perception, especially of the left side?

4 In reporting the results of the experiments concerning visual stimulation using flashing lights, why does Gazzaniga conclude that "the speech centers of the brain are located in the left hemisphere"?

5 Describe the results of the visual and tactile tests administered to split-brain patients. What happened when visual stimuli were presented to the left eye only or to the right eye only? What happened when tactile information was similarly presented (i.e., to either the right or left hand)?

6 Answer in your own words Gazzaniga's question: "Did this impotence of the right hemisphere mean that its surgical separation from the left had reduced its men-

tal powers to an imbecilic level?" Explain your answer.

7 What is "cross-cuing," and how does it complicate split-brain research?

8 Discuss the implications for second-language teaching of Gazzaniga's statement that "the extent of language present in the adult right hemisphere in no way compares with that present in the left hemisphere or, for that matter, with the extent of language present in the child's right hemisphere. Up to the age of four or so, it would appear from a variety of neurological observations, the right hemisphere is about as proficient in handling language as the left."

9 Evidence is accumulating that the right hemisphere of the human brain possesses some abilities not present in the left hemisphere and is its equal concerning some mental processes. Summarize Gazzaniga's discussion of this subject.

10 What is your reaction to Gazzaniga's statement that he and his fellow researchers have determined "that brain-bisected patients can carry out two tasks as fast as a normal person can do one"?

PROJECTS FOR "FROM ANIMAL COMMUNICATION TO THE HUMAN BRAIN"

1 Human beings, for the most part, inhabit a verbal environment. According to Edward Sapir,

Language . . . completely interpenetrates . . . direct experience. For most persons every experience, real or potential, is saturated with verbalism. This explains why so many lovers of nature, for instance, do not feel that they are truly in touch with it until they have mastered the names of a great many flowers and trees, as though the primary world of reality were a verbal one and as though one could not get close to nature unless one first mastered the terminology which somehow magically expresses it. It is this constant interplay between language and experience which removes language from the cold status of such purely and simply symbolic systems as mathematical symbolism or flag signalling.[1]

Have you ever had an experience similar to that of Sapir's "nature lover"? What does Sapir's discussion of language tell you about your experience? Write a paper in which you explore the implications of Sapir's statement.

2 *Sarah is not the only chimpanzee who has been successfully taught to communicate with human beings, and the method Sarah uses—colored tokens—is not the only means of communication that chimpanzees can be taught to utilize. Prepare a report describing the work with one or more of the other chimpanzees involved in communication experiments (Lana, for example, or the group composed of Bruno, Booee, Cindy, and Thelma). A good starting place is Eugene Linden's paperback book* Apes, Men, and Language (Pelican Books, 1976) *and its bibliography, but you should be sure to go beyond this single source.*

3 *Much fascinating work has been done with animals and their systems of communication. Using items included in the bibliography for this section, write a paper in which you review the research that has been done with either bees, birds, dolphins, or chimpanzees. You can supplement your research materials by looking in the* Reader's Guide to Periodical Literature *or* The International Index for the Social Sciences and Humanities.

4 *Examine the following conversation between Eve, a 24-month-old child, and her mother:*

Eve: Have that?
Mother: No, you may not have it.
Eve: Mom, where my tapioca?
Mother: It's getting cool. You'll have it in just a minute.
Eve: Let me have it.
Mother: Would you like to have your lunch right now?
Eve: Yeah. My tapioca cool?
Mother: Yes, It's cool.
Eve: You gonna watch me eat my lunch?
Mother: Yeah, I'm gonna watch you eat your lunch.
Eve: I eating it.
Mother: I know you are.
Eve: It time Sarah take a nap.

---

[1] Edward Sapir, "Language," *Encyclopaedia of the Social Sciences* (New York: The Macmillan Company, 1933), IX, 157.

Mother: It's time for Sarah to have some milk, yeah. And then she's gonna take a nap and you're gonna take a nap.
Eve: And you?
Mother: And me too, yeah.[2]

Compare the grammar of the child's speech with that of her mother. What elements are systematically missing from the child's speech? Now, look at Eve's speech in a conversation with her mother that was taped only three months later:

Mother: Come and sit over here.
Eve: You can sit down by me. That will make me happy. Ready to turn it.
Mother: We're not quite ready to turn the page.
Eve: Yep, we are.
Mother: Shut the door, we won't hear her then.
Eve: Then Fraser won't hear her too. Where he's going? Did you make a great big hole there?
Mother: Yes, we made a great big hole in here; we have to get a new one.
Eve: Could I get some other piece of paper?
Mother: You ask Fraser.
Eve: Could I use this one?
Mother: I suppose so.
Eve: Is Fraser goin take his pencil home when he goes?
Mother: Yes, he is.[3]

What startling changes do you note in Eve's speech? Try to describe the "grammatical rules" that govern her speech in each passage. Although Eve could not tell us of the rules she learned during the three-month interval, what rules, as evidenced implicitly by her speech, has she internalized? What conclusions can you draw about the process of language learning among children? Write a short paper dealing with these questions.

5   *It is fascinating to watch children learn language. Try taping conversations with a child at two-week intervals for several months. Share the tapes with other members of the class. Note the child's development. On the basis of one tape, plan a strategy (leading questions, etc.) for the next session with the child. Write a report in which you summarize and interpret your data.*

6   *Using the bibliography given at the end of the Farb article, prepare a report on some aspect of children's language that he discusses in "The Language of Children." For example, by reading Chomsky's review of Skinner's Verbal Behavior, you could explain in more detail than Farb has room for the objections of a transformational-generative linguist like Chomsky to the views of the behaviorists (in this case, Skinner). Other possibilities include children's acquisition of verbal-social skills; stages in language acquisition; and others that will arouse your interest.*

[2] A transcription of a taped conversation from Ursula Bellugi, "Learning the Language," *Psychology Today,* 4 (December 1970), 33.
[3] *Ibid.,* 33–34.

SELECTED BIBLIOGRAPHY

Bellugi, Ursula. "Learning the Language." *Psychology Today*, 4 (December 1970), 32–35, 66. (A study of language acquisition and the grammar of children.)

Bronowski, J., and Ursula Bellugi. "Language, Name, and Concept." *Science*, 168 (May 8, 1970), 669–673. (A comparative study of the linguistic capabilities of children and chimpanzees.)

Brown, Roger. *A First Language*. Cambridge: Harvard University Press, 1973. (A major work; readable.)

———. "How Shall A Thing Be Called?" *Psychological Review*, 85 (1958), 145–154. (A discussion of how adults teach children the names of objects.)

———. "The Comparative Psychology of Linguistic Reference." *Words and Things*. New York: The Free Press, 1958. (An historical review of research on animal communication.)

Buck, Craig. "Knowing the Left from the Right." *Human Behavior*, 5 (June 1976), 29–35. (Fascinating collection of specific examples about what each side of the brain can do.)

Carroll, John B. *The Study of Language: A Survey of Linguistics and Related Disciplines in America*. Cambridge: Harvard University Press, 1963. (Contains interesting chapters on linguistics and psychology, and on linguistics and the social sciences.)

Fishman, Joshua, ed. *Readings in the Sociology of Language*. The Hague: Mouton & Company, 1968. (A standard collection of sociolinguistic readings.)

Fleming, Joyce D. "Field Report: The State of the Apes." *Psychology Today*, 7 (January 1974), 31–38, 43–44, 46, 49–50. (Summary of research with Washoe, Lucy, Sarah, and other chimps.)

Ford, Barbara. "How They Taught a Chimp to Talk." *Science Digest*, 67 (May 1970), 10–17. (A discussion of the chimpanzee Washoe's sign language, with illustrations.)

Fromkin, Victoria. "Slips of the Tongue." *Scientific American*, 229 (1973), 110–117. (Interesting in themselves, slips of the tongue offer clues to language processing in the brain.)

———, and Robert Rodman. *An Introduction to Language*. New York: Holt, Rinehart and Winston, Inc., 1974. (See especially chapter 12, "The Gray Matter of Language: Language and the Brain," for a clear discussion and particularly helpful diagrams.)

Gardner, Allen, and Beatrice T. Gardner. "Teaching Sign Language to a Chimpanzee." *Science*, 165 (August 15, 1969), 664–672. (Teaching the infant chimpanzee Washoe the gestural language of the deaf.)

Gardner, Howard. *The Shattered Mind*. New York: Alfred A. Knopf, 1975. (See especially chapter 9, "Contrasting Mirrors," which deals with the two hemispheres of the brain.)

Geschwind, Norman. "Language and the Brain." *Scientific American*, 226 (1972), 76–83. (Aphasias and kinds of brain damage help us understand how language is organized in the brain.)

Hayes, Catherine. *The Ape in Our House*. New York: Harper & Brothers, 1951. (The story of the Hayes family's experiences with the chimpanzee Viki.)

Jakobovits, Leon A., and Murray S. Miron, eds. *Readings in the Psychology of Language*. Englewood Cliffs, New Jersey: Prentice-Hall, 1967. (Includes essays by Katz, Miller, Mowrer, Skinner, and others.)

Kagan, Jerome. "Do Infants Think?" *Scientific American*, 226 (1972), 74–82.

(Argues that cognitive development is under way as early as nine months of age.)

Krough, August. "The Language of the Bees." *Scientific American Reader.* New York: Simon & Schuster, 1953. (A summary of Karl von Frisch's classic study of communication among bees.)

Lenneberg, Eric H. *Biological Foundations of Language.* New York: John Wiley & Sons, 1967. (An interesting but technical investigation of the biological aspects of language.)

Lilly, John C. *Man and Dolphin.* New York: Pyramid Publications, 1969. (The story of man's attempt to communicate with another species.)

————. *The Mind of the Dolphin: A Nonhuman Intelligence.* New York: Avon Books, 1969. (An introduction to the controversial world of communication among dolphins.)

Linden, Eugene. *Apes, Men, and Language.* New York: Pelican Books, 1976. (A chatty survey of most of the research now being done in this country with chimpanzees.)

McNeill, David. *The Acquisition of Language: The Study of Developmental Psycholinguistics.* New York: Harper & Row, 1970. (Brief but technical discussion of language acquisition.)

Miller, George A. *The Psychology of Communication.* New York: Basic Books, 1967. (A collection of seven essays dealing with the psychology of language.)

Osgood, Charles E., and Thomas A. Sebeok, eds. *Psycholinguistics: A Survey of Theory and Research Problems.* Bloomington, Indiana: Indiana University Press, 1965. (A standard but technical collection of readings.)

Pines, Maya. *The Brain Changers: Scientists and the New Mind Control.* New York: Harcourt Brace Jovanovich, Inc., 1973. (Fascinating chapters on many aspects of the brain; see especially chapter 7, "What Half of Your Brain Is Dominant—and Can You Change It?")

Premack, David. "The Education of Sarah: A Chimp Learns the Language." *Psychology Today,* 4 (September 1970), 54–58. (Teaching a chimpanzee a non-vocal language.)

Riopelle, A. J., ed. *Animal Problem Solving.* Baltimore: Penguin Books, 1967. (A collection of reports on problem-solving experiments with animals.)

Sage, Wayne. "The Split Brain Lab." *Human Behavior,* 5 (June 1976), 25–28. (Interesting and very readable summary of split-brain research.)

Samples, Robert E. "Learning with the Whole Brain." *Human Behavior,* 4 (February 1975), 17–23. (The implications for education of our emphasis on the left half of the human brain.)

Saporta, Sol, ed. *Psycholinguistics: A Book of Readings.* New York: Holt, Rinehart & Winston, 1961. (A standard collection of introductory readings.)

Sebeok, Thomas A., and Alexandra Ramsay, eds. *Approaches to Animal Communciation.* The Hague: Mouton & Company, 1969. (A collection of essays resulting from a symposium on animal communication, or zoosemiotics.)

Shipley, Elizabeth F., Carlota S. Smith, and Lila R. Gleitman, "A Study in the Acquisition of Language: Free Responses to Commands." *Language,* 45 (1969), 322–342. (Comprehension of speech exceeds ability to produce speech in children who are at certain stages of language development.)

Slobin, Dan I. *Psycholinguistics.* Glenview, Ill.: Scott, Foresman & Co., 1971. (Good, brief introduction, especially helpful concerning language acquisition in children.)

————. "Children and Language: They Learn the Same Way All Around the

World." *Psychology Today,* 6 (July 1972), 71–74, 82. (Language acquisition by children of different cultures.)

Smith, Adam. *Powers of Mind.* New York: Random House, 1975. (Popular and interesting account of the workings of the brain, TM, EST, Rolfing, and much more. See especially "II. Hemispheres," pp. 59–182.)

Smith, Frank, and George A. Miller, eds. *The Genesis of Language: A Psycholinguistic Approach.* Cambridge: The M.I.T. Press, 1966. (Essays dealing with language development in children.)

Vetter, Harold J. "Sign Language of the Deaf." *Language Behavior and Communication: An Introduction.* Itasca, Illinois: F. E. Peacock Publishers, 1969. (A discussion of communication by a system of gestures.)

Wilson, Edward O. "Animal Communication." *Scientific American,* 227 (1972), 52–60. (From insects to mammals, animals communicate—but man's language is unique.)

PART THREE

The History of the Language

One of the most important facts to realize about any living language is that it is in a constant state of change. It is not often that we are privileged to see changes in language take place because they normally occur over great stretches of time and are frequently rather subtle. For example, the word *father* was until about 1550 written and pronounced *fader*. The history of such changes, however, constitutes the history of language itself. If one goes back far enough into the history of English, it becomes necessary, because of a lack of written records, to speculate on these changes. Such speculation, however, is not simply a matter of guesses; it is based on convincing scientific data drawn from the study of comparative grammar and from the idea that languages exist in families.

In this section, the first essay deals with Proto-Indo-European (or Indo-European, as it is more familiarly known). The following essays discuss the history of English, as it evolved within that family, and the various influences that have given American English the character it has today.

1
Language Families

James D. Gordon

The great linguistic scholars of the nineteenth century were very much interested in the ways in which languages are related and seem to exist in groups or families. From their studies of related or cognate languages grew the hypothesis that there must have been a root language from which the numerous cognate languages descended. The concept of a Proto-Indo-European language—or Indo-European, as it has come to be called—had its formal beginnings, however, in an address delivered by Sir William Jones before the Bengal Asiatic Society in 1786 in which he spoke of the historical relationship between Sanskrit and Greek, Latin, and the Germanic languages. In the following excerpt from *The English Language: An Historical Introduction*, Professor James D. Gordon briefly illustrates the relationship among several cognate languages and explains how English has evolved from Proto-Indo-European.

Cognate Languages

O NE of the important concepts in linguistic history is that of related languages, or, as they are sometimes called, *cognate* languages. These have evolved as different languages from what at a much earlier time was one language, which may be referred to as the parent or ancestral language. For example, French, Spanish, Italian, and Portuguese are modern evolutions of ancient Latin. We know this because we have preserved the knowledge of the history of the people who speak these languages as well as an abundance of texts in the parent language. If, however, we did not have the visible evidence of the parent tongue, it would still be possible to draw conclusions about it from a study of the similarities and differences in the descendant languages. This kind of study is called comparative grammar,[1] and it is one of the achievements bequeathed to us by the great linguistic scholars of the nineteenth century. Of course, since the conclusions of comparative study on the state of a prehistoric language are to some extent hypothetical, they are less certain and less detailed than the surviving evidence of a parent language and therefore subject to revision as our knowledge of history and prehistory expands.

Language Descent

The kind of relationship that exists between a language and its ancestor as well as its cognates is illustrated in the following table:

LATIN		ITALIAN	SPANISH	FRENCH
pater	"father"	*padre*	*padre*	*père*
mater	"mother"	*madre*	*madre*	*mère*
unus	"one"	*uno*	*uno*	*un*
duo	"two"	*due*	*dos*	*deux*
tres	"three"	*tre*	*tres*	*trois*
tu	"thou"	*tu*	*tu*	*tu*
venire	"come"	*venire*	*venir*	*venir*
cantare	"sing"	*cantare*	*cantar*	*chanter*
habere	"have"	*avere*	*haber*	*avoir*

Since we know that the similarities in the three modern languages are derived from a common ancestor, the records of which have been preserved, we may assume that similar likenesses in other languages point to an ancestral tongue which has not been preserved in writing. Compare, for example, the following:

GERMAN	ENGLISH
Mann	man
Vater	father
Mutter	mother
Bruder	brother
Schwester	sister
Hand	hand
Finger	finger
Fuss	foot
singen	sing
ich	I
du	thou
haben	have

[1] In the sense in which it is used here, grammar includes not only an account of conjugations, declensions, and rules of propriety, but the complete study of a language, including its sounds, inflections, lexicon, and syntax, as well as their changes with the passage of time.

Three possibilities can be adduced to explain these similarities between English and German. First, the words were borrowed from one language to the other; second, one of these languages was derived from the other; third, both languages were derived from a common source now lost. The first explanation is improbable because general observation of language behavior does not support the theory that words of such common and essential use are usually borrowed in great numbers. The second possibility is more plausible, but, when we include the evidence from still other languages like Dutch, Swedish, Danish, Norwegian, and ancient Gothic (now extinct as a living language, but surviving in writing), we are led to the third possibility, the common ancestor, as the most convincing explanation of the three. This hypothetical ancestor is called *Proto-Germanic*, or *Primitive Germanic*.

Proto-Germanic

It is even possible, by patient and detailed examination of all the extant data, to reconstruct by the comparative method the approximate form of prehistoric words. Take, for example, the English *finger*, to which the German *Finger* is so close. Among the earliest written records of the Germanic peoples we find Old English *finger*, Old Saxon and Old High German *fingar*, Old Norse *fingr*, Gothic *figgrs*; from all of these we assume the existence in Proto-Germanic of a form *fingro-z*.[2]

In Proto-Germanic, however, we have not reached the end of the comparative process, because we can discover additional likenesses between English and other languages which are not Germanic. Consider the following:

GREEK	LATIN	ENGLISH
agros	ager	acre
phratēr	frater	brother
deka	decem	ten
duo	duo	two
gonu	genu	knee
pous, podos	pes, pedis	foot
treis	tres	three

Obviously the resemblances between English on the one hand and Latin and Greek on the other are not so close as those between English and German, but extended observation of all the relevant facts from these and a number of other languages proves that these languages are indeed related. The prehistoric mother tongue, the basic forms of which

[2] Editors' note: The asterisk is conventionally used to indicate forms for which no written record exists. Forms preceded by an asterisk are reconstructed forms based on available linguistic data.

are deduced by the comparative method, is called *Proto-Indo-European*.[3] It is assumed, then, that at a very early period, not subject to precise definition but certainly several thousand years before Christ, a language spoken by a relatively small number of people, most probably in Eastern Europe,[4] began to split into dialects. Groups of these early people separated by migration from other groups, and during a time when distance or other geographical barriers made social intercourse impossible, minor differences in language became greater and greater, and eventually dialects evolved into languages. Within each of these several groups, the process of splitting was repeated in later times to such an extent that today this one ancient language has by different evolutionary routes developed into many important languages spread over Europe and Western Asia.

It is fairly easy to comprehend such a process from what we can see of the English language in the modern world. In the sixteenth century, the relatively small number of people speaking English lived in one small island. During the succeeding centuries, their language was carried by migrating groups to different parts of the world, where in the course of time the speech of these separated colonies developed special dialect features. An American, for example, though he understands his transatlantic neighbor in Britain, is aware of very prominent differences. Were it not for the fact that in modern times these differences are counteracted by a common written convention and other means of intercommunication, they would quite probably continue to grow until they made mutual understanding impossible. At that point American and British would be different languages. Moreover, within the American speech community itself we are aware of regional differences, which, under the proper conditions of time and isolation, could conceivably result in a subgroup of languages.

The Indo-European Family

In some such way, then, Indo-European has in the course of thousands of years developed in different branches, some of which are further divisible into groups and subgroups, as follows.

---

[3] Formerly called also *Indo-Germanic* by the German scholars, and earlier *Aryan*. The latter term is now old-fashioned, and has also been degraded by unpopular political uses.

[4] The first home of the Indo-Europeans was once thought to have been in Asia. A recent theory places it in Northern Europe, between the Elbe and the Vistula. See Paul Thieme, "The Indo-European Language," *Scientific American*, October 1958, pp. 63–74. A standard work on this subject is Harold Bender, *The Home of the Indo-Europeans* (Princeton, 1922).

I. *Indo-Iranian* consists of two divisions.

    A. *Indic* includes a number of languages spoken in India, the most ancient form of which is *Sanskrit*, of inestimable importance to our knowledge of Proto-Indo-European. Sanskrit was revered and preserved for religious and literary purposes, but the more popular dialects, called the *Prakrits*, are the ancestors of the modern Indic languages. One of these, *Hindi*, is now the official language of India. Another language, *Urdu*, is spoken in Pakistan. Related to them also is the language of the Gypsies, known as *Romany*.

    B. *Iranian* is preserved in two ancient forms: *Avestan*, named from the sacred book of the Zoroastrian religion, and *Old Persian*. The latter is preserved only in inscriptions, but a later form of it is the language of the *Shah Nameh*, which contains the story of Sohrab and Rustum, known to readers of English literature from Matthew Arnold's poem. From this language we have the modern forms spoken in Iran, Afghanistan, Baluchistan, and Kurdistan.

II. *Armenian* in its earliest recorded form is called *Old Armenian*, but the written remains do not go back earlier than the fifth century of the Christian era. Today it is divided into an eastern branch, found in the Soviet Union, and a western branch, in Turkey.

III. *Albanian* records from earlier times are even scantier and more recent than Armenian, the earliest dating from the fourteenth century. In both of these languages the lexicon is very heavily influenced by other languages.

IV. *Balto-Slavic*, like Indo-Iranian, has two important subdivisions.

    A. Some earlier written materials of the *Baltic* group are in a language now extinct, called *Old Prussian*.[5] The modern forms are *Lettish*, the language of Latvia, and *Lithuanian*. The latter has a special interest because of the number of primitive features it has preserved.

    B. The *Slavic* languages are the better known of the two divisions. An early form of Slavic, known as *Old Bulgarian* or *Old Church Slavic* has been preserved from the ninth century and has been the liturgical language of the Orthodox Church. The modern Slavic languages are divided geographically. The southern group comprises *Bulgarian* and three languages spoken in Yugoslavia: *Macedonian*, *Slovenian*, and *Serbo-*

---

[5] The term *Prussian* did not originally refer to the Germans, but was applied to them when they supplanted the original inhabitants of the area known as Prussia.

Croatian. The western branch includes *Polish, Czechoslovak-ian,* and *Wendish.* In the eastern group are *Great Russian, White Russian,* and *Ukrainian.* It is Great Russian that is usually meant by the term *Russian.*

V. *Hellenic,* or *Greek,* is well known in its older forms because of the antiquity of its written records. The Indo-European Greeks moved into the Greek peninsula as early as 2000 B.C., supplant-ing a more ancient culture. Their civilization, and with it their language, spread into adjoining areas. The most important of the ancient Greek dialects, that of Athens, called *Attic,* became known and was extensively used throughout the Mediterranean world as a consequence of the victories of Alexander the Great. The importance of its literature has also given it an extensive influence in the growth of Western civilization. From the com-mon Attic speech most of the dialects of modern Greece are descended.

VI. The *Italic* languages appeared in the Mediterranean world some-what later than Greek. Like Hellenic, Italic existed in several dialects, one of which, *Latin,* supplanted the others in impor-tance, became the dominant language of the ancient world, and produced the great literature which has come down to our time. The popular Latin speech, however, was carried in the days of the Roman Empire to various parts of Europe, where it became the basis of what we call today the Romance languages: *Italian, French, Spanish, Portuguese,* and *Rumanian,* as well as some others which do not now have national status, mainly *Provençal, Catalan, Sardinian,* and Romance dialects in Switzerland.

VII. *Celtic* is now of relatively minor economic and political impor-tance. It was, however, the language of those intrepid warriors known to the Romans as Gauls. At the height of their power they spread to Spain, Italy, and even Asia Minor, where they established a colony known as the Galatians, to whom St. Paul wrote his well-known epistle. As many school children know, they were subdued on the continent by Julius Caesar, and their language was eventually replaced by Latin. In Britain, however, which was also occupied at that time by Celts, the Celtic lan-guage survived. It has come down to us in two varieties: *Goi-delic,* represented by *Irish Gaelic, Scotch Gaelic,* and *Manx* (of the Isle of Man); and *Brythonic* or *Cymric,* represented by *Welsh, Cornish,* which has recently died out, and *Breton,* spoken in Brittany (France).

VIII. *Germanic* is for our purposes the most interesting, for it is the branch to which English belongs. The earliest evidences of Germanic come from the fourth century, the most important being a number of Old Norse runic inscriptions and a translation of part of the Bible by Ulfilas into *Gothic*. This ancient work has been preserved, but as a spoken language Gothic is now extinct. In the seventh century Germanic written records became more abundant. From these early writings as well as from the later surviving literature of the daughter languages we construct the parent language, *Proto-Germanic*. Like the Proto-Indo-European, of which it is a branch, Proto-Germanic has evolved into subgroups. These are usually classified as *North Germanic*, which includes the Scandinavian languages: *Danish, Swedish, Norse,* and *Icelandic; East Germanic*, all of whose members, including Gothic, are now extinct; and *West Germanic*. This last may again be subdivided into *Low* and *High West Germanic*. In this context the words "low" and "high" have no reference to social or literary prestige. They are purely geographical terms: "low" refers to the lowlands along the coast; "high" to the more elevated inland regions. High German has become what we today call simply "German"; it is the standard language of Berlin and Vienna. Low West Germanic was divided in early times into *Old Saxon*, which has come down as a regional dialect of Germany called *Plattdeutsch; Old Franconian*, which has become *Dutch* and *Flemish*; Old Frisian, which has become the *Frisian* of the Netherlands province of Friesland; and *Old English* (formerly called Anglo-Saxon), which, with important changes, has become the language of the modern English-speaking world.

It must be emphasized that the classification of these languages and the reconstruction of their prehistoric forms, Proto-Germanic and Proto-Indo-European, are based upon incomplete data from which conclusions are made by human ingenuity. As new evidence comes to light and old theories are reconsidered, important revisions of the scheme become necessary.

FOR DISCUSSION AND REVIEW

1 What is a comparative grammar? Why is it useful?

2 What are three possible conclusions that one can draw from the similarities between German and English?

3 To what do the terms *Low* and *High* Old German refer? From which type of these have present-day German and English descended?

4 In what area of the world do linguists believe that Proto-Indo-European had its origins? What evidence exists to support their view?

2
The Indo-European Family of Languages

American Heritage Dictionary

The Indo-European family of languages, of which English is a member, is descended from a prehistoric language, Proto-Indo-European, spoken in a region that has not yet been identified, possibly in the fifth millennium B.C. The chart shows the principal languages of the family, arranged in a diagrammatic form that displays their genetic relationships and loosely suggests their geographic distribution. The European groups are shown in somewhat fuller detail than the Asian ones, and in the Germanic group, to which English belongs, the intermediate historical phases of the languages are also shown.

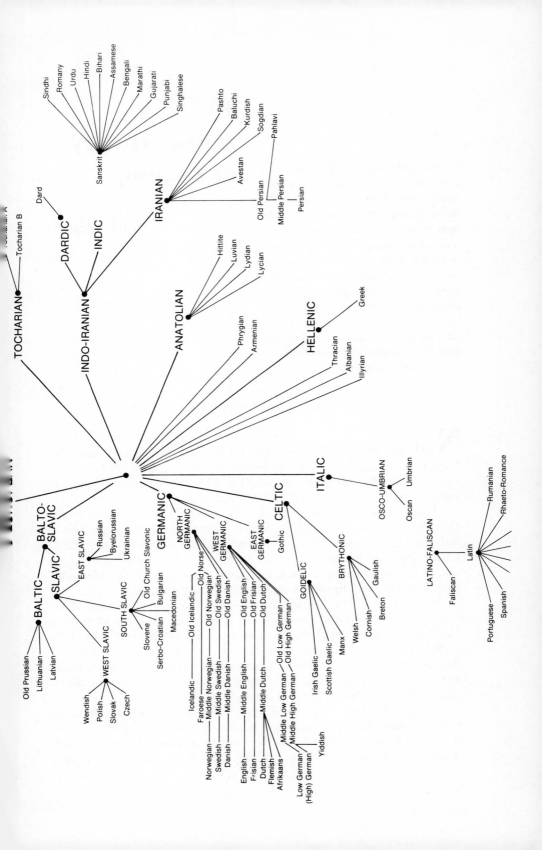

3

A Brief History of English

In this brief essay, the late Paul Roberts discusses the importance of the relationship between major events in the history of England and significant changes in vocabulary, grammar, and pronunciation that have occurred throughout the development of the English language. He shows us, first, how the people who invaded England left impressions on the language and, then, how, in recent times, the rapid spread of English has resulted in its becoming a major world language.

Paul Roberts

Historical Backgrounds

N O UNDERSTANDING of the English language can be very satisfactory without a notion of the history of the language. But we shall have to make do with just a notion. The history of English is long and complicated, and we can only hit the high spots.

The history of our language begins a little after A.D. 600. Everything before that is pre-history, which means that we can guess at it but can't prove much. For a thousand years or so before the birth of Christ our linguistic ancestors were savages wandering through the forests of northern Europe. Their language was a part of the Germanic branch of the Indo-European Family. (see chart on p. 151.)

At the time of the Roman Empire—say, from the beginning of the Christian Era to around A.D. 400—the speakers of what was to become English were scattered along the northern coast of Europe. They spoke a dialect of Low German. More exactly, they spoke several different dialects, since they were several different tribes. The names given to the tribes who got to England are *Angles, Saxons,* and *Jutes.* For convenience, we can refer to them as Anglo-Saxons.

Their first contact with civilization was a rather thin acquaintance with the Roman Empire on whose borders they lived. Probably some of the Anglo-Saxons wandered into the Empire occasionally, and certainly Roman merchants and traders traveled among the tribes. At any rate, this period saw the first of our many borrowings from Latin. Such words as *kettle, wine, cheese, butter, cheap, plum, gem, bishop, church* were borrowed at this time. They show something of the relationship of the Anglo-Saxons with the Romans. The Anglo-Saxons were learning, getting their first taste of civilization.

They still had a long way to go, however, and their first step was to help smash the civilization they were learning from. In the fourth century the Roman power weakened badly. While the Goths were pounding away at the Romans in the Mediterranean countries, their relatives, the Anglo-Saxons, began to attack Britain.

The Romans had been the ruling power in Britain since A.D. 43. They had subjugated the Celts whom they found living there and had succeeded in setting up a Roman administration. The Roman influence did not extend to the outlying parts of the British Isles. In Scotland, Wales, and Ireland the Celts remained free and wild, and they made periodic forays against the Romans in England. Among other defense measures, the Romans built the famous Roman Wall to ward off the tribes in the north.

Even in England the Roman power was thin. Latin did not become the language of the country as it did in Gaul and Spain. The mass of people continued to speak Celtic, with Latin and the Roman civilization it contained in use as a top dressing.

In the fourth century, troubles multiplied for the Romans in Britain. Not only did the untamed tribes of Scotland and Wales grow more and more restive, but the Anglo-Saxons began to make pirate raids on the eastern coast. Furthermore, there was growing difficulty everywhere in the Empire, and the legions in Britain were siphoned off to fight elsewhere. Finally, in A.D. 410, the last Roman ruler in England, bent on becoming emperor, left the islands and took the last of the legions with him. The Celts were left in possession of Britain but almost defenseless against the impending Anglo-Saxon attack.

Not much is surely known about the arrival of the Anglo-Saxons in England. According to the best early source, the eighth-century historian Bede, the Jutes came in 449 in response to a plea from the Celtic king, Vortigern, who wanted their help against the Picts attacking from the north. The Jutes subdued the Picts but then quarreled and fought with Vortigern, and, with reinforcements from the Continent, settled permanently in Kent. Somewhat later the Angles established themselves in eastern England and the Saxons in the south and west. Bede's account is plausible enough, and these were probably the main lines of the invasion.

We do know, however, that the Angles, Saxons, and Jutes were a long time securing themselves in England. Fighting went on for as long as a hundred years before the Celts in England were all killed, driven into

Wales, or reduced to slavery. This is the period of King Arthur, who was not entirely mythological. He was a Romanized Celt, a general, though probably not a king. He had some success against the Anglo-Saxons, but it was only temporary. By 550 or so the Anglo-Saxons were firmly established. English was in England.

Old English

All this is pre-history, so far as the language is concerned. We have no record of the English language until after 600, when the Anglo-Saxons were converted to Christianity and learned the Latin alphabet. The conversion began, to be precise, in the year 597 and was accomplished within thirty or forty years. The conversion was a great advance for the Anglo-Saxons, not only because of the spiritual benefits but because it reestablished contact with what remained of Roman civilization. This civilization didn't amount to much in the year 600, but it was certainly superior to anything in England up to that time.

It is customary to divide the history of the English language into three periods: Old English, Middle English, and Modern English. Old English runs from the earliest records—i.e., seventh century—to about 1100; Middle English from 1100 to 1450 or 1500; Modern English from 1500 to the present day. Sometimes Modern English is further divided into Early Modern, 1500-1700, and Late Modern, 1700 to the present.

When England came into history, it was divided into several more or less autonomous kingdoms, some of which at times exercised a certain amount of control over the others. In the century after the conversion the most advanced kingdom was Northumbria, the area between the Humber River and the Scottish border. By A.D. 700 the Northumbrians had developed a respectable civilization, the finest in Europe. It is sometimes called the Northumbrian Renaissance, and it was the first of the several renaissances through which Europe struggled upward out of the ruins of the Roman Empire. It was in this period that the best of the Old English literature was written, including the epic poem *Beowulf*.

In the eighth century, Northumbrian power declined, and the center of influence moved southward to Mercia, the kingdom of the Midlands. A century later the center shifted again, and Wessex, the country of the West Saxons, became the leading power. The most famous king of the West Saxons was Alfred the Great, who reigned in the second half of the ninth century, dying in 901. He was famous not only as a military man and administrator but also as a champion of learning. He founded and supported schools and translated or caused to be translated many books from Latin into English. At this time also much of the Northumbrian literature of two centuries earlier was copied in West Saxon. Indeed, the great bulk of Old English writing which has come down to us is in the West Saxon dialect of 900 or later.

In the military sphere, Alfred's great accomplishment was his successful opposition to the viking invasions. In the ninth and tenth centuries, the Norsemen emerged in their ships from their homelands in Denmark and the Scandinavian peninsula. They traveled far and attacked and plundered at will and almost with impunity. They ravaged Italy and Greece, settled in France, Russia, and Ireland, colonized Iceland and Greenland, and discovered America several centuries before Columbus. Nor did they overlook England.

After many years of hit-and-run raids, the Norsemen landed an army on the east coast of England in the year 866. There was nothing much to oppose them except the Wessex power led by Alfred. The long struggle ended in 877 with a treaty by which a line was drawn roughly from the northwest of England to the southeast. On the eastern side of the line Norse rule was to prevail. This was called the Danelaw. The western side was to be governed by Wessex.

The linguistic result of all this was a considerable injection of Norse into the English language. Norse was at this time not so different from English as Norwegian or Danish is now. Probably speakers of English could understand, more or less, the language of the newcomers who had moved into eastern England. At any rate, there was considerable interchange and word borrowing. Examples of Norse words in the English language are *sky, give, law, egg, outlaw, leg, ugly, scant, sly, crawl, scowl, take, thrust*. There are hundreds more. We have even borrowed some pronouns from Norse—*they, their,* and *them.* These words were borrowed first by the eastern and northern dialects and then in the course of hundreds of years made their way into English generally.

It is supposed also—indeed, it must be true—that the Norsemen influenced the sound structure and the grammar of English. But this is hard to demonstrate in detail.

A Specimen of Old English

We may now have an example of Old English. The favorite illustration is the Lord's Prayer, since it needs no translation. This has come to us in several different versions. Here is one:

Fæder ure,
þu þe eart on heofonum,
si þin nama gehalgod.
Tobecume þin rice.
Gewurþe ðin willa on eorðan swa swa on heofonum.
Urne gedæghwamlican hlaf syle us to dæg.

And forgyf us ure gyltas, swa swa we forgyfað urum gyltendum.
And ne gelæd þu us on costnunge,
ac alys us of yfele. Soþlice.

Some of the differences between this and Modern English are merely differences in orthography. For instance, the sign *æ* is what Old English writers used for a vowel sound like that in modern *hat* or *and*. The *th* sounds of modern *thin* or *then* are represented in Old English by *þ* or *ð*. But of course there are many differences in sound too. *Ure* is the ancestor of modern *our*, but the first vowel was like that in *too* or *ooze*. *Hlaf* is modern *loaf*; we have dropped the *h* sound and changed the vowel, which in *hlaf* was pronounced something like the vowel in *father*. Old English had some sounds which we do not have. The sound represented by *y* does not occur in Modern English. If you pronounce the vowel in *bit* with your lips rounded, you may approach it.

In grammar, Old English was much more highly inflected than Modern English is. That is, there were more case endings for nouns, more person and number endings for verbs, a more complicated pronoun system, various endings for adjectives, and so on. Old English nouns had four cases—nominative, genitive, dative, accusative. Adjectives had five —all these and an instrumental case besides. Present-day English has only two cases for nouns—common case and possessive case. Adjectives now have no case system at all. On the other hand, we now use a more rigid word order and more structure words (prepositions, auxiliaries, and the like) to express relationships than Old English did.

Some of this grammar we can see in the Lord's Prayer. *Heofonum*, for instance, is a dative plural; the nominative singular was *heofon*. *Urne* is an accusative singular; the nominative is *ure*. In *urum gyltendum* both words are dative plural. *Forgyfaþ* is the first person plural form of the verb. Word order is different: "urne gedæghwamlican hlaf syle us" in place of "Give us our daily bread." And so on.

In vocabulary Old English is quite different from Modern English. Most of the Old English words are what we may call native English: that is, words which have not been borrowed from other languages but which have been a part of English ever since English was a part of Indo-European. Old English did certainly contain borrowed words. We have seen that many borrowings were coming in from Norse. Rather large numbers had been borrowed from Latin, too. Some of these were taken while the Anglo-Saxons were still on the Continent (*cheese, butter, bishop, kettle,* etc.); a larger number came into English after the conversion (*angel, candle, priest, martyr, radish, oyster, purple, school, spend,* etc.). But the great majority of Old English words were native English.

Now, on the contrary, the majority of words in English are borrowed, taken mostly from Latin and French. Of the words in *The American College Dictionary* only about 14 percent are native. Most of these, to be sure, are common, high-frequency words—*the, of, I, and, because, man, mother, road,* etc.; of the thousand most common words in English, some 62 percent are native English. Even so, the modern vocabulary is very much Latinized and Frenchified. The Old English vocabulary was not.

Middle English

Sometime between the years 1000 and 1200 various important changes took place in the structure of English, and Old English became Middle English. The political event which facilitated these changes was the Norman Conquest. The Normans, as the name shows, came originally from Scandinavia. In the early tenth century they established themselves in northern France, adopted the French language, and developed a vigorous kingdom and a very passable civilization. In the year 1066, led by Duke William, they crossed the Channel and made themselves masters of England. For the next several hundred years, England was ruled by kings whose first language was French.

One might wonder why, after the Norman Conquest, French did not become the national language, replacing English entirely. The reason is that the Conquest was not a national migration, as the earlier Anglo-Saxon invasion had been. Great numbers of Normans came to England, but they came as rulers and landlords. French became the language of the court, the language of the nobility, the language of polite society, the language of literature. But it did not replace English as the language of the people. There must always have been hundreds of towns and villages in which French was never heard except when visitors of high station passed through.

But English, though it survived as the national language, was profoundly changed after the Norman Conquest. Some of the changes—in sound structure and grammar—would no doubt have taken place whether there had been a Conquest or not. Even before 1066 the case system of English nouns and adjectives was becoming simplified; people came to rely more on word order and prepositions than on inflectional endings to communicate their meanings. The process was speeded up by sound changes which caused many of the endings to sound alike. But no doubt the Conquest facilitated the change. German, which didn't experience a Norman Conquest, is today rather highly inflected compared to its cousin English.

But it is in vocabulary that the effects of the Conquest are most obvious. French ceased, after a hundred years or so, to be the native language of very many people in England, but it continued—and continues still—to be a zealously cultivated second language, the mirror of elegance and civilization. When one spoke English, one introduced not only French ideas and French things but also their French names. This was not only easy but socially useful. To pepper one's conversation with French expressions was to show that one was well-bred, elegant, *au courant*. The last sentence shows that the process is not yet dead. By using *au courant* instead of, say, *abreast of things*, the writer indicates that he is no dull clod who knows only English but an elegant person aware of how things are done in *le haut monde*.

Thus French words came into English, all sorts of them. There were words to do with government: *parliament, majesty, treaty, alliance, tax, government*; church words: *parson, sermon, baptism, incense, crucifix, religion*; words for foods: *veal, beef, mutton, bacon, jelly, peach, lemon, cream, biscuit*; colors: *blue, scarlet, vermilion*; household words: *curtain, chair, lamp, towel, blanket, parlor*; play words: *dance, chess, music, leisure, conversation*; literary words: *story, romance, poet, literary*; learned words: *study, logic, grammar, noun, surgeon, anatomy, stomach*; just ordinary words of all sorts: *nice, second, very, age, bucket, gentle, final, fault, flower, cry, count, sure, move, surprise, plain*.

All these and thousands more poured into the English vocabulary between 1100 and 1500 until, at the end of that time, many people must have had more French words than English at their command. This is not to say that English became French. English remained English in sound structure and in grammar, though these also felt the ripples of French influence. The very heart of the vocabulary, too, remained English. Most of the high-frequency words—the pronouns, the prepositions, the conjunctions, the auxiliaries, as well as a great many ordinary nouns and verbs and adjectives—were not replaced by borrowings.

Middle English, then, was still a Germanic language, but it differed from Old English in many ways. The sound system and the grammar changed a good deal. Speakers made less use of case systems and other inflectional devices and relied more on word order and structure words to express their meanings. This is often said to be a simplification, but it isn't really. Languages don't become simpler; they merely exchange one kind of complexity for another. Modern English is not a simple language, as any foreign speaker who tries to learn it will hasten to tell you.

For us Middle English is simpler than Old English just because it is closer to Modern English. It takes three or four months at least to learn to read Old English prose and more than that for poetry. But a week of good study should put one in touch with the Middle English poet Chaucer. Indeed, you may be able to make some sense of Chaucer straight off, though you would need instruction in pronunciation to make it sound like poetry. Here is a famous passage from the *General Prologue to the Canterbury Tales*, fourteenth century:

> *Ther was also a nonne, a Prioresse,*
> *That of hir smyling was ful symple and coy,*
> *Hir gretteste oath was but by Seinte Loy,*
> *And she was cleped Madame Eglentyne.*
> *Ful wel she song the service dyvyne,*
> *Entuned in hir nose ful semely.*
> *And Frenshe she spak ful faire and fetisly,*
> *After the scole of Stratford-atte-Bowe,*
> *For Frenshe of Parys was to hir unknowe.*

Early Modern English

Sometime between 1400 and 1600 English underwent a couple of sound changes which made the language of Shakespeare quite different from that of Chaucer. Incidentally, these changes contributed much to the chaos in which English spelling now finds itself.

One change was the elimination of a vowel sound in certain unstressed positions at the end of words. For instance, the words *name, stone, wine, dance* were pronounced as two syllables by Chaucer but as just one by Shakespeare. The *e* in these words became, as we say, "silent." But it wasn't silent for Chaucer; it represented a vowel sound. So also the words *laughed, seemed, stored* would have been pronounced by Chaucer as two-syllable words. The change was an important one because it affected thousands of words and gave a different aspect to the whole language.

The other change is what is called the Great Vowel Shift. This was a systematic shifting of half a dozen vowels and diphthongs in stressed syllables. For instance, the word *name* had in Middle English a vowel something like that in the modern word *father; wine* had the vowel of modern *mean; he* was pronounced something like modern *hey; mouse* sounded like *moose; moon* had the vowel of *moan*. Again the shift was thoroughgoing and affected all the words in which these vowel sounds occurred. Since we still keep the Middle English system of spelling these words, the differences between Modern English and Middle English are often more real than apparent.

The vowel shift has meant also that we have come to use an entirely different set of symbols for representing vowel sounds than is used by writers of such languages as French, Italian, or Spanish, in which no such vowel shift occurred. If you come across a strange word—say, *bine*—in an English book, you will pronounce it according to the English system, with the vowel of *wine* or *dine*. But if you read *bine* in a French, Italian, or Spanish book, you will pronounce it with the vowel of *mean* or *seen*.

These two changes, then, produced the basic differences between Middle English and Modern English. But there were several other developments that had an effect upon the language. One was the invention of printing, an invention introduced into England by William Caxton in the year 1475. Where before books had been rare and costly, they suddenly became cheap and common. More and more people learned to read and write. This was the first of many advances in communication which have worked to unify languages and to arrest the development of dialect differences, though of course printing affects writing principally rather than speech. Among other things it hastened the standardization of spelling.

The period of Early Modern English—that is, the sixteenth and seventeenth centuries—was also the period of the English Renaissance, when people developed, on the one hand, a keen interest in the past and, on the other, a more daring and imaginative view of the future. New ideas multiplied, and new ideas meant new language. Englishmen had grown accustomed to borrowing words from French as a result of the Norman Conquest; now they borrowed from Latin and Greek. As we have seen, English had been raiding Latin from Old English times and before, but now the floodgates really opened, and thousands of words from the classical languages poured in. *Pedestrian, bonus, anatomy, contradict, climax, dictionary, benefit, multiply, exist, paragraph, initiate, scene, inspire* are random examples. Probably the average educated American today has more words from French in his vocabulary than from native English sources, and more from Latin than from French.

The greatest writer of the Early Modern English period is of course Shakespeare, and the best-known book is the King James Version of the Bible, published in 1611. The Bible (if not Shakespeare) has made many features of Early Modern English perfectly familiar to many people down to present time, even though we do not use these features in present-day speech and writing. For instance, the old pronouns *thou* and *thee* have dropped out of use now, together with their verb forms, but they are still familiar to us in prayer and in Biblical quotations: "Whither thou goest, I will go." Such forms as *hath* and *doth* have been replaced by *has* and *does*; "Goes he hence tonight?" would now be "Is he going away tonight?"; Shakespeare's "Fie, on't, sirrah" would be "Nuts to that, Mac." Still, all these expressions linger with us because of the power of the works in which they occur.

It is not always realized, however, that considerable sound changes have taken place between Early Modern English and the English of the present day. Shakespearian actors putting on a play speak the words, properly enough, in their modern pronunciation. But it is very doubtful that this pronunciation would be understood at all by Shakespeare. In Shakespeare's time, the word *reason* was pronounced like modern *raisin*; *face* had the sound of modern *glass*; the *l* in *would, should, palm* was pronounced. In these points and a great many others the English language has moved a long way from what it was in 1600.

Recent Developments

The history of English since 1700 is filled with many movements and countermovements, of which we can notice only a couple. One of these is the vigorous attempt made in the eighteenth century, and the rather half-hearted attempts made since, to regulate and control the English language. Many people of the eighteenth century, not understanding very well the forces which govern language, proposed to polish and prune and restrict English, which they felt was proliferating too wildly. There was much talk of an academy which would rule on what people could and could not say and write. The academy never came into being, but the eighteenth century did succeed in establishing certain attitudes which, though they haven't had much effect on the development of the language itself, have certainly changed the native speaker's feeling about the language.

In part, a product of the wish to fix and establish the language was the development of the dictionary. The first English dictionary was published in 1603; it was a list of 2,500 words briefly defined. Many others were published with gradual improvements until Samuel Johnson published his *English Dictionary* in 1755. This, steadily revised, dominated the field in England for nearly a hundred years. Meanwhile in America, Noah Webster published his dictionary in 1828, and before long dictionary publishing was a big business in this country. The last century has seen the publication of one great dictionary: the twelve-volume *Oxford English Dictionary*, compiled in the course of seventy-five years through the labors of many scholars. We have also, of course, numerous commercial dictionaries which are as good as the public wants them to be if not, indeed, rather better.

Another product of the eighteenth century was the invention of "English grammar." As English came to replace Latin as the language of scholarship, it was felt that one should also be able to control and dissect it, parse and analyze it, as one could Latin. What happened in practice was that the grammatical description that applied to Latin was removed and superimposed on English. This was silly, because English is an entirely different kind of language, with its own forms and signals and ways of producing meaning. Nevertheless, English grammars on the Latin model were worked out and taught in the schools. In many schools they are still being taught. This activity is not often popular with school children, but it is sometimes an interesting and instructive exercise in logic. The principal harm in it is that it has tended to keep people from being interested in English and has obscured the real features of English structure.

But probably the most important force on the development of English in the modern period has been the tremendous expansion of English-speaking peoples. In 1500 English was a minor language, spoken by a few people on a small island. Now it is perhaps the greatet language of the world, spoken natively by over a quarter of a billion people and as a second language by many millions more. When we speak of English now, we must specify whether we mean American English, British English, Australian English, Indian English, or what, since the differences are considerable. The American cannot go to England or the Englishman to America confident that he will always understand and be understood. The Alabaman in Iowa or the Iowan in Alabama shows himself a foreigner every time he speaks. It is only because communication has become fast and easy that English in this period of its expansion has not broken into a dozen mutually unintelligible languages.

FOR DISCUSSION AND REVIEW

1 Roberts is very careful to describe the relationship between historical events in England and the development of the English language. Briefly review the high points of this relationship.

2 What are the three major periods in the history of English? When did each occur? On what bases have they been established?

3 During what period was the epic poem *Beowulf* written?

4 What modern sounds are represented in the Old English þ and ð?

5 How did the pronouns "they," "their," and "them" come into English?

6 When the Anglo-Saxons invaded England, their language, with some modifications, became the language of the land. How do you explain

the fact that French did not become the language of England after the invasion of William the Conqueror?

7 How would you characterize in social terms the French words that were brought into English by the Norman Conquest? In what areas of life did French have the greatest influence?

8 Explain what changes the English language underwent as a result of the Great Vowel Shift. What is the importance of this linguistic phenomenon for the history of English?

9 Early English grammars, and almost all grammars published before 1950, were modeled on Latin grammars. Why was this the case? What erroneous assumptions did these Latin-based grammars include?

4

Early American Speech:
Adoptions from Foreign Tongues

Thomas Pyles

Most languages, and especially those of Western Europe, have borrowed and continue to borrow words from other languages. Whenever new things, procedures, concepts, and ideas need to be labeled, terminology is frequently borrowed from other languages to achieve this goal. This borrowing process is particularly evident when one culture comes into contact with another, as was true during the settlement of America. In this comprehensive and detailed selection from *Words and Ways of American English,* Professor Thomas Pyles of Northwestern University discusses the various languages from which the early speakers of English in America borrowed a significant number of terms and thereby enriched their language. These borrowings from the indigenous languages of the American Indians and from the imported languages of the African, Dutch, German, French, and Spanish peoples have made, of course, a major contribution to the uniqueness of the American idiom.

BEFORE THERE was any permanent settlement of English-speaking folk in this land, a number of Indian words had made their way into the language of England by way of Spanish or Portuguese—words from Nahuatl, the tongue of the Aztecs, who were the most highly advanced of the Indians that the Spanish found in Mexico, as well as from various Indian dialects spoken in Central and South America and the West Indies. Some of these words came in time to be current in all the languages of Europe.

The English language in those exuberant days of Elizabeth, of Raleigh, Drake, Hawkins, Bacon, Marlowe, Jonson, and Shakespeare, had been particularly receptive to augmentations of its already rich word stock from foreign sources—the so-called inkhorn terms from the classical languages, along with words from French, Spanish, Italian, and Portuguese. Words from the New World must have had all the charm of lush exoticisms in a period when the language was being enriched from so many nearby Continental sources, though they seem for the most part commonplace enough today—words like *potato, tomato, chocolate, cocoa, canoe, cannibal, barbecue, maize,* and *savannah,* which must have been known to the first Englishmen to come to these shores with any intention of staying. One of them, *maize,* was by a strange perversity of linguistic fate to be replaced by *corn* in the English of America. The British use *corn* in the sense "wheat," while retaining the older meaning of "grain," as in the "Corn Laws." Another of them, *cannibal,* a modification of *Caribal* "Caribbean native," was used in slightly different form by Shakespeare in his play about the "vexed Bermoothes," for *Caliban,* if not simply a metathesized* form of *can(n)ibal,* is a variant of *Cariban,* itself a variant of *Caribal. Barbecue,* while appearing first in British English, is nevertheless much more familiar in America, and its use to designate an outdoor social or political meeting at which animals are roasted whole is exclusively American. But these words, while native to the New World, must be distinguished from those which entered the language of Englishmen who chose or were forced to transplant themselves permanently in this strange and savage land.

The colonizers of this country were confronted with a land whose topography, meteorological phenomena, trees, plants, birds, and animals were frequently quite different from what they had known in England. Inasmuch as an understanding of the principles of semantics is not congenital, people generally are wont to ask when they see some new object, "What is it?" and expect in answer to be told its name, supposing then that they have learned something really significant about it. This procedure, or something very similar to it, must have been gone through a great many times in the early days of the colonization of America when Indians were friendly enough to be asked and bright enough to divine what was being asked of them. Sometimes, too, these first white Americans made up their own names for what they saw, if there was no one to tell them the "true" names or if the "true" names were too difficult for them to pronounce. As we have seen in the preceding chapter, they frequently combined or modified English words, as

---

* Editors' note: *metathesis* is the transposition within a word of letters, sounds, or syllables (e.g., *revelant* for *relevant*).

in *bullfrog* and *jimson weed* (originally *Jamestown weed*); sometimes they made use of sound alone, as in *bobolink*.

The situation with regard to the American Indian languages, with many tribes speaking apparently unrelated languages which are in turn subdivided into dialects, is extremely complex. Fortunately it need not concern us here, for to American English only one stock, the Algonquian, is important. This huge group of tribes, comprising among others the Arapaho, Blackfoot, Cheyenne, Cree, Delaware, Fox, Micmac, Ojibwa (Chippewa), and Penobscot, formerly occupied a larger area than any other North American Indian stock. It was they whom the first English settlers in Virginia and Massachusetts came in contact with.

As early as 1608 Captain John Smith in his *True Relation of . . . Virginia Since the First Planting of That Collony* recorded *raccoon*, though he did not spell it that way. He wrote it in various ways—for instance, *raugroughcun* and later, in his *General Historie of Virginia, New-England and the Summer Isles* of 1624, *rarowcun*—in his effort to reduce to symbols, which were, incidentally, ill-adapted to that purpose, what he heard or thought he heard from the Indians. It is highly unlikely, as a matter of fact, that a single English word of Indian origin would be immediately intelligible to an Indian today, for words have been clipped, like *squash* (the vegetable), which was originally *askutasquash*, folk-etymologized like *whiskey-John* "blue jay" from *wisketjan*, or in one way or another made to conform to English speechways.

Early Indian loan words naming creatures neglected by Adam are *opossum, moose, skunk, menhaden, terrapin, woodchuck,* and *caribou*. *Opossum* usually occurs in speech and often in writing in an aphetic form as *possum*, as does *raccoon* as *coon*. *Woodchuck* is a folk-etymologizing of Cree or Ojibwa *otchek* or *odjik*. Noah Webster was quite proud, by the way, of deriving *woodchuck* from an Avestan word meaning "pig" and made frequent reference to this acute etymological discovery in lectures and prefaces. *Caribou*, as the spelling of its final syllable indicates, comes to us by way of Canadian French; an Englishman would have been more likely to write *cariboo*. These words, all of Algonquian origin, designate creatures indigenous to North America. Ojibwa *chipmunk* would seem to belong to this group, though it was first recorded considerably later, in Cooper's *Deerslayer* (1841); it was almost certainly in use much earlier.

A good many native plants, vegetables, trees, and shrubs bear names of Indian origin: *hickory, pecan, poke* (weed), *chinquapin, squash, persimmon,* and *catalpa,* all but one of which are Algonquian. That one, *catalpa,* is of Muskhogean origin. A good many Southern place names are of this linguistic stock, which includes Creek, Chickasaw, and Choctaw, but *catalpa* (with its variant *catawba*) and the topographical *bayou* (from Choctaw *bayuk* "stream," coming to us by way of Louisiana

French) are the only widely known words other than place names taken from the languages of these Indians, who formerly occupied an area of our country including most of Georgia, Alabama, and Mississippi and parts of Tennessee, Kentucky, Louisiana, and Florida.

Other early borrowings from the Indians include words denoting foods, customs, relationships, or artifacts peculiar to the Indians at the time of borrowing: *hominy, succotash, johnnycake, pone, pemmican, moccasin, tomahawk, totem, wigwam, toboggan, powwow, mackinaw, caucus* (perhaps), *wampum, sachem, papoose,* and *squaw. Toboggan* and *mackinaw* are first recorded later than the others in this group, though their earliest use in English certainly goes back considerably beyond their first recording. Both entered English by way of Canadian French; the latter word has a half-French spelling, *Mackinac,* when used as a name for the strait, the island, and the town in Michigan. The first element of *johnnycake* is probably from *jonakin* or *jonikin,* apparently of Indian origin and meaning a thin griddle cake made of corn meal. *Johnnycake* was folk-etymologized to *journey cake,* which Noah Webster thought the original form; he assumed that it meant cake to eat when one went on a journey. It has also been suggested that the word is a corruption of *Shawnee cake,* a kind of cake supposed to have been eaten by the Shawnee Indians—an explanation which Mr. Mencken in *The American Language, Supplement One* (New York, 1945) considers "much more plausible" than any other. *Jonikin* (usually spelled *johnnikin*) is still used for a corn griddle cake in the eastern part of the Carolinas and on the Eastern Shore of Maryland.

As for *caucus,* somebody suggested a good many years ago that it was from a somewhat similar Algonquian word meaning "one who advises," and more recently efforts have been made to relate it to *cockarouse,* recorded by Captain John Smith in 1624 as *caucorouse* and designating an Indian chief in Virginia, later extended to designate an influential and wealthy white colonist. It is also possible that *caucus* is a variant form of *caulkers.* The learned John Pickering in his *Vocabulary* thought so, basing his belief on a statement in the *History of the Rise and Independence of the United States* (1788) by the Reverend William Gordon, who stated that in Boston "more than fifty years ago Mr. Samuel Adams's father and twenty others, one or two from the north end of town, where all the ship business is carried on, used to meet, make a *caucus,* and lay their plan for introducing certain persons into positions of trust and power." Pickering inferred from this reference to "the north end of town, where all the ship business is carried on" that it was "not improbable that *caucus* might be a corruption of *caulkers,* the word meeting being understood." The *Dictionary of American English* suggests the possibility that *caucus* may be the name of a long-forgotten neighborhood in Boston called *West-Corcus;* indeed, the quotation given in support of this suggestion (from the Boston *Evening Post* of August 19, 1745), concerns a caucus-like meeting in that neighborhood to "take into serious consideration the conduct of those reverend clergymen who have encouraged the itineration of Mr. George Whitefield," the Calvinistic Methodist evangelist. Another etymology of *caucus* with which Pickering flirted has recently come to light: among some of his old papers there occurs an explanation to the effect that it consisted of the initials of the names of six men—Cooper, Adams, Urann, Coulson, another Urann, and Symmes. Pickering states that he got this story from "B. Russell, who had it from Sam'l Adams and Paul Revere." The etymology has a familiar ring to it; it is precisely the sort upon which the dilettante etymologist dotes. Still another theory is that the American word is simply a borrowing of Latin *caucus* "drinking vessel," which may indicate a feature of the evening's entertainment in the early American gatherings.

All the other words in this last group save *johnnycake* have made the Atlantic crossing, and most of them are now about as familiar to the English as they are to us. In fact, all of them except *mackinaw* are listed in Wyld's *Universal Dictionary*; only *succotash* and *johnnycake* are labeled "U.S.A." The usual British pronunciation of *wigwam* rimes with *big dam*, a pronunciation never heard in this country. *Pemmican*, the Indian name for dried meat pounded into paste, mixed with fat and dried fruits, and then compressed into cakes, has even acquired the figurative meaning in British English of "condensed statement." On the continent of Europe, also, most of these words are quite well known as a result of literary transmission, for generations of European children have thrilled to the novels of James Fenimore Cooper, as well as of his European imitators.

Tammany as a political designation is a well-known Americanism of Indian origin. Tammany was a Delaware chief who flourished in the latter part of the seventeenth century and who was jocularly canonized as an American saint in 1771. His name was later used to designate a political club which ultimately grew into the present powerful Democratic organization in New York City. References to *Tammany* as the name of the club, which was founded in 1789, occur from 1790 onwards. The organization uses *the Wigwam* as a designation for Tammany Hall, *sachem* for a high official of the society, and *brave* (not of Indian origin, but long used to mean an Indian warrior) for a rank-and-file member.

A good many other words of Indian origin are included in the *Dictionary of American English*, but most of them are not in wide current use: *tuckahoe* "edible part of a fungus found on roots of trees," which is also used to designate a poor white in Virginia and West Virginia, *carcajou* "wolverine," *manito* or *manitou* "a god," *quahog* or *quahaug* "hard clam," *sagamore* "chief," *samp* "corn porridge," *tamarack* "the

American larch," *mugwump* "great man," and others considerably less familiar. *Mugwump*, though known much earlier, came into real prominence in the presidential campaign of 1884, when it was applied to those independent Republicans who, affecting an attitude of superiority, refused to support James G. Blaine as their party nominee. Nowadays the word is chiefly notable for the oft-recorded definition by a Congressional wag (would there were more of his kidney!) to the effect that a mugwump was one who always had his *mug* on one side of the fence and his *wump* on the other.

Some early Americanisms were translations or supposed translations of Indian words or phrases, for example, *paleface* (first used by James Fenimore Cooper), *war paint, warpath, firewater, pipe of peace, medicine man, Great Spirit, big chief, to scalp,* and *to bury the hatchet.* Frequently *Indian* was used in conjunction with another word, as in *Indian meal, Indian file, Indian summer,* and *Indian gift,* originally a gift for which one expected something of more value in return, but later a gift which the giver took back. *Indian giver* is first recorded, as far as we know, in Bartlett's *Glossary* of 1848, with the notation that "this term is applied by children to a child who, after having given away a thing, wishes it back again," though *Indian gift* occurs much earlier. The *Dictionary of American English* lists almost a hundred such combinations, though not all are early, for instance, *honest Injun,* which is not recorded until 1875. *Indian summer* is of special interest. By 1830 it had been used in British English (by Thomas De Quincey) in the figurative sense "declining years." That the term is still perfectly familiar in England in this slightly later sense is indicated by John Galsworthy's use of it as the title of a section of the *Forsyte Saga* dealing with the last years of Jolyon Forsyte. Although the English do not have occasion to use the expression in the meteorological sense that Americans have because the phenomenon it names is much less striking in Europe than here, it is nevertheless perfectly well understood in this sense. It has been suggested that Indian summer is so called because its occurrence was predicted by the Indians to the first batch of settlers, but there is no evidence that the term, which is documented only at a comparatively late date, was ever used by the earliest settlers. Other suggestions are that the Indians were responsible for lighting the brush fires common in the late autumn or early winter; that the period constituted a last chance before the final onset of cold weather for the Indians to harass and bedevil the white settlers; and that, because the early settlers thought of the Indians as false and fickle—an idea reflected in the term *Indian giver*— the sham summer weather was called *Indian summer.* The real origin of the term remains as hazy as the weather it designates.

Before passing on to other non-English influences it is interesting to note that British English borrowed *Mohawk,* which it usually spelled *mohock*, early in the eighteenth century to designate, according to the *Oxford English Dictionary*, "one of a class of aristocratic ruffians who infested the streets of London at night," but the term has only a historical interest today. It has never had any currency in American English save among professors of eighteenth-century English literature. The *Apache* of *Apache dance*, a rowdy, sexy dance performed by a pair of dancers attired as a Parisian gangster and his "moll," did not come to us directly from the well-known American aborigines of that name. It came instead by way of French, which in the early nineteenth century borrowed the name of the Indian tribe, Gallicized its pronunciation, and used it to designate a Parisian street bully.

It is perhaps not surprising, considering the ultimate reduction of the American Indians to the status of a conquered people, that the Indian element in American English is no larger than it is. As a matter of fact, if we leave out of consideration place names, of which there are an overwhelming number—more than half of our states bear Indian names, and a large portion of our rivers, lakes, mountains, towns, and cities as well—the Indian influence on our vocabulary must be characterized as slight.

The Indian languages were not, however, the only non-European influence upon the English of America in colonial days. More than a year before the Pilgrims landed on Plymouth Rock in search of religious freedom, a group of people were against their will brought here from the west coast of Africa—principally from Senegal, Gambia, Sierra Leone, Liberia, the Gold Coast, Togo, Dahomey, Nigeria, and Angola—and forthwith sold into slavery. The traffic in Negro slaves continued until shortly before the Civil War, though slackening somewhat after 1808, when the Slave Trade Act went into effect. A great majority of these Negroes were brought direct from Africa; some, however, had previously lived in the British West Indies, where they had picked up a bare working knowledge of English.

Most of the descendants of these transplanted Africans living in the South now speak conventional American English. Because of lack of social contacts with whites and lack of schooling, relics of older standard speech may occasionally be heard from them, such as the pronunciation *deef* for *deaf* and *obleege* for *oblige*. When a colored charwoman with some embarassment informed me that her small daughter had suffered an injury in her *grine*, she was not using an un-English, "darky" pronunciation, but merely saying *groin* in a manner which went out of fashion in more sophisticated usage years ago. There is, of course, no connection whatever between race and the ability to articulate given speech sounds, though it is popularly believed that the southern Negro speaks as he does because of a peculiar conformation of speech organs, aided and abetted by indolence and stupidity. I was once gravely informed by a professor of government that the Negro does not have an *r* sound (my informant was of course referring only to *r* before a consonant sound and in final position) because the "letter *r*" did not exist in African languages—not one of which he had any acquaintance with, incidentally. When I presumed to disagree with his explanation, a corollary of which was that the speech of white southerners was *r*-less because of the linguistic influence of Negro "mammies," and to point out that an Ohio-bred Negro has no difficulty whatsoever pronouncing *r* in all positions, he was grievously offended with me. The fact is that uneducated Negroes in the South by and large differ little in their speech from the uneducated whites. As for the presence of archaisms, they may also be heard from whites who have lived for a long time in cultural isolation, for instance, the Southern mountain folk.

There are, however, communities of Negro Americans engaged largely in the cultivation of rice, cotton, and indigo along the coastal region of South Carolina and Georgia, both on the Sea Islands and on the mainland, who have lived in cultural and geographical isolation for many generations. Most of them have had little contact with whites; some, indeed, have seldom seen white people. These Negroes, numbering about a quarter of a million, speak a type of English which has been so heavily influenced by the African languages native to their remote ancestors that it is not readily intelligible to people, white or colored, from other parts of the country. Their language, Gullah or Geechee, retains a good many African characteristics in its system of sounds, its syntax, its morphology, its vocabulary, its methods of forming words, and, most striking of all to one hearing it for the first time, its intonation. The word *Gullah* is probably either from *Gola*, the name of a Liberian tribe and its language, or from *Angola*. *Geechee*, also used in the up-country of South Carolina as a derisive nickname for a low-country white, particularly one living in the Charleston area, is probably derived from the name of another Liberian tribe and language.

It was very unlikely that Africans from the same tribe or language area would find themselves thrown together on a single plantation in sufficient numbers to enable them to maintain their native languages. The chances were all that they would be considerably dispersed upon their arrival at the various southern ports. Consequently, it became necessary for them to learn English as well as they could. It is not likely that anyone helped them to do so, unless there were prototypes of Mrs. Stowe's Little Eva gliding or floating about the plantations (for Little Eva seldom merely walked) in the seventeenth and eighteenth centuries. The only English many of them ever heard from native speakers was that of the illiterate or semiliterate white indentured servants with whom they worked in the fields or who were set over them as overseers. It was for them not simply a matter of translating word for word their native idioms into English. This cannot be done successfully even with related languages, where it may result in something intelligible if un-English, like *the bread is all*, a Pennsylvania Germanism (though heard in other parts of the country) from German *das Brot ist alles*. It was for these Negroes a matter of acquiring a quite different linguistic psychology, a new attitude towards the phenomena of life as expressed by language. It is not surprising that their accomplishment fell considerably short of perfect. Their English was a sort of jargon or pidgin, which passed into use by their descendants as a native language. This type of so-called creolized language has been preserved largely in the speech of the Gullahs, Negroes who "stayed put" in a region in which they have always been far more numerous than whites and in which they have developed the only distinctive Negro speech in this country.

The principal importance of Gullah, aside from its intrinsic interest as a remarkable linguistic development, is that recent studies of it have been the means of identifying beyond doubt the African source of a number of words in Southern American English, a few of which have passed into other types of American English and one of which, *banjo*, if it is indeed of African origin, is part of the English language wherever it is spoken. Until Lorenzo Dow Turner began his investigations about twenty years ago, Gullah was traditionally regarded as "a quaint linguistic mongrel," to quote from one serious commentator; it was thought to be characterized by "intellectual indolence," "slovenly and careless," a debased form of the "peasant English" of poor whites, a sort of baby talk. One writer even went so far as to attribute its phonological characteristics to the "clumsy tongues," "flat noses," and "thick lips" of the Negroes who speak it.

Professor Turner's studies of Gullah, culminating in his *Africanisms in the Gullah Dialect* (Chicago, 1949), identify thousands of words in Gullah which have or may have African sources. Unlike earlier commentators, who assumed that many words which seemed strange to them were either nonsense words or mispronunciations of English words, Turner, himself of African descent, took the trouble to acquire a good working knowledge of West African languages. His studies and conclusions have made short shrift of some of the theories of previous writers, who assumed, for instance, that a Gullah word for "tooth" which sounded to them something like *bong* was merely a childish, clumsy-tongued, flat-nosed, thick-lipped mispronunciation of English *bone*, and that the Gullah word *det* or the expression *det rain* "a long, hard rain" was really *death rain*, which involved the further assumption that to the Gullahs a long, hard rain is an omen of death to come—as it were, folklore made to order. The fact that in the Wolof language, spoken in Senegal and Gambia, the word for "tooth" is very like *bong* (it is impossible to indicate the exact pronunciation of the un-English final sound of this word, a palatal nasal, without using phonetic symbols) and that in the same language the word for "long, hard rain" is *det* ought to dispose of the "baby talk" explanation for good and all—though of course it will not, for most people prefer "quaint" explanations of linguistic phenomena to the true ones.

From many Gullah informants, some of them bearing names which are a delight to contemplate—among them Saki Sweetwine, Prince Smith, Samuel Polite, Sanko Singleton, Balaam Walker, Scotia Washington, Shad Hall, and Paris Capers—Dr. Turner collected more than five thousand African words in the Gullah region. About four-fifths of these are now used only as personal names, but most of the remainder are everyday words in the speech of the Gullahs. Some of these words, doubtless the common possession of Negroes in all the slaveholding states, passed into the vocabulary of whites at what must have been a very early date.

How did words from the language of humble slaves get into the speech of their white masters? M. M. Mathews, who devotes the final chapter of his *Some Sources of Southernisms* (University, Ala., 1948) to Africanisms in the word stock of Southern American English, speculates with some reason that such words were transmitted by white children, who would not have resisted the influences of what their elders considered an inferior culture. Dr. Mathews cites his aged aunt's aversion to the "Negro word" *cooter* "turtle" and her regret that her brother, Mathews's father, had sullied the "purity" of his speech by ever using the word.

Actually, the African contribution is rather meager. The remarkable thing is, considering the social and economic relationship of black to white, that there should have been any contribution. Many a white southerner has imbedded in his vocabulary words whose African origin he probably never suspects. *Banjo* and *cooter* have already been cited. The first word has usually been considered as originating in a Negro mispronunciation of *bandore*, an English word of Spanish transmission denoting a musical instrument whose similarity to the banjo consisted mainly in the fact that it had strings to be plucked. According to Turner, the most probable source is Kimbundu, a language spoken in Angola, in which the word *mbanza* refers to an instrument very similar to the banjo. *Cooter* is very likely from *kuta*, a word appearing in two French West African languages, Bambara and Malinke, in which it has the same meaning as in the language of the Gullahs and in the English of many white Southerners.

Goober "peanut" is a modification of Kimbundu *nguba*, with similar forms occurring in Imbundu (also spoken in Angola) and Kongo (Belgian Congo and Angola). *Pinder*, with the same meaning, is from

Kongo *mpinda*. Both these words are freely used on a colloquial level in the South; the first has probably gained a limited national currency.

A number of gustatory and culinary terms of African origin testify to the skill of Negro cooks. Many of these, however, are local terms, like *cush* "corn meal stuffing" and *cala* "sweetened rice"—the latter term confined to the New Orleans area. *Gumbo* is confined to no locality or region, nor is *yam*, which is found also in British English and which is of Portuguese transmission; in Scotland it is used for the common white potato. If the word *yam* was brought to these shores by our early settlers, as it may have been, it is of course not to be regarded as belonging with the group of words under discussion—but there is no reason to insist that, because it occurs also in British English, we could not have got it independently. The same people from whom the Portuguese got the word were right here, and the word might well have entered the American vocabulary, as Dr. Mathews points out, from the language of the slaves. At the least, its use in American English would have been reinforced by their use of it. The word survives as an Africanism in the Gullah dialect (in the form *yambi*) to mean a red sweet potato, which is its usual meaning in southern American English.

Buckra "white man" is also of African origin, appearing as *mbakara* in Efik and Ibibio, spoken in Southern Nigeria. Loss of the initial nasal sound in the word probably occurred in Negro speech before the word was transmitted to whites and is due to the influence of English on the speech of the Negroes. Simplification of the initial consonant combinations *mb-*, *mp-*, *nd-*, *nt-*, and *ng-*, which do not occur in this position in English, is frequent in the Gullah pronunciation of African words.

The great blue heron is frequently called *poor Joe* (or *po' Joe*) in those regions of the South in which the bird is found. There can be no doubt that this is the same word as Vai (Liberia and Sierra Leone) *pojo* "heron." It is likely that *chigger* and its variant *jigger*—the dictionaries give a spelling *chigoe* which suggests a pronunciation seldom if ever heard—are of African transmission as far as their use in American English is concerned, and perhaps of African origin as well. At any rate, *jiga* "flea" is found in a number of African languages spoken in Senegal, Gambia, Togo, Dahomey, and northern and southern Nigeria. The word got into British English probably by way of the British West Indies and has been thought to be of Carib origin. It is likely, however, that its use in American English is due independently to Negro transmission, regardless of its ultimate origin.

Pickaninny, which is probably used nowadays by whites more frequently than by Negroes, is of African transmission, but its source is Portuguese *pequenino* "very little." It is not impossible that the last part of the Portuguese word may have been identified by the Negroes with the Mende (Sierra Leone) word *nini* "female breast," *pequenino* being folk-etymologized into *pickaninny* after these Negroes acquired their English. The word is not exclusively American (the same is true of *buckra, jigger,* and others), though it is probably more commonly used here than elsewhere. It is, nevertheless, recorded in British English almost a century and a half earlier than in American English.

Hoodoo and its New Orleans variant *voodoo* are Africanisms. Both forms are in use by the Gullahs. They have, however, become somewhat differentiated in meaning, the latter usually referring to the cult which flourished in the West Indies and was later introduced into this country. *Hoodoo* is applied to a person or object that is thought to bring bad luck, *to hoodoo* consequently meaning "to bring bad luck to someone." Voodoo worship was introduced into Louisiana very early by slaves from the French colonies of Martinique, Guadeloupe, and Santo Domingo, where the cult—probably of African origin, as its name would indicate— raged furiously. It would seem to have grown rather slowly at first, but was a source of worry among the whites by 1782, when the Spanish governor of Louisiana prohibited further importation of Negroes from Martinique because slaves from there were thought to be "too much given to voudouism and make the lives of the citizens unsafe." Later, and partly for the same reason, a similar prohibition was extended to Negroes from Santo Domingo. After the American occupation, however, there were no such restrictions, and with the sudden influx of Negroes into Louisiana by way of New Orleans between 1806 and 1810, voodoo began to exert a strong influence upon the Louisiana Negroes. For a long time thereafter—until well after the Civil War, in fact—voodoo "queens" and "doctors" were persons of tremendous power and prestige among the Negroes, and even to some extent among the lower-class whites.

The most famous of the queens, who were the priestesses of the cult and much more influential than the doctors who shared with them their powers of sorcery, was the remarkable Marie Laveau, a free mulatto of striking beauty in her younger years, who was by vocation a hairdresser and by avocation a procuress for white gentlemen. For more than forty years absolute ruler of the cult, she has remained a legend to this day. The visitor to New Orleans, if he is lucky, may still hear old Oscar "Papa" Celestin, a Robert Frost in ebony, sing *Marie Laveau*, an original composition which recounts some of the miracles performed by this celebrated "cunjer-lady."

Transmission into general use of African *zombi*, a word intimately associated with voodooism, is probably rather recent, though it must have been known to whites in certain areas of the South at an early date. Its present familiarity may well be credited to the cycle of "horror" films some years ago. The word originally designated the snake god which was the object of adoration in the voodoo cult. It later came to mean a supernatural force thought to restore corpses to life, and ultimately a corpse brought to life by means of this force. Recently it has been used, with an obvious appropriateness, to designate a mixed drink of (usually) rum and brandy.

Juke, which has come into general use among whites comparatively recently, mainly in the compounds *juke box* and *juke joint*, has been a part of the vocabulary of the Gullahs for a long time in the sense "disorderly," particularly in the combination *juke house*. Turner shows that the word is of African origin. In standard colloquial use its meaning has been considerably toned down, as has been that of *jazz*, which, though of unknown origin, is said to have been long used by Negroes, particularly in the New Orleans region. *Jazz* is very likely of African origin, though no African etymon has been found. These two words are included here because they have probably appeared in the English or creolized English speech of Negroes since pre-Revolutionary days even though they may have been late in reaching the standard language. Their very nature would of course sufficiently explain the fact that they were not earlier transmitted to whites. *Jazz* as a verb is, as a matter of fact, sometimes used by whites, though only on a rather low social level, in the sexual sense which it seems originally to have had among the Negroes.

It would be pleasant to be able to record that Professor Turner's researches in Gullah have cleared up the origin of *to tote*, long an etymological puzzle, but there are circumstances in respect to it which indicate that final judgment had better be reserved. It is true that no satisfactory English etymon has been found. *Tote* is one of that sizable number of words of which the dictionaries can say only "orig. uncert.," "unknown origin," or something to that effect. Professor Turner found possible African sources in Kongo and Kikongo *tota* "to pick up," with related words in other West African languages meaning "to carry." The fact that *tote* is used in Gullah does not rule out the possibility of an unknown English source, for very many English words are used by the Gullahs. It is likely, however, that if the word is not of African origin, its use has been reinforced, at least in the South and particularly among the Gullahs, by the African words. Though it is usually thought of as a southernism, *tote* is of fairly frequent occurrence in parts of New England; it has also been found in upstate New York, northern Michigan, and northern Minnesota, occurring alone and in the combinations *tote road, tote wagon, tote team,* and *tote sled*. The fact that the word crops up in parts of the country where Negro influence is highly unlikely suggests that there may after all be an English source for the word which has been lost to us. If so, the fact that words of similar sound and meaning occur in West African languages would have to be due to sheer coincidence, like the similarity in American Indian *Potomac* and Greek *potamos* "river."

Contacts with other colonizing peoples have also contributed to the American vocabulary. Relations between the English and the New Amsterdam Dutch were, it is true, never very friendly; nevertheless from the language of these Dutch settlers American English gained *coleslaw, cooky, cruller, boss, dope, hay barrack, spook, stoop* "porch," *poppycock* (from *pappekak* "soft dung"), *patroon* (which the Dutch had in turn taken from Latin *patronus*), *sleigh, scow, to snoop, bowery* "a farm" (but now more famous as the street name), *pit* "fruit stone," *boodle, Santa Claus, waffle,* and probably *Yankee.* In addition American English incorporated a number of geographical terms used in the region of the Hudson: *kill* "creek, stream, river," *dorp* "village," and *clove* "valley," which also appear in place names. Many of these Dutch words were not used by writers until well into the nineteenth century but we may be fairly sure that they occurred in English contexts much earlier; and we may be equally sure that many more Dutch words than are recorded were once in use. *Hay barrack* represents what English-speaking people did to Dutch *hooi-berg. Coleslaw* is from Dutch *koolsla* "cabbage salad"; folk etymology frequently converts it to *cold slaw. Dope* has acquired a good many slang uses, as in *to dope out, to get the dope on,* and *he's a dope* (i.e., a dolt). It seems to have begun its career in American English meaning simply a drug, later adding the connotation "narcotic." *Boss,* from *baas* "master," was a very useful word, for it allowed the American working man to enjoy the satisfying if purely verbal illusion that he had no master; only slaves had masters in early American democracy. *Father Christmas,* not *Santa Claus,* visits good English children on Christmas Eve. Our name for the jolly saint is from *Sante Klaas,* a Dutch dialect form of *Saint Nikolaas,* that is, "St. Nicholas"; it seems to have taken a long time catching on, and was probably not very common until the nineteenth century. In my childhood *Santa* was always pronounced *Santy* even by the most highly cultured; people nowadays have become much more conscious of spelling and many use a pronunciation which the spelling *Santa* seems to indicate to them.

The source of *Yankee* is uncertain, but the word is most probably from *Jan Kees* (a variant of *Jan Kaas,* which has been in Germany and Flanders a nickname of long standing for a Hollander), used by the English to designate a Dutch pirate, a sense in which it apparently came also to be used in New York as an expression of the contempt in which the English held the Dutch. Because of the final -*s,* the name seems to have been misunderstood to be a plural; the form *Yankee* is thus what is known to linguists as a back formation, like *shay* from *chaise.* It should also be noted that *j* in Dutch has the sound of English *y*; hence the initial sound of the English form of the word. It is a little difficult to understand why the word was transferred from Dutchmen to people of English descent. Perhaps the shift in application was the result of the same type of humor involved in nicknaming the fattest boy in school "Skinny"—the *lucus a non lucendo* principle.

There are, however, many rival theories, for *Yankee* has presented a fascinating problem to etymologists, both professional and lay. One of them, that *Yankee* represents an Indian effort to pronounce the word *English*, is rendered improbable by the fact that the Indians had their own words for the whites; there is no evidence that they ever attempted to use the word *English*. Because Indian etymologies have always been popular, an alternative theory has been proposed, to the effect that *Yankee* was an Indian mispronunciation of *Anglais*; this is just as improbable as the preceding etymology, and for the same reason. Still another "Indian" derivation traces the word to *Yankos*, the name of an apparently mythical Indian tribe; no trace of their existence has ever been discovered. According to Washington Irving's *History of New York . . . by Diedrich Knickerbocker* (1809), the "simple aborigines" called the whites *yanokies*, "a waggish appellation since shortened into the familiar epithet of *Yankees*." Unfortunately for Irving's reputation as an etymologist, no trace of any such Indian word has ever come to light. A nonexistent "Cherokee" word has also been cited as an etymon. Non-Indian theories attempt to derive *Yankee* from Scots dialect words, from a word in the Lancashire dialect, and from numerous Dutch words.

The meaning of *Yankee* has been anything but static. By the mid-eighteenth century its use in this country to designate a New Englander seems to have been well established. During the Civil War southerners were employing the term, usually derogatorily, for any northerner, and it was not long before it acquired what was in the usage of many southerners the inseparable prefix *dam*, as in *damyankee*.

Since the Revolutionary War the British have used the word to designate any American, with connotations no more derogatory than those of the word *American* itself as it is used by them. It is difficult to imagine any experience more painful to most deep Southerners than to be called *Yankees*; yet there is only sporadic evidence that G.I.'s of Southern origin stationed in England during either World War ever objected very vigorously to the appellation. *Yank* is about as common in British colloquial usage as the unabbreviated form; the clipped form has never been very frequent in American use, though it was the title of a magazine distributed to American soldiers and occurs in a line of the World War I song *Over There* ("The Yanks are coming").

Despite the large number of Germans in this country long before the outbreak of the Revolution, few German words entered the American vocabulary until about the middle of the nineteenth century, when many new immigrants from Germany arrived. The first large groups of Germans came from the Palatinate; they arrived on Delaware Bay in the early years of the eighteenth century, and, finding that the good lands around Philadelphia were already taken by descendants of Penn's colonists, proceeded to settle the back country. Those who subsequently moved on to other parts with the Scotch-Irish soon abandoned their native language. Those who stayed on in Pennsylvania kept pretty much to themselves—on farms and in villages where they continued speaking their dialect of German, which was in time considerably influenced by English but which had no appreciable effect upon English outside the areas in which they were settled. *Sauerkraut* appears in British as early as 1617, though neither the word nor the food it designates ever really caught on in England. It is most likely that it was borrowed independently in this country. Similarly, *noodle* is recorded in England before its first known appearance in America, but was probably reborrowed here.

It is not improbable that other words which entered American English through Pennsylvania German were known outside the immediate German settlement area before the nineteenth century, but most of them are of such a nature that we should not expect to find them recorded as early as the eighteenth century. Some of them, like *ponhaus* "scrapple," are not listed in modern abridged dictionaries, probably because lexicographers do not consider them "standard," despite the fact that they are known and used by many speakers of standard American English at the present day. *Rainworm* "earthworm" is used in settlements of German origin and is probably a translation of *Regenwurm*. It occurs in the Pennsylvania German area and in the German settlements on the Yadkin in North Carolina, as well as in Nobleboro, Maine, which was settled from the Palatinate. Old English *regenwyrm* is doubtless the ancestor of the term as it occurs elsewhere, for instance, on Buzzards Bay in Massachusetts. *Sawbuck* is now widely disseminated but it originated in German and Dutch settlements from, respectively, *Sägebock* and *zaagbock*. The fact that each end of the rack on which wood is sawed is shaped like the letter X—the Roman symbol for ten —has given rise to the slang use of the term for a ten-dollar bill. *Woodbuck* is also heard over the entire German settlement area, obviously a partial translation of German *Holzbock*. *Hex* "a witch or the spell cast by a witch" and *to hex* "to cast a spell on" are fairly well known all over the country nowadays. *Ponhaus* (also occurring as *ponhoss, ponhorse, ponehoss,* and *pondhorse*) corresponds to standard German *Pfannhase*; it is current from the Pennsylvania German area proper westward to Ohio and is also well known in northwestern Maryland and northeastern West Virginia. Other gastronomical and culinary terms of Pennsylvania German origin are *sots* "yeast," *snits* (also *schnitz*) "dried apples; pieces of fruit cut for drying" (also used as a verb "to cut into pieces"), *fat-cakes* "doughnuts" (*fettkuche*), *fossnocks* (*fasnachskuche* "Shrovetide cakes"), *thick-milk* "curdled milk" (*dickemilich*), *smear-case* "cottage cheese" (*schmierkäs*), and possibly, but by no means certainly, *applebutter. Clook* "setting hen," with its less frequent variant *cluck*, is from Pennsylvania German *kluck* (standard German *Klucke*). According to Hans Kurath's *Word Geography of the Eastern United States* (Ann Arbor, 1949), "the derogatory phrase *dumb cluck* obviously contains this word." *Belsnickel* (or *Belschnickel*) was, and still is, the southern Pennsylvanian equivalent of *Santa Claus;* the last part of the name is an affectionate diminutive form of German *Nikolaus.* Another name of long standing for the unhappily commercialized saint who rewards good children at Christmas is *Kriss Kingle* (or *Kriss Kringle*); it is a modification of *Christkindl* "Christ child." To *dunk* "to dip (doughnuts usually) into coffee or milk" is from Pennsylvania German *dunken* "to dip," corresponding to standard German *tunken.* It has not really been widely current for more than about twenty years, although it spread very rapidly once it caught on. There is no usage label for the word in the *American College Dictionary,* so that it is apparently considered standard American English nowadays. *Dunker* (or *Dunkard*) is the popular name of a member of the German Baptist Brethren, a pietistic sect which practices baptism by immersion, that is, by dunking.

From French explorers and colonizers American English acquired, usually by way of the Canadian border, such words as *prairie, bateau, voyageur, chowder, buccaneer, carryall* (vehicle), *levee, calumet,* and perhaps *gopher. Chowder* is a modification of *chaudière* "caldron." Although it is recorded first in England, *buccaneer* should probably be regarded as an Americanism by virtue of its many American historical associations; it is ultimately a Carib word, but comes to English by way of French *boucanier. Carryall* is a folk-etymologizing of *cariole. Gopher* is most likely from *gaufre* "honeycomb," in reference to the animal's burrowing habits. *Prairie* is of frequent occurrence in American English, alone and in a number of compounds such as *prairie dog, prairie wolf* "coyote," and *prairie schooner* "small covered wagon." The word is now perfectly familiar in British English also. *Levee* is a derivative of French *lever* "to raise." Its use to designate an embankment for preventing the overflow of a river is largely confined to the South, as is also its later sense "landing place for vessels." *Calumet,* ultimately a derivative of Latin *calamus* "reed," was the word used by the French explorers for the ceremonial tobacco pipe of the Indians.

A number of Spanish words, such as *mosquito* "little fly," *negro* "black" (an adjective which was soon converted into a noun), *pecadillo* "little sin," *armada* "armed (naval) forces" (originally a past participle), and *alligator* (from *el lagarto* "the lizard"), along with Nahuatl words adopted by the Spanish, such as those cited at the beginning of this chapter, entered the English language as early as the sixteenth century. These words, though some of them are more frequently used in this country than in England, should be distinguished from words taken from Spanish by English-speaking people settled on this continent. Such words are very numerous at a later date but very rare before the nineteenth century. *Calaboose* "jail" is a modification of Spanish *calabozo*, used chiefly in the southern states; it is recorded first in the latter years of the eighteenth century. *Cockroach* (as *cacarootch*) first appears in the *General Historie* of Captain John Smith, who refers to it in a somewhat ambiguous passage as "a certaine India Bug, called by the Spaniards a *Cacarootch*, the which creeping into Chests they [that is, the "cacarootches"] eat and defile with their ill-sented dung." The word used by Smith is a modification of Spanish *cucaracha* "wood louse," or possibly a variant form of it. It was later folk-etymologized to *cockroach* (just as Latin *asparagus* is converted by some speakers into *sparrow grass*) and subsequently clipped to *roach* in this country, American verbal prudery perhaps playing some part in the elimination of the first element of what deceptively appeared to be a compound of *cock* and *roach*. *Key* "reef or low island" from Spanish *cayo* was in English use before it was recorded in America, but its use is now mainly confined to this country, particularly to Florida. *Key West* is a modification of *Cayo Hueso* "bone key." The form *cay*, riming with *day*, is now more usual in British English than *key*. *Stevedore*, from Spanish *estívador*, occurs first in the form *stowadore* by association with English *to stow*.

FOR DISCUSSION AND REVIEW

1 Why is it that many of the words that we have borrowed from other languages have been culinary terms?

2 What is an "inkhorn term"? How does your desk dictionary define this term?

3 What is the first written source for *chipmunk*? What is the origin of the word?

4 What is folk etymology? Give several examples of folk etymologies from Pyles's article.

5 Define the term *metathesis*. What is the term's importance in studies of borrowings? Give several examples from Pyles's article of words said to have undergone metathesis.

6 Pyles discusses some possible etymologies for *caucus*. Which of these does your desk dictionary use? What does *Webster's Third New International Dictionary* give for an etymology for this word?

7 Does Pyles consider the American Indian languages to be a major source of borrowings? Explain.

8 What is Gullah? Briefly summarize the contribution to the study of American borrowings that Lorenzo Dow Turner has made.

9 How would you characterize the French borrowings that Pyles discusses?

PROJECTS FOR "THE HISTORY OF THE LANGUAGE"

1 Read Paul Thieme's essay "The Indo-European Language," Scientific American (October 1958), 63–74. Prepare an oral or written report on the kinds of evidence (with examples) that went into his conclusions about the Indo-European peoples.

2 The following passages are versions of the Lord's Prayer as they were written during different periods in the history of the English language. Analyze the forms that the various words have in common, and consider how each word changes from the first to the last version and, also, from one version to the next (e.g., Faeder, fadir, father, Father). Do the same kind of analysis on the various syntactical (i.e., word-order) changes that you discover (e.g., Tōcume þīn rīce, Thy kyngdom cumme to, Let thy kingdom come, Thy kingdom come). In studying the modern version, do you think that any words have completely disappeared from the language? Write an essay in which you comment on the changes that you have discovered in these excerpts. Give as many examples of the various changes as you feel are necessary to support your conclusions. Finally, draw some conclusions about the evolution of the English language as it is revealed in these passages.

1. Eornostlīce gebiddaþ ēow þus Fæder ūre þū be eart on heofonum, sie bin nama gehālgod.
2. Tōcume þīn rīce. Gewurþe þīn willa on eorþan swā swā on heofonum.
3. Ūrne daeghwæmlīcan hlāf syle ūs tōdæg.
4. And forgyf ūs ūre gyltas swā swā we forgyfaþ ūrum gyltendum.
5. And ne gelæd þū ūs on costnunge ac ālys us of yfele.
6. Witodlīce gyf gē forgyfaþ mannum hyra synna, þonne forgyfþ ēower sē heofonlīca fæder ēow ēowre gyltas.
7. Gyf gē sōþlīce ne forgyfaþ mannum, ne ēower fæder ne forgyfþ ēow ēowre synna.

Old English (ca. 1000)

1. Forsothe thus ʒe shulen preyen, Oure fadir that art in heuenes, halwid be thi name;
2. Thy kyngdom cumme to; be thi wille don as in heuen and in erthe;
3. ʒif to vs this day oure breed ouer other substaunce;
4. And forʒeue to vs oure dettis, as we forʒeue to oure dettours;
5. And leede vs nat in to temptacioun, but delyuere vs fro yuel. Amen.
6. Forsothe ʒif ʒee shulen forʒeuue to men her synnys, and ʒoure heuenly fadir shal forʒeue to ʒou ʒoure trespassis.
7. Sothely ʒif ʒee shulen forʒeue not to men, neither ʒoure fadir shal forʒeue to ʒou ʒoure synnes.

Middle English (Wycliffe, 1389)

1. After thys maner there fore praye ye, O oure father which arte in heven, halowed be thy name;
2. Let thy kingdom come; thy wyll be fulfilled as well in erth as hit ys in heven;
3. Geve vs this daye oure dayly breade;
4. And forgeve vs oure treaspases, even as we forgeve them which trespas vs;
5. Leede vs not into temptacion, but delyvre vs ffrom yvell. Amen.
6. For and yff ye shall forgeve other men there trespases, youre father in heven shal also forgeve you.
7. But and ye wyll not forgeve men there trespases, no more shall youre father forgeve youre trespases.

Early Modern English (Tyndale, 1526)

1. Pray then like this:
   Our Father who art in heaven,
   Hallowed by thy name.
2. They kingdom come,
   Thy will be done,
      On Earth as it is in heaven.
3. Give us this day our daily bread;
4. And forgive us our debts,
      As we also have forgiven our debtors;
5. And lead us not into temptation,
      But deliver us from evil.
6. For if you forgive men their trespasses, your heavenly Father also will forgive you;
7. but if you do not forgive men their trespasses, neither will your Father forgive your trespasses.

Modern English (1952)

3   The following words have interesting etymologies: algebra, anaesthetic, assassin, caucus, crocodile, tawdry, and zest. Look at their entries in the Oxford English Dictionary and then write a brief statement about each. If you have difficulty understanding the abbreviations and designations in the OED, consult the section on how to use this dictionary in the front matter.

4   In the first chapter of his All-American English: A History of the English Language in America, J. L. Dillard quotes Albert H. Marckwardt's statement in American English that the American colonists " 'were speaking and writing the English language as it was currently employed in England,' " and then he proceeds to argue against the Marckwardt thesis. Read Dillard's first chapter and the first two chapters of Marckwardt's book. Write a paper in which you summarize the views of each man. Which view do you find more persuasive?

5   Pyles discusses borrowing as applied to only the early period of our history. English has, however, continued to borrow from even more diverse sources since the period Pyles discusses. Compile a list of ten words borrowed from at least four languages that Pyles does not discuss (e.g., Italian, Yiddish, Russian, Chinese, etc.).

SELECTED BIBLIOGRAPHY

Barber, Charles L. *The Story of Speech and Language*. New York: Thomas Y. Crowell Co., 1964. (Chapters include "The Vikings in England"; "The Norman Conquest"; "English in the Scientific Age"; "English as a World Language.")

Baugh, Albert C. *A History of the English Language*. 2nd edition. New York: Appleton-Century-Crofts, Inc., 1957. (A standard text on the history of the language; first published in 1935.)

Bender, Harold H. *The Home of the Indo-Europeans*. Princeton: Princeton University Press, 1922. (The standard work on the subject.)

Brook, G. L. *A History of the English Language*. New York: W. W. Norton & Company, 1964. (Contains interesting historical studies but only a small section on the history of the language as such.)

Dillard, J. L. *All-American English: A History of the English Language in America*. New York: Random House, 1975. (Emphasizes influence of maritime English on American colonists and the later imports of Yiddish, Pennsylvania Dutch, and "Spanglish.")

Gordon, James D. *The English Language: An Historical Introduction*. New York: Thomas Y. Crowell Company, 1972. (A concisely written and clearly presented introductory text.)

Lloyd, Donald J., and Harry R. Warfel. *American English in Its Cultural Setting*. New York: Alfred A. Knopf, Inc., 1956. (Early sections, "Our Land and Our People," and "Our Language," are interesting for the history of American English.)

Marckwardt, Albert H. *American English*. New York: Oxford University Press, 1958. (A standard history.)

Myers, L. M. *The Roots of Modern English*. Boston: Little, Brown & Company, 1966. (Readable and perhaps as nontechnical as the subject will allow.)

Pyles, Thomas. *The Origins and Development of the English Language*. 2nd edition. New York: Harcourt Brace Jovanovich, Inc., 1971. (A standard text with much useful information; accompanying workbook by John Algeo is extremely useful.)

————. *Words and Ways of American English*. New York: Random House, 1952. (An introduction to American English from colonial times to the present.)

Thieme, Paul. "The Indo-European Language." *Scientific American*, 199 (October 1958), 63–74. (A brief but interesting and readable overview.)

Watkins, Calvert. "The Indo-European Origin of English," "Indo-European and the Indo-Europeans," "Indo-European Roots," *The American Heritage Dictionary of the English Language*. Ed. William Morris. Boston: American Heritage Publishing Co., Inc. and Houghton Mifflin Company, 1969. (The first two items are essays and are somewhat technical; the third item is an Indo-European root dictionary to which items in the dictionary proper are cross-referenced.)

PART FOUR

Words, Usage, and the Dictionary

The great critical debate that developed after the publication of *Webster's Third New International Dictionary* in 1961 (see the article by Albert H. Marckwardt on pp. 187–199) never really resolved any questions of lexicography. The arguments for and against the format and content of this dictionary, however, did reveal something of significance that a good many Americans had never really suspected. They showed that we are a people very much interested in words, usage, and dictionaries, and we have many firm opinions about these subjects; but we are either unaware of or strangely reluctant to admit, even to ourselves, the fascination that these subjects have for us.

The selections that follow Professor Marckwardt's essay consider the degree to which our language is inherently sexist, the history and present state of attitudes toward usage, how words in English are made, the phenomenon of euphemistic usage, and, finally, slang in both a general and a specific way.

1

Dictionaries and the English Language

Albert H. Marckwardt

Albert H. Marckwardt sets the controversy over *Webster's Third New International Dictionary* against the history of descriptive and prescriptive dictionary making. He reveals the complex nature of attitudes toward dictionaries in general and the considerable misinformation concerning them that exists even in the minds of the critics. The descriptive and prescriptive traditions are not controversial in principle, but one might usefully ask to what extent they can be put into practice in any dictionary.

NOW THAT much of the tumult and the shouting have subsided, and the controversy over *Webster's Third New International Dictionary* has attained the dignity of a casebook, it should be possible to consider both the dictionary and the varied reactions to it with a degree of detachment. Bergen Evans was quite correct in characterizing the storm of abuse provoked by the appearance of the new edition as a curious phenomenon. But how can it be explained? And more important still, what is there to be learned from it?

We must recognize, first of all, that a complete revision of our largest commercially produced dictionary of the English language has become a regularly recurring event in American life. Upon occasion the time table has varied a bit, but the following listing reveals an astonishing degree of regularity over the past century.

An American Dictionary of the English Language (Royal Quarto Edition, Unabridged)	1864	*Webster's New International Dictionary*	1909
Webster's International Dictionary	1890	*Webster's New International Dictionary* (Second edition)	1934
		Webster's Third New International Dictionary	1961

Of the five Webster editions listed above, probably none has called forth such extremes of critical comment upon its appearance as the recent Webster Third. It was characterized as "a very great calamity." Its general tone was described as "a dismaying assortment of the questionable, the perverse, the unworthy, the downright outrageous." At the same time, other reviewers spoke of the work as "an intellectual achievement of the very highest order," and "a reference work which worthily carries on a tradition of great reference works."

These extremes of praise and blame are reminiscent of the reception of the 1828 edition of *An American Dictionary of the English Language,* compiled by Webster himself and the real parent of the long line of dictionaries which bear his name. At that time a reviewer in *The Southern Literary Messenger* denounced the treatment of pronunciation as horrible and the orthography as abominable. The English *Quarterly Review* judged it "a decided failure, conducted on perverse and erroneous principles," and in much the same vein as some of the critics of the Webster Third, complained that "we do not recollect ever to have witnessed in the same compass a greater number of crudities and errors, or more pains taken to so little purpose." But Webster's 1828 work has its admirers as well, particularly among the Germans, who praised the profound learning that it reflected.

The disparate comments on Webster's early work are of interest today only as a historical phenomenon, but those which have been applied to the Webster Third still give rise to considerable confusion. It is scarcely possible for both the critics and the admirers to be right in all that they say, and one may reasonably ask what a more dispassionate evaluation might be.

Two Traditions

In approaching such an appraisal, we must understand first of all that the American lexicographer in his concern with current English faces something of a dilemma. He is the inheritor of two traditions clearly in conflict, both of which have their roots in England.

The earlier tradition is that of Samuel Johnson, the compiler of the 1755 *Dictionary of the English Language,* who lent the first touch of sheer genius to English lexicography. In the preface of this great work, he pointed out that "every language has its improprieties and absurdities, which it is the duty of the lexicographer to correct or proscribe." According to him, the function of a dictionary was one, "by which the pronunciation of our language may be fixed and its attainment facilitated; by which its purity may be preserved, its use ascertained, and its duration lengthened." That Johnson was expressing the spirit of his age is shown by comments such as that of Lord Chesterfield, who wrote, "We must have a resource to the old Roman expedient in times of confusion and choose a Dictator. Upon this principle I give my vote for Mr. Johnson to fill that great and arduous post."

This concept of the lexicographer as a linguistic legislator or arbiter, if not absolute dictator, is still strong in the United States. It is frequently reflected, and indeed encouraged, by the slogans which dictionary publishers—not the editors, let me hasten to say—choose to advertise their wares. The very phrase, "Supreme Authority," which the G. and C. Merriam Company used to employ, supported this view of the dictionary; whether intentionally or not is open to conjecture.

The slightly later and opposed tradition is that of the lexicographer as the objective recorder of the language. For the English-speaking nations this concept was first realized on a substantial scale in what is now known as *The Oxford English Dictionary* but originally entitled *A New English Dictionary on Historical Principles*. Here the purpose is stated as follows:

> The aim of this dictionary is to present in alphabetical series the words which have formed the English vocabulary from the time of the earliest records down to the present day, with all the relevant facts concerning their form, sense-history, pronunciation, and etymology. It embraces not only the standard language of literature and conversation, whether current at the moment or obsolete, or archaic, but also the main technical vocabulary, and a large measure of dialectal usage and slang.

Note that this statement contains not one word about fixing the language, about proscription or prescription of any kind. Operating on this basis, the lexicographer contents himself with setting down the record, leaving its interpretation to the reader. Needless to say, the prestige of the *Oxford English Dictionary* is enormous; it is generally conceded to be superior to the corresponding major dictionaries for the other western European languages. The principles on which it is based were formulated as early as 1859.

The conflict of principle which has been pointed out need not necessarily be troublesome. If the language involved is confined as to number of speakers and is the vehicle of a static and stabilized society, there is virtually no problem. An accurate description of the language as it is actually used, kept simple by the relative absence of variants, accurately designating social and regional status, will in itself serve prescriptive purposes. But this is not the case with English, which is spoken natively by some two hundred and seventy millions, spread over five continents of the globe. Under such circumstances, uniformity becomes a remote possibility. In the United States, at least, the language is that of a highly mobile society, both geographically and up and down the social scale. As a consequence the lines between class and regional dialects and the standard language inevitably tend to become blurred. Under such circumstances, the linguistic reporter and the legislator are more likely to seem to be working at cross purposes.

Nevertheless, it is clearly evident that as the various editions of Webster march down the century, the statements of principle which are to be found in them move steadily away from the Johnsonian or prescriptive concept toward the descriptive position of the Oxford editors. Even as early as 1864, Chauncey A. Goodrich, the chief editor of the first major revision after Webster's death, asserted that, "The chief value of a dictionary consists in its Definitions; in giving a clear, full, and accurate exhibition, of all the various shades of meaning which belong, *by established usage,* to the words of a language."

Nor was the reportorial concept limited to the Webster series of dictionaries in this country. One of the principal competitors during the early years of the present century, Dr. Isaac K. Funk, wrote in the preface of the 1913 *Standard Dictionary of the English Language,* "The chief function of a dictionary is to record usage." It is true that this forthright statement of the descriptive function was followed by a somewhat unsuccessful attempt to reconcile it with the authoritarian concept, but nevertheless the principle had been stated.

1934 Edition

The immediate predecessor of the new Webster Third was the 1934 edition. The following excerpt from its front matter (p. xvi) refers specifically to pronunciation, but it is a fair representation of the attitude of its editors toward all language matters:

> The function of a pronouncing dictionary is to record as far as possible the pronunciations prevailing in the best present usage, rather than to attempt to dictate what that usage should be. In so far as a dictionary may be known and acknowledged as a faithful recorder and interpreter of such usage, so far and no farther may it be appealed to as an authority.
>
> In the case of diverse usages of extensive prevalence, the dictionary must recognize each of them.

A somewhat broader treatment of the editorial function is to be found in the Introduction (p. xi) to the 1934 Webster:

> Both Samuel Johnson and Noah Webster conceived it to be a duty of the dictionary editor to maintain the purity of the standard language. However, with the growth in literacy of the past century, and the increase in fiction and drama, in radio and motion pictures, of the use of dialect, slang, and colloquial speech, it has become necessary for a general dictionary to record and interpret the vocabularies of geographical and occupational dialects, and of the livelier levels of the speech of the educated.

It would be difficult to imagine a more cogent or forthright exposition of the descriptive function of the dictionary than these two statements of editorial policy. The first of them apparently satisfied the editors of the Webster Third, for they repeat it in their Introduction (p. 6a) with only one minor expansion: "best present usage" of the earlier edition now reads, "General cultivated conversational usage, both formal and informal." This offers additional support for the conclusion that with respect to the conflict between opposing lexicographical concepts, the descriptive had been wholly accepted, the prescriptive completely rejected in 1934. Whatever differences there may be between the 1934 and 1961 editions, they are not matters of policy or principle. They are instead differences in the way in which a principle common to both dictionaries has been realized.

Lexicographical policy is not ordinarily a matter of absorbing interest, but it has been necessary to deal with it at some length because the Webster Third has been criticized on occasion for repudiating, even sabotaging the principles of the second edition. Such charges serve only to reveal a total lack of awareness on the part of the critic as to what these principles were, how they have developed in this country, and how they reflect a steadily changing concept of the function of the dictionary. Actually, the furor over the Webster Third is a sad commentary on how inadequately the dictionary has been presented in the English classrooms of the nation and how insufficiently English teachers are informed about one of the principal tools of their profession.

Practical Editorial Decisions

The extremes of public reaction to the new Webster must also be considered in terms of editorial decisions on a practical rather than a theoretical level. Such an understanding may best be attained by considering certain of the practical questions which confronted the editors, what the decisions on them were, and what the reasons for them may have been.

At the very outset of their preparations, the editors apparently felt an obligation to increase considerably the amount of evidence upon which the new dictionary was to be based. Dictionary evidence normally exists in the form of citation slips, the products of an extensive reading program. The citations are filed under their appropriate headwords, and in the editing process they constitute the raw material for the definitions and in fact for most of the word treatment.

At the time of the compilation of the second edition, the files in the Springfield offices held some 1,615,000 citation slips. In the years intervening between the two editions, as the result of what must have been a tremendous effort, this figure was nearly quadrupled. Just under

4,500,000 citations were added, resulting in a total of 6,000,000, a number approximately equalling the collection for the *Oxford English Dictionary*, but far more heavily concentrated on the language of the present day. In addition, the *Dictionary of American English* and the *Dictionary of Americanisms* had both been completed in the years 1944 and 1951 respectively, constituting a further increase in the size of the corpus available to the editors of the Webster Third. As a result, they found themselves with approximately 50,000 new words (words not entered in the Webster Second) and 50,000 new meanings for words already entered.

At this point physical and financial factors enter into consideration. For a number of reasons, undoubtedly based upon a century of business experience, the publishers are firmly committed to a single-volume dictionary. They had made the Webster Second as large, that is to say thick, as any one volume could possibly get and still assure a back that might withstand the rigors of long and constant use, particularly in schools and libraries. Thus it was manifestly impossible to increase the number of pages by the ten or fifteen percent necessary to accommodate the new entries. If these were to be included, something had to come out. The kind of material that was removed forms the basis of some of the criticisms of the present edition.

The first excision consisted of the materials which, in earlier editions, had been placed below the horizontal line running across the page. These included archaisms, dialect forms, variant spellings, and proper names. To quote the editors, "Many obsolete and comparatively useless or obscure words have been omitted. These include, in general, words that had become obsolete before 1755 unless found in well-known major works of a few major writers." Incidentally, the significance of the date 1755 can scarcely escape one's attention. In the first place it was the publication year of Dr. Johnson's dictionary. Moreover, as a deadline for obsolescence, it marks an advance of two centuries and a half over the corresponding date of 1500 for the Webster Second. Thus, in word selection as well as in other matters, the emphasis is clearly placed upon the current state of the language.

Getting rid of the obsolete and the obscure did not in itself solve the space problem. Still other things had to go, and these taken together constitute the parts essential to a peripheral function of the dictionary long cherished by Americans—the encyclopedic function. In the process of elimination, the editors removed among other things:

1. The gazetteer section.
2. The biographical section.
3. Titles of written works and works of art.
4. Names of characters in fiction, folklore, and mythology.

5. Names of battles, wars, organizations, cities, and states.
6. Mottoes and other familiar sayings.

There have been further excisions as well. Color plates and illustrations are reduced in a proportion somewhere between one-fourth and one-third. Even the number of pages has gone down from 3210 to 2720.

Elimination of Material

This elimination of encyclopedic material has caused anguish. "Think, if you can," complains Wilson Follett, "of an unabridged dictionary from which you cannot learn who Mark Twain was, or what were the names of the apostles, or that the Virgin was Mary, the mother of Jesus of Nazareth, or what and where the District of Columbia is." Actually, this is not at all difficult. The great Oxford comes immediately to mind, as does Henry Cecil Wyld's *Universal Dictionary of the English Language,* or any of the great academy dictionaries of such languages as French or Spanish.

Nevertheless, Follett's reaction will be shared by many Americans. In the past, dictionaries published in this country have cheerfully served an encyclopedic as well as a lexicographic function, and ironically enough it was Noah Webster himself who was primarily responsible. His first dictionary, published in 1806, included tables of the moneys of most of the commercial nations in the world, tables of weights and measures, ancient and modern, the divisions of time among the Jews, Greeks, and Romans, and an official list of the post-offices in the United States, to mention only a few of the extra features. Although the editors of the current volume have broken with their progenitor in cutting out these impedimenta, they have not at all departed from the essential principles of lexicography in so doing.

Undoubtedly they felt that the considerable increase in the number of illustrative citations would readily compensate for the loss of the peripheral material. Such citations do constitute the core of the reportorial dictionary. For instance, there were no citations for the adjective *oratorical* in the second edition; the Third has three. The second edition gave three identified citations for *chase,* verb. In the Third, there are four identified and seven unidentified citations.

According to the Preface of the current edition, "More than 14,000 different authors are quoted for their use of words or for the structural pattern of their words. . ." Many of these are contemporary. The reader is also informed that the verbal illustrations (citations apparently unidentified as to author) are "mostly from the twentieth century."

This innovation has met with something less than universal approval, a reaction not so much attributable to the editorial policy itself as to some of the advertising antics of the business office. The original brochure, announcing this edition as "one of the most remarkable literary achievements of all time," included among the list of authors cited such names as Billy Rose, Fulton Lewis, Jr., Art Linkletter, Dinah Shore, Ted Williams, and Ethel Merman. In addition there were Harry Truman, Dwight D. Eisenhower, John F. Kennedy, and Richard Nixon, whose names were undoubtedly signed to reams of material which they did not compose. To the sympathetic this signalled a conscious attempt to include a wide range of current authors. To the critical it betokened a lack of discrimination and responsibility. Actually, the citations from such sources are few in number and small in proportion.

A point which must be taken into account here is that which was made at the very outset of this essay, namely that the life of a Webster edition is roughly calculated at twenty-five years. Thus, the overriding concern of the dictionary is quite appropriately the language in its current state. It is on these grounds that the editors may logically justify the preponderance of citations from current authors, irrespective of lasting literary merit. It may be assumed that in the 1986 edition many of them will be discarded, to be replaced by others from the 1970's and early 1980's. In this respect the Webster practice will differ sharply from that of the *Oxford English Dictionary*, for which no new edition was contemplated, although certainly only a small proportion of the authors cited in that work are literary giants of lasting reputation.

Status Labels

Another departure in the Webster Third from the practice of earlier editions, which has given rise to considerable criticism, is the treatment of what are called *status labels*. Here again some of the disapproval has its source in misunderstanding. Basically, the editors have developed a terminology which is at once semantically neutral and more precise than that which has been employed in the past. The label *illiterate* has been discontinued. It has become a term of censure rather than a dispassionate indication of the inability to read and write. The current replacements, *substandard* and *nonstandard,* are matter-of-fact rather than pejorative and permit a gradation of acceptability, the latter indicating a wider range of occurrence than the former, although it is applied to a smaller number of words and expressions. American dialect ascriptions represent a great advance in precision over those of the second edition in that they reflect an adaptation of the terminology for the various dialect areas developed by Professor Hans Kurath, editor of the Linguistic Atlas and the most eminent linguistic geographer in the country. It was unfortunate, however, that the editors chose not to indicate those words current in all regions of the United States but not in England or other parts of the English-speaking world.

Another innovation in the Webster Third is the elimination of the label *colloquial*. There are two conceivable reasons for this: In the first place the term is ambivalent, signifying informality on the one hand and the spoken rather than the written medium on the other. It is customary now among students of the language to be somewhat more precise, recognizing not only colloquial but *casual* and *intimate* as further gradations of the spoken variety of the language, any of which not only may be but are regularly employed by speakers of unquestioned cultivation.

An even greater objection to the label *colloquial* is the persistence with which an unfavorable connotation has adhered to it. Dictionary users never interpreted the term in the way in which dictionary editors intended. It was not meant as a condemnation either in the Webster Second or in the various abridged dictionaries based upon it. The editors took great pains to say so, both in the prefatory material and in the definition of the word itself, but this went unheeded. So for the present edition the staff was faced with the alternative of finding an acceptable substitute less liable to misinterpretation, or of eliminating the label altogether. It chose the latter, partly perhaps because of the unsatisfactory experience of other dictionaries which had experimented with a substitute.

In general the changes in the choice and ascription of labels reflect an endeavor to achieve greater precision and objectivity. The attempt at precision undoubtedly finds some adherents, although there will be disagreements over the application of the labels in specific instances. The attempt at objectivity has, understandably enough, resulted in the disappearance of the censorious tone which for many seemed to be part of the proper function of the labels *colloquial* and *illiterate*. To such persons, the lack of censure has been understood as a lowering of standards.

Pronunciation

In dealing with pronunciation, the editors of the Webster Third had to contend with two factors which had not faced their predecessors. One was a new electronic development, namely voice amplification. The other was a new concept in the analysis of language, that of the phoneme or meaningful unit of sound.

Voice amplification affected the kind of pronunciation which the dictionary undertook to record. In pre-loud-speaker days, the second edition of Webster recorded what it called "formal platform speech," the speech of cultivated users of English, speaking formally with a view to being completely understood by their hearers. That there were other types of pronunciation wholly appropriate to less formal situations was readily conceded by the editors, but they evidently felt that their editorial responsibility could be discharged with the greatest amount of effectiveness and least confusion by indicating just the one.

The microphone has changed all this. Certain devices of articulation necessary for clarity when the speaker was forced to depend on lung power to make himself audible to the last row of a large auditorium are no longer necessary. Nor are they often employed today.

This change led the Webster editors into a complete revision of the manner in which evidence on pronunciation was collected. Where Webster Second had attempted a sampling, by means of written questionnaires, of the pronunciation of persons who did a considerable amount of public speaking, the Webster Third staff turned its attention directly to the language itself rather than to opinion about it. They listened to radio, television, and recordings; to speech in all parts of the country and in all types of situations. Again, as with the citations for word occurrences, forms, and meanings, the body of evidence was tremendously increased in range and scope, but certainly less skewed toward a single type of pronunciation.

In any English dictionary, and particularly one designed for use in the United States, a decision upon the particular system, or respelling, to indicate pronunciation always poses a problem. For a number of reasons, the American public has been unwilling to accept the International Phonetic Alphabet; nor is this a particularly economical device when a number of variants must be shown. The Webster Second continued with few changes the system of its predecessors, which was cumbersome in that a single sound was indicated by more than one transcription, and confusing in that a single character sometimes covered far more latitude than the user was likely to realize.

The editors of the current edition have attempted to take advantage of the phonemic concept, basic to present-day linguistic science. The general result has been the disappearance of a rash of diacritics which made the earlier dictionaries difficult to read and to interpret. Some useful characters have been taken over from the phonetic alphabet, notably the elongated *n* to indicate the usual sound of *ng*, and most important, the inverted *e* or schwa for the neutral vowel used in weakly stressed syllables. The latter, it must be confessed, is an innovation in which Webster followed some of its competitors. At all events, the public will no longer be misled into believing that the final vowel of *caucus* is somehow different from that of *fracas*.

Unfortunately the necessity of economizing on space has led to the excision of the authoritative treatments of the individual sounds of English which lent scholarly distinction to the second edition though perhaps read by only a few. Also, certain innovations of the Webster Third will cause annoyance until the public becomes accustomed to them. One of these may well be the indication of stress by a mark preceding rather than following the syllable. The removal of the pronunciation key from the bottom of the page is another. The use of a modified *d* character to indicate what the editors call, "the usual American pronunciation of *latter*," will seem to the critical like countenancing the slipshod, and it is possible that a *t* with a diacritic might have served quite as well without outraging quite so many sensibilities.

With pronunciation as with countless other features of the dictionary, the editors have attempted to present the facts of the language as they saw them. It is an honest presentation, maintaining the principles and the concept of the dictionary characteristic of previous editions, but carrying them out with greater consistency and basing them upon far more evidence. There have been errors of judgment, more often perhaps with respect to manner of presentation than in the interpretation of the facts which are reported, but this is inevitable in an undertaking of such magnitude.

My comments so far should have suggested, to a degree at least, the reasons for some of the changes which are to be found in the Webster Third. They have not yet given an answer to the question which was initially posed: why the extremes of praise and blame. The encomiums are easy to account for. They represent the approval of those who accept the descriptive principle and find in the current product a generally conscientious and more thorough implementation of it than is otherwise available.

Controversy

The chorus of protest is somewhat more complex in origin. It is in part the expression of a desire for linguistic authoritarianism, an attitude sincerely held by many, which can be explained only in terms of a number of complex and interrelated factors in American cultural history. Added to this is the mistaken notion that the Webster Third represents a change in lexicographical principle, an error which is fostered by the more complete coverage and greater accuracy of the edition. The excision of certain kinds of nonessential material represented a sudden departure from a time-honored practice. Moreover, there is, as always, a tendency toward careless reading and inept comparison; upon occasion a judgment objected to in the third edition was already present in the second. This reflects a not uncommon situation. Even those who are willing to concede that language standards must ultimately rest upon usage are not infrequently distressed when they encounter a detailed and factual inventory of that usage. At such a point the normal reaction is to question the accuracy of the inventory and the soundness of the method upon which it is based.

An excellent illustration of this is to be found in the treatment of the very word that has given rise to so many headlines and caused so much acid comment—*ain't*. The statement which gave rise to the excitement, namely that *ain't* is used orally in most parts of the United States by many cultivated speakers, is merely a condensation of what has already been noted in Bagby Atwood's *A Survey of Verb Forms in the Eastern United States*, a study based upon the materials of the Linguistic Atlas of the United States and Canada. "Cultivated, our foot," comments the editor of the Chicago *Daily News*; yet the cultivated informants for the various regional atlases were selected on the basis of as rigorous a set of standards in terms of family background, education, and occupation as could be established.

The presumed role of structural linguistics in the Webster Third reflects a most unfortunate confusion, and ironically it is the editor of the dictionary who is in part responsible for it. In an article in *Word Study* prior to the publication of the dictionary, Dr. Gove unintentionally left careless and uninformed readers with the mistaken impression that Leonard Bloomfield in 1926 first stated the postulate that correctness rests upon usage. Despite the fact that Dr. Gove then went on to mention any number of areas in lexicography where linguistics had had no appreciable influence, the first part of his article appears to have left many readers with the mental image of a fifth column of structuralists burrowing their way through the Merriam-Webster files in Springfield.

This notion is wrong on two counts. First, the importance of usage in the establishment of a linguistic standard had been maintained by a host of scholars from the turn of the century on. They included Thomas Lounsbury, George P. Krapp, Louise Pound, Charles C. Fries, and Sterling A. Leonard, to mention only a few of the more distinguished. The structuralists accept this as a matter of course, but they did not invent the idea. Second, except for the treatment of pronunciation, structural concepts do not appear with any great frequency in the dictionary. Words are traditionally classified as nouns, adjectives, verbs, and so on. There was no attempt to substitute a scheme consistently based either upon form or function. This is a dictionary of words rather than of morphemes. I find it difficult to detect even a hint of structuralism in the handling of the definitions. Yet Dwight Macdonald speaks of the "direct application" of structural linguistics "to making dictionaries," and the idea has been echoed by others.

It is the English-teaching profession which should be seriously disturbed by the dictionary controversy. If the Webster war has proved little or nothing about dictionaries, it has demonstrated our ineptitude, if not absolute failure, in teaching our students what a dictionary is for, how it is made, and the proper way to use it. Much of the misunderstanding of principle, of the confusion of principle and practice, of the failure to read and interpret accurately can, with considerable justice, be laid at our door. After all, the embattled critics were once our students; had our teaching of the dictionary been soundly based, this comedy of errors should have been at least somewhat less comic.

To return to the dictionary itself, however, one can only say that by a more literal acceptance of its declared function, and by running counter more obviously to what people want or think they want in a dictionary and to what they think they have been getting, the Webster Third represents a calculated risk. Depending on one's point of view, it is either a courageous or a foolhardy venture into the latter half of the twentieth century. For the staff, who in the face of the public clamor must wonder if it has been at all worthwhile, there is only the dubious comfort in Macaulay's words, "The best lexicographer may well be content if his productions are received by the world in cold esteem."

FOR DISCUSSION AND REVIEW

1 What were some of the objections made by reviewers and critics to *Webster's Third New International Dictionary?*

2 Define the words *prescriptive* and *descriptive.* How were these terms related to the controversy over *Webster's Third?*

3 Where does Marckwardt place much of the responsibility for the controversy over *Webster's Third?*

4 In what ways did the editors of *Webster's Third* reflect recent advances in linguistic science in the writing of their dictionary?

5 The word *ain't* and what *Webster's Third* said about it became a rallying point for critics of the dictionary. How does your desk dictionary describe the usage of this controversial word?

6 The editors of *Webster's Third* faced problems of pronunciation that the editors of the 1934 edition did not. What were these problems?

2

Sexism in English:

A Feminist View

Alleen Pace Nilsen

Since culture influences language and language influences culture, we cannot reasonably study one subject without also studying the other. In an effort to see what role the dictionary plays in reflecting and influencing the status of women in America, Alleen Pace Nilsen studied all the words relating to males and females in a recently published desk dictionary. She found not only that the English language is biased against women but also that this bias is preserved and consequently promoted by those who write dictionaries. Her findings raise some important questions for lexicographers and for those interested in equal rights.

DOES CULTURE shape language? Or does language shape culture? This is as difficult a question as the old puzzler of which came first, the chicken or the egg, because there's no clear separation between language and culture.

A well-accepted linguistic principle is that as culture changes so will the language. The reverse of this—as a language changes so will the culture—is not so readily accepted. This is why some linguists smile (or even scoff) at feminist attempts to replace *Mrs.* and *Miss* with *Ms.* and to find replacements for those all-inclusive words which specify masculinity, e.g., *chairman, mankind, brotherhood, freshman,* etc.

Perhaps they are amused for the same reason that it is the doctor at a cocktail party who laughs the loudest at the joke about the man who couldn't afford an operation so he offered the doctor a little something to touch up the X-ray. A person working constantly with language is likely to be more aware of how really deep-seated sexism is in our communication system.

Last winter I took a standard desk dictionary and gave it a place of honor on my night table. Every night that I didn't have anything more interesting to do, I read myself to sleep making a card for each entry that seemed to tell something about male and female. By spring I had a rather dog-eared dictionary, but I also had a collection of note cards filling two shoe boxes. The cards tell some rather interesting things about American English.

First, in our culture it is a woman's body which is considered important while it is a man's mind or his activities which are valued. A woman is sexy. A man is successful.

I made a card for all the words which came into modern English from somebody's name. I have a two-and-one-half inch stack of cards which are men's names now used as everyday words. The women's stack is less than a half inch high and most of them came from Greek mythology. Words coming from the names of famous American men include *lynch, sousaphone, sideburns, Pullman, rickettsia, Shick test, Winchester rifle, Franklin stove, Bartlett pear, teddy bear,* and *boysenberry.* The only really common words coming from the names of American women are *bloomers* (after Amelia Jenks Bloomer) and *Mae West jacket.* Both of these words are related in some way to a woman's physical anatomy, while the male words (except for *sideburns* after General Burnsides) have nothing to do with the namesake's body.

This reminded me of an earlier observation that my husband and I made about geographical names. A few years ago we became interested in what we called "Topless Topography" when we learned that the Grand Tetons used to be simply called *The Tetons* by French explorers and *The Teats* by American frontiersmen. We wrote letters to several map makers and found the following listings: *Nippletop* and *Little Nipple Top* near Mt. Marcy in the Adirondacks, *Nipple Mountain* in Archuleta County, Colorado, *Nipple Peak* in Coke County, Texas, *Nipple Butte* in Pennington, South Dakota, *Squaw Peak* in Placer County, California (and many other places), *Maiden's Peak* and *Squaw Tit* (they're the same mountain) in the Cascade Range in Oregon, *Jane Russell Peaks* near Stark, New Hampshire, and *Mary's Nipple* near Salt Lake City, Utah.

We might compare these names to Jackson Hole, Wyoming, or Pikes Peak, Colorado. I'm sure we would get all kinds of protests from the Jackson and Pike descendants if we tried to say that these topographical features were named because they in some way resembled the bodies of Jackon and Pike, respectively.

This preoccupation with women's breasts is neither new nor strictly American. I was amused to read the derivation of the word *Amazon.* According to Greek folk etymology, the *a* means "without" as in *atypical* or *amoral* while *mazon* comes from *mazōs* meaning "breast." According to the legend, these women cut off one breast so that they could better shoot their bows. Perhaps the feeling was that the women had to trade in part of their femininity in exchange for their active or masculine role.

There are certain pairs of words which illustrate the way in which sexual connotations are given to feminine words while the masculine words retain a serious, businesslike aura. For example, being a *callboy* is perfectly respectable. It simply refers to a person who calls actors when is time for them to go on stage, but being a *call girl* is being a prostitute.

Also we might compare *sir* and *madam*. *Sir* is a term of respect while *madam* has acquired the meaning of a brothel manager. The same thing has happened to the formerly cognate terms, *master* and *mistress*. Because of its acquired sexual connotations, *mistress* is now carefully avoided in certain contexts. For example, the Boy Scouts have *scoutmasters* but certainly not *scoutmistresses*. And in a dog show the female owner of a dog is never referred to as the *dog's mistress*, but rather as the *dog's master*.

Master appears in such terms as *master plan, concert master, schoolmaster, mixmaster, master charge, master craftsman*, etc. But *mistress* appears in very few compounds. This is the way it is with dozens of words which have male and female counterparts. I found two hundred such terms, e.g., *usher–usherette, heir–heiress, hero–heroine*, etc. In nearly all cases it is the masculine word which is the base with a feminine suffix being added for the alternate version. The masculine word also travels into compounds while the feminine word is a dead end; e.g., from *king–queen* comes *kingdom* but not *queendom*, from *sportsman–sportslady* comes *sportsmanship* but not *sportsladyship*, etc. There is one —and only one—semantic area in which the masculine word is not the base or more powerful word. This is in the area dealing with sex and marriage. Here it is the feminine word which is dominant. *Prostitute* is the base word with *male prostitute* being the derived term. *Bride* appears in *bridal shower, bridal gown, bridal attendant, bridesmaid*, and even in *bridegroom*, while *groom* in the sense of *bridegroom* does not appear in any compounds, not even to name the groom's attendants or his prenuptial party.

At the end of a marriage, this same emphasis is on the female. If it ends in divorce, the woman gets the title of *divorcée* while the man is usually described with a statement, such as, "He's divorced." When the marriage ends in death, the woman is a *widow* and the *-er* suffix which seems to connote masculine (probably because it is an agentive or actor type suffix) is added to make *widower*. *Widower* doesn't appear in any compounds (except for *grass widower*, which is another companion term), but *widow* appears in several compounds and in addition has some acquired meanings, such as the extra hand dealt to the table in certain card games and an undesirable leftover line of type in printing.

If I were an anthropological linguist making observations about a strange and primitive tribe, I would duly note on my tape recorder that I had found linguistic evidence to show that in the area of sex and marriage the female appears to be more important than the male, but in all other areas of the culture, it seems that the reverse is true.

But since I am not an anthropological linguist, I will simply go on to my second observation, which is that women are expected to play a passive role while men play an active one.

One indication of women's passive role is the fact that they are often identified as something to eat. What's more passive than a plate of food? Last spring I saw an announcement advertising the Indiana University English Department picnic. It read "Good Food! Delicious Women!" The publicity committee was probably jumped on by local feminists, but it's nothing new to look on women as "delectable morsels." Even women compliment each other with "You look good enough to eat," or "You have a peaches and cream complexion." Modern slang constantly comes up with new terms, but some of the old standbys for women are: cute tomato, dish, peach, sharp cookie, cheese cake, honey, sugar, and sweetie-pie. A man may occasionally be addressed as honey or described as a hunk of meat, but certainly men are not laid out on a buffet and labeled as women are.

Women's passivity is also shown in the comparisons made to plants. For example, to deflower a woman is to take away her virginity. A girl can be described as a clinging vine, a shrinking violet, or a wall flower. On the other hand, men are too active to be thought of as plants. The only time we make the comparison is when insulting a man we say he is like a woman by calling him a pansy.

We also see the active-passive contrast in the animal terms used with males and females. Men are referred to as studs, bucks, and wolves, and they go tomcatting around. These are all aggressive roles, but women have such pet names as kitten, bunny, beaver, bird, chick, lamb, and fox. The idea of being a pet seems much more closely related to females than to males. For instance, little girls grow up wearing pigtails and ponytails and they dress in halters and dog collars.

The active-passive contrast is also seen in the proper names given to boy babies and girl babies. Girls are much more likely to be given names lke Ivy, Rose, Ruby, Jewel, Pearl, Flora, Joy, etc., while boys are given names describing active roles such as Martin (warlike), Leo (lion), William (protector), Ernest (resolute fighter), and so on.

Another way that women play a passive role is that they are defined in relationship to someone else. This is what feminists are protesting when they ask to be identified as Ms. rather than as Mrs. or Miss. It is a constant source of irritation to women's organizations that when they turn in items to newspapers under their own names, that is, Susan Glascoe, Jeanette Jones, and so forth, the editors consistently rewrite the item so that the names read Mrs. John Glascoe, Mrs. Robert E. Jones.

In the dictionary I found what appears to be an attitude on the part of editors that it is almost indecent to let a respectable woman's name march unaccompanied across the pages of a dictionary. A woman's name must somehow be escorted by a male's name regardless of whether or not the male contributed to the woman's reason for being in the dictionary, or in his own right, was as famous as the woman. For example, Charlotte Brontë is identified as Mrs. Arthur B. Nicholls, Amelia Earhart is identified as Mrs. George Palmer Putnam, Helen Hayes is identified as Mrs. Charles MacArthur, Zona Gale is identified as Mrs. William Llwelyn Breese, and Jenny Lind is identified as Mme. Otto Goldschmidt.

Although most of the women are identified as Mrs. ———— or as the wife of ————, other women are listed with brothers, fathers, or lovers. Cornelia Otis Skinner is identified as the daughter of Otis, Harriet Beecher Stowe is identified as the sister of Henry Ward Beecher, Edith Sitwell is identified as the sister of Osbert and Sacheverell, Nell Gwyn is identified as the mistress of Charles II, and Madame Pompadour is identified as the mistress of Louis XV.

The women who did get into the dictionary without the benefit of a masculine escort are a group sort of on the fringes of respectability. They are the rebels and the crusaders: temperance leaders Frances Elizabeth Caroline Willard and Carry Nation, women's rights leaders Carrie Chapman Catt and Elizabeth Cady Stanton, birth control educator Margaret Sanger, religious leader Mary Baker Eddy, and slaves Harriet Tubman and Phillis Wheatley.

I would estimate that far more than fifty percent of the women listed in the dictionary were identified as someone's wife. But of all the men—and there are probably ten times as many men as women—only one was identified as "the husband of . . . ." This was the unusual case of Frederic Joliot who took the last name of Joliot-Curie and was identified as "husband of Irene." Apparently Irene, the daughter of Pierre and Marie Curie, did not want to give up her maiden name when she married and so the couple took the hyphenated last name.

There are several pairs of words which also illustrate the more powerful role of the male and the relational role of the female. For example a *count* is a high political officer with a *countess* being simply the wife of a count. The same is true for a *duke* and a *duchess* and a *king* and a *queen*. The fact that a king is usually more powerful than a queen might be the reason that Queen Elizabeth's husband is given the title of *prince* rather than *king*. Since *king* is a stronger word than *queen*, it is reserved for a true heir to the throne because if it were given to someone coming into the royal family by marriage, then the subjects might forget where the true power lies. With the weaker word of *queen*, this would not be a problem; so a woman marrying a ruling monarch is given the title without question.

My third observation is that there are many positive connotations connected with the concept of masculine, while there are either trivial or negative connotations connected with the corresponding feminine concept.

Conditioning toward the superiority of the masculine role starts very early in life. Child psychologists point out that the only area in which a girl has more freedom than a boy is in experimenting with an appropriate sex role. She is much freer to be a *tomboy* than is her brother to be a *sissy*. The proper names given to children reflect this same attitude. It's perfectly all right for a girl to have a boy's name, but not the other way around. As girls are given more and more of the boys' names, parents shy away from using boy names that might be mistaken for girl names, so the number of available masculine names is constantly shrinking. Fifty years ago *Hazel, Beverly, Marion, Frances,* and *Shirley* were all perfectly acceptable boys' names. Today few parents give these names to baby boys and adult men who are stuck with them self-consciously go by their initials or by abbreviated forms such as *Haze* or *Shirl.* But parents of little girls keep crowding the masculine set and currently popular girls' names include *Jo, Kelly, Teri, Cris, Pat, Shawn, Toni,* and *Sam.*

When the mother of one of these little girls tells her to *be a lady,* she means for her to sit with her knees together. But when the father of a little boy tells him to *be a man,* he means for him to be noble, strong, and virtuous. The whole concept of manliness has such positive connotations that it is a compliment to call a male a *he-man,* a *manly man,* or a *virile man* (*virile* comes from the Indo–European *vir,* meaning "man"). In each of these three terms, we are implying that someone is doubly good because he is doubly a man.

Compare *chef* with *cook, tailor* and *seamstress,* and *poet* with *poetess.* In each case, the masculine form carries with it an added degree of excellence. In comparing the masculine *governor* with the feminine *governess* and the masculine *major* with the feminine *majorette,* the added feature is power.

The difference between positive male and negative female connotations can be seen in several pairs of words which differ denotatively only in the matter of sex. For instance compare *bachelor* with the terms *spinster* and *old maid. Bachelor* has such positive connotations that modern girls have tried to borrow the feeling in the term *bachelor-girl. Bachelor* appears in glamorous terms such as *bachelor pad, bachelor party,* and *bachelor button.* But *old maid* has such strong negative feelings that it has been adopted into other areas, taking with it the feeling of undesirability. It has the metaphorical meaning of shriveled and unwanted kernels of pop corn, and it's the name of the last unwanted card in a popular game for children.

Patron and *matron* (Middle English for *father* and *mother*) are another set where women have tried to borrow the positive masculine connotations, this time through the word *patroness,* which literally means "female father." Such a peculiar term came about because of the high prestige attached to the word *patron* in such phrases as *"a patron of the arts"* or *"a patron saint."* *Matron* is more apt to be used in talking about a woman who is in charge of a jail or a public restroom.

Even *lord* and *lady* have different levels of connotation. *Our Lord* is used as a title for deity, while the corresponding *Our Lady* is a relational title for Mary, the moral mother of Jesus. *Landlord* has more dignity than *landlady* probably because the landlord is more likely to be thought of as the owner while the landlady is the person who collects the rent and enforces the rules. *Lady* is used in many insignificant places where the corresponding *lord* would never be used, for example, *ladies room, ladies sizes, ladies aid society, ladybug,* etc.

This overuse of *lady* might be compared to the overuse of *queen* which is rapidly losing its prestige as compared to *king.* Hundreds of beauty queens are crowned each year and nearly every community in the United States has its *Dairy Queen* or its *Freezer Queen,* etc. Male homosexuals have adopted the term to identify the "feminine" partner. And advertisers who are constantly on the lookout for euphemisms to make unpleasant sounding products salable have recently dealt what might be a death blow to the prestige of the word *queen.* They have begun to use it as an indication of size. For example, *queen-size* panty hose are panty hose for fat women. The meaning comes through a comparison with *king-size,* meaning big. However, there's a subtle difference in that our culture considers it desirable for males to be big because size is an indication of power, but we prefer that females be small and petite. So using *king-size* as a term to indicate bigness partially enhances the prestige of *king,* but using *queen-size* to indicate bigness brings unpleasant associations to the word *queen.*

Another set that might be compared are *brave* and *squaw.* The word *brave* carries with it the connotations of youth, vigor, and courage, while *squaw* implies almost opposite characteristics. With the set *wizard* and *witch,* the main difference is that *wizard* implies skill and wisdom combined with magic, while *witch* implies evil intentions combined with magic. Part of the unattractiveness of both *squaw* and *witch* is that they suggest old age, which in women is particularly undesirable. When I lived in Afghanistan (1967–1969), I was horrified to hear a proverb stating that when you see an old man you should sit down and take a lesson, but when you see an old woman you should throw a stone. I was equally startled when I went to compare the connotations of our two phrases *grandfatherly advice* and *old wives' tales*. Certainly it isn't expressed with the same force as in the Afghan proverb, but the implication is similar.

In some of the animal terms used for women the extreme undesirability of female old age is also seen. For instance consider the unattractiveness of *old nag* as compared to *filly*, of *old crow* or *old bat* as compared to *bird*, and of being *catty* as compared to being *kittenish*. The chicken metaphor tells the whole story of a girl's life. In her youth she is a *chick*, then she marries and begins feeling *cooped up*, so she goes to *hen parties* where she *cackles* with her friends. Then she has her *brood* and begins to *henpeck* her husband. Finally she turns into *an old biddy*.

FOR DISCUSSION AND REVIEW

1 Most dictionary makers try to describe accurately the way the English language is used. Can we, therefore, reasonably fault them for reflecting cultural attitudes in word definitions?

2 Nilsen provides us with an extensive catalog of words that reveal a disparaging attitude toward women. It is not her purpose, however, to offer any solutions to the problem of bias in the language. What possible improvements can you as a user of the language, lexicographers as makers of dictionaries, and women and men as leaders of the equal rights movement bring about?

3 Discuss the attempts to change social attitudes through language change (e.g., the use of *black* for *Negro*, *salesperson* for *salesman*, *genkind* for *mankind*, *otto-it* for *ottoman*, *herstory* for *history*, and *Ms.* as a title for a woman). In addition to substituting one word for another, attempts at change can be brought about by avoiding certain kinds of constructions such as the use of *his* to refer to individuals of both sexes. (Will everyone please take *his* seat? Each of the legislators voted *his* conscience.)

4 Like any attempt to change the status quo, women's attempts to change language have aroused a great deal of opposition. To what is this opposition reacting? Does the opposition seem justified? What techniques does the opposition employ?

5 According to Nilsen, in what two areas does the English language reveal the importance of women? Women are now playing new roles in American society; discuss any language changes that may result from such social changes.

3

The Trouble with Usage

Thomas J. Creswell

In the following essay, Professor Thomas J. Creswell of Chicago State University analyzes what the term *usage* means today. Of particular interest is his discussion of the concept of correctness, why such a concept is considered so important, and how all determinations of usage have been and continue to be based almost exclusively on opinions rather than on objective data. After examining more closely the principles on which the compilers of leading dictionaries and usage guides have based their conclusions regarding usage, Professor Creswell calls for a long-overdue investigation of the way our language is actually used. Only in this way, he believes, can language experts make useful statements regarding usage.

> usage . . . the way in which words and phrases are actually used (as in a particular form or sense) in a language community. —*Webster's New Collegiate Dictionary*

MANY Americans have a sense of insecurity about their use of their own language. They worry that what they say or write may be incorrect, or they believe that they regularly use "bad" English. The source of this insecurity is a belief about the nature of the English language which is tenaciously and widely held despite its inaccuracy. Simply stated, this belief is that in English any word or expression is either right or it is wrong, that there is a single, unvarying, absolute standard of correctness, and that whatever expression does not conform to that standard is wrong.

Questions of right and wrong in the use of a language by those who are native speakers and writers of that language are properly regarded as questions of usage. The study of English usage is the study of the way those who speak and write English use their language. To put it another way, English usage is concerned with the choices they make from among the many alternative ways of expression made available by the grammar and the vocabulary of English.

Although it has long been known that the observation of usage—the actual use of a language by those who speak and write it—is the *only* way of accurately determining what is "correct" in a given set of circumstances, many persist in believing otherwise. Often this other belief is not even consciously held, but it lurks somewhere in the subconscious, and it distorts the holder's view of linguistic reality. The belief is sly and subtle, tough and unyielding. Perhaps it persists because it seems to offer promise of a world more easily managed than the real world in which we live—a promise of a world with only "right" and "wrong" answers, a world with no conditional answers, no "maybe," no "possibly." Whatever the reasons, the belief persists. The belief is that there is an absolute standard of correctness in English.

Here are some sentences containing expressions sometimes condemned as bad or incorrect English.

1. It's me.
2. Between the four of us we had ten dollars.
3. Who did you see?
4. The book was rather unique.
5. I will try and find it for you.

Alternative ways of conveying the messages of sentences 1 through 5 are considered by some as the only correct ways.

1a. It's I.
2a. Among the four of us we had ten dollars.
3a. Whom did you see?
4a. The book was rather unusual.
5a. I will try to find it for you.

To believe that only the expressions in the second group, 1a through 5a, are correct is to ignore several facts of English usage. One fact is that versions 1 through 5, the so-called bad or incorrect versions, occur at least as frequently as their "correct" counterparts in all varieties of English speech—the speech of the educated and the uneducated, the speech of the prestigious and the nonprestigious. Another fact is that several of the "incorrect" versions also occur quite frequently in a number of kinds of edited, written, standard English. To ignore both their frequency of occurrence and the fact that they occur in various mediums and styles of language is to obscure a central fact about English usage.

There is no one right way. The terms *correct* and *incorrect* are not only inaccurate in characterizing such expressions, they are misleading, and it is the careless use of such terms, and the inaccurate view of the nature of English upon which arey are based, which contribute much to feelings of insecurity about language.

The wide use of such terms as *correct* and *incorrect* in discussing alternative forms of expression can only be accounted for by understanding the assumptions about the nature of English which underlie that use. Such assumptions are often offered as "reasons" for labeling certain expressions incorrect. One of the most common reasons offered for condemning an expression is that it is ungrammatical. Let us examine that reason.

If the term *ungrammatical* means anything, it must mean that the expression in question does not conform to the rules of the grammar of English. The belief that expressions which occur frequently in American speech or writing are ungrammatical is not consistent with the real nature of English grammar. The grammar of English, simply defined, is the system of devices and processes by which small units of meaning—words—are combined to make larger units—phrases and clauses. Even the most casual examination reveals that the grammar of English, in combination with the vocabulary of English, provides more than one way of expressing any meaning or message.

An event occurred some years ago which demonstrates both a failure to understand this flexibility in English grammar and the resulting tendency to draw unrealistic conclusions about an English sentence. The manufacturers of Winston cigarettes launched an advertising campaign centering upon the slogan, "Winston tastes good like a cigarette should." The uproar and indignation over the choice of slogan has still not completely subsided in some circles. Numerous "experts" and "authorities" on English heaped scorn on the sponsor and the advertising agency on the grounds that the slogan is ungrammatical. *Like*, they said, is a preposition, not a conjunction, and the construction of the slogan demands a conjunction. They insisted that only *as* would be grammatically correct in that construction.

What the experts were ignoring is the fact that the grammar of English has long made possible the use of *like* as a conjunction in such sentences. Shakespeare, for instance, used it, and in many varieties of the speech and writing of contemporary Americans, both educated and uneducated, it is so used with great frequency. It occurs rarely in highly formal varieties of writing, but it is *not*, in any reasonable sense of the word, ungrammatical. The tobacco company subsequently took advantage of the uproar and resultant publicity—like a smart advertiser should —and launched a follow-up campaign with the slogan, "What do you want, good grammar or good taste?"

The real grammatical question underlying the *like* vs. *as* controversy is whether it is possible for an English word to function as more than one part of speech. The answer is obviously that it *is* possible. Not only is it possible for words to function as more than one part of speech, it is commonplace for them to do so. *Run,* for instance, an old and common English word, is listed in *Webster's New Collegiate Dictionary* (1973) with forty-six meanings as an intransitive verb, thirty-four meanings as a transitive verb, thirty-eight as a noun, and four as an adjective. It is not the large number of different meanings that is relevant here, but the fact that the word functions as noun, adjective, and both transitive and intransitive verb. This ability of English words to function as several different parts of speech is known as functional shift. Functional shift is one of the facts of English grammar. Far from being rare, such shifts are commonplace. Most pages in an English dictionary will contain at least one example of a word which has undergone functional shift.

The notion that "bad" or "incorrect" expressions are ungrammatical will not stand up under examination. All such "errors" actually represent the functioning of options or alternatives provided by English grammar. The real error is to believe that when the grammar offers alternative modes of expression one of them is always correct and the other always incorrect.

Instead of being called ungrammatical, sometimes so-called incorrect expressions are referred to as being illogical. The "correct" forms in English, it is held, are logical, precise, and clear, while the "incorrect" forms are illogical, fuzzy, and unclear. This belief is often offered, for instance, to support the condemnation of double negatives. "I don't want none," is said to be illogical or unclear because two negatives make a positive—a statement which, even though it is true in handling the signs in algebraic multiplication, is not and has never been true in English. In English, double and even multiple negation is a well-established grammatical option. Double and multiple negatives occur in the earliest written English. One example often cited occurs in Geoffrey Chaucer's lines describing the Knight in *The Canterbury Tales:*

> He never yet no vileneye ne sayde
> In al his lyf unto no maner wight.

Transposed nearly word for word into modern English, these lines would read:

> He never yet no villainy [insults] not said
> In all his life unto no kind of man.

As can be seen, this single sentence contains four negatives. The use of multiple negatives in written English declined after Shakespeare's time, but it has never disappeared from the speech of the people. The use of double negatives is not illogical or unclear; it is simply unfashionable in certain varieties of English under certain circumstances. A study of actual usage can reveal which varieties and under what circumstances.

In addition to the beliefs that some "incorrect" English expressions are ungrammatical and that some are illogical, a third belief persists that certain English words have, or should have, absolute, unchanging meanings, and that to use those words in other senses is incorrect or bad English. Often it is argued in support of this belief that, if the words in question come to be used in other senses, somehow the English language will be weakened. Some self-appointed experts on language even contend that such weakening will lead to the early death of the language and that English will cease to be capable of producing literature or even of producing clear, unambiguous statements. This belief in the immutability of word meaning, like the others discussed here, persists in the face of much easily available evidence to the contrary.

We have already noted that *run*, for instance, is defined by a desk dictionary in 122 different meanings. On any page in any dictionary can be found words which have more than one meaning, and in any dictionary can be found word meanings labeled *obsolete*, indicating that the words in question are no longer used in the senses listed, or *archaic*, indicating that the senses are rarely so used nowadays. Every time a dictionary which bases its labels on actual observation of current practice in the use of English lists more than one meaning for a word, it provides evidence of the fact that *all* words are capable of changing their meanings. Every time such a dictionary labels a word sense as obsolete or archaic, it provides evidence that words sometimes lose meanings they once had.

Those who hold that such changes in meaning somehow make English weaker or poorer often point to the word *disinterested*. *Disinterested*, they say, means only "impartial" or "neutral"; *uninterested* means "unconcerned" or "apathetic." To use *disinterested* to mean "unconcerned" or "apathetic" as in "The teacher was totally disinterested in the children's behavior," is an error which, if persisted in, they claim, will lead to the loss of our ability to express the idea "impartial" or "neutral" in English. Even if *disinterested* were never again used in what is called its correct sense, English would in no way suffer. We still have such words as *objective, impartial, unprejudiced, neutral, unbiased, dispassionate, detached, impersonal, unopinionated, nonpartisan, open-minded*, and such phrases as *with open mind, without self interest*, and many others—all of which express with many shades of meaning the sense which some claim will be lost if *disinterested* is used to mean "unconcerned."

A study of English usage reveals that words *do* change in meaning, that they *can* cease to be used in a sense in which they have long been used, that such changes *do not* weaken the language or push it to the brink of death.

Thus far, in attempting to account for the sense of insecurity and inadequacy which many Americans have about their use of English, we have examined a central belief held, in one form or another, by many—the belief in an absolute standard of correctness. And we have examined and rejected three of the assumptions or convictions about English frequently offered to support that belief: 1) that the correct form is grammatical and the incorrect form ungrammatical; 2) that the correct form is logical and the other illogical; and 3) that certain words have fixed, permanent meanings and that to use them in other senses is to weaken English and cause its death.

The resolution of this problem seems simple. What we must do to eliminate this sense of insecurity is to discard the erroneous belief about absolute correctness, refuse to accept the "reasons" which on inspection are found incapable of accounting for the preference of one alternative over another, and turn to the study of actual English usage. We will ask the usage experts to give us the truth about how English is used. Unfortunately, that won't work. With only a few exceptions, most contemporary widely read works by usage experts are not reliable sources of accurate, up-to-date information about English usage, and many who are called usage experts hold the very views which we have just examined and rejected.

Much of what is published as usage information today is based on opinions of what English does or should do rather than on careful, detailed observations of what it actually does. The opinions—often dignified as judgments—are those of people designated by themselves or others as authorities on English usage. A recent usage guide, for instance, *The Harper Dictionary of Contemporary Usage* (1975), reports in its cover copy, "Questionnaires on contemporary usage have been answered by 136 prominent writers, editors, public speakers, educators, and commentators. The opinions of these well-known panelists on scores of the knottiest problems of disputed usage are expressed."

Some usage guides and some general purpose dictionaries which make a point of including a larger than normal amount of what they call "authoritative" information about usage also proclaim that the information they provide is based on the opinion or judgment of experts. Occasionally, an effort is made to make opinion appear to be something else. Theodore M. Bernstein, a former member of the editorial staff of *The New York Times*, member of the usage panel of *The American Heritage Dictionary*, advisor on usage to the *Random House Dictionary of the English Language*, and writer of a number of articles and books on usage, lists the sources of his statements about usage on p. viii of his usage guide, *The Careful Writer:*

> The guides to good usage presented in this book arise from six sources:
>   First, the practices of reputable writers, past and present.
>   Second, the observations and discoveries of linguistic scholars. The work of past scholars has, *when necessary* [italics here and following in this passage added], been updated. The work of contemporary scholars has been *weighed judiciously.*
>   Third, the predilections of teachers of English—whenever—*right or wrong, like it or not*—these predilections have become deeply ingrained in the language itself.
>   Fourth, *observation* of what makes for clarity, precision, and logical presentation . . .
>   Fifth, *personal preferences of the author*—and why not? . . . After all, it's my book.
>   Sixth, *experience* in the *critical* examination of the written word as an editor of *The New York Times* . . .

The underlined phrases in all but the first cited source of information indicate that, in a real sense, all but that first source are the same source —Bernstein's opinion. The "updating" and "judicious weighing" of the work of scholars, the selective acceptance of school grammar "rules," the observation, the personal preferences, and the experience—all are of or by Bernstein. As for the first source he lists—the practices of reputable writers, past and present—the samples of writing used in his work as examples are almost exclusively the work of *New York Times* reporters and writers, and those samples are almost always quoted as samples of "bad" or "incorrect" writing. Assuming that *New York Times* writers are reputable writers of the present, even in the face of their treatment by the author, that leaves us totally in the dark as to which writers of the past survive in Bernstein's memory and which rate his good opinion as reputable. What all this means is that Bernstein's six sources, upon examination, turn out to be one source—Bernstein's opinion.

But what is wrong with accepting as an accurate description of current practice in American English opinions expressed by a literate, experienced, thoughtful observer of language such as Bernstein? What is wrong is that opinion, no matter whose opinion nor how carefully expressed, is not a reliable guide to usage, and it never has been. To see why, let us look at two characteristics of opinion as a source of information about language. First, opinion is often conservative, valuing the practices of the past and rejecting change in those practices. Second, opinion is inherently unreliable.

Opinion about language and usage is usually behind the times; it is more conservative than language itself. Language changes constantly and easily; opinion, once formed, only with difficulty. Opinion often condemns or rejects an expression which has only recently come into use. Perhaps the clearest revelation of the power and obduracy with which firmly formed opinion resists change was made by Richard Grant White, an American usage expert, who wrote in *Words and Their Uses* published in the latter part of the nineteenth century, "authority of general usage, or even of the usage of great writers, is no absolute in language. There is a misuse of words which can be justified by no authority, however great, and by no usage, however general."

White's statement can only be taken to mean that, no matter what the language does, no matter what actual practice is, no matter what great writers use in their writing, if a usage expert says that an expression is wrong, then it is wrong. That this view of the source of information about usage has not died out is made clear by the following statement in Wilson Follett's *Modern American Usage* (1966): "good usage is what people who care and think about words believe good usage to be." History does not support such a view. The essential conservatism, and hence inaccuracy, of opinion has often been demonstrated by changes in the language. Many words or expressions once strongly objected to by experts have become fully accepted as standard English, but the opinions hold on doggedly. Despite nearly two centuries of schoolbook and expert insistence on a regular alternation between *shall* and *will* as future tense auxiliaries, *will* has come to be almost exclusively used in modern American English.

A most convincing demonstration of the essential conservatism of opinion was provided by the publication in 1932 of a large-scale opinion survey, *Current English Usage*, by Sterling Andrus Leonard, and, in 1938, of a follow-up study by Albert H. Marckwardt and Fred Walcott. Having collected opinions from several hundred "experts"—authors, editors, educators, and others—on some 230 expressions which were deemed controversial at the time, Leonard set up three categories for reporting the status of each item. The 71 expressions approved of by at least 75 percent of the judges were rated *Established;* the largest group of items, 121, approved of by from 25 to 75 percent of the judges were rated *Disputable,* and 38 items approved of by fewer than 25 percent were rated *Illiterate.* Suspecting that the judges' evaluations were not a reliable guide to actual usage, Marckwardt and Walcott searched the *Oxford English Dictionary, Webster's New International Dictionary,* and other sources and found that, judging by the evidence of use provided by those sources, fifty of the items rated *Disputable* in Leonard's survey were in good use as literary English, an additional thirteen as American literary English, and forty-three items as colloquial English "found in spoken or informal rather than in formal written English."

Marckwardt and Walcott concluded, "A survey of fact rather than of opinion would, in all probability, have increased the number of established usages from seventy-one to 177." They found that, if actual use was examined rather than opinions about use, there were seven chances in eight that an item found *Disputable* in the Leonard survey was wholly current in standard English, hence, hardly disputable. Language, as this study demonstrates, is far more open to change than is opinion. Opinion persists even in the face of language change.

In addition to being essentially conservative and hence out-of-date, opinion about the use of language is intrinsically and inescapably unreliable. Experts disagree, and there is no easy way of determining, when they do, whose opinion is more consistent with the facts of language. That is to say, there is no way for the nonexpert to choose from among the opinions offered the one which he should follow. The results of this essential inadequacy of opinion as a guide to usage are clearly evident in the usage notes in two modern works which offer as usage information reports of the opinions of a panel of experts.

The American Heritage Dictionary (1969) contains about 225 usage notes in which a vote by a panel of some hundred "experts" is recorded. Votes are reported as percentages of the panel of experts approving or disapproving an item of usage. The expression *to try and find*, used earlier as an example of "incorrect" usage, is, in writing, "unacceptable to 79 percent of the Usage Panel." There is not one item in all 225 or so usage notes upon which the panel of experts is in unanimous agreement. Slightly more than half of the items are approved by 50 percent or more of the experts, the other half by less than 50 percent; a purely chance distribution of votes would yield similar results. What do such percentages mean? If, on a given item, the reader is told that 60 percent of the experts approve of its use, what is he to do with the opinions of the other 40 percent? Is a simple majority vote enough to establish an expression as good or bad English? There is really no way to satisfactorily answer this question. We could arbitrarily choose a figure and say, for instance, that if more than 75 percent of the experts disapprove of an item, then it is incorrect. But, as we have seen in discussing the Leonard survey, even that kind of arbitrary weighting of opinion does not hold up under further analysis. If we look at other works reporting the opinions of experts, we find that the percentages of experts approving or disapproving a given item often do not remain stable.

The Harper Dictionary of Contemporary Usage employs a usage panel of 136 experts—25 of them persons who also served on the American Heritage usage panel. By chance, apparently, for, as far as can be seen, there is no principle underlying the selection, the Harper panel casts votes on 60 items of usage upon which the American Heritage panel has also voted. On only one item do the two panels produce identical percentages of approval/disapproval—on the use of the word *enthuse*. Seventy-six percent of both panels disapprove of this word. On one item, the use of the word *bit* in the sense "role" as in "He's doing the intellectual bit now," the panels disagree by 53 percent; 13 percent of the American Heritage panel find this usage acceptable, 66 percent of the Harper panel. On the remaining 58 items, the amount of disagreement ranges from 5 percent or less on 19 items (one-third of the total) to from 20 to 50 percent disagreement on 14 items (one-fourth of the total).

What does this disagreement both within each panel of experts and between the two panels mean? An accurate statement of the status in contemporary English of a questioned item of usage cannot be arrived at by examining the reports of votes by experts. They disagree among themselves, and there is no knowing which opinions, if any, represent an accurate description of actual practice in English. Such disagreement leads inescapably to the conclusion that *all* opinion is unreliable.

This brief survey of the trouble with usage by no means says all that needs to be said nor explains all that needs to be explained. Perhaps linguistic insecurity can never be eliminated, or even diminished. But we will never know whether it can until we abandon both misconceptions about the nature or "correctness" in English and the practice of accepting as information about usage the opinions of "experts." What are needed instead of opinions about how English works, or ought to work, are objective, unbiased, accurate descriptions of how it *does* work.

Such descriptions can be produced only by collecting large samples of actual contemporary language, studying those samples, and reporting what does, in fact, occur in them. If, for instance, it is asserted or believed that it is not "correct" to use the word *anticipate* to mean "expect" as in "I anticipate a visit from my sister," only the study of a large sample of written or spoken language can demonstrate incontrovertibly whether, and to what extent, and under what circumstances *anticipate* is used in that sense. If it is so used, then usage supports the use and there is no question as to its appropriateness.

There are problems in collecting such samples, and additional problems in reaching agreement upon which kinds of written or spoken English represent "standard" English. But the problems are not insoluble. Such procedures represent the *only* way of producing accurate, reliable, verifiable statements of what is "good" or "correct" practice.

FOR DISCUSSION AND REVIEW

1 What is the significance of the definition of usage that Creswell quotes at the beginning of his essay?

2 What are three assumptions about English frequently offered to support a belief in an absolute stan-

dard of correctness? Why does Creswell reject each assumption?

3 "Even the most casual examination reveals that the grammar of English, in combination with the vocabulary of English, provides more than one way of expressing any meaning or message." To test this statement, write at least twelve alternative forms for the following sentence: One cannot build a wall without bricks and mortar.

4 Creswell discusses in some detail the famous Winston advertising slo-

gan: "Winston tastes good like a cigarette should." Recently Winston began using a new slogan: "If it wasn't for Winston, I wouldn't smoke cigarettes." What do you find interesting about this new slogan?

5 Why does Creswell question opinion as a source of information about language?

6 Is Creswell in the final analysis advocating an "anything goes" position about usage? Explain.

4

Time Magazine

The Euphemism:

Many Americans feel that nothing is taboo anymore—that anything that can be imagined can be said or printed. The editors of *Time*, however, make clear in this essay that the euphemism is alive and well in America precisely because people often do not want to "tell it like it is." The euphemisms themselves and the aspects of life to which they are applied may change, but the euphemism as a linguistic phenomenon shows no signs of disappearing.

Telling It Like It Isn't

MODERN AMERICAN speech, while not always clear or correct or turned with much style, is supposed to be uncommonly frank. Witness the current explosion of four-letter words and the explicit discussion of sexual topics. In fact, gobbledygook and nice-Nellyism still extend as far as the ear can hear. Housewives on television may chat about their sex lives in terms that a decade ago would have made gynecologists blush; more often than not, these emancipated women still speak about their children's "going to the potty." Government spokesmen talk about "redeployment" of American troops; they mean withdrawal. When sociologists refer to blacks living in slums, they are likely to mumble about "nonwhites" in a "culturally deprived environment." The CIA may never have used the expression "to terminate with extreme prejudice" when it wanted a spy rubbed out. But in the context of a war in which "pacification of the enemy infrastructure" is the military mode of reference to blasting the Viet Cong out of a village, the phrase sounded so plausible that millions readily accepted it as accurate.

The image of a generation blessed with a swinging, liberated language is largely an illusion. Despite its swaggering sexual candor, much contemporary speech still hides behind that traditional enemy of plain talk, the euphemism.

From a Greek word meaning "to use words of good omen," euphemism is the substitution of a pleasant term for a blunt one—telling it like it isn't. Euphemism has probably existed since the beginning of language. As long as there have been things of which men thought the less said the better, there have been better ways of saying less. In everyday conversation the euphemism is, at worst, a necessary evil; at its best, it is a handy verbal tool to avoid making enemies needlessly, or shocking friends. Language purists and the blunt-spoken may wince when a young woman at a party coyly asks for direction to "the powder room," but to most people this kind of familiar euphemism is probably no more harmful or annoying than, say, a split infinitive.

On a larger scale, though, the persistent growth of euphemism in a language represents a danger to thought and action, since its fundamental intent is to deceive. As Linguist Benjamin Lee Whorf has pointed out, the structure of a given language determines, in part, how the society that speaks it views reality. If "substandard housing" makes rotting slums appear more livable or inevitable to some people, then their view of American cities has been distorted and their ability to assess the significance of poverty has been reduced. Perhaps the most chilling example of euphemism's destructive power took place in Hitler's Germany. The wholesale corruption of the language under Nazism, notes Critic George Steiner, is symbolized by the phrase *endgültige Lösung* (final solution), which "came to signify the death of 6,000,000 human beings in gas ovens."

No one could argue that American English is under siege from linguistic falsehood, but euphemisms today have the nagging persistence of a headache. Despite the increasing use of nudity and sexual innuendo in advertising, Madison Avenue is still the great exponent of talking to "the average person of good upbringing"—as one TV executive has euphemistically described the ordinary American—in ways that won't offend him. Although this is like fooling half the people none of the time, it has produced a handsome bouquet of roses by other names. Thus there is "facial-quality tissue" that is not intended for use on faces, and "rinses" or "tints" for women who might be unsettled to think they dye their hair. In the world of deodorants, people never sweat or smell; they simply "offend." False teeth sound truer when known as "dentures."

Ad men and packagers, of course, are not the only euphemizers. Almost any way of earning a salary above the level of ditchdigging is known as a profession rather than a job. Janitors for several years have been elevated by image-conscious unions to the status of "custodians"; nowadays, a teen-age rock guitarist with three chords to his credit can class himself with Horowitz as a "recording artist." Cadillac dealers refer to autos as "preowned" rather than "secondhand." Government researchers concerned with old people call them "senior citizens." Ads for bank credit cards and department stores refer to "convenient terms"

—meaning 18% annual interest rates payable at the convenience of the creditor.

Jargon, the sublanguage peculiar to any trade, contributes to euphemism when its terms seep into general use. The student New Left, which shares a taste for six-syllable words with government bureaucracy, has concocted a collection of substitute terms for use in politics. To "liberate," in the context of campus uproars, means to capture and occupy. Four people in agreement form a "coalition." In addition to "participatory democracy," which in practice is often a description of anarchy, the university radicals have half seriously given the world "anticipatory communism," which means to steal. The New Left, though, still has a long way to go before it can equal the euphemism-creating ability of government officials. Who else but a Washington economist would invent the phrase "negative saver" to describe someone who spends more money than he makes?

A persistent source of modern euphemisms is the feeling, inspired by the prestige of science, that certain words contain implicit subjective judgments, and thus ought to be replaced with more "objective" terms. To speak of "morals" sounds both superior and arbitrary, as though the speaker were indirectly questioning those of the listener. By substituting "values," the concept is miraculously turned into a condition, like humidity or mass, that can be safely measured from a distance. To call someone "poor," in the modern way of thinking, is to speak pejoratively of his condition, while the substitution of "disadvantaged" or "underprivileged," indicates that poverty wasn't his fault. Indeed, says Linguist Mario Pei, by using "underprivileged," we are "made to feel that it is all our fault." The modern reluctance to judge makes it more offensive than ever before to call a man a liar; thus there is a "credibility gap" instead.

The liberalization of language in regard to sex involves the use of perhaps a dozen words. The fact of their currency in what was once known as polite conversation raises some unanswered linguistic questions. Which, really, is the rose, and which the other name? Are the old forbidden obscenities really the crude bedrock on which softer and shyer expressions have been built? Or are they simply coarser ways of expressing physical actions and parts of the human anatomy that are more accurately described in less explicit terms? It remains to be seen whether the so-called forbidden words will contribute anything to the honesty and openness of sexual discussion. Perhaps their real value lies in the power to shock, which is inevitably diminished by overexposure. Perhaps the Victorians, who preferred these words unspoken and unprinted, will prove to have had a point after all.

For all their prudery, the Victorians were considerably more willing than modern men to discuss ideas—such as social distinctions, morality and death—that have become almost unmentionable. Nineteenth-century gentlewomen whose daughters had "limbs" instead of suggestive "legs" did not find it necessary to call their maids "housekeepers," nor did they bridle at referring to "upper" or "lower" classes within society. Rightly or wrongly, the Victorian could talk without embarrassment about "sin," a word that today few but clerics use with frequency or ease. It is even becoming difficult to find a doctor, clergyman, or undertaker (known as a "mortician") who will admit that a man has died rather than "expired" or "passed away." Death has not lost its sting; the words for it have.

There is little if any hope that euphemisms will ever be excised from mankind's endless struggle with words that, as T. S. Eliot lamented, bend, break, and crack under pressure. For one thing, certain kinds of everyday euphemisms have proved their psychological necessity. The uncertain morale of an awkward teenager may be momentarily buoyed if he thinks of himself as being afflicted by facial "blemishes" rather than "pimples." The label "For motion discomfort" that airlines place on paper containers undoubtedly helps the squeamish passenger keep control of his stomach in bumpy weather better than if they were called "vomit bags." Other forms of self-deception may not be beneficial, but may still be emotionally necessary. A girl may tolerate herself more readily if she thinks of herself as a "swinger" rather than as "promiscuous." Voyeurs can salve their guilt feelings when they buy tickets for certain "adult entertainments" on the ground that they are implicitly supporting "freedom of artistic expression."

Lexicographer Bergen Evans of Northwestern University believes that euphemisms persist because "lying is an indispensable part of making life tolerable." It is virtuous, but a bit beside the point, to contend that lies are deplorable. So they are; but they cannot be moralized or legislated away, any more than euphemisms can be. Verbal miasma, when it deliberately obscures truth, is an offense to reason. But the inclination to speak of certain things in uncertain terms is a reminder that there will always be areas of life that humanity considers too private, or too close to feelings of guilt, to speak about directly. Like stammers or tears, euphemisms will be created whenever men doubt, or fear, or do not know. The instinct is not wholly unhealthy; there is a measure of wisdom in the familiar saying that a man who calls a spade a spade is fit only to use one.

FOR DISCUSSION AND REVIEW

1   People use euphemisms, defined by *Time* as "the substitution of a pleasant term for a blunt one," when they want to avoid talking directly about subjects that make them uncomfortable, although what makes

people uncomfortable changes. For example, we have been able to talk about "legs" and "breasts" for quite a while, and "venereal disease" for a shorter time; but many people still avoid the words "die" and "death." Identify some other subjects for which euphemisms are still prevalent and list several euphemisms for each. Do you use the same euphemisms as your parents? As your grandparents?

2   Explain how our tendency to confuse words and things (mentioned by Evans) can combine with our use of euphemisms and affect both our behavior and our opinion of our behavior. Consider, for example, the following expressions used during the Vietnam war:

refugee camp
air raid
defoliation
new life hamlet
limited duration protective reaction
    strike
resources control program

List other euphemisms used by government and big business. How do they attempt to influence behavior?

3   What does *Time* mean by the "psychological necessity" of euphemisms?

5

Word-Making:

Word formation is not a haphazard procedure but one which is for the most part patterned. In this excerpt from his book *The English Language: An Introduction*, Professor W. Nelson Francis discusses the major ways, in addition to borrowing from other languages, that words are created or acquired and become a part of the vocabulary of English.

Some Sources
of New Words

W. Nelson Francis

THOUGH BORROWING has been the most prolific source of additions to the vocabulary of English, we acquire or create new words in several other ways. Those which will be discussed here, in descending order of importance, are *derivation, compounding, functional shift, back formation* and *clipping, proper names, imitation, blending,* and *original coinage.*

1. *Derivation.* The derivational process consists of using an existing word—or in some cases a bound morpheme or morphemic structure— as a stem to which affixes are attached. Thus our imaginary word *pandle* might become the stem for such derivatives as *pandler, pandlette, depandle,* and *repandlize.* Affixes like these are called *productive;* all native speakers know their meanings and feel free to add them to various kinds of stems in accordance with analogy or the rules of

Editors' note: Francis earlier tells us: "The smallest meaningful units of language —those which cannot be subdivided into smaller meaningful units—are called *morphemes.* In combinations like *rooster, greenness, lucky, widen,* and *strongly,* all of which are made up of two morphemes, one morpheme carries the principal part of the meaning of the whole. This is called the *base* (or sometimes the *root*). The bases in the examples are *roost, green, luck, wide,* and *strong.* These particular bases are capable of standing by themselves and of entering rather freely into grammatical combinations. For this reason they are called *free bases.* Other bases cannot stand alone or enter freely into grammatical combinations but must always appear in close affiliation with other morphemes. These are called *bound bases.* We can recognize a common base *turb* in such words as *disturb, perturb,* and *turbulent;* it never stands alone as the *green* of *greenness* does, so it is a bound base."

English derivation. By this process any new word, whatever its source, may almost immediately become the nucleus of a cluster of derivatives. Thus *plane*, formed by clipping from *airplane*, has produced *emplane* and *deplane*, presumably by analogy with *entrain* and *detrain*, themselves formed by analogy with *embark* and *debark*, which were borrowed from French. When *telegraph* was formed by compounding of two Greek elements, it soon gave rise to *telegrapher, telegraphy, telegraphic*, and *telegraphist*, all of which were self-explaining derivatives.

So obvious is the process of forming derivatives with productive affixes that all of us probably do it much more frequently than we realize. The words we thus "create" in most cases have been frequently used before and are listed in the dictionary, but we may not know that. This process allows us to expand our vocabulary without specifically memorizing new words. But this reliance on analogical derivation may sometimes trap us into creating new words that are unnecessary because other derivatives already exist and have become standard. The student who wrote about Hamlet's *unableness to overcome his mental undecidedness* undoubtedly was familiar with *inability* and *indecision*, but under the pressure of an examination he forgot them and created his own derivatives instead.

2. *Compounding.* In a sense, compounding is a special form of derivation in which, instead of adding affixes (bound forms) to a stem, two or more words (or in some cases bound bases) are put together to make a new lexical unit. Compounding has been a source of new words in English since earliest times, and is particularly common in present-day English. Perusal of any daily paper will turn up countless examples of compounds that are new within the last few years or months: *launching pad, blast-off, jet-port, freeway, ski-tow, free loader, feather-bedding, sit-in.* Our writing system does not indicate whether items like *weather satellite* are compounds or constructions. Many of them begin as constructions but then assume the characteristic stress patterns of compounds: some people still pronounce *ice cream* with the stress pattern of a construction (as in *iced tea*), but most treat it as a compound (as in *iceboat*). Some of the older compounds have gone through sound (and spelling) changes that have completely obscured their compound origin. Typical of these is *lord*, which began in early Old English as *hlāf-weard*, a compound of the ancestors of our *loaf* and *ward*, and passed through the stages of OE *hlāford* and ME *loverd* to its present monosyllabic form. Other examples are *woman*, originally a compound of the ancestors of *wife* and *man*, and *hussy*, from *house* and *wife*, hence etymologically a doublet of *housewife*.

The semantic relationships between the parts of compounds are very varied. If compounds are thought of as the product of a transformation process, this variety can be revealed by reconstructing the phrase from which the compound might have been created. This may range from a simple modification, in which the transformation involves only a change in stress pattern (*hot dog, blackboard, bluebird*), to complete predication, where the transformation involves complicated reordering and deletion (as in *salesman* from *man who makes sales* or *movie camera* from *camera that takes movies*). Compounds may themselves enter into compounds to produce elaborate structures like *aircraft carrier* and *real estate salesman*. These must be considered compounds, since they have the characteristic stress-pattern with the strongest stress on the first element (*áircràft càrrier, réal estàte sàlesman*), in contrast to the stress pattern of modification constructions (as in *àircràft desígner* or *rèal estàte invéstment*).

One special group of compounds, most of them of quite recent origin, includes those words—mostly technical and scientific terms—which are made up of morphemes borrowed from Greek. Many of the elements so used were free forms—words—in Greek, but must be considered bound bases in English. The practice of compounding them began in Greek: *philosophia* is compounded from *philos* "fond of" and *sophia* "wisdom." Words of this sort were borrowed into Latin in ancient times, and ultimately reached English by way of French. Renaissance scholars, who knew Greek and recognized the combining elements, began to make new combinations which did not exist in the original Greek. With the growth of scientific knowledge from the seventeenth century on, new technical and scientific terms were commonly invented this way.

Words created can be roughly divided into two groups. The first includes those which have wide circulation in the general vocabulary—like *telephone, photograph,* and *thermometer.* These are constructed out of a relatively small number of morphemes, whose meanings are well known:

tele	"far, distant"	*meter*	"measure"
phone	"sound"	*dyna*	"power"
photo	"light"	*hydro*	"water, moisture"
graph	"write, mark"	*bio*	"life"
thermo	"heat"	*morph*	"shape, form"

Inventors and manufacturers of new products often create names for their inventions from elements of this sort. Sometimes the Greek elements are combined with Latin ones, as in *automobile* (Greek *autos* "self," Latin *mobilis* "movable") and *television,* or even with native English elements, as in *dynaflow.* Recent creations in this group are *astronaut* and *cosmonaut,* from Greek *aster* "star," *kosmos* "universe," and *nautes* "sailor." Actually *cosmonaut* was first used in Russian, whence it was borrowed, but since both of its bases were already in use

in English (as in *cosmology* and *aeronaut*), it might just as well have
originated in English.

The second group of Greek-based compounds comprises the large
number of technical and scientific terms whose use is almost wholly
restricted to specialists. As in the case of *cosmonaut*, most of these
words are readily interchangeable among the languages in which scientific publication is extensive. Since it is often difficult if not impossible to determine the language in which they were first used, the
Merriam-Webster editors have recently made use of the term *International Scientific Vocabulary* (abbreviated ISV) to describe them. A few
examples of wide enough circulation to be included in an abridged dictionary, are the following:

hypsography: "recording (*graphy*) of elevation (*hypso*)"
telethermoscope: "instrument that perceives (*scope*) heat (*thermo*)
    at a distance (*tele*)"
electroencephalograph: "instrument that records (*graph*) electric
    current (*electro*) within (*en*) the head (*cephalo*)"
schizogenesis: "reproduction (*genesis*) by division (*schizo*)"

In all cases, since at least two of the combining elements are bases,
these words must be considered compounds. They may also give rise
to derivatives formed by the addition of affixes in regular patterns, such
as *electroencephalography* and *schizogenetic*. It is in this way, rather
than by direct borrowing, that Greek has made its great contribution to
the English vocabulary.

3. *Functional Shift.* Since the late Middle English period, when most
of the inflections surviving from Old English finally disappeared, it has
been easy to shift a word from one part of speech to another without
altering its form, at least in the unmarked base form. A verb like *walk*
can be turned into a noun simply by using it in a syntactic position reserved for nouns, as in *he took a walk*, where the determiner *a* marks
walk as a noun, direct object of *took*. This process, called *functional
shift*, is an important concomitant of the historical change of English
from a synthetic to an analytic language, and has greatly enlarged the
vocabulary in a very economical way. Since the words so created belong
to a different part of speech and hence have a different grammatical
distribution from that of the original, they must be considered new
words, homonymous in the base form with the words from which they
were derived, rather than merely extensions of meaning. From another
point of view, they may be thought of as derivatives with zero affixes.
In some cases they may take a different stress pattern in their new use:
the noun *implement*, with weak stress and the weak central vowel /ə/
in the last syllable, when shifted to a verb took secondary stress on the

last syllable, whose vowel was changed to /e/. Since there is overt change in pronunciation, this is true derivation rather than functional shift. But the two processes are obviously closely related.

Older instances of functional shift commonly produced nouns from verbs: in addition to *walk*, already cited, we might mention *run, steal, laugh, touch, buy, break*, and many others. In present-day English the shift from noun to verb is much in favor. In the past, short words like *brush* and *perch* were sometimes shifted from noun to verb, but today, longer nouns like *implement, position, process, contact* are often used as verbs. Even compound nouns get shifted to verbs; the secretary who said "I didn't back-file the letter, I waste-basketed it" was speaking twentieth-century English, however inelegant.

4. *Back Formation* and *Clipping* are two modes of word creation which can be classed together as different types of *reduction*. In each case, a shorter word is made from a longer one, so that the effect is the opposite of derivation and compounding. *Back formation* makes use of analogy to produce a sort of reverse derivation. The existence of *creation, create*, and *donation* readily suggests that if there is not a verb *donate* there should be. This seems so natural to us that it is hard to believe that less than a century ago *donate* was considered an American barbarism by many puristically inclined British speakers of English.[1] Other words that have come into English by back formation are *edit* (from *editor*), *burgle* (from *burglar*), *enthuse* (from *enthusiasm*), *televise* (from *television*, by analogy with pairs like *supervise: supervision*), *automate* (from *automation*), *laze* (from *lazy*), and many more. Once pairs of words like these have become established, only the historical record proving prior use of the longer forms serves to distinguish them from normal derivational pairs.

Clippings, on the other hand, are shortenings without regard to derivational analogy. They are frequent in informal language, especially spoken, as in the campus and classroom use of *exam, lab, math*, and *dorm*. They are possible because often a single syllable, usually the one bearing the main stress, is sufficient to identify a word, especially in a rather closely restricted context, so that the remaining syllables are redundant and can be dropped. Most of them preserve a colloquial flavor and are limited to the special vocabularies of occupational groups. Others, however—often over the objections of purists—attain wide circulation and may ultimately replace the longer forms on most or all levels of usage. Some that have done so are *van* (from *caravan*), *bus* (from *omnibus*), *cello* (from *violoncello*), *mob* (from Latin *mobile*

[1] See H. L. Mencken, *The American Language*, Fourth Edition (New York: Alfred A. Knopf, 1936), pp. 121, 165.

vulgus "unstable crowd"), *piano* (from *pianoforte*), and *fan* (in sense "ardent devotee," from *fanatic*). Others which are in acceptable, though perhaps characteristically informal, use alongside the longer unclipped words are *phone* (for *telephone*), *taxi* and *cab* (from *taxicab*), and *plane* (for *airplane* or older *aeroplane*). A rather special form of clipping is that which reduces long compounds or idiomatic fixed phrases to one of their elements—often the modifying element rather than the head—as in *express* from *express train, car* from *motor car*, and *outboard* from *outboard motor* (*boat*). This process often accounts for what otherwise seem strange transfers of meaning.

An extreme form of clipping is that which reduces words to their abbreviations and longer phrases to their initials. Abbreviation is, of course, a standard device of the writing system to save space by reducing the length of common or often repeated words. Usually it is confined to writing, and to rather informal writing at that. But some common abbreviations have been adopted in speech and ways have been found to pronounce them. The common abbreviations for the two halves of the day—A.M. and P.M.—which stand for the Latin phrases *ante meridiem* ("before noon") and *post meridiem* ("after noon") are frequently used in speech, where they are pronounced /é:+èm/ and /pí:èm/. These must indeed be considered words, though their spelling is that of abbreviations. The same is true of B.C. and A.D. in dates, O.K. (which has become an international word), U.S., G.I., L.P., TNT, TV, and DDT. In all these cases the pronunciation is simply the syllabic names of the letters, usually with the strongest stress on the last: /yù:+és/, /dì:+dì:+tí:/, and so on.

If the initial letters of a phrase, used as an abbreviation, happen to make a combination that is pronounceable, what results is an *acronym* —a word whose spelling represents the initial letters of a phrase. Though very popular in recent times, acronyms are by no means an innovation of the twentieth century. The early Christians made a famous one when they took the initials of the Greek phrase Ἰησοῦς Χριστὸς θεοῦ υἱὸς σωτήρ ("Jesus Christ, son of God, Savior") to make the Greek word ἰχθύς ("fish") and adopted the fish as a symbol of Christ. Acronyms have become more frequent in English since World War II. Everyone talks about NATO, UNESCO, and NASA, often without being able to supply the longer title whose initials created the acronym. In fact, acronyms have become so popular that some longer titles have been created by a kind of back formation from the desired initials. It was certainly more than a happy accident that led the Navy in World War II to call its feminine branch "Women Assigned to Volunteer Emergency Service," or WAVES. More recently an organization devoted to finding foster parents for orphan children from foreign lands

has called itself "World Adoption International Fund" so its initials
would spell WAIF.

5. *Proper Names.* The giving of individual names to persons, places,
geographic features, deities, and sometimes to animals is a universal
human practice, apparently as old as language itself. A proper name,
since it is closely restricted to a single specific referent, does not have
the general and varied distribution and reference that characterize
ordinary nouns. But there is frequent interchange across the line separating proper names from other words. Many proper names, such as
Taylor, Smith, Clark, and *Wright* are derived from common nouns
describing occupations; others like *Brown, Strong,* and *Wild* derive
from adjectives that may once have described the person so named.
Place-names also frequently show their derivation from common nouns,
as in *Northfield, Portsmouth,* and *Fairmount.*

There has also been interchange in the other direction, by which the
proper name of a person or place becomes generalized in meaning,
usually to refer to a product or activity connected with the referent of
the proper name. One famous example is the name *Caesar,* originally
a nickname coined from the Latin verb *caedo* "to cut" to describe
Julius Caesar, who was cut from his mother's womb by the operation
still called *Caesarian section.* The name was assumed by Julius's nephew
Octavius, the first Roman emperor, and then by the subsequent em-
perors, so that it became virtually a synonym for *imperator* "emperor."
In its later history it was borrowed into Germanic, ultimately becoming
German *Kaiser* (there was also a Middle English word *kayser,* now
obsolete), and into Slavonic, whence came *tsar.* Another interesting set
of words derived from names are the adjectives *mercurial, saturnine,*
and *jovial,* referring to temperaments supposed to be characteristic of
people under the dominance of the planets Mercury, Saturn, and
Jupiter. The corresponding *venereal* (from *Venus*) has been restricted
in meaning almost entirely to medical use, but *venery* is still a rather
high-flown word for love-making. Those supposed to derive instability
from the changeable moon used to be called *lunatic* (from Latin *luna,*
the moon). The punishment visited upon Tantalus, forever doomed to
be within sight of food and water that receded when he reached for it,
has given us the verb *tantalize,* formed by adding the productive suffix
-ize (itself ultimately derived from Greek) to his name. Also ultimately
Greek in origin are *hector* ("a bully, to bully") from the Trojan hero
in the *Iliad* and *mentor* ("teacher"—now often used in the sports pages
for "athletic coach") from the adviser of Telemachus in the *Odyssey.*

During the history of English since the beginning of the Middle
English period, various words have been derived from proper names.
Some earlier ones are *dunce* (from the scholastic philosopher Duns

Scotus—used in ridicule of scholastic philosophy in the later sixteenth century), *pander* (from the character Pandarus in Chaucer's *Troilus and Criseyde, c.* 1385), *mawmet* (from Mahomet; at first it meant "idol," later "puppet, doll"). The Bible, widely read from Reformation times on and frequently discussed for its symbolic as well as its literal or historical meaning, has contributed many words of this sort, such as *jeremiad* ("a denunciatory tirade"), *babel, lazar* (from Lazarus; common for *leper* in Middle English), *maudlin* (from Mary Magdalen and her noted tears), and *simony* ("taking or giving money for church offices," from Simon Magus). On the border between proper and common nouns are names of Biblical and other personages taken in figurative meanings, though usually capitalized in writing, indicating that the transfer to common noun is not complete: *the old Adam, raising Cain, a doubting Thomas, a Daniel come to judgment.*

Some proper names that have assumed general meanings have undergone pronunciation changes that obscure their origins. The adjective *tawdry* ("cheap and flashy") comes from a clipping of *Saint Audrey*, and presumably was first used to describe a kind of cheap lace sold at St. Audrey's Fair. *Bedlam*, which to us means "uproar, total confusion," was a proper name as late as the eighteenth century, when it was used as a short name for *St. Mary of Bethlehem*, a London insane asylum. The word *mawkin*, used dialectally in England for "scarecrow," comes from *Malkyn*, a girl's name, ultimately a nickname from *Mary*. The parallel nickname *Moll* gave rise to an American slang word for a criminal's girl. The history of *doll* is similar but more complicated; it passed from a clipped form of *Dorothy* to describe a miniature (usually female) figure, then to describe a small and pretty girl.

The names of historical characters—often those of unsavory reputation—have given us some rather common words. One of the most interesting of these is *guy*, from *Guy Fawkes*, used in England to describe the effigies of that notable traitor which are customarily carried in procession and burned on November 5, the anniversary of the discovery of his "Gunpowder Plot." The term came to mean "a figure of fun, a butt of scorn," and as a verb "to poke fun at, tease." In America it has become a universal colloquial term for any male not held in high respect. In phrases like *a nice guy* (when not used ironically) it has lost all of its original pejorative flavor.

Names of products derived from the names of their places of origin are rather plentiful in English. Textiles like *calico* (from *Calicut*, or *Calcutta*), *denim* (*serge de Nîmes*), *cashmere* (*Kashmir*), and *worsted* (from the name of a town in Norfolk, England) are well known. So are products like *china* (clipped from *chinaware* from *China ware*), *gin* (clipped from *Geneva*), *cognac*, and *cayenne*. Specialized and technical vocabularies are especially fond of words adapted from proper names. Skiing has its *telemark* and *christiania* (usually clipped to *christy*); librarians speak of *Dewey decimal classification* and *Cutter numbers*; horticulturalists of *fuchsia, dahlia,* and *wistaria*; physicists of *roentgen rays, curies,* and *angstrom units*; electricians of *ohms, watts,* and *amperes*; doctors of *rickettsia* and *Bright's disease*.

6. *Imitation.* A relatively small number of words in English apparently owe their origin to attempts to imitate natural sounds. *Bow-wow, meow, baa, moo,* and other words for animal cries are supposed to remind us of the noises made by dogs, cats, sheep, and cows. They are not accurate imitations, since they are pronounced with sounds characteristic of the sound-system of English, which these animals, not being native speakers of English, do not use. Other languages have other, often quite different imitative words. Both *cock-a-doodle-doo* and *kikiriki* are supposedly imitative of a rooster's crow; unless we assume that English and Greek roosters make quite different sounds, we must attribute the difference between these words to the differing sound-systems of the two languages.

Related to imitation is the phenomenon sometimes called *sound symbolism:* the habit of associating a certain type or class of meanings with a certain sound or cluster of sounds. There seems to be in English an association between the initial consonant cluster *sn-* and the nose (*snarl, sneer, sneeze, sniff, snivel, snore, snort, snout,* and *snuffle*). When slang words referring to or involving the nose are coined they may begin with this cluster, as in *snook* and *snoop*. English speakers associate the sound-combination spelled *-ash* (/æš/) with a sudden loud sound or rapid, turbulent, or destructive motion, as in *crash, dash, flash, smash,* and *splash*; and a final *-er* on verbs suggests rapidly repeated, often rhythmic motion, as in *flicker, flutter, hover, quiver, shimmer, waver*. This last example is perhaps a morpheme in its own right, though to call it one would give us a large number of bound bases that occur nowhere else. But it is well on the way to the morphemic status which certainly must be accorded to the *-le* or *-dle* of *handle, treadle,* and *spindle*.

Imitation was once considered so important as to be made the basis for a theory of the origin of language—the so-called "bow-wow theory." This theory is commonly discounted nowadays.

7. *Blending* is a combination of clipping and compounding, which makes new words by putting together fragments of existing words in new combinations. It differs from derivation in that the elements thus combined are not morphemes at the time the blends are made, though they may become so afterward as a result of the blending process, especially if several blends are made with the same element and the phenomenon of *false etymology* is present.

The poem "Jabberwocky" in Lewis Carroll's *Through the Looking Glass* contains many ingenious blends, though only a few of them (called *portmanteau words* by Humpty Dumpty in the book) have passed into the general vocabulary. Thus *slithy* (from *lithe* and *slimy*) and *mimsy* (from *miserable* and *flimsy*) are not used outside the poem, but *chortle* (*chuckle* and *snort*) and *galumphing* (*galloping* and *triumphing*) are not uncommon words, though they are usually restricted to colloquial or facetious use.

The history of *-burger* illustrates the way in which blending can give rise to a new morpheme. The name *Hamburger steak* (varying with *Hamburg steak*) was given to a kind of ground beef in America in the 1880s. It was soon shortened by phrase-clipping to *hamburger*, losing its proper-name quality in the process. The *-er* here is simply the normal German suffix for making an adjective from a proper noun (as in *Brandenburger Tor* "Brandenburg Gate"). But to those who did not know German, the word looked (and sounded) like a compound of *ham* and *burger*. So the *-burger* part was clipped and combined with various other words or parts of words to make *cheeseburger*, *deerburger*, *buffaloburger*, and many more. These have the form of compounds made up of one free base and a bound base *-burger*. Meanwhile by further clipping, *hamburger*, already short for *hamburger steak sandwich*, was cut down to *burger*, which now became a free form—a word. Thus what began as the last two syllables of a German proper adjective has become first a bound morpheme and then a full word in English.

Other morphemes which owe their origin to blending are *-rama*, *-orium*, *-teria*, and *-omat*. The first of these began with words of Greek origin like *panorama* and *cyclorama*.[2] The combining elements in Greek were *pan* "all," *kyklos* "circle, wheel," and *horama* "view," a noun derived from the verb *horan* "see." But the *-rama* part of these words was blended with *cine* (from *cinema*) to make *cinerama*, describing a type of wide-screen motion picture. Subsequently *-rama* was blended with various other elements to make new words like *colorama* and *vistarama*, as well as many trade and commercial names. It certainly must now be considered a separate morpheme, conveying a vague notion of grandeur and sweep (or so its users hope) to the words in which it is used. Similarly *-orium*, split off from *emporium* (a rather fancy Latin loan-word for "shop"), *-teria*, split off from the Spanish loan-word *cafeteria*, and *-omat*, split off from the trade name *Automat*, itself a clipping from *automatic*, have become separate morphemes, as in *lubritorium*, *valeteria*, and *laundromat*. The process of blending has thus produced not only new words but new morphemes capable of

[2] See John Lotz, "The Suffix '-rama,'" *American Speech*, 39 (1954) 156–158.

entering with some freedom into new compounds and derivatives. Many of the words thus coined never get any farther than their first application by an enterprising advertiser or proprietor, and those that do usually have a brief life. But a few seem to fill a real need and remain as part of the general vocabulary of English.

8. *Coinage.* Very few words are simply made up out of unrelated, meaningless elements. The other resources for making new words and the abundant vocabularies of other languages available for borrowing supply so many easy ways of producing new words that outright coinage seldom suggests itself. The outright coinage—unlike the compound, clipping, derivative, and blend—is also hard to remember because it has no familiar elements to aid the memory. So wholly new coinages are both harder to make and less likely to be remembered and used. It is no wonder that they are relatively rare. Some words, however, are indubitable coinages, and others for which etymologists have found no source may be tentatively assumed to be. Words like *quiz, pun, slang,* and *fun* have no cognates in other Germanic languages, cannot be traced to other languages as loan-words, and, since they are monosyllabic, are not compounds or derivatives, though they might be blends to which we have lost the key. One can imagine that *slang*—an eighteenth-century creation—combined elements from *slovenly* and *language,* but this is pure guesswork. These, together with more recent words, most of them facetious or slangy, like *hooch* and *pooch, snob* and *gob* ("sailor"), most probably originated as free coinages, sometimes involving sound symbolism.

More elaborate coinages, having more than one syllable, are likely to combine original elements with various other processes of word formation, especially derivation. Thus the stems of *segashuate, sockdologer,* and *spifflicated* seem to be coinages, but the suffixes are recognizable morphemes. In fact, it would be exceedingly unlikely for a native speaker to coin a word of more than one syllable without making use of one or more of the word-forming devices we have been discussing.

As even this brief chapter must have made obvious, the vocabulary of English is large, complex, highly diversified in origin, and constantly changing. No dictionary, however large, can contain it all. Or, if such a dictionary should be prepared, it would be out of date by the time it was printed, since new meanings, new borrowings, and new creations are being added every day. Nor can any single individual know it all. Speakers of English share a large vocabulary in common, it is true, but every individual speaker has his own unique inventory of the less commonly used words and meanings, reflecting his unique experience with language.

Many people—perhaps most people—go through life with a vocabulary adequate only to their daily needs, picking up new words when some new facet of life makes it necessary, but never indulging in curiosity and speculation about words. Others are wordlovers—collectors and connoisseurs. They like to measure one word against another, trace their etymologies and shifts of meaning, use them in new and exciting or amusing combinations. They play word-games like *Scrabble* and *Anagrams*, they do cross-word puzzles, they make puns and rhymes and nonsense jingles. Some make poems, which are the highest form of word-game. But even those who aspire no further than to the writing of good clear expository prose must become at least amateur connoisseurs of words. Only this way—not by formal exercises or courses in vocabulary-building—will they learn to make the best possible use of the vast and remarkable lexicon of English.

FOR DISCUSSION AND REVIEW

1   Francis makes references to *morphemes*. What is their importance in the study of word formation?

2   Francis tells of a student who used the words *unableness* for *inability* and *undecidedness* for *indecision* while under the pressure of an examination situation. Can you recall ever forming new words by the derivative method? Explain.

3   When settlers first came to this country, they frequently used the compounding technique to give names to specimens of the flora and fauna that were unfamiliar to them. They called unfamiliar ducks names such as *wood ducks, canvas back ducks, fan crested ducks,* and *dumpling ducks.* Naming in this particular field is no longer necessary, but science still makes great use of the compounding process. Can you give any examples of such compounds?

4   Identify the processes of word formation in the following words: *gas, contrail, happenstance, fan, elbow, peddle, ack ack, midwife, xerography, loran, positron, enthuse, piano, telecast, gin, quisling, tawdry, bang.*

6

Preface to the *Dictionary* of *American* Slang

When a fellow student asks you if you have any bread, he is most likely interested in money and not something to eat. As the following article by Stuart Berg Flexner indicates, food plays a major role in the imagery of our slang expressions. Mr. Flexner also discusses the origins of slang, its subgroups, and its place in American usage.

Stuart Berg Flexner

AMERICAN SLANG, as used in the title of this dictionary, is the body of words and expressions frequently used by or intelligible to a rather large portion of the general American public, but not accepted as good, formal usage by the majority. No word can be called slang simply because of its etymological history; its source, its spelling, and its meaning in a larger sense do *not* make it slang. Slang is best defined by a dictionary that points out who uses slang and what "flavor" it conveys.

I have called all slang used in the United States "American," regardless of its country of origin or use in other countries.

In this preface I shall discuss the human element in the formation of slang (what American slang is, and how and why slang is created and used). . . .

The English language has several levels of vocabulary:

Standard usage comprises those words and expressions used, understood, and accepted by a majority of our citizens under any circumstances or degree of formality. Such words are well defined and their most accepted spellings and pronunciations are given in our standard dictionaries. In standard speech one might say: *Sir, you speak English well.*

Colloquialisms are familiar words and idioms used in informal speech and writing, but not considered explicit or formal enough for polite conversation or business correspondence. Unlike slang, however, colloquialisms are used and understood by nearly everyone in the United States. The use of slang conveys the suggestion that the speaker and the listener enjoy a special "fraternity," but the use of colloquialisms emphasizes only the informality and familiarity of a general social situation. Almost all idiomatic expressions, for example, could be labeled colloquial. Colloquially, one might say: *Friend, you talk plain and hit the nail right on the head.*

Dialects are the words, idioms, pronunciations, and speech habits peculiar to specific geographical locations. A dialecticism is a regionalism or localism. In popular use "dialect" has come to mean the words, foreign accents, or speech patterns associated with any ethnic group. In Southern dialect one might say: *Cousin, y'all talk mighty fine.* In ethnic-immigrant "dialects" one might say: *Paisano, you speak good the English,* or *Landsman, your English is plenty all right already.*

Cant, jargon, and *argot* are the words and expressions peculiar to special segments of the population. *Cant* is the conversational, familiar idiom used and generally understood only by members of a specific occupation, trade, profession, sect, class, age group, interest group, or other sub-group of our culture. *Jargon* is the technical or even secret vocabulary of such a sub-group; jargon is "shop talk." *Argot* is both the cant and the jargon of any professional criminal group. In such usages one might say, respectively: *CQ-CQ-CQ . . . the tone of your transmission is good; You are free of anxieties related to interpersonal communication;* or *Duchess, let's have a bowl of chalk.*

Slang[1] is generally defined above. In slang one might say: *Buster, your line is the cat's pajamas,* or *Doll, you come on with the straight jazz, real cool like.*

Each of these levels of language, save standard usage, is more common in speech than in writing, and slang as a whole is no exception. Thus, very few slang words and expressions (hence very few of the entries in this dictionary) appear in standard dictionaries.

American slang tries for a quick, easy, personal mode of speech. It comes mostly from cant, jargon, and argot words and expressions whose popularity has increased until a large number of the general public uses or understands them. Much of this slang retains a basic characteristic of its origin: it is *fully* intelligible only to initiates.

Slang may be represented pictorially as the more popular portion of the cant, jargon, and argot from many sub-groups (only a few of the sub-groups are shown on page 238). The shaded areas represent only general overlapping between groups.

Eventually, some slang passes into standard speech; other slang flourishes for a time with varying popularity and then is forgotten; finally, some slang is never fully accepted nor completely forgotten. *O.K., jazz* (music), and *A-bomb* were recently considered slang, but they are now standard usages. *Bluebelly, Lucifer,* and *the bee's knees*

---

[1] For the evolution of the word "slang," see F. Klaeber, "Concerning the Etymology of Slang," *American Speech,* April, 1926.

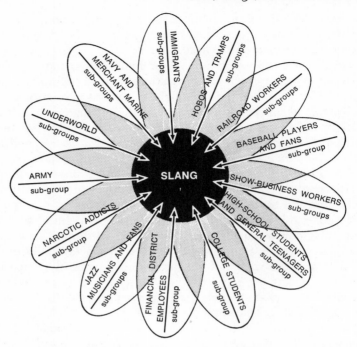

have faded from popular use. *Bones* (dice) and *beat it* seem destined to remain slang forever: Chaucer used the first and Shakespeare used the second.

It is impossible for any living vocabulary to be static. Most new slang words and usages evolve quite naturally: they result from specific situations. New objects, ideas, or happenings, for example, require new words to describe them. Each generation also seems to need some new words to describe the same old things.

Railroaders (who were probably the first American sub-group to have a nationwide cant and jargon) thought *jerk water town* was ideally descriptive of a community that others called a *one-horse town*. The changes from *one-horse town* and *don't spare the horses* to a *wide place in the road* and *step on it* were natural and necessary when the automobile replaced the horse. The automobile also produced such new words and new meanings (some of them highly specialized) as *gas buggy, jalopy, bent eight, Chevvie, convertible,* and *lube.* Like most major innovations, the automobile affected our social history and introduced or encouraged *dusters, hitch hikers, road hogs, joint hopping, necking, chicken* (the game), *car coats,* and *suburbia.*

The automobile is only one obvious example. Language always responds to new concepts and developments with new words.

Consider the following:

wars: *redcoats, minutemen, bluebelly, over there, doughboy, gold brick, jeep.*

mass immigrations: *Bohunk, greenhorn, shillalagh, voodoo, pizzeria.*

science and technology: *'gin, side-wheeler, wash-and-wear, fringe area, fallout.*

turbulent eras: *Redskin, maverick, speak, Chicago pineapple, free love, fink, breadline.*

evolution in the styles of eating: *applesauce, clambake, luncheonette, hot dog, coffee and.*

dress: *Mother Hubbard, bustle, shimmy, sailor, Long Johns, zoot suit, Ivy League.*

housing: *lean-to, bundling board, chuckhouse, W.C., railroad flat, split-level, sectional.*

music: *cakewalk, bandwagon, fish music, long hair, rock.*

personality: *Yankee, alligator, flapper, sheik, hepcat, B.M.O.C., beetle, beat.*

new modes of transportation: *stage, pinto, jitney, kayducer, hot shot, jet jockey.*

new modes of entertainment: *barnstormer, two-a-day, clown alley, talkies, d.j., Spectacular.*

changing attitudes toward sex: *painted woman, fast, broad, wolf, jail-bait, sixty-nine.*

human motivations: *boy crazy, gold-digger, money-mad, Momism, Oedipus complex, do-gooder, sick.*

personal relationships: *bunky, kids, old lady, steady, ex, gruesome two-some, John.*

work and workers: *clod buster, scab, pencil pusher, white collar, grave-yard shift, company man.*

politics: *Tory, do-nothing, mug-wump, third party, brain trust, fellow traveler, Veep.*

and even hair styles: *bun, rat, peroxide blonde, Italian cut, pony tail, D.A.*

Those social groups that first confront a new object, cope with a new situation, or work with a new concept devise and use new words long before the population at large does. The larger, more imaginative, and useful a group's vocabulary, the more likely it is to contribute slang. To generate slang, a group must either be very large and in constant contact with the dominant culture or be small, closely knit, and re-moved enough from the dominant culture to evolve an extensive, highly personal, and vivid vocabulary. Teen-agers are an example of a large sub-group contributing many words. Criminals, carnival workers, and hoboes are examples of the smaller groups. The smaller groups, because their vocabulary is personal and vivid, contribute to our general slang out of proportion to their size.

Whether the United States has more slang words than any other country (in proportion to number of people, area, or the number of words in the standard vocabulary) I do not know.[2] Certainly the French and the Spanish enjoy extremely large slang vocabularies. Americans, however, do use their general slang more than any other people.

American slang reflects the kind of people who create and use it. Its diversity and popularity are in part due to the imagination, self-confidence, and optimism of our people. Its vitality is in further part due to our guarantee of free speech and to our lack of a national acad-

---

[2] The vocabulary of the average American, most of which he knows but never uses, is usually estimated at 10,000-20,000 words. Of this quantity I estimate conservatively that 2,000 words are slang. Slang, which thus forms about 10 per cent of the words known by the average American, belongs to the part of his vocabulary most frequently *used*.

The English language is now estimated to have at least 600,000 words; this is over four times the 140,000 recorded words of the Elizabethan period. Thus over 450,000 *new words or meanings* have been added since Shakespeare's day, without counting the replacement words or those that have been forgotten between then and now. There are now approximately 10,000 slang words in American English, and about 35,000 cant, jargon, and argot words.

Despite this quantity, 25 per cent of all communication is composed of just nine words. According to McKnight's study, another 25 per cent of all speech is composed of an additional 34 words (or: 43 words comprise 50 per cent of all speech). Scholars do differ, however, on just which nine words are the most popular. Three major studies are: G. H. McKnight, *English Words and Their Background*, Appleton-Century-Crofts, Inc., 1923 (for spoken words only); Godfrey Dewey, "Relative Frequency of English Speech Sounds," *Harvard Studies in Education*, vol. IV, 1923 (for written words only); and Norman R. French, Charles W. Carter, and Walter Koenig, Jr., "Words and Sounds of Telephone Conversations," *Bell System Technical Journal*, April, 1930 (telephone speech only). Their lists of the most common nine words are:

McKnight's (speech)	Dewey's (written)	Bell Telephone (conversations)
	a	a
and	and	
be		
have		
	in	
		I
	is	is
it	it	it
		on
of	of	
	that	that
the	the	the
to	to	to
will		
you		you

emy of language or of any "official" attempt to purify our speech. Americans are restless and frequently move from region to region and from job to job. This hopeful wanderlust, from the time of the pioneers through our westward expansion to modern mobility, has helped spread regional and group terms until they have become general slang. Such restlessness has created constantly new situations which provoke new words. Except for a few Eastern industrial areas and some rural regions in the South and West, America just doesn't look or sound "lived in." We often act and speak as if we were simply visiting and observing. What should be an ordinary experience seems new, unique, or colorful to us, worthy of words and forceful speech. People do not "settle down" in their jobs, towns, or vocabularies.

Nor do we "settle down" intellectually, spiritually, or emotionally. We have few religious, regional, family, class, psychological, or philo-sophical roots. We don't believe in roots, we believe in teamwork. Our strong loyalties, then, are directed to those social groups—or sub-groups as they are often called—with which we are momentarily identified. This ever-changing "membership" helps to promote and spread slang.

But even within each sub-group only a few new words are generally accepted. Most cant and jargon are local and temporary. What persist are the exceptionally apt and useful cant and jargon terms. These be-come part of the permanent, personal vocabulary of the group members, giving prestige to the users by proving their acceptance and status in the group. Group members then spread some of this more honored cant and jargon in the dominant culture. If the word is also useful to non-group members, it is on its way to becoming slang. Once new words are introduced into the dominant culture, via television, radio, movies, or newspapers, the rapid movement of individuals and rapid communica-tion between individuals and groups spread the new word very quickly.

For example, consider the son of an Italian immigrant living in New York City. He speaks Italian at home. Among neighborhood youths of similar background he uses many Italian expressions because he finds them always on the tip of his tongue and because they give him a sense of solidarity with his group. He may join a street gang, and after school and during vacations work in a factory. After leaving high school, he joins the navy; then he works for a year seeing the country as a carnival worker. He returns to New York, becomes a longshoreman, marries a girl with a German background, and becomes a boxing fan. He uses Italian and German borrowings, some teen-age street-gang terms, a few factory terms, slang with a navy origin, and carnival, dockworker's, and boxing words. He spreads words from each group to all other groups he belongs to. His Italian parents will learn and use a few street-gang, factory, navy, carnival, dockworker's, and boxing terms; his German in-laws will learn some Italian words from his parents; his navy friends will begin to use some of his Italian expressions; his carnival friends a few navy words; his co-workers on the docks some carnival terms, in addition to all the rest; and his social friends, with whom he may usually talk boxing and dock work, will be interested in and learn some of his Italian and carnival terms. His speech may be considered very "slangy" and picturesque because he has belonged to unusual, colorful sub-groups.

On the other hand, a man born into a Midwestern, middle-class, Protestant family whose ancestors came to the United States in the eighteenth century might carry with him popular high-school terms. At high school he had an interest in hot rods and rock-and-roll. He may have served two years in the army, then gone to an Ivy League college where he became an adept bridge player and an enthusiast of cool music. He may then have become a sales executive and developed a liking for golf. This second man, no more usual or unusual than the first, will know cant and jargon terms of teen-age high-school use, hot-rods, rock-and-roll, Ivy League schools, cool jazz, army life, and some golf player's and bridge player's terms. He knows further a few slang expressions from his parents (members of the Jazz Age of the 1920's), from listening to television programs, seeing both American and British movies, reading popular literature, and from frequent meetings with people having completely different backgrounds. When he uses cool terms on the golf course, college expressions at home, business words at the bridge table, when he refers to whiskey or drunkenness by a few words he learned from his parents, curses his next-door neighbor in a few choice army terms—then he too is popularizing slang.

It is, then, clear that three cultural conditions especially contribute to the creation of a large slang vocabulary: (1) hospitality to or acceptance of new objects, situations, and concepts; (2) existence of a large number of diversified sub-groups; (3) democratic mingling between these sub-groups and the dominant culture. Primitive peoples have little if any slang because their life is restricted by ritual; they develop few new concepts; and there are no sub-groups that mingle with the dominant culture. (Primitive sub-groups, such as medicine men or magic men, have their own vocabularies; but such groups do not mix with the dominant culture and their jargon can never become slang because it is secret or sacred.)

But what, after all, are the advantages that slang possesses which make it useful? Though our choice of any specific word may usually be made from habit, we sometimes consciously select a slang word because we believe that it communicates more quickly and easily, and more personally, than does a standard word. Sometimes we resort to slang because there is no one standard word to use. In the 1940's WAC, *cold war*, and *cool* (music) could not be expressed quickly by any standard synonyms. Such words often become standard quickly, as have the first two. We also use slang because it often is more forceful, vivid, and expressive than are standard usages. Slang usually avoids the sentimentality and formality that older words often assume. Taking a girl to a *dance* may seem sentimental, may convey a degree of formal, emotional interest in the girl, and has overtones of fancy balls, fox trots, best suits, and corsages. At times it is more fun to go to a *hop*. To be *busted* or without a *hog* in one's *jeans* is not only more vivid and forceful than being penniless or without funds, it is also a more optimistic state. A *mouthpiece* (or *legal beagle*), *pencil pusher, sawbones, boneyard, bottle washer* or a course in *biochem* is more vivid and forceful than a lawyer, clerk, doctor, cemetery, laboratory assistant, or a course in biochemistry—and is much more real and less formidable than a legal counsel, junior executive, surgeon, necropolis (or memorial park), laboratory technician, or a course in biological chemistry.

Although standard English is exceedingly hospitable to polysyllabicity and even sesquipedalianism, slang is not. Slang is somet mes used not only because it is concise but just because its brevity makes it forceful. As this dictionary demonstrates, slang seems to prefer short words, especially monosyllables, and, best of all, words beginning with an explosive or an aspirate.[3]

We often use slang *fad* words as a bad habit because they are close to the tip of our tongue. Most of us apply several favorite but vague words to any of several somewhat similar situations; this saves us the time and effort of thinking and speaking precisely. At other times we purposely choose a word because it is vague, because it does not commit us too strongly to what we are saying. For example, if a friend has been praising a woman, we can reply "she's *the bee's knees*" or "she's a real *chick*," which can mean that we consider her very modern, intelligent, pert, and understanding—or can mean that we think she is one of many nondescript, somewhat confused, followers of popular fads. We can also tell our friend that a book we both have recently read is *the cat's pajamas* or *the greatest*. These expressions imply that we liked the book

[3] Many such formations are among our most frequently used slang words. As listed in this dictionary, *bug* has 30 noun meanings, *shot* 14 noun and 4 adjective meanings, *can* 11 noun and 6 verb, *bust* 9 verb and 6 noun, *hook* 8 noun and 5 verb, *fish* 14 noun, and *sack* 8 noun, 1 adjective, and 1 verb meaning. Monosyllabic words also had by far the most citations found in our source reading of popular literature. Of the 40 words for which we found the most quotations, 29 were monosyllabic. Before condensing, *fink* had citations from 70 different sources, *hot* 67, *bug* 62, *blow* and *dog* 60 each, *joint* 59, *stiff* 56, *punk* 53, *bum* and *egg* 50 each, *guy* 43, *make* 41, *bull* and *mug* 37 each, *bird* 34, *fish* and *hit* 30 each, *ham* 25, *yak* 23, *sharp* 14, and *cinch* 10. (Many of these words, of course, have several slang meanings; many of the words also appeared scores of times in the same book or article.)

for exactly the same reasons that our friend did, without having to state what these reasons were and thus taking the chance of ruining our rapport.

In our language we are constantly recreating our image in our own minds and in the minds of others. Part of this image, as mentioned above, is created by using sub-group cant and jargon in the dominant society; part of it is created by our choice of both standard and slang words. A sub-group vocabulary shows that we have a group to which we "belong" and in which we are "somebody"—outsiders had better respect us. Slang is used to show others (and to remind ourselves of) our biographical, mental, and psychological background; to show our social, economic, geographical, national, racial, religious, educational, occupational, and group interests, memberships, and patriotisms. One of the easiest and quickest ways to do this is by using counter-words. These are automatic, often one-word responses of like or dislike, of acceptance or rejection. They are used to counter the remarks, or even the presence, of others. Many of our fad words and many student and quasi-intellectual slang words are counter-words. For liking: *beat, the cat's pajamas, drooly, gas, George, the greatest, keen, nice, reet, smooth, super, way out*, etc. For rejection of an outsider (implying incompetence to belong to our group): *boob, creep, dope, drip, droop, goof, jerk, kookie, sap, simp, square, weird*, etc. Such automatic counters are overused, almost meaningless, and are a substitute for thought. But they achieve one of the main purposes of speech: quickly and automatically they express our own sub-group and personal criteria. Counter-words are often fad words creating a common bond of self-defense. All the rejecting counters listed above could refer to a moron, an extreme introvert, a birdwatcher, or a genius. The counters merely say that the person is rejected—he does not belong to the group. In uttering the counter we don't care what the person is; we are pledging our own group loyalty, affirming our identity, and expressing our satisfaction at being accepted.

In like manner, at various periods in history, our slang has abounded in words reflecting the fear, distrust, and dislike of people unlike ourselves. This intolerance is shown by the many derogatory slang words for different immigrant, religious, and racial groups: *Chink, greaser, Heinie, hunkie, mick, mockie, nigger, spik*. Many counters and derogatory words try to identify our own group status, to dare others to question our group's, and therefore our own, superiority.

Sometimes slang is used to escape the dull familiarity of standard words, to suggest an escape from the established routine of everyday life. When slang is used, our life seems a little fresher and a little more personal. Also, as at all levels of speech, slang is sometimes used for the pure joy of making sounds, or even for a need to attract attention by making noise. The sheer newness and informality of certain slang words produces a pleasure.

But more important than this expression of a more or less hidden esthetic motive on the part of the speaker is slang's reflection of the personality, the outward, clearly visible characteristics of the speaker. By and large, the man who uses slang is a forceful, pleasing, acceptable personality. Morality and intellect (too frequently not considered virtues in the modern American man) are overlooked in slang, and this has led to a type of reverse morality: many words, once standing for morally good things, are now critical. No one, for example, though these words were once considered complimentary, wants to be called a *prude* or *Puritan*. Even in standard usage they are mildly derisive.

Moreover, few of the many slang synonyms for drunk are derogatory or critical. To call a person a standard drunk may imply a superior but unsophisticated attitude toward drinking. Thus we use slang and say someone is *boozed up, gassed, high, potted, stinking, has a glow on,* etc., in a verbal attempt to convey our understanding and awareness. These slang words show that we too are human and know the effects of excessive drinking.

In the same spirit we refer to people sexually as *big ass man, fast, John, sex pot, shack job, wolf,* etc., all of which accept unsanctioned sexual intercourse as a matter of fact. These words are often used in a complimentary way and in admiration or envy. They always show acceptance of the person as a "regular guy." They are never used to express a moral judgment. Slang has few complimentary or even purely descriptive words for "virgin," "good girl," or "gentleman." Slang has *bag, bat, ex, gold digger, jerk, money mad, n.g., old lady, square,* etc.; but how many words are there for a good wife and mother, an attractive and chaste woman, an honest, hard-working man who is kind to his family, or even a respected elderly person? Slang—and it is frequently true for all language levels—always tends toward degradation rather than elevation. As slang shows, we would rather share or accept vices than be excluded from a social group. For this reason, for self-defense, and to create an aura (but not the fact) of modernity and individuality, much of our slang purposely expresses amorality, cynicism, and "toughness."

Reverse morality also affects slang in other ways. Many use slang just because it is not standard or polite. Many use slang to show their rebellion against *boobs, fuddy-duddies, marks,* and *squares.* Intellectuals and politicians often use slang to create the "common touch" and others use slang to express either their anti-intellectualism or avant-garde leanings. Thus, for teen-agers, entertainers, college students, beatniks, jazz fans, intellectuals, and other large groups, slang is often used in preference to standard words and expressions. Slang is the "official" modern language of certain vociferous groups in our population.

In my work on this dictionary, I was constantly aware that most American slang is created and used by males. Many types of slang words—including the taboo and strongly derogatory ones, those referring to sex, women, work, money, whiskey,[4] politics, transportation, sports, and the like—refer primarily to male endeavor and interest. The majority of entries in this dictionary could be labeled "primarily masculine use." Men belong to more sub-groups than do women; men create and use occupational cant and jargon; in business, men have acquaintances who belong to many different sub-groups. Women, on the other hand, still tend to be restricted to family and neighborhood friends. Women have very little of their own slang. The new words applied to women's clothing, hair styles, homes, kitchen utensils and gadgets are usually created by men. Except when she accompanies her boy friend or husband to *his* recreation (baseball, hunting, etc.) a woman seldom mingles with other groups. When women do mingle outside of their own neighborhood and family circles, they do not often talk of the outside world of business, politics, or other fields of general interest where new feminine names for objects, concepts, and viewpoints could evolve.

Men also tend to avoid words that sound feminine or weak. Thus there are sexual differences in even the standard vocabularies of men and women. A woman may ask her husband to set the table for dinner, asking him to put out the *silver, crystal,* and *china*—while the man will set the table with *knives, forks, spoons, glasses,* and *dishes.* His wife might think the *table linen attractive,* the husband might think the *tablecloth* and *napkins* pretty. A man will buy a *pocketbook* as a gift for his wife, who will receive a *bag.* The couple will live under the same roof, the wife in her *home,* the man in his *house.* Once outside of their domesticity the man will begin to use slang quicker than the woman. She'll get into the *car* while he'll get into the *jalopy* or *Chevvie.* And so they go: she will learn much of her general slang from him; for any word she associates with the home, her personal belongings, or any female concept, he will continue to use a less descriptive, less personal one.

Males also use slang to shock. The rapid tempo of life, combined with the sometimes low boiling point of males, can evoke emotions— admiration, joy, contempt, anger—stronger than our old standard vocabulary can convey. In the stress of the moment a man is not just in a standard "untenable position," he is *up the creek.* Under strong anger

---

[4] It would appear that the word having the most slang synonyms is *drunk.*

a man does not feel that another is a mere "incompetent"—he is a *jerk* or a *fuck-off*.

Men also seem to relish hyperbole in slang. Under many situations, men do not see or care to express fine shades of meaning: a girl is either a *knockout* or a *dog*, liquor either *good stuff* or *panther piss*, a person either has *guts* or is *chicken*, a book is either *great* or nothing but *crap*. Men also like slang and colloquial wording because they express action or even violence: we *draw pay, pull a boner, make a score, grab some sleep, feed our face, kill time*—in every instance we tend to use the transitive verb, making ourselves the active doer.

The relation between a sub-group's psychology and its cant and jargon is interesting, and the relation between an individual's vocabulary and psychological personality is even more so. Slang can be one of the most revealing things about a person, because our own personal slang vocabulary contains many words used by choice, words which we use to create our own image, words which we find personally appealing and evocative—as opposed to our frequent use of standard words merely from early teaching and habit. Whether a man calls his wife *baby, doll, honey, the little woman, the Mrs.*, or *my old lady* certainly reveals much about him. What words one uses to refer to a mother (*Mom, old lady*), friend (*buddy, bunkie, old man*), the bathroom (*can, John, little boy's room*), parts of the body and sex acts (*boobies, gigi, hard, laid, score*), being tired (*all in, beat*), being drunk (*clobbered, high, lit up like a Christmas tree, paralyzed*), and the like, reveal much about a person and his motivations.[5]

The basic metaphors, at any rate, for all levels of language depend on the five senses. Thus *rough, smooth, touch; prune, sour puss, sweet; fishy, p.u., rotten egg; blow, loud; blue, red, square*. In slang, many metaphors refer to touch (including the sense of heat and cold) and to taste.

Food is probably our most popular slang image. Food from the farm, kitchen, or table, and its shape, color, and taste suggest many slang metaphors. This is because food can appeal to taste, smell, sight, and touch, four of our five senses; because food is a major, universal image to all people, all sub-groups; because men work to provide it and women devote much time to buying and preparing it; because food is before our eyes three times every day.

Many standard food words mean money in nonstandard use: *cab-*

---

[5] For just the last example, *clobbered* may indicate that a drinker is punishing himself, *high* that he is escaping, *lit up like a Christmas tree* that he is seeking attention and a more dominant personality, and *paralyzed* that he seeks punishment, escape or death.

bage, kale, lettuce. Many apply to parts of the body: *cabbage head, cauliflower ear, meat hooks, nuts, plates of meat.* Many food words refer to people: *apple, cold fish, Frog, fruitcake, honey, sweetie pie.* Others refer to general situations and attitudes: to *brew* a plot, to receive a *chewing out,* to find oneself *in a pickle* or something *not kosher,* to be unable to *swallow* another's story, to ask *what's cooking?* Many drunk words also have food images: *boiled, fried, pickled;* and so do many words for nonsense: *applesauce, banana oil, spinach.* Many standard food words also have sexual meanings in slang. The many food words for money, parts of the body, people, and sex reveal that food means much more to us than mere nourishment. When a *good egg brings home the bacon* to his *honey,* or when a *string bean* of a *sugar daddy* takes his *piece* of *barbecue* out to get *fried* with his hard-earned *kale,* food images have gone a long way from the farm, kitchen, and table.

Sex has contributed comparatively few words to modern slang,[6] but these are among our most frequently used. The use of sex words to refer to sex in polite society and as metaphors in other fields is increasing. Sex metaphors are common for the same conscious reasons that food metaphors are. Sex appeals to, and can be used to apply to, most of the five senses. It is common to all persons in all sub-groups, and so we are aware of it continually.

Slang words for sexual attraction and for a variety of sexual acts, positions, and relationships are more common than standard words. Standard non-taboo words referring to sex are so scarce or remote and scientific that slang is often used in referring to the most romantic, the most obscene, and the most humorous sexual situations. Slang is so universally used in sexual communication that when "a man meets a maid" it is best for all concerned that they know slang.[7] Slang words for sex carry little emotional connotation; they express naked desire or mechanical acts, devices, and positions. They are often blunt, cynical and "tough."

The subconscious relating of sex and food is also apparent from reading this dictionary. Many words with primary, standard meanings of food have sexual slang meanings. The body, parts of the body, and descriptions of each, often call food terms into use: *banana, bread, cheese cake, cherry, jelly roll, meat,* etc. Beloved, or simply sexually attractive, people are also often called by food names: *cookie, cup of tea,*

---

[6] Many so-called bedroom words are not technically slang at all, but are sometimes associated with slang only because standard speech has rejected them as taboo. However, many of these taboo words do have further metaphorical meanings in slang: *fucked, jerk, screw you,* etc.

[7] On the other hand, Madame de Staël is reported to have complimented one of her favorite lovers with "speech is not his language."

honey, peach, quail, tomato, etc. This primary relation between sex and food depends on the fact that they are man's two major sensuous experiences. They are shared by all personalities and all sub-groups and they appeal to the same senses—thus there is bound to be some overlapping in words and imagery. However, there are too many standard food words having sexual meanings in slang for these conscious reasons to suffice. Sex and food seem to be related in our subconscious.

Also of special interest is the number of slang expressions relating sex and cheating. Used metaphorically, many sex words have secondary meanings of being cheated, deceived, swindled, or taken advantage of, and several words whose primary meaning is cheating or deceiving have further specific sexual meanings: *cheating, fucked, make, royal screwing, score, turn a trick,* etc. As expressed in slang, sex is a trick somehow, a deception, a way to cheat and deceive us. To curse someone we can say *fuck you* or *screw you,* which expresses a wish to deprive him of his good luck, his success, perhaps even his potency as a man.[8] Sex is also associated with confusion, exhausting tasks, and disaster: *ball buster, screwed up, snafu,* etc. It seems clear, therefore, that, in slang, success and sexual energy are related or, to put it more accurately, that thwarted sexual energy will somehow result in personal disaster.

Language is a social symbol. The rise of the middle class coincided with the period of great dictionary makers, theoretical grammarians, and the "correct usage" dogma. The new middle class gave authority to the dictionaries and grammarians in return for "correct usage" rules that helped solidify their social position. Today, newspaper ads still implore us to take mail-order courses in order to "learn to speak like a college graduate," and some misguided English instructors still give a good speaking ability as the primary reason for higher education.

The gap between "correct usage" and modern practice widens each day. Are there valid theoretical rules for speaking good English, or should "observed usage" be the main consideration? Standard words do not necessarily make for precise, forceful, or useful speech. On the other

---

[8] See F. P. Wood, "The Vocabulary of Failure," *Better English,* Nov., 1938, p. 34. The vocabulary of failure is itself very revealing. Failure in one's personality, school, job, business, or an attempted love affair are all expressed by the same vocabulary. One gets the *brush off,* the *gate,* a *kiss off,* or *walking papers* in both business and personal relationships. As the previous discussion of counterwords demonstrates, slang allows no distinction or degree among individual failures. Incompetence does not apply to just one job or facet of life—either one belongs or is considered unworthy. This unworthiness applies to the entire personality, there are no alternate avenues for success or happiness. One is not merely of limited intelligence, not merely an introvert, not merely ugly, unknowing, or lacking in aggression—but one is a failure in all these things, a complete *drip, jerk,* or *square.* The basic failure is that of personality, the person is not a mere failure— he is an outcast, an untouchable; he is taboo.

hand, "observed usage" can never promise logic and clarity. Today, we have come to depend on "observed usage," just as eighteenth- and nine-teenth-century social climbers depended on "correct usage," for social acceptance.

Because it is not standard, formal, or acceptable under all conditions, slang is usually considered vulgar, impolite, or boorish. As this dictionary shows, however, the vast majority of slang words and expressions are neither taboo, vulgar, derogatory, nor offensive in meaning, sound, or image. There is no reason to avoid any useful, explicit word merely because it is labeled "slang." Our present language has not decayed from some past and perfect "King's English," Latin, Greek, or pre-Tower of Babel tongue. All languages and all words have been, are, and can only be but conventions mutually agreed upon for the sake of communicating. Slang came to America on the Mayflower. In general, it is not vulgar, new, or even peculiarly American: an obvious illustration of this is the polite, old French word *tête*, which was originally slang from a Latin word *testa*—cooking pot.

Cant and jargon in no way refer only to the peculiar words of undesirable or underworld groups. Slang does not necessarily come from the underworld, dope addicts, degenerates, hoboes, and the like. Any cultural sub-group develops its own personal cant and jargon which can later become general slang. All of us belong to several of these specific sub-groups using our own cant and jargon. Teen-agers, steel workers, soldiers, Southerners, narcotic addicts, churchgoers, truck drivers, advertising men, jazz musicians, pickpockets, retail salesmen in every field, golf players, immigrants from every country, college professors, baseball fans—all belong to typical sub-groups from which slang originates. Some of these sub-groups are colorful; most are composed of prosaic, average people.

Many people erroneously believe that a fundamental of slang is that it is intentionally picturesque, strained in metaphor, or jocular. Picturesque metaphor (and metonymy, hyperbole, and irony) does or should occur frequently in all levels of speech. Picturesque metaphor is a frequent characteristic of slang, but it does not define slang or exist as an inherent part of it. The picturesque or metaphorical aspect of slang is often due to its direct honesty or to its newness. Many standard usages are just as picturesque, but we have forgotten their original metaphor through habitual use. Thus slang's *jerk* and *windbag* are no more picturesque than the standard *incompetent* and *fool*. *Incompetent* is from the Latin *competens* plus the negating prefix *in-* and = "unable or unwilling to compete"; *fool* is Old French, from the Latin *follis* which actually = "bellows or wind bag"; slang's *windbag* and the standard *fool* actually have the same metaphor.

As for picturesque sounds, I find very few in slang. Onomatopoeia, reduplications, harsh sounds and pleasing sounds, even rhyming terms, exist on all levels of speech. Readers of this dictionary will find no more picturesque or unusual sounds here than in a similar length dictionary of standard words. Many slang words are homonyms for standard words.

As has been frequently pointed out, many slang words have the same meaning. There seems to be an unnecessary abundance of counter-words, synonyms for "drunk," hundreds of fad words with almost the same meaning, etc. This is because slang introduces word after word year after year from many, many sub-groups. But slang is a scatter-gun process; many new words come at the general public; most are ignored; a few stick in the popular mind.

Remember that "slang" actually does not exist as an entity except in the minds of those of us who study the language. People express themselves and are seldom aware that they are using the artificial divisions of "slang" or "standard." First and forever, language is language, an attempt at communication and self-expression. The fact that some words or expressions are labeled "slang" while others are labeled "jargon" or said to be "from the Anglo-Saxon" is of little value except to scholars. Thus this dictionary is a legitimate addition to standard dictionaries, defining many words just as meaningful as and often more succinct, useful, and popular than many words in standard dictionaries.

FOR DISCUSSION AND REVIEW

1 What distinctions does Flexner make in discussing the terms *argot, slang, colloquial, cant, jargon,* and *dialect*?

2 How is slang created?

3 According to Flexner, what are the three cultural conditions that contribute to the creation of a large slang vocabulary?

4 Why is food imagery so prevalent in slang usage?

5 Flexner's essay was first published in 1960; at that time he claimed that "women have very little of their own slang" because they "still tend to be restricted to family and neighborhood friends." Is this still a fair assessment? Is there an increasing tendency on the part of women to use slang for its shock value? Explain.

6 In the last few years, the drug subculture, the Vietnam War, and the women's movement have produced many slang terms. More recently, the citizens' band radio craze has generated so much slang that dictionaries of CB terms are being published (e.g., *CB Slanguage*). What other areas of American life are now contributing to the corpus of American slang? Discuss some of these areas and the slang associated with them.

7

Course Names:

Another Aspect of College Slang

Paul A. Eschholz and Alfred F. Rosa

Many slang terms used on college campuses today are carried over from other subcategories of American slang, and so the question of how to define collegiate slang has become a difficult one. One area of slang that is unique to the college setting, however, consists of the familiar and sometimes facetious names that students give their courses. The following article, published in a recent issue of *American Speech*, discusses, and categorizes by word-formation processes, such names as they have been used on the campus of the University of Vermont and concludes that, in addition to being often quite humorous, they are an essential component of collegiate slang. Finally, the names that students give the courses they take in college may suggest something about their attitudes toward higher education in general.

C OLLEGE SLANG has a subcategory that consists of the names students give their courses. Richard K. Seymour, in briefly discussing such items, states that "a very frequent type of semantic transfer is that of facetious descriptions of courses to the names of the big courses."[1] Seymour, however, deals only with a few names for courses taken by large numbers of students or for the whole curriculum of a department or school. The use of such names as *dirt farming* for "History of American Democracy" or *God* for courses in a divinity school (to cite two of his examples) is a noteworthy departure from clipped forms such as

[1] "Collegiate Slang: Aspects of Word Formation and Semantic Change," *Publication of the American Dialect Society*, no. 51 (April 1969), 20.

bio, econ, psych, chem, poli sci, and *trig* that traditionally have been used by high school and college students.

With the belief that the phenomenon of students giving bynames to courses is widespread and complex, we set out to study the whole area more extensively, albeit in a limited context. During the past two years we have gathered by questionnaire a large sample of students' names for courses so that we could see more particularly what the data would reveal. The course names were used at the University of Vermont during the academic years 1970–1972, and our informants were students in the "Introduction to the English Language" course offered by the English Department and in an interdepartmental linguistics course. These students provided us with 263 different course names, which were then discussed in our classes in an effort to eliminate any idiosyncratic terms.

Our study of this data revealed that students use familiar patterns in creating slang names for courses. In addition, their names seem to reveal their biases about and attitudes toward particular courses and toward education in general. A wide variety of word-formation processes (such as shortening, acronymy, reduplication, rhyme formation, punning, derivation, blending, and alliteration) is exhibited in our data. The following is a description of these processes with examples, although categorizing is often difficult because several processes are at work in the formation of a course name. The names used in the following discussion are representative of larger categories of data in our study.

Shortening

Brevity is the soul of slang; the short word is easier to remember, is more forceful, and is more frequently used. In addition to the traditional clipped forms mentioned earlier that are still in use today, such as *Trig* for *Trigonometry* and *Calc* for *Calculus,* students have provided new clipped forms for individual courses:

Anal /enəl/	Fundamental Concepts of Mathematical Analysis
	Analytic Geometry and Calculus
Oral Interp	Oral Interpretation of Literature
Con Law	Constitutional Law
Cart	Cartography
Hip Lit	Literature of the Counter-Culture
Brit Lit	British Literature
Stat	Elementary Statistics
Comp and Con	(French) Composition and Conversation
Astrogut	Introductory Meteorology

The only two important words left intact in this list are *oral* and *law,* short words. *Hip* and *gut* are substitutions for *counter-culture* and *intro-*

ductory, respectively. In *Astrogut*, we see not only a clipping (Astronomy) but also a compounding. Also worthy of note are the assonance, rhyme, and alliteration in *Hip Lit, Brit Lit*, and *Comp and Con*.

Acronymy

The proliferation of new organizations and institutions with long, complicated names has spawned a great number of initialisms and acronyms—abbreviations made up of the initials of the original multiword titles.[2] Every year at the University of Vermont the students have their own version of Sadie Hawkins week, when the girls pay all expenses on dates. While it is formally titled "Men's Economic Recovery Program," students affectionately refer to it as *MERP* Week. Student organizations that utilize an easy-to-remember acronym for their names include *DART* (Drug Abuse Research Team) and *BEAM* (Burlington Ecumenical Action Ministry). Although acronyms are more often used for students' social and political organizations, several have found their way into the titles of courses. A still frequent abbreviation is *ROTC* (Reserve Officers Training Corps), which may be pronounced either as an initialism /ar o ti si/ or an acronym /ratsi/ with the spelling variations *R.O.T.C.* and *Rotsy*. A frequently used initialism is *R&R* (Readings and Research), which enjoys widespread popularity because such a course is offered in many departments. Quite possibly this initialism is a carry-over from the Army's "Rest and Recreation." A less frequently used but interesting acronym is *FOC* /fak/ (Foundations of Oral Communication). Students playfully reverse the acronym procedure to yield such variations of the original course name as "Fools Obsessed with Communication" and "Fun on Campus." Whereas government and business, which are responsible for the creation of a great number of acronyms, tend to think in acronymic terms when naming new organizations and agencies, college faculty and administration rarely name courses with such abbreviations in mind. This may explain the sparsity of acronyms for course names; more often than not they seem to be accidental.

Rhyming Pair Formation

Students often use pairs of names to designate their courses. The basic formula for pairs of nouns or verbs, "X and Y" or "X for Y," can be used in several ways. Often the key words rhyme:

---

[2] "The Agonies of Acronymania," *Time*, 20 July 1970, pp. 58, 61.

Priests and Beasts	Introduction to the Study of Western Religion
Trees and Bees	Dendrology
Socks and Jocks	General Physical Education
Slums and Bums	Urban Local Government
Nuts and Sluts	Abnormal Psychology
Gabs and Blabs	Foundations of Oral Communication
Stars and Mars	The Solar System
Struck and Fuck	(Zoology) General Structure and Functions
Trees and Leaves	Dendrology
Hicks and Sticks	Rural Local Government
Stones and Bones	(Anthropology) World Pre-History
Places and Spaces	World Geography
Cuts and Guts	Principles of Biology
Flicks and Tricks	Development of the Motion Picture
Weeds and Seeds	Introduction to Plant Biology
Trains and Planes	Transportation and Public Utilities
Maps and Naps	Introduction to Physical Geography
Spaces and Races	Introduction to Human Geography
Rocks for Jocks	Introductory Geology
Drugs for Thugs	(Psychology) The Drug Culture
Choke and Croak	First Aid and Safety Education
Cut 'em and Gut 'em	Mammalian Anatomy and Physiology
Bag 'em and Tag 'em	Field Zoology
Seed and Breed	Advanced Livestock Production

Several rhyme formations that follow the analogy of "hit the pit" (go to the all-night study area in the basement of the library) include *Mug the Bug* (Principles of Pest Control) and *Play with Clay* ([Art] Basic Design).

A variation on the rhyming pair formation, without the conjunction, is reduplication. Examples are: *Blabber Jabber* (Public Speaking), *Mumble Jumble* (Public Speaking), and *Frig Trig* (Plane Trigonometry).

Nonrhyming Coordinations

Although rhymed pairs are popular because they are easy to remember and have an aura of nursery-school childishness about them, some courses do not easily lend themselves to the rhyming process. The formula of coordinated nouns or verbs is nevertheless used:

Secants and Sines	Plane Trigonometry
Cowboys and Indians	(English) Regional Writing in America
Paper and Pulp	Forest Products
Wind and Rain	Climate
Ice and Snow	Glacial Geology
Needles and Pins	Clothing Selection and Construction
Needles and Thread	Tailoring
Nuts and Bolts	Household Equipment

Tricks and Puzzles	Fundamentals of Mathematics
Food and Nuts	Basic Concepts of Nutrition
Hills and Curves	Highway Geometric Design
Prove 'em and Learn 'em	Fundamental Concepts of Mathematics
Think and Write	Written Expression
Touch and Go	(Psychology) Sensory Perception
Divide and Multiply	Mechanisms of Cell Division
Show and Tell	Public Speaking

Analogical Derivation

The word ending -*ology* "science or study of" is a familiar constituent of college course names (for example, Immunology, Virology, Sedimentary Petrology, Advanced Paleontology); students by analogy have utilized this ending in devising new names for courses. For example, students have taken the forms *cow* and *barf* and applied them to courses entitled "Introductory Dairy Technology" and "Principles of Biology" respectively; to these they have added -*ology* to lend a degree of facetious respectability and academic stuffiness to the new names. The results are humorous incongruities: *Cowology* and *Barfology*. Another example of the same process is the appellation *zerology*, which students apply to any course that is, in their own terms, "a nothing course."

Punning

A play on words is manifested in the following examples:

Where's my fodder?	Fundamentals of Livestock Feeding
Stumping	Introduction to Forestry
Super Bull	Animal Breeding
Confusion	Chinese Religion and Thought
Gut Course	Principles of Biology
Bach to Rock	Survey of Musical Literature

Stumping operates on three levels: the literal "reducing to or removing stumps," the oratorical "speaking as from a stump," and the academic "challenging or perplexing." *Confusion* plays upon the name of Confucius. The last two puns are particularly interesting. *Gut Course*, a label usually reserved for easy or basic courses, is ironically applied to a course that has usually been considered difficult at the University of Vermont. This particular use derives from the subject matter of the course and is related to pair formations *Cut 'em and Gut 'em* and *Cuts of Guts*. *Bach to Rock* is a good pun because it gives a sense of the historical orientation of the course and seems to be related to the expressions "Back to Back" and "Back to Bach."

Synecdoche

Naming a course on the basis of a characteristic part is a form of synecdochic creation. Although synecdoche is evident in some of the other categories, especially pair formation, there are many other examples:

Cottage Cheese	Manufactured Dairy Products
Hoof and Mouth	Animal Diseases
Threads	Introduction to Textiles and Clothing
Loom	Weaving
Secants and Sines	Plane Trigonometry
God	Introduction to the Study of Religion
Sheet Folding	Introductory Nursing
Bedpan	Intermediate Nursing
Diaper Rash	Maternal-Child Nursing
Cat	Mammalian Anatomy and Physiology
Milk	Milk Processing
Steel	(Civil Engineering) Advanced Structural Design
Strength	(Civil Engineering) Mechanics of Materials
Cement	Reinforced Concrete
Water	Hydraulics
Crap	Sanitary Engineering
Clay	Introduction to Ceramics

While synecdoche often uses an important part that is directly associated with the subject to stand for the whole, students may take an unattractive, distasteful, and seemingly insignificant aspect of the course as the part to signify the whole, as in *Bedpan, Sheet Folding, Cottage Cheese,* and *Threads.*

Borrowing

One major category of course names comes from the world of advertising and television. Students borrow program names, the names of famous personalities, and key advertising phrases; they feel that such names are particularly apt for the impression that certain courses give.

Get Smart	(Education) The Slow Learner
Sea Hunt	Geological Oceanography
Edge of Night	Medieval European Civilization
The Lighted Path	Introductory Meteorology
Another World	The Solar System
As the World Turns	History of the United States
Our Changing World	Contemporary History
Ding-Dong Time	(Religion) Myth, Symbol, and Ritual
F Troop	Introduction to Tactics: American Military History
Bright Promise	(Sociology) Social Movements

All in the Family	(Sociology) The Family
Smokey the Bear	Forest Fire Control
Mickey Mouse Math	College Algebra
Roberts' Rules	Parliamentary Procedure
Robin Hood	General Physical Education: Archery
Newton's Menagerie	General Physics
Politics with Tricky Dicky	(Political Science) The National Executive
Blood, Sweat, and Tears	Mammalian Anatomy and Physiology
The Un-Math	Plane Analytic Geometry and Calculus
TV Guide	Advanced Television Production
Fight Now, Pay Later	American Foreign Policy
A & P	Mammalian Anatomy and Physiology
The Elephant and the Ass	Political Parties

The analogy that students make between television programs and courses has some validity. Just like serial television programs, college courses have a main character, a supporting cast, a theme, regular meetings, a generally similar yearly schedule, and a major statement for each installment.

Conclusion

Student bynames for courses, as examples of purely collegiate slang, express student attitudes, which seem to us to be satiric and anti-intellectual. Most of the course names solicited from students reflect their negative or cynical attitudes toward specific courses, education, and society in general. More important, these names are indicative of what appears to be a new wave of criticism directed at higher education. With greater public scrutiny of education has come the cry for accountability and more practicality, if not relevance, in courses, and this trend is also quite evident in our study. Although there are exceptions, in general we found courses that seemed to students to have a practical or utilitarian purpose did not elicit pejorative names.

The items include the vulgar and the witty, with a great deal of skepticism and satire throughout. In addition to the names already cited, the following ones are representative of student attitudes: *Physucks, FOC-off, Grow Your Own Grass, Supergut, American Gutterment, Sadistics, Orgasmic Chem, Flunk Fast, Sex for Credit, Bull for Credit,* and *Dunderology*. Although there has always been a strain of anti-intellectualism in American culture, this trend seems to be more pronounced today.

Much of the slang that college students use can also be found in other subcultures. It is, however, unlikely that the names students give their courses have any use outside the college ambience. Such names, tied as they are to the academic side of college life, seem to be genuine examples of college slang.

FOR DISCUSSION AND REVIEW

1 What are some of the important characteristics of slang? How are these characteristics of slang revealed in college-course names?

2 Do you and the members of your class use unofficial course names? Discuss the various reasons why you do or do not use such names.

3 What types of word-formation processes are revealed in college-course names? Can you think of a course name used by students on your campus that fits each of the word-formation categories?

4 In the "Preface to the *Dictionary of American Slang*" (pp. 236–251), Stuart Berg Flexner discusses the fact that slang is always changing. What are some of the reasons why such change is particularly true of slang names for college courses?

PROJECTS FOR "WORDS, USAGE, AND THE DICTIONARY"

1 There are many different kinds of dictionaries published today. Dictionaries of foreign languages, artists, slang, psychology, and music are only a few. Consult the reference section of your library and list the different dictionaries it contains. In three or four sentences, describe each dictionary.

2 A worthwhile and enjoyable project for the class as a whole is a dictionary debate. Each of three or four groups is asked to become familiar with one of the various recently published desk dictionaries. In turn, individual members of each group are responsible for knowing about particular aspects of their dictionary (e.g., number of entries, usage labels, adequacy of etymology, illustrations, information about synonyms and antonyms, front matter, encyclopedic information, and appendices). It is probably a good idea for all the groups to consider the treatment of a particular word (e.g., *fun*). After the necessary research is completed, the groups meet and debate the merits of their dictionaries. Care should be taken to avoid comparisons between abridged and unabridged dictionaries.

3 If you were compiling a dictionary and had before you only the following quotations, what definition would you write for the word *lasto*? Do not try to find a one-word synonym; write a ten- to twenty-word definition:

a. A lasto is sometimes difficult to clean.

b. Mary put too much food into her lasto and it overflowed.

c. A knife will do many of the jobs that a lasto will do, but the knife cannot do them as efficiently.

d. The blades on a lasto must be bent for it to work well.

e. Some lastos have only three speeds; others have as many as ten.

4   Write a paper on how the Random House, American Heritage, and
    Webster's New World dictionaries have responded to criticisms di-
    rected at Webster's Third New International Dictionary. Reviews of
    these dictionaries would be the most helpful place to begin your study,
    and the Book Review Digest will provide you with references. For re-
    views of Webster's Third, see: James Sledd and Wilma R. Ebbitt, eds.
    Dictionaries and THAT Dictionary (Glenview, Illinois: Scott, Foresman
    and Company, 1962).

5   In her article "Sexism in English: A Feminist View," Nilsen has claimed
    that the English language is inherently sexist. Those in the women's
    movement are not the only ones to have made such a charge regarding
    prejudice; blacks have asserted that English is also inherently prejudi-
    cial on racial grounds. Read William Walter Duncan's essay "How
    'White' Is Your Dictionary?" ETC.: A Review of General Semantics,
    27, no. 1, 89–91; write a brief summary of the article and present it to
    the class for discussion.

6   Find twenty-five words in your desk dictionary that have some relation
    to males and females and study the words in the way Nilsen studied
    her words. Using Nilsen's article "Sexism in English: A Feminist View"
    as a model, write a short paper in which you discuss the biases that you
    see in the language. If some of your words were also used by Nilsen
    (try to avoid excessive overlap), discuss any similarities and differences
    you see in the treatment of the words.

7   In her article "American Euphemisms for Dying, Death, and Burial: An
    Anthology," American Speech, 11, no. 3 (October 1936), 195–202,
    Louise Pound has compiled an impressive list of euphemisms relating to
    death. Other areas of American life that are taboo—and regarding
    which a great number of euphemistic terms are used—include money,
    sex, and disease (anything from acne to cancer). Using Pound's article
    as a model, choose a taboo subject and compile a list of euphemisms
    that are frequently used in treatments of the subject.

8   Study a copy of the New York Times for its use of euphemisms in edi-
    torials, news articles, commercial ads, classified ads, etc. Write an
    essay based on what you find in the newspaper, and then draw some
    conclusions regarding the frequency and types of euphemisms you
    have found. For what purposes are the euphemisms used in the different
    parts of the newspaper?

9   Either as a class project or individually, compile a lexicon of slang (or
    of short-order cooking terms, skiing words, etc.) used on your campus.
    If the project is to be done by the whole class, care should be taken in
    defining words to include the variety of usages offered by all members
    of the class. A related project could center on the principles of word
    making revealed by these efforts. (Some of the difficulty of writing
    definitions may be seen in project 3 above.)

10 *Your class may find it interesting to redo the study done by Eschholz
    and Rosa on slang names for college courses. The students in your
    school should provide many new names; some names, however, may be
    the same. After you have compiled the list of course names, analyze
    them and try to categorize them according to the types of word-making
    processes they reveal.*

11 *Each of the following items is normally discussed as a question of usage
    by usage guides and dictionaries. Consult three or four usage guides in
    the reference room of your library for information about each item.
    What advice does each guide offer? How does the advice given by
    one guide compare with that given by another? What conclusions can
    you draw about the usefulness of such usage guides?*

      1. *hopefully*
      2. *nauseous*
      3. *imply/infer*
      4. *contact (as a verb)*
      5. *ain't*
      6. *among/between*
      7. *enthuse*
      8. *irregardless*
      9. *lay/lie*
     10. *uninterested/disinterested*

SELECTED BIBLIOGRAPHY

Adler, Mortimer. "How To Read A Dictionary." *Saturday Review of Literature*, 24,
    no. 34 (13 December 1941), 3–4, 18–20. (A brief but interesting perusal of
    the dictionary with some historical references.)

Anon. "The Agonies of Acronymania." *Time*, 20 July 1970. (A brief article on the
    rapid growth of acronyms and initialisms in recent years.)

Barnhart, C. L. "Problems in Editing Commercial Dictionaries." *Problems in
    Lexicography*. Ed. Fred W. Householder and Sol Saporta. Bloomington: Publi-
    cation twenty-one of the Indiana Research Center in Anthropology, Folklore,
    and Linguistics, 1962. (Analyzes technical problems facing dictionary editors
    and discusses ways these problems have been solved.)

Bolinger, Dwight. "Structure in Language: The Higher Levels." *Aspects of Lan-
    guage*. New York: Harcourt, Brace & World, 1958. (Excellent introductory
    section on morphemes and their role in word formation.)

————. "The Life and Death of Words." *The American Scholar*, 22, no. 3 (Sum-
    mer 1953), 323–335. (Discusses attempts to see words as being affected by
    the families in which they exist and argues against "straight-line" etymologiz-
    ing.)

Bradley, Henry. "Word-Making in English." *The Making of English*. New York:
    Collier-Macmillan Ltd. and St. Martin's Press, Inc., 1904. (Analyzes the word-
    formation processes of composition, derivation, back-formation, shortening,
    and root-creation.)

Chapman, Robert L. "A Working Lexicographer Appraises Webster's III." *American Speech*, 42, no. 3 (October 1967), 202–210. (Concise criticisms of *Webster's Third* by a lexicographer who used it for three years.)

Current Slang. Published by the English Department at the University of South Dakota, Vermillion, South Dakota, 1969–1971. (Attempted to keep up-to-date on the latest slang usage in America.)

Dieterich, Daniel. *Teaching About Doublespeak*. Urbana, Illinois: NCTE, 1976. (Essays dealing with the theoretical background of doublespeak as well as with teaching it on the elementary, secondary, and college levels.)

Duncan, William Walter. "How 'White' Is Your Dictionary?" *ETC.: A Review of General Semantics*, 27, no. 1, 89–91. (Investigates the use of the words *white* and *black* in *Webster's Third* and concludes that *Webster's Third* is not descriptive in its treatment of these words.)

Eschholz, Paul A., Alfred F. Rosa, and Virginia P. Clark, eds. *Language Awareness*. New York: St. Martin's Press, 1974. (A collection of essays designed to make students more aware of how language affects their lives and how their writing reflects and shapes the world around them.)

ETC.: A Review of General Semantics. San Francisco, California: International Society for General Semantics. (A popular journal of semantics founded by S. I. Hayakawa.)

Farb, Peter. *Word Play: What Happens When People Talk*. New York: Alfred A. Knopf, Inc., 1974; paperback by Bantam, 1974. (A highly readable popularization of recent linguistic work and attitudes toward language; particularly good on language at the word level.)

Gove, Philip B., ed. *The Role of the Dictionary*. Indianapolis: The Bobbs-Merrill Company, Inc., 1967. (A short but readable collection of essays including two useful ones on repetition in defining and usage in the dictionary.)

Gray, Jack, ed. *Words, Words, and Words About Dictionaries*. San Francisco: Chandler Publishing Company, 1963. (A book of readings with considerable sample material.)

Greenough, James, B., and George L. Kittredge. *Words and Their Ways in English Speech*. New York: Crowell-Collier and Macmillan, Inc., 1901; paperback by Beacon Press, 1962. (An older book but still valuable especially on meaning changes and slang.)

Hayakawa, S. I. *Language in Thought and Action*. 3rd edition. New York: Harcourt Brace Jovanovich, Inc., 1972. (A classic introduction to general semantics.)

Hockett, Charles F. "Analogical Creation." *A Course in Modern Linguistics*. New York: The Macmillan Company, 1958. (A description of a specific type of word formation used particularly by children.)

Kolin, Philip C. "The Language of Nursing." *American Speech*, 48, nos. 3–4 (Fall–Winter 1973), 192–210. (A brief but thorough survey of the jargon of the nursing profession.)

Laird, Charlton. "Words and Their Waywardnesses in Present-Day Speech." *College Composition and Communication*, 22, no. 3 (October 1971), 221–228. (Discusses the tendency toward phrase making and specialization in present-day English.)

Lloyd, Donald J., and Harry R. Warfel. "The Dictionary." *American English in Its Cultural Setting*. New York: Alfred A. Knopf, Inc., 1956. (The best short history of the American dictionary.)

Lodwig, Richard R., and Eugene F. Barrett. *The Dictionary and the Language*. New York: Hayden Book Companies, 1967. (Good section on the making of a modern dictionary.)

McNeill, David. "Speaking of Space." *Science,* 152 (May 1966), 875–880. (Discusses the great number of nominal compounds found in technical and space language and the structures that underlie them.)

Mathews, Mitford M. "The Freshman and His Dictionary." *College Composition and Communication,* 6 (December 1955), 187–190. (Discusses the ways in which the dictionary is a useful tool.)

Maurer, David W., and Victor H. Vogel. "The Argot of Narcotics Addicts." *Narcotics and Narcotic Addiction.* 3rd edition. Springfield, Illinois: Charles C. Thomas, 1967. (A discussion of argot formation followed by a glossary of terms.)

Mencken, H. L. *The American Language: The Fourth Edition and the Two Supplements.* Abridged and ed. Raven I. McDavid, Jr. New York: Alfred A. Knopf, Inc., 1963. (A classic study on the subject with an interesting section on euphemisms.)

Pound, Louise. "American Euphemisms for Dying, Death, and Burial: An Anthology." *American Speech,* 11, no. 3 (October 1936), 195–202. (An exhaustive and impressive thematic collection of euphemisms; very little on the psychological implications of euphemistic usage.)

Pyles, Thomas. "Words and Meaning." *The Origins and Development of the English Language.* New York: Harcourt, Brace & World, 1971. (An examination of how and why meanings change.)

Rank, Hugh, ed. *Language and Public Policy.* Urbana, Illinois: NCTE, 1974. (A basic text on public doublespeak published under the auspices of the NCTE Committee on Public Doublespeak.)

Roberts, Paul. "How to Find Fault with a Dictionary." *Understanding English.* New York: Harper & Row, Inc., 1958. (Useful on both the history of dictionaries and how to use them.)

Seymour, Richard K. "Collegiate Slang: Aspects of Word Formation and Semantic Change." *Publication of the American Dialect Society,* no. 51 (April 1969), 13–22. (Somewhat dated but still useful in showing how slang relies on basic word-formation processes.)

Sledd, James, and Wilma R. Ebbitt. *Dictionaries and THAT Dictionary.* Glenview, Illinois: Scott, Foresman and Company, 1962. (A casebook on the controversy concerning the publication of *Webster's Third New International Dictionary.*)

Trippett, B. L. "Profile of a Best Seller." *Technical Communications.* (1970, 3rd quarter). (Discusses some of the reasons behind the great success of the *American Heritage Dictionary.*)

Whitehall, Harold. "The Development of the English Dictionary." *Webster's New World Dictionary of the English Language.* New York: The World Publishing Company, 1958. (A basic historical survey.)

Wilson, Kenneth G., R. H. Hendrickson, and Peter Alan Taylor. *Harbrace Guide to Dictionaries.* New York: Harcourt, Brace & World, Inc., 1963. (Thorough, but does not treat recently published dictionaries.)

PART FIVE

The Systems of Grammar

Investigation of language and its structure has always interested
some scholars, but the last thirty years have brought an amazing
growth of that interest. Linguistics has experienced an explosion
of knowledge similar to that which has occurred in many other
fields. Stimulated by the work of anthropologists with the
American Indian and also by the need for language-study
programs during World War II, scholars began a still uncompleted
reexamination of the nature of language and of particular
languages. In America, this reexamination involved new analyses

of English quite unlike the traditional Latin-based grammar that had been accepted almost without question. And this reexamination led eventually to the introduction into the public schools of several "new" grammars and to the growth in many universities of departments of linguistics.

The initial articles in this section describe the sources of traditional English grammar and some typical attitudes of many native speakers of English toward grammar. Subsequent articles illustrate the development of linguistics in America since World War II. Structural linguistics, the earliest approach described, aroused misgivings in many Americans, who still liked their grammar prescriptive—as the 1961 controversy about *Webster's Third New International Dictionary* revealed. Then, in the late 1950s, another grammatical theory, the transformational-generative one, began to gain increasing acceptance. The emphasis that it placed on cognitive processes and on linguistic universals seemed wholly new, although it in fact had its roots in centuries-old ideas. The last two articles in the section focus on transformational-generative grammar and how it has changed since Noam Chomsky published *Syntactic Structures* in 1957.

Linguists do not yet fully understand human language and how it works, nor do they agree about what form a grammatical description should take. What they all do share, however, is the constant challenge that the study of the complexities of human language offers.

1
Trouble
in Linguistic
Paradise

An allegory, like Bunyan's *Pilgrim's Progress* or Spenser's *The Faerie Queene*, arouses our interest both in the characters and events that are actually described and also in what lies behind them, what they represent. In this short allegorical piece, Professor Charlton Laird describes the feelings of many people in the United States in the mid 1950s as they became aware of the differences between structural linguistics, by then taught in many schools, and the traditional grammar which they had accepted since childhood. Especially disturbing to many was the apparent erosion of standards.

Charlton Laird

ONCE UPON a time the User of English dwelt in a paradise known as the Eden of Linguistic Authority, which the Gods of Prescriptive Grammar had made to wall him from the sins of Doubt, Thought, and Unsanctioned Innovation. The plants in the garden were neatly trimmed, freed of all weedy vulgarisms which might suggest the Vulgus, a many-headed beast, who was to be kept out of the garden. Furthermore, the Great I-Decide of Prescriptive Grammar had provided a Rulebook for the Policing of English, and a Usage Ukase Unifier to enforce it, so that there would never be any uncertainty or irregularity about anything, and the garden would retain its beauty and order forever. The Usage Unifier had put labels on the plants identifying them as they had come from the Celestial Inflectional Syntactical Lexicographical Nursery.

There was, for example, the Lexicographical Tree, which bore all the words in the world. True, these words did not grow quite on the tree itself, but they were in the dictionaries, and the dictionaries hung from the boughs of the tree, and in these works the irrefragable facts about the words were culled and recorded, forever to remain unchanged, *saecula saeculorum*. Each of these words the Gods of Prescriptive Grammar had made in their own images, and the user of English could trust the words because once they had been hung from the boughs of the Lexicographical Tree, that was all he knew and all he would ever need to know.

There was also the Trellis of the Authoritarian Decalogue, a rambling vine draped on a series of handsome signs: "Thou shalt not say 'Ain't,'" "Thou shalt not end a sentence with a preposition," "Thou shalt not use the gauche word *get*, which is inelegant," "Thou shalt not say 'It's me,' which is illogical," and many more. By its name the trellis should have had only ten signs, but time out of mind there seemed to have been an infinity of them, and every time the User of English looked at the trellis he noticed some new ones: "Thou shalt not say 'I will' when 'I shall' is correct"; "Thou shalt not confuse *like* and *as* or say 'Everybody took their hats.'"

Then there were the Hedges of Preferred Usage, which were perhaps the most wonderful plants in the garden, for they surrounded everything. True, they seemed to get nowhere but they kept the more circumspect dwellers in the garden from straying into inelegant locutions. They bore few flowers of poetry, and even the fruits of prose might wither on the durable redundancies that proliferated like suckers from the hedges, but they had a consistency that would cry out strumpet-tongued against the deep damnation of their digging up. The User of English was occasionally irked with them since they got in his way, but he hesitated to root any of them out lest he thereby disrupt some ancient symmetry which the Great I-Decide would feel was very real, although not to the vulgar eye.

Now, there were in the Garden creeping and crawling things, which would skitter under the Hedges of Preferred Usage and go where they pleased, or they would stray outside the walls of the Garden and bring back ways of saying things which were not in the dictionaries on the Lexicographical Tree, and what concourse they had with these Lilith-like locutions of dubious virtue, it were perhaps best not to inquire. One of the cleverest of these creatures was a serpent known as the Modern Linguist, a pernicious fellow, always up to mischief. He would entice the Termites of Research to riddle the signs in the Trellis of the Authoritarian Decalogue, and would whisper slyly to the fat, well-dressed words in the dictionaries, "Did you know, my dear, that your occasional linguistic slips are showing?"

Naturally, the conduct of this serpent troubled the User of English, and one day when he caught the reptile slithering out of a sort of den he had concocted out of multigraphed monographs, linguistic institutes, and rejected allophones, the User accosted him, saying "Look here. I want a conference with you."

"You mean you wish to transform a few morphemes?" the serpent asked slyly, knowing full well that the words *phoneme* and *morpheme* always made the User of English blush for shame.

But the User was not abashed. Recalling his course in English Minus 1, The Principles and Practice of Approved Jargon, he said firmly, "You are featuring a position of maintaining an uncooperative attitude toward certain aspects of the circumstances involving conditions not approved in the regulations, and accordingly I am about to emphasize taking under consideration the expediting of a report."

During this speech the serpent had had plenty of time to twist himself up the Tree of Knowledge of Good and Evil Speech. "The trouble with you, my friend," he said, "is that you have too little poetry in your soul. Even a bit of doggerel would do you no harm. For whatever good it may do, here is a jingle I have been puttering with." Then he recited as follows:

> Oh, purist with zeal thermostatic,
> Devoted to forms hieratic,
>   Degoggle your eyes
>   And try on for size,
> Something morphophonematic.

The serpent disappeared among the leaves, but the User of English could still hear him muttering, as though to himself,

> A pedagogue aptly called Domsky,
> Never got loose from his Momsky,
>   He approached his demise
>   With Carpenter Fries,
> But wait till he hears about Chomsky!

The User of English was outraged. He assumed that these limericks were not intended for him, but there was that crack about the goggles. He was outraged, but he was also intrigued. True, he was wearing goggles, and the Great I-Decide had strictly forbidden him to remove them. Still, I-Decide did not come around as often as he used to, and accordingly the User slipped the goggles sideways for just a peep. Then in amazement he took them off and stared.

The Garden was no longer there. Or it was so changed that at first it seemed not to be there. He could stroll through the Hedges of Preferred Usage, which were full of holes. Even the neat little Parts of Speech were lopping every which way, having little to stand on. The dictionaries still dangled from the Lexicographical Tree, but the definitions in them no longer looked like the codification of eternal truth. And now the User of English was taken with a staggering surmise. Suppose there were no Gods of Prescriptive Grammar, and the Great I-Decide himself a quack or a hoax? Suppose that language had not been made in the images of the Gods of anything, but that he himself, the User of English, had made his language in his own image, not even in his best image, but had blundered into much of it, as it were accidentally, when he was not thinking at all, so that it reflected, along with other things, that little unselfconscious self of dubious repute with Freudian overtones—and the Lord knew what undertones—which another serpent, the Modern Psychologist, had been telling him about?

By the time such questions had been asked, the User of English found himself well outside anything which could any longer be called an Eden of Linguistic Authority. Like Milton's Adam and Eve, "some natural tears he shed, but wiped them soon; the world was all before him." If he could discover nowhere the order and symmetry which he had once supposed existed in the garden of his mother tongue, he found that the more human his language appeared to be, the more interesting it became. It was a bit like a charming baby, his own offspring, which he could chuck under the chin, while listening to it gurgle. Accordingly, he set to examining it, and in the last half century he has discovered a good bit. Meanwhile, he found that his old enemy, the Modern Linguist, was quite a chummy fellow, and what they found together has considerable importance for teachers of English. Let us have a look at some of it.

FOR DISCUSSION AND REVIEW

1 Prepare a brief, nonallegorical summary of Professor Laird's tale. Try to describe very specifically the beliefs of the begoggled "User of English."

2 Throughout this essay, allusions are made to the story of the Garden of Eden. Why does that story work in this context? Explain.

3 Almost at the end of the allegory, the "User of English" removes his goggles. List, in nonallegorical form, the changes he notices in the Garden of Eden. What are his reactions to these changes? Give a contemporary example of each of the kinds of change that he notices.

2

Where Our Grammar Came From

The fact that English grammar has a history going back at least as far as Plato surprises many people, but it is nevertheless true. In the following article, Karl W. Dykema traces this long and complex history from the Graeco-Latinate origins and up through the Middle Ages. In the process of describing the origins of traditional English grammar, Dykema reveals where many of our contemporary misconceptions about grammar and language originated.

Karl W. Dykema

THE TITLE of this paper is too brief to be quite accurate. Perhaps with the following subtitle it does not promise too much: A partial account of the origin and development of the attitudes which commonly pass for grammatical in Western culture and particularly in English-speaking societies.

The etymology of *grammar* shows rather sharp changes in meaning: it starts with Greek *gramma, letter* (of the alphabet), itself a development from *graphein, draw* or *write*. The plural *grammata* develops in meaning through *letters* to *alphabet* to the *rudiments of writing,* to *the rudiments of learning.* The adjective form *grammatike* with *techne* meant the art of knowing one's letters. From this form comes the Latin *grammaticus.* The medieval vernacular forms with *r* are something of a mystery, appearing first in Old Provençal as *gramaira* and developing in English with a variety of spellings, often with only one *m* and ending in *er.* One of the more amusing forms is that with the first *r* dissimilated to *l, glamour.*

In present usage at least four senses can be distinguished which have an application to language: (1) The complete structural pattern of a language learned unconsciously by the child as he acquires his native tongue; (2) an attempt to describe objectively and systematically this fundamental structure, usually called descriptive grammar; (3) a partial description of the language based on puristic or pedagogical objectives, usually called prescriptive grammar; (4) a conviction held by a good many people that somewhere there is an authoritative book called a grammar, the conscientious memorization of which will eliminate all difficulties from their use of language. This I call grammar as remedy. It is mainly with the last two of these notions of grammar that I shall concern myself, prescriptive grammar and grammar as remedy, and how the earlier conceptions of grammar were metamorphosed into them.

As the etymology of the word suggests, Western grammar begins with the ancient Greeks. As early as Plato we find in the *Sophist* the statement that a word describing action is a verb (rhema), one which performs the action is a noun (onoma). Aristotle adds conjunctions (syndesmoi), recognizes that sentences have predicates, and is aware of three genders and of inflection (*Rhetoric*, etc.). The Stoics attempted to separate linguistic study from philosophy and made important contributions to the discipline. In their writings we find terms which are approximately equivalent to *noun, verb, conjunction, article, number, gender, case, voice, mood,* and *tense*.[1] But the direct source of most of our widely used grammatical terms is Dionysius Thrax's little *Techne Grammatike*, which Gilbert Murray recollects his great-uncle still using at the Merchants Taylors' School in the nineteenth century to learn Greek from.[2]

A few quotations from this little work will illustrate how close many of our school grammars still are to their source of more than 2000 years ago:

> A sentence is a combination of words, either in prose or verse, making complete sense. . . . Of discourse there are eight parts: noun, verb, participle, article, pronoun, preposition, adverb, and conjunction. . . . A noun is a part of discourse having cases, indicating a body (as "stone") or a thing (as "education"), and is used in a common and a peculiar way (i.e., is common or proper). . . . A verb is a word without case, admitting tenses, persons, and numbers, and indicating action and passion (i.e., being-acted-upon). . . . A pronoun is a word indicative of definite persons and is used in place of a noun. . . . The adverb is an uninflected part of discourse, used of a verb or subjoined to a verb. . . . The conjunction is a word conjoining or connecting thought in some order and filling a gap in the expression.[3]

The few examples I have given emphasize analysis by meaning, because that is the aspect of classical grammar which our traditional grammar

---

[1] R. H. Robins, *Ancient and Medieval Grammatical Theory in Europe* (London, 1951), pp. 20–35.
[2] Gilbert Murray, *Greek Studies* (Oxford, 1946), p. 181.
[3] "The Grammar of Dionysius Thrax," translated by Thos. Davidson, *Journal of Speculative Philosophy*, 8 (1874): 326–339.

has dwelt upon. But the definitions of noun and verb, it should be observed, begin with formal distinctions—case and tense—and throughout the work there is clearly an awareness of the importance of structure in the functioning of the language. The contribution of the Greeks to linguistics was a great one, as Gilbert Murray and others have pointed out. But for twenty centuries their work was carried on by slavish and unimaginative imitators incapable of developing the work of their predecessors. Especially in the less highly inflected languages like English and French it did not occur to them that the inflectional devices of Latin and Greek must have some counterpart in the structure of the modern language.

Though today there are a few scholars in universities who assert that they pursue grammar for its own sake as an academic discipline, most people conceive of grammar only as a utilitarian thing, as a means of learning to use a language correctly. This notion was certainly completely absent from the thinking of Plato, Aristotle, and the Stoics, and probably from that of Dionysius Thrax. Grammar began as a philosophical inquiry into the nature of language. Now, for most people, it is merely a dogmatic means of achieving correctness. It is this transformation that I am mainly concerned with.

How the transformation took place is not easy to document. Perhaps the most plausible explanation lies in the familiar desire of younger teachers to regurgitate undigested fragments of what they have swallowed in the course of their higher education. All too often a high school teacher just out of college will use his college lecture notes as the foundation of his high school teaching, or a teacher of undergraduates tries to give them exactly what he got in his graduate seminar.

Then there is the fundamental difference between the prevailing purposes of elementary and advanced instruction. Primary education is severely utilitarian; and though it can hardly be denied that, especially in our society, graduate instruction is often infected by utilitarianism, the speculative approach does persist, and inquiry for its own sake plays a major role. The curriculum at all levels of education is and has been determined partly by tradition, partly by immediate utilitarian objectives, partly by a desire to perpetuate the best elements of the cultural heritage. The application of these criteria is of ascending difficulty. Easiest is to accept without question the practice of one's predecessors; not much harder is to accept a limited practical goal and provide instruction intended to achieve it. Most difficult is to select critically what is most valuable in the cultural heritage, and the Romans weren't up to it.

Because of Greek prestige in the ancient world, less developed cultures borrowed extensively from that of Greece. The influence of Greek art, philosophy, and literature on Rome is familiar, but Greek grammar was quite as influential and became the model not only for grammars

of Latin but of Syriac, Armenian, Hebrew, and possibly Arabic as well.
It could not be a good model. The structure of every language is
peculiar to itself—though there are, of course, similarities between members of the same linguistic family—and the best description of it derives
from a careful examination of the language itself, not from an attempt
to fit it into the pattern of another. To be sure, both Greek and Latin
are rich in inflections and the Latin of Varro was not much further
away from the parent Indo-European than was the Greek of Dionysius
Thrax; so the deformation imposed by the model was less distorting
than when the same procedure was followed many centuries later and
attempts were made to strait-jacket the modern vernaculars of Europe
within the model of Latin grammar. For example, Greek had a definite
article, Latin had none, though in Varro's *De Lingua Latina*, the term
articuli is applied to the demonstratives *is* and *hic* (VIII, 45, 51). Latin
has more cases but a different tense system and no dual. English has
only two inflected active tenses against six for Latin, but many more
periphrastic verbal constructions than had Latin.

The attention given to grammar by the ancients seems to have been
considerable. Susemihl in his *History of Greek Literature in the Alexandrian Period* discusses over fifty grammarians. One of them, Aristophanes of Byzantium (ca. 257–ca. 180 B.C.), was librarian to Ptolomy
Epiphanius, who imprisoned him to prevent the king of Pergamum
from hiring him away.

Among the Romans, grammarians were also in demand. The slave
Lutatius Daphnis, a grammarian, was bought for 700,000 sesterces, perhaps $35,000, which puts him about in the class of a lesser baseball
player. Caesar put this Lutatius Daphnis in charge of the public libraries, though it was not until much later, according to Suetonius, that
a regular salary of 100,000 sesterces was paid from the privy purse for
Latin and Greek teachers of rhetoric (Suetonius, *Lives of the Caesars*,
VIII, xviii). Caesar himself took part in one of the persisting grammatical quarrels of the time, that of the analogists and the anomalists, by
producing a work called *De Analogia*, known to us only in fragments.
Though he favored the analogists, who demanded complete inflectional
consistency, it is significant that he wanted no radical departures from
usage.[4] Suetonius also states that Claudius "invented three new letters
and added them to the [Latin] alphabet, maintaining that they were
greatly needed; he published a book on their theory when he was still
in private life, and when he became emperor had no difficulty in bringing about their general use" (Suetonius, *Lives of the Caesars*, V, xli).
Theodore Roosevelt was less successful when he tried to impose a few

[4] Jean Collart, *Varron, Grammairien Latin* (Paris, 1954), pp. 10, 19, 146; Robins,
p. 58.

spelling reforms on the Government Printing Office; Congress refused to permit the changes.

Though Caesar favored the analogists, he was unwilling to depart from established usage. His position was that of many of his cultivated contemporaries, as it has been of many cultivated people ever since. The appeal of analogy is the appeal of logic, a creation of the Greeks and a tool that has been used with interesting and surprising effects in most areas of Western thought ever since. The foundation of Aristotelian logic is the syllogism. As the analogists applied the syllogism to language it worked like this: the form of the personal pronoun determines the form of the verb of which the pronoun is the subject. The form *you* is plural; therefore the form of the verb *be* which follows it must be plural; hence *you were*, not *you was*. So we have in cultivated English today only *you were*. But the cultivated dare not apply this syllogism to the intensive or reflexive, where the eighteenth-century practice of agreement with the notional number of the pronoun still persists. The eighteenth century had both *you was there yourself* and *you were there yourselves*; while we have *you were there yourselves* when the notional number of *you* is plural, but *you were there yourself* when it is singular.

Language has its own logic, which it is the function of the descriptive grammarian to discover if he can. Whatever it may be, it is not Aristotelian logic. But for two millennia our attitudes toward language have been colored by the assumption that the system of a language can be analyzed and prescribed by an intellectual tool that is inapplicable.

Conformity to a standard, or correctness if you like, is, of course, socially of the greatest importance. There is a long record of the penalties imposed on those who deviate from the standard, the earliest I know of being the account given in *Judges* (12, 4–6) of the forty and two thousand Ephraimites who were slain by the Gileadites because they pronounced *shibboleth sibboleth*. Later examples are less gory. Aristophanes in the *Lysistrata* (lines 81–206) ridicules the dialect of the Spartan women, though they are the allies of the Athenian women in their campaign of sexual frustration. Stephen Runciman in his *Byzantine Civilization* says "the Patriarch Nicetas in the Eleventh Century was laughed at for his Slavonic accent, and the statesman Margarites treated with disrespect in the Thirteenth because he spoke with a rough rustic voice."[5] And Chaucer's nun spoke the provincial French of the Benedictine nunnery of Stratford-Bow, the French of Paris—standard French—being to her unknown.

Conformity to the standard is what matters. But how is the standard to be determined? Quintilian, whom Professor T. W. Baldwin calls

[5] Stephen Runciman, *Byzantine Civilization* (Meridian Books, New York, 1956), pp. 173, 176.

"The Supreme Authority" in his *Shakespeare's Small Latine and Lesse Greeke*, provides a most illuminating basis for discussion. In the *Institutes* Quintilian tells us that:

> Language is based on reason, antiquity, authority and usage. Reason finds its chief support in analogy and sometimes in etymology. As for antiquity, it is commended to us by the possession of a certain majesty, I might almost say sanctity. Authority as a rule we derive from orators and historians. For poets, owing to the necessities of metre, are allowed a certain licence. . . . The judgment of a supreme orator is placed on the same level as reason, and even error brings no disgrace, if it results from treading in the footsteps of such distinguished guides. Usage however is the surest pilot in speaking, and we should treat language as currency minted with the public stamp. But in all cases we have need of a critical judgment, . . . (I.vi. 1–3)

This is fuller than Horace's neater statement: "Use is the judge, and law, and rule of speech" (*De Arte Poetica*, 72: *Quem* [*usus*] *penes arbitrium est et ius et norma loquendi*.) and shows more clearly why we have troubles. Usage "is the surest pilot" but "we have need of a critical judgment."

Quintilian has more to say on the matter:

> Usage remains to be discussed. For it would be almost laughable to prefer the language of the past to that of the present day, and what is ancient speech but ancient usage of speaking? But even here the critical faculty is necessary, and we must make up our minds what we mean by usage. If it be defined merely as the practice of the majority, we shall have a very dangerous rule affecting not merely style but life as well, a far more serious matter. For where is so much good to be found that what is right should please the majority? The practices of depilation, of dressing the hair in tiers, or of drinking to excess at the baths, although they may have thrust their way into society, cannot claim the support of usage, since there is something to blame in all of them (although we have usage on our side when we bathe or have our hair cut or take our meals together). So too in speech we must not accept as a rule of language words and phrases that have become a vicious habit with a number of persons. To say nothing of the language of the uneducated, so we are all of us well aware that whole theatres and the entire crowd of spectators will often commit *barbarisms* in the cries which they utter as one man. I will therefore define usage in speech as the agreed practice of educated men, just as where our way of life is concerned I should define it as the agreed practice of all good men. (I.vi. 43–45)

But Quintilian makes it quite apparent from the many examples he cites that educated men are not entirely agreed on their practice, and that they lean heavily on the authority of Greek usage:

> More recent scholars have instituted the practice of giving Greek nouns their Greek declension, although this is not always possible. Personally I prefer to follow the Latin method, so far as grace of diction will permit. For I should not like to say *Calypsonem* on the analogy of *Iunonem*, although Gaius Caesar in deference to antiquity does adopt this way of declining it. Current practice has however prevailed over his authority. In other words which can be declined in either way without impropriety, those who prefer it can employ the Greek form: they will not be speaking Latin, but will not on the other hand deserve censure. (I.v. 63–64)

A thorough knowledge of Greek, learned from slave-tutors, had long been common among educated Romans, but it was Varro who transferred the entire body of Greek grammatical scholarship to Latin in his *De Lingua Latina*, written between 57 and 45 B.C. Though of the original 25 books of that work only V through X survive relatively intact, we have a fairly good account of what was in the rest because Varro is the source which all later Latin grammarians follow, and they have apparently borrowed from him most faithfully.

Greek grammar, is, then, a development of Greek philosophy, an attempt to treat systematically an important aspect of human behavior. It is a late development which in Alexandrian culture is given a practical application through its use in the editing, elucidation, and interpretation of texts, especially that of Homer; and in the correction of solecisms. Since there was little of the speculative in the Romans, Varro's encyclopedic treatment of Latin language and literature was the ultimate source of a host of school texts.

What has been presented so far is a partial account of the development of philology, though this ancient term has been an ambiguous one for almost as long as it has existed—naturally enough, since it derives from the Greek roots usually translated as *love* and *word*. Some people love words as the means of argument, others because they are the foundation of literature, others still for their forms and relations in discourse. All these senses have been designated by the word since it first appeared in Greek, and in nineteenth-century France and Germany it normally included literary history, textual and literary criticism, and linguistics. (We might well revive the word; it would provide a single term by which we could describe ourselves along with chemists, historians, and the rest; we are philologists.)

The ancients called the various aspects of this study by a variety of names: *philologos, grammatikos, grammatistes, kritikos* in Greek; *philo-*

logus, grammaticus, litterator, criticus in Latin. They were evidently no more certain of exactly what the terms signified than we are today with similar terms. Suetonius writes:

> The term *grammaticus* became prevalent through Greek influence, but at first such men were called *litterati*. Cornelius Nepos, too, in a little book in which he explains the difference between *litteratus* and *eruditus* says that the former is commonly applied to those who can speak or write on any subject accurately, cleverly and with authority; but that it should strictly be used of interpreters of the poets, whom the Greeks call *grammatici*. That these were also called *litteratores* is shown by Messala Corvinus in one of his letters, in which he says, "I am not concerned with Furius Bibaculus, nor with Ticidas either, or with the *litterator* Cato." For he unquestionably refers to Valerius Cato, who was famous both as a poet and as a grammarian. Some however make a distinction between *litteratus* and *litterator*, as the Greeks do between *grammaticus* and *grammatista*, using the former of a master of his subject, the latter of one moderately proficient. Orbilius too supports this view by examples, saying: "In the days of our forefathers, when anyone's slaves were offered for sale, it was not usual except in special cases to advertise any one of them as *litteratus* but rather as *litterator*, implying that he had a smattering of letters, but was not a finished scholar."
>
> The grammarians of early days taught rhetoric as well, and we have treatises from many men on both subjects. It was this custom, I think, which led those of later times also, although the two professions had now become distinct, nevertheless either to retain or to introduce certain kinds of exercises suited to the training of orators, such as problems, paraphrases, addresses, character sketches and similar things; doubtless that they might not turn over their pupils to the rhetoricians wholly ignorant and unprepared. But I observe that such instruction is now given up, because of the lack of application and the youth of some of the pupils; for I do not believe that it is because the subjects are underrated. I remember that at any rate when I was a young man, one of these teachers, Princeps by name, used to declaim and engage in discussion on alternate days; and that sometimes he would give instruction in the morning, and in the afternoon remove his desk and declaim. I used to hear, too, that within the memory of our forefathers some passed directly from the grammar school to the Forum and took their place among the most eminent advocates. (*On Grammarians, iv*)

Another writer who provides evidence on the Roman attitudes towards language is Aulus Gellius in his *Attic Nights*. Gellius represents the aristocrat's conviction that what he himself does must be right coupled with the conservative attitude that older practice is to be preferred:

> Valerius Probus was once asked, as I learned from one of his friends, whether one ought to say *has urbis* or *has urbes* and *hanc turrem* or *hanc turrim*. "If," he replied, "you are either composing verse or writing prose and have to use those words, pay no attention to the musty, fusty rules of the grammarians, but consult your own ear as to what is to be said in any given place. What it favors will surely be the best." Then the one who had asked the question said: "What do you mean by 'consult my ear'?" and he told me that Probus answered: "Just as Vergil did his, when in different passages he has used *urbis* and *urbes*, following the taste and judgment of his ear. For in the first *Georgic*, which," said he, "I have read in a copy corrected by the poet's own hand, he wrote *urbis* with an *i*. . . .
>
> But turn and change it so as to read *urbes*, and somehow you will make it duller and heavier. On the other hand, in the third *Aeneid* he wrote *urbes* with an *e*: . . .
>
> Change this too so as to read *urbis* and the word will be too slender and colorless, so great indeed is the different effect of combination in the harmony of neighboring sounds. . . .
>
> These words have, I think, a more agreeable lightness than if you should use the form in *e* in both places." But the one who had asked the question, a boorish fellow surely and with untrained ear, said: "I don't just understand why you say that one form is better and more correct in one place and the other in the other." Then Probus, now somewhat impatient, retorted: "Don't trouble then to inquire whether you ought to say *urbis* or *urbes*. For since you are the kind of man that I see you are and err without detriment to yourself, you will lose nothing whichever you say." (XIII. xxi. 3–8)

And his attitude toward grammarians is expressed quite as explicitly in this passage:

> Within my memory Aelius Melissus held the highest rank among the grammarians of his day at Rome; but in literary criticism he showed greater boastfulness and sophistry than real merit. Besides many other works which he wrote, he made a book which at the time when it was issued seemed to be one of remarkable learning. The title of the book was designed to be especially attractive to readers, for it was called *On Correctness in Speech*. Who, then would suppose that he could speak correctly or with propriety unless he had learned those rules of Melissus?
>
> From that book I take these words: "*Matrona*, 'a matron,' is a woman who has given birth once; she who has done so more than once is called *mater familias*, 'mother of a family'; just so a sow

which has had one litter is called *porcetra;* one which has had more, *scrofa.*" But to decide whether Melissus thought out this distinction between *matrona* and *mater familias* and that it was his own conjecture, or whether he read what someone else had written, surely requires soothsayers. For with regard to *porcetra* he has, it is true, the authority of Pomponius in the Atellan farce which bears that very title; but that "matron" was applied only to a woman who had given birth once, and "mother of the family" only to one who had done so more than once, can be proved by the authority of no ancient writer. . . . (XVIII. vi. 1–7)

By the Middles Ages the aristocrats were unlikely to have had much education, and the classical heritage was perpetuated by the grammarians, whose dogmatic victory was complete. Donatus (fl. 400) and Priscian (fl. 500) are the dominating figures. The name of the first, shortened to Donat or Donet, became synonymous with "grammar" or "lesson" in Old French and Middle English, and the grammar of the second survives in over a thousand manuscripts.[6] He also has the distinction of being consigned to Hell by Dante (*Inferno,* 15:110).

As an example of Priscian, here is the beginning of an analysis of the *Aeneid*—this is not from his big grammar, which was in eighteen books, but from a smaller one, *Partitiones Duodecim Versuum Aeneidos Principalium:*

Scan the verse, *Arma vi/rumque ca/no Tro/iae qui/primus ab/oris.* How many caesuras does it have? Two. What are they? Semiquinaria (penthemimeral) and semiseptenaria (hephthemimeral). How? The semiquinaria is *arma virumque cano* and the semiseptenaria is *arma virumque cano Troiae.* How many figures are there? Ten. For what reason? Because it consists of three dactyls and two spondees. How many parts of speech has this verse? Nine. How many nouns? Six: *arma, virum, Troiae, qui, primus, oris.* How many verbs? One: *cano.* How many prepositions? One: *ab.* How many conjunctions? One, *que.* Discuss each word; *arma,* what part of speech is it? Noun. Of what sort? Appelative (or common). What is its species? General. Its gender? Neuter. Why neuter? Because all nouns which end in *a* in the plural are unquestionably of neuter gender. Why is the singular not used? Because this noun signifies many and various things. . . .[7]

And this is not the end of the catechism on the opening line of Virgil.

---

[6] John Edwin Sandys, A *History of Classical Scholarship* (Cambridge, 1920), vol. 1, p. 230, note; p. 274.
[7] Heinrich Keil, *Grammatici Latini* (Leipzig, 1859), vol. 3, p. 459.

Evidently this sort of drill was to accompany the study of the poem from beginning to end, if the end was ever reached.

Increasingly in the Middle Ages the written heritage of Greece and Rome was accepted unquestioningly because literate men did not have a cultural background which would permit them to ask pertinent questions. We learn, for example, that one of the best sources for the text of Diogenes Laertius is a manuscript of about 1200 written by a scribe "who obviously knew no Greek."[8] To be sure, there were sometimes conflicts between the Christian heritage and the classical, usually resolved in favor of the Christian. In a medieval manuscript is the comment: "Concerning the words *scala* (step), and *scopa* (broom), we do not follow Donatus and the others who claim they are plural because we know that the Holy Ghost has ruled that they are singular." And it was comforting when the traditions of classical grammar could be given divine corroboration. For example: "The verb has three persons. This I hold to be divinely inspired, for our belief in the Trinity is thereby manifested in words." Or this: "Some maintain that there are more, some that there are fewer parts of speech. But the world-encircling church has only eight offices [Presumably Ostiariat, Lektorat, Exorzistat, Akolythat, Subdiakonat, Diakonat, Presbyterat, Episkopat]. I am convinced that this is through divine inspiration. Since it is through Latin that those who are chosen come most quickly to a knowledge of the Trinity and under its guidance find their way along the royal road into their heavenly home, it was necessary that the Latin language should be created with eight parts of speech."[9]

On the other hand, St. Boniface's (675–754) "sense of grammatical accuracy was so deeply shocked when he heard an ignorant priest administering the rite of baptism *in nomine Patria et Filia et Spiritus sancti* [that is, with complete disregard of the required case endings] that he almost doubted the validity of the rite."[10]

Up to about the twelfth century Donatus and Priscian, whose grammars were based ultimately on classical Latin, were followed unquestioningly except where there seemed to be a conflict with sacred texts. The Vulgate and various theological writings were in a later Latin which might disagree with classical grammar, as in the more frequent use of the personal pronouns.[11]

[8] Diogenes Laertius, *Lives of Eminent Philosophers*, with an English translation by R. D. Hicks (Loeb Classical Library) (Cambridge & London, 1925), vol. 1, p. xxxv. (The quotations from Suetonius, Varro, Quintilian, and Aulus Gellius are from the translations in the Loeb Classical Library editions.)
[9] J. J. Baebler, *Beiträge zu einer Geschichte der lateinischen Grammatik im Mittelalter* (Halle a. S., 1885), p. 22/Hans Arens, *Sprachwissenschaft, der Gang ihrer Entwicklung von der Antike bis zur Gegenwart* (Munich, 1955), pp. 30, 31.
[10] Sandys, p. 469.
[11] Baebler, p. 22.

But in the twelfth century the reintroduction of Greek philosophy had a tremendous impact on medieval thought, as is best illustrated by the Aristotelianism of Aquinas. And St. Thomas, as might be expected, deals with philological matters in the *Summa Theologica*, and again as might be expected through the syllogism:

> It seems that in Holy Writ a word cannot have several senses, historical or literal, allegorical, tropological or moral, and anagogical. For many different senses in one text produce confusion and deception and destroy all force of argument. Hence no argument, but only fallacies, can be deduced from a multiplicity of propositions. But Holy Writ ought to be able to state the truth without any fallacy. Therefore in it there cannot be several senses to a word. (First Part, Question One, Article 10, Objection 1)

A more explicitly grammatical example is this one from the thirteenth century:

> For a complete sentence, two things are necessary, namely a subject and a predicate. The subject is that which is being discussed; it is what determines the person of the verb. The predicate is that which is expressed by the subject. Nouns were invented to provide subjects. . . . Verbs were invented to provide predicates.

This concept of grammar being something created is found in another thirteenth-century writer:

> Was he who invented grammar a grammarian? No, because the creation of grammar cannot be based on teaching since that would presuppose its existence. Grammar was invented. For the invention of grammar must precede grammar. So it was not the grammarian but the philosopher who created grammar, for the philosopher studies the nature of things and recognizes their essential qualities.[12]

The authority of the grammarian was occasionally challenged. In a seventeenth-century German satirical treatment of schoolmasters is this account of a fifteenth-century episode:

> The Emperor Sigismund came to the Council of Constance and said: "Videte patres, ut eradicetis schismam Hussitarium." There sat an old Bohemian pedant in the Council who was convinced that with this box on the ear to Priscian the Emperor had sinned against the Catholic Church as gravely as had John Hus and Hieronymus of Prague. So he said [in Latin]: "Most Serene Highness, *schisma* is neuter gender." The emperor said [in German]: "How do you know

12 Arens, pp. 32, 34.

that?" The old Bohemian pedant answered [now in German]: "Alexander Gallus says so." The emperor said: "Who is Alexander Gallus?" The Bohemian pedant answered: "He is a monk." "Yes," said Sigismund, "I am the Roman emperor, and my word is worth at least that of a monk." (Joh. Balthaser Schupp, *Der Teutsche Schulmeister*, 1663)[13]

It now remains to consider the transfer of these attitudes to the modern vernacular languages. But first a brief review of the three preceding stages. The first is the unique situation in Greece, which differed from that of any of the succeeding cultures in two significant ways: it was essentially a monolingual society, and at least during the period of its greatest intellectual and artistic achievement it knew nothing of formal grammar. Rome differed in both essentials. The cultivated Roman was educated in Greek, and formal grammar was a part of his Latin education, though this does not mean that he learned Greek through formal grammar. In the Middle Ages the two-language requirement for the educated, which was characteristic of Rome, was continued, but with an important difference. Whereas for the Roman, Latin was a respectable language with a respectable literature, for the educated man of the Middle Ages his native vernacular was not respectable and at least at first had no important literature. Also he learned the language of scholarship and literature in a way quite different from that used by the Roman. He learned it with the aid of formal grammar.

Of these three stages, the third, the medieval, is much the longest; in formal education and scholarship it lasts well into the eighteenth century and therefore has a duration of well over a thousand years. Of course during the last two or three hundred of those years a great change had come over Europe, due partly to an intimate reacquaintance with the heritage of Greece and Rome. But in the field of philology this meant largely a return to the attitudes of the ancients. It also meant the transference of the whole philological approach—ancient and medieval —to the modern vernacular languages.

The history of vernacular grammars and of English grammars in particular comes next in this development, but there is no space for it here.

One consequence of this transfer must be illustrated: the ambivalence it has given us toward language. Here are some examples. Trollope in his *Autobiography* writes:

The ordinary talk of ordinary people is carried on in short sharp expressive sentences, which very frequently are never completed,—

13 Baebler, p. 118.

the language of which even among educated people is often incorrect. The novel-writer in constructing his dialogue must so steer between absolute accuracy of language—which would give to his conversation an air of pedantry, and the slovenly inaccuracy of ordinary talkers, which if closely followed would offend by an appearance of grimace—as to produce upon the ear of his readers a sense of reality. If he be quite real he will seem to attempt to be funny. If he be quite correct he will seem to be unreal.[14]

The nineteenth-century German philologist Wilhelm Scherer, discussing the great dramatist Heinrich Kleist, remarks that "he did distinguished work in all forms. There dwells in his language an individual magic, though he has an uncertain control of German grammar."[15] And in a recent review in the TLS is this sentence: "He [Leonard Clark] died after completing the first draft of his book, *Yucatan Adventure*, which would have gained some grammar, while losing some of the punch of its author's virile enthusiasm, if it had been more carefully revised."[16]

In a detective story, Rex Stout has Archie Goodwin make this comment after one of the principal characters has said, "Yes. . . . We shall see.": "But what really settled it was her saying, 'We shall see.' He [Nero Wolfe] will always stretch a point, within reason, for people who use words as he thinks they should be used."[17] But in another story Wolfe is made to say, "If it's her again. . . ."[18]

And Mark Twain, who took Cooper severely to task for his "ungrammatical" English, did what was perhaps his best work, in *Huckleberry Finn*, by using a narrative device which relieved him of all responsibility for conforming to standard usage.

One of the most eloquent and emphatic in condemnation of the Latin grammatical tradition was Macaulay but, as you might guess, he is much too long to quote here.[19]

I conclude by returning to the four senses of the term grammar outlined at the beginning. Contemporary philologists who specialize in linguistics have, it seems to me, attempted to strip away the accretions

---

[14] Anthony Trollope, *An Autobiography* (World's Classics, Oxford, 1953), p. 206.
[15] Wilhelm Scherer, *Geschichte der deutschen Literatur* (Knaur, Berlin, n.d.), p. 752.
[16] *Times Literary Supplement*, March 20, 1959, p. 156.
[17] Rex Stout, "Murder Is No Joke," *And Four to Go, A Nero Wolfe Foursome* (New York: Viking, 1958), p. 155.
[18] Rex Stout, "Too Many Women," *All Aces, A Nero Wolfe Omnibus* (New York: Viking, 1958), p. 237.
[19] T. B. Macaulay, "The London University," Edinburgh Review, February 1826, in *Critical, Historical and Miscellaneous Essays and Poems* (Philadelphia: Porter and Coats, n.d.), vol. 3, pp. 631–634.

of two thousand years and are turning to a rigorously descriptive approach, the seeds of which are to be found in the Greeks. Other philologists have other interests, such as literary history, literary criticism, and, of course, the problem of getting freshmen to write better. As an inescapable burden of their academic heritage, they have to bear the weight of the ancient and medieval grammatical tradition, which survives in the other two senses, prescriptive grammar and grammar as remedy. What I have tried to do is to give some account of how that tradition developed, how it was transmitted, and why much of it is essentially irrelevant to the problems the philologist faces today.[20]

[20] A somewhat shorter version of this paper was read to the Northeastern Ohio College English Group, Akron, 5 November 1960.

FOR DISCUSSION AND REVIEW

1 In the first paragraph of his article, Dykema facetiously suggests an elaborate subtitle. In this subtitle he refers to "the attitudes which commonly pass for grammatical in Western culture and particularly in English-speaking societies." Why does he feel that such a qualification is necessary?

2 What does Dykema mean when he states that "grammar began as a philosophic inquiry into the nature of language" but is now mostly "a dogmatic means of achieving correctness"? What causes for this change does he suggest?

3 What etymology does Dykema give for the word *grammar*? Consult your desk dictionary to see how much of this information is available there. On the basis of this comparison, what can you say about the etymologies in desk dictionaries?

4 What four meanings of *grammar* does Dykema say can presently be distinguished? In what sense do you usually use the word *grammar*?

5 Summarize the similarities and differences between traditional English grammar and the grammar of the ancient Greeks.

6 Why was Greek grammar a bad model for the grammars of other languages (e.g., Latin, Hebrew, the modern European languages)?

7 Recognizing the social importance of correct usage, Dykema states, "Conformity to the standard is what matters." He immediately asks, however, "But how is the standard to be determined?" What possibilities does he suggest for determining correct usage? Do you agree with any of the possibilities that he describes?

8 Dykema notes the multiple meanings that the word *philology* has had. Does your desk dictionary indicate that the word is still ambiguous?

9 Who were the following men and why are they important in the history of the study of grammar: Dionysius Thrax, Varro, Donatus, Priscian?

10 Briefly summarize, with respect to grammatical studies, the attitudes toward grammar and the duration of those attitudes in ancient Greece, in Rome, and in the Middle Ages.

11 Dykema speaks of our "ambivalence" toward language caused by "the transference of the whole philological approach—ancient and medieval—to the modern vernacular languages." Explain.

3
Revolution
in Grammar

"Revolution" is not too strong a word to describe the effects that structural linguistics had on language analysis and teaching. Writing in 1954, Professor W. Nelson Francis sets forth the basic premises of the structuralists concerning the characteristics of human language and the appropriate methods of analyzing it. Since the structuralists objected to the inadequacies of traditional grammar, Francis discusses these and briefly traces the history of this grammar; he concludes that "It is now as unrealistic to teach 'traditional' grammar of English as it is to teach 'traditional' (i.e., pre-Darwinian) biology or 'traditional' (i.e., four-element) chemistry." Three years after the original publication of this article, the arrival of another grammatical revolution, that of the transformationalists, was signaled by the appearance of Noam Chomsky's *Syntactic Structures*.

W. Nelson Francis

I

A LONG overdue revolution is at present taking place in the study of English grammar—a revolution as sweeping in its consequences as the Darwinian revolution in biology. It is the result of the application to English of methods of descriptive analysis originally developed for use with languages of primitive peoples. To anyone at all interested in language, it is challenging; to those concerned with the teaching of English (including parents), it presents the necessity of radically revising both the substance and the methods of their teaching.

A curious paradox exists in regard to grammar. On the one hand it is felt to be the dullest and driest of academic subjects, fit only for those in whose veins the red blood of life has long since turned to ink. On the other, it is a subject upon which people who would scorn to be professional grammarians hold very dogmatic opinions, which they will defend with considerable emotion. Much of this prejudice stems from the usual sources of prejudice—ignorance and confusion. Even highly educated people seldom have a clear idea of what grammarians do, and there is an unfortunate confusion about the meaning of the term "grammar" itself.

Hence it would be well to begin with definitions. What do people mean when they use the word "grammar"? Actually the word is used to refer to three different things, and much of the emotional thinking about matters grammatical arises from confusion among these different meanings.

The first thing we mean by "grammar" is "the set of formal patterns in which the words of a language are arranged in order to convey larger meanings." It is not necessary that we be able to discuss these patterns self-consciously in order to be able to use them. In fact, all speakers of a language above the age of five or six know how to use its complex forms of organization with considerable skill; in this sense of the word—call it "Grammar 1"—they are thoroughly familiar with its grammar.

The second meaning of "grammar"—call it "Grammar 2"—is "the branch of linguistic science which is concerned with the description, analysis, and formulization of formal language patterns." Just as gravity was in full operation before Newton's apple fell, so grammar in the first sense was in full operation before anyone formulated the first rule that began the history of grammar as a study.

The third sense in which people use the word "grammar" is "linguistic etiquette." This we may call "Grammar 3." The word in this sense is often coupled with a derogatory adjective: we say that the expression "he ain't here" is "bad grammar." What we mean is that such an expression is bad linguistic manners in certain circles. From the point of view of "Grammar 1" it is faultless; it conforms just as completely to the structural patterns of English as does "he isn't here." The trouble with it is like the trouble with Prince Hal in Shakespeare's play—it is "bad," not in itself, but in the company it keeps.

As has already been suggested, much confusion arises from mixing these meanings. One hears a good deal of criticism of teachers of English couched in such terms as "they don't teach grammar any more." Criticism of this sort is based on the wholly unproved assumption that teaching Grammar 2 will increase the student's proficiency in Grammar 1 or improve his manners in Grammar 3. Actually, the form of Grammar 2 which is usually taught is a very inaccurate and misleading analysis of the facts of Grammar 1; and it therefore is of highly questionable value in improving a person's ability to handle the structural patterns of his language. It is hardly reasonable to expect that teaching a person some inaccurate grammatical analysis will either improve the effectiveness of his assertions or teach him what expressions are acceptable to use in a given social context.

These, then, are the three meanings of "grammar": Grammar 1, a form of behavior; Grammar 2, a field of study, a science; and Grammar 3, a branch of etiquette.

II

Grammarians have arrived at some basic principles of their science, three of which are fundamental to this discussion. The first is that a language constitutes a set of behavior patterns common to the members of a given community. It is a part of what the anthropologists call the culture of the community. Actually it has complex and intimate relationships with other phases of culture such as myth and ritual. But for purposes of study it may be dealt with as a separate set of phenomena that can be objectively described and analyzed like any other universe of facts. Specifically, its phenomena can be observed, recorded, classified, and compared; and general laws of their behavior can be made by the same inductive process that is used to produce the "laws" of physics, chemistry, and the other sciences.

A second important principle of linguistic science is that each language or dialect has its own unique system of behavior patterns. Parts of this system may show similarities to parts of the systems of other languages, particularly if those languages are genetically related. But different languages solve the problems of expression and communication in different ways, just as the problems of movement through water are solved in different ways by lobsters, fish, seals, and penguins. A couple of corollaries of this principle are important. The first is that there is no such thing as "universal grammar," or at least if there is, it is so general and abstract as to be of little use. The second corollary is that the grammar of each language must be made up on the basis of a study of that particular language—a study that is free from preconceived notions of what a language should contain and how it should operate. The marine biologist does not criticize the octopus for using jet-propulsion to get him through the water instead of the methods of self-respecting fish. Neither does the linguistic scientist express alarm or distress when he finds a language that seems to get along quite well without any words that correspond to what in English we call verbs.

A third principle on which linguistic science is based is that the analysis and description of a given language must conform to the requirements laid down for any satisfactory scientific theory. These are (1) simplicity, (2) consistency, (3) completeness, and (4) usefulness for predicting the behavior of phenomena not brought under immediate observation when the theory was formed. Linguistic scientists who have recently turned their attention to English have found that, judged by these criteria, the traditional grammar of English is unsatisfactory. It falls down badly on the first two requirements, being unduly complex and glaringly inconsistent within itself. It can be made to work, just as the Ptolemaic earth-centered astronomy can be, but at the cost of great elaboration and complication. The new grammar, like the Copernican sun-centered astronomy, solves the same problems with greater elegance, which is the scientist's word for the simplicity, compactness, and tidiness that characterize a satisfactory theory.

III

A brief look at the history of the traditional grammar of English will make apparent the reasons for its inadequacy. The study of English grammar is actually an outgrowth of the linguistic interest of the Renaissance. It was during the later Middle Ages and early Renaissance that the various vernacular languages of Europe came into their own. They began to be used for many kinds of writing which had previously always been done in Latin. As the vernaculars, in the hands of great writers like Dante and Chaucer, came of age as members of the linguistic family, a concomitant interest in their grammars arose. The earliest important English grammar was written by Shakespeare's contemporary, Ben Jonson.

It is important to observe that not only Ben Jonson himself but also those who followed him in the study of English grammar were men deeply learned in Latin and sometimes in Greek. For all their interest in English, they were conditioned from earliest school days to conceive of the classical languages as superior to the vernaculars. We still sometimes call the elementary school the "grammar school"; historically the term means the school where Latin grammar was taught. By the time the Renaissance or eighteenth-century scholar took his university degree, he was accustomed to use Latin as the normal means of communication with his fellow scholars. Dr. Samuel Johnson, for instance, who had only three years at the university and did not take a degree, wrote poetry in both Latin and Greek. Hence it was natural for these men to take Latin grammar as the norm, and to analyze English in terms of Latin. The grammarians of the seventeenth and eighteenth centuries who formulated the traditional grammar of English looked for the devices and distinctions of Latin grammar in English, and where they did not actually find them they imagined or created them. Of course, since English is a member of the Indo-European family of languages, to which Latin and Greek also belong, it did have many grammatical elements in common with them. But many of these had been obscured or wholly lost as a result of the extensive changes that had taken place in English—changes that the early grammarians inevitably conceived of as degeneration. They felt that it was their function to resist further change, if not to repair the damage already done. So preoccupied were they with the grammar of Latin as the ideal that they overlooked in large part the exceedingly complex and delicate system that English had substituted for the Indo-European grammar it had abandoned. Instead they stretched unhappy English on the Procrustean bed of Latin. It is no wonder that we commonly hear people say, "I didn't really understand grammar until I began to study Latin." This is eloquent testimony to the fact that the grammar "rules" of our present-day textbooks are largely an inheritance from the Latin-based grammar of the eighteenth century.

Meanwhile the extension of linguistic study beyond the Indo-European and Semitic families began to reveal that there are many different ways in which linguistic phenomena are organized—in other words, many different kinds of grammar. The tone-languages of the Orient and of North America, and the complex agglutinative languages of Africa, among others, forced grammarians to abandon the idea of a universal or ideal grammar and to direct their attention more closely to the individual systems employed by the multifarious languages of mankind. With the growth and refinement of the scientific method and its application to the field of anthropology, language came under more rigorous scientific scrutiny. As with anthropology in general, linguistic science at first concerned itself with the primitive. Finally, again following the lead of anthropology, linguistics began to apply its techniques to the old familiar tongues, among them English. Accelerated by the practical need during World War II of teaching languages, including English, to large numbers in a short time, research into the nature of English grammar has moved rapidly in the last fifteen years. The definitive grammar of English is yet to be written, but the results so far achieved are spectacular. It is now as unrealistic to teach "traditional" grammar of English as it is to teach "traditional" (i.e., pre-Darwinian) biology or "traditional" (i.e., four-element) chemistry. Yet nearly all certified teachers of English on all levels are doing so. Here is a cultural lag of major proportions.

IV

Before we can proceed to a sketch of what the new grammar of English looks like, we must take account of a few more of the premises of linguistic science. They must be understood and accepted by anyone who wishes to understand the new grammar.

First, the spoken language is primary, at least for the original study of a language. In many of the primitive languages,[1] of course, where writing is unknown, the spoken language is the *only* form. This is in many ways an advantage to the linguist, because the written language may use conventions that obscure its basic structure. The reason for the primary importance of the spoken language is that language originates as speech, and most of the changes and innovations that occur in the history of a given language begin in the spoken tongue.

Secondly, we must take account of the concept of dialect. I suppose most laymen would define a dialect as "a corrupt form of language spoken in a given region by people who don't know any better." This introduces moral judgments which are repulsive to the linguistic scholar. Let us approach the definition of a dialect from the more objective end, through the notion of a speech community. A speech community is merely a group of people who are in pretty constant intercommunication. There are various types of speech communities: local ones, like "the people who live in Tidewater Virginia"; class ones, like "the white-collar class"; occupational ones, like "doctors, nurses, and other people who work in hospitals"; social ones, like "clubwomen." In a sense, each of these has its own dialect. Each family may be said to have its own dialect; in fact, in so far as each of us has his own vocabulary and particular quirks of speech, each individual has his own dialect. Also, of course, in so far as he is a member of many speech communities, each individual is more or less master of many dialects and shifts easily and almost unconsciously from one to another as he shifts from one social environment to another.

In the light of this concept of dialects, a language can be defined as a group of dialects which have enough of their sound-system, vocabulary, and grammar (Grammar 1, that is) in common to permit their speakers to be mutually intelligible in the ordinary affairs of life. It usually happens that one of the many dialects that make up a language comes to have more prestige than the others; in modern times it has

---

[1] "Primitive languages" here is really an abbreviated statement for "languages used by peoples of relatively primitive culture"; it is not to be taken as implying anything simple or rudimentary about the languages themselves. Many languages included under the term, such as native languages of Africa and Mexico, exhibit grammatical complexities unknown to more "civilized" languages.

usually been the dialect of the middle-class residents of the capital, like Parisian French and London English, which is so distinguished. This comes to be thought of as the standard dialect; in fact, its speakers become snobbish and succeed in establishing the belief that it is not a dialect at all, but the only proper form of the language. This causes the speakers of other dialects to become self-conscious and ashamed of their speech, or else aggressive and jingoistic about it—either of which is an acknowledgment of their feelings of inferiority. Thus one of the duties of the educational system comes to be that of teaching the standard dialect to all so as to relieve them of feelings of inferiority, and thus relieve society of linguistic neurotics. This is where Grammar 3, linguistic etiquette, comes into the picture.

A third premise arising from the two just discussed is that the difference between the way educated people talk and the way they write is a dialectical difference. The spread between these two dialects may be very narrow, as in present-day America, or very wide, as in Norway, where people often speak local Norwegian dialects but write in the Dano-Norwegian *Riksmaal*. The extreme is the use by writers of an entirely different language, or at least an ancient and no longer spoken form of the language—like Sanskrit in northern India or Latin in western Europe during the later Middle Ages. A corollary of this premise is that anyone setting out to write a grammar must know and make clear whether he is dealing with the spoken or the written dialect. Virtually all current English grammars deal with the written language only; evidence for this is that their rules for the plurals of nouns, for instance, are really spelling rules, which say nothing about pronunciation.

This is not the place to go into any sort of detail about the methods of analysis the linguistic scientist uses. Suffice it to say that he begins by breaking up the flow of speech into minimum sound-units, or phones, which he then groups into families called phonemes, the minimum significant sound-units. Most languages have from twenty to sixty of these. American English has forty-one: nine vowels, twenty-four consonants, four degrees of stress, and four levels of pitch. These phonemes group themselves into minimum meaningful units, called morphemes. These fall into two groups: free morphemes, those that can enter freely into many combinations with other free morphemes to make phrases and sentences; and bound morphemes, which are always found tied in a close and often indissoluble relationship with other bound or free morphemes. An example of a free morpheme is "dog"; an example of a bound morpheme is "un-" or "ex-". The linguist usually avoids talking about "words" because the term is very inexact. Is "instead of," for instance, to be considered one, two, or three words? This is purely a matter of opinion; but it is a matter of fact that it is made up of three morphemes.

In any case, our analysis has now brought the linguist to the point where he has some notion of the word-stock (he would call it the "lexicon") of his language. He must then go into the question of how the morphemes are grouped into meaningful utterances, which is the field of grammar proper. At this point in the analysis of English, as of many other languages, it becomes apparent that there are three bases upon which classification and analysis may be built: form, function, and meaning. For illustration let us take the word "boys" in the utterance "the boys are here." From the point of view of form, "boys" is a noun with the plural ending "s" (pronounced like "z"), preceded by the noun-determiner "the," and tied by concord to the verb "are," which it precedes. From the point of view of function, "boys" is the subject of the verb "are" and of the sentence. From the point of view of meaning, "boys" points out or names more than one of the male young of the human species, about whom an assertion is being made.

Of these three bases of classification, the one most amenable to objective description and analysis of a rigorously scientific sort is form. In fact, many conclusions about form can be drawn by a person unable to understand or speak the language. Next comes function. But except as it is revealed by form, function is dependent on knowing the meaning. In a telegraphic sentence like "ship sails today"[2] no one can say whether "ship" is the subject of "sails" or an imperative verb with "sails" as its object until he knows what the sentence means. Most shaky of all bases for grammatical analysis is meaning. Attempts have been made to reduce the phenomena of meaning to objective description, but so far they have not succeeded very well. Meaning is such a subjective quality that it is usually omitted entirely from scientific description. The botanist can describe the forms of plants and the functions of their various parts, but he refuses to concern himself with their meaning. It is left to the poet to find symbolic meaning in roses, violets, and lilies.

At this point it is interesting to note that the traditional grammar of English bases some of its key concepts and definitions on this very subjective and shaky foundation of meaning. A recent English grammar defines a sentence as "a group of words which expresses a complete thought through the use of a verb, called its predicate, and a subject, consisting of a noun or pronoun about which the verb has something to say."[3] But what is a complete thought? Actually we do not identify sentences this way at all. If someone says, "I don't know what to do," dropping his voice at the end, and pauses, the hearer will know that it is quite safe for him to make a comment without running the risk of

[2] This example is taken from C. C. Fries, *The Structure of English* (New York, 1952), p. 62. This important book will be discussed below.
[3] Ralph B. Allen, *English Grammar* (New York, 1950), p. 187.

interrupting an unfinished sentence. But if the speaker says the same words and maintains a level pitch at the end, the polite listener will wait for him to finish his sentence. The words are the same, the meaning is the same; the only difference is a slight one in the pitch of the final syllable—a purely formal distinction, which signals that the first utterance is complete, a sentence, while the second is incomplete. In writing we would translate these signals into punctuation: a period or exclamation point at the end of the first, a comma or dash at the end of the second. It is the form of the utterance, not the completeness of the thought, that tells us whether it is a whole sentence or only part of one.

Another favorite definition of the traditional grammar, also based on meaning, is that of "noun" as "the name of a person, place, or thing"; or, as the grammar just quoted has it, "the name of anybody or anything, with or without life, and with or without substance or form."[4] Yet we identify nouns, not by asking if they name something, but by their positions in expressions and by the formal marks they carry. In the sentence, "The slithy toves did gyre and gimble in the wabe," any speaker of English knows that "toves" and "wabe" are nouns, though he cannot tell what they name, if indeed they name anything. How does he know? Actually because they have certain formal marks, like their position in relation to "the" as well as the whole arrangement of the sentence. We know from our practical knowledge of English grammar (Grammar 1), which we have had since before we went to school, that if we were to put meaningful words into this sentence, we would have to put nouns in place of "toves" and "wabe," giving something like "The slithy snakes did gyre and gimble in the wood." The pattern of the sentence simply will not allow us to say "The slithy arounds did gyre and gimble in the wooden."

One trouble with the traditional grammar, then, is that it relies heavily on the most subjective element in language, meaning. Another is that it shifts the ground of its classification and produces the elementary logical error of cross-division. A zoologist who divided animals into invertebrates, mammals, and beasts of burden would not get very far before running into trouble. Yet the traditional grammar is guilty of the same error when it defines three parts of speech on the basis of meaning (noun, verb, and interjection), four more on the basis of function (adjective, adverb, pronoun, conjunction), and one partly on function and partly on form (preposition). The result is that in such an expression as "a dog's life" there can be endless futile argument about whether "dog's" is a noun or an adjective. It is, of course, a noun from the point of view of form and an adjective from the point of view

4 *Ibid.*, p. 1.

of function, and hence falls into both classes, just as a horse is both a mammal and a beast of burden. No wonder students are bewildered in their attempts to master the traditional grammar. Their natural clear- ness of mind tells them that it is a crazy patchwork violating the ele- mentary principles of logical thought.

V

If the traditional grammar is so bad, what does the new grammar offer in its place?

It offers a description, analysis, and set of definitions and formulas —rules, if you will—based firmly and consistently on the easiest, or at least the most objective, aspect of language, form. Experts can quibble over whether "dog's" in "a dog's life" is a noun or an adjective, but anyone can see that it is spelled with "s" and hear that it ends with a "z" sound; likewise anyone can tell that it comes in the middle be- tween "a" and "life." Furthermore he can tell that something impor- tant has happened if the expression is changed to "the dog's alive," "the live dogs," or "the dogs lived," even if he doesn't know what the words mean and has never heard of such functions as modifier, sub- ject, or attributive genitive. He cannot, of course, get very far into his analysis without either a knowledge of the language or access to some- one with such knowledge. He will also need a minimum technical vo- cabulary describing grammatical functions. Just so the anatomist is better off for knowing physiology. But the grammarian, like the anat- omist, must beware of allowing his preconceived notions to lead him into the error of interpreting before he describes—an error which often results in his finding only what he is looking for.

When the grammarian looks at English objectively, he finds that it conveys its meanings by two broad devices: the denotations and con- notations of words separately considered, which the linguist calls "lexi- cal meaning," and the significance of word-forms, word-groups, and arrangements apart from the lexical meanings of the words, which the linguist calls "structural meaning." The first of these is the domain of the lexicographer and the semanticist, and hence is not our present concern. The second, the structural meaning, is the business of the structural linguist, or grammarian. The importance of this second kind of meaning must be emphasized because it is often overlooked. The man in the street tends to think of the meaning of a sentence as being the aggregate of the dictionary meanings of the words that make it up; hence the widespread fallacy of literal translation—the feeling that if you take a French sentence and a French-English dictionary and write down the English equivalent of each French word you will come out with an intelligible English sentence. How ludicrous the results can be, anyone knows who is familiar with Mark Twain's retranslation from the French of his jumping frog story. One sentence reads, "Eh bien! I no saw not that that frog has nothing of better than each frog." Upon which Mark's comment is, "if that isn't grammar gone to seed, then I count myself no judge."[5]

The second point brought out by a formal analysis of English is that it uses four principal devices of form to signal structural meanings:

1. Word order—the sequence in which words and word-groups are arranged.

2. Function-words—words devoid of lexical meaning which indicate relationships among the meaningful words with which they appear.

3. Inflections—alterations in the forms of words themselves to signal changes in meaning and relationship.

4. Formal contrasts—contrasts in the forms of words signaling greater differences in function and meaning. These could also be considered inflections, but it is more convenient for both the lexicographer and the grammarian to consider them separately.

Usually several of these are present in any utterance, but they can be separately illustrated by means of contrasting expressions involving minimum variation—the kind of controlled experiment used in the scientific laboratory.

To illustrate the structural meaning of word order, let us compare the two sentences "man bites dog" and "dog bites man." The words are identical in lexical meaning and in form; the only difference is in sequence. It is interesting to note that Latin expresses the difference between these two by changes in the form of the words, without necessarily altering the order: "homo canem mordet" or "hominem canis mordet." Latin grammar is worse than useless in understanding this point of English grammar.

Next, compare the sentences "the dog is the friend of man" and "any dog is a friend of that man." Here the words having lexical meaning are "dog," "is," "friend," and "man," which appear in the same form and the same order in both sentences. The formal differences between them are in the substitution of "any" and "a" for "the," and in the insertion of "that." These little words are function-words; they make quite a difference in the meanings of the two sentences, though it is virtually impossible to say what they mean in isolation.

Third, compare the sentences "the dog loves the man" and "the

5 Mark Twain, "The Jumping Frog; the Original Story in English; the Retranslation Clawed Back from the French, into a Civilized Language Once More, by Patient and Unremunerated Toil," 1601 . . . and Sketches Old and New (n.p., 1933), p. 50.

dogs loved the men." Here the words are the same, in the same order, with the same function-words in the same positions. But the forms of the three words having lexical meaning have been changed: "dog" to "dogs," "loves" to "loved," and "man" to "men." These changes are inflections. English has very few of them as compared with Greek, Latin, Russian, or even German. But it still uses them; about one word in four in an ordinary English sentence is inflected.

Fourth, consider the difference between "the dog's friend arrived" and "the dog's friendly arrival." Here the difference lies in the change of "friend" to "friendly," a formal alteration signaling a change of function from subject to modifier, and the change of "arrived" to "arrival," signaling a change of function from predicate to head-word in a noun-modifier group. These changes are of the same formal nature as inflections, but because they produce words of different lexical meaning, classifiable as different parts of speech, it is better to call them formal contrasts than inflections. In other words, it is logically quite defensible to consider "love," "loves," "loving," and "loved" as the same word in differing aspects and to consider "friend," "friendly," "friendliness," "friendship," and "befriend" as different words related by formal and semantic similarities. But this is only a matter of convenience of analysis, which permits a more accurate description of English structure. In another language we might find that this kind of distinction is unnecessary but that some other distinction, unnecessary in English, is required. The categories of grammatical description are not sacrosanct; they are as much a part of man's organization of his observations as they are of the nature of things.

If we are considering the spoken variety of English, we must add a fifth device for indicating structural meaning—the various musical and rhythmic patterns which the linguist classifies under juncture, stress, and intonation. Consider the following pair of sentences:

Alfred, the alligator is sick!
Alfred the alligator is sick.

These are identical in the four respects discussed above—word order, function-words, inflections, and word-form. Yet they have markedly different meanings, as would be revealed by the intonation if they were spoken aloud. These differences in intonation are to a certain extent indicated in the written language by punctuation—that is, in fact, the primary function of punctuation.

VI

The examples so far given were chosen to illustrate in isolation the various kinds of structural devices in English grammar. Much more commonly the structural meaning of a given sentence is indicated by a combination of two or more of these devices: a sort of margin of safety which permits some of the devices to be missed or done away with without obscuring the structural meaning of the sentence, as indeed anyone knows who has ever written a telegram or a newspaper headline. On the other hand, sentences which do not have enough of these formal devices are inevitably ambiguous. Take the example already given, Fries's "ship sails today." This is ambiguous because there is nothing to indicate which of the first two words is performing a noun function and which a verb function. If we mark the noun by putting the noun-determining function-word "the" in front of it, the ambiguity disappears; we have either "the ship sails today" or "ship the sails today." The ambiguity could just as well be resolved by using other devices: consider "ship sailed today," "ship to sail today," "ship sail today," "shipping sails today," "shipment of sails today," and so on. It is simply a question of having enough formal devices in the sentence to indicate its structural meaning clearly.

How powerful the structural meanings of English are is illustrated by so-called "nonsense." In English, nonsense as a literary form often consists of utterances that have a clear structural meaning but use words that either have no lexical meaning, or whose lexical meanings are inconsistent one with another. This will become apparent if we subject a rather famous bit of English nonsense to formal grammatical analysis:

> All mimsy were the borogoves
> And the mome raths outgrabe.

This passage consists of ten words, five of them words that should have lexical meaning but don't, one standard verb, and four function-words. In so far as it is possible to indicate its abstract structure, it would be this:

> All . . . .y were the . . . . .s
> And the . . .   . . .s   . . . .

Although this is a relatively simple formal organization, it signals some rather complicated meanings. The first thing we observe is that the first line presents a conflict: word order seems to signal one thing, and inflections and function-words something else. Specifically, "mimsy" is in the position normally occupied by the subject, but we know that it is not the subject and that "borogoves" is. We know this because there is an inflectional tie between the form "were" and the "s" ending of "borogoves," because there is the noun-determiner "the" before it, and because the alternative candidate for the subject, "mimsy," lacks both of these. It is true that "mimsy" does have the function-word "all" before it, which may indicate a noun; but when it does, the noun is either plural (in which case "mimsy" would most likely end in "s"), or else the noun is what grammarians call a mass-word (like "sugar," "coal," "snow"), in which case the verb would have to be "was," not "were." All these formal considerations are sufficient to counteract the effect of word order and show that the sentence is of the type that may be represented thus:

All gloomy were the Democrats.

Actually there is one other possibility. If "mimsy" belongs to the small group of nouns which don't use "s" to make the plural, and if "borogoves" has been so implied (but not specifically mentioned) in the context as to justify its appearing with the determiner "the," the sentence would then belong to the following type:

[In the campaign for funds] all alumni were the canvassers.
[In the drought last summer] all cattle were the sufferers.

But the odds are so much against this that most of us would be prepared to fight for our belief that "borogoves" are things that can be named, and that at the time referred to they were in a complete state of "mimsyness."

Moving on to the second line, "And the mome raths outgrabe," the first thing we note is that the "And" signals another parallel assertion to follow. We are thus prepared to recognize from the noun-determiner "the," the plural inflection "s," and the particular positions of "mome" and "outgrabe," as well as the continuing influence of the "were" of the preceding line, that we are dealing with a sentence of this pattern:

And the lone rats agreed.

The influence of the "were" is particularly important here; it guides us in selecting among several interpretations of the sentence. Specifically, it requires us to identify "outgrabe" as a verb in the past tense, and thus a "strong" or "irregular" verb, since it lacks the characteristic past-tense ending "d" or "ed." We do this in spite of the fact that there is another strong candidate for the position of verb: that is, "raths," which bears a regular verb inflection and could be tied with "mome" as its subject in the normal noun-verb relationship. In such a case we should have to recognize "outgrabe" as either an adverb of the kind not marked by the form-contrast ending "ly," an adjective, or the past participle of a strong verb. The sentence would then belong to one of the following types:

And the moon shines above.
And the man stays aloof.
And the fool seems outdone.

But we reject all of these—probably they don't even occur to us—because they all have verbs in the present tense, whereas the "were" of the first line combines with the "And" at the beginning of the second to set the whole in the past.

We might recognize one further possibility for the structural meaning of this second line, particularly in the verse context, since we are used to certain patterns in verse that do not often appear in speech or prose. The "were" of the first line could be understood as doing double duty, its ghost or echo appearing between "raths" and "outgrabe." Then we would have something like this:

All gloomy were the Democrats
And the home folks outraged.

But again the odds are pretty heavy against this. I for one am so sure that "outgrabe" is the past tense of a strong verb that I can give its present. In my dialect, at least, it is "outgribe."

The reader may not realize it, but in the last four paragraphs I have been discussing grammar from a purely formal point of view. I have not once called a word a noun because it names something (that is, I have not once resorted to meaning), nor have I called any word an adjective because it modifies a noun (that is, resorted to function). Instead I have been working in the opposite direction, from form toward function and meaning. I have used only criteria which are objectively observable, and I have assumed only a working knowledge of certain structural patterns and devices known to all speakers of English over the age of six. I did use some technical terms like "noun," "verb," and "tense," but only to save time; I could have got along without them.

If one clears his mind of the inconsistencies of the traditional grammar (not so easy a process as it might be), he can proceed with a similarly rigorous formal analysis of a sufficient number of representative utterances in English and come out with a descriptive grammar. This is just what Professor Fries did in gathering and studying the material for the analysis he presents in the remarkable book to which I have already referred, *The Structure of English*. What he actually did was to put a tape recorder into action and record about fifty hours of telephone conversation among the good citizens of Ann Arbor, Michigan. When this material was transcribed, it constituted about a quarter of a million words of perfectly natural speech by educated middle-class Americans. The details of his conclusions cannot be presented here, but they are sufficiently different from the usual grammar to be revolutionary. For instance, he recognizes only four parts of speech among the words with lexical meaning, roughly corresponding to what the traditional grammar calls substantives, verbs, adjectives, and adverbs, though to avoid preconceived notions from the traditional grammar Fries calls them Class 1, Class 2, Class 3, and Class 4 words. To these he adds a relatively small group of function-words, 154 in his materials, which he divides into fifteen groups. These must be memorized by anyone learning the language; they are not subject to the same kind of general rules that govern the four parts of speech. Undoubtedly his conclusions will be developed and modified by himself and by other linguistic scholars, but for the present his book remains the most complete treatment extant of English grammar from the point of view of linguistic science.

VII

Two vital questions are raised by this revolution in grammar. The first is, "What is the value of this new system?" In the minds of many who ask it, the implication of this question is, "We have been getting along all these years with traditional grammar, so it can't be so very bad. Why should we go through the painful process of unlearning and relearning grammar just because linguistic scientists have concocted some new theories?"

The first answer to this question is the bravest and most honest. It is that the superseding of vague and sloppy thinking by clear and precise thinking is an exciting experience in and for itself. To acquire insight into the workings of a language, and to recognize the infinitely delicate system of relationship, balance, and interplay that constitutes its grammar, is to become closely acquainted with one of man's most miraculous creations, not unworthy to be set beside the equally beautiful organization of the physical universe. And to find that its most complex effects are produced by the multi-layered organization of relatively simple materials is to bring our thinking about language into accord with modern thought in other fields, which is more and more coming to emphasize the importance of organization—the fact that an organized whole is truly greater than the sum of all its parts.

There are other answers, more practical if less philosophically valid. It is too early to tell, but it seems probable that a realistic, scientific grammar should vastly facilitate the teaching of English, especially as a foreign language. Already results are showing here; it has been found that if intonation contours and other structural patterns are taught quite early, the student has a confidence that allows him to attempt to speak the language much sooner than he otherwise would.

The new grammar can also be of use in improving the native speaker's proficiency in handling the structural devices of his own language. In other words, Grammar 2, if it is accurate and consistent, *can* be of use in improving skill in Grammar 1. An illustration is that famous bugaboo, the dangling participle. Consider a specific instance of it, which once appeared on a college freshman's theme, to the mingled delight and despair of the instructor:

Having eaten our lunch, the steamboat departed.

What is the trouble with this sentence? Clearly there must be something wrong with it, because it makes people laugh, although it was not the intent of the writer to make them laugh. In other words, it produces a completely wrong response, resulting in total breakdown of communication. It is, in fact, "bad grammar" in a much more serious way than are mere dialectical divergences like "he ain't here" or "he never seen none," which produce social reactions but communicate effectively. In the light of the new grammar, the trouble with our dangling participle is that the form, instead of leading to the meaning, is in conflict with it. Into the position which, in this pattern, is reserved for the word naming the eater of the lunch, the writer has inserted the word "steamboat." The resulting tug-of-war between form and meaning is only momentary; meaning quickly wins out, simply because our common sense tells us that steamboats don't eat lunches. But if the pull of the lexical meaning is not given a good deal of help from common sense, the form will conquer the meaning, or the two will remain in ambiguous equilibrium—as, for instance, in "Having eaten our lunch, the passengers boarded the steamboat." Writers will find it easier to avoid such troubles if they know about the forms of English and are taught to use the form to convey the meaning, instead of setting up tensions between form and meaning. This, of course, is what English teachers are already trying to do. The new grammar should be a better weapon in their arsenal than the traditional grammar, since it is based on a clear understanding of the realities.

The second and more difficult question is, "How can the change from one grammar to the other be effected?" Here we face obstacles of a formidable nature. When we remember the controversies attending on revolutionary changes in biology and astronomy, we realize what a tenacious hold the race can maintain on anything it has once learned, and the resistance it can offer to new ideas. And remember that neither astronomy nor biology was taught in the elementary schools. They were, in fact, rather specialized subjects in advanced education. How then change grammar, which is taught to everybody, from the fifth grade up through college? The vested interest represented by thousands upon thousands of English and Speech teachers who have learned the traditional grammar and taught it for many years is a conservative force comparable to those which keep us still using the chaotic system of English spelling and the unwieldy measuring system of inches and feet, pounds and ounces, quarts, bushels, and acres. Moreover, this army is constantly receiving new recruits. It is possible in my state to become certified to teach English in high school if one has had eighteen credit hours of college English—let us say two semesters of freshman composition (almost all of which is taught by people unfamiliar with the new grammar), two semesters of a survey course in English literature, one semester of Shakespeare, and one semester of the contemporary novel. And since hard-pressed school administrators feel that anyone who can speak English can in a pinch teach it, the result is that many people are called upon to teach grammar whose knowledge of the subject is totally inadequate.

There is, in other words, a battle ahead of the new grammar. It will have to fight not only the apathy of the general public but the ignorance and inertia of those who count themselves competent in the field of grammar. The battle is already on, in fact. Those who try to get the concepts of the new grammar introduced into the curriculum are tagged as "liberal" grammarians—the implication being, I suppose, that one has a free choice between "liberal" and "conservative" grammar, and that the liberals are a bit dangerous, perhaps even a touch subversive. They are accused of undermining standards, of holding that "any way of saying something is just as good as any other," of not teaching the fundamentals of good English. I trust that the readers of this article will see how unfounded these charges are. But the smear campaign is on. So far as I know, neither religion nor patriotism has yet been brought into it. When they are, Professor Fries will have to say to Socrates, Galileo, Darwin, Freud, and the other members of the honorable fraternity of the misunderstood, "Move over, gentlemen, and make room for me."

FOR DISCUSSION AND REVIEW

1   According to Francis, what meanings may the word *grammar* have? Compare the meanings of *grammar* listed by Francis with those suggested by Dykema (pp. 271–272).

2   List five or six basic premises underlying the "new grammar."

3   What objections does the structuralist have to traditional grammar?

4   What devices does English use to signal structural meaning? Give an example of each.

5   Of what value does Professor Francis find the new grammar? What obstacles did it face in 1954?

6   What do your reactions to Francis' statements suggest about your own attitudes toward language and "correctness"?

4

Transformational-Generative Grammar

Lyda E. LaPalombara

The "happy unanimity" of linguists in the 1950s, to borrow the late Paul Roberts's felicitous phrase, was shattered by the appearance in 1957 of Noam Chomsky's *Syntactic Structures*. This book started what Roberts called "the revolt of the transformationalists." Transformational-generative grammar caused a revolt partly because it asks very different questions about language than did earlier grammars; it is no wonder, therefore, that it arrives at very different answers. In the following selection, Lyda E. LaPalombara traces the development of transformational-generative grammar from its early form as set forth in *Syntactic Structures* (1957), through the so-called standard theory of *Aspects of the Theory of Syntax* (1965), to the contemporary model, which is far from being complete. Finally, she considers in detail the much-debated question of linguistic universals, showing why this question is central both to transformational-generative theory itself and to an understanding of it.

Historical Background

IN 1957, at the height of structuralism's influence on linguistic studies, a young professor of modern languages at the Massachusetts Institute of Technology published a book which challenged many of the basic beliefs of the linguistic "establishment." The professor was A. Noam Chomsky, and his book, a 108-page monograph entitled *Syntactic Structures*, was soon to have a profound effect on language studies.[1]

[1] Chomsky's book was based on his Ph.D. dissertation, written in 1955 at the Uni-

In this small volume, Chomsky leveled major criticisms at the structuralist approach to language study—criticisms which ranged from a general charge that the entire structuralist theory had been built upon "wrong" assumptions to the rejection of such specific structuralist methods as their taxonomic data-gathering techniques and their belief in the adequacy of "discovery procedures."

We should recognize, of course, that the very best of the structuralists had often modified the rigid requirements of structural linguistics to make use of specific insights. One linguist who did this was Zellig Harris, who recently had begun to express the hope that structural grammarians might find a way to move beyond the classification and description of utterances. He felt that linguists ought to extend their research in an effort to arrive at more far-reaching theories concerning the "logic" of language regularities. In fact, during the early fifties, Harris and his student Noam Chomsky had worked together to develop a phrase-structure grammar which, although modeled along the rigorous lines set down by the structuralists, also made some use of scholarly traditional notions which the structural purists had for some time rejected.[2]

It seems fairly clear, then, that Harris's views played a role in encouraging (if not in actually seeding) Chomsky's doubts about the adequacy of the structuralist approach. Whatever the catalyst, Chomsky's own inquiring mind seems early on to have begun to harbor serious misgivings about the theoretical assumptions, the methods, and the future possibilities of the "Bloomfieldian" school of structural linguistics in which he had received his earliest training. It is important for us to understand that despite Chomsky's having come to his views, as is often said, "through" structuralism, his own thinking has been much more closely allied from the beginning with that of the philosophical traditional grammarians from Plato through Humboldt. He does not elaborate on his belief in the existence of a universal grammar in *Syntactic Structures*. But the concept is certainly there: one of his most compelling arguments is for the need, in developing grammars of specific lan-

---

versity of Pennsylvania under the direction of Zellig Harris. The dissertation was based on research conducted by Chomsky while he was a Harvard Fellow (1951–1955). It is said by some that the dissertation contains the seeds of everything Chomsky has done since.

2 At the time when Chomsky wrote *Syntactic Structures*, certain of his views had not yet departed radically from those of the Bloomfieldians. Nevertheless, from the very outset, he strongly criticized the structuralists' taxonomic approach.

In his "Preface," Chomsky acknowledges his considerable indebtedness to Zellig Harris for many ideas and suggestions. (Harris, for example, had already done some early work on transformational structure and had developed a number of string transformations.) Chomsky adds, however, that in this book he proceeds from a somewhat different point of view.

guages, to be certain that these particular grammars fall within the framework of a *general* linguistic theory. This interest in the general nature of language is to be one increasingly emphasized in Chomsky's later work. Here he merely states that it is a "crucial topic."

Chomsky confines himself in *Syntactic Structures* to laying a careful foundation and to outlining the direction in which he believes linguistic study ought to proceed. His first chapter is devoted to carefully defining —and in some cases, redefining—a number of linguistic terms. Next, he states his aim: that of determining the basic underlying principles of a "successful" grammar. He then proceeds to examine a number of generative grammars and to demonstrate that no particular grammar thus far formulated meets his standards of adequacy. Last, he presents a new formulation, phase structure rules plus transformation rules, which he believes is more accurate and more useful. In the process, Chomsky argues that an adequately formulated *grammar* of a language *is*, in fact, a *theory* of that language.

Chomsky believes that the first problem in developing a correct theory (grammar) is that of selecting criteria. Certainly an adequate grammar should be one that is capable of producing grammatical sentences and ruling out ungrammatical ones. But beyond this, a grammar should be able to produce (or to project) *all* of the grammatical sentences possible in a language. Thus, Chomsky argues, it is entirely proper to begin with the assumption that a grammar's adequacy can be tested against the intuitions of a mature native speaker. This is an important point. What Chomsky is saying is that utterances cannot be identified as "grammatical" solely on the basis of their having been spoken—and then collected by a linguistic field worker. An adequate grammar should be able to explain, rather, what the speaker *knows to be possible*. No grammar can be said to be adequate unless it is able to mirror the speaker's ability both to produce and to understand an unlimited number of grammatical utterances—even, and crucially, ones which he has never spoken or heard before.[3] Beyond everyday clichés and speech formulas, the native speaker's typical utterances are completely novel. (The possibility of their ever having occurred before or their ever occurring again is close to zero.) A grammar, then, should somehow be able to reflect this phenomenon; and this is the chief reason that Chomsky is opposed to the kind of grammar which is based on what he considers an unrealistic, high statistical probability of sentence occurrence—the inevitable outcome if one is to consider only those utterances which have been collected.

---

[3] In *Syntactic Structures* Chomsky does not mention that the mature speaker's competence is not necessarily always reflected in grammatical performance. In later works, however, he discusses this "problem" at length.

To illustrate this contention, Chomsky asks the reader to consider this now-famous pair of sentences:

1. Colorless green ideas sleep furiously.
2. Furiously sleep ideas green colorless.

Not only are both of these sentences unfamiliar (in the sense that they have never been spoken or heard before), but they are also "nonsense." Yet, despite the fact that neither sentence has "'meaning," every native speaker of English can recognize that the first sentence is grammatical English, while the second is not. An adequate grammar of English should be able to account for this ability.

These examples suggest another interesting fact: a native speaker can distinguish "grammatical" and "ungrammatical" sentences even when the utterances themselves are devoid of semantic "meaning." Chomsky concludes, accordingly, that a grammar model should be based on syntax rather than on semantics. Syntax is an independent component of a grammar system, and one which is primary.[4]

Before proceeding to the examination and evaluation of grammar models, Chomsky adds one more condition which must be met by an adequate grammar: a correct grammar must be able to account for recursiveness, a process whereby the repeated application of a small number of rules permits the generation of infinitely long sentences. It is apparently a property of all human languages.

Having thus laid the groundwork, so to speak, Chomsky next proceeds to examine and evaluate two known grammar models, and after he finds each of them lacking, to suggest a third, more powerful model. The first of these grammar models, an "elementary linguistic theory," is known mathematically as a "finite state Markov process." It is a simple, linear, left-to-right model which can be graphically represented by the following diagram:

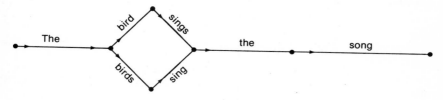

This model can be thought of as a kind of language-generating machine.[5] Beginning at the left and proceeding always to the right in

---

[4] Chomsky's early insistence on the autonomy of syntax is, no doubt, a legacy inherited from Bloomfieldian structuralism, in which he received his earliest linguistic training. As you will see, Chomsky gradually changed his views in the years that followed.

[5] The term "machine" is a mathematical term, not to be confused with a mechan-

the direction of the arrows, each node represents a state where, a choice having been made, the machine "switches" to a new state. At the final node a complete, grammatical sentence will have been generated.

The model can now be expanded by providing a lexicon (a list of words) from which, at any given point, one choice must be made. For example, in the enlarged model below, one must first choose between *a* or *the;* that choice having been made, the machine switches to the next state where one word must be chosen from among the three choices listed. Notice, however, that at the stage where the second lexical choice is made, the speaker is committed to a particular path. Thus, if *boy, girl,* or *bird* is chosen, the next choice has to be either *likes* or *sings.* When the final choice is made, the machine switches to its final state, and a complete sentence has been generated:

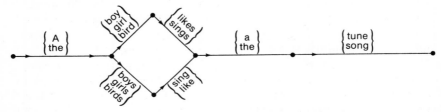

The model can be even further extended by the device of including one or more "closed loops" at various points along the path. One then has the option of going around any closed loop once, twice, or any number of times before proceeding to the next state and eventually to the final state:

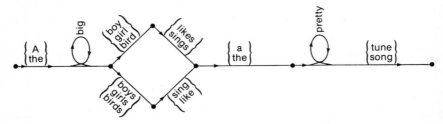

As you can see, by adding closed loops we can construct a model grammar which is able to account for recursiveness and thus to derive infinitely long sentences. Moreover, it is possible to construct similar models for all varieties of sentences in a language and to provide a huge lexicon which includes entries for all possible word choices. Theoretically, at least, it should be possible to provide enough separate models

---

ical device that turns out products assembly-line fashion. Rather, mathematicians refer to their models as machines which give instructions for the generation of an infinite number of correct answers.

to account for an infinite number of the grammatical sentences in a language.

If we grant that the formulation of such a model is possible, complex though it would obviously have to be, we are forced to admit that it is a very powerful grammar indeed. And yet, argues Chomsky, it will not be good enough. Aside from its complexity, a Markov grammar is still not adequate, for there is no conceivable way that such a grammar can account for *all* possible sentences in a language. Precisely because each state along the prescribed left-to-right path is determined by that state immediately preceding it, there is simply no method for explaining grammatical interdependencies between nonadjacent, discontinuous elements. Yet, human languages do have this "mirror-image" characteristic. Consider the English sentence below as an illustration:

Mary, **who,** *although she is pretty,* **thinks herself ugly,** *is pathetic.*
  a   *b*   *c*   *b*   *a*

Notice that in this sentence *a* is dependent on *a*, and *b* is dependent on *b*, for subject-verb agreement.

We must therefore reject a Markov grammar model, for it cannot explain a linguistic characteristic like subject-verb agreement when other words intervene between the subject and the verb. Yet this sort of interdependence between discontinuous elements is, as already pointed out, a characteristic common to natural languages. We therefore need a more powerful grammar—one which will fit into the framework of a general linguistic theory. Although a Markov model can explain *much* of what is true about English sentences, it ultimately leads to a dead end.

Even if it should be possible to devise some highly complex method by which a linear grammar model could overcome this difficulty, it would still be inadequate. If a model could be constructed which would generate only English sentences, such a grammar would not be able to explain all possible sentences. If, on the other hand, it were possible to construct a model that could generate all possible sentences, it would also generate a great many nonsentences.

The second grammar model which Chomsky examines is a phrase-structure grammar (also called constituent or IC grammar). For a number of years linguists, including Chomsky himself, had been attempting with only limited success to write a satisfactory model for an IC grammar. It is in *Syntactic Structures* that Chomsky shows, for the first time, that it is possible to construct a formal, mathematical phrase-structure grammar model. Having seen an analogy between mathematical and linguistic systems, he demonstrates that language, like mathematics, is a system in which a finite number of rules are able to generate an infinite number of correct results.

The "set theory" of mathematics is a particularly useful device, because it can handle syntactic relations between certain discontinuous elements in a string, a phenomenon which cannot be explained with a linear model that describes only individual phonemes, morphemes, and words. A simple arithmetic example might help to make the set theory clear to you. Consider the following two problems:

$$(3 + 4) \times 10 = 70$$
$$3 + (4 \times 10) = 43$$

Notice how the device of bracketing several separate constituents into a single set enlarges and changes an explanation.

The phrase-structure grammar which Chomsky presents in *Syntactic Structures* consists, then, of a limited number of formal rules which explain the linguistic processes involved in generating simple English sentences. Then, borrowing still another mathematical device, he shows how a derivation generated from these "rewriting" rules can be graphically represented in a branching tree diagram.

By formalizing phrase-structure rules in this way, Chomsky is able to demonstrate formally what their strong points and their weaknesses are. He can prove, for example, that a phrase-structure model constructed along these lines is a far more powerful grammar than was the simpler linear model. Yet, though it is superior to the Markov model, it is still lacking, for like the earlier model, a phrase-structure rule is completely dependent upon the string immediately preceding it for its next step in a derivation.

What we need then is a still more powerful model, a model which makes use of phrase-structure rules but is then able to go beyond them. The solution, he thinks, is to add a transformational component to the grammar—a higher level which contains rules for scanning and converting entire derivations. It is this kind of grammar model which Chomsky outlines in *Syntactic Structures*. He calls his model a transformational-generative grammar theory.

But before we continue, several things should be stressed. First, the grammar model presented in *Syntactic Structures* is admittedly incomplete. Chomsky contents himself in his first book with describing the broad outlines of his theory and in presenting arguments to prove that such a theory is better than any previous grammar systems.

It is important also that you avoid the mistake, made by many linguists at the time, of viewing Chomsky's transformational grammar as an extended structuralist theory. Although his grammar is like the grammar of the structuralists in being syntactically based, his goals have been, from the beginning, fundamentally different from those of the structuralists. Basic to Chomsky's argument is his insistence that a grammar theory, if it is to be adequate, must be able to explain a native speaker's linguistic intuitions. It is a description and explanation of mature language competence that Chomsky is after: a theory which is able to account for the grammar knowledge that every speaker has in his head.

These views were quite daring ones for a serious language scholar to voice in the 1950s. Remember, this was the period in American academics which was dominated by the behavioral scientists' empirical methodologies. It was a time when expressions like *insight, mind,* and *intuition* were considered dirty words.

Standard TG Grammar Theory: *Aspects* Model

Overview of the System

In *Syntactic Structures* and in other early work with TG grammar theory, Chomsky, like the structuralists, still viewed language study as an independent and autonomous discipline. However, by the time he wrote *Aspects of the Theory of Syntax* some ten years later, he had come to regard linguistics as a branch of cognitive psychology. To be sure, he still thought a grammar theory should contain a syntax as the principal mediating component, but he was no longer willing to ignore the influence of semantics. This, as you will see, was an important and far-reaching change.

Before we examine the revised TG model,[6] it needs, I think, to be emphasized that a transformational-generative grammar model is *not* to be viewed as the actual process speakers go through to produce the sentences of their language. In the early years this view was a commonly— and mistakenly—held one, possibly because of Chomsky's use of the word *generative*. Actually, the term is one borrowed from mathematics and refers not at all to the actual production of a result—of sentences, in the case of a grammar model. In mathematics, a generative model is one which, taken together with a general theory about mathematics, tries to define explicitly and precisely a particular set of mathematical relations using a process model of description. A transformational-generative grammar, then, is a theory which attempts to explain what speakers *have in their heads,* not what they do.

The *Aspects* TG grammar model has three major components: a *syntax,* a *semantics,* and a *phonology.* Of these three, the syntax is central. It contains a base component and a transformational component.

---

[6] The grammar model presented here is basically the same one that was given in *Aspects*. However, several points which were shortly to supplement the *Aspects* theory have been added.

The base component contains a finite set of phrase-structure rules (both branching rules and subcategorization rules), a lexicon or dictionary (also finite), and some preliminary context-free lexical insertion rules (L rules). The transformational component contains context-sensitive transformational rules of three types: lexical insertion rules, general transformation rules (these are the familiar optional T rules of the *Syntactic Structures* grammar), and two kinds of local transformation rules: affix-incorporation and segment structure T rules. The rules of the base component are said to be context-free, which means that each one of them applies "in ignorance" of any other rules. The transformation rules, on the other hand, are by their very nature context-sensitive: they apply only in certain restricted environments.

The semantic component and the phonological component of the *Aspects* grammar are said to be interpretive. The semantic component operates on the deep structure level; it determines a semantic interpretation of a sentence generated by the rules of the syntactic component. (For example, the semantic component must be consulted for information concerning the inherent semantic features of words: whether a noun, for instance, is common or proper, abstract or concrete, animate or inanimate, and so on—all of which information has syntactic consequences.) In other words, the semantic component takes as "input" the information generated by the base rules of the grammar and assigns a semantic or "meaning" interpretation to the string.

The function of the phonological component is also interpretive. It provides information concerning the pronunciation of constituents. That is, once all transformations have been performed, the phonological component of the grammar finishes the job of converting a deep structure to a surface structure (an actual spoken sentence) by assigning pronunciation features to it.

Although this general explanation is somewhat complicated and difficult to follow, it is important for you to have a preview of what the completed grammar model will look like before we proceed to study the *Aspects* grammar theory in more detail. On the page immediately following, you will find both an outline and a diagram of the overall grammar.

The Search for Linguistic Universals

The notion of linguistic universals developed very early in the history of Western language study and has persisted, in one form or another, ever since. As we have seen, however, the meaning of the term *universal* has varied through the ages. The Ancient Greek scholars debated the universal "rightness" of word meanings, and later, the Greek Stoics speculated that the outer forms of language reveal universal inner

THE TOTAL GRAMMAR SYSTEM

I. SYNTACTIC COMPONENT
   The Base (Context-Free)
   A. Phrase-Structure Rules
      1. Branching Rules
      2. Subcategorization Rules
         a. Strict Subcategorization Rules
         b. Selectional Rules
   B. The Lexicon and Preliminary Lexical Insertion Rules
   C. Transformation Rules (Context-Sensitive)
      1. Final Lexical Insertion T Rules
      2. General T Rules
      3. Local T Rules
         a. Segment Transformations
         b. Other Local Transformations

II. SEMANTIC COMPONENT
   Operates on the base component. Influences subcategorization rules
   and lexicon, and assigns a semantic interpretation to the deep structure generated by the PS rules.

III. PHONOLOGICAL COMPONENT
   Contributes phonological feature matrix information to the lexicon.
   After application of all T rules, provides a phonological interpretation
   for the surface structure.

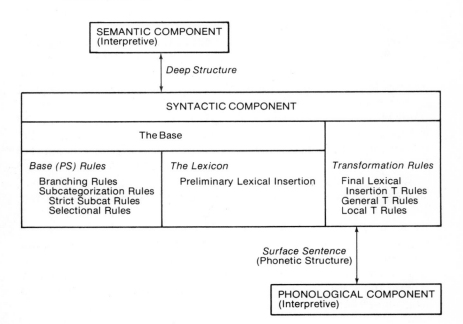

truths about human nature. The beliefs of both groups were based solely, however, on their observations of Greek, which they considered to be the only perfect language.

Certain language scholars of the Middle Ages and the Renaissance (Helias, Sanctius, Huarte, Ramus, and others) also hypothesized about language universals, but their speculations were based on comparisons of the European vernacular languages.

Until the seventeenth century, speculations about language universals seem to have been widely scattered and somewhat random. As a result of the philosophical musings of Descartes and his disciples, interest in linguistic universals was at that time renewed and in fact became the consuming fascination of a great many philosophers and language scholars. The debate between the Rationalists and the Empiricists was destined not to die down until it was overshadowed by the work of the nineteenth-century historical-comparative linguists.

For nearly two centuries thereafter, empirical language research dominated the linguistic scene, conducted first by the European historical and comparative field workers and later by the American structural linguists. The American structuralists in particular came to question nearly every previous assumption concerning language universals, for in studying the exotic American Indian languages, scholars like Bloomfield and Whorf were impressed by the great diversity they observed among languages. In fact, they concluded that every language was separate and independent, most often bearing little or no resemblance to any other language.

We now know that the very methods of the structuralists' linguistic investigations, unavoidably occasioned by their complete unfamiliarity with the tongues they were deciphering, caused them to concentrate exclusively on the surface forms of Indian languages. The consequent confining of their linguistic descriptions to actual utterances understandably led them to exaggerate surface language differences and to fail to see deeper linguistic similarities. Despite their rejection of the concept of language universality, the structuralists nevertheless contributed a number of useful generalizations about language. They became convinced, for example, that there is no such thing as a "primitive" language, that all languages have equally complex grammars, and that every language is capable of expressing whatever needs to be expressed within a given culture. Moreover, the structuralists insisted that any language is capable of being expanded, by the addition of new vocabulary words for example, to handle any new situation which might arise. They further stated that every language has its own rules of phonology, syntax, and semantics, even though such rules often vary greatly from language to language.

We see, therefore, that regardless of the particular linguistic focus of language scholars throughout the entire history of language study, various hypotheses about the nature of language in general have persisted. It is only in recent years, however, that the work of the transformational generative linguists has for the first time made it possible to offer scientific, empirical evidence in support of an explicit theory of linguistic universals.

In *Syntactic Structures*, although Chomsky did not dwell on a discussion of the concept of linguistic universals, he argued that an adequate grammar theory must necessarily be constructed within the framework of a *general* linguistic theory. Indeed, it was precisely Chomsky's insistence that a grammar theory should seek to explain the intuitions of the mature normal native speaker-listener that drew the original fire of the structuralists. They accused Chomsky of being a "mentalist" who simply ignored all of the available scientific evidence—evidence which proved that no claim of language universality could be reasonably made.

In the years since Chomsky's original book, the work of the transformational-generative linguists has made it clear that the really striking observation about languages is how alike they are in their deep structures, despite their superficial differences. The current dispute focuses on the precise nature of linguistic universals, some claiming they are primarily phonological, others claiming that they are chiefly syntactic, and still others arguing that they are semantic.

As Chomsky pointed out in his original book, there are two ways to go about the process of investigating universals. One is to conduct comparative studies of the grammar systems of a great many languages. The second method—and this is the one Chomsky urged—is to conduct in-depth investigations of particular languages, always with the unformulated general goal in mind of explaining the grammar rules of a specific language within the larger framework of a general language theory. Only after a great many detailed generative grammars of particular languages have been analyzed will the linguist be able to determine that corpus of general and specific characteristics which all languages have in common.

In his earliest book, Chomsky argued that syntactic grammar study was an independent, autonomous discipline. But he gradually came to be less certain about this original assumption. In subsequent years, Chomsky and his followers have become interested in the process of language acquisition, and in an explanation for the fact that every language learner inevitably ends up knowing more than could possibly have been learned from the information contained in the primary "input" data. Thus, the whole enterprise of investigating speaker-hearer intuition has had broad philosophical consequences, and has prompted transformational-generative linguists to conclude that mature linguistic competence must be largely attributable to human genetic endowment of a highly specific nature.

General Linguistic Universals

All languages are now known to have sentences, and these sentences are invariably constructed of a sequence of words which are ordered according to a complex system of grammar rules. The sentences of all languages are recursive, and the grammars of all languages exploit redundant grammar signals. All languages have sentences which are transformations of simpler sentences. Moreover, transformation rules universally involve some method of conjoining, or nesting, or both. And T rules are universally performed by means of a limited number of grammatical operations: addition (insertion) rules, reduction or deletion rules, and rearranging or permutation rules.

Because the same grammatical operations occur in all natural human languages, it follows, according to the generative linguists, that certain qualities of mind cannot be ignored. Indeed, it is just such mental properties that must offer explanations for the remarkable sameness of languages, even when they are clearly unrelated either geographically or historically. All language learners must possess a number of innate mental qualities which enable them to learn a language in the first place.

For example, speakers of languages everywhere "know" whether a sentence is put together properly or not, i.e., whether or not a sentence is grammatical. Although speakers cannot necessarily assign label names like *noun* or *verb* to the words of their language, they have some way of distinguishing between word classes, as can be demonstrated by the nature of children's mistakes. An English-speaking child might say, for instance, "John *hitted* me," or "John is *badder* than Jane," but never says anything like "He *spinached* me," or "Jane is *girlest* than me." In other words, a child knows which word classes call for particular inflectional suffixes, and knows these rules before he has learned the irregular forms.

Furthermore, as evidenced by actual linguistic performance, it is clear that all speakers have some means of determining syntactic relationships. For instance, they know the difference between the subject and object of a given verb, for they never interchange such nominals with the subject or object of a verb in another clause.

Speakers also know which elements are modifiers and which nouns or verbs they modify. And given whole sentences, they know that certain structurally dissimilar strings have the same meaning, whereas certain similarly structured strings have different meanings. The fact that mature speakers of all languages have these abilities suggests to the generative linguist that all human beings have similarly "programmed" brains.

Recent studies of language acquisition by children are providing evidence that children everywhere, regardless of language, go through exactly the same language-learning stages. Interestingly, the very kinds of mistakes which children characteristically make at certain stages in the language-learning process indicate that a child's grammar is its own and not that of the mature speaker. Asked to repeat a sentence like "Where can I put this?" a child at a certain stage invariably says, "Where I can put this?" Such a sentence is clearly the child's own production, not an imitation of adult speech. It is as if the child cannot help "processing" the utterance according to its own inner system of "rules." Two transformation operations are called for in the sentence he has been asked to repeat (the addition of a question word in the sentence-initial position, and the transposition of "I" and "can"), but at the particular stage of learning where a sentence like "Where I can put this?" occurs, the child is not yet able to perform more than one transformation operation in a single sentence.

At a later stage in the learning process, a child will be able to perform two operations in a single sentence, but not three. That is, if the interviewer says, "Ask me where you can find the book," the child answers correctly, "Where can I find the book?" The addition of a third operation, however, such as a negative transformation, will result in a mistake. That is, when the interviewer says, "Ask me why you can't find the book," the child, who is capable of only two but not three transformation operations, will answer, "Why I can't find the book?"[7]

Eventually, usually by the age of five or six, children reach a more mature level of competence. At this stage, they "know" the basic grammar rules of their language. Chomsky and other transformationalists have concluded that the only possible answer to such uniformity of learning stages and such uniform results is that certain innate, biologically determined structures and organization principles already reside in the human brain at birth. How else would a language learner be able to sort out from the vast number of syntactic, sound, and meaning signals which actually occur in the sentences of all languages only those few that are significant? How does a language learner arrive at the decision to choose some signals but to reject others? And how explain the obvious fact that all such choosing and rejecting is accomplished at a below-awareness level? Speakers are able to do these things, but they cannot

[7] Detailed results of child language-acquisition studies will not be given here. If you are interested in reading more on this subject, a good general source of information is Dan I. Slobin's monograph, *Psycholinguistics* (Scott, Foresman Basic Psychological Concept Series, 1971).

explain how they do them. Nor are they even aware of the enormous complexity of the task.

For very much the same reasons, Descartes and his rationalist disciples arrived at similar conclusions. Humans, they reasoned, must be genetically endowed with language-learning principles or propensities. Chomsky, however, has gone even further, for he believes that the human brain contains something more than capacity; he believes that it contains innate ideas, principles, and actual structures: a fixed, predetermined set of possible sounds, meanings, and syntactic structures that determine and limit the actual form that any natural human language *must* take.

What the generative linguists are interested in, then, is discovering just what is involved in the cognitive process which determines that every language is cut to the same pattern. Generational linguists now believe that all languages are alike in their deep structures, despite the fact that surface sentences do not resemble each other in point by point language comparisons. Many linguists are also coming to believe that even the grammar rules whereby deep structures are transformed to surface manifestations closely follow a restricted number of universal linguistic tendencies.

Linguistic universals seem to be of two broad types: substantive and formal. When the older grammars mentioned universals at all, they generally referred to substantive ones, such as that the sentences of all languages contain nouns and verbs. Formal universals, on the other hand, are much more abstract and deeply general. They include the kind of phenomena implied in statements regarding the specific form which every language *must* take—the restricted set of possible structures and grammar rules which, because they are already "fixed" in the human mind, any natural human language must be limited to. The following list will give you a general idea of the difference between substantive and formal universals:

SUBSTANTIVE UNIVERSALS	FORMAL UNIVERSALS
Syntax	
Certain fixed universal syntactic categories, like nouns and verbs, exist in all languages.	The grammar of every language contains transformation rules, probably applicable in a least-to-most-dominant, cyclic, hierarchical order.
Semantics	
Certain fixed universal semantic features, like [±Animate], [±Human], exist in all languages.	Every language has a lexicon. More specifically, every language has lexical words to represent proper names. The nature of thought predetermines the terms of word representation.

Phonology

Certain fixed universal phonetic features exist in all languages.	The grammar of every language contains phonological rules, probably applicable in a cyclic hierarchical order from least to most dominant.

As the list above might suggest, it is not always easy to draw a sharp line between substantive and formal universals, nor is it easy to distinguish between semantic and syntactic features. There also appear to be both absolute universals and universal tendencies. Those specific forms of grammar rules which occur in all languages are universal absolutes, whereas those structures or rules which are found in many but not all languages are strong universal tendencies.

In the next few pages, as we discuss more specifically some of these universal absolutes and tendencies, we shall follow the usual practice of lumping syntactic and semantic features together.

Syntactic and Semantic Universals

All languages contain sentences, and the simple sentences of all languages contain the following universal semantic concepts:

1. Sentences of all languages can make positive declarative statements.
2. Negative assertions are possible in all languages.
3. The sentences of all languages can pose questions.
4. Certain sentences of all languages can give commands.

All languages make use of transformations of the more elementary sentences, always by means of conjoining, nesting, or both. Furthermore, transformation rules universally perform a limited number of "fixed" operations out of all conceivable possibilities: insertion of additional elements; reduction or deletion of elements; and rearrangement or permutation of elements. Transformation rules are probably also universally applied in a fixed, least-to-most-dominant cyclic order.

Certain specific rules of syntax are common to all (or most) languages. For example, it is probably a universal absolute that a syntactic plural exists in one form or another in all languages. Similarly, the existence of a syntactic past tense appears to be an absolute linguistic universal, although again the specific method of indicating pastness varies among languages. Although only one past-tense form is present in some languages, there seems to be a strong universal tendency toward different degrees of pastness. Yet another kind of syntactic rule which probably is an absolute is the existence of some form of concord or "agreement" between certain sentence elements.

As for semantic features, not only does every language possess a lexicon of words, but every language so far studied has been found to contain complex lexical items constructed from simpler ones. This phenomenon is accomplished in one of two ways (or both): by compounding or by the addition of affixes. Among affix types, present information indicates that the infix is the least common, while the suffix is the most prevalent. Compounding, on the other hand, most frequently appears to be binary, singularly in the case of the compounding of only two lexical elements, hierarchically in the case of multiple compounding. (Thus, *streetcar conductor* consists first of the two elements, *streetcar* and *conductor*; and at the next level down, *streetcar* consists of the elements, *street* and *car*.)

The clauses of complex sentences tend toward the same structural forms. Equally dominant clauses tend to be ones that are compounded or clauses which are in apposition (i.e., a first clause followed by a second, complement clause). Embedded clauses, on the other hand, tend to be of a restricted number of types: relative clauses, adjectival modifier clauses, adverbial modifier clauses, and the like.

The sequential order of elements within a clause differs fairly widely among languages. Yet, there are certain tendencies, the strongest of which seems to favor the occurrence of subject before verb in the simplest sentences of most languages. Many linguists also believe that some form of verb auxiliary or auxiliaries are present in all languages, and further, that the form of auxiliaries is according to one or both of two methods: verb suffix forms and separate verb-related elements.

Languages seem to be about evenly divided as regards the sequential order of a verb and its objects, some being "verb-initial" and others being "verb-final" languages. Interestingly, however, as Ronald W. Langacker points out, the sequential order of verb-final languages seems to be the exact reverse of that in verb-initial languages.[8] That is, in verb-initial languages, the order is usually Verb + Direct Object + Oblique Object; in verb-final languages, the order is Oblique Object + Direct Object + Verb. Langacker also points out certain reverse parallels between verb-initial and verb-final languages. In verb-initial languages like Samoan or English, for example, pre-positions seem to dominate over post-positions; conjunctions tend to attach to the second or following element rather than to the preceding one; modifiers—especially complex, larger-than-word ones—tend to follow the nouns they modify; and suffix-addition is used only infrequently as a grammatical device.

In verb-final languages like Japanese or Turkish, however, post-positions seem to dominate over pre-positions, conjunctions tend to

---

[8] See chapter 9 of Ronald W. Langacker, *Language and Its Structure*, 2nd edition (Harcourt, 1973).

attach to the preceding rather than to the following element; modifiers of all kinds, both simple and complex, usually precede the nouns they modify; and suffix-addition is heavily exploited as a grammatical device.

Such observations lead Langacker to conclude that, considering the total range of theoretical possibilities for clause construction, the methods toward which human languages universally tend are highly restrictive.

As for specific grammar rules of substitution, deletion, reduction, insertion, and permutation, it appears that certain of these are absolute universals. No language has yet been found, for example, which does not permit the substitution of a pronoun form for a second co-referential noun or noun phrase (a second noun phrase which is identical to an earlier noun phrase within the same clause). Also prevalent, and probably an absolute, is a grammar rule which permits the deletion of a noun or noun phrase when it occurs in a conjoined or embedded clause in the same syntactic position as that of an identical noun phrase in the dominant clause.

Grammar insertion rules across languages also possess strong universal tendencies. It is common to find grammar rules which call for the insertion of a lexically "empty" element in certain transformations (for example, "it" in the transformation, "It is raining"; or the insertion of an "empty" element as a subordination marker, such as the use of "that" in a nominal transformation like "That he is late is true.")

A grammar rule like the English rule which requires that personal pronouns be marked for case (I, she, he, for a subject pronoun; but me, her, or him for an object pronoun) also tends to occur in many languages. In fact, in many languages nouns are similarly marked for subjective or objective case.

As with reduction, deletion, substitution, and insertion rules, linguists have also discovered universal tendencies among permutation rules. One such rule, which has a strong tendency to occur among verb-initial languages especially, requires that relative pronouns and question words be in clause-initial positions. No exceptions to this last rule have yet been found among verb-initial languages, so that in all probability it represents a kind of universal absolute.

The truly significant thing about the recurrent tendency toward or actual use of certain specific grammar rules in language after language is that out of the entire range of possibilities, only a limited few seem to occur. Moreover, as was mentioned earlier, there is no apparent connection between the occurrence of certain rules and historical relatedness or geographical proximity of languages.

As Chomsky pointed out in his radio interview with Stuart Hampshire, many seemingly rational, simple, efficient grammatical operations never occur, while those which do occur are more often than not complex in the extreme. There exists no natural language, for instance, which makes use of such an obviously conceivable operation as that used in "Pig Latin," whereby every word beginning with a consonant deletes the initial consonant and moves it to the end of the word as the first sound in an "-ay" suffix (*fix = ixfay; land = andlay*). Likewise, no language has a rule which requires a noun to "agree" with any element other than its own modifier, or a verb to "agree" with an element other than its own subject or object.

So unlikely, in fact, are many apparently simple operations, such as the transformation of a declarative statement to a question by some elementary process like exactly reversing the word order or reversing the order of every two words; so unlikely is a rule which requires that the first word of every sentence be a noun with an initial consonant; so unlikely are any number of easily imagined elementary processes, as to suggest that certain operations are linguistic impossibilities. The investigations of linguistic universals to date thus strongly support the conclusion that the human brain is "programmed" to look for certain possibilities and to unconsciously reject other processes as insignificant, even when they show up accidentally.

Phonological Universals

Just as all sentences in all languages are composed of strings of words which are put together according to universal concatenation rules, never randomly, so the words of all languages appear to be composed of an extremely limited number of combined sounds. No language has yet been found whose words cannot be subdivided into morphemes, and whose morphemes in turn cannot be further subdivided down to the point of minimal, inherently meaningless sound components or phonemes. Moreover, out of all the possible sounds the human vocal apparatus is capable of producing, only a small number constitute the fixed set of sounds from which the particular phonemes of specific languages are drawn.

As with syntactic and semantic rules, linguists are now able to isolate specific phonological rules which are either linguistic absolutes or universal linguistic tendencies. That is, evidence is accumulating to suggest the existence of a small, fixed number of universal rules of sound combination and organization. Moreover, many linguists now have strong reason to believe that phonological transformation processes are determined by phonological rules that apply in a cyclic sequential order from least to most dominant sounds.

Among the possible phonological universals, the following are some that have been suggested as either phonological absolutes or as strong phonological tendencies:

GENERAL, MOSTLY SUBSTANTIVE
PHONOLOGICAL UNIVERSALS

1. All languages use combinations of minimal, meaningless sounds (phonemes) to form meaningful word components (morphemes), which in turn combine to form the words of languages.

2. All languages make use of both consonant and vowel sounds.

3. All languages seem to make use of three nasal phonemes.

4. All languages make use of "glides" between certain sounds.

5. The phonemes of all languages are chosen from a fixed, restricted list of possible sounds which might conceivably be exploited in human languages.

6. No morpheme in any language has yet been discovered to consist of as many as, say, nine consecutive vowel sounds or nine consecutive consonant sounds.

7. For those languages which are "tone" languages, no morpheme has yet been discovered which consists of more than six "tones"; usually, in fact, a language will exploit only four or five different tones.

MORE SPECIFIC FORMAL PHONOLOGICAL UNIVERSALS

There appear to exist certain phonological rules which determine which sounds may occur next to other sounds. For instance:

8. A phonological transformation rule which may be an absolute but which certainly represents a strong universal tendency requires the mutation or the deletion of unstressed vowels. English examples of such a vowel sound mutation principle can be illustrated with such word pairs as *realize/realization; senile/senility; fancy/fanciful*. The sound deletion principle can be illustrated with the English combinations, *I am/I'm; do not/don't; was not/wasn't*.

9. Another recurring phonological transformation rule calls for the aspiration of a voiceless consonant (like the /p/ of *tap*) when it occurs in a sound-initial position: *pat*.

10. There seems to exist a common phonological rule that requires the insertion of a consonant sound segment between two separate and distinct vowel sounds, as in the English words *a + apple*, which becomes *an apple*.

11. Yet another apparently universal phonological rule calls for the nasalization of a vowel sound when it occurs before a nasal consonant like /ŋ/. An example is the English word pair: *sin/sing*.

12. The linguist would never expect to find certain consonant sounds transformed to other consonant sounds, as for example, a /k/ sound changed to /m/ or /l/. On the other hand, it is very common in all languages to find an /s/ or a /t/ sound changed to /š/ sound: *face/facial; part/partial.*

Summary Comments

Work has only just begun in the search for linguistic universals. All linguists understand that their present conclusions must be regarded as tentative, for at any time new evidence may surface which disproves some of their current hypotheses. Nevertheless, enough progress has been made to allow for the conclusion that in all probability, linguistic universals exist as a reality—not only as extremely general, substantive statements concerning phenomena which all languages share in common, but also as more specific statements of formal universal principles that determine the grammar rules of all human languages.

Certainly, the assumption of the existence of such language universals goes a long way toward explaining both human linguistic creativity and the language acquisition process in the first place. From the infinite number of ways the earth might have come into existence, only one was needed. This one means of creation having taken place, evolutionary events followed certain patterns. It is certainly more useful and more interesting to study those patterns than to stand in awe of the fact that one course of events was followed rather than any other. The same applies to the origins and study of language. The evident truth simply cannot be ignored: that of all the myriad conceivable ways that languages could be structured, natural human languages seem to be confined to a limited and apparently fixed number of grammatical processes.

Still, in spite of the distance over which linguists have advanced their knowledge, we are a long way from reaching complete answers. Even if we accept the concept of innate linguistic specifications, there still remain a host of unanswered questions. Exactly what, for example, must language learners discover beyond that which is genetically specified in their own brains? How much of language learning is attributable to external observation and experience with a particular language? Are there precise, predetermined, specific phases through which every child must go before it discovers the grammar rules of its own native language? And to what extent are linguistic abilities and cognition dependent upon other innate psychological restraints? Can we, in fact, separate linguistic cognition from other equally unique human learning abilities?

Clearly, we will not learn all the answers for a very long time. That would require at least the development of an adequate theory of specific universal linguistic structure and a more general theory of human psychological organization, neither of which is currently available. We have learned a great deal, but what we can be reasonably sure of is minuscule compared to that which we still need to know.

Language is difficult to study and in some ways difficult to teach, because in spite of the progress which has been made, we still do not know enough. There seems to be small doubt that linguistic competence is just one part of a much larger psychological phenomenon about which we still have only superficial understanding. It is clear that before we have all or even nearly all the answers, we shall have to know a great deal more about the whole subject of human cognition—a subject about which some of the best modern scholarly minds are in substantial disagreement.

FOR DISCUSSION AND REVIEW

1 What are three of Chomsky's criticisms of the structuralists in *Syntactic Structures*? Try to give a concrete example of each kind of criticism.

2 What reason does LaPalombara give for her assertion that Chomsky's ideas have from the outset been closer to those of "the philosophical traditional grammarians from Plato through Humboldt" than to those of the structural linguists?

3 In *Syntactic Structures*, Chomsky argues that a grammar must meet certain criteria. What are these criteria?

4 Chomsky asserts in *Syntactic Structures* that a Markov-type grammar is an inadequate model. What type(s) of sentences and/or constructions does this type of grammar fail to account for? Give a few examples of sentences or constructions that a Markov grammar could not account for.

5 Chomsky also argues in *Syntactic Structures* that phrase-structure grammars, although more powerful than Markov grammars, are not adequate. What are his arguments? What kind of addition to a phrase-structure grammar does he

suggest in order to eliminate its limitations?

6 In what sense does Chomsky use the term *generative* in "transformational-generative grammar"?

7 Explain the three major components of the transformational grammar described in *Aspects of the Theory of Syntax*. Which of them is central?

8 Which components of the *Aspects* grammar model are called "interpretive"? What does this term mean in this context?

9 Although the structuralists objected to the idea of linguistic universals that had attracted many scholars from the time of the ancient Greeks until the nineteenth century, they did, as LaPalombara says, contribute "a number of useful generalizations about language." List at least three such contributions; try to give some concrete examples of the generalizations.

10 As LaPalombara indicates, the work of the transformational-generative linguists has greatly stimulated interest in linguistic universals. There is no agreement as to whether phonological, syntactic, or semantic universals are primary;

but there is agreement on the nature of some general linguistic universals. List five such universals. Where possible, give an example of each in English (and in another language if you know one well).

11   What explanation do transformational-generative linguists offer for the existence of linguistic universals?

12   Why are studies of language acquisition in children of particular interest to transformational linguists?

13   Explain LaPalombara's statement that "linguistic universals seem to be of two broad types: substantive and formal." Give two specific examples of each type. How would you explain the basic difference(s) between the two types?

14   Distinguish between "absolute universals" and "universal tendencies." Give six examples of each, three phonological and three syntactic/semantic. (Notice that it is quite often difficult to make a clear-cut distinction between what is an "absolute universal" and what is a "universal tendency.")

15   What does LaPalombara say is "the truly significant thing about the recurrent tendency toward or actual use of certain specific grammar rules in language . . ."? Why is it so significant?

16   What advantages do you see to the theory of linguistic universals?

5

Language and the Mind

Noam Chomsky

Transformational-generative grammar is inextricably linked with the name Noam Chomsky, the M.I.T. linguist whose 1957 book *Syntactic Structures* first brought this theory extensive attention. Chomsky himself, however, points to the connection between his ideas and those of rationalist, as opposed to empiricist, philosophy. For example, in the early nineteenth century Wilhelm von Humboldt saw the necessity for describing speech production and interpretation through "a generative system of rules" in the human mind. In the following article, Chomsky discusses reasons for believing that the human mind contains "innate ideas and principles" that enable all normal children to acquire language. Far from being free to organize their linguistic experiences in all possible ways, children are predisposed to structure the data only in accordance with these innate principles, principles common to all human languages. Evident in Chomsky's article is the coming together of ideas from philosophy and psychology as well as linguistics.

How DOES the mind work? To answer this question we must look at some of the work performed by the mind. One of its main functions is the acquisition of knowledge. The two major factors in acquisition of knowledge, perception and learning, have been the subject of study and speculation for centuries. It would not, I think, be misleading to characterize the major positions that have developed as outgrowths of classical rationalism and empiricism. The rationalist theories are marked by the importance they assign to *intrinsic* structures in mental operations—to central processes and organizing principles in perception, and to innate ideas and principles in learning. The empiricist approach, in contrast, has stressed the role of experience and control by environmental factors.

The classical empiricist view is that sensory images are transmitted to the brain as impressions. They remain as ideas that will be associated in various ways, depending on the fortuitous character of experience. In this view a language is merely a collection of words, phrases, and sentences, a habit system, acquired accidentally and extrinsically. In the formulation of Willard Quine, knowledge of a language (and, in fact, knowledge in general) can be represented as "a fabric of sentences variously associated to one another and to nonverbal stimuli by the mechanism of conditioned response." Acquisition of knowledge is only a matter of the gradual construction of this fabric. When sensory experience is interpreted, the already established network may be activated in some fashion. In its essentials, this view has been predominant in modern behavioral science, and it has been accepted with little question by many philosophers as well.

The classical rationalist view is quite different. In this view the mind contains a system of "common notions" that enable it to interpret the scattered and incoherent data of sense in terms of objects and their relations, cause and effect, whole and part, symmetry, gestalt properties, functions, and so on. Sensation, providing only fleeting and meaningless images, is degenerate and particular. Knowledge, much of it beyond immediate awareness, is rich in structure, involves universals, and is highly organized. The innate general principles that underlie and organize this knowledge, according to Leibniz, "enter into our thoughts, of which they form the soul and the connection . . . although we do not at all think of them."

This "active" rationalist view of the acquisition of knowledge persisted through the romantic period in its essentials. With respect to language, it achieves its most illuminating expression in the profound investigations of Wilhelm von Humboldt. His theory of speech perception supposes a generative system of rules that underlies speech production as well as its interpretation. The system is generative in that it makes infinite use of finite means. He regards a language as a structure of forms and concepts based on a system of rules that determine their interrelations, arrangement, and organization. But these finite materials can be combined to make a never-ending product.

In the rationalist and romantic tradition of linguistic theory, the normal use of language is regarded as characteristically innovative. We construct sentences that are entirely new to us. There is no substantive notion of "analogy" or "generalization" that accounts for this creative aspect of language use. It is equally erroneous to describe language as a "habit structure" or as a network of associated responses. The innovative element in normal use of language quickly exceeds the bounds of such marginal principles as analogy or generalization (under any substantive interpretation of these notions). It is important to emphasize this fact because the insight has been lost under the impact of the behaviorist assumptions that have dominated speculation and research in the twentieth century.

In Humboldt's view, acquisition of language is largely a matter of maturation of an innate language capacity. The maturation is guided by internal factors, by an innate "form of language" that is sharpened, differentiated, and given its specific realization through experience. Language is thus a kind of latent structure in the human mind, developed and fixed by exposure to specific linguistic experience. Humboldt believes that all languages will be found to be very similar in their grammatical form, similar not on the surface but in their deeper inner structures. The innate organizing principles severely limit the class of possible languages, and these principles determine the properties of the language that is learned in the normal way.

The active and passive views of perception and learning have elaborated with varying degrees of clarity since the seventeenth century. These views can be confronted with empirical evidence in a variety of ways. Some recent work in psychology and neurophysiology is highly suggestive in this regard. There is evidence for the existence of central processes in perception, specifically for control over the functioning of sensory neurons by the brain-stem reticular system. Behavioral counterparts of this central control have been under investigation for several years. Furthermore, there is evidence for innate organization of the perceptual system of a highly specific sort at every level of biological organization. Studies of the visual system of the frog, the discovery of specialized cells responding to angle and motion in the lower cortical centers of cats and rabbits, and the somewhat comparable investigations of the auditory system of frogs—all are relevant to the classical questions of intrinsic structure mentioned earlier. These studies suggest that there are highly organized, innately determined perceptual systems that are adapted closely to the animal's "life space" and that provide the basis for what we might call "acquisition of knowledge." Also relevant are certain behavioral studies of human infants, for example those showing the preference for faces over other complex stimuli.

These and other studies make it reasonable to inquire into the possibility that complex intellectual structures are determined narrowly by innate mental organization. What is perceived may be determined by mental processes of considerable depth. As far as language learning is concerned, it seems to me that a rather convincing argument can be made for the view that certain principles intrinsic to the mind provide invariant structures that are a precondition for linguistic experience. In the course of this article I would like to sketch some of the ways such conclusions might be clarified and firmly established.

There are several ways linguistic evidence can be used to reveal properties of human perception and learning. In this section we consider one research strategy that might take us nearer to this goal.

Let us say that in interpreting a certain physical stimulus a person constructs a "percept." This percept represents some of his conclusions (in general, unconscious) about the stimulus. To the extent that we can characterize such percepts, we can go on to investigate the mechanisms that relate stimulus and percept. Imagine a model of perception that takes stimuli as inputs and arrives at percepts as "outputs." The model might contain a system of beliefs, strategies for interpreting stimuli, and other factors, such as the organization of memory. We would then have a perceptual model that might be represented graphically.

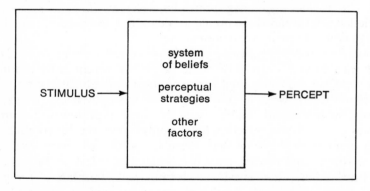

Consider next the system of beliefs that is a component of the perceptual model. How was this acquired? To study this problem, we must investigate a second model, which takes certain data as input and gives as "output" (again, internally represented) the system of beliefs operating in the perceptual model. This second model, a model of learning, would have its own intrinsic structure, as did the first. This structure might consist of conditions on the nature of the system of beliefs that can be acquired, of innate inductive strategies, and again, of other factors such as the organization of memory.

Under further conditions, which are interesting but not relevant here, we can take these perceptual and learning models as theories of the acquisition of knowledge, rather than of belief. How then would the models apply to language? The input stimulus to the perceptual model is a speech signal, and the percept is a representation of the

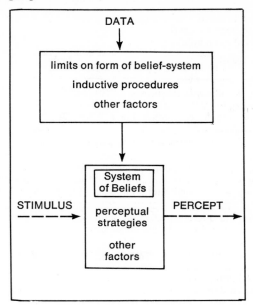

utterance that the hearer takes the signal to be and of the interpretation he assigns to it. We can think of the percept as the structural description of a linguistic expression which contains certain phonetic, semantic, and syntactic information. Most interesting is the syntactic information, which best can be discussed by examining a few typical cases.

The three sentences in the example seem to be the same syntactic structure. Each contains the subject *I*, and the predicate of each consists of a verb (*told, expected, persuaded*), a noun phrase (*John*), and an embedded predicate phrase (*to leave*). This similarity is only superficial, however—a similarity in what we may call the "surface structure" of these sentences, which differ in important ways when we consider them with somewhat greater care.

The differences can be seen when the sentences are paraphrased or subjected to certain grammatical operations, such as the conversion from active to passive forms. For example, in normal conversation the sentence "I told John to leave" can be roughly paraphrased as "What I told John was to leave." But the other two sentences cannot be paraphrased as "What I persuaded John was to leave" or "What I expected John was to leave." Sentence 2 can be paraphrased as: "It was expected by me that John would leave." But the other two sentences cannot undergo a corresponding formal operation, yielding: "It was persuaded by me that John would leave" or "It was told by me that John should leave."

(1)	I told John to leave
(2)	I expected John to leave
(3)	I persuaded John to leave

FIRST PARAPHRASE:

(1a)	What I told John was to leave (ACCEPTABLE)
(2a)	What I expected John was to leave (UNACCEPTABLE)
(3a)	What I persuaded John was to leave (UNACCEPTABLE)

SECOND PARAPHRASE:

(1b)	It was told by me that John would leave (UNACCEPTABLE)
(2b)	It was expected by me that John would leave (ACCEPTABLE)
(3b)	It was persuaded by me that John would leave (UNACCEPTABLE)

| (4) | I expected the doctor to examine John |
| (5) | I persuaded the doctor to examine John |

PASSIVE REPLACEMENT AS PARAPHRASE:

| (4a) | I expected John to be examined by the doctor (MEANING RETAINED) |
| (5a) | I persuaded John to be examined by the doctor (MEANING CHANGED) |

Sentences 2 and 3 differ more subtly. In Sentence 3 *John* is the direct object of *persuade,* but in Sentence 2 *John* is not the direct object of *expect.* We can show this by using these verbs in slightly more complex sentences: "I persuaded the doctor to examine John" and "I expected the doctor to examine John." If we replace the embedded proposition *the doctor to examine John* with its passive form *John to be examined by the doctor,* the change to the passive does not, in itself, change the meaning. We can accept as paraphrases "I expected the doctor to examine John" and "I expected John to be examined by the doctor." But we cannot accept as paraphrases "I persuaded the doctor to examine John" and "I persuaded John to be examined by the doctor."

The parts of these sentences differ in their grammatical functions. In "I persuaded John to leave" *John* is both the object of *persuade* and the subject of *leave.* These facts must be represented in the percept since they are known, intuitively, to the hearer of the speech signal. No special training or instruction is necessary to enable the native speaker to understand these examples, to know which are "wrong" and which "right," although they may all be quite new to him. They are interpreted by the native speaker instantaneously and uniformly, in accordance with structural principles that are known tacitly, intuitively, and unconsciously.

These examples illustrate two significant points. First, the surface structure of a sentence, its organization into various phrases, may not reveal or immediately reflect its deep syntactic structure. The deep structure is not represented directly in the form of the speech signal; it is abstract. Second, the rules that determine deep and surface structure and their interrelation in particular cases must themselves be highly abstract. They are surely remote from consciousness, and in all likelihood they cannot be brought to consciousness.

A study of such examples, examples characteristic of all human languages that have been carefully studied, constitutes the first stage of the linguistic investigation outlined above, namely the study of the percept. The percept contains phonetic and semantic information related through the medium of syntactic structure. There are two aspects to this syntactic structure. It consists of a surface directly related to the phonetic form, and a deep structure that underlies the semantic interpretation. The deep structure is represented in the mind and rarely is indicated directly in the physical signal.

A language, then, involves a set of semantic-phonetic percepts, of sound-meaning correlations, the correlations being determined by the kind of intervening syntactic structure just illustrated. The English language correlates sound and meaning in one way, Japanese in another, and so on. But the general properties of percepts, their forms and mechanisms, are remarkably similar for all languages that have been carefully studied.

Returning to our models of perception and learning, we can now take up the problem of formulating the system of beliefs that is a central component in perceptual processes. In the case of language, the "system of beliefs" would now be called the "generative grammar," the system of rules that specifies the sound-meaning correlation and generates the class of structural descriptions (percepts) that constitute the language in question. The generative grammar, then, represents the speaker-hearer's knowledge of his language. We can use the term *grammar of a language* ambiguously, as referring not only to the speaker's internalized, subconscious knowledge but to the professional linguist's representation of this internalized and intuitive system of rules as well.

How is this generative grammar acquired? Or, using our learning model, what is the internal structure of the device that could develop a generative grammar?

We can think of every normal human's internalized grammar as, in effect, a theory of his language. This theory provides a sound-meaning correlation for an infinite number of sentences. It provides an infinite set of structural descriptions; each contains a surface structure that determines phonetic form and a deep structure that determines semantic content.

In formal terms, then, we can describe the child's acquisition of language as a kind of theory construction. The child discovers the theory of his language with only small amounts of data from that language. Not only does his "theory of the language" have an enormous predictive scope, but it also enables the child to reject a great deal of the very data on which the theory has been constructed. Normal speech consists, in large part, of fragments, false starts, blends, and other distortions of the underlying idealized forms. Nevertheless, as is evident from a study of the mature use of language, what the child learns is the underlying ideal theory. This is a remarkable fact. We must also bear in mind that the child constructs this ideal theory without explicit instruction, that he acquires this knowledge at a time when he is not capable of complex intellectual achievements in many other domains, and that this achievement is relatively independent of intelligence or the particular course of experience. These are facts that a theory of learning must face.

A scientist who approaches phenomena of this sort without prejudice or dogma would conclude that the acquired knowledge must be determined in a rather specific way by intrinsic properties of mental organization. He would then set himself the task of discovering the innate ideas and principles that make such acquisition of knowledge possible.

It is unimaginable that a highly specific, abstract, and tightly organized language comes by accident into the mind of every four-year-old child. If there were not an innate restriction on the form of grammar, then the child could employ innumerable theories to account for his linguistic experience, and no one system, or even small class of systems, would be found exclusively acceptable or even preferable. The child could not possibly acquire knowledge of a language. This restriction on the form of grammar is a precondition for linguistic experience, and it is surely the critical factor in determining the course and result of language learning. The child cannot know at birth which language he is going to learn. But he must "know" that its grammar must be of a predetermined form that excludes many imaginable languages.

The child's task is to select the appropriate hypothesis from this restricted class. Having selected it, he can confirm his choice with the evidence further available to him. But neither the evidence nor any process of induction (in any well-defined sense) could in themselves have led to this choice. Once the hypothesis is sufficiently well confirmed, the child knows the language defined by this hypothesis; consequently, his knowledge extends vastly beyond his linguistic experience, and he can reject much of this experience as imperfect, as resulting from the interaction of many factors, only one of which is the ideal grammar that determines a sound-meaning connection for an infinite class of linguistic expressions. Along such lines as these one might outline a theory to explain the acquisition of language.

As has been pointed out, both the form and meaning of a sentence are determined by syntactic structures that are not represented directly in the signal and that are related to the signal only at a distance, through a long sequence of interpretive rules. This property of abstractness in grammatical structure is of primary importance, and it is on this property that our inferences about mental processes are based. Let us examine this abstractness a little more closely.

Not many years ago, the process of sentence interpretation might have been described approximately along the following lines. A speech signal is received and segmented into successive units (overlapping at the borders). These units are analyzed in terms of their invariant phonetic properties and assigned to "phonemes." The sequence of phonemes, so constructed, is then segmented into minimal grammatically functioning units (morphemes and words). These are again categorized. Successive operations of segmentation and classification will lead to what I have called "surface structure"—an analysis of a sentence into phrases, which can be represented as a proper bracketing of the sentence, with the bracketed units assigned to various categories. Each segment—phonetic, syntactic or semantic—would be identified in terms of certain invariant properties. This would be an exhaustive analysis of the structure of the sentence.

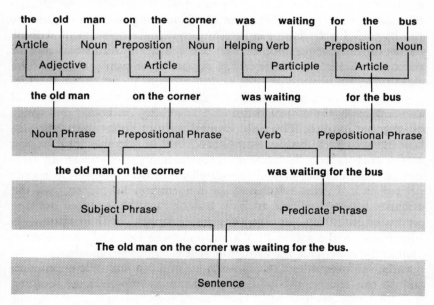

With such a conception of language structure, it made good sense to look forward hopefully to certain engineering applications of linguistics—for example, to voice-operated typewriters capable of segmenting an expression into its successive phonetic units and identifying these, so that speech could be converted to some form of phonetic writing in a mechanical way; to mechanical analysis of sentence structure by fairly straight-forward and well-understood computational techniques; and perhaps even beyond to such projects as machine translation. But these hopes have by now been largely abandoned with the realization that this conception of grammatical structure is inadequate at every level, semantic, phonetic, and syntactic. Most important, at the level of syntactic organization, the surface structure indicates semantically significant relations only in extremely simple cases. In general, the deeper aspects of syntactic organization are representable by labeled bracketing, but of a very different sort from that seen in surface structure.

There is evidence of various sorts, both from phonetics and from experimental psychology, that labeled bracketing is an adequate representation of surface structure. It would go beyond the bounds of this paper to survey the phonetic evidence. A good deal of it is presented in a forthcoming book, *Sound Pattern of English*, by myself and Morris Halle. Similarly, very interesting experimental work by Jerry Fodor and his colleagues, based on earlier observations by D. E. Broadbent and Peter Ladefoged, has shown that the disruption of a speech signal (for example, by a superimposed click) tends to be perceived at the boundaries of phrases rather than at the point where the disruption actually occurred, and that in many cases the bracketing of surface structure can be read directly from the data on perceptual displacement. I think the evidence is rather good that labeled bracketing serves to represent the surface structure that is related to the perceived form of physical signals.

Deep structures are related to surface structures by a sequence of certain formal operations, operations now generally called "grammatical transformations." At the levels of sound, meaning, and syntax, the significant structural features of sentences are highly abstract. For this reason they cannot be recovered by elementary data-processing techniques. This fact lies behind the search for central processes in speech perception and the search for intrinsic, innate structure as the basis for language learning.

How can we represent deep structure? To answer this question we must consider the grammatical transformations that link surface structure to the underlying deep structure that is not always apparent.

Consider, for example, the operations of passivization and interrogation. In the sentences (1) John was examined by the doctor, and (2) did the doctor examine John, both have a deep structure similar to the paraphrase of Sentence 1, (3) the doctor examined John. The same network of grammatical relations determines the semantic interpretation in each case. Thus two of the grammatical transformations of English must be the operations of passivization and interrogation that form such surface structures as Sentences 1 and 2 from a deeper structure which in its essentials also underlies Sentence 3. Since the transformations ultimately produce surface structures, they must produce labeled bracketings [see illustration p. 180]. But notice that these operations can apply in sequence: we can form the passive question "was John examined by the doctor" by passivization followed by interrogation. Since the result of passivization is a labeled bracketing, it follows that the interrogative transformation operates on a labeled bracketing and forms a new labeled bracketing. Thus a transformation such as interrogation maps a labeled bracketing into a labeled bracketing.

By similar argument, we can show that all grammatical transformations are structure-dependent mappings of this sort and that the deep structures which underlie all sentences must themselves be labeled bracketings. Of course, the labeled bracketing that constitutes deep structure will in general be quite different from that representing the surface structure of a sentence. Our argument is somewhat oversimplified, but it is roughly correct. When made precise and fully accurate it strongly supports the view that deep structures, like surface structures, are formally to be taken as labeled bracketings, and that grammatical transformations are mappings of such structures onto other similar structures.

Recent studies have sought to explore the ways in which grammatical structure of the sort just described enters into mental operations. Much of this work has been based on a proposal formulated by George Miller as a first approximation, namely, that the amount of memory used to store a sentence should reflect the number of transformations used in deriving it. For example, H. B. Savin and E. Perchonock investigated this assumption in the following way: they presented to subjects a sentence followed by a sequence of unrelated words. They then determined the number of these unrelated words recalled when the subject attempted to repeat the sentence and the sequence of words. The more words recalled, the less memory used to store the sentence. The fewer words recalled, the more memory used to store the sentence. The results showed a remarkable correlation of amount of memory and number of transformations in certain simple cases. In fact, in their experimental material, shorter sentences with more transformations took up more "space in memory" than longer sentences that involved fewer transformations.

Savin has extended this work and has shown that the effects of deep structure and surface structure can be differentiated by a similar technique. He considered paired sentences with approximately the same deep structure but with one of the pair being more complex in surface structure. He showed that, under the experimental conditions just described, the paired sentences were indistinguishable. But if the sequence of unrelated words precedes, rather than follows, the sentence being tested, then the more complex (in surface structure) of the pair is more difficult to repeat correctly than the simpler member. Savin's very plausible inference is that sentences are coded in memory in terms of deep structure. When the unrelated words precede the test sentence, these words use up a certain amount of short-term memory, and the sentence that is more complex in surface structure cannot be analyzed with the amount of memory remaining. But if the test sentence precedes the unrelated words, it is, once understood, stored in terms of deep structure, which is about the same in both cases. Therefore the same amount of memory remains, in the paired cases, for recall of the following words. This is a beautiful example of the way creative experimental studies can interweave with theoretical work in the study of language and of mental processes.

In speaking of mental processes we have returned to our original problem. We can now see why it is reasonable to maintain that the linguistic evidence supports an "active" theory of acquisition of knowledge. The study of sentences and of speech perception, it seems to me, leads to a perceptual theory of a classical rationalist sort. Representative of this school, among others, were the seventeenth-century Cambridge Platonists, who developed the idea that our perception is guided by notions that originate from the mind and that provide the framework for the interpretation of sensory stimuli. It is not sufficient to suggest that this framework is a store of "neural models" or "schemata" which are in some manner applied to perception (as is postulated in some current theories of perception). We must go well beyond this assumption and return to the view of Wilhelm von Humboldt, who attributed to the mind a system of rules that generates such models and schemata under the stimulation of the senses. The system of rules itself determines the content of the percept that is formed.

We can offer more than this vague and metaphoric account. A generative grammar and an associated theory of speech perception provide a concrete example of the rules that operate and of the mental objects that they construct and manipulate. Physiology cannot yet explain the physical mechanisms that affect these abstract functions. But neither physiology nor psychology provides evidence that calls this account into question or that suggests an alternative. As mentioned earlier, the most exciting current work in the physiology of perception shows that even the peripheral systems analyze stimuli into the complex properties of objects, and that central processes may significantly affect the information transmitted by the receptor organs.

The study of language, it seems to me, offers strong empirical evidence that empiricist theories of learning are quite inadequate. Serious efforts have been made in recent years to develop principles of induction, generalization, and data analysis that would account for knowledge of a language. These efforts have been a total failure. The methods and principles fail not for any superficial reason such as lack of time or data. They fail because they are intrinsically incapable of giving rise to the system of rules that underlies the normal use of language. What evidence is now available supports the view that all human languages share deep-seated properties of organization and structure. These properties—these linguistic universals—can be plausibly assumed to be an innate mental endowment rather than the result of learning. If this is true, then the study of language sheds light on certain long-standing issues in the theory of knowledge. Once again, I see little reason to doubt that what is true of language is true of other forms of human knowledge as well.

There is one further question that might be raised at this point. How does the human mind come to have the innate properties that underlie acquisition of knowledge? Here linguistic evidence obviously provides no information at all. The process by which the human mind has achieved its present state of complexity and its particular form of innate organization are a complete mystery, as much of a mystery as the analogous questions that can be asked about the processes leading to the physical and mental organization of any other complex organism. It is perfectly safe to attribute this to evolution, so long as we bear in mind that there is no substance to this assertion—it amounts to nothing more than the belief that there is surely some naturalistic explanation for these phenomena.

There are, however, important aspects of the problem of language and mind that can be studied sensibly within the limitations of present understanding and technique. I think that, for the moment, the most productive investigations are those dealing with the nature of particular grammars and with the universal conditions met by all human languages. I have tried to suggest how one can move, in successive steps of increasing abstractness, from the study of percepts to the study of grammar and perceptual mechanisms, and from the study of grammar to the study of universal grammar and the mechanisms of learning.

In this area of convergence of linguistics, psychology, and philosophy, we can look forward to much exciting work in coming years.

FOR DISCUSSION AND REVIEW

1 Distinguish between rationalist and empiricist theories concerning perception and learning.
2 Compare and contrast the empiricist and the rationalist view of the nature of knowledge, including language. In his article on the acquisition of language by children, which position does Lewis (pp. 100–109) support?
3 Summarize von Humboldt's view of language acquisition.

4 What does Chomsky mean by *percept*? On what basis can he assert that "the general properties of percepts . . . are remarkably similar for all languages that have been carefully studied"? If percepts are similar, what does vary from language ∜to language?

5 According to Chomsky, how does a child acquire language? How does Chomsky support this view?

6 Why does Chomsky describe "abstractness in grammatical structure" as "of primary importance"?

7 Define *deep* and *surface structures*. How are deep and surface structures related? How does this relationship affect comprehension of a sentence? (You may find it helpful to refer to Lewis's discussion of deep and surface structure, p. 106, and to LaPalombara's outline and diagram, p. 312.)

8 What are *linguistic universals* and why are they important? Consider not only Chomsky's discussion but also those by Miller (p. 132) and Postal (p. 149).

PROJECTS FOR "THE SYSTEMS OF GRAMMAR"

1 *Prepare a short questionnaire designed to reveal people's experiences with grammar during their school years and their attitudes toward it. Some questions that you may want to ask include: In what grades was grammar taught under the rubric of grammar? What exactly was taught? How much time was devoted to it? What were the attitudes of the teachers toward grammar? What were the attitudes of the students? What kind of grammar was presented? Do you think your previous study of grammar enhanced your understanding of English or of other languages? If so, try to explain how; be specific. A final question could be: How would you define the term grammar? Ask at least ten people to complete the questionnaire. You may want to include not only those in your age group but also some older people—of your parents' or even your grandparents' generations. Organize your findings. You may wish to compare them with those of others in your class. Prepare a report in which you summarize your conclusions.*

2 *Several of the articles in this book (Chomsky, LaPalombara, Farb, Lewis) assert that children have an innate ability to acquire language and, in effect, "build" their own grammars on the basis of whatever linguistic data surround them. Observe several children of kindergarten age or younger. How far has their grammar-building process progressed? Consider such things as vocabulary, sounds, the ability to adjust language to situation (functional variation), and both production and comprehension of a variety of syntactic structures. Write a paper summarizing your observations.*

3 *The articles in this section deal with developments in American linguistics since World War II. The study of English grammar, however, has a much longer history. Write a paper or prepare an oral report on one of the following topics: summarize the development of English grammar*

from its beginnings in the eighteenth century; describe the eighteenth-century attitudes toward "ain't" and the double negative; compare eighteenth-century prescriptive statements with statements in modern handbooks. You may want to begin by reading chapter 4, "English Grammar," in H. A. Gleason, Jr., Linguistics and English Grammar (New York: Holt, Rinehart & Winston, 1965), pp. 67–87.

4 *In "Revolution in Grammar" (pp. 286–303), W. Nelson Francis lists four main ways in which grammatical meaning is signaled in English. Examine the following: "These foser glipses have volbicly merfed the wheeple their preebs."[1] Although you do not know the meaning of any of the italicized words (How big is a "wheeple"? How does one "merf"? Are "glipses" good to eat?), you do know a great deal about them. On the basis of the devices Francis lists, what can you say about the form, function, and meaning of the words?*

5 *Read the following paragraph:*

The hunter crept through the leaves. The leaves had fallen. The leaves were dry. The hunter was tired. The hunter had a gun. The gun was new. The hunter saw a deer. The deer had antlers. A tree partly hid the antlers. The deer was beautiful. The hunter shot at the deer. The hunter missed. The shot frightened the deer. The deer bounded away.

Without changing important words or the meaning, rewrite the paragraph so as to avoid the many short, choppy sentences. Compare your rewritten version with those prepared by other members of the class. Are they alike? If they are not, describe the differences. How do you account for the fact that passages that appear different can have the same meaning?

6 *Some nonlinguists wrongly accuse the "new grammars" of being permissive. They are not; but they are descriptive rather than prescriptive —that is, they are attempts to describe language as accurately as possible. Do you think most Americans are ready to accept the descriptive approach to language? Collect evidence to support your conclusion. Good sources will be letters-to-the-editor columns; vocabulary sections in certain popular magazines, "how to" paperback books, and some regular newspaper features dealing with language. Write a paper summarizing your findings.*

7 *As a native speaker of English, you have an internalized knowledge of the language—call it a "native-speaker intuition" if you will. For example, you can recognize a grammatical English sentence, you can interpret a sentence, you can perceive ambiguity, and you can determine when strings are synonymous. Examine the following groups of sentences; what can you tell about each group?*

[1] This example comes from Kenneth G. Wilson, "English Grammars and the Grammar of English," which appears in the front matter of Funk & Wagnalls Standard College Dictionary: Text Edition (New York: Harcourt, Brace & World, 1963).

A 1 *The path ran around the fountain.*
   2 *The soldiers were told to stop marching on the parade ground.*
   3 *The chicken is too hot to eat.*

B 1 *That student continually sleeps in class.*
   2 *Student in class continually that sleeps.*
   3 *In class that student continually sleeps.*

C 1 *The Pittsburgh Pirates beat the Baltimore Orioles in the World Series.*
   2 *The ones that the Pittsburgh Pirates beat in the World Series were the Baltimore Orioles.*
   3 *The Baltimore Orioles were beaten by the Pittsburgh Pirates in the World Series.*

D 1 *Sam asked the students to build a display.*
   2 *Sam promised the students to build a display.*
   3 *Sam told the students to build a display.*

Do your statements about these groups of sentences support the claims made by LaPalombara (pp. 304–325) and Chomsky (pp. 327–339)? Consider especially the validity of such concepts as competence, performance, and deep and surface structures. Write a short paper describing your conclusions.

SELECTED BIBLIOGRAPHY

Bolinger, Dwight. *Aspects of Language.* 2nd edition. New York: Harcourt Brace Jovanovich, Inc., 1975. (A thoroughly readable and complete introduction to the study of language.)

Cattell, N. R. *The New English Grammar: A Descriptive Introduction.* Cambridge: The M.I.T. Press, 1969. (Outstanding introduction to transformational grammar up to 1968.)

Chomsky, Noam. *Aspects of the Theory of Syntax.* Cambridge: The M.I.T. Press, 1965. (The first major revision of TG theory as originally described in *Syntactic Structures.*)

————. *Syntactic Structures.* The Hague: Mouton & Company, 1957. (Essential but difficult study; where it all began.)

Emig, Janet A., James T. Fleming, and Helen M. Popp, eds. *Language and Learning.* New York: Harcourt, Brace & World, 1966. (Excellent collection of articles on different aspects of language.)

Faust, George P. "Something of Morphemics." *College Composition and Communication,* 5 (1954), 65–69. (Introductory discussion of the smallest meaningful units of language.)

————. "Terms in Phonemics." *College Composition and Communication,* 5 (1954), 30–34. (Introductory discussion of the concept of the phoneme, important in structural linguistics.)

Francis, W. Nelson. *The Structure of American English*. New York: Ronald Press, 1958. (Influential structural linguistics text.)

Fromkin, Victoria, and Robert Rodman. *An Introduction to Language*. New York: Holt, Rinehart & Winston, Inc., 1974. (An outstanding and readable text for introductory courses in linguistics.)

Gleason, H. A., Jr. *Linguistics and English Grammar*. New York: Holt, Rinehart & Winston, 1965. (Excellent study; extensive general and topical bibliographies.)

Hall, Robert A., Jr. *Linguistics and Your Language*. Garden City, N.Y.: Doubleday and Co., 1960. (A readable, popular introduction to linguistics, excluding developments during the last decade.)

Herndon, Jeanne H. *A Survey of Modern Grammars*. New York: Holt, Rinehart & Winston, 1970. (An introductory book dealing with structural and the early form of transformational-generative grammar, directed toward inservice and preservice teachers.)

Jacobs, Roderick A., and Peter S. Rosenbaum, eds. *Readings in English Transformational Grammar*. Waltham, Mass.: Ginn and Company, 1970. (Anthology of theoretical and descriptive articles; excellent bibliography.)

Johnson, Nancy Ainsworth. *Current Topics in Language: Introductory Readings*. Cambridge: Winthrop Publishers, Inc., 1976. (Essays with a practical orientation dealing with language acquisition, language variation, modern grammars, and the reading process.)

Joos, Martin, ed. *Readings in Linguistics*. Chicago: University of Chicago Press, 1966. (Traces the development of linguistics in the U.S. since 1925.)

Lamberts, J. J. "Basic Concepts for Teaching from Structural Linguistics." *English Journal*, 49 (1960), 172–176. (Good introduction to basic ideas.)

Langacker, Ronald W. *Language and Its Structure: Some Fundamental Linguistic Concepts*. 2nd edition. New York: Harcourt Brace Jovanovich, Inc., 1973. (Like the Bolinger book, a readable, complete, and up-to-date introduction.)

Leiber, Justin. *Noam Chomsky: A Philosophic Overview*. New York: St. Martin's Press, 1975. (Chomsky comments about this book: "It is the book that I would recommend to people who ask me what I'm up to. In fact, I think it is a good general introduction to recent work in linguistics. . . ." Contains a bibliography of Chomsky's works to 1971.)

Lester, Mark, ed. *Readings in Applied Transformational Grammar*. New York: Holt, Rinehart & Winston, 1970. (Intended for a nontechnical audience and including articles about psycholinguistic questions and the applications of transformational grammar.)

Levin, Samuel R. "Comparing Traditional and Structural Grammar." *College English,* 21 (1960), 260–265. (Short discussion pointing to weaknesses of traditional grammar.)

Lyons, John. *Noam Chomsky*. New York: The Viking Press, 1970. (Clear and complete account of Chomsky's central ideas. Contains a bibliography of Chomsky's works to 1970.)

Reibel, David A., and Sanford A. Schane, eds. *Modern Studies in English: Readings in Transformational Grammar*. Englewood Cliffs, N.J.: Prentice-Hall, 1969. (Anthology of articles on the transformational analysis of English.)

Roberts, Paul. "Foreword." *A Linguistics Reader*. Ed. Graham Wilson. New York: Harper & Row, 1967. (Entertaining and informative introduction to the study of language.)

Robins, R. H. *Ancient and Mediaeval Grammatical Theory in Europe*. London: Bell, 1951. (A short but thorough history of ideas about grammar.)

Thomas, Owen. "Generative Grammar: Toward Unification and Simplification." *English Journal,* 51 (1962), 94–99. (Introductory article describing some advantages of generative grammar.)

————. " Grammatici Certant." *English Journal,* 52 (1963), 322–326. (Brief but helpful comparison of traditional, historical, structural, and generative grammars.)

Thomas, Owen, and Eugene Kintgen. *Transformational Grammar and the Teacher of English.* 2nd edition. New York: Holt, Rinehart & Winston, Inc., 1974. (Thorough, and not too difficult for a determined beginner.)

Wilkinson, Andrew. *The Foundations of Language.* New York and London: Oxford University Press, 1971. (Fascinating discussion of basic linguistic concepts and language acquisition in children.)

Wilson, Kenneth G. "English Grammars and the Grammar of English." *Funk and Wagnalls Standard College Dictionary: Text Edition.* New York: Harcourt, Brace & World, 1963. 'Introductory comparison of traditional, structural, and early transformational grammar.)

PART SIX

Regional
Varieties
of English

Dialect study, especially with its recent historical and educational applications, is a fascinating and integral part of linguistics. The word *dialect*, however, is widely misunderstood, largely as a result of the negative connotations it has acquired.

Many Americans mistakenly view dialects as ignorant corruptions of the English language; little do they realize that they and their close associates speak a regional variety of English that can be called a dialect. Furthermore, in a strict sense, each person has his or her own unique dialect, an *idiolect*. A dialect, then, is simply a variety of a language; it differs from other varieties in certain features of pronunciation, vocabulary, and grammar. Since the majority of the native speakers in any given region share many features of pronunciation, vocabulary, and grammatical usage, linguistic geographers can make general statements about regional dialect distribution.

The first article in this section first introduces the student to the concept of regional dialects and to linguistic geographers and their work—the systematic study of language variation within a country or other specified area. The next selection examines the field methods used by dialectologists to obtain accurate information about the pronunciation, vocabulary, and grammar of speakers in a particular area. Finally, a specific study in geographical variation is presented.

1
Regional Variations

Albert H. Marckwardt

In this excerpt from *American English,* Professor Albert H. Marckwardt presents an overview of regional dialects in the United States. He provides a brief sketch of the history of dialect study and describes the monumental efforts of Hans Kurath and other researchers in compiling the *Linguistic Atlas of New England,* the first unit of the projected *Linguistic Atlas of the United States and Canada.* In addition, Marckwardt identifies the distinctive differences in the vocabulary, pronunciation, and grammar of the various regional dialects and the numerous factors that help account for the different regional varieties of English. Until his death in 1975, Marckwardt was director of the *Linguistic Atlas of the North-Central States* and emeritus professor of English at Princeton University.

THE ENGLISH LANGUAGE is spoken natively in America by no less than 145 million persons over an area of some three million square miles. Various parts of the United States differ considerably from each other with respect to climate, topography, plant and animal life, economic conditions, and social structure. Sociologists and historians recognize at least six regional cultures within the continental borders of the country. The same a priori grounds that led us to assume the existence of a series of differences between British and American English at the outset of this work will justify the inference that the language is likely not to be uniform throughout the country. The American novelist John Steinbeck in his *Grapes of Wrath* offers convincing evidence of the plausibility of this assumption:

"I knowed you wasn't Oklahomy folks. You talk queer kinda—
That ain't no blame, you understan'."

"Ever'body says words different," said Ivy. "Arkansas folks says
'em different, and Oklahomy folks says 'em different. And we seen a
lady from Massachusetts, an' she said 'em differentest of all. Couldn'
hardly make out what she was sayin'."

Early travelers to America and native commentators on the language
agree on the existence of regional differences at an early period in our
national history. Mrs. Anne Royal called attention to various southernisms in the works which she wrote during the second quarter of the
nineteenth century, and as early as 1829, Dr. Robley Dunglison had
identified many of the Americanisms, in the glossary he compiled, with
particular portions of the country. Charles Dickens recognized regional
differences in the English he encountered in his first tour of the United
States, and William Howard Russell, reporting on Abraham Lincoln's
first state banquet, at which he was a guest, mentions his astonishment
at finding "a diversity of accent almost as great as if a number of foreigners had been speaking English."

A number of other observers, however, were sufficiently impressed
by the uniformity of the language throughout the country to make this
a matter of comment. De Tocqueville, in a rather extended treatment
of the language of the young republic, flatly declared, "There is no
patois in the New World," and John Pickering, along with Noah Webster easily the most distinguished of our early philologists, also remarked
on the great uniformity of dialect through the United States, "in consequence," as he said, "of the frequent removals of people from one part
of our country to another."

There is truth in both types of comment. People in various parts of
the United States do not all speak alike, but there is greater uniformity
here than in England or in the countries of Western Europe, and this
makes the collection of a trustworthy body of information upon the
regional variations in American English a somewhat difficult and delicate matter.

The gathering of authentic data on the dialects of many of the
countries of Western Europe began in the latter decades of the nineteenth century. The *Atlas linguistique de la France* followed closely
upon the heels of the *Sprachatlas des deutschen Reichs*, and the activities of the English Dialect Society were initiated about the same time.
In 1889 a group of American scholars organized the American Dialect
Society, hoping that the activities of this organization might result in a
body of material from which either a dialect dictionary or a series of
linguistic maps, or both, might be compiled. The society remained relatively small, however, and although some valuable information appeared

in its journal *Dialect Notes,* a systematic survey of the regional varieties of American English has not yet resulted from its activities.

The past quarter of a century, however, has seen the development of such a survey. Beginning in 1928, a group of researchers under the direction of Professor Hans Kurath, now of the University of Michigan, undertook the compilation of a *Linguistic Atlas of New England* as the first unit of a projected *Linguistic Atlas of the United States and Canada.* The New England atlas, comprising a collection of some 600 maps, each showing the distribution of a single language feature throughout the area, was published over the period from 1939 to 1943. Since that time, field work for comparable atlases of the Middle Atlantic and of the South Atlantic states has been completed, and the materials are awaiting editing and publication. Field records for atlases of the North Central states and the Upper Middle West are virtually complete, and significant beginnings have been made in the Rocky Mountain and the Pacific Coast areas. Surveys in Louisiana, in Texas, and in Ontario are also under way.* It is perhaps not too optimistic to predict that within the next twenty-five years all of the United States and Canada as well will have been covered in at least an initial survey.

For a number of reasons it is not easy to collect a body of valid and reliable information on American dialects. The wide spread of education, the virtual extinction of illiteracy, the extreme mobility of the population—both geographically and from one social class to another—and the tremendous development of a number of media of mass communication have all contributed to the recession of local speech forms. Moreover, the cultural insecurity of a large portion of the American people has caused them to feel apologetic about their language. Consequently, they seldom display the same degree of pride or affection that many an English or a European speaker has for his particular patois. Since all dialect research is essentially a sampling process, this means that the investigator must take particular pains to secure representative and comparable samples from the areas which are studied. Happily, the very care which this demands has had the result of developing the methodology of linguistic geography in this country to a very high level.

In general, the material for a linguistic atlas is based upon the natural responses of a number of carefully selected individuals representing

---

* Editors' note: Since the original publication of this article, *The Linguistic Atlas of the Upper Midwest,* edited by Harold B. Allen, has been published, and the fieldwork for the middle and south Atlantic states, the north central states, the Gulf states, California, Washington, Arkansas, Colorado, Oklahoma, and Tennessee has been completed or is near completion. Under the direction of Frederic G. Cassidy, the *Dictionary of American Regional English,* a project sponsored by the American Dialect Society, is currently being edited and should be published in 1980.

certain carefully chosen communities, which in themselves reflect the principal strains of settlement and facets of cultural development in the area as a whole. Since the spread of education generally results in the disappearance of local or regional speech forms, and since the extension of schooling to virtually all of the population has been an achievement of the past seventy-five years, it became necessary for the American investigator to differentiate between the oldest generation, for whom schooling beyond the elementary level is not usual, and a middle-aged group who is likely to have had some experience with secondary schools. In addition, it is highly desirable to include some representatives of the standard or cultivated speech in each region, that their language may serve as a basis for comparison with the folk speech. Accordingly, in the American atlases, from each community represented, the field worker will choose at least two, and sometimes three representatives, in contrast to the usual practice of European researchers, who may safely content themselves with one. Moreover, it is equally necessary to make certain that the persons chosen in any community have not been subject to alien linguistic influences; consequently, only those who have lived there all of their lives, and preferably those who represent families who have long been identified with the area in question, are interviewed, although as one moves westward into the more recently settled areas this is not always possible.

Since complete materials are available only for the eastern seaboard and for the area north of the Ohio River as far west as the Mississippi, tentative conclusions relative to the regional variations in American English can be presented only for the eastern half of the country. The principal dialect areas presented in Kurath's *Word Geography of the Eastern United States*, are indicated on the accompanying map.

The three major dialect boundaries, it will be noted, cut the country into lateral strips and are labeled by Professor Kurath *Northern*, *Midland*, and *Southern* respectively. The line which separates the Northern and Midland areas begins in New Jersey a little below Sandy Hook, proceeds northwest to the east branch of the Susquehanna near Scranton, Pennsylvania, then goes westward through Pennsylvania just below the northern tier of counties. In Ohio the boundary dips below the Western Reserve, then turns northwest again, passing above Fort Wayne, Indiana. When it approaches South Bend it dips slightly to the southwest and cuts through Illinois, reaching the Mississippi at a point slightly above Quincy. The other principal boundary, that separating the Southern and Midland areas, begins at a point somewhat below Dover in Delaware, sweeps through Baltimore in something of an arc, turns sharply southwest north of the Potomac, follows the crest of the Blue Ridge in Virginia, and south of the James River swerves out into the

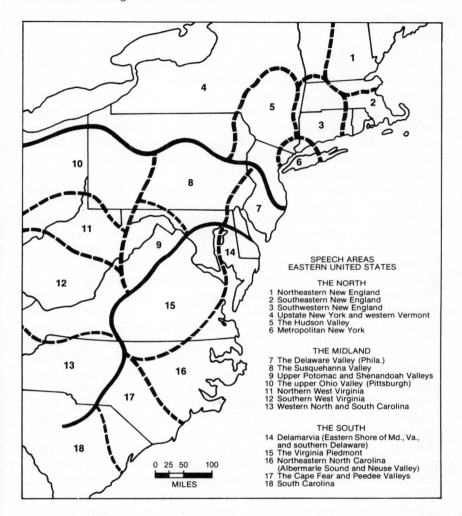

SPEECH AREAS
EASTERN UNITED STATES

THE NORTH
1 Northeastern New England
2 Southeastern New England
3 Southwestern New England
4 Upstate New York and western Vermont
5 The Hudson Valley
6 Metropolitan New York

THE MIDLAND
7 The Delaware Valley (Phila.)
8 The Susquehanna Valley
9 Upper Potomac and Shenandoah Valleys
10 The upper Ohio Valley (Pittsburgh)
11 Northern West Virginia
12 Southern West Virginia
13 Western North and South Carolina

THE SOUTH
14 Delamarvia (Eastern Shore of Md., Va.,
   and southern Delaware)
15 The Virginia Piedmont
16 Northeastern North Carolina
   (Albermarle Sound and Neuse Valley)
17 The Cape Fear and Peedee Valleys
18 South Carolina

0 25 50 100
MILES

North Carolina Piedmont. As we approach the lower part of South Carolina and Georgia the boundary is as yet unknown.

Even these necessarily incomplete results of the survey carried on under Professor Kurath and his associates have modified considerably our previous conceptions of the regional distribution of American speech forms. This modification is brought about principally by adding one concept and eliminating another. The concept thus eliminated has been variously known as Middle Western, Western, or General American. The older view of American dialects, reduced to its simplest terms, recognized the existence of a New England type of speech, a Southern type, and the remainder was generally blanketed by some such term as General American.

It seems clear now that what is neither New England nor Southern —which includes, of course, something between three-quarters and nine-tenths of the continental United States—is far too diverse and lacking in homogeneity to be considered a single major dialect. We know, for example, that there are a significant number of differences, both in vocabulary and in verb inflections, between the folk speech of most of Pennsylvania and that of New York State, and between Michigan and Wisconsin on the one hand, and most of Indiana and large portions of Illinois and Ohio on the other. As our information for the rest of the country becomes available, there can be little doubt that this conclusion will be strengthened.

The concept which has been added is the recognition of a Midland type of speech as distinct from [that of] both North and South. An examination of the evidence which Professor Kurath presents in his *Word Geography* leaves no doubt that the speech of this area, though it is by no means uniform, is sufficiently differentiated from [that of] both North and South to justify its classification as a major dialect area. This conclusion is supported not only by Atwood's study of the verb forms in the eastern portion of the country but by the available materials from the North Central States.

The map shown on page 351 includes also a few, but not all, of the subdialect areas which merit recognition. In the North the principal area is that which separates coastal New England from western New England, New York State, and the territory to the west. In general, this boundary follows the line of the Green Mountains, the Berkshire Hills, and the Connecticut River. The Metropolitan New York area consists of a broad circle with the city itself at the center; the Hudson Valley area encompasses the original Dutch settlements in New York and northern New Jersey, spreading into northeastern Pennsylvania. The Midland area is divided into northern and southern sub-areas, the line of demarcation being just a little south of the Old National Road in Ohio, Indiana, and Illinois. Within the Southern dialect region, the Virginia Piedmont and the Delmarva peninsula constitute distinct sub-areas.

Thus far it is the lexical materials gathered in connection with the various atlas projects which have been analyzed most extensively, and as the title of Professor Kurath's work indicates, his plotting of the major dialect areas is based upon vocabulary evidence. For example, characteristic Northern expressions that are current throughout the area include *pail, swill, whiffletree* or *whippletree, comforter* or *comfortable* for a thick quilt, *brook, co-boss* or *come-boss* as a cow call, *johnnycake, salt pork,* and *darning needle* for a dragonfly. In the Midland area we find *blinds* for roller shades, *skillet, spouting* or *spouts* for eaves, a *piece* for food taken between meals, *snake feeder* for a dragonfly, *sook* as the call to calves, *armload* for an armful of wood; and one *hulls* beans when he takes off the shells. A quarter *till* the hour is a typical Midland expression, as is the elliptical *to want off*, or *out*, or *in*. The South has *lightwood* as the term for kindling, a *turn* of wood for an armful; stringbeans are generally *snap beans*; *hasslet* is the term for the edible inner organs of a pig, *chittlins* for the small intestine; and in this area cows are said to *low* at feeding time.

The subdialect areas also have their characteristic forms. In coastal New England, for instance, *pigsty* is the normal term for pigpen, *bonny clapper* for curdled sour milk, *buttonwood* for a sycamore, and *pandowdy* for a cobbler type of dessert. Eastern Virginia has *cuppin* for a cowpen, *corn house* for a crib. *Lumber room* survives as the term for a storeroom. A grasshopper is known as a *hopper grass*, and *batter bread* is used for a soft cornbread containing egg.

As far as the sectors of the American lexicon which reflect regional differences are concerned, the matter is trenchantly summarized in Kurath's *Word Geography*, where the author points out first of all that the vocabularies of the arts and sciences, of industries, commercial enterprises, social and political institutions, and even many of the crafts, are national in scope because the activities they reflect are organized on a national basis. He then goes on to say:

> Enterprises and activities that are regionally restricted have, on the other hand, a considerable body of regional vocabulary which, to be sure, may be known in other parts of the country, even if it is not in active use. The cotton planter of the South, the tobacco grower, the dairy farmer, the wheat grower, the miner, the lumberman, and the rancher of the West have many words and expressions that are strictly regional and sometimes local in their currency.
>
> Regional and local expressions are most common in the vocabulary of the intimate everyday life of the home and the farm—not only among the simple folk and the middle class but also among the cultured. . . . Food, clothing, shelter, health, the day's work, play, mating, social gatherings, the land, the farm buildings, implements, the farm stocks and crops, the weather, the fauna and flora—these are the intimate concern of the common folk in the countryside, and for these things expressions are handed down in the family and the neighborhood that schooling and reading and a familiarity with regional or national usage do not blot out.

It is not only in the vocabulary that one finds regional differences in American speech. There are pronunciation features as well. Throughout the Northern area, for example, the distinction between [o] and [ɔ] in such word pairs as *hoarse* and *horse, mourning* and *morning* is generally maintained; [s] regularly occurs in *grease* (verb) and *greasy*, and *root* is pronounced by many with the vowel of *wood*. Within the Northern area such subdialects as coastal New England and Metropolitan New York also show many characteristic forms; the treatment of the vowel of *bird* is only one of these, and words of the *calf, pass, path, dance* group constitute another. In the Midland area speakers fail to distinguish between *hoarse* and *horse*. Rounding is characteristic of the vowels of *hog, frog, log, wasp* and *wash*, and in the last of these words an *r* often intrudes in the speech of the not too highly educated. The vowels of *due* and *new* will resemble that of *food* rather than *feud*. In the South, *r* is "lost" except before vowels, as it is in eastern New England and New York City but not in the Northern area generally. Words like *Tuesday, due*, and *new* have a y-like glide preceding the vowel, and final [z] in *Mrs.* is the normal form.

Among the older, relatively uneducated group and even to some extent among the middle-aged informants who have had some secondary schooling there are also regional differences in inflectional forms and syntax. For example, *hadn't ought* for "oughtn't," *see* as a past-tense form, *clim* for "climbed" among the oldest sector of the population, *wan't* for "wasn't," *be* in such expressions as *How be you?*, and the choice of the preposition *to* in *sick to his stomach* are all characteristic of the Northern area. *Clum* for "climbed," *seen* for "saw," *all the further* and *I'll wait on you* are to be found in the Midlands, whereas *belongs to be, heern* for "heard," *seed* as the past tense of "to see," *holp* for "helped," *might could* and *mought have* are characteristic of the South.

All of this raises the question as to how the regional forms of American English developed in our three and one-half centuries of linguistic history. The first factor which must be taken into account is settlement history. Where did our earliest settlers come from, and what dialects did they speak? . . . At the time of the earliest settlements, English local and regional dialects were in a stronger position than they are today in that they constituted the natural speech of a greater portion of the English-speaking population and were in customary use farther up the social scale.

Moreover, it is quite unlikely that any single local settlement, even at the outset, ever consisted entirely of speakers of the same dialect. Of ten families of settlers gathered in any one place, two might well have spoken London English, three or four others one of the southern or southeastern county dialects. There would be in addition a couple of families speaking northern English and another two or three employing a western dialect. In the course of their being in constant contact with each other, compromises for the everyday terms in which their dialects differed would normally have developed, and one could reasonably expect to find a southern English term for a water receptacle, a northern word for earthworm, and a western designation for sour milk. Matters of pronunciation would eventually, perhaps after a slightly longer time, be compromised in much the same manner. Moreover, the resultant compromises for various localities would be different. In the first place, no two localities would have had exactly the same proportions of speakers of the various English dialects, and even if they had, the two localities would not have arrived at precisely the same set of compromises. Thus, early in our history we developed, at various points on the Atlantic seaboard, a number of local cultures, each with distinctive social characteristics of its own—including a dialect which was basically a unique blend of British types of speech, supplemented in its vocabulary by borrowings from the Indians and from Dutch and German neighbors.

With the beginning of the nineteenth century, three changes occurred which were to have a profound effect upon the language situation in America. First, the industrial revolution resulted in the growth of a number of industrial centers, uprooting a considerable proportion of the farm population and concentrating it in the cities. The development of the railroad and other mechanical means of travel increased greatly the mobility of the average person. The large-scale migrations westward also resulted in some resettlement and shifting, even among those who did not set out on the long trek. All of this resulted in a general abandonment of narrowly local speech forms in favor of fewer, more or less general, regional types. Some local speech forms have remained even to the present day. These are usually known as relics, particularly when they are distributed in isolated spots over an area rather than in concentration. *Open stone peach*, for example, is a relic for freestone peach, occurring in Maryland. *Smurring up*, "getting foggy," survives as a relic in eastern Maine and more rarely on Cape Cod and Martha's Vineyard.

Even prior to the shifts in population and changes in the culture pattern, certain colonial cities such as Boston, Philadelphia, and Charleston had acquired prestige by developing as centers of trade and foci of immigration. They became socially and culturally outstanding, as well as economically powerful, thus dominating the areas surrounding them. As a consequence, local expressions and pronunciations peculiar to the countryside came to be replaced by new forms of speech emanating from these centers. A fairly recent instance of this is to be found in the New England term *tonic* for soda water, practically coextensive with the area served by Boston wholesalers. Professor Kurath considers the influence of these centers as second only to the influence of the original settlement in shaping the regional types of speech on the Atlantic seaboard and in determining their geographic boundaries.

Nor was the general process of dialect formation by any means completed with the settlement of the Atlantic seaboard. As the land to the west came to be taken up in successive stages (for example, western New York, Michigan, Wisconsin in the North; southern Ohio, Indiana, and southern Illinois in the Midland area) the same mixtures of speech forms among the settlers were present at first, and the same linguistic compromises had to be worked out. The same processes occurred in the interior South, in Texas, and later on in the Far West. Consequently, the complete linguistic history, particularly with respect to regional forms, of the United States will not be known until all of the facts concerning the present regional distribution of speech forms have been collected, and until these facts have been collated with the settlement history of the various areas and the speech types employed by the settlers at the time they moved in. In its entirety this would necessitate a greater knowledge of the local dialects of seventeenth-century England than we have at present.

Moreover, such environmental factors as topography, climate, and plant and animal life also play their parts in influencing the dialect of an area, just as they did in the general transplanting of the English language to America. The complexity and size of the network of fresh-water streams will affect the distribution and meaning of such terms as *brook, creek, branch,* and *river.* In parts of Ohio and Pennsylvania, for example, the term *creek* is applied to a much larger body of water than in Michigan. It is even more obvious that in those parts of the country where snow is a rarity or does not fall at all, there will be no necessity for a battery of terms to indicate coasting face down on a sled. It is not surprising that those areas of the country where cows can be milked outside, for at least part of the year, will develop a specific term for the place where this is done: witness *milk gap* or *milking gap* current in the Appalachians south of the James River. The wealth of terms for various types of fences throughout the country is again dependent, in part at least, on the material which is available for building them, be it stones, stumps, or wooden rails.

Different types of institutions and practices which developed in various parts of the country also had their effect upon regional vocabulary. Those settlements which did not follow the practice of setting aside a parcel of land for common grazing purposes had little use for such terms as *green* or *common.* The meaning of *town* will vary according to the place and importance of township and county respectively in the organization of local government. The same principle applies equally well to foods of various kinds, which reflect not only materials which are readily available but folk practices as well. The German custom of preparing raised doughnuts as Lenten fare survives in the Pennsylvania term *fossnocks*, shortened from *Fastnachtskuchen*.

Finally, a new invention or development introduced into several parts of the country at the same time will acquire different names in various places. The baby carriage, for example, seems to have been a development of the 1830s and 1840s, and this is the term which developed in New England. Within the Philadelphia trade area, however, the article became known as a *baby coach*, whereas *baby buggy* was adopted west of the Alleghenies and *baby cab* in other regions throughout the country. Nor have we necessarily seen an end to this process. Within the last two decades the building of large, double-lane, limited-access automobile highways has been undertaken in various parts of the country, yet the terminology for them differs considerably. In eastern New York, Connecticut, and Rhode Island these are *parkways*, but *turnpikes* in Pennsylvania, New Jersey, New Hampshire, Maine, Massachusetts, Ohio, and Indiana. In New York *thruway* is used, and they are *expressways* in Michigan and *freeways* in California. These would seem to be regionalisms in the making. . . .

FOR DISCUSSION AND REVIEW

1 Early visitors to America commented upon the distinct regional differences in speech they noticed and also upon the uniformity of the language throughout the country. Why, according to Marckwardt, is there "truth in both types of comment"?

2 Briefly describe the processes involved in the making of a linguistic atlas.

3 What, according to Marckwardt, are the three aspects of American speech in which one finds regional differences? Give several examples of each aspect.

4 To what factors does Marckwardt attribute the development of re-gional forms of American English during our three and one-half centuries of linguistic history? How have these factors affected the part of the country with which you are most familiar?

5 Marckwardt cites *parkways, turnpikes, thruways, expressways,* and *freeways* as "regionalisms in the making." What are some other relatively recent inventions or developments that have been introduced into various parts of the United States and that have acquired different names in various places?

2

Dialects: How They Differ

In the preceding selection by Albert H. Marckwardt, you learned of the distinctive regional differences in American speech and of the ongoing work on the *Linguistic Atlas of the United States and Canada.* Roger W. Shuy, in the following excerpt from *Discovering American Dialects,* discusses in some detail regional variations in pronunciation, vocabulary, and grammar, and explains the methods used by fieldworkers to collect dialect data. Shuy is professor of linguistics at Georgetown University.

Roger W. Shuy

SPEAKERS of one dialect may be set off from speakers of a different dialect by the use of certain pronunciations, words, and grammatical forms. The frequent first reaction of a person who hears an unfamiliar dialect is that the strange sounds and words are a chaotic mess. This is similar to the feeling an American has when he sees British motorists driving "on the wrong side of the street," or to the bewildered feeling we have upon hearing a foreign language for the first time. Surely, we feel, there is no system in that sort of behavior!

Mankind apparently views all unfamiliar human behavior as suspicious and unsystematic. If you have ever watched a bird build a nest on a window sill or in a bush within the range of any passing alley cat, you have probably not questioned the intelligence of the bird. Most people accept even apparently erratic animal behavior and assume that, no matter how foolish the act may seem, it probably makes sense to the animal. But as soon as a human being is seen to behave "differently," he is frequently considered foolish or uncooperative. Language, in this case a dialect, is also a form of behavior. That people speak different dialects in no way stems from their intelligence or judgment. They speak the dialect which enables them to get along with the other members of their social and geographical group.

Differences in Pronunciation

Differences in pronunciation are of two types: totally patterned and partially patterned. A totally patterned difference is one in which the sound behaves consistently in a particular situation. For example, in some parts of the country, particularly in eastern New England, the pronunciation of "r" is lost before consonants and in word-final position. Thus a Midwesterner's "park the car" becomes the New Englander's "pahk the cah." From the New Englander's point of view, it might be equally valid to say that Midwesterners insert r's before consonants (park) and following a vowel at the ends of words (car). That the words in question have r's in their spellings is really not important here, for spellings remain fixed long after pronunciations change, and letters may have different sound values in different dialects. But whether we say the New Englander *drops* an r or the Midwesterner *inserts* one, the fact remains that the difference is totally patterned in most speech styles. Recent dialect research has shown that a person may shift his pattern slightly, depending upon his relationship to his audience and on whether he is reading aloud or speaking impromptu. Professor William Labov of Columbia University has observed, for example, that New York working-class people tend to say *dis* for *this* and *dese* for *these* when they are talking about a bad accident or about a personal brush with death. They say *dis* and *dese* less frequently when talking with teachers and even less frequently when reading aloud.

The second kind of variation in pronunciation, a partially patterned difference, may occur in a few words or even in only one. The partially patterned sound is not consistent throughout the dialect. It was mentioned above that the eastern New Englander "drops" an r before consonants and in word-final position in a totally patterned way. Now let us cite the Midwesterner who inserts an *r* in certain words but in no particular phonetic pattern. In most of Ohio, Indiana, and Illinois (except for a few northern counties), *wash* is pronounced "*worsh*" by a large number of speakers, particularly by those with no more than a high school education. If this were totally patterned, these speakers would also say "borsh" instead of *bosh* and "jorsh" instead of *josh* (many of them do say "gorsh" instead of *gosh*).

Other examples of partially patterned differences (still sticking with r problems) include "lozengers" for *lozenges*, "framiliar" for *familiar*, "quintruplets" for *quintuplets*, and "surpress" for *suppress*. This phenomenon, sometimes referred to as the "intrusive r," is most noticeable in someone else's dialect. Midwesterners are amused at the Bostonian's pronunciation of "Cuber" and "Asiar" for *Cuba* and *Asia* before words beginning with vowels, failing to hear their own intrusive r's in *worsh* and *lozengers*. Likewise, the Bostonian tends to hear the Midwesterner's intrusive r's but not his own.[1]

Our standard alphabet cannot record the many sounds in American English pronunciation. The dialectologist uses a highly detailed phonetic alphabet to record the most minute audible features of speech. The student can easily learn and use a simpler set of symbols to record the variations he meets in his dialect studies. Below is a chart which should enable you to record pronunciations yourself.

Consonants

Most of the consonant letters of our standard alphabet may be used to approximate the sounds we hear. Some new symbols are necessary, however, and these will be set off to the right and identified by a convenient label. Note that a key word is given to illustrate each sound.

SYMBOL		KEY WORD	
p		*p*in	
b		*b*in	
t		*t*in	
d		*d*in	
k		*k*in	
g		*g*et	
m		*m*an	
n		*n*an	
	ŋ (eng)		si*ng*
l		*l*ip	
r		*r*ip	
h		*h*at	
w		*w*in	
y		*y*ellow	
	θ (theta)		*th*in
	ð (eth)		*th*en
f		*f*ish	
v		*v*ery	
s		*s*it	
z		*z*ip	
	č (c wedge)		*ch*ur*ch*
	ǰ (j wedge)		*j*ail
	š (s wedge)		*sh*are
	ž (z wedge)		a*z*ure

---

[1] The "intrusive r" is not limited here to word structure but may be found in a string of sounds in a sentence. The Bostonian's "intrusive r" is either the last sound of a word which comes before a word beginning with a vowel or the last sound of an utterance.

Vowels

The vowels of English are much more difficult to represent because our alphabet provides only five symbols for a great many sounds. To understand why we need more phonetic symbols than letters in our alphabet, a cutaway drawing of the mouth may be helpful (example 1).

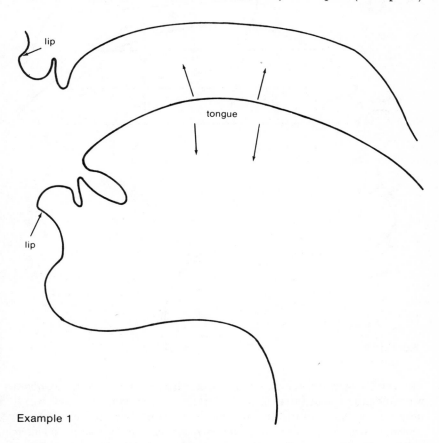

lip

tongue

lip

Example 1

Differences in vowels are made by raising, lowering, fronting, and backing the tongue and by spreading or rounding the lips. Thus a high front vowel is made with the tongue raised and fronted (see the upper dotted line in example 2). A low back vowel is made with the tongue drawn back and flattened as low as possible (see the lower dotted line in example 2).

A systematic way to identify vowels, then, is to describe the relative position of the tongue while they are being made. The following chart will show these positions and illustrate conventional symbols used for them. In order to better realize the sounds presented in example 3, we

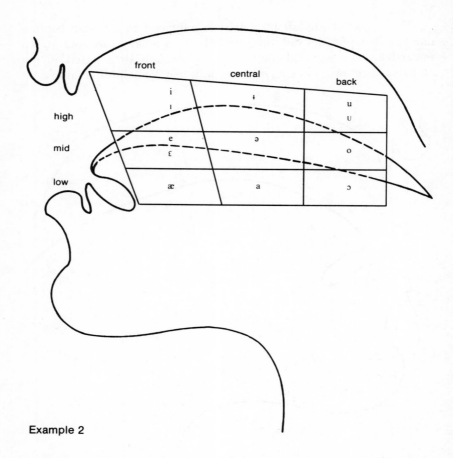

Example 2

can insert key words which may illustrate these sounds. Several words of warning must precede such an undertaking, however. The key words may not perfectly illustrate the sounds in your own dialect. The low central vowel, [ɑ], is used in *father* in most dialects, but some speakers will say it with an [ɔ]. Likewise, few speakers of American English can keep from gliding from [e] to [ɪ] in words like *say* or *bait*, or from gliding from [o] to [ʊ] in *over* or *boat*. But, for purposes of convenience, our key words will not reflect the natural tendency to glide these words.

Certain vowel sounds of English are made up of combinations of the preceding sounds (example 3). These are often called dipthongs or glides. Note the examples in figure 1 (p. 364). As your ability to hear and record speech sounds improves, you will be able to distinguish other glides such as the Midland [æʊ] in *cow* [kæʊ] as opposed to the Northern pronunciation [kɑʊ].

Pronunciation Fieldwork

As you practice writing the sounds you hear with the symbols listed on preceding pages, you can start to determine certain things about other speakers. Begin by writing short words, dictated by your teacher or your classmates. *Do not be influenced by the spelling of the word.* Listen only for its sound and write it using the phonetic symbols. People do not hear sounds in exactly the same ways, so it should not surprise you if the students in a given class produce several different acceptable transcriptions. The following words will provide good practice for you:

coat	dogs	hike
cats	how	then
boom	boil	should
beans	ringing	money
catches	wilt	rumor
thick	late	joy
sox		judges

Example 3

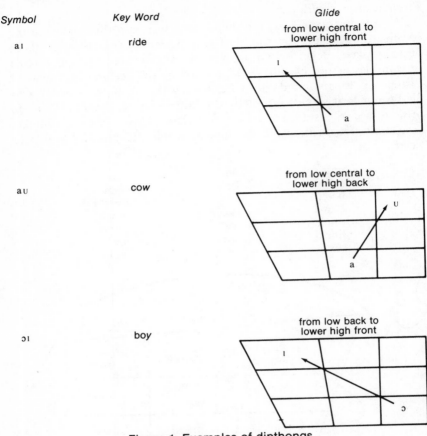

Figure 1. Examples of dipthongs.

Remember that a good ear for sounds is not developed right away. You may wish to practice with other transcription exercises, or you may simply write phonetically the words used by teachers, classmates, television performers, or members of your family. If classmates or friends from a different part of the country are willing to serve as informants, have them pronounce the following words:

WORD	NORTHERN	MIDLAND	SOUTHERN
1. creek	ɪ and i	ɪ (north Midland) i (south Midland)	i
2. penny	ε	ε	ɪ—(Southwest)
3. Mary	ε e (parts of eastern New England)	ε	e

WORD	NORTHERN	MIDLAND	SOUTHERN
4. married	æ (east of Appalachians) ɛ (elsewhere)	ɛ	ɛ
5. cow	aʊ	æʊ	æʊ or aʊ
6. sister	ɪ	ɨ (eastern)	ɨ (eastern)
7. foreign	ɔ	ɑ	ɑ
8. orange	ɑ (east of Alleghenies) ɔ	ɑ and ɔ	ɑ and ɔ
9. tomato	o	ə	o or ə
10. coop	u	u (NM), ʊ (SM)	ʊ
11. roof	ʊ	u and/or ʊ	u
12. bulge	ə	ə or ʊ	ə or ʊ
13. farm	ɑ	ɑ or ɔ	ɑ or ɔ
14. wire	ɑɪ	ɑɪ or ɑ	ɑ
15. won't	ə o (urban)	o	o
16. fog	ɑ (New England) ɑ and ɔ (Midwest)	ɔ ɔ	ɔ ɔ
17. hog	ɑ (New England) ɑ and ɔ (Midwest)	ɔ	ɔ
18. on	ɑ	ɔ	ɔ
19. long	ɔ	ɔ	ɑ (eastern Virginia) ɔ (elsewhere)
20. careless	ɪ	ə	ɨ
21. stomach	ə	ɪ	ə

The vowels of these words are pronounced differently in the various parts of our country. The major variants are listed beside the words along with their general distributions.

Consonants sometimes will give clues to the dialect a person speaks. The following generalizations may be helpful:

WORD	NORTHERN	MIDLAND	SOUTHERN
1. humor	hɪumər	yumər	hɪumər or yumər
2. wash	waš or wɔš	wɔrš or wɔɪš	wɔš or wɔɪš or waš
3. with	wɪð and wɪθ (N.Y., Chicago, Detroit=wɪt working class)	wɪθ	wɪθ
4. greasy	grisɪ	grizɪ	grizɪ

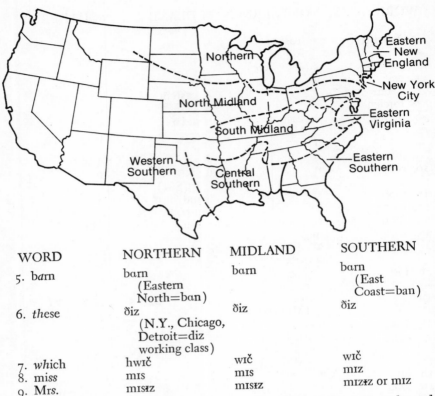

WORD	NORTHERN	MIDLAND	SOUTHERN
5. barn	barn (Eastern North=ban)	barn	barn (East Coast=ban)
6. these	ðiz (N.Y., Chicago, Detroit=diz working class)	ðiz	ðiz
7. which	hwɪč	wɪč	wɪč
8. miss	mɪs	mɪs	mɪz
9. Mrs.	mɪsɪz	mɪsɪz	mɪzɨz or mɪz

With the mobility of the American population today, we are bound to discover exceptions to generalizations like these. Also, . . . settlement history has caused some curious mixtures of speech patterns in our country. On the whole, however, the generalizations may be useful in helping you to recognize the dialect of your informant.

One bit of advice as you get your informants to say these words— *try for a natural situation.* One way professional fieldworkers have done this is to ask, for example, for what the person calls a small stream of water that runs through a farm. *Creek* is a likely response. You can easily invent similar questions for other words. It might be interesting, furthermore, to compare a person's response in conversation with his pronunciation when he reads the word in a sentence or in a list of such words. You may discover that your classmates have different pronunciations for different occasions. . . .

Differences in Vocabulary

Words are interesting to almost everyone. Through his vocabulary a person may reveal facts about his age, his sex, his education, his occupation, and his geographical and cultural origins. Our first reaction may be to imagine that all speakers of English use the same words. Nothing could be further from the truth; our language contains a vast number of synonyms to show different shades of meaning or reveal as much of our inner feelings as we want to. Some of these vocabulary choices are made deliberately. We use other words, however, without really knowing that our vocabulary is influenced by our audience.

Age

Certain words tell how old we are. For example, many people refer to an electric refrigerator as an *ice box* despite the fact that in most parts of our country ice boxes have not been in common use for many years. Older natives of some Northern dialect areas still may call a frying pan a *spider*, a term which remained in the vocabulary of the older generation long after the removal of the four legs which gave the descriptive title. Frying pans no longer look like four-legged spiders, but the name remains fixed in the vocabulary of certain people.

Sex

Our vocabulary may also identify whether we are male or female. Most high school boys, for example, are not likely to use *lovely, peachy, darling*, and many words ending in *-ie*. Adult males are not apt to know or use very many words concerned with fabrics, color shadings, sewing, or women's styles. Women of all ages are not likely to use the specialized vocabulary of sports, automobile repair, or plumbing.

Education

A person also reveals his educational background through his choice of words. It is no secret that learning the specialized vocabulary of psychology, electronics, or fishing is necessary before one becomes fully accepted as an "insider," and before he can fully participate in these areas. Much of what a student learns about a course in school is shown in his handling of the vocabulary of the subject. It is also true, however, that a person's choice of words is not nearly as revealing of education as his grammar and pronunciations are.

Occupation

The specialized vocabulary of occupational groups also appears in everyday language. Truck drivers, secretaries, tirebuilders, sailors, farmers, and members of many other occupations use such words. Linguists who interview people for *The Linguistic Atlas of the United States and Canada* have found that the calls to certain animals, for example, illustrate what might be called farm vocabulary, particularly for the older generation of farmers (city dwellers obviously have no particular way of calling sheep or cows from pasture). Even within farming areas, furthermore, vocabulary will reveal specialization. Recent Illinois language studies showed that a male sheep was known as a *buck* only to farmers who had at some time raised sheep.

Origins

It is common knowledge that certain words indicate where we are from. Northerners use *pail* for a kind of metal container which Mid-landers refer to as a *bucket. Pits* are inside cherries and peaches of Northerners; *seeds* are found by some Midlanders. It is amusing to some people, furthermore, that as a general rule horses are said to *whinny* or *whinner* in Northern dialect areas, whereas they *nicker* in some of the Midland parts of our country.

Customs are also revealed in our vocabulary. The *county seat* is relatively unknown in rural New England, where local government is handled at the town meeting.

The special names for various ethnic or national groups, whether joking or derogatory, are an indication of the settlement patterns of an area. If a person has the terms *Dago, Kraut,* or *Polack* in his active vocabulary, it is quite likely that he lives among or near Italians, Germans, or Polish people. Sometimes the nickname of a specific immigrant group becomes generalized to include most or all newcomers. Such a case was recently noted in Summit County, Ohio, where some natives refer to almost all nationality groups as *Hunkies,* regardless of whether or not they come from Hungary. That this practice has been with us for many years is shown in a comment by Theodore Roosevelt that anything foreign was referred to as *Dutch.* One nineteenth century politician even referred to Italian paintings as "Dutch daubs from Italy."[2]

Vocabulary Fieldwork

To show some of the ways a speaker's vocabulary may reveal his age, sex, occupation, or regional and cultural origins, let us do a dialect vocabulary project as it might be done by a linguist (called a fieldworker in this case) who interviews people (called informants) for *The Linguistic Atlas.*

The Atlas fieldworker gathers his information in face-to-face interviews. He may supplement his interview data, however, with questionnaires such as the one which follows. Sometimes these questionnaires are mailed; sometimes the fieldworker distributes them personally. Whatever method of distribution is used, one thing is certain: The questionnaires have been extremely helpful, reliable, and accurate indications of vocabulary in use.

[2] H. L. Mencken, *The American Language,* abridged and revised by Raven I. Mc-David, Jr. (New York: Knopf, 1963), p. 371.

A Checklist of Regional Expressions

Directions

1. Please put a circle around the word or words in each group which you ordinarily use (don't circle words you have heard—just those you actually use).
2. IF the word you ordinarily use is not listed in the group, please write it in the space by the item.
3. IF you never use any word in the group, because you never need to refer to the thing described, do not mark the word.

EXAMPLE

CENTER OF A PEACH: pit, seed, ⟨stone,⟩ kernel, heart

Household

1. TO PUT A SINGLE ROOM OF THE HOUSE IN ORDER: clean up, do up, redd up, ridd up, straighten up, tidy up, put to rights, slick up
2. PAPER CONTAINER FOR GROCERIES, ETC.: bag, poke, sack, toot
3. DEVICE FOUND ON OUTSIDE OF THE HOUSE OR IN YARD OR GARDEN: faucet, spicket, spigot, hydrant, tap
4. WINDOW COVERING ON ROLLERS: blinds, curtains, roller shades, shades, window blinds, window shades
5. LARGE OPEN METAL CONTAINER FOR SCRUB WATER: pail, bucket
6. OF PEAS: to hull, to pod, to shell, to shuck
7. WEB HANGING FROM CEILING OF A ROOM: cobweb, dust web, spider's web, web
8. METAL UTENSIL FOR FRYING: creeper, fryer, frying pan, fry pan, skillet, spider
9. OVER A SINK: faucet, hydrant, spicket, spigot, tap
10. OVERLAPPING HORIZONTAL BOARDS ON OUTSIDE OF HOUSE: clapboards, siding, weatherboards, weatherboarding
11. LARGE PORCH WITH ROOF: gallery, piazza, porch, portico, stoop, veranda
12. SMALL PORCH, OFTEN WITH NO ROOF: deck, platform, porch, portico, step, steps, stoop, veranda, piazza
13. DEVICES AT EDGES OF ROOF TO CARRY OFF RAIN: eaves, eaves spouts, eavestroughs, gutters, rain troughs, spouting, spouts, water gutter

14. RUBBER OR PLASTIC UTENSIL FOR SCRAPING DOUGH OR ICING FROM A MIXING BOWL: scraper, spatula, kid-cheater, bowl scraper

15. VEHICLE FOR SMALL BABY: baby buggy, baby cab, baby carriage, baby coach

16. TO _____ THE BABY (IN SUCH A VEHICLE): ride, roll, wheel, push, walk, stroll

17. FURRY STUFF WHICH COLLECTS UNDER BEDS AND ON CLOSET FLOORS: dust, bunnies, dust kittens, lint balls, pussies

Family

18. FAMILY WORD FOR FATHER: dad, daddy, father, pa, papa, pappy, paw, pop

19. FAMILY WORD FOR MOTHER: ma, mama, mammy, maw, mom, mommer, mommy, mother

20. IMMEDIATE FAMILY: my family, my folks, my parents, my people, my relatives, my relations, my kin, my kinfolks

21. OTHERS RELATED BY BLOOD: my family, my folks, my kind, my kinfolks, my people, my relation, my relatives, my relations, my kin

22. OF A CHILD: favors (HIS MOTHER), features, looks like, resembles, takes after, is the spitting image of

23. OF CHILDREN: brought up, fetched up, raised, reared

24. THE BABY *MOVES ON ALL FOURS* ACROSS THE FLOOR: crawls, creeps

Automotive

25. PLACE IN FRONT OF DRIVER WHERE INSTRUMENTS ARE: dash, dashboard, instrument panel, panel, crash panel

26. AUTOMOBILE DEVICE FOR MAKING THE CAR GO FASTER: accelerator, gas, gas pedal, pedal, throttle

27. PLACE WHERE FLASHLIGHT AND MAPS MAY BE KEPT: glove compartment, compartment, shelf, cabinet

28. AUTOMOBILE WITH TWO DOORS: tudor, coupe, two-door

29. THE CAR NEEDS _____: a grease job, greased, lubrication, a lube job, to be greased, to be lubed, greasing, servicing, to be serviced

30. LARGE TRUCK WITH TRAILER ATTACHED: truck, truck and trailer, semi, rig, trailer-truck

Urban

31. NEW LIMITED ACCESS ROAD: turnpike, toll road, freeway, parkway, pay road, tollway, thruway, expressway

32. SERVICE AND EATING AREAS ON THE ABOVE: service stop, service area, oasis, rest area

33. GRASS STRIP IN THE CENTER OF A DIVIDED ROAD: median, center strip, separator, divider, barrier, grass strip, boulevard

34. PLACE WHERE FIRE ENGINES ARE KEPT: fire hall, fire house, fire station

35. PLACE WHERE SCHEDULED AIRLINES OPERATE: airport, port, terminal, air terminal (by proper name), air field, field

36. PLACE WHERE TRAIN STOPS: station, railway station, depot, train stop, train station, railroad station

37. PLACE WHERE FIREMEN ATTACH HOSE: fire hydrant, fire plug, plug, hydrant, water tap

38. GRASS STRIP BETWEEN SIDEWALK AND STREET: berm, boulevard, boulevard strip, parking, parking strip, parkway, sidewalk plot, tree lawn, neutral ground, devil strip, tree bank, city strip

39. CALL TO HAIL A TAXI: taxi!, cab!, cabbie!, hack!, hey!, (wave arm), (whistle)

40. POLICEMAN: cop, policeman, copper, fuzz, dick, officer, bull

41. THE ROAD IS _____: slick, slippery

42. PLACE WHERE PACKAGED GROCERIES CAN BE PURCHASED: grocery store, general store, super market, store, delicatessen, grocery, market, food market, food store, super mart

43. A PIECE OF PAVEMENT BETWEEN TWO HOUSES ON A CITY BLOCK: gangway, walk, path, sidewalk

44. PLACE WHERE YOU WATCH TECHNICOLOR FEATURES IN A CAR: drive-in, drive-in movie, outdoor movie, outdoor theater, open-air movie, open-air theater, passion pit

Nature

45. ANIMAL WITH STRONG ODOR: polecat, skunk, woodspussy, woodpussy

46. SMALL, SQUIRREL-LIKE ANIMAL THAT RUNS ALONG THE GROUND: chipmunk, grinnie, ground squirrel

47. WORM USED FOR BAIT IN FISHING: angledog, angleworm,

bait worm, eace worm, earthworm, eelworm, fish bait, fishing worm, fishworm, mudworm, rainworm, redworm

48. LARGER WORM: dew worm, night crawler, night walker, (Georgia) wiggler, town worm

49. DOG OF NO SPECIAL KIND OR BREED: common dog, cur, cur dog, fice, feist, mongrel, no-count, scrub, heinz, sooner, mixed dog, mutt

50. INSECT THAT GLOWS AT NIGHT: fire bug, firefly, glow worm, june bug, lightning bug, candle bug

51. LARGE WINGED INSECT SEEN AROUND WATER: darning needle, devil's darning needle, dragon fly, ear-sewer, mosquito hawk, sewing needle, snake doctor, snake feeder, sewing bug

52. FRESHWATER SHELLFISH WITH CLAWS; SWIMS BACKWARD: crab, craw, crawdad(die), crawfish, crayfish

53. CENTER OF A CHERRY: pit, seed, stone, kernel, heart

54. CENTER OF A PEACH: pit, seed, stone, kernel, heart

55. HARD INNER COVER OF A WALNUT: hull, husk, shell, shuck

56. GREEN OUTER COVER OF A WALNUT: hull, husk, shell, shuck

57. BUNCH OF TREES GROWING IN OPEN COUNTRY (PARTICULARLY ON A HILL): motte, clump, grove, bluff

58. WEB FOUND OUTDOORS: cobweb, dew web, spider nest, spider's nest, spider web, web

59. TREE THAT PRODUCES SUGAR AND SYRUP: hard maple, rock maple, sugar maple, sugar tree, maple tree, candy tree, sweet maple

Foods

60. MELON WITH YELLOW OR ORANGE INSIDES: muskmelon, melon, mushmelon, lope, cantaloup, mussmellon

61. A SPREADABLE LUNCHEON MEAT MADE OF LIVER: liver sausage, braunschweiger, liverwurst

62. A CARBONATED DRINK: pop, soda, soda pop, tonic, soft drink

63. A GLASS CONTAINING ICE CREAM AND ROOT BEER: a float, a root beer float, a black cow, a Boston cooler

64. DISH OF COOKED FRUIT EATEN AT THE END OF A MEAL: fruit, sauce, dessert, compote

65. PEACH WHOSE MEAT STICKS TO SEED: cling, cling peach, clingstone, clingstone peach, hard peach, plum-peach, press peach

66. FOOD EATEN BETWEEN REGULAR MEALS: a bite, lunch, a piece, piece meal, a snack, a mug-up, munch, nash, nosh

67. CORN SERVED ON COB: corn-on-the-cob, garden corn, green corn, mutton corn, roasting ears, sugar corn, sweet corn

68. BEANS EATEN IN PODS: green beans, sallet beans, snap beans, snaps, string beans, beans

69. EDIBLE TOPS OF TURNIPS, BEETS, ETC: greens, salad, sallet

70. A WHITE LUMPY CHEESE: clabber cheese, cottage cheese, curd cheese, curd(s), dutch cheese, home-made cheese, pot cheese, smear-case, cream cheese

71. ROUND, FLAT CONFECTION WITH HOLE IN CENTER, MADE WITH BAKING POWDER: crull, cruller, doughnut, fat-cake, fried cake, cake doughnut, raised doughnut

72. BREAD MADE OF CORN MEAL: corn bread, corn dodger(s), corn pone, hoe cake(s), johnnycake, pone bread

73. COOKED MEAT JUICES POURED OVER MEAT, POTATOES, OR BREAD: gravy, sop, sauce, drippings

74. GROUND BEEF IN A BUN: hamburg, hamburger, burger

75. LARGE SANDWICH DESIGNED TO BE A MEAL IN ITSELF: hero, submarine, hoagy, grinder, poor-boy

Games

76. CHILDREN'S CRY AT HALLOWEEN TIME: trick or treat!, tricks or treats!, beggar's night!, help the poor!, Halloween!, give or receive!

77. FAST MOVING AMUSEMENT PARK RIDE (ON TRACKS): coaster, roller coaster, rolly-coaster, shoot-the-chutes, the ride of doom

78. CALL TO PLAYERS TO RETURN BECAUSE A NEW PLAYER WANTS TO JOIN: allie-allie-in-free, allie-allie-oxen free, allie-allie-ocean free, bee-bee bumble bee, everybody in free, newcomer-newcomer!

79. CALL TO PASSER-BY TO RETURN A BALL TO THE PLAYGROUND: little help!, ball!, hey!, yo!, ball up!

80. TO COAST ON SLED LYING DOWN FLAT: belly-booster,

belly-bump, belly-bumper, belly-bunker, belly-bunt, belly-bust, belly buster, belly-down, belly-flop, belly-flopper, belly-grinder, belly-gut, belly-gutter, belly-kachug, belly-kachuck, belly-whack, belly-whop, belly-whopper, belly-slam, belly-smacker

81. TO HIT THE WATER WHEN DIVING: belly-flop, belly-flopper, belly-bust, belly-buster

82. TO STOP A GAME YOU CALL: time!, time out!, times!, pax!, fins!

School

83. TO BE ABSENT FROM SCHOOL: bag school, bolt, cook jack, lay out, lie out, play hookey, play truant, run out of school, skip class, skip school, slip off from school, ditch, flick, flake school, blow school

84. WHERE SWINGS AND PLAY AREAS ARE: school yard, playground, school ground, yard, grounds

85. HOLDS SMALL OBJECTS TOGETHER: rubber band, rubber binder, elastic binder, gum band, elastic band

86. DRINKING FOUNTAIN: cooler, water cooler, bubbler, fountain, drinking fountain

87. THE AMOUNT OF BOOKS YOU CAN CARRY IN BOTH ARMS: armful, armload, load, turn

Clothing

88. SHORT KNEE-LENGTH OUTER GARMENT WORN BY MEN: shorts, bermuda shorts, bermudas, walking shorts, knee (length) pants, pants, knee-knockers

89. SHORT KNEE-LENGTH OUTER GARMENT WORN BY WOMEN: shorts, bermudas, walking shorts, pants

90. OUTER GARMENT OF A HEAVY MATERIAL WORN BY MALES AS THEY WORK: levis, overalls, dungarees, jeans, blue jeans, pants

91. GARMENT WORN BY WOMEN AT THE SEASHORE: swim suit, swimming suit, bathing suit

92. GARMENT WORN BY MEN AT THE SEASHORE: swim suit, swimming suit, bathing suit, swimming trunks, trunks, bathing trunks, swimming shorts

Miscellaneous

93. A TIME OF DAY: quarter before eleven, quarter of eleven, quarter till eleven, quarter to eleven, 10:45

94. SOMEONE FROM THE COUNTRY: backwoodsman, clod-hopper, country gentleman, country jake, countryman, hayseed, hick, hoosier, hillbilly, jackpine savage, mossback, mountain-boomer, pumpkinhusker, railsplitter, cracker, redneck, rube, share-cropper, stump farmer, swamp angel, yahoo, yokel, sodbuster

95. SOMEONE WHO WON'T CHANGE HIS MIND IS: bull-headed, contrary, headstrong, ornery, otsny, owly, pig-headed, set, sot, stubborn, mulish, muley

96. WHEN A GIRL STOPS SEEING A BOY FRIEND SHE IS SAID TO: give him the air, give him the bounce, give him the cold shoulder, give him the mitten, jilt him, kick him, throw him over, turn him down, shoot him down, give him the gate, brush him off, turn him off, break up with him

97. BECOME ILL: be taken sick, get sick, take sick, be taken ill, come down

98. BECOME ILL WITH A COLD: catch a cold, catch cold, get a cold, take cold, take a cold, come down with a cold

99. SICK _____: at his stomach, in his stomach, on his stomach, to his stomach, of his stomach, with his stomach

100. I ——— YOU'RE RIGHT: reckon, guess, figger, figure, suspect, imagine

The preceding vocabulary questionnaire, frequently called a check-list, is only suggestive of what might be asked for in a particular community. Of the hundred items in ten general fields, you may find some questions more interesting and useful to study than others. Further-more, you may add other words to this list, or you may find other an-swers to questions listed here.

Let us suppose, however, that you wish to make a vocabulary survey of your community using this checklist. If your school has ample facili-ties and supplies, you could reproduce all or part of this questionnaire, distribute it to various neighbors, let them fill it out at their leisure, and then have them return it to you for tabulation and analysis.

One last matter of data must be included, however, if the checklist is to be meaningful. The dialectologist needs to know certain things about the people who fill out the checklists. The following questions should be answered if the data are to be interpreted meaningfully.

Let us look for a moment at the personal data sheet. We note that dialectologists think it important to keep a record of the informant's age, sex, race, education, mobility, travel, ancestry, language skills, and occupation. People from the same general area may use different words,

Personal Data Sheet

Sex _____ Race _____

Have you filled out this same   Age _____ Highest grade level

questionnaire before? Yes __ No __ reached in school _____

State _____ County _____ Town _____

How long have you lived here? _____ years

Birthplace _____
                     (town)   (state)

Other towns, states, or nations you have lived in (please give
approximate years for each place)

_____
_____
_____

Have you traveled much outside your native state? ____ (Yes or No)
If so, where? _____

_____

Parents' birthplace (state or nation):

Father _____ Grandfather _____

                                          Grandmother _____

Mother _____ Grandfather _____

                                          Grandmother _____

Do you speak any non-English language? ____ If so, which? ____
                                                    (yes or no)
Occupation _____

If retired, former occupation _____

If housewife, husband's occupation _____

Name (optional) _____

and this personal data sheet will help us find out why. In parts of Michigan, for example, the older generation may still use the term *spider* for what younger informants may call *frying pan*. This is an indication of current language change. It is never a surprise to us to hear that our parents' generation did things differently. Nor should we be surprised to note that they use different words.

There are any number of things you may be able to discover by making a vocabulary survey in your community. What you should remember as you gather your data is the principle of constants and variables, a principle familiar to you, no doubt, from mathematics. You may gather your data in any way you wish, but chances are you will not be able to get a representation of all ages, ethnic groups, religions, and occupations of the people in your area, especially if you live in an urban community. A somewhat narrower approach would be easier and more successful, for example:

1. *Age Contrast:* Collect checklists from three or four people who have lived all their lives in your community. This gives you two constants: the checklist and the native born residents. The most interesting variables will be their age and education along with, of course, their answers. If you select older people and younger people of roughly the same education and social status, chances are that any vocabulary differences will stem from the contrast in ages.

2. *Education Contrast:* Collect checklists from three or four people who have different educational backgrounds. College graduates, for example, may be contrasted with people who have had less than a high school education. If your informants are of roughly the same age, and if their personal data sheets are otherwise similar, the differences which you note may be attributable to their contrasting educations.

3. *Describe the Local Dialect Area:* Collect checklists from three or four people who have lived all their lives in your community. Try to get older, middle-aged, and younger people who have educational backgrounds characteristic of your community (in some parts of our country, for example, college graduates are simply not frequently found). Then note the responses of these informants to some or all of the following questions: 1, 2, 3, 5, 8, 9, 10, 13, 24, 45, 46, 47, 50, 51, 53, 54, 64, 67, 69, 70, 71, 72, 87, 93, 97, 98, 99. For each of these questions there is a response which research has shown to be characteristic of one side of the dialect map shown on page 366 (of course, the term may be used elsewhere, too, but not as generally). The following chart will indicate some of the words you may expect to find *in certain parts* of the Northern, Midland, and Southern dialect areas:

QUESTION	ITEM	NORTH-ERN	MID-LAND	SOUTH-ERN
1	TO PUT ROOM IN ORDER:		redd up ridd up	
2	PAPER CONTAINER:	bag	sack	sack
3	ON OUTSIDE OF HOUSE:	faucet	spigot spicket hydrant	spigot spicket hydrant
5	CONTAINER:	pail	bucket	bucket
8	METAL UTEN-SIL: (frying pan common everywhere)	spider	skillet	skillet spider
9	OVER A SINK:	faucet	spigot spicket	spigot spicket

QUESTION	ITEM	NORTH-ERN	MID-LAND	SOUTH-ERN
10	BOARDS: (siding common every-where)	clapbords	weather-boards	
13	DEVICES AT ROOF:	gutters (ENE) eaves spouts eaves-troughs	gutters spouting spouts	gutters
24	BABY MOVES:	creeps	crawls	crawls
45	ANIMAL:	skunk	skunk polecat woodspussy woodpussy	polecat
46	ANIMAL: (note: for some people, chipmunk and ground squirrel are two different animals)	chipmunk	ground squirrel	ground squirrel
47	WORM:	angleworm	fish(ing) worm	fish(ing) worm
50	INSECT:	firefly (urban) lightning bug (rural)	lightning bug fire bug	lightning bug
51	INSECT:	(devil's) darning needle sewing bug dragon fly	snake feeder snake doctor dragon fly	snake feeder snake doctor dragon fly mosquito hawk
53	CHERRY:	pit stone	seed stone	seed stone
54	PEACH:	pit stone	seed stone	seed stone
64	DISH:	dessert sauce fruit	dessert fruit	dessert fruit
67	CORN:	corn-on-the-cob green corn sweet corn	corn-on-the-cob sweet corn roasting ears	roasting ears sweet corn
69	TOPS:		greens	greens salad salat

QUESTION	ITEM	NORTH-ERN	MID-LAND	SOUTH-ERN
70	CHEESE: (cottage cheese common everywhere)	dutch cheese pot cheese	smear-case	clabber cheese curds
71	CONFECTION:	doughnut fried cake	doughnut	doughnut
72	BREAD:	johnny cake corn bread	corn bread	corn bread corn pone
87	TO CARRY:	armful	armload	armload
93	QUARTER—:	to of	till	till to
97	BECOME ILL:	get sick	take sick	take sick
98	WITH A COLD:	catch a cold	take a cold	take a cold
99	SICK—: (at his stomach common everywhere)	to his stomach	on his stomach in his stomach	

Many of the suggested checklist items have not been surveyed nationally (the automotive terms, for example), and so we cannot show their regional distributions. This should not prevent you from checking them in your own community to discover what term is characteristic there.

4. *Contrast Regional Dialects:* Have two natives of your area and two newcomers from other parts of the country fill out all or part of the checklist. Note the contrasts which are evidence of geographical differences. Your conclusions will be more certain if your informants are roughly the same age and have roughly the same educational background. This will help rule out age or education as the cause of the vocabulary difference.

Differences in Grammar

In addition to pronunciation and vocabulary differences in dialects, there are differences which involve matters of grammar. In grammar we include such things as past tenses of verbs, plural nouns, and word order (syntax) patterns. For example, many people use *dived* as the past tense of the verb *dive*. Others use *dove*. Still others use both forms. Likewise, some people say *this is as far as I go*. Others habitually say *this is all the farther I go*. These forms are used by educated and respectable people, and their English is considered equally educated and respectable. If one or two of the above examples sound strange or wrong to you, then you are probably living in an area which uses the alternative form. This does not mean that your way is better or worse—only that it is different.

On the other hand, some variants of grammatical items are used by relatively uneducated people. For the past tense of *dive* they might use the forms *duv* or *div*. For the distance statement they might say *this is the furtherest I go* or *this is the fartherest I go*.

Thus we can see that grammatical items may indicate place of origin or social level. The following chart shows how people in two theoretical areas differ internally, because of social class, and externally, because of where they live.

	AREA X		AREA Y
Speaker	*Grammatical item used*	*Speaker*	*Grammatical item used*
higher social status:	dove	higher social status:	dived
middle social status:	dove	middle social status:	dived
lower social status:	dove, duv	lower social status:	dived, div

Contrary to what some people think, even people of higher social classes do not make the same grammatical choices in different parts of our country. Well-educated natives of Wisconsin tend to say *dove*; their counterparts from Kentucky favor *dived*.

For determining social levels, grammatical choices are as important as pronunciation and vocabulary choices. Regional distributions of grammatical choice, however, are not as clearly marked as other differences. Of particular interest to American fieldworkers are the following items:[3]

1. *Prepositions*
   Trouble comes all _____ once. (to = N, at)
   It's half _____ six. (past, after)
   It's quarter _____ four. (of, to = N, till = M, before, until)
   It's _____ the door. (behind, hindside, in back of, back of)
   He isn't _____. (at home, to home, home)
   It's coming right _____ you. (at, toward, towards)
   Guess who I ran _____. (into, onto, up against, upon, up with, against, again, afoul of = NE, across)
   They named the baby _____ him. (after, for, at, from)
   I fell _____ the horse. (off, off of, offen, off from, from)
   I wonder what he died _____. (of, with, from, for)
   He's sick _____ his stomach. (to = N, at = M, S, of, on = M, in = M, with)
   He came over _____ tell me. (to, for to = SM, S, for = S)

---

[3] Whenever ϕ appears, it signifies that nothing is added to the statement. N stands for Northern, M for Midland, S for Southern and NE for New England. For a map of these dialect areas, see page 366.

I want this _____ of that. (instead, stead, in room, in place)

We're waiting _____ John. (on = M, for)

The old man passed _____. (away, on, out, φ)

He did it _____ purpose. (on, a, for, φ)

I want _____ the bus. (off = M, to get off)

He was _____ (singing, a-singing) and _____. (laughing, a-laughing)

How big _____ (a, of a) house is it?

2. *Matters of agreement*

Here _____ your pencils. (is, are)

The oats _____ thrashed. (is = M, are = N)

These cabbages _____ (is, are) for sale.

3. *Plural formations*

I have two _____ of shoes. (pair = N, S, pairs = M)

They had forty _____ of apples. (bushel = N, bushels = M)

He has two _____ of butter. (pound = S, pounds = M)

The fence has twenty _____. (posts, post, postis, poss)

He likes to play _____. (horseshoe, horseshoes)

Put your feet in the _____. (stirrup, stirrups)

Let's spray for _____. (moth, moths, mothis)

I bought two _____ of lettuce. (head, heads)

That's a long _____. (way = N, ways = M)

That's a short _____. (way = N, ways = M)

It's nine _____ high. (foot, feet)

We have three _____. (desks, desk, deskis, desses, dess)

4. *Pronouns*

It wasn't _____. (me, I)

This is _____. (yours, yourn)

This is _____. (theirs, theirn)

Are _____ (pl.) coming over? (you, youse, yuz, youns, you-all)

_____ boys are all bad. (those, them, them there)

He's the man _____ owns the car. (that, who, what, which, as, φ)

He's the boy _____ father is rich. (whose, that his, that the, his)

"I'm not going!" "_____." (Me either, Me neither, Neither am I, Nor I either, Nor I neither)

It is _____. (I, me)

It is _____. (he, him)

He's going to do it _____. (himself, hisself)

Let them do it _____. (themselves, themself, theirselves, theirself)

I'll go with _____. (φ, you)

5. *Adjectives*

The oranges are all _____. (φ, gone)

Some berries are _____. (poison, poisonous)

6. *Adverbs*

You can find these almost _____. (anywhere, anywheres, anyplace)

This is _____ I go. (as far as, as fur as, all the farther, all the further, the farthest, the furthest, the fartherest, the furtherest)

7. *Conjunctions*

It seems _____ we'll never win. (as though, like, as if)

I won't go _____ he does. (unless, without, lessen, thouten, douten,
  less, else)
I like him _____ he's funny. (because, cause, on account of, count,
  owing to)
Do this _____ I eat lunch. (while, whiles, whilst)
This is not _____ long as that one. (as, so)

8. *Articles*
   John is _____ university. (in, in the)
   She is _____ hospital. (in, in the)
   I have _____ apple. (a, an)
   John has _____. (flu, the flu)
   Do you have _____? (mumps, the mumps)

9. *Verbs*

Past tense forms:	began, begun, begin
	blew, blowed
	climbed, clim (N), clum (M)
	came, come, comed
	could, might could (SM, S)
	dived, dove (N)
	drank, drunk, drinked
	did, done
	drowned, drownded
	ate, et, eat
	gave, give (M)
	grew, growed
	learned, learnt, larnt, larnd
	lay, laid
	rode, rid
	ran, run
	saw, seen (M), seed (M), see (N)
	sat, set
	spoiled, spoilt
	swam, swim
	threw, throwed
	wore, weared
	wrote, writ
Past participles:	tore up, torn up
	wore out, worn out
	rode (M), ridden
	drank, drunk
	bit, bitten
Negative:	hadn't ought (N), ought not, oughtn't,
	didn't ought

Some of the preceding grammatical choices may seem appropriate
to you; others may appear to be undesirable. But in unguarded moments you may find yourself using more than one of the choices. What
is particularly interesting to linguists is the fact that many forces contribute to our shift from one variant to another.

Grammar Fieldwork

People tend to be much more self-conscious about their use of verb forms, prepositions, pronouns, and so on, than they are about their vocabulary or pronunciation. Consequently, no simple checklist will be given here. However, you can observe the above items in the casual conversations of your acquaintances, in the speech of television actors (especially those who portray Westerners, hillbillies, blue collar urbanites, farmers, well-heeled tycoons, and other special "types"), in the dialogue of novels or short stories, and in the speech of out-of-staters who have recently moved to your community. You must remember, however, that people are very sensitive about their grammar. The good fieldworker is tactful and objective. He does not ridicule the grammar of other areas or other social levels; in fact, he does not even seem to be especially interested in the grammar of his subject's responses. Much of the time he contents himself with getting details of grammar in conversation, without direct questioning.

FOR DISCUSSION AND REVIEW

1 What are the two types of pronunciation differences? Explain how they differ.

2 Using the phonetic symbols provided by Shuy in the charts for consonants and vowels, carefully transcribe your pronunciation of each of the following words. Discuss any differences between your pronunciations and those of other members of the class.

     a. folk
     b. pneumonia
     c. scent
     d. pear
     e. judgment
     f. constitution
     g. horse
     h. please
     i. women
     j. cushion

3 Pronounce each of the vowels in Shuy's "example 3." Explain what happens to your tongue and lips as you pronounce each vowel. How does this information help explain why certain combinations of sounds in English (e.g., *sixths*, *prompts*) are difficult to pronounce?

4 Discuss with specific examples how vocabulary can reveal facts about a person's age, sex, education, occupation, and geographical and cultural origins.

5 Complete the vocabulary questionnaire on pages 369–375. Compare your responses with those of other members of the class and with those provided on pages 377–379. Are the responses patterned? How do you account for any deviations from the patterns?

6 Shuy cites the examples of *spider* and *frying pan* to illustrate differences in vocabulary from one generation to another. Prepare a list of words that your parents or grandparents use that you do not use. What words do you use in their place?

7 Why does Shuy feel that a checklist or questionnaire is inappropriate as the only means for determining grammatical choices of informants? What are the alternatives to a questionnaire?

3

Grease and Greasy:

A Study of Geographical Variation

Using data from the field records of the *Linguistic Atlas* project, Professor E. Bagby Atwood examines the different pronunciations of *grease* and *greasy*. This classic study of geographical variation not only determines the distribution of the various pronunciations of *grease* and *greasy* in the eastern United States but also proves that the differences are dependent on the geographical location of the speakers—and not on their social or educational levels. Atwood was professor of English at the University of Texas and director of the Texas dialect project until his death in 1963.

E. Bagby Atwood

T HE FACT that the verb *to grease* and the adjective *greasy* are pronounced by some Americans with [s] and by others with [z] has long been well known even to amateur observers of speech.[1] It has also been pretty well accepted that the incidence of [s] or [z] in the words in question is primarily dependent on the geographical location of the speaker rather than on his social or educational level—that [s] is, in general, "Northern," [z] "Southern."

[1] Webster's *New International Dictionary* states that [z] in *grease* is found "esp. Brit. and Southern U.S."; [z] in *greasy* is "perhaps more general in England and the southern U.S. than in the North and East." Kenyon and Knott, *Pronouncing Dictionary* (Springfield, Mass., 1944), give [s] and [z] for the country as a whole, only [z] for the South. *The Century, Funk and Wagnalls New Standard,* and the *American College Dictionary* merely give [s] or [z] for both words. Kenyon and Knott state that "['grizɪ] and [tə griz] are phonetically normal; ['grisɪ] and [tə gris] imitate the noun *grease* [gris]." Certainly many verbs since Middle English times have been distinguished from the corresponding nouns by voicing the final fricative; cf. *house: to house, proof: to prove, wreath: to wreathe, abuse: to abuse* —and (with vowel change) *bath: to bathe, breath: to breathe, grass: to graze,* etc. This paper will not be concerned with the origin or history of the feature.

The pronunciation of the vowels is of no significance in our study. For convenience I am using the symbol [i] for both the stressed and the unstressed vowels in *greasy*.

As early as 1896, George Hempl published a study[2] of these two words, based on a rather widely circulated written questionnaire. His returns enabled him to divide the country into four major areas, according to the percentages of [s] in *to grease* and *greasy* respectively. The "North"[3]—extending from New England to the Dakotas—showed 88 and 82 percent of [s] pronunciations; the "Midland," comprising a fairly narrow strip extending from New York City to St. Louis,[4] 42 and 34 percent; the "South,"[5] 12 and 12 percent; and the "West"—an ever-widening area extending westward from St. Louis—56 and 47 percent. The material which Hempl was able to collect was admittedly "insufficient";[6] moreover, he had no means of selecting strictly representative informants;[7] and the answers may not always have been correct, since, it seems to me, an understanding of the questions would have required a certain degree of linguistic sophistication.[8] Still, in spite of these handicaps, Hempl's study has not been greatly improved upon by later writers. Most authorities content themselves by stating that [z] in *to grease* and *greasy* is predominantly Southern, and that either [s] or [z] may occur elsewhere.[9] Few investigators have gathered material that would enable them to draw clearer lines between [s] and [z] than Hempl was able to do.[10]

---

[2] *"Grease* and *Greasy," Dialect Notes,* I (1896), 438–444.

[3] In addition to New England, this area includes New Brunswick, Quebec, Ontario, New York, Michigan, Wisconsin, North Dakota, South Dakota, Minnesota, and the northern portions of Pennsylvania, Ohio, Indiana, Illinois, and Iowa.

[4] This includes New York City, New Jersey, Delaware, the District of Columbia, southern Pennsylvania, southern Ohio, northern West Virginia, middle Indiana, middle Illinois, and St. Louis, Missouri.

[5] This includes everything to the south of the Midland, as far west as Texas.

[6] Op. cit., p. 438.

[7] For example, he urged his colleagues, especially "teachers of English in colleges, normal schools, and young ladies' seminaries to use the questions as an exercise in English." Ibid., p. 444.)

[8] Question 45 reads: "In which (if any) of the following does *s* have the sound of *z*: '*the grease,*' '*to grease,*' '*greasy*'?" (Hempl, "American Speech Maps," *Dialect Notes,* I [1896], 317.) Judging from my experience in teaching phonetic transcription to college seniors and graduate students, a considerable proportion of a class would simply not know whether [s] or [z] was used in such words; certainly many students unhesitatingly write [s] in words like *rose* and *has* simply because the *letter s* is used in standard spelling.

[9] See footnote 1. It is sometimes pointed out that the same speaker may use both ['grisi] and ['grizi] with a distinction in meaning. This point will be discussed below.

[10] A. H. Marckwardt was able to draw a fairly clean line through Ohio, Indiana, and Illinois, though on the basis of relatively little data. See "Folk Speech in Indiana and Adjacent States," *Indiana History Bulletin,* XVII (1940), 120–140. Henry L. Smith has long been using the word *greasy* as a test word in his demonstrations of regional variation and to determine the origins of speakers, though

The field records that have been gathered for the *Linguistic Atlas of the United States and Canada*[11] provide us with an excellent basis for delimiting the geographical and social spread of speech forms in the eastern United States. A number of features of the *Atlas* methodology[12] are conducive to an accurate picture of native and normal speech. The informants, though relatively few,[13] were carefully chosen, each being both native to and representative of his community. The answers to questions were elicited, so far as possible, in a conversational atmosphere, and thus the occurrence of ungenuine forms was minimized. Finally, the forms were recorded by trained phoneticians, who would be very unlikely to make such errors as to write [s] when the informant actually uttered [z].

A few words should be said regarding the cartographical representation of linguistic atlas data. In such works as the *Atlas Linguistique de la France*,[14] in which each community, or "point" on the map, is represented by a single speaker, it is usually possible to draw lines, or *isoglosses*, separating those communities where a form occurs from those where it does not occur. Often these isoglosses set off a large block of "points," forming a solid area—as, for example, the southern French territory marked by initial [k] in the word *chandelle*.[15] A more complex presentation is sometimes required, as in the case of the northern French occurrences of [k] in this same word: After setting off our solid

---

he has not published his material. I presume that Dr. Smith's observations are the source of Mario Pei's statement: " 'greazy' . . . would place the speaker south of Philadelphia, while 'greassy' would place him north of Trenton." (*The Story of Language* [Philadelphia and New York, 1949], p. 51.) C. K. Thomas considers the word *greasy* in his survey of the regional speech types, but comes to the strange conclusion that "the choice between [s] and [z] in words like *discern, desolate, absorb, absurd*, and *greasy* seems to be more personal than regional." (*An Introduction to the Phonetics of American English* [New York, 1947], p. 154). G. P. Krapp is likewise at fault when he states that, in *greasy*, "popular usage and, in general, standard speech have only the form with [z]." (*The Pronunciation of Standard English in America* [New York, 1919], p. 119.)

11 The New England materials have been published as the *Linguistic Atlas of New England*, ed. Hans Kurath and Bernard Bloch, 3 vols., Providence, R.I., 1939–1943. Field records for most of the Middle Atlantic and South Atlantic states were gathered by the late Guy S. Lowman; recently (summer 1949) Dr. Raven I. McDavid, Jr., completed the work for the eastern seaboard. The records, in an unedited but usable state, are filed at the University of Michigan, where they were made available to me through the courtesy of Professor Kurath.

12 See *Handbook of the Linguistic Geography of New England*, ed. H. Kurath and others (Providence, R.I., 1939), for a complete account of the *Atlas* methodology.

13 Something like 1600 informants have been interviewed, representing communities from New Brunswick to northern Florida, approximately as far west as Lake Erie.

14 Ed. J. Gilliéron and E. Edmont, 7 vols., Paris, 1902–1910.

15 See Karl Jaberg, "Sprachgeographie," *Siebenunddreissigstes Jahresheft des Vereins Schweiz. Gymnasiallehrer* (Aarau, 1908), pp. 16–42; also Plate III.

area we find outside it a number of scattered communities where the feature in question occurs; these must be indicated by additional lines encircling the "points" where the form is found.[16] In still other cases, the communities where a given speech form occurs (for example, *conin* for "rabbit") are so scattered that it is impossible to connect them; in such cases our isoglosses must consist merely of scattered circles here and there on the map.[17] When this situation obtains we would prob- ably do better to assign a symbol (say, a cross, or a dot, or a triangle) to the scattered form in question, lest the labyrinth of lines become too much for the reader to cope with.

Now, in presenting data from the American *Atlas*, we are faced with all these complications, plus others arising from the fact that more than one informant was chosen to represent each community. That is, at nearly every "point" the American fieldworkers recorded the usage of one elderly, poorly educated informant and one younger, more modern informant. In certain key communities a third type was included—a well-educated, or "cultured," speaker who presumably represented the cultivated usage of the area. Thus, at the same point on the map we often find such variants as *sot down* (preterite), representing rustic usage, *set* or *sit down*, representing more modern popular usage, and *sat down*, representing cultivated usage.[18] It is obviously impossible to draw isoglosses separating *sot* from *set* or *sat*; it is even impractical to set off the *sot* areas, since the form occurs in about every other commu- nity through considerable areas. In other cases, of course, it is quite easy to mark off an area where a certain form is current. *Holp* (for *helped*), for example, occupies a very clearcut area south of the Poto- mac.[19] Yet a line marking off this area would by no means constitute a dividing line between *holp* and *helped*, since most of the younger in- formants within the *holp* area use the standard form *helped*. My point is that an isogloss based on American *Atlas* materials *should in all cases be regarded as an outer limit, not as a dividing line between two speech forms.*

The examples hitherto adduced have, of course, illustrated the inci- dence of "nonstandard" as against "standard" speech forms. What of those instances of two forms which are equally "standard," each within

---

[16] Ibid., Plate III.

[17] Ibid., Plate X.

[18] In addition, the same informant often uses more than one form; all of these are of course entered at that point on the map. On at least one occasion McDavid picked up from the same informant, as the preterite of *see*, *I seen, I seed, I see,* and *I saw*.

[19] This verb, as well as the others mentioned, is treated in my *Survey of Verb Forms in the Eastern United States,* 1953.

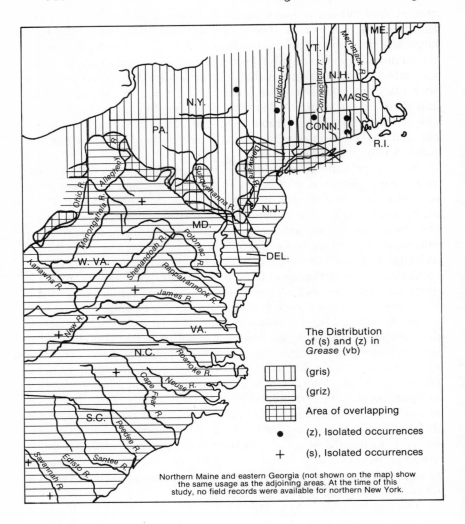

The Distribution
of (s) and (z) in
Grease (vb)

	(gris)
	(griz)
	Area of overlapping
●	(z), Isolated occurrences
+	(s), Isolated occurrences

Northern Maine and eastern Georgia (not shown on the map) show
the same usage as the adjoining areas. At the time of this
study, no field records were available for northern New York.

its area? Kurath's map of *pail* and *bucket* provides an example.[20] Here
too we must follow the same principle: We must first draw the outer
limit of one form, then of the other. The two lines will lap over each
other at some points, enclosing certain communities of mixed usage.[21]

[20] A *Word Geography of the Eastern United States* (Ann Arbor, Mich., 1949),
Figure 66.

[21] Even after drawing the lines we would find a good many scattered, or "stray,"
occurrences of *pail* within the *bucket* area and vice versa. Kurath's lines, which
are all outer limits, do not attempt to indicate the presence of stray forms or
small patches which occur outside the main area; however, since he also publishes
maps on which each occurrence of each word is recorded by a symbol, the reader
can easily check and interpret his isoglosses.

Thus, *a dividing line is a double isogloss,* each line being the outer limit of one of the two speech forms in question. The areas of overlapping between the two lines may be wide or narrow, depending on many social, geographical, and historical considerations.

Let us return to *grease* and *greasy.* The variations between [s] and [z] in these words furnishes an almost ideal example of geographical (as against social) distribution. Consider first the verb *grease.* It is unnecessary to describe in detail the incidence of [s] and [z], since the accompanying map tells its own story. The northern line of the [z]-form, it may be observed, takes in the southwestern corner of Connecticut (west of the Housatonic); from there it passes westward just to the north of New Jersey; then it dips sharply southward to Philadelphia, to the west of which it again rises gradually northward to the northwestern corner of Pennsylvania. The transition area (where both [s] and [z] are used) is relatively narrow to the west of Philadelphia; to the northeast, however, it widens considerably so as to include most of northern New Jersey, as well as New York City and eastern Long Island.

Outside our pair of isoglosses there is a surprisingly small number of "stray" forms. All together, there are only six occurrences of [z] in the [s] area and only six of [s] in the [z] area.[22] (It will be observed, of course, that there is a second area, or island, of [s] along the Ohio River extending northeastward from the vicinity of Marietta, Ohio.) There is no sign whatever of social variation within the solid [s] and [z] areas; cultivated usage is in strict agreement with popular usage.[23] Within the areas of overlapping there is naturally some variation between older and more modern informants—yet the general trend is not at all clear. In the communities of divided usage to the west of Philadelphia the more modern informant uses [s] in six out of eight instances; in such communities to the northeast of Philadelphia the modern preference is for [s] in six instances, for [z] in six others. As for cultured informants within the areas of overlapping, ten use [griz], five use [gris], and one offers both [s] and [z] forms. One might state, very tentatively, that cultivated usage has tended to favor [griz], particularly in New York City and northern New Jersey.

For the adjective *greasy,* the pronunciations [grisi] and [grizi] show almost precisely the same isoglosses as those for [gris] and [griz]. The northern limit of [z] pushes further northward at three points in Pennsylvania;[24] correspondingly, the southern limit of [s] retreats northward

---

22 This amounts to less than one percent of the informants. Most of the informants who show exceptional usage also give the "normal" form; that is, they use both [s] and [z] forms.

23 Although the preterite form of the verb was not called for in the work sheets, Lowman picked up some five instances of *grez* [grɛz] in the [z] area; and a number of other informants reported having heard this form.

24 Lehigh, Columbia, and Lancaster counties.

at one point in Ohio, three in Pennsylvania, and two in northern New Jersey.[25] Within the [s] area, there are ten stray forms with [z], scattered through New England and the Hudson Valley; six of these occur in the cultured type of informant. Within the [z] area, we again find six stray occurrences of [s]; and precisely the same island of [s] occurs along the Ohio River. In short, a few more eastern informants use [z] in *greasy* than in *grease*, though the difference is not great. Within the areas of overlapping we find almost exactly the same social distribution as in the case of *grease*. Cultured informants prefer [grizi] by eleven to four; this fact, together with the six "stray" northern uses of [z] in the cultured type, inclines us to believe that [z] in *greasy* has penetrated into northeastern cultivated speech a little more palpably than in the case of *grease*—though still to a very slight extent.

After describing the incidence of the speech forms in question, we are still faced with a number of questions, to which our data can provide only partial answers.

What becomes of our isoglosses in the areas west of Pennsylvania? The materials being gathered for the Great Lakes atlas (under the direction of Professor A. H. Marckwardt) will undoubtedly provide an answer. I have not been able to examine the latest of these materials; but judging from preliminary information, as well as from a map already published by Professor Marckwardt,[26] the northern limit of [z] in *greasy* passes through central Ohio, then swings northward so as to take in almost the whole of Indiana, then bends southward through central Illinois in the direction of St. Louis. Whether the areas of transition are wide or narrow we can probably not determine with accuracy, since, in general, only one social type (the elderly, or rustic) is included in the Great Lakes survey.

Why should the isoglosses run where they do? The answer, in part, is relatively simple. Of the two sets of variants, the [s] forms were evidently generalized in the New England colonies, the [z] forms in the Middle and South Atlantic colonies. The westward migrations and settlements of the New Englanders covered New York State, northern Pennsylvania, Michigan, Wisconsin, and the northern portions of Ohio, Indiana, and Illinois.[27] Many speech features mark off this Northern area from the "Midland"—the area occupied primarily by Pennsylvanians.[28] Most of the northern lines, to be sure, pass further to the

---

25 Columbia, Armstrong, Blair, Cumberland, Hunterdon, and Morris counties.

26 "Folk Speech of Indiana and Adjacent States," op. cit., p. 128.

27 Kurath, *Word Geography*, pp. 1–7; see also Lois K. M. Rosenberry, *The Expansion of New England*, Boston and New York, 1909. Even the island of [s] forms around Marietta, Ohio, is to be explained on the basis of early settlement; this area was first settled by New Englanders as early as the 1780s. See Rosenberry, pp. 175ff.

28 Examples of Northern words (from Kurath) are *whiffletree, pail, darning needle*

north in Pennsylvania than do those of the [s] in *grease* and *greasy*. Yet the penetration of northern forms to the area of Philadelphia is occasionally to be observed in other instances; for example, the line of Northern *clapboards* (as against Midland and Southern *weatherboards*) dips sharply southward so as to take in Philadelphia and northern Delaware. Another explanation for the prevalence of [gris] and ['grisi] in east central Pennsylvania might be the fact that much of the area was occupied in the early 18th century by Palatine Germans, whose native dialect had no [z] phoneme at all[29] and who may, for this reason, have favored [s] in any English words where variation between [s] and [z] occurred.

What is the British practice with regard to the pronunciation of *grease* and *greasy?* No complete survey has been made; but there seems no doubt that London usage, as well as "Received Standard" usage throughout southern England, is mixed.[30] The questionnaires which Hempl circulated in England (for his study cited above) showed that in London only 25 and 33 percent of the informants used [s] in *grease* and *greasy;* but that in England exclusive of London the percentages of [s] were 84 and 74.[31] We have no ground, even yet, for rejecting these figures; but it should be pointed out that folk speech in England, just as in the United States, shows its isoglosses. A survey of the linguistic atlas type conducted by Guy S. Lowman in 1934[32] shows that the [z] in *grease* (I have no information on *greasy*) occupies East Anglia and a small adjoining area; that [s] is universal in the remainder of southern England (we are speaking strictly of the rustic type of speaker). Since the line passes through (or very near) London, it is easy to see why the metropolitan area should show a mixture of usage.

Is there any evidence of a differentiation in meaning between ['grisi] and ['grizi]? The *Atlas* provides no answer to this question, since, in the interest of obtaining comparable data, the words were always called for in the same context ("grease the car, axle, etc." and "my hands are greasy"). In general, such differentiations in meaning are characteristic of areas of mixed usage, not of those where one pronunciation or an-

("dragonfly"), and *co, boss!* (cow call). Verb forms which I have found to have similar distributions are *hadn't ought* ("oughtn't"), *how be you?, clim* ("climbed"), and *see* as a preterite of *to see.* Note that Kurath's definition of "Midland" does not coincide with that of Hempl; the area, according to the former, extends much farther to the southwestward of Pennsylvania than Hempl indicated. (See *Word Geography,* pp. 27–37.)

29 See Carroll E. Reed, *The Pennsylvania German Dialect Spoken in the Counties of Lehigh and Berks: Phonology and Morphology* (Seattle, Wash., 1949), pp. 20, 29.

30 See Daniel Jones, *An English Pronouncing Dictionary,* 9th ed., London, 1948.

31 Hempl, op. cit., pp. 442–443.

32 Lowman's British field records are filed in an unedited state at the University of Michigan.

other is definitely established. The distinction usually given in dictionaries is that ['grisi] may mean literally "covered with grease," while ['grizi] may be used with less literal, and sometimes unpleasant, connotations.[33] What we can say with confidence is that speakers to the south of our isoglosses do not follow this practice: ['grizi] is universal with the literal meaning "covered with grease"; whether or not more speakers in the area of overlapping, and to the north of it, would have used ['grizi] had the context been different, we are unable to determine.

How should we evaluate the *Atlas* data as a picture of reality? What is most important to realize is that the *Atlas* makes no attempt whatever to record the usage of non-native speakers, or even of those natives who have resided for long periods outside their home communities. Such speakers are rather uncommon in some communities, fairly numerous in others; in a few of the latter, the *Atlas* may even reflect the usage of a minority of old-timers. In view of this, we might be inclined to wonder whether the percentage method might not give a truer picture of prevalent usage than the isogloss method. The proportion of non-native speech forms in a community would, of course, roughly correspond to the proportion of non-native residents; such data would certainly be valuable, though to collect it on a large enough scale (say, 100 or so informants from each county) would be so difficult as to be practically impossible. Few investigators are qualified to make extensive phonetic observations, and those few must take their informants from such captive groups as college classes, whose usage may or may not be spontaneous or representative. Another feature of the *Atlas* that must be considered is the preponderance of rather old informants. Since the interviews were conducted several years ago, many of the forms shown to be current among the aged may now be rare or even obsolete; moreover, the *Atlas* records would not reflect the most recent trends, fads, and innovations—some of which are rapid, others extremely slow. It seems unlikely to me that the lines on *grease* and *greasy* have shifted radically in the last few years, yet I have no doubt that usage may have changed

[33] Daniel Jones, *English Pronouncing Dictionary:* "Some speakers use the forms . . . with a difference of meaning, ['griːsi] having reference merely to the presence of grease and ['griːzi] having reference to the slipperiness caused by grease." *Webster's NID* state: ". . . many people in all sections use ['grisi] in some connotations and ['grizi] in others, the first esp. in the literal sense, covered with grease." Cf. Kenyon and Knott: "Some distinguish ['grisi] 'covered with grease' from ['grizi] 'slimy' " (op. cit.). G. P. Krapp states: "A distinction is sometimes made in the meaning of ['griːsi] and ['griːzi], the later being regarded as a word of unpleasant connotation" (op. cit., p. 119). *Webster's* implies that this distinction is fairly general throughout the country—a very dubious proposition. T. Larsen and F. C. Walker simply prescribe [s] for the meaning "sticky" and [z] for the meaning "slippery"—as though this feature were standard and universal (See *Pronunciation* [Oxford Press, 1931], p. 92.)

in certain individual communities.[34] All things considered, the *Linguistic Atlas* offers the most reliable body of data as yet assembled, or likely to be assembled in the near future, on American speech; isoglosses based on it reflect the usage of a highly important segment of our population, and they are, moreover, of the highest value in a study of our cultural and settlement history.

[34] Dr. Smith expresses the opinion that the younger generation in New York City has gone over almost entirely to the [s] in *greasy*.

FOR DISCUSSION AND REVIEW

1 What were the results of the 1896 study undertaken by George Hempl? What does Atwood's study add to Hempl's results?

2 Why does Atwood feel that the data from the field records of the *Linguistic Atlas* project provide an excellent basis for "delimiting the geographical and social spread of speech forms in the eastern United States"?

3 Explain Atwood's use of the terms *isogloss* and *dividing line*.

4 Why, according to Atwood, do the isoglosses for *grease* and *greasy* occur where they do?

5 How do you pronounce *grease* and *greasy*? Do your pronunciations agree with Atwood's statements about geographical distributions? If not, can you account for the discrepancy?

6 What are two important conclusions to be drawn from Atwood's study?

PROJECTS FOR "REGIONAL VARIETIES OF ENGLISH"

1 Prepare a report on the purposes, methods, and progress of the Linguistic Atlas of the United States and Canada project. Use the library card catalogue, Hans Kurath's Handbook of the Linguistic Geography of New England, Lee Pederson's A Manual for Dialect Research in the Southern States, the Newsletter of the American Dialect Society, the PMLA Bibliography, and the International Index to the Social Sciences and Humanities to locate materials for this project.

2 As evidenced by Roger Shuy's discussion of methodology (pp. 358–383) and E. Bagby Atwood's study (pp. 384–393), word geography is a fascinating aspect of dialect study. Using Shuy's "Checklist of Regional Expressions" (pp. 369–375) and his "Personal Data Sheet" (p. 376), survey your class, your campus, or your community. Before you actually collect any data, you will want to consider such matters as the size and nature of the population to be studied, the selection of reliable and representative informants, and the possible influences of factors in the college's or community's history. Tabulate your results. Do any local or regional patterns emerge?

3   Study the history of your community so that you can write a report in
    which you discuss the ways in which settlement patterns, population
    shifts, and physical geography have influenced the speech of the area.
4   The names of cities, towns, rivers, and mountains often provide clues to
    settlement and migration patterns. Using a map of your area, list some
    important local place names and discuss their significance. For example,
    you may wish to find out the meaning of each name and whether or not
    any of the names appear elsewhere in the country (and, if so, whether or
    not they are related). You will find the following references useful: Kelsie
    B. Harder's Illustrated Dictionary of Place Names (1976) and George R.
    Stewart's American Place-Names (1970).
5   Compose a questionnaire that is designed to ascertain vocabulary items
    of an urban dialect. You may wish to consult the extensive questionnaire
    compiled by Frederic G. Cassidy ("A Method for Collecting Dialect,"
    Publication of the American Dialect Society, no. 20 [November 1953],
    19–96) for examples of how to frame different types of questions or Lee
    A. Pederson's "An Approach to Urban Word Geography" (American
    Speech, 46 [Spring–Summer 1971], 73–86) for suggestions about par-
    ticular types of vocabulary items. Distribute your questionnaire to
    selected informants on your campus or in your community and tabulate
    your results. Discuss any patterns that emerge.
6   Dialect differences in pronunciation abound. Here are some words for
    which there are distinct regional pronunciations. Compare your pro-
    nunciation of these items with those of others in your class:

collar	cot	wash
car	apricot	paw
empty	dog	tomato
door	clientele	marry
garage	mangy	Mary
oil	house	roof
can	very	sorry
greasy	either	fog
lot	caller	water
caught	horse	almond
hurry	class	idea

What pronunciation differences do you note among the members of your
class? Are any regional patterns of pronunciation evident? Compare
your results with the regional pronunciations discussed by Roger W. Shuy
(pp. 358–383).

SELECTED BIBLIOGRAPHY

Allen, Harold B. The Linguistic Atlas of the Upper Midwest. Vol. 1, "Regional
    Speech Distribution." Minneapolis: University of Minnesota Press, 1973; vol.
    2, "Grammar." Minneapolis: University of Minnesota Press, 1975; vol. 3,

"Pronunciation." Minneapolis: University of Minnesota Press, 1976. (Invaluable reference for study of speech in the Upper Midwest.)

―――. "The Linguistic Atlases: Our New Resource." English Journal, 45 (April 1956), 188–194. (A discussion of Linguistic Atlas data and their applications.)

―――. "The Primary Dialect Areas of the Upper Midwest." Studies in Language and Linguistics in Honor of Charles C. Fries. Ed. Albert H. Marckwardt. Ann Arbor: The English Language Institute, The University of Michigan, 1964. (A study of the lexical, phonological, and morphological features of the speech in the Upper Midwest region.)

―――. "Two Dialects in Contact." American Speech, 48 (Spring–Summer 1973), 54–66. (A study of dialect boundaries in Upper Midwest based on Atlas materials.)

―――, and Gary N. Underwood, eds. Readings in American Dialectology. New York: Appleton-Century-Crofts, 1971. (An anthology of essays dealing with important regional and social aspects of American dialectology.)

Atwood, E. Bagby. A Survey of Verb Forms in the Eastern United States. Ann Arbor: University of Michigan Press, 1953. (A fundamental work in linguistic geography.)

Cassidy, Frederic G. Dictionary of American Regional English. Cambridge: Belknap Press, Harvard University, forthcoming. (A long-awaited reference and research work.)

―――. "A Method for Collecting Dialect." Publication of the American Dialect Society, no. 20 (November 1953), 5–96. (Entire issue devoted to a discussion of field methods and the presentation of a comprehensive dialect questionnaire.)

Daivs, A. L. "Developing and Testing the Checklist." American Speech, 46 (Spring–Summer 1971), 34–37. (Discussion of problems associated with developing a vocabulary questionnaire.)

―――. "Dialect Distribution and Settlement Patterns in the Great Lakes Region." The Ohio State Archeological and Historical Quarterly, 60 (January 1951), 48–56. (A study showing many interesting correlations between linguistic features and settlement patterns in the Great Lakes region.)

Drake, James A. "The Effect of Urbanization upon Regional Vocabulary." American Speech, 36 (February 1961), 17–33. (A study of regional dialect items and urbanization in Cleveland, Ohio.)

Duckert, Audrey R. "The Second Time Around: Methods in Dialect Revisiting." American Speech, 46 (Spring–Summer 1971), 66–72. (Methods for studying areas previously surveyed by the Atlas project—with emphasis on New England.)

Francis, W. Nelson. The English Language: An Introduction. New York: W. W. Norton & Company, 1965. (See pp. 223–244 for a consideration of regional variety in English.)

Harder, Kelsie B., ed. Illustrated Dictionary of Place Names: United States and Canada. New York: Van Nostrand Reinhold Company, 1976. (Invaluable reference work for North American place names.)

Kurath, Hans. Studies in Area Linguistics. Bloomington: Indiana University Press, 1972. (An examination of regional and social dialectology, American and foreign.)

―――. A Word Geography of the Eastern United States. Ann Arbor: University of Michigan Press, 1949. (A basic book in linguistic geography.)

―――, Miles L. Hanley, Bernard Block, et al. Linguistic Atlas of New England.

3 vols. in 6 parts. Providence, R.I.: Brown University Press, 1939–1943; re-issued New York: AMS Press, 1972. (Indispensable research and reference work for the study of speech in New England and for comparative studies. Should be used with companion *Handbook*.)

McMillan, James B. *Annotated Bibliography of Southern American English*. Coral Gables: University of Miami Press, 1971. (A valuable reference work for the study of speech in southern states.)

Marckwardt, Albert H. *American English*. New York: Oxford University Press, 1958. (An introduction to American dialects from an historical point of view.)

————. "Principal and Subsidiary Areas in the North-Central States." *Publication of the American Dialect Society*, no. 27 (April 1957), 3–15. (A regional study of dialect variation—includes seven maps.)

Pederson, Lee A. "An Approach to Urban Word Geography." *American Speech*, 46 (Spring–Summer 1971), 73–86. (Presentation of vocabulary questionnaire suitable for urban testing—namely, in Chicago.)

Pyles, Thomas. *Words and Ways of American English*. New York: Random House, 1952. (An introduction to American English from colonial times to present.)

Reed, Carroll E. *Dialects of American English*. 2nd edition. Amherst: The University of Massachusetts Press, 1973. (An introduction to dialect study with units devoted to sectional atlas studies and to urban dialect studies.)

————. "The Pronunciation of English in the Pacific Northwest." *Language*, 37 (October–December 1961), 559–564. (A description of the pronunciation of vowels and consonants by residents of the Pacific Northwest.)

Underwood, Gary N. "Vocabulary Change in the Upper Midwest." *Publication of the American Dialect Society*, no. 49 (April 1968), 8–28. (An investigation of language change that utilizes four generations of informants.)

Williamson, Juanita V., and Virginia M. Burke, eds. *A Various Language: Perspectives on American Dialects*. New York: Holt, Rinehart & Winston, Inc., 1971. (An anthology of essential articles dealing with American dialects.)

Wood, Gordon R. "Word Distribution in the Interior South." *Publication of the American Dialect Society*, no. 35 (April 1961), 1–16. (A regional dialect study for the southern United States.)

PART SEVEN

Social
Varieties
of English

Dialectology is concerned with the social variations of language as well as with the regional ones. It is important to recognize the interrelationships between social and regional variations: social variations exist within regional dialect areas. Although the majority of native speakers in any given area share numerous features of pronunciation, vocabulary, and grammatical usage that identify them as being from that particular region, they do not necessarily share social features that can reflect class, socioeconomic, and educational levels.

In the past, social variations were often looked upon as

corruptions of or departures from "correct" English. Today, however, much attention is focused on the careful and thoughtful study of nonstandard dialects within American society. The first selections in this section introduce the student to the concept of social speech communities and to a classification of functional varieties of English. The subsequent readings illustrate specific studies and applications of research that has been undertaken with respect to functional and social varieties of American English. Scholars have explored and sought to explain not only the social, regional, and educational aspects of dialect but also the linguistic problems encountered by the speaker of nonstandard English.

1
Speech
Communities

In addition to geography, age, education, occupation, and social position are factors that shape dialect variations within a language. Professor Roberts, in this excerpt from his book *Understanding English*, discusses the effects of speech communities upon the language patterns of persons who come into contact with them. Recall your own experiences with childhood and adolescent speech communities while reading this selection.

Paul Roberts

Directions of Change in Language

IMAGINE a village of a thousand people all speaking the same language and never hearing any language other than their own. As the decades pass and generation succeeds generation, it will not be very apparent to the speakers of the language that any considerable language change is going on. Oldsters may occasionally be conscious of and annoyed by the speech forms of youngsters. They will notice new words, new expressions, "bad" pronunciations, but will ordinarily put these down to the irresponsibility of youth, and decide piously that the language of the younger generation will revert to decency when the generation grows up.

It doesn't revert, though. The new expressions and the new pronunciations persist, and presently there is another younger generation with its own new expressions and its own pronunciations. And thus the language changes. If members of the village could speak to one another across five hundred years, they would probably find themselves unable to communicate.

Now suppose that the village divides itself and half the people move away. They move across the river or over a mountain and form a new village. Suppose the separation is so complete that the people of New Village have no contact with the people of Old Village. The language of both villages will change, drifting away from the language of their common ancestors. But the drift will not be in the same direction. In both villages there will be new expressions and new pronunciations, but not the same ones. In the course of time the language of Old Village and New Village will be mutually unintelligible with the language they both started with. They will also be mutually unintelligible with one another.

An interesting thing—and one for which there is no perfectly clear explanation—is that the rate of change will not ordinarily be the same for both villages. The language of Old Village changes faster than the language of New Village. One might expect that the opposite would be true—that the emigrants, placed in new surroundings and new conditions, would undergo more rapid language changes. But history reports otherwise. American English, for example, despite the violence and agony and confusion to which the demands of a new continent have subjected it, is probably essentially closer to the language of Shakespeare than London English is.

Suppose one thing more. Suppose Old Village is divided sharply into an upper class and a lower class. The sons and daughters of the upper class go to preparatory school and then to the university; the children of the lower class go to work. The upper-class people learn to read and write and develop a flowering literature; the lower-class people remain illiterate. Dialects develop, and the speech of the two classes steadily diverges. One might suppose that most of the change would go on among the illiterate, that the upper-class people, conscious of their heritage, would tend to preserve the forms and pronunciations of their ancestors. Not so. The opposite is true. In speech, the educated tend to be radical and the uneducated conservative. In England one finds Elizabethan forms and sounds not among Oxford and Cambridge graduates but among the people of backward villages.

A village is a fairly simple kind of speech community—a group of people steadily in communication with one another, steadily hearing one another's speech. But the village is by no means the basic unit. Within the simplest village there are many smaller units—groupings based on age, class, occupation. All these groups play intricately on one another and against one another, and a language that seems at first a coherent whole will turn out on inspection to be composed of many differing parts. Some forces tend to make these parts diverge; other forces hold them together. Thus the language continues in tension.

The Speech Communities of the Child

The child's first speech community is ordinarily his family. The child learns whatever kind of language the family speaks—or, more precisely, whatever kind of language it speaks to him. The child's language learning, now and later, is governed by two obvious motives: the desire to communicate and the desire to be admired. He imitates what he hears. More or less successful imitations usually bring action and reward and tend to be repeated. Unsuccessful ones usually don't bring action and reward and tend to be discarded.

But since language is a complicated business it is sometimes the unsuccessful imitations that bring the reward. The child, making a stab at the word *mother*, comes out with *muzzer*. The family decides that this is just too cute for anything and beams and repeats *muzzer*, and the child, feeling that he's scored a bull's eye, goes on saying *muzzer* long after he has mastered *other* and *brother*. Baby talk is not so much invented by the child as sponsored by the parent.

Eventually the child moves out of the family and into another speech community—other children of his neighborhood. He goes to kindergarten and immediately encounters speech habits that conflict with those he has learned. If he goes to school and talks about his *muzzer*, it will be borne in on him by his colleagues that the word is not well chosen. Even *mother* may not pass muster, and he may discover that he gets better results and is altogether happier if he refers to his female parent as his ma or even his old lady.

Children coming together in a kindergarten class bring with them language that is different because it is learned in different homes. It is all to some degree unsuccessfully learned, consisting of not quite perfect imitations of the original. In school all this speech coalesces, differences tend to be ironed out, and the result differs from the original parental speech and differs in pretty much the same way.

The pressures on the child to conform to the speech of his age group, his speech community, are enormous. He may admire his teacher and love his mother; he may even—and even consciously—wish to speak as they do. But he *has* to speak like the rest of the class. If he does not, life becomes intolerable.

The speech changes that go on when the child goes to school are often most distressing to parents. Your little Bertram, at home, has never heard anything but the most elegant English. You send him to school, and what happens? He comes home saying things like "I done real good in school today, Mom." But Bertram really has no choice in the matter. If Clarence and Elbert and the rest of the fellows customarily say "I done real good," then Bertram might as well go around with three noses as say things like "I did very nicely."

Individuals differ of course, and not all children react to the speech community in the same way. Some tend to imitate and others tend to force imitation. But all to some degree have their speech modified by forces over which neither they nor their parents nor their teachers have any real control.

Individuals differ too in their sensitivity to language. For some, language is always a rather embarrassing problem. They steadily make boners, saying the right thing in the wrong place or the wrong way.

They have a hard time fitting in. Others tend to change their language slowly, sticking stoutly to their way of saying things, even though their way differs from that of the majority. Still others adopt new language habits almost automatically, responding quickly to whatever speech environment they encounter.

Indeed some children of five or six have been observed to speak two or more different dialects without much awareness that they are doing so. Most commonly, they will speak in one way at home and in another on the playground. At home they say, "I did very nicely" and "I haven't any"; these become, at school, "I done real good" and "I ain't got none."

The Class as a Speech Community

Throughout the school years, or at least through the American secondary school, the individual's most important speech community is his age group, his class. Here is where the real power lies. The rule is conformity above all things, and the group uses its power ruthlessly on those who do not conform. Language is one of the chief means by which the school group seeks to establish its entity, and in the high school this is done more or less consciously. The obvious feature is high school slang, picked up from the radio, from other schools, sometimes invented, changing with bewildering speed. Nothing is more satisfactory than to speak today's slang; nothing more futile than to use yesterday's.

There can be few tasks more frustrating than that of the secondary school teacher charged with the responsibility of brushing off and polishing up the speech habits of the younger generation. Efforts to make *real* into *really*, *ain't* into *am not*, *I seen him* into *I saw him*, *he don't* into *he doesn't* meet at best with polite indifference, at worst with mischievous counterattack.

The writer can remember from his own high school days when the class, a crashingly witty bunch, took to pronouncing the word *sure* as *sewer*. "Have you prepared your lesson, Arnold?" Miss Driscoll would ask. "Sewer, Miss Driscoll," Arnold would reply. "I think," said Miss Driscoll, who was pretty quick on her feet too, "that you must mean 'sewerly,' since the construction calls for the adverb not the adjective." We were delighted with the suggestion and went about saying "sewerly" until the very blackboards were nauseated. Miss Driscoll must have wished often that she had left it lay.

Confronting the Adult World

When the high school class graduates, the speech community disintegrates as the students fit themselves into new ones. For the first time in the experience of most of the students the speech ways of adult communities begin to exercise real force. For some people the adjustment is a relatively simple one. A boy going to work in a garage may have a good deal of new lingo to pick up, and he may find that the speech that seemed so racy and won such approval in the corridors of Springfield High leaves his more adult associates merely bored. But a normal person will adapt himself without trouble.

For others in other situations settling into new speech communities may be more difficult. The person going into college, into the business world, into scrubbed society may find that he has to think about and work on his speech habits in order not to make a fool of himself too often.

College is a particularly complicated problem. Not only does the freshman confront upperclassmen not particularly disposed to find the speech of Springfield High particularly cute, but the adult world, as represented chiefly by the faculty, becomes increasingly more immediate. The problems of success, of earning a living, of marriage, of attaining a satisfactory adult life loom larger, and they all bring language problems with them. Adaptation is necessary, and the student adapts.

The student adapts, but the adult world adapts too. The thousands of boys and girls coming out of the high schools each spring are affected by the speech of the adult communities into which they move, but they also affect that speech. The new pronunciation habits, developing grammatical features, different vocabulary do by no means all give way before the disapproval of elders. Some of them stay. Elders, sometimes to their dismay, find themselves changing their speech habits under the bombardment of those of their juniors. And then of course the juniors eventually become the elders, and there is no one left to disapprove.

The Space Dimension

Speech communities are formed by many features besides that of age. Most obvious is geography. Our country was originally settled by people coming from different parts of England. They spoke different dialects to begin with and as a result regional speech differences existed from the start in the different parts of the country. As speakers of other languages came to America and learned English, they left their mark on the speech of the sections in which they settled. With the westward movement, new pioneers streamed out through the mountain passes and down river valleys, taking the different dialects west and modifying them by new mixtures in new environments.

Today we are all more or less conscious of certain dialect differences in our country. We speak of the "southern accent," "the Brooklyn accent," the "New England accent." Until a few years ago it was often said that American English was divided into three dialects: Southern American (south of the Mason-Dixon line); Eastern American (east of the Connecticut River); and Western American. This description suggests certain gross differences all right, but recent research shows that it is a gross oversimplification.

The starting point of American dialects is the original group of colonies. We had a New England settlement, centering in Massachusetts; a Middle Atlantic settlement, centering in Pennsylvania; a southern settlement, centering in Virginia and the Carolinas. These colonies were different in speech to begin with, since the settlers came from different parts of England. Their differences were increased as the colonies lived for a century and a half or so with only thin communication with either Mother England or each other. By the time of the Revolution the dialects were well established. Within each group there were of course subgroups. Richmond speech differed markedly from that of Savannah. But Savannah and Richmond were more like each other than they were like Philadelphia or Boston.

The Western movement began shortly after the Revolution, and dialects followed geography. The New Englanders moved mostly into upper New York State and the Great Lakes region. The Middle Atlantic colonists went down the Shenandoah Valley and eventually into the heart of the Midwest. The southerners opened up Kentucky and Tennessee, later the lower Mississippi Valley, later still Texas and much of the Southwest. Thus new speech communities were formed, related to the old ones of the seaboard, but each developing new characteristics as lines of settlement crossed.

New complications were added before and after the Revolution by the great waves of immigration of people from countries other than England: Swedes in Delaware, Dutch in New York, Germans and Scots-Irish in Pennsylvania, Irish in New England, Poles and Greeks and Italians and Portuguese. The bringing in of Negro slaves had an important effect on the speech of the South and later on the whole country. The Spanish in California and the Southwest added their mark. In this century movement of peoples goes on: the trek of southern Negroes to northern and western cities, the migration of people from Arkansas, Oklahoma, and Texas to California. All these have shaped and are shaping American speech.

We speak of America as the melting pot, but the speech communities of this continent are very far from having melted into one. Linguists today can trace very clearly the movements of the early settlers in the still living speech of their descendants. They can follow an eighteenth century speech community West, showing how it crossed this pass and followed that river, threw out an offshoot here, left a pocket there, merged with another group, halted, split, moved on once more.

If all other historical evidence were destroyed, the history of the country could still be reconstructed from the speech of modern America.

Social Differences

The third great shaper of speech communities is the social class. This has been, and is, more important in England than in America. In England, class differences have often been more prominent than those of age or place. If you were the blacksmith's boy, you might know the son of the local baronet, but you didn't speak his language. You spoke the language of your social group, and he that of his, and over the centuries these social dialects remained widely separated.

England in the twentieth century has been much democratized, but the language differences are far from having disappeared. One can still tell much about a person's family, his school background, his general position in life by the way he speaks. Social lines are hard to cross, and language is perhaps the greatest barrier. You may make a million pounds and own several cars and a place in the country, but your vowels and consonants and nouns and verbs and sentence patterns will still proclaim to the world that you're not a part of the upper crust.

In America, of course, social distinctions have never been so sharp as they are in England. We find it somewhat easier to rise in the world, to move into social environments unknown to our parents. This is possible, partly, because speech differences are slighter; conversely, speech differences are slighter because this is possible. But speech differences do exist. If you've spent all your life driving a cab in Philly and, having inherited a fortune, move to San Francisco's Nob Hill, you will find that your language is different, perhaps embarrassingly so, from that of your new acquaintances.

Language differences on the social plane in America are likely to correlate with education or occupation rather than with birth—simply because education and occupation in America do not depend so much on birth as they do in other countries. A child without family connection can get himself educated at Harvard, Yale, Princeton. In doing so, he acquires the speech habits of the Ivy League and gives up those of his parents.

Exceptions abound. But in general there is a clear difference between the speech habits of the college graduate and those of the high school graduate. The cab driver does not talk like the Standard Oil executive, the college professor like the carnival pitch man, or an Illinois merchant like a sailor shipping out of New Orleans. New York's Madison Avenue and Third Avenue are only a few blocks apart, but they are widely separated in language. And both are different from Broadway.

It should be added that the whole trend of modern life is to reduce rather than to accentuate these differences. In a country where college

education becomes increasingly everybody's chance, where executives
and refrigerator salesmen and farmers play golf together, where a college
professor may drive a cab in the summertime to keep his family alive,
it becomes harder and harder to guess a person's education, income,
and social status by the way he talks. But it would be absurd to say that
language gives no clue at all.

Good and Bad

Speech communities, then, are formed by many features: age,
geography, education, occupation, social position. Young people speak
differently from old people, Kansans differently from Virginians, Yale
graduates differently from Dannemora graduates. Now let us pose a
delicate question: aren't some of these speech communities better than
others? That is, isn't better language heard in some than in others?

Well, yes, of course. One speech community is always better than
all the rest. This is the group in which one happens to find oneself.
The writer would answer unhesitatingly that the noblest, loveliest, pur-
est English is that heard in the Men's Faculty Club of San Jose State
College, San Jose, California. He would admit, of course, that the
speech of some of the younger members leaves something to be desired;
that certain recent immigrants from Harvard, Michigan, and other foreign parts need to work on the laughable oddities lingering in their
speech; and that members of certain departments tend to introduce a
lot of queer terms that can only be described as jargon. But in general
the English of the Faculty Club is ennobling and sweet.

As a practical matter, good English is whatever English is spoken by
the group in which one moves contentedly and at ease. To the bum on
Main Street in Los Angeles, good English is the language of other
L.A. bums. Should he wander onto the campus of UCLA, he would
find the talk there unpleasant, confusing, and comical. He might agree,
if pressed, that the college man speaks "correctly" and he doesn't. But
in his heart he knows better. He wouldn't talk like them college jerks
if you paid him.

If you admire the language of other speech communities more than
you do your own, the reasonable hypothesis is that you are dissatisfied
with the community itself. It is not precisely other speech that attracts
you but the people who use the speech. Conversely, if some language
strikes you as unpleasant or foolish or rough, it is presumably because
the speakers themselves seem so.

To many people, the sentence "Where is he at?" sounds bad. It is
bad, they would say, in and of itself. The sounds are bad. But this is
very hard to prove. If "Where is he at?" is bad because it has bad
sound combinations, then presumably "Where is the cat?" or "Where

is my hat?" are just as bad, yet no one thinks them so. Well, then, "Where is he at?" is bad because it uses too many words. One gets the same meaning from "Where is he?" so why add the *at?* True. Then "He going with us?" is a better sentence than "Is he going with us?" You don't really need the *is*, so why put it in?

Certainly there are some features of language to which we can apply the terms *good* and *bad, better* and *worse.* Clarity is usually better than obscurity; precision is better than vagueness. But these are not often what we have in mind when we speak of good and bad English. If we like the speech of upper-class Englishmen, the presumption is that we admire upper-class Englishmen—their characters, culture, habits of mind. Their sounds and words simply come to connote the people themselves and become admirable therefore. If we knew the same sounds and words from people who were distasteful to us, we would find the speech ugly.

This is not to say that correctness and incorrectness do not exist in speech. They obviously do, but they are relative to the speech community—or communities—in which one operates. As a practical matter, correct speech is that which sounds normal or natural to one's comrades. Incorrect speech is that which evokes in them discomfort or hostility or disdain. . . .

FOR DISCUSSION AND REVIEW

1 Identify the factors which, according to Roberts, shape speech communities.

2 Does education have an influence on dialect? If so, what exactly is the nature of this influence?

3 Roberts feels that there is a marked difference between the speech communities of one generation and the next. Observe and describe speech differences between students and faculty in your school. Compare your findings with those of your teacher. Does a similar situation exist between you and your parents?

4 Do men and women speak different dialects? Try to describe the language of the opposite sex. Compare your results with those of other members of the class. What generalizations can you make about the language of women and the language of men? You may find it helpful to review Flexner's discussion (p. 246).

5 Roberts talks of the "enormous pressures" on a person to conform to the speech of his age group and his speech community. Discuss the pressures that you felt while growing up.

6 What does Roberts mean when he states that "correctness and incorrectness . . . are relative to the speech community—or communities —in which one operates"? Do you agree with him? Explain.

2

The Styles of the Five Clocks

In this excerpt from The Five Clocks, *Martin Joos, director of the Linguistic Centre at the University of Toronto, explores the complex ways in which speakers adjust their language to the various contexts in which they employ it. He identifies five styles, forms of language chosen to meet certain social expectations, and accurately describes the setting, audience, and linguistic features associated with each style. As you read, consider how many of the five styles you have had occasion to use.*

Martin Joos

THAT more than one kind of English is likely to be in use at the same time and place is a notorious fact. So is sex, for that matter, or the weather. But our accommodations to those facts are not equally realistic. We have easily understood that evolution has so shaped our planet's flora and fauna that agriculture is best served by fluctuating weather and cyclical seasons. With a great deal more effort, we are coming to understand that sex is here to stay and may even have a sort of survival value—that its seasons and its vagaries may conceivably be essential to the business of being human.

Long ago taught to give weather its highest praise by calling it "seasonable," we have been learning recently to treat sex with the same respect for facts. The intellectual gain is great, however few may value it. Much greater, some say, is the profit that comes from not sending children into adulthood with useless burdens of guilt.

English-usage guilt feelings have not yet been noticeably eased by the work of linguistic scientists, parallel to the work done by the psychiatrists. It is still our custom unhesitatingly and unthinkingly to demand that the clocks of language all be set to Central Standard Time. And each normal American is taught thoroughly, if not to keep accurate time, at least to feel ashamed whenever he notices that a clock of his is out of step with the English department's tower clock. Naturally he avoids looking aloft when he can. Then his linguistic guilt hides deep

in his subconscious mind and there secretly gnaws away at the under-
pinnings of his public personality. . . .

English, like national languages in general, has five clocks. And the
times that they tell are not simply earlier and later; they differ sidewise,
too, and in several directions. Naturally. A community has a complex
structure, with variously differing needs and occasions. How could it
scrape along with only one pattern of English usage? . . .

We have not yet learned to speak of English as we speak of the
weather and agriculture, and as we are slowly learning to speak of sex
and survival. In the school folklore called "grammar" for lack of effective challenge—a sort of numerology taught in high schools instead of
algebra, an astrology masquerading as astronomy in our colleges—we
are bound to speak of English usage only in a simplistic way, like a
proper Victorian maiden lady speaking of Men. . . .

Style

Here are the five clocks to which we shall principally devote our
attention. They may be called "higher" and "lower" for convenience in
referring to the tabulation; but that doesn't mean anything like relative
superiority. More later.

STYLE

frozen
formal
consultative
casual
intimate

With a single exception, there is no law requiring a speaker to confine himself to a single style for one occasion; in general, he is free to
shift to another style, perhaps even within the sentence. But normally
only two neighboring styles are used alternately, and it is antisocial to
shift two or more steps in a single jump, for instance from casual to
formal. When the five styles have been separately and comparatively
described, the details of shifting will be obvious. . . .

The two defining features of consultative style are: (1) The speaker
supplies background information—he does not assume that he will be
understood without it. . . . (2) The addressee participates continuously. Because of these two features, consultative style is our norm for
coming to terms with strangers—people who speak our language but
whose personal stock of information may be different.

But treating the listener as a stranger is hard work in the long run;
therefore we sooner or later try to form a social group with him. Our

most powerful device for accomplishing this is the use of casual style. Casual style is for friends, acquaintances, insiders; addressed to a stranger, it serves to make him an insider simply by treating him as an insider. Negatively, there is absence of background information and no reliance on listeners' participation. This is not rudeness; it pays the addressee the compliment of supposing that he will understand without those aids. On the positive side, we have two devices which do the same job directly: (1) ellipsis, and (2) slang, the two defining features of casual style. . . .

The purpose of ellipsis and the purpose of slang is the same; but they are opposite in their description and opposite in their history. Ellipsis is a minus feature and is very stable historically; slang is a plus feature and is absolutely unstable. Yet both signify the same: that the addressee, an insider, will understand what not everybody would be able to decipher.

Ellipsis (omission) makes most of the difference between casual grammar and consultative grammar. "I believe that I can find one" is proper (though not required) in consultative grammar, but casual English requires a shorter form, say "I believe I can find one" if not the still more elliptical "Believe I can find one." All the weak words of English can be omitted at the beginning of a casual sentence: "Been a good thing if . . ." for "It would have been a good thing if . . ." and similarly "[A] friend of mine . . ." or "[The] coffee's cold." Some ellipsis is only phonological: "Can I help you?" is consultative and "C'n I help you?" is casual. Modern "cute" from original "acute" and "fence" from "defence" are two out of many words which originated in casual style and have since been promoted; similarly, "Thank you" from "I thank you" has been promoted all the way to formal style, while "Thanks" from "Many thanks" or "Much thanks" (Shakespeare) has been promoted only to consultative. Aside from such little shifts in the tradition, ellipsis is stable: the elliptical expressions in use today can nearly all be found in Shakespeare, for instance "Thanks."

As an institution, slang is also ancient; but each individual slang expression is, on the contrary, necessarily unstable. The reason is obvious. Because the utility of any slang expression for classing the addressee as an insider (or excluding an unwanted listener as an outsider) depends on the fact—or at least the polite fiction—that only a minority of the population understands this bit of slang, each slang expression is necessarily ephemeral; for when that fiction has become transparent with age, its purpose is foiled. and then the useless slang is abandoned while new slang has to be created to take its place—not new slang of the same meaning, of course, but just enough new slang to maintain a normal supply. The abandoned slang is then "dead slang," a few items of which may still be resurrected as period-pieces for jocular or nostalgic employment, for instance "kiddo" or "for crying out loud." . . .

Besides these two pattern devices—ellipsis and slang—casual style is marked by an arbitrary list of formulas, all very stable, which are learned individually and used to identify the style for the hearer's convenience. "Come on!" has been one of these identifiers since before the time of Shakespeare (*The Tempest*, I, ii, 308); and all this while, every adult native speaker of English to whom it was addressed has unconsciously known that the speaker was using casual style and has reacted accordingly—and the speaker, without knowing why he did it, has used it to procure that reaction. It is all automatic, unconscious, just as the speaker of a falsehood is not aware that his motive for saying "as a matter of fact" is to label it as false—a Freudian confession which is institutional in English. . . .

Each style has its own list of such conventional formulas, which we may call "code labels" because they serve both to carry part of the message and to identify the style. The identifying function of a code label is uniformly effective; its message-bearing function varies freely from nothing at all to a full message-fraction. Thus "Come on!" means anything from "Consider yourself among friends" to "You're invited"; while "Come on, cheer up!" means nothing but "Cheer up because you're among friends." There is of course a long list of casual code labels, but "Come on!" is one of the commonest.

Consultative code labels include the standard list of listener's insertions "yes [professorial for *yeah*], yeah, unhunh, that's right, oh, I see, yes I know" and a very few others, plus the "well" that is used to reverse the roles between listener and speaker. . . .

Both colloquial styles—consultative and casual—routinely deal in a public sort of information, though differently: casual style takes it for granted and at most alludes to it, consultative style states it as fast as it is needed. Where there happens to be no public information for a while, a casual conversation (among men) lapses into silences and kidding, a consultative one is broken off or adjourned. These adjustments help to show what sort of role public information plays in the two colloquial styles: it is essential to them both.

Now in intimate style, this role is not merely weakened; rather, it is positively abolished. Intimate speech excludes public information.

Definition: An intimate utterance pointedly avoids giving the addressee information from outside of the speaker's skin. Example: "Ready" said in quite a variety of situations, some of them allowing other persons to be present; note that this could be equivalent to either a statement or a question. . . .

The systematic features of intimate style are two, just as in the other styles: (1) extraction; (2) jargon. Both are stable, once the intimate group (normally a pair) has been formed. Extraction has just been illustrated: the speaker extracts a minimum pattern from some conceivable casual sentence. Extraction is not ellipsis. An elliptical sentence still has wording, grammar, and intonation. Intimate extraction employs only part of this triplet. Our printed "Engh" represents an empty word, one that has no dictionary meaning but serves as a code label for intimate style. (The parallel word in casual style, spelled "unh," has a different vocal quality.) There is, however, a message-meaning; this is conveyed by the intonation, the melody, with which "Engh" is spoken. The speaker has extracted this intonation from a possible casual sentence, and that is all he uses of the grammatical triplet "wording, grammar, intonation." . . . Once more, this is not rudeness; this pays the addressee the highest complement possible among mature people. . . .

Intimate style tolerates nothing of the system of any other style: no slang, no background information, and so on. Any item of an intimate code that the folklore calls "slang" is not slang but jargon—it is not ephemeral, but part of the permanent code of this group—it has to be, for intimacy does not tolerate the slang imputation that the addressee needs to be told that she is an insider. The imputations of all other styles are similarly corrosive. Accordingly, intimate codes, or jargons, are severely limited in their use of public vocabulary. Each intimate group must invent its own code. Somehow connected with all this is the cozy fact that language itself can never be a topic in intimate style. Any reaction to grammar, for instance, promptly disrupts intimacy. . . .

Describing formal style by departure from consultative style, the crucial difference is that participation drops out. This is forced whenever the group has grown too large: the insertions then may overlap, causing semantic confusion, or each listener must space his insertions out beyond the biological limit of about thirty seconds; either of these results then causes this or that group-member to withdraw by becoming catatonic or absent, or to begin speaking in formal style and thus to render the others catatonic or absent. This homeostasis, then, either reduces the size of the group so that it may remain consultative or splits the group into one manic speaker and a set of catatonic hearers. A competent manic is able to convert a tête-à-tête into a formal assembly; but normal persons maintain consultation up to a group size of approximately six, which sets the limits on the size and composition of a "committee" in the English-speaking sense. Beyond that, parliamentary law is requisite, i.e., a division into active and chair-warming persons.

Nonparticipation is also forced whenever a speaker is entirely uncertain of the prospective response. Thus conversations between strangers begin in formal style; among urbane strangers in English-speaking cultures, the formal span is only the ceremony of introduction, whose function is to insure that no real business shall be impeded by formality; it then lasts for one consultative speech-span, approximately six seconds. Within a consultation, a similar formal span is instituted whenever embarrassment arises or is imminent. The rupture of consultation is marked either by formal leave-taking or by casual leave-taking; adjournment of consultation is marked by consultative leave-taking, e.g., "I might not be back for a while."

Formal style is designed to inform: its dominating character, something which is necessarily ancillary in consultation, incidental in casual discourse, absent in intimacy. The formal code labels inform each hearer that he is in a formal frame, is not to make insertions but must wait until authorized to speak, and is being given time to plan reactions —as much as half a century. The leading code label is "may"; any message requiring either "might" or "can" in other styles is suppressed or paraphrased, giving "May I help you?" and "We may not see one another for some time," the consultative equivalent of which was cited previously. We may most economically label an introduction as formal by saying "May I present Mr. Smith?"—or petrify a child by saying "No, you may not." Originally, the well-placed "may" was as effective as a hat pin.

Beyond its code labels, formal style is strictly determined by the absence of participation. This absence infects the speaker also. He may speak as if he were not present, avoiding such allusions to his own existence as "I, me, mine," with the possible exception of "one"—a formal code label—or "myself" in desperate situations. The speaker protects both the text and himself from involvement; presumably he will be absent if the roof collapses.

Lacking all personal support, the text must fight its own battles. Form becomes its dominant character. Robbed of personal links to reality, it scorns such other links as the stone painfully kicked to refute an idealist philosopher; instead, it endeavors to employ only logical links, kept entirely within the text, and displays those logical links with sedulous care. The pronunciation is explicit to the point of clattering; the grammar tolerates no ellipsis and cultivates elaborateness; the semantics is fussy. Background information is woven into the text in complex sentences. Exempt from interruption, the text organizes itself into paragraphs; the paragraphs are linked explicitly: thus this is the third of a quadruplet. Formal text therefore demands advance planning. . . .

The defining features of formal style are two: (1) detachment; (2) cohesion. One feature, of the highest importance, is retained from the basal styles: intonation. Since the audience hears the text just once, any deficiency in the intonation is dangerous, any major defect is disastrous. Lack of intonation, as in print, is simply a blank check; but false intonation will mulct the listener in triple damages. . . .

That list of words in sequence is all that is left in frozen style. Punctuation is of very little help towards an adequate intonation, and good frozen style never relies on it. Frozen style—a style for print and for declamation—is defined by the absence of authoritative intonation in the text, as also by the fact that the reader or hearer is not permitted to cross-question the author. Relative to the other styles, these peculiarities clearly are defects in the frozen style, preventing it from functioning as they do. Freed from those other functions, frozen style develops its own functions, by common consent surpassing the others. From the surpassing excellence of good frozen style, our folklore has derived the mistaken theory that it is the ideal of all language.

Is not good writing the highest type of language? Yes, in its own way. But if we approach it through the Grove of Academe, we see nothing but trees labeled "best" and "correct" and "classic" and the rest. It is not possible to discern the nature of excellence in memorable writing from the standpoint that fine printable style is a complex of correct forms and superior formulas. If that were true, it could be learned; the truth is that it can only be invented.

Frozen style can indeed be understood on its own terms, but only if the way is cleared of the prejudice that it does what other discourse does but does it better. To do that, we swiftly approach it twice from the other end of the style scale. Good intimate style fuses two personalities. Good casual style integrates disparate personalities into a social group which is greater than the sum of its parts, for now the personalities complement each other instead of clashing. Good consultative style produces cooperation without the integration, profiting from the lack of it. Good formal style informs the individual separately, so that his future planning may be the more discriminate. Good frozen style, finally, lures him into educating himself, so that he may the more confidently act what role he chooses.

Each of the latter four does its own work by making a virtue out of necessity—a necessity that springs from its own deficiencies in comparison to one or two basal styles. Personal disparities are over-compensated in social integration by casual devices designed out of the mere fact that one person is not another person. Each lack of shared information is over-compensated in consultation, because two heads are better than one and consultation makes them more than twice as good. Each loss from lack of participation is over-compensated in good formal communication by giving several hours of preparation to one hour of discourse.

Frozen style is for people who are to remain social strangers. Our direct compensation for remaining strangers is consultative style. By comparison, frozen style lacks two things, participation and intonation. It gains two things of which this is one: the reader can reread.

FOR DISCUSSION AND REVIEW

1 What are the five styles that Joos identifies? What are the specific characteristics of each?

2 Which of the five styles do you use most often? Least often? Why? Describe situations in which you would use each of the five styles.

3 Identify the style of the following statement:

The chairperson wishes to make several announcements before the meeting commences, so she would appreciate your undivided attention.

Now, rewrite the sentence in any two of the other four styles.

4 Does Joos's article help overcome what the author himself calls the "English-usage guilt feelings" of the average American? Explain.

5 Imagine that you just received a traffic ticket for speeding. How would you describe the incident to your roommate, to your parents, to the judge? Compare the various styles of English in your respective descriptions.

3

Sociolinguistic Factors in the History of American Negro Dialects

William A. Stewart, a leading authority on American Negro dialects,
examines nonstandard Negro dialects from an historical point of
view. The logical, coherent, and
grammatical nature of the Negro's
nonstandard speech is soundly documented by Stewart. In addition, he
addresses the dialect-based problems that today's educators must
confront. The pedagogical implications of the differences between
standard English and nonstandard
Negro dialects are crucial for the
prospective "inner city" teacher.

William A. Stewart

Within the last few years, the increased national commitment
to bettering the lot of socially and economically underprivileged groups
of Americans—the so-called "disadvantaged"—has caused educators to
consider ways in which the schools may involve themselves in this task.
Of the many possibilities, certainly one of the most obvious is to deal
with the chronic language problems associated with many of the disadvantaged. Yet, although there is a general awareness that certain of the
disadvantaged do have language problems, there is at the same time a
lack of agreement as to what these problems entail, and therefore what
to do about them. Some investigators (often educational psychologists)
have maintained that the disadvantaged characteristically do not use
verbal communication to the extent that members of the middle class
do, and are thus impoverished in "communicative skills." To alleviate
this situation, they have recommended programs aimed at encouraging
the use of verbal communication of a variety of kinds by disadvantaged
pupils. A few investigators have theorized that members of disadvantaged groups may even engage less in abstract thinking than do middle-
class persons. For this there have been suggested programs designed to
teach more perception and conceptualization on the part of the disadvantaged pupils.

On the other hand, linguists have tended to emphasize one other
type of language problem which some disadvantaged groups often have,
and for which evidence is quite accessible—being encountered every
day in the nation's classrooms. This is the purely structural conflict be-

tween on the one hand the patterns of a non-standard dialect which an individual may have learned at home or in peer-group interaction, and on the other hand the equivalent patterns of standard English—the language of modern technology and of the middle class. This is one kind of problem which many of the nation's schools ought to be ready and willing to cope with. One indication of the readiness of the schools is the fact that traditional English teachers are rapidly abandoning the older "sloppy speech" and "lazy tongue" views of non-standard speech in favor of a realization that it usually represents the speaker's use of some language system which, though it may differ from standard English in form and sometimes even in function, is nevertheless logical, coherent, and (in its own way) grammatical. Another indication of the readiness of schools to cope with the problem of dialect differences is the growth of a cadre of specialists in the teaching of English to speakers of other languages. With them, there has come into being a set of new techniques for teaching English to persons coming from a different language background.

Just as they are ready, America's schools certainly ought to be willing to deal with dialect-based problems, since there are a number of ways in which, by themselves, they can render a non-standard speaker dysfunctional in exchanges with standard-English-speaking members of the middle class. One way is for minor pronunciation differences between a non-standard dialect and standard English—each one perhaps trivial by itself—to pile up in an utterance to such an extent that the non-standard version becomes unintelligible to a middle-class listener, even though in grammar and vocabulary it may be quite similar to its standard equivalent. Thus, a non-standard version of "I don't know where they live" might, in one dialect, become cryptic to the standard-speaking listener, merely because of its being pronounced something like *Ah 'own know wey 'ey lib*. Or, a standard English speaker may misunderstand a non-standard utterance, even though he thinks he has deciphered it correctly, because it contains non-standard grammatical constructions which are unknown to him. For example, a middle-class listener may take a non-standard sentence *Dey ain't like dat* to mean "they aren't like that," when it really means "They didn't like that." The standard-English speaker is simply unaware that *ain't* is this particular dialect's way of negating verbs in the past tense, as he is unaware that the usual equivalent in the same dialect of "They aren't like that" would be either *Dey not like dat* or *Dey don't be like dat* (the two variants indicating a difference in meaning which is not easily expressed in standard English). Of course, similar breakdowns in intelligibility may also occur in the other direction, when the non-standard speaker tries to understand standard English. Finally, even when he does succeed in making himself understood by his middle-class listeners, the non-standard speaker may still fall victim to the difference in social prestige between his dialect and standard English. In other words, although middle-class persons may understand what he is saying, they may still consider him uncouth for saying it the way he does.

Professionally able though the schools may now be to embark on programs which would deal effectively with this kind of problem, the likelihood of their actually doing so in the near future is certainly not increased by the unwillingness of many educators and even some applied linguists to approach the problem in any but the most general terms. For, unfortunately, the technical know-how necessary to teach standard English to speakers of non-standard dialects is simply not embodied in an awareness of the problem at the level of "Some children should probably be taught standard English as a second dialect"—no matter how true such statements may be. The necessary know-how will begin to be adequate when and only when applied linguists can give, and educators will take seriously, details of the type "The verb system of such-and-such a non-standard dialect operates in such-and-such a way, and the verb system of standard English operates in such-and-such a way, so that structural interference is most likely to occur at points *a*, *b*, and *c*. Therefore, the following lessons and drills in the standard English verb system is what children who speak this non-standard dialect will need."[1]

One reason why there is little remedial English now being taught based upon a systematic comparison of the differences between non-standard dialects and standard English is that information about one of the pedagogically most important features of non-standard dialects—their grammatical systems—is still largely lacking. This lack is due in great part to the fact that American dialect studies have traditionally emphasized differences in pronunciation and vocabulary, at the expense of information on systematic grammatical differences.

Now that linguists have begun to fill this information gap, however, they are finding their observations on language variation among the disadvantaged received with uneasiness and even hostility by many teachers, administrators, and community leaders. The reason for this is undoubtedly that the accurate description of dialect variation in American communities—particularly in urban centers—is turning out to show a disturbing correlation between language behavior on the one hand and socio-economic and ethnic stratification on the other.[2] The

---

[1] See William A. Stewart, editor, *Non-Standard Speech and the Teaching of English* (Washington, D.C., Center for Applied Linguistics, 1964).

[2] The American Dream notwithstanding, it is well known to social scientists that American society is stratified into a number of social classes and ethnic groups, and that each of these exhibits a "characteristic" configuration of customs, attitudes, roles, life-ways and, as it turns out, speech patterns. The literature on social

correlation is particularly controversial insofar as it involves the speech of large numbers of American Negroes, since at the present time Negro leadership (and this includes most Negro educators) is probably more achievement-oriented than any other. Because of this orientation, Negro elites tend not to welcome any evidence of uniform or stable behavioral differences between members of their own group (even lower-class ones) and those of the white-dominated middle class. Yet the fact is that Negroes account for most of the most pedagogically problematic non-standard dialect speakers in the larger cities, and also include within their group speakers of the most radically non-standard dialects of natively-spoken English in the entire country.[3] Furthermore, because de facto segregation in housing has caused non-standard-dialect-speaking Negroes to predominate in many schools and because these Negroes appear in many cases to have different kinds of problems with standard English than non-standard-dialect-speaking whites have (even in the same area), the sweeping, for political purposes, of Negro dialect descriptions under the white-oriented geographic dialect rug would probably be more detrimental to disadvantaged Negro children than it would be advantageous to Negro elites.[4]

On the other hand, linguists should realize that the fears and anxieties of Negro leaders about public discussion of ethnically correlated behavioral differences may have some foundation. It is possible, for example, that quite objective and innocently-made statements about dialect differences between whites and Negroes might be interpreted by white racists as evidence of Negro cultural backwardness or mental inferiority, or even seized upon by black racists as evidence of some sort of mythical Negro "soul." Linguists should not censor their data, but they should make sure that their statements about Negro-white

---

and ethnic stratification is extensive, but good introductions are Egon Ernest Bergel, *Social Stratification* (New York, McGraw-Hill Book Co., 1962), and Tamotsu Shibutani and Kian M. Kwan, *Ethnic Stratification* (New York, The Macmillan Co., 1965). For an exhaustively documented study of the correlation between language variation and social class, ethnicity, and age in an American metropolis, see William Labov, *The Social Stratification of English in New York City* (Washington, D.C., The Center for Applied Linguistics, 1966).

[3] These two facts may not be entirely unrelated. For a graphic indication of the relatively more non-standard grammatical norms of Negro children over white children in a single city, see Figure 18 (page 53) in Walter Loban, *Problems in Oral English: Kindergarten Through Grade Nine* (Champaign, Ill., National Council of Teachers of English, 1966).

[4] For a discussion of Negro dialect in one urban community, see William A. Stewart, "Urban Negro Speech: Sociolinguistic Factors Affecting English Teaching" in Roger W. Shuy, editor, *Social Dialects and Language Learning* (Champaign, Ill., National Council of Teachers of English, 1965). The non-standard dialect patterns cited earlier in the present article are also Negro dialect.

differences are not divorced from an awareness of the historical, social, and linguistic reasons why such differences may have come into existence and been maintained. Perhaps it would serve that end to point out here some of the sociolinguistic factors involved in the evolution of American Negro dialects, factors which explain why certain kinds of American Negro dialects are both different from the non-standard dialects of American whites, and more radically deviant from standard English.

Although the linguistic history of the Negro in the United States can be reconstructed from the numerous literary attestations of the English of New World Negroes over the last two and a half centuries, and by comparing these with the English of Negroes in the United States, the Caribbean, and West Africa today, this has never been done for the English teaching profession. In presenting a historical sketch of this type, I realize that both the facts presented and my interpretations of them may embarrass or even infuriate those who would like to whitewash American Negro dialects by claiming that they do not exist —that (in spite of all sorts of observable evidence to the contrary) they are nothing but Southern white dialects, derived directly from Great Britain. I will simply make no apologies to those who regard human behavior as legitimate only if observed in the white man, since I feel that this constitutes a negation of the cultural and ethnic plurality which is one of America's greatest heritages. On the other hand, I do regret that such a historical survey, although linguistically interesting, may at times conjure up out of the past memories of the Negro-as-slave to haunt the aspirations of the Negro-as-equal.

Of those Africans who fell victim to the Atlantic slave trade and were brought to the New World, many found it necessary to learn some kind of English. With very few exceptions, the form of English which they acquired was a pidginized one, and this kind of English became so well established as the principal medium of communication between Negro slaves in the British colonies that it was passed on as a creole language to succeeding generations of the New World Negroes, for whom it was their native tongue.[5] Some idea of what New World

[5] In referring to types of languages, linguists use the terms *pidgin* and *creole* in a technical sense which has none of the derogatory or racial connotations of popular uses of these terms. When a linguist says that a variety of language is pidginized, he merely means that it has a markedly simplified grammatical structure compared with the "normal" (i.e., unpidginized) source-language. This simplification may be one way in which speakers of different languages can make a new language easier to learn and use—particularly if they have neither the opportunity nor the motivation to learn to speak it the way its primary users do. In addition, some of the unique characteristics of a pidgin language may be due, not to simplification, but to influences on it from the native languages of its users. What is important to realize, however, is that pidginized languages do have grammatical

Negro English may have been like in its early stages can be obtained
from a well-known example of the speech of a fourteen-year-old Negro
lad given by Daniel DeFoe in *The Family Instructor* (London, 1715).
It is significant that the Negro, Toby, speaks a pidginized kind of English to his boy master, even though he states that he was born in the
New World. A sample of his speech is:[6]

Toby. Me be born at Barbadoes.
Boy. Who lives there, Toby?
Toby. There lives white mans, white womans, negree mans, negree
womans, just so as live here.
Boy. What and not know God?
Toby. Yes, the white mans say God prayers,—no much know God.
Boy. And what do the black mans do?
Toby. They much work, much work,—no say God prayers, not at all.
Boy. What work do they do, Toby?
Toby. Makee the sugar, makee the ginger,—much great work, weary
work, all day, all night.

Even though the boy master's English is slightly non-standard (e.g.
black mans), it is still quite different from the speech of the Negro.

An idea of how widespread a pidginized form of English had become among the Negro population of the New World by the end of
the Seventeenth Century can be gathered from the fact that it had
even become the language of the coastal plantations in the Dutch
colony of Surinam (i.e., Dutch Guiana), in South America. In an early
description of that colony, the chapter on the Negro ends with a sample

---

structure and regularity, even though their specific patterns may be different from
those of the related unpidginized source-language of higher prestige. Thus, the
fact that the sentence *Dem no get-am* in present-day West African Pidgin English
is obviously different from its standard English equivalent "They don't have it"
does not necessarily indicate that the Pidgin English speaker "talks without grammar." In producing such a sentence, he is unconsciously obeying the grammatical
rules of West African Pidgin English, and these determine that *Dem no get-am*
is the "right" construction, as opposed to such ungrammatical or "wrong" combinations as *No dem get-am, No get dem-am, Get-am dem no*, etc. If a pidgin
finally becomes the native language of a speech community (and thereby becomes
by definition a creole language), it may expand in grammatical complexity to the
level of "normal" or unpidginized languages. Of course, the resulting creole language may still exhibit structural differences from the original source-language,
because the creole has gone through a pidginized stage. For more details, see
Robert A. Hall, Jr., *Pidgin and Creole Languages* (Ithaca, N.Y., Cornell U. Press,
1966).

[6] The same citation is given in a fuller form, along with a number of other attestations of early New World Negro speech, in George Philip Krapp, *The English
Language in America* (New York, The Century Co., 1925), Vol. I, pp. 255–265.
Other attestations are cited in Tremaine McDowell, "Notes on Negro Dialect in
the American Novel to 1821," *American Speech*, V (1930), pp. 291–296.

conversation in the local Negro English dialect. The dialogue includes such sentences as *Me bella well* "I am very well," *You wantee siddown pinkininne?* "Do you want to sit down for a bit?", and *You wantee go walka longa me?* "Do you want to take a walk with me?"[7] In these sentences, the use of the enclitic vowel in *wantee* recalls the same in De-Foe's example *makee*. Also, the speaker, like Toby, uses *me* as a subject pronoun. In the first Surinam sentence, we see an early example of a construction without any equivalent of the standard English verb "to be." Toby also would probably have said *Me weary*, since the *be* in his first sentence was in all likelihood a past-tense marker (as it is in present-day West African Pidgin English)—the sentence therefore meaning "I was born in Barbadoes." In the last Surinam sentence, a reflex of English *along* is used with the meaning of standard English "with." It may or may not be accidental that in the Gullah dialect, spoken by the Negroes along the South Carolina coastal plain, the same phenomenon occurs, e.g., *Enty you wantuh walk long me?* "Do you want to take a walk with me?" Some Gullah speakers even still use *me* as a subject pronoun, e.g., *Me kyaan bruk-um* "I can't break it," and enclitic final vowels seem to have survived in such Gullah forms as *yerry, yeddy* "to hear."

Early examples of Negro dialect as spoken in the American colonies show it to be strikingly similar to that given by DeFoe for the West Indies and by Herlein for Surinam. In John Leacock's play, *The Fall of British Tyranny* (Philadelphia, 1776), part of the conversation between a certain "Kidnapper" and Cudjo, one of a group of Virginia Negroes, goes as follows:[8]

> *Kidnapper.* . . . what part did you come from?
> *Cudjo.* Disse brack man, disse one, disse one, disse one, come from Hamton, disse one, disse one, come from Nawfok, me come from Nawfok too.
> *Kidnapper.* Very well, what was your master's name?
> *Cudjo.* Me massa name Cunney Tomsee.
> *Kidnapper.* Colonel Thompson—eigh?
> *Cudjo.* Eas, massa, Cunney Tomsee.
> *Kidnapper.* Well then I'll make you a major—and what's your name?
> *Cudjo.* Me massa cawra me Cudjo.

[7] J. D. Herlein, *Beschryvinge van de volksplantinge Zuriname* (Leeuwarden, 1718), pp. 121–123. Herlein gives the Negro English dialogues in Dutch orthography. I have retranscribed these sentences in the kind of spelling which his English contemporaries would have used in order to show better the relationship between the Surinam dialect and the other examples. In the Dutch spelling, these sentences appear as *My belle wel, Jou wantje sie don pinkinine?*, and *Jo wantje gaeu wakke lange mie?*

[8] This citation also occurs in Krapp, and with others in Richard Walser, "Negro Dialect in Eighteenth-Century American Drama," *American Speech*, XXX (1955), pp. 269–276.

Again, the enclitic vowels (e.g., *disse*) and the subject pronoun *me* are prominent features of the Negro dialect. In the sentence *Me Massa name Cunney Tomsee* "My master's name is Colonel Thompson," both the verb "to be" and the standard English possessive suffix *-s* are absent. Incidentally, Cudjo's construction is strikingly similar to sentences like *My sister name Mary* which are used by many American Negroes today.

One possible explanation why this kind of pidginized English was so widespread in the New World, with widely separated varieties resembling each other in so many ways, is that it did not originate in the New World as isolated and accidentally similar instances of random pidginization, but rather originated as a *lingua franca* in the trade centers and slave factories on the West African coast.[9] It is likely that at least some Africans already knew this pidgin English when they came to the New World, and that the common colonial policy of mixing slaves of various tribal origins forced its rapid adoption as a plantation *lingua franca*.

In the course of the Eighteenth Century, some significant changes took place in the New World Negro population, and these had their effect on language behavior. For one thing, the number of Negroes born in the New World came to exceed the number of those brought over from Africa. In the process, pidgin English became the creole mother-tongue of the new generations, and in some areas it has remained so to the present day.[10]

In the British colonies, the creole English of the uneducated Negroes and the English dialects of both the educated and uneducated whites were close enough to each other (at least in vocabulary) to allow the speakers of each to communicate, although they were still different enough so that the whites could consider creole English to be "broken" or "corrupt" English and evidence, so many thought, of the mental limitations of the Negro. But in Surinam, where the European settlers spoke Dutch, creole English was regarded more objectively. In fact, no less than two language courses specifically designed to teach creole English to Dutch immigrants were published before the close of the Eighteenth Century.[11]

[9] See, for example, Basil Davidson, *Black Mother; The Years of the African Slave Trade* (Boston, Little, Brown and Co., 1961), particularly p. 218.

[10] In the West Indies, creole English is usually called *patois*, while in Surinam it is called *Taki-Taki*. In the United States, the only fairly "pure" creole English left today is Gullah, spoken along the coast of South Carolina.

[11] These were Pieter van Dijk, *Nieuwe en nooit bevoorens gexiende onderwijzinge in het Bastert Engeles, of Neeger Engels* (Amsterdam, undated, but probably 1780), and G. C. Weygandt, *Gemeenxame leerwijze om het Basterd of Neger-Engelsch op een gemakkelijke wijze te leeren verstaan en spreeken* (Paramaribo, 1798).

Another change which took place in the New World Negro population primarily during the course of the Eighteenth Century was the social cleavage of the New World-born generations into underprivileged field hands (a continuation of the older, almost universal lot of the Negro slave) and privileged domestic servants. The difference in privilege usually meant, not freedom instead of bondage, but rather freedom from degrading kinds of labor, access to the "big house" with its comforts and "civilization," and proximity to the prestigious "quality" whites, with the opportunity to imitate their behavior (including their speech) and to wear their clothes. In some cases, privilege included the chance to get an education and, in a very few, access to wealth and freedom. In both the British colonies and the United States, Negroes belonging to the privileged group were soon able to acquire a more standard variety of English than the creole of the field hands, and those who managed to get a decent education became speakers of fully standard and often elegant English. This seems to have become the usual situation by the early 1800's, and remained so through the Civil War. In Caroline Gilman's *Recollections of a Southern Matron* (New York, 1838), the difference between field-hand creole (in this case, Gullah) and domestic servant dialect is evident in a comparison of the gardener's "He tief one sheep—he run away las week, cause de overseer gwine for flog him" with Dina's " 'Scuse me, missis, I is gitting hard o'hearing, and yes is more politer dan no" (page 254). A more striking contrast between the speech of educated and uneducated Negroes occurs in a novel written in the 1850's by an American Negro who had traveled extensively through the slave states. In Chapter XVII, part of the exchange between Henry, an educated Negro traveler, and an old "aunty" goes as follows:[12]

> 'Who was that old man who ran behind your master's horse?'
> 'Dat Nathan, my husban'.'
> 'Do they treat him well, aunty?'
> 'No, chile, wus an' any dog, da beat 'im foh little an nothin'.'
> 'Is uncle Nathan religious?'
> 'Yes, chile, ole man an' I's been sahvin' God dis many day, fo yeh baun! Wen any on 'em in de house git sick, den da sen foh 'uncle Nathan' come pray foh dem; 'uncle Nathan' mighty good den!'

After the Civil War, with the abolition of slavery, the breakdown of the plantation system, and the steady increase in education for poor

---

[12] Martin R. Delany, *Blake; or the Huts of America*, published serially in *The Anglo-African Magazine* (1859). The quotation is from Vol. I, No. 6 (June 1859), page 163.

as well as affluent Negroes, the older field-hand creole English began to lose many of its creole characteristics, and take on more and more of the features of the local white dialects and of the written language. Yet, this process has not been just one way. For if it is true that the speech of American Negroes has been strongly influenced by the speech of whites with whom they came into contact, it is probably also true that the speech of many whites has been influenced in some ways by the speech of Negroes.[13]

Over the last two centuries, the proportion of American Negroes who speak a perfectly standard variety of English has risen from a small group of privileged house slaves and free Negroes to persons numbering in the hundreds of thousands, and perhaps even millions. Yet there is still a sizeable number of American Negroes—undoubtedly larger than the number of standard-speaking Negroes—whose speech may be radically non-standard. The non-standard features in the speech of such persons may be due in part to the influence of the non-standard dialects of whites with whom they or their ancestors have come in contact, but they also may be due to the survival of creolisms from the older Negro field-hand speech of the plantations. To insure their social mobility in modern American society, these non-standard speakers must undoubtedly be given a command of standard English; that point was made in the early part of this paper. In studying non-standard Negro dialects and teaching standard English in terms of them, however, both the applied linguist and the language teacher must come to appreciate the fact that even if certain non-standard Negro dialect patterns do not resemble the dialect usage of American whites, or even those of the speakers of remote British dialects, they may nevertheless be as old as African and European settlement in the New World, and therefore quite widespread and well-established. On various occasions, I have pointed out that many speakers of non-standard American Negro dialects make a grammatical and semantic distinction by means of *be*, illustrated by such constructions as *he busy* "He is busy (momentarily)" or *he workin'* "he is working (right now)" as opposed to *he be busy* "he is (habitually) busy" or *he be workin'* "he is working (steadily)," which the grammar of standard English is unable to make.[14] Even this distinction goes back well over a century. One observer in the 1830's noted a request by a slave for a permanent supply of soap as "(If) Missis only give we, we be so clean forever," while *be* is absent

---

[13] See Raven I. McDavid, Jr. and Virginia Glenn McDavid, "The Relationship of the Speech of American Negroes to the Speech of Whites," *American Speech*, XXVI (1951), pp. 3–17.

[14] See, for example, *The Florida FL Reporter*, Vol. 4, No. 2 (Winter 1965–1966), page 25.

in a subsequent report of someone's temporary illness with "She jist sick for a little while."[15]

Once educators who are concerned with the language problems of the disadvantaged come to realize that non-standard Negro dialects represent a historical tradition of this type, it is to be hoped that they will become less embarrassed by evidence that these dialects are very much alike throughout the country while different in many ways from the non-standard dialects of whites, less frustrated by failure to turn non-standard Negro dialect speakers into standard English speakers overnight, less impatient with the stubborn survival of Negro dialect features in the speech of even educated persons, and less zealous in proclaiming what is "right" and what is "wrong." If this happens, then applied linguists and educators will be able to communicate with each other, and both will be able to communicate with the non-standard-speaking Negro child. The problem will then be well on its way toward a solution.

[15] Frances Anne Kemble, *Journal of a Residence on a Georgian Plantation in 1838–1839* (New York, 1862). The first quotation is from page 52, and the second is from page 118.

FOR DISCUSSION AND REVIEW

1   What, according to Stewart, are some common misconceptions about nonstandard dialects? How has the work of the linguist helped to correct these misconceptions?

2   What distinctions does Stewart make in discussing *pidgin language*, *creole language*, and *dialect*?

3   Stewart concludes that "nonstandard Negro dialects represent a historical tradition." What evidence does he utilize to arrive at this conclusion?

4   According to Stewart, why should educators be less concerned with "proclaiming what is 'right' and what is 'wrong' " and more concerned with trying to understand the pronunciation, vocabulary, and grammatical forms of nonstandard speech?

4

Should
Ghettoese
Be Accepted?

William Raspberry, a columnist for the *Washington Post*, discusses a question that educators are facing at present. On the basis of the evidence available, how does one approach the conflict between patterns of a nonstandard dialect which the child learns either at home or from his peers and the equivalent patterns of standard English? Raspberry advocates the desirability of making slum children bidialectal. In order to implement such a program, he feels that teachers sensitive to nonstandard language are needed in ghetto schools.

William Raspberry

BY THE time I get there, he will have gone."

"Time I git dere, he be done gone."

You and I were taught to recognize the first example as good English and the second as bad. According to a growing number of linguists, we were taught wrong.

The two sentences, these linguists tell us, don't represent proper and improper usage; they represent two distinct languages, equally consistent and, in that they communicate meaning, equally valid.

The first is standard American English; the second, the nonstandard English of the black slums. These linguists, who include some of the leading lights at Washington's Center for Applied Linguistics, are attempting to build on the validity of the second as a means of teaching the first.

English teachers don't find it necessary to make a Spanish-speaking child feel that his native language is bad in order to get him to learn English. But when confronting children who speak the native tongue of the black slums, too many of them do precisely that. One unfortunate result, the linguists tell us, is that slum children become ashamed of their language and, therefore, ashamed of themselves.

The child who points to the rose on his teacher's desk and says, "Dere go a flyvuh," will too frequently be told flatly that a rose is a *flower* and that it isn't going anywhere.

Such instruction is more likely to confuse than help. The child knows very well that his meaning would be unmistakable at home; his mother might have put it just the same way. Furthermore, if his efforts at free expression are criticized too often, he may simply shut up and say nothing at all.

And so the teacher dubs him "nonverbal," a typical label for the ghetto child.

Nonverbal, hell! Follow him out the schoolhouse door and listen while his playmate tries to get a word in edgewise.

The teacher has made a classical error. He has tried to teach his pupil a new language by condemning the pupil's old one. And the result is that the child shrinks from the teacher, making it very difficult if not impossible for him to teach the pupil anything at all.

Wouldn't it be better, the linguists ask, to accept the validity of the child's native language if that facilitates teaching him a new one?

The answer would be obvious if the child's native tongue were French or Spanish. The difference is that French and Spanish are respected languages *and they don't sound like standard English.* Thus, *voici and voilà* aren't wrong; they simply aren't English. Their exact equivalent in ghettoese, "here go" and "dere go" are just close enough to standard English that teachers are tempted to brand them as bad standard English rather than good nonstandard.

Nonstandard English, or ghettoese, it must be admitted, is a lot easier to recognize than to describe. (Try describing *standard* English!)

The linguists emphasize two things about ghettoese: First, it is the language spoken almost universally among low-income black Americans (and understood by almost all black Americans) and second, it is consistent in syntax.

Ghettoese is not slang: The latter is little more than a one-for-one substitution of nonstandard words for standard ones. Nor is it simply mispronunciation of standard English words.

"Sue is a boss chick" is slang. Boss is a synonym for "fine" and chick for "girl." But the sentence isn't ghettoese, although something very like it might be heard among ghetto residents.

On the other hand, the statement, "Dat Sue sho a boss chick," is ghettoese—but not solely because of the mispronunciation of "that" and "sure," for "Sue a boss chick" is also ghettoese, although each word may be given the standard pronunciation. It is ghettoese because of the missing "is," a feature common to ghetto speech patterns.

The linguists make another point: Ghettoese is not necessarily less *precise* than standard English. In some instances, it may be more precise than the standard.

Ask a slum child why his father missed last night's meeting, and the answer might be, "He sick." Ask him why his father misses so many meetings, and he might answer, "He be sick." The first describes a temporary illness; the second, a chronic or recurring one. No such distinction exists in standard English. The answer to both questions in standard English would be, "He is sick."

This example seems to be a favorite among the linguists who want standard English taught as a foreign language, which has led me on occasion to refer to them as the he-be-sick school.

This designation suggests, unfairly, that the linguists who have been addressing themselves to the language problems of slum children are of a single mind. Not so. There is something less than unanimity among them even on the notion of teaching standard English as a foreign language.

For some, it is a direct analogy to the teaching of English to a Spanish-speaking child. For others, it means using some of the techniques that are used in the teaching of foreign languages.

It is pointed out, for instance, that one reason middle-class children learn to read more easily than slum children is that the former have to make but a single translation: from print to sound. A slum child, on the other hand, has to make a second translation: from the standard English to his native nonstandard, just as a French-speaking youngster would have to make the additional translation to his native French.

The argument loses a little in light of the fact that translation increasingly is thought of as a rather poor way of teaching foreign languages. Total immersion is the current trend. If you want to learn Russian in a hurry, you might find yourself in a classroom where only Russian is spoken. No tedious translations. You learn to speak Russian because you have to speak Russian to get along in the class.

The method has a lot to recommend it. After all, isn't that how you learned English?

If the total immersion system is an effective way of teaching foreign languages and if our linguist friends want to teach English as a foreign language, then why not total immersion in standard English?

As a matter of fact, that is what almost always happens. Good teachers don't spend their time reminding their pupils that the "flyvuh" isn't going anywhere. They are careful to say, "Here is a flower." They believe that if they say something in standard English distinctly enough and often enough the child will learn to say it that way, too.

That is a very great deal different from translating from nonstandard into standard, which some of the linguists seem to be suggesting.

At least one of them, William A. Stewart, explicitly makes that suggestion. He tells of the time a young "problem reader" from the inner city happened across his ghettoese translation of *The Night Before Christmas*:

It's the night before Christmas, and here in our house
It ain't nothing moving, not even no mouse.
There go we-all stockings, hanging high up off the floor,
So Santa Claus can full them up, if he walk in through our door.

Says Stewart:

Lenora was one of the "problem readers" of the public schools;
she read school texts haltingly, with many mistakes and with little
ability to grasp the meaning of what she read. Yet, when she began
to read the nonstandard version of the poem, her voice was steady,
her word reading [was] accurate, and her sentence intonation was
natural. . . .

This unexpected success in reading so surprised Lenora that she
began to discuss the experience with her little brother. They decided that there was something different about the text, but were
unable to tell exactly what it was.

To compare, I then had Lenora read the standard English version
of the poem. . . . When she did, all the "problem reader" behavior
returned.

Stewart's point goes far beyond pronunciation; its essence is grammar. His translation closely approximated the grammar of Lenora's
native ghettoese, leaving her to make the single print-to-sound translation. Clement Moore's original required her to make the second stan-
dard-to-nonstandard translation and, thus, exposed her as being a
problem reader.

It is for this reason that some linguists have proposed that early
reading material for inner-city children be written in the slum dialect.
They point to experiments, notably in Sweden, which indicate that
children who are introduced to reading through their own nonstandard
dialects and then are switched to standard surpass those who use standard materials from the beginning.

If this is so, they suggest, then we should be able to improve dras-
tically the reading abilities of young slum dwellers simply by first
teaching them to read in their native tongue.

The theory makes a good deal of sense, but it may be asking too
much to expect the average classroom to implement it effectively. The
more likely result is either to hopelessly confuse such children or to
reinforce their nonstandard speech patterns.

But more is involved here than the teaching of reading. Involved,
too, is the assessment of a child's intelligence, an assessment often
based on his language proficiency in standard English.

Joan C. Baratz of the Education Study Center makes that point in
the September 1969 issue of *Child Development*:

"If the criterion for language development is the use of a well-ordered systematic code," she says, "then the continued use of measures of language development that have standard English as the criterion of a developed form will only continue to produce the results that the Negro, lower-class child is delayed in language development because he has not acquired the rules that the middle-class child has been able to acquire. . . ."

What that means, I think, is that there are two distinct questions to be asked: To what degree has this child developed language skills? To what degree has this child developed facility *in standard English?*

Most of our written tests pretend to ask the first question, when in fact they ask the second. The answer to the first question is obviously a more valid measure of intelligence. But that is not the end of it.

What you, I, and the linguists want is to have slum children learn the language that will help them get along in the American society. That means standard English.

It may be academically interesting to be aware that, from a purely linguistic point of view, nonstandard is just as valid as standard. Interesting, but not particularly useful.

If employers, personnel officers, and the others whom we find it useful to impress with our intelligence were fluent in nonstandard English and understood its validity and if books and newspapers were written in nonstandard, then it would be unnecessary to teach standard (But in that case, nonstandard would, by definition, be standard!)

The reason we want slum children to learn standard is that nonstandard is a good deal less negotiable—just as trading stamps are less negotiable than cash.

But that doesn't mean that trading stamps are *bad*. It is here that the linguists make the heart of their case. The way we speak is such an integral part of who we are that to deprecate our speech is to deprecate us.

What the linguists want to do is to give slum children facility with standard English without forcing them to forget their native nonstandard—to give them cash without confiscating their trading stamps. The nonstandard, lest we forget, may be *the* negotiable language back home in the slum neighborhood or within the family or on the playground. After all, you can't pay cash for that lamp at the redemption center.

What we are talking about, then, is the desirability of making slum children bilingual, just as most educated blacks are bilingual. (Forget the black teacher, recently escaped from the slums, who pretends she doesn't understand when Johnny says, "I'mo take me a brick an' bus' you upsi' yo' head." Her kind, happily, is disappearing.) Giving slum children this kind of bilinguality has far less to do with understanding the inner workings of ghettoese than with being sensitive to the inner workings of people.

No teacher expects a pupil to learn arithmetic if he calls him a dunderhead every time the child delivers himself of a wrong answer. Nor should the teacher expect him to learn standard English (or anything else, for that matter) if, by his attitude, he conveys "you are a dunderhead" every time the child opens his mouth. (This, however, is simply psychology, not linguistics.)

In that light, linguists who emphasize the beauties of ghettoese may be showing their contempt for teachers. Their implication is that teachers are too stupid to distinguish between form and substance, that if a child says something really clever—but in ghettoese—the teacher will hear nothing but the ghettoese.

If that is the case, if substantial numbers of teachers believe nonstandard equals stupid, then forget linguistics. Forget everything, for any teacher so insensitive that he will shame a child into silence every time he opens his mouth is beyond the help even of the Center for Applied Linguistics.

FOR DISCUSSION AND REVIEW

1 Why does Raspberry believe that "ghettoese" should be accepted? Does he set limits to this acceptance?

2 According to Raspberry, why should slum children be given facility with standard English?

3 In an article entitled "Sense and Nonsense about American Dialects," Raven I. McDavid advises that "the first principle of any language program is that, whatever the target, it must respect the language that the students bring with them to the classroom." If you were establishing a program to make slum children bidialectal, would you heed this advice? Why or why not?

5

A Checklist of Significant Features for Discriminating Social Dialects[1]

Raven I. McDavid, Jr.

Professor Raven I. McDavid, Jr., is among a growing number of linguists who are exploring the various social and educational implications of American dialects. McDavid, as well as the other authors who propose programs advocating functional bidialectalism—William A. Stewart (pp. 416–426), William Raspberry (pp. 427–432), and William Labov (pp. 439–446), recognizes the problems associated with implementing such a program in the classroom. As an aid to teachers who want to teach a standard variety of English to speakers of a nonstandard variety, McDavid compiled the following checklist concerned with significant features of social dialects. The list is valuable not only as a diagnostic tool but also as the basis for patterned drills in Standard English. McDavid is Professor of English at the University of Chicago and director-editor of *The Linguistic Atlas of the Middle and South Atlantic States.*

A S AN AID to the teacher who is interested in a more efficient approach to the problem of teaching a standard variety of English—for public roles—to those who use non-standard varieties at home, the following list of features, all of which are both systematic and significant, has been drawn up, partly from the collections of the regional linguistic atlases, partly from more intensive local studies.

[1] This list will be incorporated in a manual of social dialects being prepared by Alva L. Davis of the Illinois Institute of Technology under a grant from the U.S. Office of Education.

The emphasis is on those features of the language that recur frequently and are therefore most amenable to pattern drills. It must not
be inferred that other, less well-patterned features of English are unimportant as social markers, but only that they do not lend themselves to
productive drill. Discriminating the principal parts of irregular verbs, as
past tense *saw* and past participle *seen*, is a part of the linguistic behavior that constitutes Standard English, but the pattern *see-saw-seen* is
duplicated only by such compounds of *see* as *foresee*. On the other
hand, the discrimination between *I see* and *he sees* is a part of a pattern
of subject-verb concord that is faced every time a subject is used with
a present tense verb.

The list is concerned with social dialects of English and does not
include all the problems faced by the native speaker of some other language. For each such situation one needs special contrastive studies like
those currently being published by the University of Chicago Press. Native speakers of Spanish, for instance, have special difficulties with the
English consonant clusters /sp-, st-, sk-/ at the beginnings of words;
native speakers of Czech or Finnish need to learn the accentual patterns
of English; native speakers of continental European languages need to
master the perfect phrase in such expressions of time as *I have been in
Chicago for five years;* native speakers of almost every other language
need to learn a finer meshed set of vowel distinctions, as between *peach*
and *pitch, bait* and *bet* and *but, pool* and *pull, boat* and *bought, hot*
and *hut.*

The origins of these features are of indirect concern here; that they
are of social significance is what concerns us. In general, however, it is
clear that most of them may be traced back to the folk speech of England, and that in the United States none of them is exclusively identified with any racial group, though in any given community some of
them may be relatively more frequent among whites or among Negroes.

This list is restricted to features that occur in speech as well as in
writing. It is recognized that regional varieties of English differ in the
distance between standard informal speech and standard formal writing. They vary considerably in the kinds of reductions of final consonant clusters, either absolutely or when followed by a word beginning
with a consonant. The plural of sixth may be /sɪks/, homonymous with
the cardinal numeral; *burned a hole* may be pronounced /bə̂rnd ə hól/
but *burned my pants* /bərn mài pǽnts/. Similarly, the copula may not
appear in questions as *They ready? That your boy? We going now? She
been drinking?* The auxiliary *have* may not appear even as a reflex of /v/
in such statements as *I been thinking about it* or *we been telling you
this.* In families where the conventions of written and printed English
are learned early as a separate subsystem, differences of this kind cause
little trouble but for speakers of non-standard dialects who have little

home exposure to books, these features may provide additional problems in learning to write. It is often difficult for the teacher to overcome these problems in the students' writing without fostering an unnatural pronunciation.

It should be recognized, of course, that cultural situations may change in any community. To take the southern dialectal situation, with which I am most familiar. Forty years ago there was a widespread social distinction in the allophones of /ai/. The monophthongal [a·] was used by all classes finally, as in *rye*, or before voiced consonants as in *ride*; before voiceless consonants, however, educated speakers had a diphthong and any uneducated speakers used the monophthong, so that *nice white rice* became a well known social shibboleth.[2] In recent years, however, the shibboleth has ceased to operate, and many educated Southerners now have the monophthong in all positions, and their numbers are increasing. This observation was also made last spring by James B. McMillan, of the University of Alabama, who added that in his experience the falling together of /ai/ and /a/ before /-r/, so that *fire* and *far*, *hired* and *hard*, become homonymous, was still restricted to non-standard speech. Yet last August I noticed that this homonymy was common on the Dallas radio, in the formal speech of the editor of the women's hour.

It should not be assumed, furthermore, that one will not find other systematic features discriminating local dialects. Nor should we be so naive as to expect the speakers of any community to cease regarding the speech of outsiders as *ipso facto* inferior because it is different—even though these outsiders may be superior in education and social standing.

We are all ethnocentric after our own fashion; in our localities, we may consider some differences important whether they are or not—and if enough people worry about them some of these may become important. This is the traditional origin of neuroses. Meanwhile, it is probably good sense as well as good humor to recognize that though the white middle-class Chicagoan often considers the loss of /r/ in *barn* and the like a lower-class feature, the cultivated Southerner associates the middle western /r/ in such words with the speech of poor whites— and that the distinction between *wails* and *whales* is socially diagnostic nowhere in the English-speaking world. The features here are diagnostic everywhere, though not all of them occur in every situation where differences in social dialects are important.

---

[2] This observation was made, *inter alia*, in my analyses of the pronunciation of English in the Greenville, S.C., metropolitan area, at meetings of the Linguistic Society in New York City (December 1938) and Chapel Hill, N.C. (July 1941).

Pronunciation

1. The distinction between /θ/ as in *thin* and /t/ in *tin*, /f/ in *fin*, /s/ in *sin*.

2. Failure to make the similar distinction between /ð/ in *then* and /d/, /v/, /z/.

3. Failure to make the distinction between the vowels of *bird* and *Boyd*, *curl* and *coil*.

   A generation ago this contrast was most significant among older speakers of the New York metropolitan area. It has become less important, since few younger speakers confuse these pairs. But it still should be noted, not only for New York City but for New Orleans as well.[3]

   At one time a monophthongal /ai/ in the South was standard in final position and before voiced consonants, as in *rye* and *ride*, but substandard before voiceless consonants as in *right*. This is no longer true; many educated Southerners have monophthongal /ai/ in all positions and the number is increasing.

4. The omission of a weak stressed syllable preceding the primary stress, so that in substandard speech *professor* may become *fessor*, *reporter* become *porter*, and *insurance* become *shoo-ance* or *sho-unce*.

5. A statistically disproportionate front-shifting of the primary stress giving such forms as *po*-lice, *in*-surance, *ee*-ficiency and *gui*-tar, etc.

   Front-shifting is characteristic of English borrowings from other languages; in *bal*cony it is completely acceptable, in *ho*tel and *Ju*ly, acceptability is conditioned by position in the sentence.

6. Heavy stress on what is a weak stressed final syllable in standard English, giving accid*ent*, elem*ent*, presid*ent*, evid*ence*, etc.

Inflection

Noun

7. Lack of the noun plural: Two *boy* came to see me.

8. Lack of the noun genitive: This is *Mr. Brown* hat.

Pronoun

9. Analogizing of the /-n/ of *mine* to other absolute genitives, yielding *ourn*, *yourn*, *hisn*, *hern*, *theirn*.

10. Analogizing of the compound reflexives, yielding *hisself*, *theirselves*.

Demonstratives

11. Substitution of *them* for *those*, as *them* books.

12. Compound demonstratives: *these-here* dogs, *them-(th)ere* cats.

---

[3] The monophthongal southern /ai/ disturbs many easterners and middlewesterners. Some Philadelphians, for instance, allege that southerners confuse *ride* and *rod*; some Detroiters, that they confuse *right* and *rat*. They do not; the confusion exists in the mind of the eastern and middlewestern observer.

Adjectives

13. Analogizing of inflected comparisons: the *wonderfullest* time, a *lovinger* child.

14. Double comparisons: a *more prettier* dress, the *most ugliest* man.

Verb

15. Unorthodox person-number concord of the present of *to be*. This may be manifest in generalizing of *am* or *is* or *are*, or in the use of *be* with all persons.

16. Unorthodox person-number concord of the past of *be*: I *were* or we *was*.

17. Failure to maintain person-number concord of the present indicative of other verbs: *I does, he do*. (This is perhaps the most clearly diagnostic feature.)

    Note that three third person singular forms of common verbs are irregular: *has, does* /dʌz/, *says* /sɛz/; in the last two the spelling conceals the irregularity, but many speakers who are learning this inflection will say /duz/ and /sez/.

18. Omission of /-ɪŋ/ of the present participle: He was *open* a can of beer.

    Note that both /ɪŋ/ and /ɪn/ may be heard in standard speech, depending on region and styles.

19. Omission of /-t, -d, -əd/ of the past tense: *I burn a hole* in my pants yesterday.

    Note that before a word beginning with a consonant the /-d/ may be omitted in speech in *I burned my* pants. Those who have this contextual loss of the sound need to learn the special conventions of writing.

20. Omission of /-t, -d, -əd/ of the past participle.

21. Omission of the verb *to be* in statements before a predicate nominative. *He a good boy.*

    Note that in questions this omission may occur in standard oral English, though it would never be written in standard expository prose.

22. Omission of *to be* in statements before adjectives: *They ready.*

23. Omission of *to be* in statements before present participles: *I going* with you.

24. Omission of *to be* in statements before past participle: *The window broken.*

25. Omission of the /-s, -z, -əz/ reflex of *has* before *been* in statements: *He been drinking.*

    Note that this omission may occur in questions in standard oral English, and also that in standard oral English many educated speakers may omit the /-v/ reflex of *have*: *I been thinking about it; we been tell you this*, though it would not be omitted in standard expository prose.

26. Substitution of *been, done,* or *done been* for *have*, especially with a third person singular subject: *He done been finished.* In other situations the /-v/ may be lost, as in #25 (the preceding situation).

FOR DISCUSSION AND REVIEW

1   What does McDavid mean when he says that the features in his checklist are "both systematic and significant"?

2   What are the implications of Mc-
    David's statement that his check-
    list is designed "as an aid to the
    teacher who is interested in a more
    efficient approach to the problem
    of teaching a standard variety of
    English—for public roles—to those
    who use nonstandard varieties at
    home"?

3   McDavid states that "the features
    here are diagnostic everywhere,
    though not all of them occur in
    every situation where differences
    in social dialects are important."
    Of the twenty-six features for dis-
    criminating social dialects, which
    are important in your area? Ex-
    plain by citing specific examples of
    speech in your locale.

4   Many authors, in order to enhance
    the aura of realism, try to repre-
    sent dialect in their writing. Con-
    sider the following passage from
    Mark Twain's *The Adventures* of
    Huckleberry Finn:

    "Why, Huck, doan' de French
    people talk de same way we
    does?"

    "No, Jim; you couldn't under-
    stand a word they said—not a
    single word."

    "Well, now, I be ding-busted!
    How do dat come?"

    "I don't know; but it's so. I
    got some of their jabber out of
    a book. S'pose a man was to
    come to you and say *Polly-voo-
    franzy*—what would you think?"

    "I wouldn' think nuff'n; I'd
    take en bust him over de head.
    Dat is, if he warn't white. I
    wouldn't 'low no nigger to call
    me dat."

    "Shucks, it ain't calling you
    anything. It's only saying do you
    know how to talk French."

    "Well, den, why couldn't he
    say it?"

    "Why, he *is* a-saying it. That's a

Frenchman's *way* of saying it."

    "Well, it's a blame' ridicklous
    way, en I doan' want to hear no
    mo' 'bout it. Dey ain' no sense
    in it."

    "Looky here, Jim; does a cat
    talk like we do?"

    "No, a cat don't."

    "Well, does a cow?"

    "No, a cow don't, nuther."

    "Does a cat talk like a cow,
    or a cow talk like a cat?"

    "No, dey don't."

    "It's natural and right for 'em
    to talk different from each other,
    ain't it?"

    "Course."

    "And ain't it natural and right
    for a cat and a cow to talk dif-
    ferent from *us?*"

    "Why, mos' sholy it is."

    "Well, then, why ain't it natu-
    ral and right for a *Frenchman* to
    talk different from *us?* You an-
    swer me that."

    "Is a cat a man, Huck?"

    "No."

    "Well, den, dey ain't no sense
    in a cat talkin' like a man. Is a
    cow a man?—er is a cow a cat?"

    "No, she ain't neither of
    them."

    "Well, den, she ain' got no
    business to talk like either one
    er the yuther of 'em. Is a French-
    man a man?"

    "Yes."

    "*Well,* den! Dad blame it,
    why doan' he *talk* like a man?
    You answer me *dat!*"

    I see it warn't no use wasting
    words—you can't learn a nigger
    to argue. So I quit.

Using McDavid's checklist, identify
the significant features in the speech
of both Huck and Jim. What conclusions can be drawn from your
analysis?

6

The Study of Nonstandard English

William Labov

Professor Labov is well known for his studies of New York City speech, especially Negro speech. In this selection, he argues for the need to study nonstandard dialect, explains some of its distinguishing characteristics, and discusses the relationship between nonstandard dialect and standard English. In other studies, Labov advocates functional bidialectalism for speakers of a nonstandard dialect. He urges Negroes to learn standard English because of its value for coping with social situations and operating in the business world.

Three Reasons for Studying Nonstandard Language

SINCE LANGUAGE learning does take place outside of the classroom, and the six-year-old child does have great capacity for learning new language forms as he is exposed to them, it may be asked why it should be necessary for the teacher to understand more about the child's own vernacular. First, we can observe that automatic adjustment does *not* take place in all cases. Even the successful middle class student does not always master the teacher's grammatical forms; and in the urban ghettos we find very little adjustment to school forms. Students continue to write *I have live* after ten or twelve years in school; we will describe below failures in reading the *-ed* suffix which show no advance with years in school. Second, knowledge of the underlying structure of the nonstandard vernacular will allow the most efficient teaching. If the teacher knows the general difference between standard negative attraction and nonstandard negative concord, he can teach a hundred different standard forms with the simple instruction: *The negative is attracted only to the first indefinite.* Thus by this one rule we can make many corrections:

He don't know nothing	⟶	He doesn't know anything
Nobody don't like him	⟶	Nobody likes him
Nobody hardly goes there	⟶	Hardly anybody goes there
Can't nobody do it	⟶	Nobody can do it

Third, the vernacular must be understood because ignorance of it leads to serious conflict between student and teacher. Teachers in ghetto schools who continually insist that *i* and *e* sound different in *pin* and *pen* will only antagonize a great number of their students. The knowledge that *i* and *e* actually sound the same before *m* and *n* for most of their students (and "should" sound the same if they are normal speakers) will help avoid this destructive conflict. Teachers who insist that a child meant to say *He is tired* when he said *He tired* will achieve only bewilderment in the long run. Knowledge that *He tired* is the vernacular equivalent of the contracted form *He's tired* will save teacher and student from this frustration.

Granted that the teacher wishes to learn about the student's language, what methods are available for him to do so? Today, a great many linguists study English through their own intuitions; they operate "out of their own heads" in the sense that they believe they can ask and answer all the relevant questions themselves. But even if a teacher comes from the same background as his students, he will find that his grammar has changed, that he no longer has firm intuitions about whether he can say *Nobody don't know nothing about it* instead of *Nobody knows nothing about it*. He can of course sit down with a student and ask him all kinds of direct questions about his language, and there are linguists who do this. But one cannot draw directly upon the intuitions of the two major groups we are interested in, children and nonstandard speakers. Both are in contact with a superordinate or dominant dialect, and both will provide answers which reflect their awareness of this dialect as much as of their own. One can of course engage in long and indirect conversations with students, hoping that all of the forms of interest will sooner or later occur, and there are linguists who have attempted to study nonstandard dialects in this way. But these conversations usually teach the subject more of the investigator's language than the other way around. In general, one can say that whenever a speaker of a nonstandard dialect is in a subordinate position to a speaker of a standard dialect, the rules of his grammar will shift in an unpredictable manner towards the standard. The longer the contact, the stronger and more lasting is the shift. Thus adolescent speakers of a vernacular make very unreliable informants when they are questioned in a formal framework. The investigator must show considerable sociolinguistic sophistication to cope with such a situation, and indeed the teacher will also need to know a great deal about the social forces which affect linguistic behavior if he is to interpret his students' language.

Nonstandard Dialects as "Self-Contained" Systems

The traditional view of nonstandard speech as a set of isolated deviations from standard English is often countered by the opposite view:

that nonstandard dialect should be studied as an isolated system in its own right, without any reference to standard English. It is argued that the system of grammatical forms of a dialect can only be understood through their internal relations. For example, nonstandard Negro English has one distinction which standard English does not have: there is an invariant form *be* in *He always be foolin' around* which marks habitual, general conditions, as opposed to the unmarked *is, am, are,* etc., which do not have any such special sense. It can be argued that the existence of this distinction changes the value of all other members of the grammatical system and that the entire paradigm of this dialect is therefore different from that of standard English. It is indeed important to find such relations within the meaningful set of grammatical distinctions, if they exist, because we can then *explain* rather than merely describe behavior. There are many co-occurrence rules which are purely descriptive—the particular dialect just happens to have X' *and* Y' where another has X and Y. We would like to know if a special nonstandard form X' *requires* an equally nonstandard Y' because of the way in which the nonstandard form cuts up the entire field of meaning. This would be a tremendous help in teaching, since we would be able to show what sets of standard rules have to be taught together to avoid confusing the student with a mixed, incoherent grammatical system.

The difficulty here is that linguistics has not made very much progress in the analysis of semantic systems. There is no method or procedure which leads to reliable or reproducible results—not even among those who agree on certain principles of grammatical theory. No one has yet written a complete grammar of a language—or even come close to accounting for all the morphological and syntactic rules of a language. And the situation is much more primitive in semantics; for example, the verbal system of standard English has been studied now for many centuries, yet there is no agreement at all on the meaning of the auxiliaries *have . . . ed* and *be . . . ing.* The meaning of *I have lived here,* as opposed to *I lived here,* has been explained as a) relevant to the present, b) past *in* the present, c) perfective, d) indefinite, e) causative, and so on. It is not only that there are many views; it is that in any given discussion no linguist has really found a method by which he can reasonably hope to persuade others that he is right. If this situation prevails where most of the investigators have complete access to the data, since they are native speakers of standard English, we must be more than cautious in claiming to understand the meaning of *I be here* as opposed to *I am here* in nonstandard Negro English, and even more cautious in claiming that the meaning of nonstandard *I'm here* therefore differs from standard *I'm here* because of the existence of the other form. Most teachers have learned to be cautious in accepting a grammarian's statement about the meaning of their own native forms, but they have no way of judging statements made about a dialect which they do not speak, and they are naturally prone to accept such statements on the authority of the writer.

There is, however, a great deal that we can do to show the internal relations in the nonstandard dialect as a system. There are a great many forms which seem different on the surface but can be explained as expressions of a single rule, or the absence of a single rule. We observe that in nonstandard Negro English it is common to say *a apple* rather than *an apple*. This is a grammatical fault from the point of view of standard speakers, and the school must teach *an apple* as the written, standard form. There is also a rather low-level, unimportant feature of pronunciation which is common to southern dialects: in *the apple*, the word *the* has the same pronunciation as in *the book* and does not rhyme with *be*. Finally, we can note that, in the South, educated white speakers keep the vocalic schwa which represents *r* in *four*, but nonstandard speakers tend to drop it (registered in dialect writing as *fo' o'clock*). When all these facts are put together, we can begin to explain the nonstandard *a apple* as part of a much broader pattern. There is a general rule of English which states that we do not pronounce two (phonetic) vowels in succession. Some kind of semi-consonantal glide or consonant comes in between: an *n* as in *an apple*, a *"y"* as in *the apple*, an *r* as in *four apples*. In each of these cases, this rule is not followed for nonstandard Negro English. A teacher may have more success in getting students to write *an apple* if he presents this general rule and connects up all of these things into a single rational pattern, even if some are not important in themselves. It will "make sense" to Negro speakers, since they do not drop *l* before a vowel, and many rules of their sound system show the effect of a following vowel.

There are many ways in which an understanding· of the fundamental rules of the dialect will help to explain the surface facts. Some of the rules cited above are also important in explaining why nonstandard Negro speakers sometimes delete *is*, in *He is ready*, but almost always delete *are*, in *You are ready*; or why they say *they book* and *you book* but not *we book*. It does not always follow, though, that a grammatical explanation reveals the best method for teaching standard English.

Systematic analysis may also be helpful in connecting up the nonstandard form with the corresponding standard form and in this sense understanding the meaning of the nonstandard form. For example, nonstandard speakers say *Ain't nobody see it*. What is the nearest standard equivalent? We can connect this up with the standard negative "foregrounding" of *Scarcely did anybody see it* or, even more clearly, the literary expression *Nor did anybody see it*. This foregrounding fits in with the general colloquial southern pattern with indefinite subjects:

Didn't anybody see it, nonstandard *Didn't nobody see it*. In these cases, the auxiliary *didn't* is brought to the front of the sentence, like the *ain't* in the nonstandard sentence. But there is another possibility. We could connect up *Ain't nobody see it* with the sentence *It ain't nobody see it*, that is, "There isn't anybody who sees it"; the dummy *it* of nonstandard Negro English corresponds to standard *there*, and, like *there*, it can be dropped in casual speech. Such an explanation is the only one possible in the case of such nonstandard sentences as *Ain't nothin' went down*. This could not be derived from **Nothin' ain't went down*, a sentence type which never occurs. If someone uses one of these forms, it is important for the teacher to know what was intended, so that he can supply the standard equivalent. To do so, one must know a great deal about many underlying rules of the nonstandard dialect, and also a great deal about the rules of English in general.

Nonstandard English as a Close Relative of Standard English

Differences between standard and nonstandard English are not as sharp as our first impressions would lead us to think. Consider, for example, the socially stratified marker of "pronominal apposition"—the use of a dependent pronoun in such sentences as

My oldest sister she worked at the bank.

Though most of us recognize this as a nonstandard pattern, it is not always realized that the "nonstandard" aspect is merely a slight difference in intonation. A standard speaker frequently says the same thing, with a slight break after the subject: *My oldest sister—she works at the bank, and she finds it very profitable.* There are many ways in which a greater awareness of the standard colloquial forms would help teachers interpret the nonstandard forms. Not only do standard speakers use pronominal apposition with the break noted above, but in casual speech they can also bring object noun phrases to the front, "foregrounding" them. For example, one can say

My oldest sister—she worked at the Citizens Bank in Passaic last year.
The Citizens Bank, in Passaic—my oldest sister worked there last year.
Passaic—my oldest sister worked at the Citizens Bank there last year.

Note that if the foregrounded noun phrase represents a locative—the "place where"—then its position is held by *there*, just as the persons are represented by pronouns. If we are dealing with a time element, it can be foregrounded without replacement in any dialect: *Last year, my oldest sister worked at the Citizens Bank in Passaic.*

It is most important for the teacher to understand the relation between standard and nonstandard and to recognize that nonstandard

English is a system of rules, different from the standard but not necessarily inferior as a means of communication. All of the teacher's social
instincts, past training, and even faith in his own education lead him
to believe that other dialects of English are merely "mistakes" without
any rhyme or rationale.

In this connection, it will be helpful to examine some of the most
general grammatical differences between English dialects spoken in the
United States. One could list a very large number of "mistakes," but
when they are examined systematically the great majority appear to be
examples of a small number of differences in the rules. The clearest
analysis of these differences has been made by Edward Klima (1964).
He considers first the dialect in which people say sentences like

> Who could she see?
> Who did he speak with?
> He knew who he spoke with.
> The leader who I saw left.
> The leader who he spoke with left.

What is the difference between this dialect and standard English? The
usual schoolbook answer is to say that these are well-known mistakes
in the use of *who* for *whom*. But such a general statement does not add
any clarity to the situation; nor does it help the student to learn standard English. The student often leaves the classroom with no more
than an uneasy feeling that *who* is incorrect and *whom* is correct. This
is the state of half-knowledge that leads to hypercorrect forms such as
Whom did you say is calling? In the more extreme cases, *whom* is seen
as the only acceptable, polite form of the pronoun. Thus a certain re-
ceptionist at a hospital switchboard regularly answers the telephone:
"Whom?"

The nonstandard dialect we see here varies from standard English
by one simple difference in the order of rules. The standard language
marks the objective case—the difference between *who* and *whom*—in a
sentence form which preserves the original subject-object relation:

> Q—She could see WH-someone.

The WH-symbol marks the point to be questioned in this sentence.
When cases are marked in this sentence, the pronoun before the verb
receives the unmarked subjective case and the pronoun after the verb
the marked objective case.

> Q—she(subjective case)—could—see—WH-someone(objective case)

The combination of WH, indefinite pronoun, and objective case is to
be realized later as *whom*. At a later point, a rule of WH-*attraction* is
applied which brings the WH-word to the beginning of the sentence:

> Q—Whom—she—could—see

and finally the Q-marker effects a reversal of the pronoun and auxiliary, yielding the final result:

Whom could she see?

Here the objective case of the pronoun refers to the underlying position of the questioned pronoun as object of the verb.

The nonstandard dialect also marks cases: *I, he, she, they* are subjective forms, and *me, him, her, them* are objective. But the case marking is done after, rather than before, the WH-attraction rule applies. We begin with the same meaningful structure, *Q-She could see WH-someone,* but the first rule to consider is WH-*attraction*:

Q—WH someone—she—could—see

Now the rule of case marking applies. Since both pronouns are before the verb, they are both unmarked:

Q—WH-someone(unmarked)—she(unmarked)—could see.

Finally, the question flip-flop applies, and we have

Who could she see?

The same mechanism applies to all of the nonstandard forms given above.

We can briefly consider another nonstandard grammatical rule, that which yields *It's me* rather than *It's I.* The difference here lies again in the rule of case marking. As noted above, this rule marks pronouns which occur after verbs; but the copula is not included. The nonstandard grammar which gives us *It's me* differs from standard English in only one simple detail—the case-marking rule includes the verb *to be* as well as other verbs. It is certainly not true that this nonstandard grammar neglects the case-marking rule; on the contrary, it applies the rule more generally than standard English here. But the order of the rules is the same as that for the nonstandard grammar just discussed: we get *Who is he?* rather than *Whom is he?* Like the other verbs, the copula marks the pronoun only after WH-attraction has applied.

In all of the examples just given, we can observe a general tendency towards simplification in the nonstandard grammars. There is a strong tendency to simplify the surface subjects—that is, the words which come before the verb. This is most obvious in pronominal apposition. The foregrounded part identifies the person talked about, *my oldest sister;* this person is then "given," and the "new" predication is made with a pronoun subject: *she worked at the Citizens Bank.*

A parallel tendency is seen in the nonstandard grammars which confine the objective marker to positions after the verb. But this tendency to simplify subjects is not confined to standard colloquial English. Sentences such as the following are perfectly grammatical but are seldom if ever found in ordinary speech:

For him to have broken his word so often was a shame.

Most often we find that the rule of "extraposition" has applied, moving the complex subject to the end of the sentence:

It was a shame for him to have broken his word so often.

In general, we find that nonstandard English dialects are not radically different systems from standard English but are instead closely related to it. These dialects show slightly different versions of the same rules, extending and modifying the grammatical processes which are common to all dialects of English.

Any analysis of the nonstandard dialect which pretends to ignore other dialects and the general rules of English will fail (1) because the nonstandard dialect is *not* an isolated system but a part of the sociolinguistic structure of English, and (2) because of the writer's knowledge of standard English. But it would be unrealistic to think that we can write anything but a superficial account of the dialect if we confine our thinking to this one subsystem and ignore whatever progress has been made in the understanding of English grammar.

FOR DISCUSSION AND REVIEW

1 According to Labov, why is it important to study nonstandard language?

2 Labov states that "nonstandard English dialects are not radically different systems from standard English but are instead closely related to it." What evidence does Labov present to document this conclusion?

3 In what ways would an understanding of nonstandard dialect be of value to a teacher in an urban school system?

4 "Nonstandard English," according to Labov, "is a system of rules, different from the standard but not necessarily inferior as a means of communication." What are some of these rules? Illustrate them. How does an understanding of the fundamental rules of Black English help to explain the speech patterns of blacks?

PROJECTS FOR "SOCIAL VARIETIES OF ENGLISH"

1 *Embarrassing situations can arise, according to Roberts (pp. 399–407), when a person moves to a new area and discovers that his or her language is different from that of new acquaintances. Silas Lapham, the rustic hero of William Dean Howells's The Rise of Silas Lapham, moves his family from rural Vermont to Boston's exclusive Beacon Street. Read chapter 14 of Howells's novel, and discuss the embarrassing situations that the Laphams encounter at the dinner party as a result of speech*

differences. Do the Laphams' experiences remind you of any awkward situations in your own life? Describe them, particularly the language involved.

2 *Having read the arguments by William Labov (pp. 439–446), William A. Stewart (pp. 416–426), and William Raspberry (pp. 427–432) in favor of functional bidialectalism, read James Sledd's argument against it in "Bi-Dialectalism: The Linguistics of White Supremacy," English Journal, 58 (1969), 1307–1315. Discuss their ideas. Do you consider the sociologic and economic factors raised by the various authors important? What issues do not appear to be relevant? From an educational point of view, which argument is the strongest? Defend your position in an essay.*

3 *According to Paul Roberts (pp. 399–407), you are presently a member of a college speech community. As a class or individual project, collect vocabulary items that are either unique to your student community or used in an unusual way by the community. Compare your listing with lexicons of collegiate slang in back issues of Current Slang or with items in the Dictionary of American Slang (Wentworth and Flexner).*

4 *In an article entitled "Sense and Nonsense About American Dialects" (PMLA, 81 [1966], 7–17), Raven I. McDavid, Jr., says that "the surest social markers in American English are grammatical forms." Collect examples of grammatical forms used in your community. What social classes are represented?*

5 *The concept of "Standard English" has caused much misunderstanding and debate. For many Americans, "standard" implies that one variety of English is more correct or more functional than other varieties. Research the concept of "Standard English." How, for example, did the concept develop? How do various linguists define it? Is "Standard English" a social dialect? What exactly is the power or mystique of "Standard English"?*

6 *Read John S. Kenyon's "Cultural Levels and Functional Varieties of English" (College English, 10 [October 1948], 31–36) and J. J. Lamberts' "Another Look at Kenyon's Levels" (College English, 24 [November 1962], 141–143). Discuss these classifications of language usage in light of Martin Joos's "The Styles of the Five Clocks" (pp. 408–414).*

7 *Select the work of an author whose characters speak a social or regional variety of English—e.g., William Dean Howells, The Rise of Silas Lapham; Mark Twain, Roughing It (particularly "Buck Fanshaw's Funeral"); Bret Harte, The Luck of Roaring Camp and Other Sketches; Sarah Orne Jewett, The Country of the Pointed Firs; Joel Chandler Harris, Uncle Remus and Br'er Rabbit; William Faulkner, The Sound and the Fury; Willa Cather, My Antonia; or John Steinbeck, The Grapes of Wrath. Identify the dialect presented and discuss the devices that the author uses to represent dialect. Read a passage aloud; how closely does it approximate actual speech?*

SELECTED BIBLIOGRAPHY

Allen, Harold B., and Gary N. Underwood, eds. *Readings in American Dialectology.* New York: Appleton-Century-Crofts, 1971. (An anthology of essays dealing with important regional and social aspects of American dialectology.)

Brasch, Ila Wales, and Walter Milton Brasch. *A Comprehensive Annotated Bibliography of American Black English.* Baton Rouge: Louisiana State University, 1974. (Invaluable bibliography on the subject of Black English.)

Brown, Claude. "The Language of Soul." *Esquire,* April 1968, pp. 88ff. (An examination of one variety of Afro-American speech.)

Cordasco, Frank M. "Knocking Down the Language Walls." *Commonweal,* October 6, 1967, pp. 6–8. (A discussion of legislation to establish bilingual American education programs.)

Dillard, J. L. *All-American English: A History of the English Language in America.* New York: Random House, 1975. (Stresses "Maritime English" and its influence on the American colonists.)

————. *Black English: Its History and Usage in the United States.* New York: Random House, 1972. (An investigation of the ways in which Black English differs from other varieties of American English.)

Fasold, Ralph W. "Distinctive Linguistic Characteristics of Black English." *Linguistics and Language Study: 20th Roundtable Meeting.* Ed. James E. Alatis. Washington, D.C.: Georgetown University Press, 1970. (An examination of the distinctive differences between the nonstandard speech of poor blacks and the speech of whites.)

————, and Walt Wolfram. *Teaching Standard English in the Inner City.* Washington, D.C.: Center for Applied Linguistics, 1970. (Discussion of the problems of teaching Standard English—interesting chapter on "Some Linguistic Features of Negro Dialect.")

Francis, W. Nelson. *The English Language: An Introduction.* New York: W. W. Norton & Company, 1965. (See pp. 244–263 for a consideration of social and educational varieties of English.)

Hernandez-Chavez, Eduardo, Andrew D. Cohen, and Anthony F. Beltramo, eds. *El Lenguaje de los Chicanos.* Washington, D.C.: Center for Applied Linguistics, 1975. (Collection of twenty articles that examine the dynamic coming together of Spanish and English in the Southwest.)

Hinton, Norman D. "The Language of Jazz Musicians." *Publication of the American Dialect Society,* no. 30 (November 1958), 38–48. (A glossary of words used by jazz musicians in their everyday speech.)

Hoffman, Melvin J. "Bi-dialectalism Is Not the Linguistics of White Supremacy: Sense Versus Sensibilities." *The English Record,* 21 (April 1971), 95–102. (An argument supporting the bidialectal approach to the teaching of Standard English and refuting James Sledd's position.)

Houston, Susan. "A Sociolinguistic Consideration of the Black English of Children in Northern Florida." *Language,* 45 (September 1969), 599–607. (A linguistic and sociolinguistic examination of Black English as spoken in one of Florida's northern counties.)

————. "Black English." *Psychology Today,* 6 (March 1973), 45–48. (Describes the two "registers" of Black English—one for in-class use and one for the home environment.)

Ives, Sumner. "Dialect Differentiation in the Stories of Joel Chandler Harris." *American Literature,* 17 (March 1955), 88–96. (A study of the social implications of Harris's dialects.)

————. "A Theory of Literary Dialect." *Tulane Studies in English,* 2 (1950), 137–182. (An essential reference for all students doing work in literary dialects.)

Kenyon, John S. "Cultural Levels and Functional Varieties of English." *College English,* 10 (October 1948), 31–36. (A classification of language that recognizes, first, levels having cultural or social associations and, second, formal and familiar varieties of language usage.)

Labov, William. "The Logic of Nonstandard English." *Linguistics and Language Study: 20th Roundtable Meeting.* Ed. James E. Alatis. Washington, D.C.: Georgetown University Press, 1970. (Refutes theories that Black English lacks logic and sophistication and reveals mental inferiority.)

————. *The Nonstandard Vernacular of the Negro Community: Some Practical Suggestions.* Washington, D.C.: Education Resources Information Center, 1967. (Some advice to teachers concerning bidialectalism for the speaker of a nonstandard dialect.)

————. *The Social Stratification of English in New York City.* Washington, D.C.: Center for Applied Linguistics, 1966. (A landmark sociolinguistic study of New York City speech.)

————. "Stages in the Acquisition of Standard English." *Social Dialects and Language Learning.* Ed. Roger W. Shuy. Champaign, Illinois: NCTE, 1964. (An investigation of the acquisition of Standard English by children in New York City.)

Lamberts, J. J. "Another Look at Kenyon's Levels." *College English,* 24 (November 1962), 141–143. (A reassessment of John S. Kenyon's classification of cultural levels and functional varieties of English.)

McDavid, Raven I., Jr. "Sense and Nonsense about American Dialects." *PMLA,* 81 (1966), 7–17. (Exposes several widespread misconceptions about American dialects.)

McDowell, Tremaine. "The Use of Negro Dialect by Harriet Beecher Stowe." *American Speech,* 6 (June 1931), 322–326. (A study in literary dialect.)

Mencken, H. L. *The American Language: The Fourth Edition and the Two Supplements.* Abridged and ed. Raven I. McDavid, Jr. New York: Alfred A. Knopf, 1963. (A classic study of American English.)

Miller, Mary R. "Bilingualism in Northern New England." *Publication of the American Dialect Society,* no. 52 (November 1969), 1–23. (A detailed study of French-English bilingualism.)

Nash, Rose. "Englañol: More Language Contact in Puerto Rico." *American Speech,* 46 (Spring–Summer 1971), 106–122. (A discussion of Spanish-influenced English.)

————. "Spanglish: Language Contact in Puerto Rico." *American Speech,* 45 (Fall–Winter 1970), 223–233. (A study of the linguistic dilemma caused by the mixing of two languages in Puerto Rico.)

O'Neil, Wayne. "The Politics of Bidialectalism." *College English,* 33 (1972), 433–438. (Argues that bidialectalism is aimed at maintaining the social status quo—the inequality of blacks in a predominantly white society.)

Ortego, Philip D. "Schools for Mexican-Americans: Between Two Cultures." *Saturday Review,* April 17, 1971, pp. 62–64, 80–81. (A discussion of bilingual education for Mexican-American children.)

Pederson, Lee A. "Negro Speech in *The Adventures of Huckleberry Finn.*" *Mark Twain Journal,* 13 (1966), 1–4. (An examination of the literary representation of Negro dialect in Twain's classic novel.)

————. "Terms of Abuse for Some Chicago Social Groups." *Publication of the*

American Dialect Society, no. 42 (November 1964), 26–48. (A detailed study of terms of abuse and contempt for members of racial, religious, and nationality groups in Chicago.)

Pixton, William H. "A Contemporary Dilemma: The Question of Standard English." *College Composition and Communication,* 5 (1974), 247–253. (Argues for the use of Standard English by blacks.)

Rawles, Myrtle Read. " 'Boontling'—Esoteric Speech of Boonville, California." *Western Folklore,* 25 (1966), 93–103. (A discussion of the lingo used by the people of Boonville.)

Sawyer, Janet B. "Social Aspects of Bilingualism in San Antonio, Texas." *Publication of the American Dialect Society,* no. 41 (April 1964), 7–15. (A study of the frustrations and social pressures experienced by Mexican-Americans as a result of being caught between two cultures.)

Shuy, Roger W. "Detroit Speech: Careless, Awkward, and Inconsistent, or Systematic, Graceful, and Regular?" *Elementary English,* 45 (May 1968), 565–569. (A discussion of nonstandard speech in Detroit, Michigan.)

————. "Some Useful Myths in Social Dialectology." *The Florida FL Reporter,* 11 (Spring–Fall 1973), 17–20, 55. (Identifies several myths that, though oversimplifications, are useful to social dialectologists.)

Sledd, James. "Bi-Dialectalism: The Linguistics of White Supremacy." *English Journal,* 58 (1969), 1307–1315. (Argues against linguists and teachers who advocate bidialectal programs.)

Smith, Riley B. "Research Perspectives on American Black English: A Brief Historical Sketch." *American Speech,* 49 (Spring–Summer 1974), 24–39. (A bibliographical essay with a historical perspective.)

Stewart, William A. "Continuity and Change in American Negro Dialects." *The Florida FL Reporter,* 6, i (1968), 3–4, 14–16, 18. (An examination of some syntactic features of black speech.)

Stockton, Eric. "Poe's Use of Negro Dialect in 'The Gold-Bug.' " *Studies in Language and Linguistics in Honor of Charles C. Fries.* Ed. Albert H. Marckwardt. Ann Arbor: The English Language Institute, The University of Michigan, 1964. (An analysis of Jupiter's speech as an example of literary dialect used by pre-Civil War writers.)

Teschner, Richard V., Garland Bills, and Jerry R. Craddock. *Spanish and English of United States Hispanos: A Critical, Annotated, Linguistic Bibliography.* Washington, D.C.: Center for Applied Linguistics, 1975. (An invaluable research tool for studies in this area.)

Williamson, Juanita V., and Virginia M. Burke, eds. *A Various Language: Perspectives on American Dialects.* New York: Holt, Rinehart & Winston, Inc., 1971. (An anthology of essential articles dealing with American dialects, regional and social.)

Wolfram, Walt. *Sociolinguistic Aspects of Assimilation: Puerto Rican English in New York City.* Washington, D.C.: Center for Applied Linguistics, 1974. (A thorough study of the language problems encountered by Puerto Ricans in New York City.)

————, and Ralph W. Fasold. *The Study of Social Dialects in American English.* Englewood Cliffs, N.J.: Prentice-Hall, 1974. (An introduction to the linguist's view of social variation in language—special attention given to possible educational applications.)

PART EIGHT

The Language of the Body: Kinesics and Proxemics

When people think of language, they tend to consider it primarily in terms of the words that they say or write. To look at language in this way, however, is to ignore the significant role played by nonverbal communication. For example, it has been estimated that in a conversation between two people, only 35 percent of the message is conveyed by the words. The remaining 65 percent is communicated nonverbally by how they speak, move, gesture, and by how they handle spatial relationships. Thus, both *kinesics*, the study of movement (related to Greek *kinēsis*, movement), and *proxemics*, the study of the ways in which space is handled (related to Latin *proximus*, nearest), are important aspects of nonverbal communication. Awareness of their importance is not really new—writers and artists have long effectively utilized their observations of nonverbal communication. But for most of us, the idea that "language is more than words" *is* new; we have not sufficiently realized the importance of kinesics and proxemics to all kinds of interpersonal relationships. We need to study them systematically, especially because of their many practical applications in medicine, diplomacy, education, race relations, business negotiations—any situation in which people interact and need to understand one another. The first articles in this section provide a general introduction to nonverbal communication; they are followed by more detailed studies of specific kinds of kinesic and proxemic situations.

1

The Sounds
of Silence

Until recently, most Americans were largely unaware of the existence, let alone the importance, of nonverbal communication. Yet it is omnipresent in interpersonal situations and powerfully affects our judgments about other people and theirs about us. One of the men who has pioneered in the study of nonverbal communication is anthropologist Edward Hall. In this article, Edward and Mildred Hall discuss the crucial effects that "your posture, gestures, facial expression, costume, the way you walk, even your treatment of time and space and material things" may have, and emphasize the importance of respecting the power and diversity of "the sounds of silence."

Edward T. Hall and
Mildred Reed Hall

BOB LEAVES his apartment at 8:15 A.M. and stops at the corner drugstore for breakfast. Before he can speak, the counterman says, "The usual?" Bob nods yes. While he savors his Danish, a fat man pushes onto the adjoining stool and overflows into his space. Bob scowls and the man pulls himself in as much as he can. Bob has sent two messages without speaking a syllable.

Henry has an appointment to meet Arthur at 11 o'clock; he arrives at 11:30. Their conversation is friendly, but Arthur retains a lingering hostility. Henry has unconsciously communicated that he doesn't think the appointment is very important or that Arthur is a person who needs to be treated with respect.

George is talking to Charley's wife at a party. Their conversation is entirely trivial, yet Charley glares at them suspiciously. Their physical proximity and the movements of their eyes reveal that they are powerfully attracted to each other.

José Ybarra and Sir Edmund Jones are at the same party and it is important for them to establish a cordial relationship for business reasons. Each is trying to be warm and friendly, yet they will part with mutual distrust and their business transaction will probably fall through. José, in Latin fashion, moved closer and closer to Sir Edmund as they spoke, and this movement was miscommunicated as pushiness to Sir Edmund, who kept backing away from this intimacy, and this was miscommunicated to José as coldness. The silent languages of Latin and English cultures are more difficult to learn than their spoken languages.

In each of these cases, we see the subtle power of nonverbal communication. The only language used throughout most of the history of humanity (in evolutionary terms, vocal communication is relatively recent), it is the first form of communication you learn. You use this preverbal language, consciously and unconsciously, every day to tell other people how you feel about yourself and them. This language includes your posture, gestures, facial expressions, costume, the way you walk, even your treatment of time and space and material things. All people communicate on several different levels at the same time but are usually aware of only the verbal dialog and don't realize that they respond to nonverbal messages. But when a person says one thing and really believes something else, the discrepancy between the two can usually be sensed. Nonverbal-communication systems are much less subject to the conscious deception that often occurs in verbal systems. When we find ourselves thinking, "I don't know what it is about him, but he doesn't seem sincere," it's usually this lack of congruity between a person's words and his behavior that makes us anxious and uncomfortable.

Few of us realize how much we all depend on body movement in our conversation or are aware of the hidden rules that govern listening behavior. But we know instantly whether or not the person we're talking to is "tuned in" and we're very sensitive to any breach in listening etiquette. In white middle-class American culture, when someone wants to show he is listening to someone else, he looks either at the other person's face or, specifically, at his eyes, shifting his gaze from one eye to the other.

If you observe a person conversing, you'll notice that he indicates he's listening by nodding his head. He also makes little "Hmm" noises. If he agrees with what's being said, he may give a vigorous nod. To show pleasure or affirmation, he smiles; if he has some reservations, he looks skeptical by raising an eyebrow or pulling down the corners of his mouth. If a participant wants to terminate the conversation, he may start shifting his body position, stretching his legs, crossing or uncrossing them, bobbing his foot or diverting his gaze from the speaker. The more he fidgets, the more the speaker becomes aware that he has lost his audience. As a last measure, the listener may look at his watch to indicate the imminent end of the conversation.

Talking and listening are so intricately intertwined that a person cannot do one without the other. Even when one is alone and talking to oneself, there is part of the brain that speaks while another part listens. In all conversations, the listener is positively or negatively reinforcing the speaker all the time. He may even guide the conversation without knowing it, by laughing or frowning or dismissing the argument with a wave of his hand.

The language of the eyes—another age-old way of exchanging feelings—is both subtle and complex. Not only do men and women use their eyes differently but there are class, generation, regional, ethnic and national cultural differences. Americans often complain about the way foreigners stare at people or hold a glance too long. Most Americans look away from someone who is using his eyes in an unfamiliar way because it makes them self-conscious. If a man looks at another man's wife in a certain way, he's asking for trouble, as indicated earlier. But he might not be ill mannered or seeking to challenge the husband. He might be a European in this country who hasn't learned our visual mores. Many American women visiting France or Italy are acutely embarrassed because, for the first time in their lives, men really look at them—their eyes, hair, nose, lips, breasts, hips, legs, thighs, knees, ankles, feet, clothes, hairdo, even their walk. These same women, once they have become used to being looked at, often return to the United States and are overcome with the feeling that "No one ever really looks at me anymore."

Analyzing the mass of data on the eyes, it is possible to sort out at least three ways in which the eyes are used to communicate: dominance *vs.* submission, involvement *vs.* detachment and positive *vs.* negative attitude. In addition, there are three levels of consciousness and control, which can be categorized as follows: (1) conscious use of the eyes to communicate, such as the flirting blink and the intimate nose-wrinkling squint; (2) the very extensive category of unconscious but learned behavior governing where the eyes are directed and when (this unwritten set of rules dictates how and under what circumstances the sexes, as well as people of all status categories, look at each other); and (3) the response of the eye itself, which is completely outside both awareness and control—changes in the cast (the sparkle) of the eye and the pupillary reflex.

The eye is unlike any other organ of the body, for it is an extension of the brain. The unconscious pupillary reflex and the cast of the eye have been known by people of Middle Eastern origin for years—although most are unaware of their knowledge. Depending on the context, Arabs and others look either directly at the eyes or deeply *into* the eyes of their interlocutor. We became aware of this in the Middle East several years ago while looking at jewelry. The merchant suddenly started to push a particular bracelet at a customer and said, "You buy this one."

What interested us was that the bracelet was not the one that had been consciously selected by the purchaser. But the merchant, watching the pupils of the eyes, knew what the purchaser really wanted to buy. Whether he specifically knew *how* he knew is debatable.

A psychologist at the University of Chicago, Eckhard Hess, was the first to conduct systematic studies of the pupillary reflex. His wife remarked one evening, while watching him reading in bed, that he must be very interested in the text because his pupils were dilated. Following up on this, Hess slipped some pictures of nudes into a stack of photographs that he gave to his male assistant. Not looking at the photographs but watching his assistant's pupils, Hess was able to tell precisely when the assistant came to the nudes. In further experiments, Hess retouched the eyes in a photograph of a woman. In one print, he made the pupils small, in another, large; nothing else was changed. Subjects who were given the photographs found the woman with the dilated pupils much more attractive. Any man who has had the experience of seeing a woman look at him as her pupils widen with reflex speed knows that she's flashing him a message.

The eye-sparkle phenomenon frequently turns up in our interviews of couples in love. It's apparently one of the first reliable clues in the other person that love is genuine. To date, there is no scientific data to explain eye sparkle; no investigation of the pupil, the cornea or even the white sclera of the eye shows how the sparkle originates. Yet we all know it when we see it.

One common situation for most people involves the use of the eyes in the street and in public. Although eye behavior follows a definite set of rules, the rules vary according to the place, the needs and feelings of the people, and their ethnic background. For urban whites, once they're within definite recognition distance (16–32 feet for people with average eyesight), there is mutual avoidance of eye contact—unless they want something specific: a pickup, a handout or information of some kind. In the West and in small towns generally, however, people are much more likely to look at and greet one another, even if they're strangers.

It's permissible to look at people if they're beyond recognition distance; but once inside this sacred zone, you can only steal a glance at strangers. You *must* greet friends, however; to fail to do so is insulting. Yet, to stare too fixedly even at them is considered rude and hostile. Of course, all of these rules are variable.

A great many blacks, for example, greet each other in public even if they don't know each other. To blacks, most eye behavior of whites has the effect of giving the impression that they aren't there, but this is due to white avoidance of eye contact with *anyone* in the street.

Another very basic difference between people of different ethnic backgrounds is their sense of territoriality and how they handle space.

This is the silent communication, or miscommunication, that caused friction between Mr. Ybarra and Sir Edmund Jones in our earlier example. We know from research that everyone has around himself an invisible bubble of space that contracts and expands depending on several factors: his emotional state, the activity he's performing at the time and his cultural background. This bubble is a kind of mobile territory that he will defend against intrusion. If he is accustomed to close personal distance between himself and others, his bubble will be smaller than that of someone who's accustomed to greater personal distance. People of North European heritage—English, Scandinavian, Swiss and German—tend to avoid contact. Those whose heritage is Italian, French, Spanish, Russian, Latin American or Middle Eastern like close personal contact.

People are very sensitive to any intrusion into their spatial bubble. If someone stands too close to you, your first instinct is to back up. If that's not possible, you lean away and pull yourself in, tensing your muscles. If the intruder doesn't respond to these body signals, you may then try to protect yourself, using a briefcase, umbrella or raincoat. Women—especially when traveling alone—often plant their pocketbook in such a way that no one can get very close to them. As a last resort, you may move to another spot and position yourself behind a desk or a chair that provides screening. Everyone tries to adjust the space around himself in a way that's comfortable for him; most often, he does this unconsciously.

Emotions also have a direct effect on the size of a person's territory. When you're angry or under stress, your bubble expands and you require more space. New York psychiatrist Augustus Kinzel found a difference in what he calls Body-Buffer Zones between violent and nonviolent prison inmates. Dr. Kinzel conducted experiments in which each prisoner was placed in the center of a small room and then Dr. Kinzel slowly walked toward him. Nonviolent prisoners allowed him to come quite close, while prisoners with a history of violent behavior couldn't tolerate his proximity and reacted with some vehemence.

Apparently, people under stress experience other people as looming larger and closer than they actually are. Studies of schizophrenic patients have indicated that they sometimes have a distorted perception of space, and several psychiatrists have reported patients who experience their body boundaries as filling up an entire room. For these patients, anyone who comes into the room is actually inside their body, and such an intrusion may trigger a violent outburst.

Unfortunately, there is little detailed information about normal people who live in highly congested urban areas. We do know, of course, that the noise, pollution, dirt, crowding and confusion of our cities induce feelings of stress in most of us, and stress leads to a need for greater space. The man who's packed into a subway, jostled in the street, crowded into an elevator and forced to work all day in a bull pen or in a small office without auditory or visual privacy is going to be very stressed at the end of his day. He needs places that provide relief from constant overstimulation of his nervous system. Stress from over-crowding is cumulative and people can tolerate more crowding early in the day than later; note the increased bad temper during the evening rush hour as compared with the morning melee. Certainly one factor in people's desire to commute by car is the need for privacy and relief from crowding (except, often, from other cars); it may be the only time of the day when nobody can intrude.

In crowded public places, we tense our muscles and hold ourselves stiff, and thereby communicate to others our desire not to intrude on their space and, above all, not to touch them. We also avoid eye con-tact, and the total effect is that of someone who has "tuned out." Walking along the street, our bubble expands slightly as we move in a stream of strangers, taking care not to bump into them. In the office, at meetings, in restaurants, our bubble keeps changing as it adjusts to the activity at hand.

Most white middle-class Americans use four main distances in their business and social relations: intimate, personal, social and public. Each of these distances has a near and a far phase and is accompanied by changes in the volume of the voice. Intimate distance varies from direct physical contact with another person to a distance of six to eighteen inches and is used for our most private activities—caressing another person or making love. At this distance, you are overwhelmed by sen-sory inputs from the other person—heat from the body, tactile stimula-tion from the skin, the fragrance of perfume, even the sound of breathing —all of which literally envelop you. Even at the far phase, you're still within easy touching distance. In general, the use of intimate dis-tance in public between adults is frowned on. It's also much too close for strangers, except under conditions of extreme crowding.

In the second zone—personal distance—the close phase is one and a half to two and a half feet; it's at this distance that wives usually stand from their husbands in public. If another woman moves into this zone, the wife will most likely be disturbed. The far phase—two and a half to four feet—is the distance used to "keep someone at arm's length" and is the most common spacing used by people in conversation.

The third zone—social distance—is employed during business trans-actions or exchanges with a clerk or repairman. People who work to-gether tend to use close social distance—four to seven feet. This is also the distance for conversations at social gatherings. To stand at this dis-tance from someone who is seated has a dominating effect (e.g., teacher to pupil, boss to secretary). The far phase of the third zone—seven to twelve feet—is where people stand when someone says, "Stand back so I can look at you." This distance lends a formal tone to business or social discourse. In an executive office, the desk serves to keep people at this distance.

The fourth zone—public distance—is used by teachers in classrooms or speakers at public gatherings. At its farthest phase—25 feet and beyond—it is used for important public figures. Violations of this distance can lead to serious complications. During his 1970 U.S. visit, the president of France, Georges Pompidou, was harassed by pickets in Chicago, who were permitted to get within touching distance. Since pickets in France are kept behind barricades a block or more away, the president was outraged by this insult to his person, and President Nixon was obliged to communicate his concern as well as offer his personal apologies.

It is interesting to note how American pitchmen and panhandlers exploit the unwritten, unspoken conventions of eye and distance. Both take advantage of the fact that once explicit eye contact is established, it is rude to look away, because to do so means to brusquely dismiss the other person and his needs. Once having caught the eye of his mark, the panhandler then locks on, not letting go until he moves through the public zone, the social zone, the personal zone and, finally, into the intimate sphere, where people are most vulnerable.

Touch also is an important part of the constant stream of communication that takes place between people. A light touch, a firm touch, a blow, a caress are all communications. In an effort to break down barriers among people, there's been a recent upsurge in group-encounter activities, in which strangers are encouraged to touch one another. In special situations such as these, the rules for not touching are broken with group approval and people gradually lose some of their inhibitions.

Although most people don't realize it, space is perceived and distances are set not by vision alone but with all the senses. Auditory space is perceived with the ears, thermal space with the skin, kinesthetic space with the muscles of the body and olfactory space with the nose. And, once again, it's one's culture that determines how his senses are programmed—which sensory information ranks highest and lowest. The important thing to remember is that culture is very persistent. In this country, we've noted the existence of culture patterns that determine distance between people in the third and fourth generations of some families, despite their prolonged contact with people of very different cultural heritages.

Whenever there is great cultural distance between two people, there are bound to be problems arising from differences in behavior and expectations. An example is the American couple who consulted a psychiatrist about their marital problems. The husband was from New England and had been brought up by reserved parents who taught him to control his emotions and to respect the need for privacy. His wife was from an Italian family and had been brought up in close contact with all the members of her large family, who were extremely warm, volatile and demonstrative.

When the husband came home after a hard day at the office, dragging his feet and longing for peace and quiet, his wife would rush to him and smother him. Clasping his hands, rubbing his brow, crooning over his weary head, she never left him alone. But when the wife was upset or anxious about her day, the husband's response was to withdraw completely and leave her alone. No comforting, no affectionate embrace, no attention—just solitude. The woman became convinced her husband didn't love her and, in desperation, she consulted a psychiatrist. Their problem wasn't basically psychological but cultural.

Why has man developed all these different ways of communicating messages without words? One reason is that people don't like to spell out certain kinds of messages. We prefer to find other ways of showing our feelings. This is especially true in relationships as sensitive as courtship. Men don't like to be rejected and most women don't want to turn a man down bluntly. Instead, we work out subtle ways of encouraging or discouraging each other that save face and avoid confrontations.

How a person handles space in dating others is an obvious and very sensitive indicator of how he or she feels about the other person. On a first date, if a woman sits or stands so close to a man that he is acutely conscious of her physical presence—inside the intimate-distance zone— the man usually construes it to mean that she is encouraging him. However, before the man starts moving in on the woman, he should be sure what message she's really sending; otherwise, he risks bruising his ego. What is close to someone of North European background may be neutral or distant to someone of Italian heritage. Also, women sometimes use space as a way of misleading a man and there are few things that put men off more than women who communicate contradictory messages—such as women who cuddle up and then act insulted when a man takes the next step.

How does a woman communicate interest in a man? In addition to such familiar gambits as smiling at him, she may glance shyly at him, blush and then look away. Or she may give him a real come-on look and move in very close when he approaches. She may touch his arm and ask for a light. As she leans forward to light her cigarette, she may brush him lightly, enveloping him in her perfume. She'll probably continue to smile at him and she may use what ethologists call preening gestures —touching the back of her hair, thrusting her breasts forward, tilting her hips as she stands or crossing her legs if she's seated, perhaps even exposing one thigh or putting a hand on her thigh and stroking it.

She may also stroke her wrists as she converses or show the palm of her hand as a way of gaining his attention. Her skin may be unusually flushed or quite pale, her eyes brighter, the pupils larger.

If a man sees a woman whom he wants to attract, he tries to present himself by his posture and stance as someone who is self-assured. He moves briskly and confidently. When he catches the eye of the woman, he may hold her glance a little longer than normal. If he gets an encouraging smile, he'll move in close and engage her in small talk. As they converse, his glance shifts over her face and body. He, too, may make preening gestures—straightening his tie, smoothing his hair or shooting his cuffs.

How do people learn body language? The same way they learn spoken language—by observing and imitating people around them as they're growing up. Little girls imitate their mothers or an older female. Little boys imitate their fathers or a respected uncle or a character on television. In this way, they learn the gender signals appropriate for their sex. Regional, class and ethnic patterns of body behavior are also learned in childhood and persist throughout life.

Such patterns of masculine and feminine body behavior vary widely from one culture to another. In America, for example, women stand with their thighs together. Many walk with their pelvis tipped slightly forward and their upper arms close to their body. When they sit, they cross their legs at the knee or, if they are well past middle age, they may cross their ankles. American men hold their arms away from their body, often swinging them as they walk. They stand with their legs apart (an extreme example is the cowboy, with legs apart and thumbs tucked into his belt). When they sit, they put their feet on the floor with legs apart and, in some parts of the country, they cross their legs by putting one ankle on the other knee.

Leg behavior indicates sex, status and personality. It also indicates whether or not one is at ease or is showing respect or disrespect for the other person. Young Latin-American males avoid crossing their legs. In their world of *machismo*, the preferred position for young males when with one another (if there is no older dominant male present to whom they must show respect) is to sit on the base of their spine with their leg muscles relaxed and their feet wide apart. Their respect position is like our military equivalent; spine straight, heels and ankles together— almost identical to that displayed by properly brought up young women in New England in the early part of this century.

American women who sit with their legs spread apart in the presence of males are *not* normally signaling a come-on—they are simply (and often unconsciously) sitting like men. Middle-class women in the presence of other women to whom they are very close may on occasion throw themselves down on a soft chair or sofa and let themselves go. This is a signal that nothing serious will be taken up. Males, on the other hand, lean back and prop their legs up on the nearest object.

The way we walk, similarly, indicates status, respect, mood and ethnic or cultural affiliation. The many variants of the female walk are too well known to go into here, except to say that a man would have to be blind not to be turned on by the way some women walk—a fact that made Mae West rich before scientists ever studied these matters. To white Americans, some French middle-class males walk in a way that is both humorous and suspect. There is a bounce and looseness to the French walk, as though the parts of the body were somehow unrelated. Jacques Tati, the French movie actor, walks this way; so does the great mime, Marcel Marceau.

Blacks and whites in America—with the exception of middle- and upper-middle-class professionals of both groups—move and walk very differently from each other. To the blacks, whites often seem incredibly stiff, almost mechanical in their movements. Black males, on the other hand, have a looseness and coordination that frequently makes whites a little uneasy; it's too different, too integrated, too alive, too male. Norman Mailer has said that squares walk from the shoulders, like bears, but blacks and hippies walk from the hips, like cats.

All over the world, people walk not only in their own characteristic way but have walks that communicate the nature of their involvement with whatever it is they're doing. The purposeful walk of North Europeans is an important component of proper behavior on the job. Any male who has been in the military knows how essential it is to walk properly (which makes for a continuing source of tension between blacks and whites in the Service). The quick shuffle of servants in the Far East in the old days was a show of respect. On the island of Truk, when we last visited, the inhabitants even had a name for the respectful walk that one used when in the presence of a chief or when walking past a chief's house. The term was *sufan,* which meant to be humble and respectful.

The notion that people communicate volumes by their gestures, facial expressions, posture and walk is not new; actors, dancers, writers and psychiatrists have long been aware of it. Only in recent years, however, have scientists begun to make systematic observations of body motions. Ray L. Birdwhistell of the University of Pennsylvania is one of the pioneers in body-motion research and coined the term kinesics to describe this field. He developed an elaborate notation system to record both facial and body movements, using an approach similar to that of the linguist, who studies the basic elements of speech. Birdwhistell and other kinesicists such as Albert Sheflen, Adam Kendon and William Condon take movies of people interacting. They run the film over and over again, often at reduced speed for frame-by-frame analysis, so that they can observe even the slightest body movements not perceptible at normal interaction speeds. These movements are then recorded in notebooks for later analysis.

To appreciate the importance of nonverbal-communication systems, consider the unskilled inner-city black looking for a job. His handling of time and space alone is sufficiently different from the white middle-class pattern to create great misunderstandings on both sides. The black is told to appear for a job interview at a certain time. He arrives late. The white interviewer concludes from his tardy arrival that the black is irresponsible and not really interested in the job. What the interviewer doesn't know is that the black time system (often referred to by blacks as C. P. T.—colored people's time) isn't the same as that of whites. In the words of a black student who had been told to make an appointment to see his professor: "Man, you *must* be putting me on. I never had an appointment in my life."

The black job applicant, having arrived late for his interview, may further antagonize the white interviewer by his posture and his eye behavior. Perhaps he slouches and avoids looking at the interviewer; to him, this is playing it cool. To the interviewer, however, he may well look shifty and sound uninterested. The interviewer has failed to notice the actual signs of interest and eagerness in the black's behavior, such as the subtle shift in the quality of the voice—a gentle and tentative excitement—an almost imperceptible change in the cast of the eyes and a relaxing of the jaw muscles.

Moreover, correct reading of black-white behavior is continually complicated by the fact that both groups are comprised of individuals—some of whom try to accommodate and some of whom make it a point of pride *not* to accommodate. At present, this means that many Americans, when thrown into contact with one another, are in the precarious position of not knowing which pattern applies. Once identified and analyzed, nonverbal-communication systems can be taught, like a foreign language. Without this training, we respond to nonverbal communications in terms of our own culture; we read everyone's behavior as if it were our own, and thus we often misunderstand it.

Several years ago in New York City, there was a program for sending children from predominantly black and Puerto Rican low-income neighborhoods to summer school in a white upper-class neighborhood on the East Side. One morning, a group of young black and Puerto Rican boys raced down the street, shouting and screaming and overturning garbage cans on their way to school. A doorman from an apartment building nearby chased them and cornered one of them inside a building. The boy drew a knife and attacked the doorman. This tragedy would not have occurred if the doorman had been familiar with the behavior of boys from low-income neighborhoods, where such antics are routine and socially acceptable and where pursuit would be expected to invite a violent response.

The language of behavior is extremely complex. Most of us are lucky to have under control one subcultural system—the one that reflects our sex, class, generation and geographic region within the United States. Because of its complexity, efforts to isolate bits of nonverbal communication and generalize from them are in vain; you don't become an instant expert on people's behavior by watching them at cocktail parties. Body language isn't something that's independent of the person, something that can be donned and doffed like a suit of clothes.

Our research and that of our colleagues has shown that, far from being a superficial form of communication that can be consciously manipulated, nonverbal-communication systems are interwoven into the fabric of the personality and, as sociologist Erving Goffman has demonstrated, into society itself. They are the warp and woof of daily interactions with others and they influence how one expresses oneself, how one experiences oneself as a man or a woman.

Nonverbal communications signal to members of your own group what kind of person you are, how you feel about others, how you'll fit into and work in a group, whether you're assured or anxious, the degree to which you feel comfortable with the standards of your own culture, as well as deeply significant feelings about the self, including the state of your own psyche. For most of us, it's difficult to accept the reality of another's behavioral system. And, of course, none of us will ever become fully knowledgeable of the importance of every nonverbal signal. But as long as each of us realizes the power of these signals, this society's diversity can be a source of great strength rather than a further—and subtly powerful—source of division.

FOR DISCUSSION AND REVIEW

1 Give some examples of nonverbal positive and negative reinforcement in talking and listening situations.

2 Describe the phenomenon the Halls call "pupillary reflex." Have you ever noticed any examples of it? Explain.

3 To what extent, according to the Halls, does ethnic background produce differences in nonverbal communication behavior? Give some examples of situations in which these differences may be of great importance.

4 What do the Halls mean by the "invisible bubble of space" surrounding each of us? What factors may affect its size at any given time?

5 What are the four distances used by most white middle-class Americans in social and business situations? Describe the varying sensory inputs at each distance (auditory, olfactory, tactile, visual, etc.). Are there significant cross-cultural differences? Explain.

6 According to the Halls, how and when do people learn body lan-

guage? Why have nonverbal communication systems developed?

7 What are "preening gestures"? Give some examples. Are they used only by humans? (Before answering, be sure you know what an *ethologist* is.)

8 How important is "leg behavior"? How much does it vary between men and women and among different cultures?

9 Discuss the implications of the Halls' statement: "Once identified and analyzed, nonverbal-communication systems can be taught, like a foreign language. Without this training, we respond to nonverbal communications in terms of our own culture; we read everyone's behavior as if it were our own, and thus we often misunderstand it."

2

Learning to Read Gestures

In this informative essay, Gerard I. Nierenberg and Henry H. Calero, practicing consultants in the field of labor negotiations, discuss the importance of the nonverbal component of the communication process. They stress the need to understand such basic concepts as gesture clusters, contextual readings, and congruence if one is to learn to understand gestures. In addition to comments on the psychological complexities of gestures, the authors suggest some practical exercises for learning to interpret body language.

Gerard I. Nierenberg
and Henry H. Calero

A N AIRPORT is an excellent spot for viewing the entire human emotional spectrum. As travelers arrive and depart, you can see the woman who is very apprehensive about flying pinching the fleshy part of her hand for reassurance, as if she were saying to herself, "It's going to be all right." In the same manner people say, "I had to pinch myself to make sure that it wasn't a dream." A male waiting for departure time may also be unsure about flying. However, he is sitting in a rigid, upright position with his ankles locked. His hands are clenched together, making one big fist, while he rhythmically massages one thumb against the other on top of his interlocked hands. These gestures indicate a nervous attitude.

Walking away from the departure area, you see three men in telephone booths. One of them (Figure 1) is standing with his body at attention. His coat is buttoned. He gives the impression that whoever he is talking to is very important to him. He might be a salesman talking to a customer on the telephone as if he were actually in his presence.

The second caller's body is relaxed (Figure 2). He slouches over, shifts his weight from foot to foot, and rests his chin on his chest. He appears to be looking at the floor and nods his head as if saying, "Yeah, yeah." Reading this person further, you get the impression that he is comfortable but possibly bored with the conversation and attempting to hide the fact. The receiver of the call can be taken for granted. It is probably his wife or an old friend.

From these clues, can you visualize how a third caller might look as he talks to his girlfriend? This caller's face is hidden. His hunched shoulder may be concealing it from view or his body may be completely turned away from passers-by. His head is probably tilted to one side, and he handles the phone as if it were the object of his affection (Figure 3).

As you move toward the baggage-claim area, you may see a family group, which you can identify by the striking similarity in the way they all walk. Others on their way to the baggage-claim counter who have been met by family or friends usually appear the happiest and walk with a great deal of enthusiasm. Those who are waiting to be met keep rising on their toes and looking around.

During our brief visit to the airport we have become aware of the different actions of people. Merely by noting a variety of gestures we have been able to make guesses about people: attitudes, relationships, and situations. We have even conjured up an image of the person on the other end of the telephone line. Our observations have been of people acting and reacting in the real world, not in an isolated laboratory situation. In short, we have been exposed to the vast field of nonverbal communication that complements and supplements and can even displace verbal exchange. . . .

Life, the True Testing Ground

Automobile manufacturers subject any new car accessory to extensive testing. However, it is not until the accessory is exposed to real-life situations that its success or failure can be definitely determined. Some years ago the Ford Motor Company decided to improve the safety of its automobile by adding an accessory called the vacuum automatic door lock, a device designed to lock the door automatically as soon as the car reached a speed of 9 m.p.h. After cars with the new locks were on the market, however, Ford began receiving complaint after complaint.

Whenever the buyers of these cars went to automatic car-washing stations they had trouble. As the automobile went down the washing line, the wheels were spun on the whitewall automatic washers and the car reached a relative speed of 9 m.p.h. The doors automatically locked, and at the end of the car-wash production line the drivers had to get a locksmith to pick the lock so they could get back into their own automobiles. So Ford went back to the drawing board and back to manually operated door locks.

In the same manner, life situations also offer better tests for the

1. The salesman

2. The husband

3. The lover

interpretation of gestures. The comprehension of gestures has not been achieved through the limited behavioral-laboratory approach, one which attempts to study individual parts abstracted from meaningful groups of gestures. It is a human process, and the methods that men have intuitively used for hundreds of thousands of years to understand one another naturally lend themselves as techniques for understanding gestures.

Our own awareness of nonverbal communications was an outgrowth of our interest in developing and teaching the art of negotiating. When we met and joined together to present workshops and seminars on negotiating to top executives in the United States and abroad, we were both aware of the vital role nonverbal communications play in every negotiating situation. We found that verbal exchange does not operate in a vacuum; rather, it is a complex process involving people, words, and body movements. It was only by considering these elements together that we could follow the progress of a negotiation.

We found that one limiting factor to studying gestures has been the lack of a simple system of transcribing or reproducing an actual situation where individuals could be thoroughly observed and the interaction or expressive behavior between subjects studied systematically. With the videotape recorder we were able to eliminate this first difficulty.

Ray Birdwhistell, senior research scientist at Eastern Pennsylvania Research Institute, is presently engaged in filming encounters and noting them through kinesics, a science that sets out to analyze individual gestures by considering their component parts. This book considers the problem of nonverbal communication in a different manner. We have considered Norbert Wiener's admonition in *Cybernetics:* "Many a missionary has fixed his own misunderstanding of a primitive language as law eternal in the process of reducing it to writing. There is much in the social habits of a people which is dispersed and distorted by the mere act of making inquiries about it." In addition to viewing individual gestures we present the myriad of attitudes expressed by not one gesture but a series of related ones. These we call gesture-clusters. They are groups of nonverbal communications associated with different attitudes. The gestures that comprise a cluster can occur at the same time, as locking arms and ankles and making a fist, or occur one after the other. In videotape recording we have a useful tool for capturing and preserving these gesture-clusters, and the seminar participants' role-playing for gesture-analysis in negotiating situations have provided us with our raw material.

We have held hundreds of seminars with thousands of participants and have recorded 2,500 negotiating situations. Our audiences have not only provided the research material on gestures but also acted as the researchers. We presented the gestures to them individually and in videotaped clusters and then asked our seminar audiences what they recognized, what the feeling or message of the nonverbal communication was. We first merely wanted the audience to recognize the gestures by separating them from nonmeaningful body movements. We then wanted the audience to give gestures their meaning.

As a result of many discussions it came to our attention that when the audiences began to recognize the meaning of certain gestures, they more or less relied upon getting the meaning by a subconscious empathy. That is, the viewer would empathize with the observed, empathize with his body tensions and positions, and understand the gesture's meaning by putting himself in the place of the person he was viewing. However, when gestures are merely read subconsciously, only unconscious assumptions about them can be made. Sigmund Freud wrote, "The unconscious of one human being can react upon that of another without passing through the conscious." These unconscious reactions then become untested "facts" to which we respond. If we subconsciously conceive of the gesture as unfriendly, without conscious control we bring about a belligerent reaction that degenerates into a vicious cycle of hostility. As thinking men, we should be able to evaluate most stimuli before reacting to them.

If we could stop and read gestures consciously, if we could subject them to examination and verification, it is possible that before communications degenerate we could elevate the process to a different plane. We might read our own gestures and find that we are precipitating the other person's reactions. Or the gestures that we find undesirable might be found to be merely the result of the other person's physical idiosyncrasies. For example, a certain judge grimaced and blinked at lawyers appearing before him, causing considerable alarm among those inclined to be self-conscious or nervous. The judge suffered from the results of a stroke that left him with gestural scars. There are also misunderstandings because the same gesture can produce completely different responses in different cultures. Still other gestures may be repeated merely because of habit and do not signal a currently held attitude, whatever their origin. Gestures, then, appear to be made more meaningful by being brought out of the subconscious and recognized on the conscious level. We can term this *thinking through to the subconscious*. In this way we get a message rather than just a subconscious empathetic feeling.

Gestures Come in Clusters

The understanding of gestures is very difficult when the various elements are separated from their context. However, when gestures are fitted together into their composite positions, a complete picture evolves.

Each gesture is like a word in a language. In order to be understood in a language, one must structure his words into units, or "sentences," that express complete thoughts. It is not unusual for attendees at our seminars to attempt to bridge this word/sentence gap quickly. Some sincerely believe that a cursory exposure to the world of nonverbal communication equips them to speak the "language" fluently. On the contrary, this serves only to bring their awareness to a conscious level, not to make them experts. We attempt to discourage individuals from jumping to immediate conclusions based on the observation and comprehension of isolated gestures. Understanding the congruence of gestures in harmony with one another is far more important. A static gesture lasting several seconds might be contradicted by a prior body movement (incongruence), which in turn might be further repudiated by a subsequent gesture.

The so-called nervous laugh is a good example of incongruity. In every instance that we have recorded of the nervous laugh there has been an incongruity between the sound, which should indicate amusement, and the rest of the gesture-cluster, which signals extreme discomfort. Not only are there nervous arm and leg movements, but the entire body shifts as though trying to escape from an unpleasant situation. This gesture-cluster seldom results from a humorous statement. It indicates that the laugher is unsure of himself or even somewhat frightened by a situation.

By mentally matching congruent gestures that form clusters we can understand the attitudes expressed and discover some meaning. Indeed, what we should look for are similar attitudinal gestures that not only endorse one another but serve to make a cluster. As an example, a congruent set of gestures for a salesman who is very anxious and enthusiastic about his product might be sitting on the edge of his chair, feet apart, possibly on the toes in a sprinter's position, hand on the table, body leaning forward. Facial congruence might amplify the posture: eyes alert, a slight smile, and probably, no furrow on the brow.

Understanding congruency of gestures serves as a monitoring device for discovering a person's attitude and then giving his actions meaning. It serves as an "anti-assumption" control that forces us to observe further before jumping to a conclusion. Initially, it appears very easy to read individual gestures and have fun determining what they may mean. However, the serious student of gestures soon understands that each gesture can quickly be countered, amplified, and confused by another. At various times, people without nonverbal-communication-awareness training have probably made quick judgments concerning gestural meaning without considering congruency. From our experience these were the instances that proved most disastrous to them.

One of our fellow researchers in England, Dr. D. A. Humphries, asked us about the reliability of nonverbal elements in verbal exchanges. We mentioned that in our early research we sometimes found a dichotomy between obvious verbal and nonverbal meanings. It was only after a later, fuller evaluation of the situations that we found that the nonverbal gesture proved to be the more truthful. So the congruence of gestures not only concerns us with matching gesture with gesture but with verbal/gesture evaluation. It is the gesture-endorsing spoken word that is important for total communication. Politicians can win or lose campaigns depending on whether they maintain congruence. Now that television plays such a prominent part in political campaigns, the congruence of gesticulation becomes extremely important in presenting arguments. Unfortunately, however, we still can see many a high-ranking politician using gestures that are incongruent with his speech. While saying, "I'm sincerely receptive to a dialogue with the young people," for example, he shakes his finger and then his fist at his audience. Or he attempts to convince his audience of his warm, humane approach while using short, violent karate hand chops at the lectern.

Here is a test to determine how congruence can assist you. The following passage from Charles Dickens's *Great Expectations* is a scene for the reader to visualize:

> Casting my eyes along the street at a certain point of my progress, I beheld Trabb's boy approaching, lashing himself with an empty blue bag. Deeming that a serene and unconscious contemplation of him would best beseem me, and would be most likely to quell his evil mind, I advanced with that expression of countenance, and was rather congratulating myself on my success, when suddenly the knees of Trabb's boy smote together, his hair uprose, his cap fell off, he trembled violently in every limb, staggered out into the road, and crying to the populace, "Hold me! I'm so frightened!" feigned to be in a paroxysm of terror and contrition, occasioned by the dignity of my appearance. As I passed him, his teeth loudly chattered in his head, and with every mark of extreme humiliation, he prostrated himself in the dust.

After having read this passage, attempt, without rereading, to visualize the people and the scene. Picture in your mind's eye what the writer described and then write down what you saw. Then reread the paragraph to see how accurately you remembered it. Now see if you can remember more. Having in mind a congruence of gestures that the author is very much aware of, try the same visualization experiment with the next paragraph, but tie the gestures together, forming a memory chain:

> This was a hard thing to bear, but this was nothing. I had not ad-

vanced another two hundred yards, when to my inexpressible terror, amazement, and indignation, I again beheld Trabb's boy approaching. He was coming round a narrow corner. His blue bag was slung over his shoulder, honest industry beamed in his eyes, a determination to proceed to Trabb's with cheerful briskness was indicated in his gait. With a shock he became aware of me, and was severely visited as before; but this time his motion was rotatory, and he staggered round and round me with knees more afflicted, and with uplifted hands as if beseeching for mercy. His sufferings were hailed with the greatest joy by a knot of spectators, and I felt utterly confounded.

Congruence can provide a structure on which human actions can be ordered and thereby recalled more easily. The problem with observing congruence is that we tend to "tune in and out" not only verbal communication but also nonverbal messages. As an example, imagine an individual briskly walking into your office. He says good morning, unbuttons his coat, sits down with his body relaxed, legs spread apart, slight smile on his face, hands lightly resting on the arms of the chair. Thus far, all congruent gestures indicate that the person is receptive, open, not defensive, and probably at ease or comfortable with the environment. Once having organized the initial gestures into a composite attitude or feeling, you will find it easy to turn off your visual reception in favor of the audio and relax into a complacent belief that everything is going well. The rude awakening comes when you are jarred from your lethargy by an awareness that something has gone wrong. The person is now talking with his fists clenched, or he is shaking his index finger at you. In addition to scowling, he is getting red in the face either from heat or anger. The environment has quickly deteriorated into a rather sticky situation from which you must either extricate yourself or face a hostile friend, client, or customer.

Although at first it is difficult to concentrate on seeing gestures objectively, by exercising our awareness daily it becomes much easier, as in learning any language. And as for congruity, if instead of concentrating on gestures as mere parts that must be fitted together for meaning we concentrate upon the gesture-clusters, then congruity of body movements and gestures becomes considerably simpler to understand. This contributes greatly to *seeing* the overall meaning.

The Benefits of Understanding Gestures

People can communicate different types of information at different levels of understanding. The communication process consists of more than the spoken or written language. When you are trying to communicate with a person, sometimes you get through and sometimes you do not—not because of what you said or how you said it or the logic of your thoughts, but because many times the reception of your communication is based upon the degree of the listener's empathy for your nonverbal communication. A husband turning his back on his wife and slamming the front door without a word is heralding a significant message. It is therefore not very difficult to understand what benefits a person can derive from understanding nonverbal language, since we communicate in a multiprocess manner. Keep in mind, however, that your emotional relations, mannerisms, habits, and gestures are separate and distinct from those of the person sitting next to you at a business conference or party, at a ballgame or bar, or on the subway or bus. Also, dealing with people by lumping them into one category or another has more dangers than rewards.

Observing and becoming aware of gestures is fairly simple, but interpreting them is something else. As an example, we have recorded, observed, and had corroborated by other researchers the gesture of covering one's mouth while speaking. There is agreement that this is an indication that one is unsure of what he is saying. If you then find yourself listening to an individual who suddenly starts to speak through his hands, is he lying? unsure? doubting what he is saying? Possibly any of these. But before you jump to a conclusion, recall (if you can) whether the person has previously spoken in that manner. What were the circumstances? If not, consider that he may have had some recent dental work that might cause him to become self-conscious when talking, or that someone may have told him he has bad breath. If he has a track record of covering his mouth while speaking, continue to Phase II of the analysis. After he says something that you would like to test, ask him, "Are you sure?" Such a direct question can be answered with a simple yes. It can also make him very defensive, in which case you will know that he is not sure of what he has said. Or he will react to your question by saying something like, "Now that you mention it, I guess I'm really not sure." As with verbal understanding, we must consider more than the individual unit out of context. Experience, alternative verification, and congruency are important ingredients. However, in situations where one cannot use the usual methods of confirmation, consideration should be given to a consensus on the meaning of the hand-over-mouth gesture: The many law-enforcement people who have attended our seminars state without exception that the gesture indicates that the person is doubtful, unsure, lying, or distorting the truth.

One of the participants in our seminar, in discussing nonverbal communication, reported the following: "On returning from the Chicago seminar I was seated next to a woman who explained that she was a registered nurse. She then proceeded to tell me all that was wrong with the medical profession. From my point of view she was overgeneralizing and drew conclusions that I believed to be false. The point of all this is that while I was attempting to listen I had my arms folded high on my chest, feeling very stubbornly that she didn't know what she was talking about. When I discovered myself in this position, I understood what was taking place within me. I tried a different approach. I uncrossed my arms and proceeded to listen without evaluating. As a result I was able to listen more intently. I became less defensive and was able to realize that although I disagreed, she was saying something I was now able to listen to more fully and appreciate."

The folded-arms gesture can be understood and utilized in another way: While trying to communicate with someone, we may notice him taking this position like some bygone cigarstore Indian. This is one of the gestures that indicate he is not going to listen and is very adamant about it. In many conversations, rather than recognizing this and coping with it by trying alternative methods and courses open to us, we proceed in the same conversational pattern and talk a blue streak. Therefore, instead of helping the individual to cooperate in the communication, we tend to drive him further away.

Feedback plays a major role in the full communication process, and gesture-clusters are an important feedback. They indicate from moment to moment and movement to movement exactly how individuals or groups are reacting nonverbally. We can learn whether what we are saying is being received in a positive manner or a negative one, whether the audience is open or defensive, self-controlled or bored. Speakers call this audience-awareness, or relating to a group. Nonverbal feedback can warn you that you must change, withdraw, or do something different in order to bring about the result that you desire. If you are *not* aware of feedback, then there is a strong possibility that you will fail to communicate your believability or sincerity to an individual or to an audience.

An attorney who attended one of our seminars sent us a letter in which he explained the benefits he had derived from consciously considering nonverbal communication. He said in the course of an office visit his client crossed his arms and legs "in a defensive position" and proceeded to spend the next hour admonishing him. Noticing the nonverbal implications of the client's gestures, he let his client talk it out of his system. Only after this did the lawyer offer professional advice on how to handle the difficult situation the client found himself in. The attorney stated that had he not attended our seminar he would not have given his client a chance to be receptive to him, since he would not have read his client's needs and would probably have attempted immediately to give him unheeded advice.

A common observation seminar attendees make is, "I feel frustrated because despite the fact that I'm aware that gestures exist, I find myself tuned out for periods of as long as fifteen minutes where I'm absolutely unaware of what's going on." The art of thoroughly seeing nonverbal communications is a learning process almost as difficult as acquiring fluency in a foreign language. In addition to maintaining a conscious awareness of your own gestures and the meaning you are conveying to your audience, we recommend that you set aside at least ten minutes a day during which you consciously "read" the gestures of others. Anywhere that people gather is an excellent "reading" ground. Social and business gatherings that permit freely expressed emotions and the possibility of polarization of attitudes are especially well-suited for doing thorough research. The attitudes of people attending these functions are usually so intense that each tends to be "wearing his feelings on his sleeve." However, you do not have to leave your home to do homework. Television offers a fertile field for reading nonverbal communication, particularly the interview and discussion programs. Try to understand what is happening by just watching the picture. Turn on the sound at five-minute intervals to check the verbal communication against your reading of the gestures. Be sure to watch for congruency and gesture-clusters.

FOR DISCUSSION AND REVIEW

1 Why do the authors feel that "life situations" offer better tests for the interpretation of nonverbal communication than the "behavioral-laboratory approach"?

2 What are gesture-clusters? Why are they considered so important?

3 What is congruence? Why is it considered to be so essential in interpreting gestures?

4 What role does the subconscious play in our gestures and in the interpretation of gestures in general?

5 To what does the expression *thinking through to the unconscious* refer?

6 Describe the basic metaphor that the authors use in their discussion of gestures, gesture-clusters, and the interpretation of gestures. How effective is the metaphor?

3

The Effects of Physical Appearance on Human Communication

Mark L. Knapp

Although people have always known that physical appearance plays an important role in interpersonal relations, it is only recently that researchers have begun to describe in detail the specific nature of that role. In this selection from *Nonverbal Communication in Human Interaction*, Mark L. Knapp reviews some of the research dealing with physical appearance/attractiveness, body types, tallness or height, and self-image as influenced by body image. Most of the research confirms what people have intuitively sensed to be true; other research, however, offers interesting contradictions to strongly held beliefs.

PICTURE the following scene: Mr. and Mrs. American awake and prepare to start the day. Mrs. American takes off her "nighttime" bra and replaces it with a "slightly-padded-uplift" bra. After removing her chin strap, she further pulls herself together with her girdle. Then she begins to "put on her face." This involves an eyebrow pencil, mascara, lipstick, rouge, eye liner, and false eye lashes. Then she removes the hair under her arms and on her legs and places a hairpiece on her head. False fingernails, nail polish, and tinted contact lenses precede the deodorant, perfume, and endless decisions concerning clothes. Mr. American shaves the hair on his face, puts a toupee on his head and carefully attaches his newly purchased sideburns. He removes his false teeth from a solution used to whiten them, gargles with a breath sweetener, selects his after shave lotion, puts on his elevator shoes, and begins making his clothing decisions. This hypothetical example represents an extreme, but it is, nonetheless, true that people go to great lengths to make themselves "attractive." Why? Does it may any difference to our interpersonal contacts?

Our Body: Its General Attractiveness

While it is not uncommon to hear people muse about how "inner beauty" is the only thing that really counts, research suggests that "outer beauty" or physical attractiveness plays an influential role in determining responses for a broad range of interpersonal encounters.

Consider, for instance, a fascinating study by Singer concerning the use of physical attractiveness by females as a manipulative device to obtain higher grades from college professors.[1] This phase of Singer's research occurred after he found no difference between scores of males and females on a Machiavellian scale,[2] but could not identify the specific ways in which Machiavellian females expressed these attitudes behaviorally. He hypothesized that there were many sociocultural factors which militated against females using obviously devious, deceitful, or exploitative tactics; and that, therefore, they adopted a more socially acceptable method—capitalizing on their good looks! To test this, he first obtained 192 pictures of freshman girls and had the pictures rated by 40 faculty members—with each picture being rated five times. When he compared these ratings with grade point averages and birth order, Singer found a positive relationship between being firstborn, attractive, and female, and grade point average. Naturally, he then asked, why was this true of firstborn girls and not those born later? He reasoned that if firstborns engaged in more "exhibiting" behavior, professors would be more likely to remember them and give them the benefit of the doubt on grades.

Observations of actual behavior and self-reports confirmed that first-born girls tend to sit in the front of the room, come up more frequently after class, and make more frequent appointments to see instructors during office hours. Singer also sought to find out whether the higher grades given to attractive females were due to luck or whether there was manipulation by the girls involved. Singer thought that if he could show that firstborns were more aware of, and socially concerned about, their looks, this finding would tend to support his attractiveness-manipulation interpretation. He, therefore, asked females to estimate ideal body measurements *and* their own measurements.[3] One group was told actual measurements would be taken after the paper and pencil estimates; another group was not told this would be done. Estimates were made of

---

[1] J. E. Singer, "The Use of Manipulative Strategies: Machiavellianism and Attractiveness," *Sociometry* 27 (1964): 128–151.

[2] Machiavellianism is generally associated with the use of any means necessary, no matter how unscrupulous, to achieve a goal. It is frequently associated with cunning, duplicity, or bad faith.

[3] J. E. Singer and P. F. Lamb, "Social Concern, Body Size, and Birth Order," *Journal of Social Psychology* 68 (1966): 143–151.

height, weight, bust, waist, and hips. Neck, ankle, and wrist size were added as control items. The results supported Singer's "manipulative intent" hypothesis because: (1) firstborns had more accurate information about their body measurements, (2) they were more accurate in stating norms for the ideal female figure, and (3) they were more likely to distort their measurements in the direction of the ideal norms than were later borns. Singer's conclusion is worth noting:

> In some respects the results are not at all surprising. The suggestion that men live by their brains and women by their bodies was made as far back as Genesis. Although not astoundingly new, the implications are rather frightening. The documentation of the utility of manipulative skills was obtained from a population of freshmen in a university setting, with a criterion of academic success. The results imply that the poor college professor is a rather put-upon creature, hoodwinked by the male students (later born) and enticed by the female students (first born) as he goes about his academic and personal responsibilities. He is seemingly caught in a maelstrom of student intrigue and machination. The picture is bleak. In defense we can only offer the consolation that when 22 male members of the faculty at The Pennsylvania State University were administered the Machiavellian scale, their mean score was 10.44. When compared with the total sample values from the 994 subject study . . . the faculty appear significantly more manipulative than the students ($t = 2.43$, $p > 0.02$). It is hoped that the academicians are fighting stratagem with stratagem.[4]

Other persuasive studies also show attractiveness to be important. Mills and Aronson found an attractive female could modify attitudes of male students more than an unattractive girl could.[5] Actually one girl was made up to look different under two conditions. In the unattractive condition she was rated repulsive by independent observers; she wore loose fitting clothing; her hair was messy, makeup was conspicuously absent, a trace of a mustache was etched on her upper lip, and her complexion was oily and unwholesome looking. The experimenter suggested to a group of students that they would more quickly complete some measuring instruments if a volunteer would read the questions aloud and indicate what they meant. The "volunteer" was either the attractive or unattractive girl. It might be that Mills and Aronson's results

---

[4] Singer, "The Use of Manipulative Strategies: Machiavellianism and Attractiveness," p. 150.

[5] J. Mills and E. Aronson, "Opinion Change as a Function of the Communicator's Attractiveness and Desire to Influence," *Journal of Personality and Social Psychology* 1 (1965): 73–77.

would not have been so clear cut with a female audience, but Widgery and Webster[6] offer some evidence that attractive persons, regardless of sex, will be rated high on the character dimension of credibility scales. While more work needs to be done, attractiveness does seem to be an influential factor on perception of initial credibility—hence an influential factor in one's ultimate persuasiveness.

Physical attractiveness also seems to be an extremely important factor in courtship and marriage decisions. Numerous studies provide testimony from unmarried men and women that physical attractiveness is a critical factor in mate selection. One early study asked students if they would marry a person who ranked low in such qualities as economic status, good looks, disposition, family religion, morals, health, education, intelligence, or age.[7] Men most frequently rejected women who were deficient in good looks, disposition, morals, and health. Women did not seem to worry as much about marrying a man who was deficient in good looks. On the other hand, gender seemed to make little difference in a study which asked persons to evaluate strangers of the same or opposite sex—strangers who had previously been rated as either physically attractive or unattractive.[8] Interpersonal attraction was greatest toward the physically attractive strangers—regardless of sex. In this phase of the study, subjects had no other information about the stranger; through subsequent study, the same researchers found that physical attractiveness was still an important determinant of attraction when subjects had additional information about the strangers—e.g., information on several of the strangers' attitudes. These traits do not seem limited to the United States. A study conducted in India found that men wanted wives who were more physically beautiful than themselves, and women wanted husbands who were equal to them in physical beauty.[9]

More recently, the effect of physical attractiveness on dating behavior was studied. Walster and her colleagues randomly paired 752 college students for a freshman dance.[10] A great deal of information was gathered from each student—including self-reports about popularity,

[6] R. N. Widgery and B. Webster, "The Effects of Physical Attractiveness Upon Perceived Initial Credibility," *Michigan Speech Journal* 4 (1969): 9–15.

[7] R. E. Baber, *Marriage and Family* (New York: McGraw-Hill, 1939).

[8] D. Byrne, O. London, and K. Reeves, "The Effects of Physical Attractiveness, Sex, and Attitude Similarity on Interpersonal Attraction," *Journal of Personality* 36 (1968): 259–272.

[9] B. N. Singh, "A Study of Certain Personal Qualities as Preferred by College Students in Their Marital Partners," *Journal of Psychological Researches* 8 (1964): 37–48.

[10] E. Walster, V. Aronson, D. Abrahams, and L. Rohmann, "Importance of Physical Attractiveness in Dating Behavior," *Journal of Personality and Social Psychology* 4 (1966): 508–516.

religious preference, height, race, expectations for the date, self-esteem, high school academic percentile rank, scholastic aptitude score, and personality test scores. In addition, each student was rated by several judges for attractiveness. Physical attractiveness was by far the most important determinant of how much a date would be liked by his or her partner. It appears that physical attractiveness was just as important an asset for a man as for a woman, since it was a reliable predictor for both groups. Brislin and Lewis replicated this study with 58 unacquainted men and women and again found a strong correlation (.89) between "desire to date again" and "physical attractiveness."[11] In addition, this study asked each person whether they would like to date anyone else at the dance. Of the 13 other people named, all had previously, and independently, been rated very attractive.

It seems that in many situations everyone prefers the most attractive date possible regardless of his or her own attractiveness and regardless of the possibility of being rejected by the most attractive date. There are obvious exceptions. Some gigolos argue that if they approach a girl who is somewhat less attractive—particularly in the company of some who are very attractive—their chances of succeeding are greatly increased. Another exception might be cases in which males are low in self-esteem. Kiesler and Baral report research which suggests that males with high self-esteem are more apt to display romantic behavior toward highly attractive females while low-esteem males seek out less attractive females.[12]

The whole question of "what is sex appeal" seems relevant at this point.[13] The answer is far from clear-cut because so many aspects vary with the situation, the time (both time in a person's life and time in history), and the experiences and preferences of each individual. For instance, one may make different evaluations of another's sex appeal depending on whether the person is known or a stranger. A student attending a university, isolated from an urban environment, may consider another person particularly sexy—only to find his judgment changed when he returns to the city where he has a greater variety to choose from. Others may label *sexy* those with whom they feel they have some chance of "success" in a sexual encounter. They may react to cues which suggest "readiness" or "openness." Still others may identify sex appeal with pleasant early love experiences (with parents and relatives) and select people with the same pleasantness, the same interests, or the

11 R. W. Brislin and S. A. Lewis, "Dating and Physical Attractiveness: Replication," *Psychological Reports* 22 (1968): 976.

12 Cited in E. Berscheid and E. H. Walster, *Interpersonal Attraction* (Reading, Mass.: Addison-Wesley, 1969): 113–114.

13 B. I. Murstein, W. J. Gadpaille, and D. Byrne, "What Makes People Sexually Appealing?" *Sexual Behavior* 1 (1971): 75–77.

same values. Possibly the most familiar reaction to the question, "what constitutes sex appeal?" involves judgments about physical features— e.g., "I'm a breast man," or "He's got a rugged face," or "I'm a leg man," or "He looks like a stud." Frequently, these responses to physical characteristics are defined by one's reference group or the mass media (e.g., movie idols)—and have relatively little to do with sexual expertise.

While some people would like to believe that "everything is beautiful in its own way"—as a 1970 pop song put it— it should also be recognized that some people are beautiful in much the same way to large segments of the population. The stereotypes of American beauty promoted by *Playboy* and the Miss America Pageant, among numerous others, seem to be very influential in setting cultural norms. Their recognition of this influence caused members of the women's liberation movement to condemn *Playboy's* portrayal of ideal womanhood and prompted some Negro leaders to organize a Miss Black America Pageant. It is not surprising to find that in one case over 4,000 judges, differing in age, sex, occupation, and geographical location, exhibited high levels of agreement concerning "prettiness" in young women's faces.[14] Physical attractiveness seems to play an important role in persuading and/or manipulating others—whether in courtship, a classroom, or a public speaking situation. Certainly it is very influential on first impressions and expectations for an encounter. What specific aspects of another person's appearance do we respond to? Does it make any difference how we perceive our own body and appearance? The answers to these questions will be the focus for the remainder of this chapter.

Body Shape

In order to add a personal dimension to some of the theory and research in this section, a short Self-description Test is provided. By taking this test, you can gather some data on yourself which can be compared with others who have taken it.[15]

Self-description Test

Instructions: Fill in each blank with a word from the suggested list following each statement. For any blank, three in each statement, you may select any word from the list of twelve immediately below. An exact word to fit you may not be in the list, but select the words that seem to fit *most closely* the way you are.

[14] A. M. Iliffe, "A Study of Preferences in Feminine Beauty," *British Journal of Psychology* 51 (1960): 267–273.
[15] J. B. Cortes and F. M. Gatti, "Physique and Self-Description of Temperament," *Journal of Consulting Psychology* 29 (1965): 434.

1   I feel most of the time _____, _____, and _____.

calm	relaxed	complacent
anxious	confident	reticent
cheerful	tense	energetic
contented	impetuous	self-conscious

2   When I study or work, I seem to be _____, _____, and _____.

efficient	sluggish	precise
enthusiastic	competitive	determined
reflective	leisurely	thoughtful
placid	meticulous	cooperative

3   Socially, I am _____, _____, and _____.

outgoing	considerate	argumentative
affable	awkward	shy
tolerant	affected	talkative
gentle-tempered	soft-tempered	hot-tempered

4   I am rather _____, _____, and _____.

active	forgiving	sympathetic
warm	courageous	serious
domineering	suspicious	soft-hearted
introspective	cool	enterprising

5   Other people consider me rather _____, _____, and _____.

generous	optimistic	sensitive
adventurous	affectionate	kind
withdrawn	reckless	cautious
dominant	detached	dependent

6   Underline *one* word out of the three in each of the following
    lines which most closely describes the way you are.
    (a)   assertive, relaxed, tense   (e)   dependent, dominant,
    (b)   hot-tempered, cool, warm   detached
    (c)   withdrawn, sociable, active   (f)   enterprising, affable,
    (d)   confident, tactful, kind   anxious

This test has been given to numerous individuals participating in
studies concerned with the relationship between certain personality and
temperament characteristics and certain body types or builds. Generally,
these studies are concerned with a person's physical similarity to three
extreme varieties of human physique. These are shown in Figure 1.

Naturally, most of us do not fit these extremes exactly. So a system
has been developed for specifying body type based on the assumption
that we may have some features of all three types. Sheldon's work

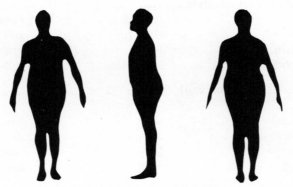

(a) The endomorph: soft, round, fat

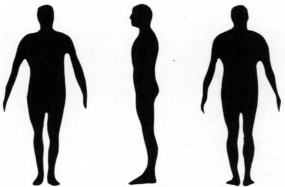

(b) The mesomorph: bony, muscular, athletic

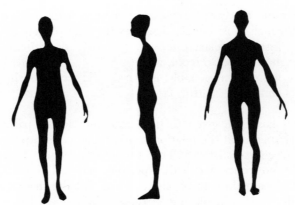

(c) The ectomorph: tall, thin, fragile

Figure 1.

helps to explain this system.[16] A person's physical characteristics are rated on a scale from 1 to 7—7 representing the highest correspondence with one of the three extreme body types. An individual's "*somatype*" is represented by three numbers—the first referring to the degree of endomorphy, the second referring to degree of mesomorphy and the third to degree of ectomorphy. A grossly fat person would be 7/1/1; a broad-shouldered, athletic person would be 1/7/1; and a very skinny person would be a 1/1/7. It is reported that Jackie Gleason is roughly 6/4/1. Muhammad Ali 2/7/1 and Abraham Lincoln 1/5/6. Scientific criticism of Sheldon's work has been plentiful. His work has, however, been the basis for many studies investigating the same general question —and in spite of critical errors in Sheldon's methodology, many of the later studies—using more precise measurements and research designs— have confirmed many of his early conclusions.

Now to the test you took earlier. Cortes and Gatti used this test to measure temperament. When they correlated the results with measures of physique, they found a very high correspondence. In other words, on the basis of this work we would expect to have a pretty good idea of your body build by the answers you gave on the Self-description Test. To calculate your score on the test, simply add up the number of adjectives you chose from each of the endomorph, mesomorph and ectomorph categories listed in Table 1.

If you chose six adjectives from the endomorph category, twelve from the mesomorph, and three from the ectomorph lists, your temperament score would be 6/12/3. If we assume a high correlation with body features we would assume you are primarily mesomorphic with a leaning toward endomorphism. This test and the body-personality research allow us to make some predictions based on probabilities, but, of course, in individual cases there may be exceptions. Nor can we assume from this work that the body causes temperament traits. The high correspondence between certain temperament traits and body builds may be due to life experiences, environmental factors, self-concept, and a host of other variables.

The obvious question at this point is, "What does all this have to do with human communication?" Simply this: If a case can be made that there are clearly defined and generally accepted physique-temperament stereotypes, we can reason that they will have a lot to do with the way you are perceived and responded to by others, and with the personality traits expected of you by others. Wells and Siegel uncovered some data

16 W. H. Sheldon, *Atlas of Man: A Guide for Somatyping the Adult Male At All Ages* (New York: Harper and Row, 1954); W. H. Sheldon, *The Varieties of Human Physique* (New York: Harper and Row, 1940); W. H. Sheldon, *The Varieties of Temperament* (New York: Harper and Row, 1942).

TABLE 1   ADJECTIVES RELATED TO BODY SHAPES

Endomorphic	Mesomorphic	Ectomorphic
dependent	dominant	detached
calm	cheerful	tense
relaxed	confident	anxious
complacent	energetic	reticent
contented	impetuous	self-conscious
sluggish	efficient	meticulous
placid	enthusiastic	reflective
leisurely	competitive	precise
cooperative	determined	thoughtful
affable	outgoing	considerate
tolerant	argumentative	shy
affected	talkative	awkward
warm	active	cool
forgiving	domineering	suspicious
sympathetic	courageous	introspective
soft-hearted	enterprising	serious
generous	adventurous	cautious
affectionate	reckless	tactful
kind	assertive	sensitive
sociable	optimistic	withdrawn
soft-tempered	hot-tempered	gentle-tempered

supporting the existence of such stereotypes.[17] One hundred twenty adult subjects were shown silhouette drawings of the endomorph, ectomorph, and mesomorph, and asked to rate them on a set of 24 bipolar adjective scales such as: lazy-energetic; fat-thin; intelligent-unintelligent; dependent–self-reliant; etc. The investigators deliberately chose people who had not been to college—assuming these people would not be contaminated with information from previous studies which might structure their answers. Their results show: (1) the *endomorph* was rated fatter, older, shorter (silhouettes were the same height), more old-fashioned, less strong physically, less good looking, more talkative, more warmhearted and sympathetic, more good-natured and agreeable, more dependent on others, and more trusting of others; (2) the *mesomorph* was rated stronger, more masculine, better looking, more adventurous, younger, taller, more mature in behavior, more self-reliant; (3) the *ectomorph* was rated thinner, younger, more ambitious, taller, more suspicious of others, more tense and nervous, less masculine, more stubborn

[17] W. Wells and B. Siegel, "Stereotyped Somatypes," *Psychological Reports* 8 (1961): 77–78. Another study, using a written description of body extremes, asked personality questions about the written descriptions and found similar results. Cf. K. T. Strongman and C. J. Hart, "Stereotyped Reactions to Body Build," *Psychological Reports* 23 (1968): 1175–1178.

and inclined to be difficult, more pessimistic and quieter. Several reports suggest that the relationship between body build and temperament also holds for young children.[18] For example, thin ectomorphic boys and girls were more anxious, more conscientious and more meticulous than children with other body builds. The reactions to endomorphs, or obese individuals, are encountered frequently. They are discriminated against when seeking to obtain life insurance, adopt children, obtain jobs, and even in entrance to college.[19] One author suggests obesity is stamped with a stigma of moral turpitude.[20]

We have been trained for so long to believe that stereotypes are harmful distortions of the truth, we often fail to consider another equally plausible explanation—that a particular stereotype may be the result of a distillation of ages of social experience. In other words, a stereotype may be more accurate than we wish to admit—there may be some reason for the stereotype other than prejudicial whims. Clearly, the evidence shows we do associate certain personality and temperament traits with certain body builds. These expectations may or may not be accurate, but they do exist; they are a part of the psychological mortar in interpersonal communication. We must recognize these stereotypes as potential stimuli for communication responses, so we can deal with them more effectively.

Another dimension of body build which may influence interpersonal responses is tallness or height. In American society there seems to be a preference for the taller man. The ideal lover is not *short*, dark, and handsome; romantic leads in movies are tall; the taller of the two national presidential candidates seems to be a consistent winner since 1900; and a survey at the University of Pittsburgh shows shorter men are shortchanged on job opportunities and salaries. Pittsburgh graduates 6 ft. 2 in. to 6 ft. 4 in. received average starting salaries 12.4% higher than those men under 6 ft. Further support for discrimination against the short man comes from a study of 140 corporate recruiters who were asked to make a choice between two men just by reading their application for employment. Applications were exactly the same except one listed a height of 6 ft. 1 in. and the other 5 ft. 5 in. Only about 1 percent favored the short man. Does a tall person have a natural advantage in persuading people? Some preliminary evidence indicates he does

[18] R. N. Walker, "Body Build and Behavior in Young Children: II. Body Build and Parents' Ratings," *Child Development* 34 (1963): 1–23. See also R. W. Parnell, *Behavior and Physique: An Introduction to Practical and Applied Somatometry* (London: Edward Arnold, 1958).

[19] H. Channing and J. Mayer, "Obesity—Its Possible Effect on College Acceptance," *New England Journal of Medicine* 275 (1966): 1172–1174.

[20] W. J. Cahnman, "The Stigma of Obesity," *Sociological Quarterly* 9 (1968): 283–299.

not.[21] Photographs were taken of the same person from two different angles—one designed to make him look short; one to make him look tall. These pictures plus a tape-recorded persuasive speech were the stimuli for various student groups. Attitude measures indicated there was no statistically significant difference between the "tall" and "short" speakers. It is more likely that tallness interacts with other factors such as general body size, girth, facial features, and numerous other variables. In your own experience, you can probably recall some individuals who seemed almost frighteningly "overpowering," while others of the same height did not have this quality. Another investigator looked at height from the standpoint of the receiver—rather than the communicator or sender.[22] Will receivers perceive differences in height of people they think to be different in status? Again, only tentative conclusions can be drawn from some early work. A single individual was introduced to five similar groups of students. Each time he was introduced as a person with a different status—e.g., student, lecturer, doctor, full professor. Students were then told they needed numerical data for their statistics lesson, so they were asked to estimate the height of the person just introduced. Results seem to suggest there is some perceptual distortion of height—the higher the ascribed status, the higher the judgments of height.

So far we have been discussing our perceptions of others. An equally important dimension of interpersonal communication is what we think of ourselves—our self-image. The self-image is the root system from which all of our overt communication behavior grows and blossoms. Our overt communication behavior is only an extension of the accumulated experiences which have gone into making up our understanding of self. In short, what you are, or think you are, organizes what you say and do. An important part of your self-image is body image—perhaps the first part formed in very young children. Given the social role of the American female, it seems likely that physical attractiveness and its component parts are of major importance. Some females, then, may be more secure about, and more accepting of, their bodies than males because they can relate their body attributes to a woman's primary social role. Jourard and Secord found males most satisfied with their bodies when they were somewhat larger than normal; females most satisfied when their bodies were smaller than normal—but when their busts were larger than average.[23] Sex researchers have frequently noted emotional

---

21 E. E. Baker and W. C. Redding, "The Effects of Perceived Tallness in Persuasive Speaking; An Experiment," *Journal of Communication* 12 (1962): 51–53.

22 P. R. Wilson, "Perceptual Distortion of Height as a Function of Ascribed Academic Status," *Journal of Social Psychology* 74 (1968): 97–102.

23 S. M. Jourard and P. F. Secord, "Body Cathexis and Personality," *British Journal of Psychology* 46 (1955): 130–138.

problems in males resulting from perceived incongruence between their genital size and the supposed masculine ideal perpetuated by our literary and oral heritage. As we develop, we learn the cultural ideal of what the body should be like, and this results in varying degrees of satisfaction with the body—particularly during adolescence.[24]

[24] For an extensive treatment of body image research, see: F. C. Shontz, *Perceptual and Cognitive Aspects of Body Experience* (New York: Academic Press, 1969); and W. Gorman, *Body Image and the Image of the Brain* (St. Louis: W. H. Green, 1969).

FOR DISCUSSION AND REVIEW

1 Why do people go to such great lengths to make themselves physically attractive? Do you and your parents define "attractiveness" in the same way? Explain.

2 According to Knapp, can physical attractiveness be used as a manipulative device? Why or why not?

3 What is the relationship between the self-esteem of males and the attractiveness of female partners?

4 What are the three body types discussed by Knapp? Briefly describe each. What is an individual's somatype, and how is it determined?

5 Complete the short Self-description Test on pp. 482–483. Using Table 1, calculate your score on the test. Simply add up the number of adjectives you choose from each of the endomorph, mesomorph, and ectomorph categories listed in the table. Do you agree with the results of your test? Why or why not?

6 Do you agree that dominance through height exists in most situations? Explain your position.

4
Winking, Blinking and Nods

It is a widely-held belief that our eyes are capable of communicating a vast range of emotions, and many examples from literature, the arts, and popular belief can be cited to support this observation. Our eyes, however, do not communicate by themselves; they operate in conjunction with other facial and body movements to convey a person's feelings. In this selection from *Body Language,* Julius Fast discusses just how telling our eyes are, how we can learn to read them, and how eye movements are culturally related.

Julius Fast

The Stare that Dehumanizes

THE COWPUNCHER sat his horse loosely and his fingers hovered above his gun while his eyes, ice cold, sent chills down the rustler's back.

A familiar situation? It happens in every western novel, just as in every love story the heroine's eyes *melt* while the hero's eyes *burn* into hers. In literature, even the best literature, eyes are *steely, knowing, mocking, piercing, glowing* and so on.

Are they really? Are they ever? Is there such a thing as a burning glance, or a cold glance or a hurt glance? In truth there isn't. Far from being windows of the soul, the eyes are physiological dead ends, simply organs of sight and no more, differently colored in different people to be sure, but never really capable of expressing emotion in themselves.

And yet again and again we read and hear and even tell of the eyes being wise, knowing, good, bad, indifferent. Why is there such confusion? Can so many people be wrong? If the eyes do not show emotion, then why the vast literature, the stories and legends about them?

Of all parts of the human body that are used to transmit information, the eyes are the most important and can transmit the most subtle nuances. Does this contradict the fact that the eyes do not show emotion? Not really. While the eyeball itself shows nothing, the emotional impact of the eyes occurs because of their use and the use of the face around them. The reason they have so confounded observers is because by length of glance, by opening of eyelids, by squinting and by a dozen little manipulations of the skin and eyes, almost any meaning can be sent out.

But the most important technique of eye management is the look, or the stare. With it we can often make or break another person. How? By giving him human or nonhuman status.

Simply, eye management in our society boils down to two facts. One, we do not stare at another human being. Two, staring is reserved for a non-person. We stare at art, at sculpture, at scenery. We go to the zoo and stare at the animals, the lions, the monkeys, the gorillas. We stare at them for as long as we please, as intimately as we please, but we do not stare at humans if we want to accord them human treatment.

We may use the same stare for the side-show freak, but we do not really consider him a human being. He is an object at which we have paid money to stare, and in the same way we may stare at an actor on a stage. The real man is masked too deeply behind his role for our stare to bother either him or us. However, the new theater that brings the actor down into the audience often gives us an uncomfortable feeling. By virtue of involving us, the audience, the actor suddenly loses his non-person status and staring at him becomes embarrassing to us.

As I said before, a Southern white may stare at a black in the same way, making him, by the stare, into an object rather than a person. If we wish pointedly to ignore someone, to treat him with an element of contempt, we can give him the same stare, the slightly unfocused look that does not really see him, the cutting stare of the socially elite.

Servants are often treated this way as are waiters, waitresses and children. However, this may be a mutually protective device. It allows the servants to function efficiently in their overlapping universe without too much interference from us, and it allows us to function comfortably without acknowledging the servant as a fellow human. The same is true of children and waiters. It would be an uncomfortable world if each time we were served by a waiter we had to introduce ourselves and indulge in social amenities.

A Time for Looking

With unfamiliar human beings, when we acknowledge their humanness, we must avoid staring at them, and yet we must also avoid ignoring them. To make them into people rather than objects, we use a deliberate and polite inattention. We look at them long enough to make it quite clear that we see them, and then we immediately look away. We are saying, in body language, "I know you are there," and a moment later we add, "But I would not dream of intruding on your privacy."

The important thing in such an exchange is that we do not catch the eye of the one whom we are recognizing as a person. We look at him without locking glances, and then we immediately look away. Recognition is not permitted.

There are different formulas for the exchange of glances depending on where the meeting takes place. If you pass someone in the street you may eye the oncoming person till you are about eight feet apart, then you must look away as you pass. Before the eight foot distance is reached, each will signal in which direction he will pass. This is done with a brief look in that direction. Each will veer slightly, and the passing is done smoothly.

For this passing encounter Dr. Erving Goffman in *Behavior in Public Places* says that the quick look and the lowering of the eyes is body language for, "I trust you. I am not afraid of you."

To strengthen this signal, you look directly at the other's face before looking away.

Sometimes the rules are hard to follow, particularly if one of the two people wears dark glasses. It becomes impossible to discover just what they are doing. Are they looking at you too long, too intently? Are they looking at you at all? The person wearing the glasses feels protected and assumes that he can stare without being noticed in his staring. However, this is a self-deception. To the other person, dark glasses seem to indicate that the wearer is always staring at him.

We often use this look-and-away technique when we meet famous people. We want to assure them that we are respecting their privacy, that we would not dream of staring at them. The same is true of the crippled or physically handicapped. We look briefly and then look away before the stare can be said to be a stare. It is the technique we use for any unusual situation where too long a stare would be embarrassing. When we see an interracial couple we use this technique. We might use it when we see a man with an unusual beard, with extra long hair, with outlandish clothes, or a girl with a minimal mini-skirt may attract this look-and-away.

Of course the opposite is also true. If we wish to put a person down we may do so by staring longer than is acceptably polite. Instead of dropping our gazes when we lock glances, we continue to stare. The person who disapproves of interracial marriage or dating will stare rudely at the interracial couple. If he dislikes long hair, short dresses or beards he may show it with a longer-than-acceptable stare.

The Awkward Eyes

The look-and-away stare is reminiscent of the problem we face in adolescence in terms of our hands. What do we do with them? Where do we hold them? Amateur actors are also made conscious of this. They are suddenly aware of their hands as awkward appendages that must somehow be used gracefully and naturally.

In the same way, in certain circumstances, we become aware of our glances as awkward appendages. Where shall we look? What shall we do with our eyes?

Two strangers seated across from each other in a railway dining car have the option of introducing themselves and facing a meal of inconsequential and perhaps boring talk, or ignoring each other and desperately trying to avoid each other's glance. Cornelia Otis Skinner, describing such a situation in an essay, wrote, "They re-read the menu, they fool with the cutlery, they inspect their own fingernails as if seeing them for the first time. Comes the inevitable moment when glances meet, but they meet only to shoot instantly away and out the window for an intent view of the passing scene."

This same awkward eye dictates our looking behavior in elevators and crowded buses and subway trains. When we get on an elevator or train with a crowd we look briefly and then look away at once without locking glances. We say, with our look, "I see you. I do not know you, but you are a human and I will not stare at you."

In the subway or bus where long rides in very close circumstances are a necessity, we may be hard put to find some way of not staring. We sneak glances, but look away before our eyes can lock. Or we look with an unfocused glance that misses the eyes and settles on the head, the mouth, the body—for any place but the eyes is an acceptable looking spot for the unfocused glance.

If our eyes do meet we can sometimes mitigate the message with a brief smile. The smile must not be too long or too obvious. It must say, "I am sorry we have looked, but we both know it was an accident."

Bedroom Eyes

The awkward eye is a common enough occurrence for all of us to have experienced it at one time or another. Almost all actions and interactions between humans depend on mutual glances. The late Spanish philosopher José Ortega y Gasset, in his book *Man and People*, spoke of "the look" as something that comes directly from within a man "with the straight-line accuracy of a bullet." He felt that the eye, with its lids and socket, its iris and pupil, was equivalent to a "whole theatre with its stage and actors."

The eye muscles, Ortega said, are marvelously subtle and because of this every glance is minutely differentiated from every other glance. There are so many different looks that it is nearly impossible to name them, but he cited, "the look that lasts but an instant and the insistent look; the look that slips over the surface of the thing looked at and the look that grips it like a hook; the direct look and the oblique look whose extreme form has its own name, 'looking out of the corner of one's eye.' "

He also listed the "sideways glance" which differs from any other oblique look although its axis is still on the bias.

Every look, Ortega said, tells us what goes on inside the person who gives it, and the intent to communicate with a look is more genuinely revealing when the sender of the look is unaware of just how he sends it.

Like other researchers into body language Ortega warned that a look in itself does not give the entire story, even though it has a meaning. A word in a sentence has a meaning too, but only in the context of the sentence can we learn the complete meaning of the word. So too with a look. Only in the context of an entire situation is a look entirely meaningful.

There are also looks that want to see but not be seen. These the Spanish philosopher called sideways glances. In any situation we may study someone and look as long as we wish, providing the other person is not aware that we are looking, providing our look is hidden. The moment his eyes move to lock with ours, our glance must slide away. The more skilled the person, the better he is at stealing these sideways glances.

In a charming description Ortega labels one look "the most effective, the most suggestive, the most delicious and enchanting." He called it the most complicated because it is not only furtive, but it is also the very opposite of furtive, because it makes it obvious that it is looking. This is the look given with lidded eyes, the sleepy look or calculating look or appraising look, the look a painter gives his canvas as he steps back from it, what the French call les yeux en coulisse.

Describing this look, Ortega said the lids are almost three-quarters closed and it appears to be hiding itself, but in fact the lids compress the look and "shoot it out like an arrow."

"It is the look of eyes that are, as it were, asleep but which behind the cloud of sweet drowsiness are utterly awake. Anyone who has such a look possesses a treasure."

Ortega said that Paris throws itself at the feet of anyone with this look. Louis XV's DuBarry was supposed to have had it, and so was Lucien Guitry. In our own Hollywood, Robert Mitchum certainly had it and it set him up for years as a masculine sex symbol. Mae West copied it and the French actress Simone Signoret has it so perfectly controlled that even in middle age she comes across as a very sexy and attractive woman.

Other Cultures, Other Looks

The recognition of the eye as a means of communication, or of a look as having special significance is nothing new. Looking is something that has always had strong emotions attached to it and has been forbidden, under certain circumstances, in prehistory and legend. Lot's wife was turned to a pillar of salt for looking back, and Orpheus lost Eurydice by looking at her. Adam, when he tasted the fruit of knowledge, was afraid to look at God.

The significance of looking is universal, but usually we are not sure of just how we look or how we are looked at. Honesty demands, in our culture, that we look someone straight in the eye. Other cultures have other rules, as a principal in a New York City high school recently discovered.

A young girl at the high school, a fifteen-year-old Puerto Rican, had been caught in the washroom with a group of girls suspected of smoking. Most of the group were known troublemakers, and while this young girl, Livia, had no record, the principal after a brief interview was convinced of her guilt and decided to suspend her with the others.

"It wasn't what she said," he reported later. "It was simply her attitude. There was something sly and suspicious about her. She just wouldn't meet my eye. She wouldn't look at me."

It was true. Livia at her interview with the principal stared down at the floor in what was a clear-cut guilty attitude and refused to meet his eyes.

"But she's a good girl," Livia's mother insisted. Not to the school, for she was too much of a "troublemaker" the principal felt, to come to the authorities with her protest. Instead, she turned to her neighbors and friends. As a result there was a demonstration of Puerto Rican parents at the school the next morning and the ugly stirrings of a threatened riot.

Fortunately, John Flores taught Spanish literature at the school, and John lived only a few doors from Livia and her family. Summoning his own courage, John asked for an interview with the principal.

"I know Livia and her parents," he told the principal. "And she's a good girl. I am sure there has been some mistake in this whole matter."

"If there was a mistake," the principal said uneasily, "I'll be glad to rectify it. There are thirty mothers outside yelling for my blood. But I questioned the child myself, and if ever I saw guilt written on a face— she wouldn't even meet my eyes!"

John drew a sigh of relief, and then very carefully, for he was too new in the school to want to tread on toes, he explained some basic facts of Puerto Rican culture to the principal.

"In Puerto Rico a nice girl, a good girl," he explained, "does not meet the eyes of an adult. Refusing to do so is a sign of respect and obedience. It would be as difficult for Livia to look you in the eye as it would be for her to misbehave, or for her mother to come to you with a complaint. In our culture, this is just not accepted behavior for a respectable family."

Fortunately the principal was a man who knew how to admit that he was wrong. He called Livia and her parents and the most vocal neighbors in and once again discussed the problem. In the light of John Flores' explanation it became obvious to him that Livia was not avoiding his eyes out of defiance, but out of a basic demureness. Her slyness, he now saw, was shyness. In fact, as the conference progressed and the parents relaxed, he realized that Livia was indeed a gentle and sweet girl.

The outcome of the entire incident was a deeper, more meaningful relationship between the school and the community—but that of course is another story. What is of particular interest in this story is the strange confusion of the principal. How did he so obviously misinterpret all the signals of Livia's behavior?

Livia was using body language to say, "I am a good girl. I respect you and the school. I respect you too much to answer your questions, too much to meet your eyes with shameless boldness, too much to defend myself. But surely my very attitude tells you all this."

How could such a clear-cut message be interpreted as, "I defy you. I will not answer your questions. I will not look you in the eyes because I am a deceitful child. I will evade your questions slyly—"

The answer of course is a cultural one. Different cultures have different customs and, of course, different body language. They also have different looks and different meanings to the same looks.

In America, for instance, a man is not supposed to look at a woman for any length of time unless she gives him her permission with a body language signal, a smile, a backward glance, a direct meeting of his eye. In other countries different rules apply.

In America, if a woman looks at a man for too long a period of time, she commits herself to a verbal approach. Her signal says, "I am interested. You can approach me." In Latin countries, though freer body movements are permissible, such a look might be a direct invitation to a physical "pass." It becomes obvious then why a girl like Livia would not look the principal in the eye.

Again, in our country, two men are not allowed to stare at each other for more than a brief period of time unless they intend to fight or to become intimate. Any man who looks at another man for too long embarrasses and annoys him and the other man begins to wonder just what he wants.

This is another example of the rigidity of the rules of looking. If someone stares at us and we meet his eye and catch him staring, it is his duty to look away first. If he does not look away as we engage his eye, then we become uncomfortable and aware that something is wrong. Again we become embarrassed and annoyed.

A Long Look at Oneself

In an attempt to discover just how some of these rules for visual communication work, Dr. Gerhard Neilson of Copenhagen analyzed the "looks" of the subjects in his self-confrontation studies. To discover just how long, and when, the people being interviewed looked at the interviewer, he filmed interviews and replayed them a number of times in slow motion.

While he started with no clear-cut idea of how long one man would look at another during an interview, he was surprised to find how little looking there actually was. The man who looked at his interviewer the most, still looked away 27 percent of the time. The man who looked at his interviewer the least looked away 92 percent of the time. Half of the people interviewed looked away for half of the time they were being interviewed.

Dr. Neilson found that when people spoke a lot they looked at their partners very little; when they listened a lot they also looked a lot. He reports that he expected people to look at each other more when they listened more, but he was surprised to find them looking less when they spoke more.

He found that when people start to speak, they look away from their partners at first. There is a subtle timing, he explains, in speaking, listening, looking and looking away. Most people look away either immediately before or after the beginning of one out of every four speeches they make. A few look away at the beginning of half their speeches. As they finish speaking, half the people look at their partners.

As to why so many people refuse to meet the eyes of their partners during a conversation, Dr. Neilson believes this is a way of avoiding distraction.

How Long Is a Glance?

Another study, carried out by Dr. Ralph V. Exline at the University of Delaware, involved 40 men and 40 women, all freshmen and sophomores. In the study a man interviewed 20 men and 20 women and a woman interviewed the other 20 of each sex. Half the students were questioned by both interviewers about intimate subjects, their plans, desires, needs and fears. The other half were asked about recreational interests, reading, movies, sports.

Dr. Exline found that when the students were interviewed about personal subjects, they didn't look at the interviewer as often as they did when they were interviewed about recreational subjects. Women, however, in both types of interview, looked at the interviewers more frequently than men did.

What seems to come across from both these studies, and others of a similar nature, is that when someone looks away while he's speaking, it generally means he's still explaining himself and doesn't want to be interrupted.

A locking of his gaze with his partner's at this point would be a signal to interrupt when he paused. If he pauses and is not looking at his conversational partner, it means he hasn't yet finished. He is signaling, "This is what I want to say. What is your answer?"

If you look away from the person who is speaking to you while you are listening, it is a signal, "I am not completely satisfied with what you are saying. I have some qualifications."

If you look away while you are speaking it may mean, "I am not certain of what I am saying."

If while you are listening, you look at the speaker, you signal, "I agree with you," or "I am interested in what you are saying."

If while you are speaking, you look at the listener, you may be signaling, "I am certain of what I am saying."

There are also elements of concealment in looking away from your partner. If you look away while he is speaking, you signal, "I don't want you to know what I feel." This is particularly true if the partner is critical or insulting. It is something like an ostrich burying his head in the sand. "If I cannot see you, you cannot hurt me." This is the reason children will often refuse to look at you when you are scolding them.

However, there are more complexities here than meet the eye . . . or the glance. Looking away during a conversation may be a means of concealing something. Therefore when someone else looks away, we may think he is concealing something. To practice deceit we may sometimes deliberately look at our partner instead of refusing to meet his glance.

In addition to length and direction of glances, there is a good deal of signaling involved in the act of closing the lid. In addition to the half-lidded look Ortega described, Birdwhistell states that five young nurses, in a series of tests, reported twenty-three different positions of lid closure that they could distinguish.

But they all agreed that only four out of the twenty-three "meant anything." Retesting allowed Dr. Birdwhistell to label these four positions, "open-eyed, droopy-lidded, squinting, eyes-closed-tight."

Working from the opposite end, trying to get the girls to reproduce the lid positions, was not so successful. All could reproduce five of the twenty-three positions, but only one could reproduce more than five.

Using a group of men in the same type of experiment, he found that all could reproduce at least ten positions. Unexpectedly men were more facile at winking. Some of the men could reproduce fifteen different positions, and one—fantastically eloquent in body language—came up with thirty-five different eyelid positions.

Branching out into cultural comparisons Dr. Birdwhistell found that among the Japanese both sexes were similar in the number of eyelid positions they could reproduce. But even the Japanese could recognize, in others, more positions than they could assume themselves.

When movement of the eyebrows is added to movement of the lids, many more recognizable signals are produced. Some scientists have found as many as forty different positions of the brows alone, though most agree that less than half of them are significant. It is only when the significant eyebrow movements are combined with the significant lid movements and we add forehead creases that the permutations and combinations are endless.

If each combination has a different implication, then there is no end to the number of signals we can transmit with our eyes and the skin around them.

FOR DISCUSSION AND REVIEW

1 What does the ability to stare at an object or person tell you about your attitude toward that person or object?

2 Why is it often considered impolite to wear dark glasses? Do dark glasses annoy you? Explain.

3 What does Fast mean by awkward eyes?

4 What are les yeux en coulisse? What do they tell us about the observer and the observed?

5 According to Dr. Neilson, why in a conversation do speakers not look at their partners more often than

they do? Do you agree with his interpretation? Explain.

6 What does a meeting of the eyes in a conversation say to the person who is not talking?

7 The claim has been made that it is easier to lie verbally than kinesically. Do you think the Halls (pp. 453–470) and Fast would agree with this statement? Do you agree? Explain.

8 Analyze each of the following movie stills. What emotions do you think are expressed by each face? What do the eyes, in particular, tell you?

5
Communication by Gesture in the Middle East

In the preceding selection, Julius Fast related an anecdote that illustrated how eye movements are linked to culture and how a misunderstanding was avoided when this fact was realized. In this essay on gesture in the Arab world, Leo Hamalian offers a more complete picture of body language in a foreign culture. His analysis of the belly dance, the Arab handshake, the courting gestures of Arab males and females, and the influence of social position and education on such gestures is interesting as a study in itself. It is also significant for the contrast it provides in the study of our own body language.

Leo Hamalian

I T WAS, I believe, an Englishman with an eye for epigram as well as for ethnology who remarked that Arabs fight with their mouths and talk with their hands. Even if the events of the next few years in the Middle East should invalidate the first half of this observation, nevertheless the second half will remain true for sometime to come. Of course, Arabs also talk with their mouths, but they have attained such an eloquence of gesture that often words seem superfluous in a conversation. Watching two Arabs conduct a conversation, you begin to feel that you do not have to understand their tongue in order to understand their conversation.

During the first months of my stay in the Middle East (chiefly in Syria, but with frequent visits to Lebanon and Jordan), it seemed to me that these gestures were not subject to classification or generalization, and therefore perhaps without much significance to the semanticist. However, as I continued my observations over the following months, certain patterns began to emerge and now I believe that I can risk several broad statements that may prove useful or interesting to the semanticist who is concerned with the ways of communication in other parts of the world. These statements, incidentally, have been subject to the scrutiny of some of my colleagues at the Syrian University, and while they took issue with a particular point here and there, they agreed in general with the conclusions drawn below.

• Gestures in the Arab world are apparently confined to the hands—although an expert knows how to use all parts of the body to communicate.

• The gestures are usually sex-linked; that is, certain gestures are associated exclusively with men, others with women; also, women seem to depend upon gesture far less than men do.

• Gesture is associated with the level of education—educated Arabs use gesture far less than uneducated Arabs.

• Gestures appear to be associated with expressions of three main emotions: of friendly feelings, of hostile feelings and of erotic feelings.

Most gesture language seems to be confined to the hands, but in that most expressive form of gesture, the dance, the Arab uses the shoulders, the torso, and the legs "to speak"; these gestures often signify an invitation to sexual encounter, but sometimes they express rejection as well. For instance, slowly raising the leg apparently expresses the desire to copulate; the manipulation of the arms may suggest loveplay; and the movement of the hips in a certain manner indicates that the dancer has arrived at a climax. The use of the body to communicate in the so-called "belly dance" (a corruption of the *hareem* dance) is an elaborate art as practiced by the expert; and one of the most baffling yet fascinating experiences for a Westerner fresh to the Middle East is watching an audience respond to the gestures of the dancer. There is conducted, in effect, a dialogue, half in gesture, half in words: the calls of the audience will encourage the dancer to attain new peaks of frenzied movement, which in turn will drive the audience into a state of wild cries and clapping. In panting pantomime, the dancer beckons, tempts, accepts, and consummates, her arms, bosom, hips, and thighs blending in a series of fluid undulations that convey meaning to admiring males as words never could.

For Arab men, this experience is often the only outlet for sexual feelings permitted by the mores of the society, and thus a skilled "belly dancer" holds the same status with them as Marilyn Monroe once had among American men. The varied movements and positions of the "belly dancer" is a subject for a separate paper, preferably by a specialist in the field of dance, but I wanted to indicate briefly in this paper that silent communication is far from limited to the hands.

Certain gestures which correspond to the vocabulary of the men's room are almost never practiced by women. (This is a carry-over from spoken Arabic). Other gestures associated with masculinity are considered to be unsuited to the image of soft femininity. Often this seems to be a matter related to social class: the closer a woman is to the working class, the more likely she is to move into the domain of masculine gesture. For example, sometimes you will see a woman who conducts a stall in the *souq* ball her hand and thrust it with a twist in the direction of a potential purchaser who has haggled too long over price: the gesture plainly says in the Middle East as elsewhere in the Mediterranean area, "Your offer is too low—go screw yourself, friend."

The most common of gestures in the Middle East, lifting the chin upwards to indicate the negative, has been given several nuances by women. The defiant toss of the head usually means "Absolutely not!" A more temperate tilt of the eyebrows while widening the eyes (without any gesture of the head itself) can mean, "I think it is not likely, but you may try to persuade me otherwise." Men use the gesture also, but without the ability to bestow it with the range of meanings that women do. There are, I am sure, many other gestures connected with gender that an experienced anthropologist might bring to light, but I myself found that women of this part of the world are loathe to discuss intimate customs. The fact that there is no literature on the subject does not help such investigation.

Arabs are people of passion who need to express their feelings through gesture as well as words; but the more educated an Arab is, the less he uses gesture, possibly because he has been conditioned by education to inhibit the expression of extravagant feelings. Thus, one of my Syrian colleagues who read this paper discovered much in it that he had not known before. Also, Arabs who have learned Western ways regard communication by gesture as a form of vulgarity, an extension of "lower class" manners. In Damascus, the *souq Hamadiyeh* or the shops lining "The Street Called Straight" are the best places to see Arab conversation in action.

In the Arab world, people like to express their feelings of friendship or antagonism—traditionally among the most important relationships here—in a manner more dramatic than words allow. For example, if an Arab accepts you as a friend, he will place his two index fingers side by side as a sign that he considers you to be his equal in all respects. (From this meaning, the gesture has taken on a secondary significance: "The two things we are talking about are the same.") In Jordan, if a bedouin extends his little finger and invites you to lock pinkies, he is offering friendship; the same gesture involving the second finger means that you are henceforth his enemy. In Syria and Lebanon, these meanings seem to be reversed.

There is also a special way of shaking hands to denote the degree of friendship. Between close friends, the hand is held up and out, as though prepared to make a fast gun-draw, then brought down in an arc to meet the hand of the friend in what becomes an explosive contact of flesh. No one can mistake the warmth and vigor of feeling that two friends put into this gesture. When the same friends take leave of each other, each will place a hand over his heart to indicate that he is sincerely grieved by the parting. The same gesture is used when one refuses the proffer of food or drink. Again, it carries the implication of sincere sorrow.

If one can read signs of friendship clearly, then the signs of antagonism are no less distinct. Perhaps it is necessary for Arabs, who value friendship above anything else, to communicate this basic emotion in a simple, unmistakable language understood everywhere in the Arab world. For example, the index fingers pointing at each other in opposition is one way by which hostility is expressed. If the speaker has passed beyond this stage into open animosity, he will join his index finger and thumb in a circle, draw back his lips in a snarl, and thus silently convey his sentiments: "Watch out, you son of a dog; I'll break your neck if you continue to provoke me." Taxi drivers frequently flash this sign at one another, knowing that they could never make their anger heard above the din of an Arab city.

When one feels happiness or joy at the expense of another person or wishes to show that he is rejoicing in the misfortune of an enemy, he will grind coffee in pantomime or turn his hands into a mortar-and-pestle.

If an Arab feels neither friendly nor hostile, he makes another gesture: he places his thumbs behind the lapels of his jacket and lifts the jacket gently backwards and forwards. A sign of lack of interest, this gesture says: "It is no skin off my nose" or "This matter has nothing to do with me."

The bunched finger-tips, that familiar Mediterranean gesture, has received skillful variations in the hands of the Arabs. Vibrated back and forth, bunched finger-tips can mean, "What is the matter with you, stupid son of a donkey?" Held towards the speaker and drawn back towards his body gradually, it means, "Please—go more slowly" or "Relax, friend, Rome was not built in a century." Tilted out towards the listener, bunched fingers may mean, "What would you like?" or, in our familiar idiom, "What's yours, bud?"

In the domain of sex, which between two unmarried people requires a more covert approach in the Middle East than anywhere else in the world, gesture appears to be indispensable for the tryst. A man who encounters a young lady in public may run his hand over his hair as a way of saying, "Hello, you cool chick." If the response is the same from the young lady, it signifies a willingness to improve relationships. Having struck up an acquaintance, the young man may be emboldened to twist his moustache and close one eye slightly, his way of saying, "I would now like to sleep with you if you don't mind." The young lady who does not draw her veil up indignantly and flee from the premises insulted is apparently ready to hear or see more. Should the young man carry out a successful assignation, he may boast about his conquest to his friends with a scrub-brush motion of his fingers: it usually means, "I slept with her and I am willing to go shares with you." Or the young man may silently signal to his friends, by lifting his leg, stiff-kneed, that the lady is free with her favors. However, if none of his advances were successful, then he may mimic a man turning a light bulb on the wall at hip-level. This generally means, "Well, that's how the cookie crumbles —nothing doing there."

As S. I. Hayakawa says, there are occasions "when it is felt that language is not sufficiently affective by itself to produce the results wanted." On such occasions, the Arab has an unusually rich storehouse of nonverbal communication to draw upon. It gives Middle Eastern life a colorful and exciting quality and perhaps deserves more careful study in the future than it has received in the past. For instance, it is interesting to ask to what extent the success of a Nasser depends upon his mastery of nonverbal communication.

FOR DISCUSSION AND REVIEW

1 What general emotional categories are represented through gesture in the Arab world?

2 According to Hamalian, is gesture in the Middle East confined to a particular area of the body? Explain.

3 What is the relationship between sex and social class in the use of gesture in the Middle East?

4 Does education in the Arab world eliminate gesture or does it change it? Explain.

6

Space Speaks

Edward T. Hall

When we observe a man and a woman whispering to each other, we should realize that they are also communicating something to us. That is, we should recognize that there is a certain degree of intimacy between them because they are close together. We have not in the past considered this kind of information to be communication, nor, until recently, have we attempted to study how space speaks to us. In this chapter from his book *The Silent Language*, Edward T. Hall examines the subject of proxemics and its principles, the concept of territoriality, how Americans view space in a personal and equalitarian manner, and how cultures vary in their use of space.

E VERY LIVING thing has a physical boundary that separates it from its external environment. Beginning with the bacteria and the simple cell and ending with man, every organism has a detectable limit which marks where it begins and ends. A short distance up the phylogenetic scale, however, another, non-physical boundary appears that exists outside the physical one. This new boundary is harder to delimit than the first but is just as real. We call this the "organism's territory." The act of laying claim to and defending a territory is termed territoriality. It is territoriality with which this chapter is most concerned. In man, it becomes highly elaborated, as well as being very greatly differentiated from culture to culture.

Anyone who has had experience with dogs, particularly in a rural setting such as on ranches and farms, is familiar with the way in which the dog handles space. In the first place, the dog knows the limits of his master's "yard" and will defend it against encroachment. There are also certain places where he sleeps: a spot next to the fireplace, a spot in the kitchen, or one in the dining room if he is allowed there. In short, a dog has fixed points to which he returns time after time depending upon the occasion. One can also observe that dogs create zones around them. Depending upon his relationship to the dog and the zone he is in, a trespasser can evoke different behavior when he crosses the invisible lines which are meaningful to the dog.

This is particularly noticeable in females with puppies. A mother who has a new litter in a little-used barn will claim the barn as her territory. When the door opens she may make a slight movement or stirring in one corner. Nothing else may happen as the intruder moves ten or fifteen feet into the barn. Then the dog may raise her head or get up, circle about, and lie down as another invisible boundary is crossed. One can tell about where the line is by withdrawing and watching when her head goes down. As additional lines are crossed, there will be other signals, a thumping of the tail, a low moan or a growl.

One can observe comparable behavior in other vertebrates—fish, birds, and mammals. Birds have well-developed territoriality, areas which they defend as their own and which they return to year after year. To those who have seen a robin come back to the same nest each year this will come as no surprise. Seals, dolphin, and whales are known to use the same breeding grounds. Individual seals have been known to come back to the same rock year after year.

Man has developed his territoriality to an almost unbelievable extent. Yet we treat space somewhat as we treat sex. It is there but we don't talk about it. And if we do, we certainly are not expected to get technical or serious about it. The man of the house is always somewhat apologetic about "his chair." How many people have had the experience of coming into a room, seeing a big comfortable chair and heading for it, only to pull themselves up short, or pause and turn to the man and say, "Oh, was I about to sit in your chair?" The reply, of course, is usually polite. Imagine the effect if the host were to give vent to his true feelings and say, "Hell, yes, you're sitting in my chair, and I don't like anybody sitting in my chair!" For some unknown reason, our culture has tended to play down or cause us to repress and dissociate the feelings we have about space. We relegate it to the informal and are likely to feel guilty whenever we find ourselves getting angry because someone has taken our place.

Territoriality is established so rapidly that even the second session in a series of lectures is sufficient to find a significant proportion of most audiences back in the same seats. What's more, if one has been sitting in a particular seat and someone else occupies it, one can notice a fleeting irritation. There is the remnant of an old urge to throw out the interloper. The interloper knows this too, because he will turn around or look up and say, "Have I got your seat?" at which point you lie and say, "Oh no, I was going to move anyway."

Once while talking on this subject to a group of Americans who were going overseas, one very nice, exceedingly mild-mannered woman raised her hand and said, "You mean it's natural for me to feel irritated when another woman takes over my kitchen?" Answer: "Not only is it natural, but most American women have very strong feelings about their kitchens. Even a mother can't come in and wash the dishes in her daughter's kitchen without annoying her. The kitchen is the place where 'who will dominate' is settled. All women know this, and some can even talk about it. Daughters who can't keep control of their kitchen will be forever under the thumb of any woman who can move into this area."

The questioner continued: "You know that makes me feel so relieved. I have three older sisters and a mother, and every time they come to town they march right into the kitchen and take over. I want to tell them to stay out of my kitchen, that they have their own kitchens and this is my kitchen, but I always thought I was having unkind thoughts about my mother and sisters, thoughts I wasn't supposed to have. This relieves me so much, because now I know I was right."

Father's shop is, of course, another sacred territory and best kept that way. The same applies to his study, if he has one.

As one travels abroad and examines the ways in which space is handled, startling variations are discovered—differences which we react to vigorously. Since none of us is taught to look at space as isolated from other associations, feelings cued by the handling of space are often attributed to something else. In growing up people learn literally thousands of spatial cues, all of which have their own meaning in their own context. These cues "release" responses already established in much the same way as Pavlov's bells started his dogs salivating. Just how accurate a spatial memory is has never been completely tested. There are indications, however, that it is exceedingly persistent.

Literally thousands of experiences teach us unconsciously that space communicates. Yet this fact would probably never have been brought to the level of consciousness if it had not been realized that space is organized differently in each culture. The associations and feelings that are released in a member of one culture almost invariably mean something else in the next. When we say that some foreigners are "pushy," all this means is that their handling of space releases this association in our minds.

What gets overlooked is that the response is there *in toto* and has been there all along. There is no point in well-meaning people feeling guilty because they get angry when a foreigner presents them with a spatial cue that releases anger or aggression. The main thing is to know what is happening and try to find out which cue was responsible. The next step is to discover, if possible, whether the person really intended to release this particular feeling or whether he intended to engender a different reaction.

Uncovering the specific cues in a foreign culture is a painstaking and laborious process. Usually it is easier for the newcomer to listen to the observations of old-timers and then test these observations against his own experience. At first he may hear, "You're going to have a hard time getting used to the way these people crowd you. Why, when you are trying to buy a theater ticket, instead of standing in line and waiting their turn they all try to reach in and get their money to the ticket seller at once. It's just terrible the way you have to push and shove just to keep your place. Why, the last time I got to the ticket window of the theater and poked my head up to the opening, there were five arms and hands reaching over my shoulder waving money." Or he may hear the following: "It's as much as your life is worth to ride the streetcars. They're worse than our subways. What's more, these people don't seem to mind it at all." Some of this stems from the fact that, as Americans we have a pattern which discourages touching, except in moments of intimacy. When we ride on a streetcar or crowded elevator we will "hold ourselves in," having been taught from early childhood to avoid bodily contact with strangers. Abroad, it's confusing when conflicting feelings are being released at the same time. Our senses are bombarded by a strange language, different smells, and gestures, as well as a host of signs and symbols.

However, the fact that those who have been in a foreign country for some time talk about these things provides the newcomer with advance warning. Getting over a spatial accent is just as important, sometimes more so, than eliminating a spoken one. Advice to the newcomer might be: Watch where people stand, and don't back up. You will feel funny doing it, but it's amazing how much difference it makes in people's attitudes toward you.

How Different Cultures Use Space

Several years ago a magazine published a map of the United States as the average New Yorker sees it. The details of New York were quite clear and the suburbs to the north were also accurately shown. Hollywood appeared in some detail while the space in between New York and Hollywood was almost a total blank. Places like Phoenix, Albuquerque, the Grand Canyon, and Taos, New Mexico, were all crowded into a hopeless jumble. It was easy to see that the average New Yorker knew little and cared less for what went on in the rest of the country. To the geographer the map was a distortion of the worst kind. Yet to the student of culture it was surprisingly accurate. It showed the informal images that many people have of the rest of the country.

As a graduate student I lived in New York, and my landlord was a first-generation American of European extraction who had lived in New York all his life. At the end of the academic year as I was leaving, the landlord came down to watch me load my car. When I said goodby, he remarked, "Well, one of these Sunday afternoons I put my family in the car and we drive out to New Mexico to see you."

The map and the landlord's comment illustrate how Americans treat space as highly personalized. We visualize the relationship between places we know by personal experience. Places which we haven't been to and with which we are not personally identified tend to remain confused.

Traditionally American space begins with "a place." It is one of the oldest sets, comparable to, but not quite the same as, the Spanish *lugar*. The reader will have no difficulty thinking up ways in which place is used: "He found a place in her heart," "He has a place in the mountains," "I am tired of this place," and so on. Those who have children know how difficult it is to get across to them the whole concept of place—like Washington, or Boston, or Philadelphia, and so on. An American child requires between six and seven years before he has begun to master the basic concepts of place. Our culture provides for a great variety of places, including different classes of places.

Contrasted with the Middle East, our system is characterized by fine gradations as one moves from one space category to the next. In the world of the Arab there are villages and cities. That is about all. Most non-nomadic Arabs think of themselves as villagers. The actual villages are of varying population, from a few families up to several thousands.

The smallest place category in the United States is not covered by a term like hamlet, village, or town. It is immediately recognizable as a territorial entity, nevertheless, because such places are always named. They are areas with no recognizable center where a number of families live—like Dogpatch of the funny papers.

Our Dogpatches present the basic American pattern in uncomplicated form. They have scattered residences with no concentration of buildings in one spot. Like time, place with us is diffused, so that you never quite know where its center is. Beyond this the naming of place categories begins with the "crossroads store" or "corner" and continues with the "small shopping center," the "county seat," the "small town," "large town," "metropolitan center," "city," and "metropolis." Like much of the rest of our culture, including the social ranking system, there are no clear gradations as one moves from one category to the next. The "points" are of varying sizes, and there are no linguistic cues indicating the size of the place we are talking about. The United States, New Mexico, Albuquerque, Pecos are all said the same way and used the same way in sentences. The child who is learning the language has no way of distinguishing one space category from another by listening to others talk.

The miracle is that children eventually are able to sort out and pin down the different space terms from the meager cues provided by others. Try telling a five-year-old the difference between where you live in the suburbs and the town where your wife goes to shop. It will be a frustrating task, since the child, at that age, only comprehends where *he* lives. His room, his house, his place at the table are the places that are learned early.

The reason most Americans have difficulty in school with geography or geometry stems from the fact that space as an informal cultural system is different from space as it is technically elaborated by classroom geography and mathematics. It must be said in fairness to ourselves that other cultures have similar problems. Only the very perceptive adult realizes that there is anything really difficult for the child to learn about space. In reality, he has to take what is literally a spatial blur and isolate the significant points that adults talk about. Sometimes adults are unnecessarily impatient with children because they don't catch on. People do not realize that the child has heard older people talking about different places and is trying to figure out, from what he hears, the difference between this place and that. In this regard it should be pointed out that the first clues which suggest to children that one thing is different from another come from shifts in tone of voice which direct attention in very subtle but important ways. Speaking a fully developed language as we do, it is hard to remember that there was a time when we could not speak at all and when the whole communicative process was carried on by means of variations in the voice tone. This early language is lost to consciousness and functions out of awareness, so that we tend to forget the very great role it plays in the learning process.

To continue our analysis of the way a child learns about space, let us turn to his conception of a road. At first a road is whatever he happens to be driving on. This doesn't mean that he can't tell when you take a wrong turn. He can, and often will even correct a mistake which is made. It only means that he has not yet broken the road down into its components and that he makes the distinction between this road and that road in just the same way that he learns to distinguish between the phoneme *d* and the phoneme *b* in initial position in the spoken language.

Using roads for cross-cultural contrast, the reader will recall that Paris, being an old city as well as a French city, has a street-naming system that puzzles most Americans. Street names shift as one progresses. Take Rue St.-Honoré, for example, which becomes Rue du Faubourg St.-Honoré, Avenue des Ternes, and Avenue du Roule. A child growing up in Paris, however, has no more difficulty learning his system than one of our children learning ours. We teach ours to watch the intersections and the directions and that when something happens—that is,

when there is a change of course at one of these points—you can expect
the name to change. In Paris the child learns that as he passes certain
landmarks—like buildings that are well known, or statues—the name of
the street changes.

It is interesting and informative to watch very young children as
they learn their culture. They quickly pick up the fact that we have
names for some things and not for others. First, they identify the whole
object or the set—a room, for instance; then they begin to fixate on
certain other discrete objects like books, ashtrays, letter openers, tables,
and pencils. By so doing they accomplish two things. First, they find
out how far down the scale they have to go in identifying things. Second, they learn what are the isolates and patterns for handling space
and object nomenclature. First children are often better subjects than
second children, because, having learned the hard way, the first one will
teach the second one without involving the parents.

The child will ask, "What's this?" pointing to a pencil. You reply,
"A pencil." The child is not satisfied and says, "No, this," pointing to
the shaft of the pencil and making clear that she meant the shaft. So
you say, "Oh, that's the shaft of the pencil." Then the child moves her
finger one quarter inch and says, "What's this?" and you say, "The
shaft." This process is repeated and you say, "That's still the shaft; and
this is the shaft, and this is the shaft. It's all the shaft of the pencil.
This is the shaft, this is the point, and this is the eraser, and this is the
little tin thing that holds the eraser on." Then she may point to the
eraser, and you discover that she is still trying to find out where the
dividing lines are. She manages to worm out the fact that the eraser
has a top and sides but no more. She also learns that there is no way to
tell the difference between one side and the next and that no labels are
pinned on parts of the point, even though distinctions are made between the lead and the rest of the pencil. She may glean from this that
materials make a difference some of the time and some of the time
they do not. Areas where things begin and end are apt to be important,
while the points in between are often ignored.

The significance of all this would undoubtedly have escaped me if
it hadn't been for an experience on the atoll of Truk. In a rather detailed series of studies in technology I had progressed to the point of
having to obtain the nomenclature of the canoe and the wooden food
bowl. At this point it was necessary for me to go through what children
go through—that is, point to various parts after I thought I had the
pattern and ask if I had the name right. As I soon discovered, their system of carving up microspace was radically different from our own. The
Trukese treat open spaces, without dividing lines (as we know them),
as completely distinct. Each area has a name. On the other hand, they
have not developed a nomenclature for the edges of objects as elab-

orately as Westerners have done. The reader has only to think of rims
and cups and the number of different ways in which these can be referred to. There is the rim itself. It can be square or round or elliptical
in cross section; straight, flared, or curved inward; plain or decorated,
and wavy or straight. This doesn't mean that the Trukese don't elaborate rims. They do; it just means that we have ways of talking about
what we do and not as many ways of talking about what happens to an
open area as they do. The Trukese separate parts which we think of as
being "built in" to the object.

A certain decoration or carving at either end of a canoe-shaped food
bowl is thought of as being separate or distinct from the rim in which
it has been carved. It has an essence of its own. Along the keel of the
canoe the carving, called the *chunefatch,* has characteristics with which
it endows the canoe. The canoe is one thing, the chunefatch something
else. Open spaces without obvious markers on the side of the bowl have
names. Such distinctions in the dividing up of space make the settling
of land claims unbelievably complicated in these islands. Trees, for instance, are considered separate from the soil out of which they grow.
One man may own the trees, another the soil below.

Benjamin Whorf, describing how Hopi concepts of space are reflected in the language, mentions the absence of terms for interior
three-dimensional spaces, such as words for room, chamber, hall, passage, interior, cell, crypt, cellar, attic, loft and vault. This does not alter
the fact that the Hopi have multi-room dwellings and even use the
rooms for special purposes such as storage, grinding corn, and the like.

Whorf also notes the fact that it is impossible for the Hopi to add
a possessive pronoun to the word for room and that in the Hopi scheme
of things a room in the strict sense of the word is not a noun and does
not act like a noun.

Since there is a wealth of data on how strongly the Hopi feel about
holding onto things which are theirs, one has to rule out the possessive
factor in Whorf's references to their inability to say "my room." It's
just that their language is different. One might be led to assume by this
that the Hopi would then lack a sense of territoriality. Again, nothing
could be farther from the truth. They just use and conceive of space
differently. We work from points and along lines. They apparently do
not. While seemingly inconsequential, these differences caused innumerable headaches to the white supervisors who used to run the Hopi
reservation in the first part of this century.

I will never forget driving over to one of the villages at the end of
a mesa and discovering that someone was building a house in the
middle of the road. It later developed that the culprit (in my eyes) was
a man I had known for some time. I said, "Paul, why are you building
your house in the middle of the road? There are lots of good places on

either side of the road. This way people have to knock the bottoms out of their cars driving around on the rocks to get to the village." His reply was short and to the point: "I know, but it's my right." He did have a right to a certain area laid down long before there was a road. The fact that the road had been used for many years meant nothing to him. Use and disuse of space in our terms had nothing to do with his ideas of possession.

Space as a Factor in Culture Contact

Whenever an American moves overseas, he suffers from a condition known as "culture shock." Culture shock is simply a removal or distortion of many of the familiar cues one encounters at home and the substitution for them of other cues which are strange. A good deal of what occurs in the organization and use of space provides important leads as to the specific cues responsible for culture shock.

The Latin house is often built around a patio that is next to the sidewalk but hidden from outsiders behind a wall. It is not easy to describe the degree to which small architectural differences such as this affect outsiders. American Point Four technicians living in Latin America used to complain that they felt "left out" of things, that they were "shut off." Others kept wondering what was going on "behind those walls." In the United States, on the other hand, propinquity is the basis of a good many relationships. To us the neighbor is actually quite close. Being a neighbor endows one with certain rights and privileges, also responsibilities. You can borrow things, including food and drink, but you also have to take your neighbor to the hospital in an emergency. In this regard he has almost as much claim on you as a cousin. For these and other reasons the American tries to pick his neighborhood carefully, because he knows that he is going to be thrown into intimate contact with people. We do not understand why it is that when we live next to people abroad the sharing of adjacent space does not always conform to our own pattern. In France and England, for instance, the relations between neighbors are apt to be cooler than in the United States. Mere propinquity does not tie people together. In England neighbor children do not play as they do in our neighborhoods. When they do play, arrangements are sometimes made a month in advance as though they were coming from the other side of town!

Another example has to do with the arrangement of offices. In this case one notices great contrast between ourselves and the French. Part of our over-all pattern in the United States is to take a given amount of space and divide it up equally. When a new person is added in an office, almost everyone will move his desk so that the newcomer will have his share of the space. This may mean moving from positions that have been occupied for a long time and away from favorite views from the window. The point is that the office force will make its own adjustments voluntarily. In fact, it is a signal that they have acknowledged the presence of the new person when they start rearranging the furniture. Until this has happened, the boss can be sure that the new person has not been integrated into the group.

Given a large enough room, Americans will distribute themselves around the walls, leaving the center open for group activities such as conferences. That is, the center belongs to the group and is often marked off by a table or some object placed there both to use and save the space. Lacking a conference table, members will move their chairs away from their desks to form a "huddle" in the middle. The pattern of moving from one's place to huddle is symbolized in our language by such expressions as, "I had to take a new position on that point," or "The position of the office on this point is . . ."

The French, by contrast, do not make way for each other in the un-. spoken, taken-for-granted way that we do. They do not divide up the space with a new colleague. Instead they may grudgingly give him a small desk in a dark corner looking toward the wall. This action speaks eloquently to Americans who have found themselves working for the French. We feel that not to "make a place" accents status differences. If the rearrangement which says, "Now we admit you to the group, and you are going to stay," fails to take place, Americans are likely to feel perilously insecure. In French offices the key figure is the man in the middle, who has his fingers on everything so that all runs smoothly. There is a centralized control. The French educational system runs from the middle, so that all students all over France take the same class at the same time.

It has already been mentioned that ordering is an important element in American patterns. As a general rule, whenever services are involved we feel that people should queue up in order of arrival. This reflects the basic equalitarianism of our culture. In cultures where a class system or its remnants exist, such ordinality may not exist. That is, where society assigns rank for certain purposes, or wherever ranking is involved, the handling of space will reflect this.

To us it is regarded as a democratic virtue for people to be served without reference to the rank they hold in their occupational group. The rich and poor alike are accorded equal opportunity to buy and be waited upon in the order of arrival. In a line at the theater Mrs. Gotrocks is no better than anyone else. However, apart from the English, whose queueing patterns we share, many Europeans are likely to look upon standing in line as a violation of their individuality. I am reminded of a Pole who reacted this way. He characterized Americans as sheep, and the mere thought of such passiveness was likely to set him off crashing into a line at whatever point he pleased. Such people can't stand the idea of being held down by group conformity as if they were an automaton. Americans watching the Pole thought he was "pushy." He didn't bother to hide the fact that he thought we were much too subdued. He used to say, "What does it matter if there is a little confusion and some people get served before others?"

Formal Space Patterns

Depending upon the culture in question, the formal patterning of space can take on varying degrees of importance and complexity. In America, for example, no one direction takes precedence over another except in a technical or utilitarian sense. In other cultures one quickly discovers that some directions are sacred or preferred. Navajo doors must face east, the mosques of the Moslems must be oriented toward Mecca, the sacred rivers of India flow south. Americans pay attention to direction in a technical sense, but formally and informally they have no preference. Since our space is largely laid out by technical people, houses, towns, and main arteries are usually oriented according to one of the points of the compass. The same applies to roads and main highways when the topography allows, as it does in the flat expanses of Indiana and Kansas. This technical patterning allows us to locate places by co-ordinates (a point on the line). "He lives at 1321 K Street, N.W." tells us that he lives in the northwest part of town in the thirteenth block west of the line dividing the town into east-west halves and eleven blocks north of the line dividing the town into north-south halves, on the left side of the street, about one quarter of the way up the block.

In the country we will say, "Go out of town ten miles west on Highway 66 until you get to the first paved road turning north. Turn right on that road and go seven miles. It's the second farm on your left. You can't miss it."

Our concept of space makes use of the edges of things. If there aren't any edges, we make them by creating artificial lines (five miles west and two miles north). Space is treated in terms of a co-ordinate system. In contrast, the Japanese and many other people work within areas. They name "spaces" and distinguish between one space and the next or parts of a space. To us a space is empty—one gets into it by intersecting it with lines.

A technical pattern which may have grown out of an informal base is that of positional value or ranking. We have canonized the idea of the positional value in almost every aspect of our lives, so much so that even children four years old are fully aware of its implications and are apt to fight with each other as to who will be first.

In addition to positional value, the American pattern emphasizes equality and standardization of the segments which are used for measuring space or into which space is divided, be it a ruler or a suburban subdivision. We like our components to be standard and equal. American city blocks tend to have uniform dimensions whereas towns in many other parts of the world are laid out with unequal blocks. This suggests that it was no accident that mass production, made possible by the standardization of parts, had its origins in the Untied States. There are those who would argue that there are compelling technological reasons for both mass production and parts standardization. However, an examination of actual practice indicates that Europeans have produced automobiles in the past—and very good ones too—in which the cylinders were all of different sizes. The difference in dimensions was not great, of course, a matter of a very few thousands of an inch. This, however, was enough to cause the car to make noise and use too much oil if it was repaired by an American mechanic unfamiliar with the European patterns that lack the uniformity isolate.

Japan, too, has a passion for uniformity, though it is somewhat different from ours. All mats (*tatami*) on the floors of Japanese houses and all windows, doors, and panels are usually of identical dimensions in a given district. In newspaper advertisements of houses for sale or rent the dimensions are usually given in terms of the number of mats of a specific area. Despite this example of uniformity, the Japanese differ from us in a way which can have considerable economic results. In one case, for example, they manufactured a very large order of electronics parts according to rigid specifications which they were quite able to meet. When the product arrived in the United States, it was discovered that there were differences between various batches of these parts. The customer subsequently discovered that while the whole internal process of manufacture had been controlled, the Japanese had failed to standardize their gauges! It is no accident that in the United States there is a Bureau of Standards. Much of the success of this country's technical skill and productivity, which we are trying to pass on to other nations, rests on these and similar unstated patterns.

How Space Communicates

Spatial changes give a tone to a communication, accent it, and at times even override the spoken word. The flow and shift of distance between people as they interact with each other is part and parcel of the communication process. The normal conversational distance between strangers illustrates how important are the dynamics of space interaction. If a person gets too close, the reaction is instantaneous and automatic—the other person backs up. And if he gets too close again, back we go again. I have observed an American backing up the entire length of a long corridor while a foreigner whom he considers pushy tries to catch up with him. This scene has been enacted thousands and thousands of times—one person trying to increase the distance in order to be at ease, while the other tries to decrease it for the same reason, neither one being aware of what was going on. We have here an example of the tremendous depth to which culture can condition behavior.

One thing that does confuse us and gets in the way of understanding cultural differences is that there are times in our own culture when people are either distant or pushy in their use of space. We, therefore, simply associate the foreigner with the familiar; namely those people who have acted in such a way that our attention was drawn to their actions. The error is in jumping to the conclusion that the foreigner feels the same way the American does even though his overt acts are identical.

This was all suddenly brought into focus one time when I had the good fortune to be visited by a very distinguished and learned man who had been for many years a top-ranking diplomat representing a foreign country. After meeting him a number of times, I had become impressed with his extraordinary sensitivity to the small details of behavior that are so significant in the interaction process. Dr. X. was interested in some of the work several of us were doing at the time and asked permission to attend one of my lectures. He came to the front of the class at the end of the lecture to talk over a number of points made in the preceding hour. While talking he became quite involved in the implications of the lecture as well as what he was saying. We started out facing each other and as he talked I became dimly aware that he was standing a little too close and that I was beginning to back up. Fortunately I was able to suppress my first impulse and remain stationary because there was nothing to communicate aggression in his behavior except the conversational distance. His voice was eager, his manner intent, the set of his body communicated only interest and eagerness to talk. It also came to me in a flash that someone who had been so successful in the old school of diplomacy could not possibly let himself communicate something offensive to the other person except outside of his highly trained awareness.

By experimenting I was able to observe that as I moved away slightly, there was an associated shift in the pattern of interaction. He had more trouble expressing himself. If I shifted to where I felt comfortable (about twenty-one inches), he looked somewhat puzzled and hurt, almost as though he were saying: "Why is he acting that way? Here I am doing everything I can to talk to him in a friendly manner and he suddenly withdraws. Have I done anything wrong? Said something that I shouldn't?" Having ascertained that distance had a direct effect on his conversation, I stood my ground, letting him set the distance.

Not only is a vocal message qualified by the handling of distance, but the substance of a conversation can often demand special handling of space. There are certain things which are difficult to talk about unless one's is within the proper conversational zone.

Not long ago I received a present of some seeds and chemicals along with the information that if I planted the seeds the chemicals would make them grow. Knowing little about hydroponics except that the plants should be suspended above the fluid in which chemicals are dissolved, I set out to find a suitable flowerpot. At every flower shop I was met with incredulity and forced to go through a routine involving a detailed explanation of just what it was I wanted and how hydroponics worked.

My ignorance of both hydroponics and florist shops made me feel somewhat ill at ease, so that I did not communicate in the manner that I use when I am speaking on a familiar subject in a familiar setting. The role that distance plays in a communication situation was brought home to me when I entered a shop in which the floor was filled with benches spaced at about twenty-inch intervals. On the other side of the benches was the female proprietor of the shop. As I entered, she craned her neck as though to reach over the benches, raised her voice slightly to bring it up to the proper level, and said, "What was it you wanted?" I tried once. "What I'm looking for is a *hydroponic* flowerpot." "What kind of flowerpot?" still with the neck craned. At this point I found myself climbing over benches in an effort to close up the space. It was simply impossible for me to talk about such a subject in a setting of this sort at a distance of fifteen feet. It wasn't until I got to within three feet that I was able to speak with some degree of comfort.

Another example is one that will be familiar to millions of civilians who served in the Army during World War II. The Army, in its need to get technical about matters that are usually handled informally, made a mistake in the regulations on distance required for reporting to a superior officer. Everyone knows that the relationship between officers and men has certain elements which require distance and impersonality. This applied to officers of different ranks when they were in command relationship to each other. Instructions for reporting to a superior officer were that the junior officer was to proceed up to a point three paces in front of the officer's desk, stop, salute, and state his rank, his name, and his business: "Lieutenant X, reporting as ordered, sir." Now, what cultural norms does this procedure violate, and what does it communicate? It violates the conventions for the use of space. The distance is too great, by at least two feet, and does not fit the situation. The normal speaking distance for business matters, where impersonality is involved at the beginning of the conversation, is five and a half to eight feet. The distance required by the army regulations borders on the edge of what we would call "far." It evokes an automatic response to shout. This detracts from the respect which is supposed to be shown to the superior officer. There are, of course, many subjects which it is almost impossible to talk about at this distance, and individual army officers recognize this by putting soldiers and junior officers at ease, asking them to sit down or permitting them to come closer. However, the first impression was that the Army was doing things the hard way.

For Americans the following shifts in the voice are associated with specific ranges of distances:

1. *Very close* (3 in. to 6 in.)   Soft whisper; top secret
2. *Close* (8 in to 12 in.)   Audible whisper; very confidential
3. *Near* (12 in. to 20 in.)   Indoors, soft voice; outdoors, full voice; confidential
4. *Neutral* (20 in. to 36 in.)   Soft voice, low volume; personal subject matter
5. *Neutral* (4½ ft. to 5 ft.)   Full voice; information of nonpersonal matter
6. *Public Distance* (5½ ft. to 8 ft.)   Full voice with slight overloudness; public information for others to hear
7. *Across the room* (8 ft. to 20 ft.)   Loud voice; talking to a group
8. *Stretching the limits of distance*   20 ft. to 24 ft. indoors; up to 100 ft. outdoors; hailing distance, departures

In Latin America the interaction distance is much less than it is in the United States. Indeed, people cannot talk comfortably with one another unless they are very close to the distance that evokes either sexual or hostile feelings in the North American. The result is that when they move close, we withdraw and back away. As a consequence, they think we are distant or cold, withdrawn and unfriendly. We, on the other hand, are constantly accusing them of breathing down our necks, crowding us, and spraying our faces.

Americans who have spent some time in Latin America without learning these space considerations make other adaptations, like barricading themselves behind their desks, using chairs and typewriter tables to keep the Latin American at what is to us a comfortable distance. The result is that the Latin American may even climb over the obstacles until he has achieved a distance at which he can comfortably talk.

FOR DISCUSSION AND REVIEW

1 What are some of the ways in which territoriality communicates?

2 What is culture shock, and what does the use of space have to do with it? How might a lack of awareness of the ways in which foreign cultures use space create embarrassing situations?

3 What is the connection between Hall's discussion of the territoriality of an individual and commuting by car as opposed to public transportation? How does the concept of territoriality help explain irritability caused by rush-hour traffic?

4 It has been theorized that the concept of American equality is related to the way in which we use space. What is the basis of this theory?

5 Review the article by Woolfson (pp. 28–35). What are some of the possible implications of the Whorfian hypothesis on the study of space?

6 The next time you go to a movie or watch television, carefully note the utilization of space by the characters involved. How do people react when their territory is invaded? What defenses do they employ against invasion? How does the invader act?

7 What is the relationship between space and personality? In what ways can this information be valuable to a parent? A teacher? A psychiatrist? A prison warden?

8 Each of the following photographs illustrates the proxemic principles discussed by Professor Hall. Analyze each of the pictures in terms of spatial relationships and gestural activity. Explain your findings, and be prepared to discuss your interpretations.

PROJECTS FOR "THE LANGUAGE OF THE BODY: KINESICS AND PROXEMICS"

1 Study the following illustration of a typical buyer-seller relationship; the buyer is on the left and the seller on the right. Discuss the interaction

between the buyer and the seller in terms of their gestures, their personal appearances, and their proxemic arrangement. What general statements can you make about the buyer? About the seller?

2 Study a short movie while the sound is turned off. Make notes on your observations of proxemics and body language and what you learn from these aspects of behavior. Turn on the sound and make notes on your findings once again. Write a paper that discusses the quantitative and qualitative differences in what you learned from both viewings. Ideally, you should try to determine the relative importance of body language, verbal communication, and proxemics.

3 Using the following diagrams of common classroom seating arrange-

"row-by-row"   "horseshoe"   "circle"

OOOOOOOOOOOOOOO

X

O = student
X = teacher

ments, devise an experiment that will test the effects on behavior of the various arrangements. You may wish to poll the feelings of members of a number of classes and elicit reasons for their feelings. Which arrangement was judged most comfortable? Least comfortable? Why? Is there any relationship between seating arrangements and class size? Between seating arrangements and class or grade level? Between seating arrangements and types of classroom activities or subject matter? **Explain.**

4   Play a game that involves body language. For example, divide players into groups to act out situations involving body language—a tough cop ticketing a motorist; one person trying to give directions to another but not succeeding; a man trying to be friendly with a woman who really does not wish to be bothered but who also does not wish to be impolite. Performances should be judged by the group as a whole on the basis of the degree to which performers illustrate a knowledge of body language.

5   Collect a dozen printed advertisements for the purpose of determining the degree to which they illustrate principles of body language and proxemics. You should limit your study to various advertisements dealing with one particular product (e.g., perfume, stockings, cars, cigarettes, etc.).

5   Ray L. Birdwhistell, a pioneer in the field of kinesics, has claimed that a trained observer can tell where a person is from by the body language he or she uses. Study a foreigner or a person who lives in a part of the country different from your own to see if you can identify characteristics of nonverbal language to support Birdwhistell's statement.

'   It has been estimated that 65 percent of communication is extraverbal, whereas only 35 percent is verbal. Study a dramatic presentation of a play or a movie made from a novel and test the accuracy of this claim. For example, locate a specific scene in the written work in which the thoughts and feelings of a character are revealed through an omniscient narrator. Study how these feelings and thoughts are conveyed to you in the dramatic version.

Body language as a science may be new, but authors as far back in history as Homer were aware of how important the descriptions of characters could be. Some critics say that in his short story "Clay" in Dubliners, James Joyce describes Maria as having witch-like characteristics, the recognition of which is central to the meaning of his story. Joyce does not tell us that Maria is a witch; he shows her to be one, and that method is very effective. Herman Melville in his short story "Bartleby the Scrivener" makes use of his knowledge of proxemics. The story's subtitle is "A Story of Wall Street," and it is indeed a story of walls and the frustrations that they symbolize in Bartleby, the main character. Study a scene from a work of literature for what *it tells you through its use of kinesics and proxemics. You may wish to consider scenes from such works as Twain's Pudd'nhead Wilson, James's The American, or Nathanael West's The Day of The Locust.*

9   *The following advertisement was used to promote the "Metropolitan Museum of Art Seminars in the Home" series. It features two paintings by Holbein the Younger, both commissioned by Henry VIII. Carefully read the text of the advertisement.*

     Artists have long utilized a knowledge of body language in making their work more communicative and effective. "Every major work of art," as the advertisement says, "contains clues to what the artist is trying to reveal." Carefully analyze for kinesic and proxemic "clues" Titian's "Venus," da Vinci's "The Last Supper," or a painting of your choice in which human figures play an important role. Explain how the "clues" help you interpret the work of art.

10   *In Body Language, Julius Fast states that "when a man's territorial defenses are weakened or intruded upon, his self-assurance tends to grow weaker." As an experiment, try invading the territory of a friend or roommate. For example, look over his or her shoulder while he or she is typing. What happens? Think of other situations in which you can invade territory claimed by one or more people. Do your experiences in invading these territories confirm Fast's generalization? Explain.*

SELECTED BIBLIOGRAPHY

Ardrey, Robert. *The Territorial Imperative.* New York: Atheneum, 1966. (An examination of the concept of territoriality, the relationship of men and animals to space.)

Baker, Stephen. *Visual Persuasion.* New York: McGraw-Hill, 1961. (An analysis of "picture-talk" in modeling, advertising and corporate business.)

Birdwhistell, Ray L. *Introduction to Kinesics.* Louisville: University of Louisville Press, 1952. (Introduction to the field of kinesics, with kinegraphs and what they symbolize.)

————. "Kinesics." *International Encyclopaedia of Social Sciences.* Ed. David L. Sills. New York: Macmillan and The Free Press, 1968. (A brief but technical introduction.)

————. *Kinesics and Context: Essays on Body Motion Communication.* Philadelphia: University of Pennsylvania Press, 1970. (An interesting collection of Birdwhistell's essays on nonverbal human communication; excellent bibliography.)

Blackmon, Rosemary. "How Much Do You Tell When You Talk?" *Vogue,* July 1961, pp. 40–41, 100–101. (A readable discussion of paralinguistic speech features.)

Bosmajian, Haig A. *The Rhetoric of Nonverbal Communication: Readings.* Glenview, Illinois: Scott, Foresman and Company, 1971. (An introduction to the rhetoric of nonverbal communication and its powers of persuasion.)

If you were Henry VIII, which princess would you marry?

Here are details from two famous portraits of [noble] young princesses, Christina of Denmark on the left [and] Anne of Cleves on the right. Holbein the Younger [painted] both for Henry VIII, to help the English king [choose] his fourth wife without making a tedious trip across [Europe] to meet the princesses in person.

Holbein wanted his patron to know something [about] each girl's personality, as well as her appearance.

And so, as John Canaday points out in the [Metropolitan] Museum Seminars in Art, the artist painted [subtly], intelligent Christina in a subdued costume that does [little] to distract attention from the girl herself. In contrast, [he portrayed] the sweet but rather dull Anne in an elabo-[rately] jeweled headdress and robe, far more interesting than [her] face. Christina looks forthrightly at us, while Anne's [eyes] evade us. Christina's hands are full of graceful move-[ment], while Anne's are submissively folded.

What Holbein suggested about the contrasting [personalities] of the two princesses, through the details [and] composition of their portraits, turned out to be true. [The more discerning Christina was not charmed by Henry's [reputation] as a husband, and turned down the thrice-[married] king. Placid, obedient Anne then accepted—but a [bored] Henry divorced her with indecent haste.

Every major work of art contains clues to what the artist is trying to reveal. Yet a surprising number of well-educated people are blind to these clues. It was to help such people that the Metropolitan Museum and John Canaday, now art critic of The New York Times, created the Seminars in Art.

Each seminar is a handsome portfolio, the core of which is a lecture on one aspect of painting. Each is illustrated with many black-and-white pictures and twelve large separate full-color reproductions of notable paintings. As you compare these masterpieces, Mr. Canaday's lectures clarify their basic differences and similarities, and so reveal what to look for in any painting you may see.

Soon, paintings will be more than just "good" or "bad" to you. You will be able to talk knowledgeably when you visit a gallery or museum. And parents will find themselves sharing their understanding with their children, providing a foundation for a lifelong interest in art.

You can study the first seminar by mailing the coupon to the Book-of-the-Month Club, which administers the program for the Museum. You will receive the first of the twelve portfolios, What Is a Painting?, for a two week trial examination. Subsequent portfolios, sent at the rate of ap-proximately one a month, are devoted to realism, expressionism, abstraction, composition, painting techniques and the role of the artist as social critic and visionary.

If you choose not to continue, return the portfolio, canceling your subscription. There's no obligation. Otherwise, you pay only $5.50, plus postage and handling, for this and each portfolio you accept.

Metropolitan Museum of Art Seminars in the Home

c/o Book-of-the-Month Club, Inc.
280 Park Avenue, New York, N.Y. 10017

Please enroll me as a subscriber and send me Portfolio I, What Is a Painting? If after two weeks I decide not to continue, I may return it, canceling my subscription. If I retain it, bill me $5.50 for it and for each of the remaining portfolios as they are received. I may cancel this subscription at any time. A postage and handling charge is added to all shipments.

PRINT NAME_____

ADDRESS_____

CITY_____STATE_____ZIP_____
PLEASE NOTE: IN CANADA, PRICE OF EACH PORTFOLIO IS $6.00 PLUS MAILING.

Chaitanya. "The School of Silence." *Quest,* 59 (Autumn 1968), 48–51. (Gesture, movement, and silence as means of dramatic expression and communication.)

Chase, Stuart. *The Proper Study of Mankind* . . . New York: Harper & Row, 1956. (See pp. 276–289; an informative chapter on the communication sciences, twelve disciplines pursuing communication study.)

Critchley, M. *The Language of Gesture.* London: Arnold, 1939. (A valuable early study.)

————. *Silent Language.* London: Butterworths, 1975. (A thorough study of gestural language—emphasis given to sign languages, rhetoric, and dance.)

Darwin, Charles R. *The Expression of the Emotions in Man and Animals.* London: J. Murray, 1873. (A germinal work.)

Davis, Flora. "The Way We Speak 'Body Language.' " *New York Times Magazine,* May 31, 1970, section 6, pp. 8–9, 29, 31–32, 34, 41–42. (An introductory essay on the work with kinesics of Birdwhistell, Scheflen, Goffman, and Kendon; illustrated.)

Duke, Charles R. "Nonverbal Communication: Activities to Stimulate Awareness." *Exercise Exchange,* 18 (Spring 1974), 21–25. (A listing of classroom exercises involving nonverbal communication—includes bibliography of films useful in the study of gestures.)

Eisenberg, Abne M., and Ralph R. Smith. *Nonverbal Communication.* Indianapolis: The Bobbs-Merrill Company, Inc., 1971. (Introductory text on nonverbal communication—includes fascinating section on "Exercises in Nonverbal Communication.")

Ekman, Paul. "Communication through Nonverbal Behavior: A Source of Information about an Interpersonal Relationship." *Affect, Cognition, and Personality.* Ed. Silvan S. Tomkins and Carroll E. Izard. New York: Springer Publishing Company, 1965, pp. 391–442. (A discussion of how nonverbal expressions provide additional information to assist in the interpretation of verbal symbols.)

Eschholz, Paul A. "Mark Twain and the Language of Gesture." *Mark Twain Journal,* 17 (Winter 1973–1974), 5–8. (An examination of Twain's use of nonverbal communication in his novels—emphasis given to Pudd'nhead Wilson.)

————, and Alfred F. Rosa. "Evaluating Seating Arrangements in the English Classroom." *Classroom Practices in Teaching English.* Champaign, Illinois: NCTE, 1972, pp. 75–79. (A study of classroom seating arrangements and their relationship to classroom activities.)

Fabun, Donald. "The Silent Languages." *Communications: The Transfer of Meaning.* New York: The Macmillan Company, 1968. (An introductory discussion of the languages of time, color, and space.)

Goffman, Erving. *Behavior in Public Places.* New York: The Free Press of Glencoe, 1963. (A psychiatrist's analysis of public behavior.)

————. *The Presentation of Self in Everyday Life.* Edinburgh: University of Edinburgh, Social Sciences Research Center, 1956. (An analysis of an individual's impressions of himself when appearing before others.)

Hall, Edward T. *Beyond Culture.* Garden City, New York: Doubleday, 1976. (A study of how some of the basic cultural systems such as time and space are used to organize human behavior.)

————. "Proxemics." *Current Anthropology,* 9 (April–June 1968), 83–104. (A good introduction to proxemics with charts, comments by authorities, and bibliography.)

————. *The Hidden Dimension.* Garden City, New York: Doubleday, 1966. (A fascinating discussion of human and animal use of space.)

Harris, Christie, and Moira Johnston. *Figleafing Through History: The Dynamics of Dress.* New York: Atheneum, 1971. (An entertaining historical discussion of clothes and how they affect the self-conceptions of individuals in different societies.)

Hayes, Francis. "Gestures: A Working Bibliography." *Southern Folklore Quarterly,* 21 (December 1957), 218–317. (Extensive references to books and articles on gestures; annotated.)

Hazard, John N. "Furniture Arrangement as a Symbol of Judicial Roles." *ETC.,* 19 (1962), 181–188. (A case study in proxemics.)

Hewes, Gordon W. "World Distribution of Certain Postural Habits." *American Anthropologist, 57* (April 1955), 231–244. (Distribution and significance of certain standing and sitting positions.)

Hinde, Robert A., ed. *Non-Verbal Communication.* Cambridge: Cambridge University Press, 1972. (An informative collection of fifteen essays on the nature of communication, communication in animals, and nonverbal communication in man.)

Johnson, Kenneth R. "Black Kinesics—Some Non-Verbal Communication Patterns in the Black Culture." *The Florida FL Reporter, 9* (Spring—Fall 1971), 17–20, 57. (A description of some of the nonverbal communication patterns of blacks and the meanings that these patterns convey.)

Key, Mary Ritchie. *Paralanguage and Kinesics (Nonverbal Communication).* Metuchen, New Jersey: The Scarecrow Press, Inc., 1975. (Useful study of nonverbal communication—includes excellent bibliography.)

Knapp, Mark L. *Nonverbal Communication in Human Interaction.* New York: Holt, Rinehart & Winston, Inc., 1972. (A discussion of and review of research for six major nonverbal variables that influence the process of human communication.)

————. "Nonverbal Communication: The Interview." *Exercise Exchange,* 17 (Fall 1972), 26–29. (Interesting classroom exercise involving the interview situation.)

Mehrabian, Albert. "Communication Without Words." *Psychology Today,* 2 (September 1968), 52–55. (A basic discussion of nonverbal forms of communication.)

Michael, G., and F. N. Willis, Jr. "The Development of Gestures as a Function of Social Class, Education, and Sex." *Psychological Record,* 18 (October 1968), 515–519. (A study of eight groups of children differing in social class, education, and sex.)

Morris, Desmond. *The Human Zoo.* New York: McGraw-Hill, 1969. (A zoologist's analysis of the sociological implications of population clusters.)

Nierenberg, Gerard I. *The Art of Negotiating.* New York: Hawthorn Books, 1968. (Practical application of kinesics to interpersonal relationships.)

————, and Henry H. Calero. *How To Read a Person Like a Book.* New York: Hawthorn Books, 1971. (A profusely illustrated, popular treatment of kinesics and proxemics.)

————. *Meta-Talk: The Guide to Hidden Meanings in Conversation.* New York: Simon & Schuster, 1973. (A study of meaning in relation to the speaker, listener, and circumstance.)

"Parting Shots: What Are The Politicians Really Saying?—Body Language Tells You." *Life,* October 9, 1970, pp. 82–84. (Selected pictures of politicians with interpretative remarks.)

Pittenger, Robert E., Charles F. Hackett, and John J. Danehy. *The First Five Minutes: A Sample of Microscopic Interview Analysis*. Ithaca, New York: Paul Martineau, Publisher, 1960. (An in-depth analysis with emphasis on paralinguistic features of a five-minute interview between a psychiatrist and a young female patient.)

Ruesch, Jurgen, and Weldon Kees. *Nonverbal Communication: Notes on the Visual Perception of Human Relations*. Berkeley and Los Angeles: University of California Press, 1956. (An investigation of nonverbal forms of communication; dated illustrations.)

Scheflen, Albert E. *Body Language and the Social Order: Communication as Behavioral Control*. Englewood Cliffs, New Jersey: Prentice-Hall, 1972. (A discussion of the uses of body language for purposes of social control.)

————. "The Significance of Posture in Communications Systems." *Psychiatry*, 27 (November 1964), 316–331. (A psychiatrist's analysis of the significance of postural activities and markers in interview and group situations; illustrated.)

Smith, Henry Lee, Jr. "Language and the Total System of Communication." *Linguistics Today*. Ed. A. A. Hill. New York: Basic Books, 1968. (An interesting, readable analysis of the totality of communication.)

Sommer, Robert. *Personal Space*. Englewood Cliffs, New Jersey: Prentice-Hall, 1969. (A guide to the design of physical spaces based on research of people's use of personal space.)

"Teacher's Desk." *Psychology Today*, 5 (September 1971), 12. (Brief review of some research on classroom seating arrangements.)